His Divine Grace
A.C. BHAKTIVEDANTA SWAMI PRABHUPĀDA
*Founder-*Ācārya *of the International Society for Krishna Consciousness*

Plate 1 The great saint Nārada became very compassionate upon the King and decided to instruct him about spiritual life. (*page 1135*)

Plate 2 Lord Kṛṣṇa imparted the imperishable science of *yoga* to the sun-god, Vivasvān, who instructed it to Manu, the father of mankind, who in turn instructed it to Ikṣvāku. (*page 1323*)

Plate 3 The Supreme Lord is the Supreme Spirit, the Supersoul. (*page 1358*)

Plate 4 The perfect result of an education is the fixing of one's mind on the lotus feet of Kṛṣṇa. (*page 1428*)

Plate 5 Consulting a bona fide spiritual master is the same as consulting the Supreme Personality of Godhead personally. (*page 1430*)

Plate 6 The Personality of Godhead, appearing on the shoulder of Garuda, dissipated all the darkness of the universe. (*page 1491*)

Plate 7 The remaining trees, being very much afraid of the Pracetās, immediately delivered their daughter at the advice of Lord Brahmā. (*page 1548*)

ALL GLORY TO ŚRĪ GURU AND GAURĀṄGA

Śrīmad-Bhāgavatam

of

KṚṢṆA-DVAIPĀYANA VYĀSA

अपि स्मरसि चात्मानमविज्ञातसखं सखे ।
हित्वा मां पदमन्विच्छन् भौमभोगरतो गतः ॥५३॥

api smarasi cātmānam
avijñāta-sakhaṁ sakhe
hitvā māṁ padam anvicchan
bhauma-bhoga-rato gataḥ (p. 1348)

BOOKS by

His Divine Grace A.C. Bhaktivedanta Swami Prabhupāda

Bhagavad-gītā As It Is
Śrīmad-Bhāgavatam, Cantos 1-4 (13 Vols.)
Śrī Caitanya-caritāmṛta (3 Vols.)
Teachings of Lord Caitanya
The Nectar of Devotion
Śrī Īśopaniṣad
Easy Journey to Other Planets
Kṛṣṇa Consciousness: The Topmost Yoga System
Kṛṣṇa, The Supreme Personality of Godhead (2 Vols.)
Transcendental Teachings of Prahlād Mahārāja
Transcendental Teachings of Caitanya Mahāprabhu
Kṛṣṇa, the Reservoir of Pleasure
The Perfection of Yoga
Beyond Birth and Death
On the Way to Kṛṣṇa
Rāja-vidyā: The King of Knowledge
Elevation to Kṛṣṇa Consciousness
Lord Caitanya in Five Features
Back to Godhead Magazine (Founder)

A complete catalogue is available upon request.

International Society for Krishna Consciousness
3764 Watseka Avenue
Los Angeles, California 90034

Puranas. Bhāgavatapurāṇa.

Śrīmad-Bhāgavatam

Fourth Canto

"The Creation of the Fourth Order"

(Part Four—Chapters 25-31)

With the Original Sanskrit Text,
Its Roman Transliteration, Synonyms,
Translation and Elaborate Purports by

His Divine Grace
A.C. Bhaktivedanta Swami Prabhupāda
Founder-Ācārya of the International Society for Krishna Consciousness

THE BHAKTIVEDANTA
BOOK TRUST
New York · Los Angeles · London · Bombay

Readers interested in the subject matter of this book
are invited by the International Society for Krishna Consciousness
to correspond with its Secretary.

International Society for Krishna Consciousness
3764 Watseka Avenue
Los Angeles, California 90034

Library of Congress Catalogue Card Number: 75-189067
International Standard Book Number: 0912776-49-8

Printed in the United States of America

TABLE OF CONTENTS

CHAPTER TWENTY-NINE

Talks Between Nārada and
King Prācīnabarhi

CHAPTER TWENTY-FIVE

The Descriptions of the Characteristics of King Purañjana

TEXT 1

मैत्रेय उवाच
इति सन्दिश्य भगवान् बार्हिषदैरभिपूजितः ।
पश्यतां राजपुत्राणां तत्रैवान्तर्दधे हरः ॥ १ ॥

maitreya uvāca
iti sandiśya bhagavān
bārhiṣadair abhipūjitaḥ
paśyatāṁ rāja-putrāṇāṁ
tatraivāntardadhe haraḥ

maitreyaḥ uvāca—the great sage Maitreya continued to speak; *iti*—thus; *sandiśya*—giving instruction; *bhagavān*—most powerful lord; *bārhiṣadaiḥ*—by the sons of King Barhiṣat; *abhipūjitaḥ*—being worshiped; *paśyatām*—while they were looking on; *rāja-putrāṇām*—the sons of the King; *tatra*—there; *eva*—certainly; *antardadhe*—became invisible; *haraḥ*—Lord Śiva.

TRANSLATION

The great sage Maitreya continued speaking to Vidura: My dear Vidura, in this way Lord Śiva instructed the sons of King Barhiṣat. The sons of the King also worshiped Lord Śiva with great devotion and respect. Finally, Lord Śiva became invisible to the princes.

PURPORT

This chapter contains a great lesson concerning the monarchical kingdom in the days of yore. When King Barhiṣat was considering retiring from the royal duties, he sent his sons to perform austerities in order to become perfect kings for the welfare of the citizens. At the same time King Barhiṣat was being instructed by the great sage Nārada about the material world and the living entity who wants to enjoy it. It is therefore very clear how the kings and princes were trained to take charge of a kingdom. Welfare activities for the benefit of the citizens were aimed at understanding the Supreme Personality of Godhead. The human form of life is especially meant for understanding God, our relationship with Him and our activities in His service. Because the kings took charge of the spiritual education of the citizens, both the king and the citizens were happy in Kṛṣṇa consciousness. In this regard, we should remember that the monarchical hierarchy of Prācīnabarhiṣat comes from Mahārāja Dhruva, a great devotee of the Lord and the most celebrated disciple of Nārada Muni. King Prācīnabarhiṣat was then too much engaged in fruitive activities due to performing different types of *yajñas.* One can actually be promoted to higher planetary systems or to the heavenly kingdoms by performing various *yajñas,* but there is no question of liberation or going back home, back to Godhead. When the great sage Nārada saw that a descendant of Mahārāja Dhruva was being misled by fruitive activities, he took compassion upon him and personally came to instruct him about the ultimate benediction of life, *bhakti-yoga.* How Nārada Muni indirectly introduced the *bhakti-yoga* system to King Prācīnabarhiṣat is very interestingly described in this Twenty-fifth Chapter.

TEXT 2

रुद्रगीतं भगवतः स्तोत्रं सर्वे प्रचेतसः ।
जपन्तस्ते तपस्तेपुर्वर्षाणामयुतं जले ॥ २ ॥

rudra-gītaṁ bhagavataḥ
stotraṁ sarve pracetasaḥ
japantas te tapas tepur
varṣāṇām ayutaṁ jale

rudra-gītam—the song sung by Lord Śiva; *bhagavataḥ*—of the Lord; *stotram*—prayer; *sarve*—all; *pracetasaḥ*—the princes known as the Pracetās; *japantaḥ*—reciting; *te*—all of them; *tapaḥ*—austerity; *tepuḥ*—executed; *varṣāṇām*—of years; *ayutam*—10,000; *jale*— within the water.

TRANSLATION

All the Pracetā princes simply stood in the water for ten thousand years and recited the prayers given to them by Lord Śiva.

PURPORT

Of course in the modern age one may be amazed how the princes could stand in the water for ten thousand years. However, living within air or living within water is the same process; one simply has to learn how to do it. The aquatics live within water for their whole life span. Certain favorable conditions are created to enable them to live within water. In those days, however, people used to live for 100,000 years. Out of so many years, if one could spare ten thousand years for the sake of austerity, he would be assured of success in his future life. This was not very astonishing. Although such a feat is impossible in this age, it was quite possible in Satya-yuga.

TEXT 3

प्राचीनबर्हिषं क्षत्तः कर्मस्वासक्तमानसम् ।
नारदोऽध्यात्मतत्त्वज्ञः कृपालुः प्रत्यबोधयत् ॥ ३ ॥

prācīnabarhiṣaṁ kṣattaḥ
karmasv āsakta-mānasam
nārado 'dhyātma-tattva-jñaḥ
kṛpāluḥ pratyabodhayat

prācīnabarhiṣam—unto King Prācīnabarhiṣat; *kṣattaḥ*—O Vidura; *karmasu*—in fruitive activities; *āsakta*—attached; *mānasam*—with this mentality; *nāradaḥ*—the great sage Nārada; *adhyātma*—spiritualism; *tattva-jñaḥ*—one who knows the truth; *kṛpāluḥ*—being compassionate; *pratyabodhayat*—gave instructions.

TRANSLATION

While the princes were undergoing severe austerities in the water, their father was performing different types of fruitive activities. At this time the great saint Nārada, master and teacher of all spiritual life, became very compassionate upon the King and decided to instruct him about spiritual life.

PURPORT

As pointed out by Prabodhānanda Sarasvatī Ṭhākura, a great devotee of Lord Caitanya, *kaivalya*, or merging into the Brahman effulgence, is just like going to hell. He similarly states that elevation to the upper planetary systems for the enjoyment of heavenly life is just so much phantasmagoria.

This means that a devotee does not give any importance to the ultimate goal of the *karmīs* and *jñānīs*. The ultimate goal of the *karmīs* is promotion to the heavenly kingdom, and the ultimate goal of the *jñānīs* is merging into the Brahman effulgence. Of course the *jñānīs* are superior to the *karmīs*, as confirmed by Lord Caitanya: *koṭi-karmaniṣṭha-madhye eka 'jñānī' śreṣṭha.* "One *jñānī*, or impersonalist, is better than many thousands of fruitive actors." (Cc. *Madhya* 19.147) Therefore a devotee never enters upon the path of *karma*, or elevation by fruitive activities. Nārada Muni took compassion upon King Prācīnabarhiṣat when he saw the King engaged in fruitive activity. In comparison to mundane workers, however, those who are trying to be elevated to the higher planetary systems by performing *yajñas* are undoubtedly superior. In pure devotional service, however, both *karma* and *jñāna* are considered to be bewildering features of the illusory energy.

TEXT 4

श्रेयस्त्वं कतमद्राजन् कर्मणाऽऽत्मन ईहसे ।
दुःखहानिः सुखावाप्तिः श्रेयस्तन्नेह चेष्यते ॥ ४ ॥

śreyas tvaṁ katamad rājan
karmaṇātmana īhase
duḥkha-hāniḥ sukhāvāptiḥ
śreyas tan neha ceṣyate

śreyaḥ—ultimate benediction; *tvam*—you; *katamat*—what is that; *rājan*—O King; *karmaṇā*—by fruitive activities; *ātmanaḥ*—of the soul; *īhase*—you desire; *duḥkha-hāniḥ*—disappearance of all distresses; *sukha-avāptiḥ*—attainment of all happiness; *śreyaḥ*—benediction; *tat*—that; *na*—never; *iha*—in this connection; *ca*—and; *iṣyate*—is available.

TRANSLATION

Nārada Muni asked King Prācīnabarhiṣat: My dear King, what do you desire to achieve by performing these fruitive activities? The chief aim of life is to get rid of all miseries and enjoy happiness, but these two things cannot be realized by fruitive activity.

PURPORT

In this material world there is a great illusion which covers real intelligence. A man in the mode of passion wants to work very hard to derive some benefit, but he does not know that time will never allow him to enjoy anything permanently. Compared to the work one expends, the gain is not so profitable. Even if it is profitable, it is not without its distresses. If a man is not born rich, and he wants to purchase a house, cars and other material things, he has to work hard day and night for many years in order to possess them. Thus happiness is not attained without undergoing some distress.

Actually pure happiness cannot be had within this material world. If we wish to enjoy something, we must suffer for something else. On the whole, suffering is the nature of this material world, and whatever enjoyment we are trying to achieve is simply illusion. After all, we have to suffer the miseries of birth, old age, disease and death. We may discover many fine medicines, but it is not possible to stop the sufferings of disease or death. Actually medicine is not the counteracting agent for either disease or death. On the whole there is no happiness in this material world, but an illusioned person works very hard for so-called happiness. Indeed, this process of working hard is actually taken for happiness. This is called illusion.

Therefore Nārada Muni asked King Prācīnabarhiṣat what he desired to attain by performing so many costly sacrifices. Even if one attains a heavenly planet, he cannot avoid the distresses of birth, old age, disease and death. Someone may argue that even devotees have to undergo many distresses in executing austerities and penances connected with devotional service. Of course for the neophytes the routine of devotional service may be very painful, but at least they have the hope that they will ultimately be able to avoid all kinds of distresses and achieve the highest perfectional stage of happiness. For the common *karmīs*, there is no such hope because even if they are promoted to the higher planetary systems, they are not guaranteed freedom from the miseries of birth, old age, disease and death. Even Lord Brahmā, who is situated in the highest planetary system (Brahmaloka), has to die. Lord Brahmā's birth and death may be different from an ordinary man's, but within this material world he cannot avoid the distresses of birth, old age, disease and death. If one is at all serious about attaining liberation from these miseries, he must take to devotional service. This is confirmed by the Lord Himself in *Bhagavad-gītā:*

janma karma ca me divyam
evaṁ yo vetti tattvataḥ
tyaktvā dehaṁ punar janma
naiti mām eti so 'rjuna

"One who knows the transcendental nature of My appearance and activities does not, upon leaving the body, take his birth again in this material world, but attains My eternal abode, O Arjuna." (Bg. 4.9)

Thus after attaining full Kṛṣṇa consciousness, the devotee does not return to this material world after death. He goes back home, back to Godhead. That is the perfect stage of happiness, unblemished by any trace of distress.

TEXT 5

राजोवाच
न जानामि महाभाग परं कर्मापविद्धधीः ।
ब्रूहि मे विमलं ज्ञानं येन मुच्येय कर्मभिः ॥ ५ ॥

rājovāca
na jānāmi mahā-bhāga
paraṁ karmāpaviddha-dhīḥ
brūhi me vimalaṁ jñānaṁ
yena mucyeya karmabhiḥ

rājā uvāca—the King replied; *na*—not; *jānāmi*—I know; *mahā-bhāga*—O great soul; *param*—transcendental; *karma*—by fruitive activities; *apaviddha*—being pierced; *dhīḥ*—my intelligence; *brūhi*—please tell; *me*—to me; *vimalam*—spotless; *jñānam*—knowledge; *yena*—by which; *mucyeya*—I can get relief; *karmabhiḥ*—from the fruitive activities.

TRANSLATION

The King replied: O great soul, Nārada, my intelligence is entangled in fruitive activities; therefore I do not know the ultimate goal of life. Kindly instruct me in pure knowledge so that I can get out of the entanglement of fruitive activities.

PURPORT

Śrī Narottama dāsa Ṭhākura has sung:

sat-saṅga chāḍi' kainu asate vilāsa
te-kāraṇe lāgila ye karma-bandha-phāṅsa

As long as a person is entangled in fruitive activities, he is bound to accept one body after another. This is called *karma-bandha-phāṅsa*—entanglement in fruitive activities. It does not matter whether one is engaged in pious or impious activities, for both are causes for further entanglement in material bodies. By pious activities one can take birth in a rich family and get a good education and a beautiful body, but this does not mean that the distresses of life are ultimately eliminated. In the Western countries it is not unusual for one to take birth in a rich aristocratic family, nor is it unusual for one to have a good education and a very beautiful body, but this does not mean that Westerners are free from the distresses of life. Although at the present moment the younger generation in Western countries has sufficient education, beauty and wealth, and although there is enough food, clothing and facilities for sense gratification, they are in distress. Indeed, they are so distressed that they become "hippies," and the laws of nature force them to accept a wretched life. Thus they go about unclean and without shelter or food, and they are forced to sleep in the street. It can be concluded that one cannot become happy by simply performing pious activities. It is not a fact that those who are born with a silver spoon in their mouths are free from the material miseries of birth, old age, disease and death. The conclusion is that one cannot be happy by simply executing pious or impious activities. Such activities simply cause entanglement and transmigration from one body to another. Narottama dāsa Ṭhākura calls this *karma-bandha-phāṅsa.*

King Prācīnabarhiṣat admitted this fact and frankly asked Nārada Muni how he could get out of this *karma-bandha-phāṅsa,* entanglement in fruitive activities. This is actually the stage of knowledge indicated in the first verse of *Vedānta-sūtra: athāto brahma-jijñāsā* (Vs. 1.1.1). When one actually reaches the platform of frustration in an attempt to discharge *karma-bandha-phāṅsa,* he inquires about the real value of life, which is called *brahma-jijñāsā.* In order to inquire about the ultimate goal of life, the *Vedas* enjoin: *tad vijñānārthaṁ sa gurum evābhigacchet* (*Muṇḍaka Up.* 1.2.12). "In order to understand the transcendental science, one must approach a bona fide spiritual master."

King Prācīnabarhiṣat found the best spiritual master, Nārada Muni, and he therefore asked him about that knowledge by which one can get out of the entanglement of *karma-bandha-phāṅsa,* fruitive activities. This is the actual business of human life. *Jīvasya tattva-jijñāsā nārtho yaś ceha karmabhiḥ* (*Bhāg.* 1.2.10). As stated in the Second Chapter of the First Canto of *Śrīmad-Bhāgavatam,* a human being's only business is inquiring from a bona fide spiritual master about extrication from the entanglement of *karma-bandha-phāṅsa* .

TEXT 6

गृहेषु कूटधर्मेषु पुत्रदारधनार्थधीः ।
न परं विन्दते मूढो भ्राम्यन् संसारवर्त्मसु ॥ ६ ॥

gṛheṣu kūṭa-dharmeṣu
putra-dāra-dhanārtha-dhīḥ
na paraṁ vindate mūḍho
bhrāmyan saṁsāra-vartmasu

gṛheṣu—in family life; *kūṭa-dharmeṣu*—in false occupational duties; *putra*—sons; *dāra*—wife; *dhana*—wealth; *artha*—the goal of life; *dhīḥ*—one who considers; *na*—not; *param*—transcendence; *vindate*—achieves; *mūḍhaḥ*—rascal; *bhrāmyan*—wandering; *saṁsāra*—of material existence; *vartmasu*—on the paths.

TRANSLATION

Those who are only interested in a so-called beautiful life—namely remaining as a householder entangled by sons and a wife and searching after wealth—think that such things are life's ultimate goal. Such people simply wander in different types of bodies throughout this material existence without finding out the ultimate goal of life.

PURPORT

Those who are too much attached to family life—which consists of entanglement with wife, children, wealth and home—are engaged in *kūṭa-dharma,* pseudo-duties. Prahlāda Mahārāja has likened these pseudo occupational duties to a dark well *(andha-kūpa).* Prahlāda has purposefully spoken of this dark well because if one falls into this well, he will die. He may cry for help, but no one will hear him or come to rescue him.

The words *bhrāmyan saṁsāra-vartmasu* are significant. In *Caitanya-caritāmṛta,* Śrī Caitanya Mahāprabhu very clearly explains: *brahmāṇḍa bhramite kona bhāgyavān jīva* (Cc. *Madhya* 19.151). All living entities are wandering in different types of bodies throughout different planets, and if, in the course of their wanderings, they come in contact with a devotee by the direction of the Supreme Personality of Godhead, their lives become successful. Even though King Prācīnabarhiṣat was engaged in fruitive activity, the great sage Nārada appeared before him. The King was very fortunate to be able to associate with Nārada, who enlightened him in spiritual knowledge. It is the duty of all saintly persons to follow in the footsteps of Nārada Muni and travel all over the world to every country and village just to instruct illusioned persons about the goal of life and to save them from the entanglement of *karma-bandha,* fruitive activity.

TEXT 7

नारद उवाच
भो भोः प्रजापते राजन् पशून् पश्य त्वयाध्वरे ।
संज्ञापिताञ्जीवसङ्घान्निर्घृणेन सहस्रशः ॥ ७ ॥

nārada uvāca
bho bhoḥ prajā-pate rājan
paśūn paśya tvayādhvare
saṁjñāpitāñ jīva-saṅghān
nirghṛṇena sahasraśaḥ

nāradaḥ uvāca—the great sage Nārada replied; *bhoḥ bhoḥ*—hello; *prajā-pate*—O ruler of the citizens; *rājan*—O King; *paśūn*—animals; *paśya*—please see; *tvayā*—by you; *adhvare*—in the sacrifice; *saṁjñāpitān*—killed; *jīva-saṅghān*—groups of animals; *nirghṛṇena*—without pity; *sahasraśaḥ*—in thousands.

TRANSLATION

The great saint Nārada said: O ruler of the citizens, my dear King, please see in the sky those animals which you have sacrificed without compassion and without mercy in the sacrificial arena.

PURPORT

Because animal sacrifice is recommended in the *Vedas,* there are animal sacrifices in almost all religious rituals. However, one should not be satisfied simply by killing animals according to the directions of the scriptures. One should transcend the ritualistic ceremonies and try to understand the actual truth, the purpose of life. Nārada Muni wanted to instruct the King about the real purpose of life and invoke a spirit of renunciation in his heart. Knowledge and the spirit of renunciation *(jñāna-vairāgya)* are the ultimate goal of life. Without knowledge, one cannot become detached from material enjoyment, and without being detached from material enjoyment, one cannot make spiritual advancement. *Karmīs* are generally engaged in sense gratification, and for this end they are prepared to commit so many sinful activities. Animal sacrifice is but one such sinful activity. Consequently, by his mystic power Nārada Muni showed King Prācīnabarhiṣat the dead animals which he had sacrificed.

TEXT 8

एते त्वां सम्प्रतीक्षन्ते स्मरन्तो वैशसं तव ।
सम्परेतमयः - कूटैश्छिन्दन्त्युत्थितमन्यवः ॥ ८ ॥

ete tvāṁ sampratīkṣante
smaranto vaiśasaṁ tava
samparetam ayaḥ-kūṭaiś
chindanty utthita-manyavaḥ

ete—all of them; *tvām*—you; *sampratīkṣante*—are awaiting; *smarantaḥ*—remembering; *vaiśasam*—injuries; *tava*—of you; *samparetam*—after your death; *ayaḥ*—made of iron; *kūṭaiḥ*—by the horns; *chindanti*—pierce; *utthita*—enlivened; *manyavaḥ*—anger.

TRANSLATION

All these animals are awaiting your death so that they can avenge the injuries you have inflicted upon them. After you die, they will angrily pierce your body with iron horns.

PURPORT

Nārada Muni wanted to draw King Prācīnabarhiṣat's attention to the excesses of killing animals in sacrifices. It is said in the *śāstras* that by killing animals in a sacrifice, one immediately promotes them to human birth. Similarly, by killing their enemies on a battlefield, the *kṣatriyas* who fight for a right cause are elevated to the heavenly planets after death. In *Manu-saṁhitā* it is stated that it is necessary for a king to execute a murderer so that the murderer will not suffer for his criminal actions in his next life. On the basis of such understanding, Nārada Muni warns the King that the animals killed in sacrifices by the King await him at his death in order to avenge themselves. Nārada Muni is not contradicting himself here. Nārada Muni wanted to convince the King that overindulgence in animal sacrifice is risky because as soon as there is a small discrepancy in the execution of such a sacrifice, the slaughtered animal may not be promoted to a human form of life. Consequently the person performing sacrifice will be responsible for the death of the animal, just as much as a murderer is responsible for killing another man. When animals are killed in a slaughterhouse, six people connected with the killing are responsible for the murder. The person who gives permission for the killing, the person who kills, the person who helps, the person who purchases the meat, the person who cooks the flesh and the person who eats it, all become entangled in the killing. Nārada Muni wanted to draw the King's attention to this fact. Thus animal killing is not encouraged even in a sacrifice.

TEXT 9

अत्र ते कथयिष्येऽमुमितिहासं पुरातनम् ।
पुरञ्जनस्य चरितं निबोध गदतो मम ॥ ९ ॥

atra te kathayiṣye 'mum
itihāsaṁ purātanam
purañjanasya caritaṁ
nibodha gadato mama

atra—herewith; *te*—unto you; *kathayiṣye*—I shall speak; *amum*—on this subject matter; *itihāsam*—history; *purātanam*—very old; *purañjanasya*—in the matter of Purañjana; *caritam*—his character; *nibodha*—try to understand; *gadataḥ mama*—while I am speaking.

TRANSLATION

In this connection I wish to narrate an old history connected with the character of a king called Purañjana. Please try to hear me with great attention.

PURPORT

The great sage Nārada Muni turned toward another topic—the history of King Purañjana. This is nothing but the history of King Prācīnabarhiṣat told in a different way. In other words, this is an allegorical presentation. The word *purañjana* means "one who enjoys in a body." This is clearly explained in the next few chapters. Because a person entangled in material activities wants to hear stories of material activities, Nārada Muni turned to the topics of King Purañjana, who is none other than King Prācīnabarhiṣat. Nārada Muni did not, however, deprecate the value of performing sacrifices in which animals are sacrificed. Lord Buddha, however, directly rejected all animal sacrifice. Śrīla Jayadeva Gosvāmī has stated: *nindasi yajña-vidher ahaha śruti-jātam.* The word *śruti-jātam* indicates that in the *Vedas* animal sacrifice is recommended, but Lord Buddha directly denied Vedic authority in order to stop animal sacrifice. Consequently Lord Buddha is not accepted by the followers of the *Vedas.*

Because he does not accept the authority of the *Vedas,* Lord Buddha is depicted as an agnostic or atheist. The great sage Nārada cannot decry the authority of the *Vedas,* but he wanted to indicate to King Prācīnabarhiṣat that the path of *karma-kāṇḍa* is very difficult and risky.

Foolish persons accept the difficult path of *karma-kāṇḍa* for the sake of sense enjoyment, and those who are too much attached to sense enjoyment are called *mūḍhas* (rascals). It is very difficult for a *mūḍha* to understand the ultimate goal of life. In the propagation of the Kṛṣṇa consciousness movement, we actually see that many people are not attracted because they are *mūḍhas* engaged in fruitive activity. It is said: *upadeśo hi mūrkhāṇāṁ prakopāya na śāntaye (Hitopadeśa).* If good instructions are given to a foolish rascal, he simply becomes angry and turns against the instructions instead of taking advantage of them. Because Nārada Muni knew this very well, he indirectly instructed the King by giving him the history of his entire life. In order to wear a gold or diamond nose pin or earring, one has to pierce the ear or nose. Such pain endured for the sake of sense gratification is endured on the path of *karma-kāṇḍa,* the path of fruitive activity. If one wishes to enjoy something in the future, he has to endure trouble in the present. If one wants to become a millionaire in the future and enjoy his riches, he has to work very hard at the present moment in order to accumulate money. This is *karma-kāṇḍīya.* Those who are too much attached to such a path undergo the risk anyway. Nārada Muni wanted to show King Prācīnabarhiṣat how one undergoes great troubles and miseries in order to engage in fruitive activity. A person who is very much attached to material activity is called *viṣayī.* A *viṣayī* is an enjoyer of *viṣaya,* which means eating, sleeping, mating and defending. Nārada Muni is indirectly indicating through the story of King Purañjana that eating, sleeping, mating and defending are troublesome and risky.

The words *itihāsam* (history) and *purātanam* (old) indicate that although a living entity lives within the material body, the history of the living entity within the material body is very old. In this regard, Śrīla Bhaktivinoda Ṭhākura has sung: *anādi karama-phale, paḍi' bhavārṇava-jale, taribāre nā dekhi upāya.* "Due to my past fruitive activities I have fallen into the water of material existence, and I cannot find any way to get out of it." Every living entity is suffering in this material existence from past activities; therefore everyone has a very old history. Foolish material scientists have manufactured their own theories of evolution, which are simply concerned with the material body. But actually this is not the real evolution. The real evolution is the history of the living entity, who is *purañjana,* living within the body. Śrī Nārada Muni will explain this evolutionary theory in a different way for the understanding of sane persons.

TEXT 10

आसीत्पुरञ्जनो नाम राजा राजन् बृहच्छ्रवाः ।
तस्याविज्ञातनामाऽऽसीत्सखाविज्ञातचेष्टितः ॥१०॥

āsīt purañjano nāma
rājā rājan bṛhac-chravāḥ
tasyāvijñāta-nāmāsīt
sakhāvijñāta-ceṣṭitaḥ

āsīt—there was; *purañjanaḥ*—Purañjana; *nāma*—named; *rājā*—king; *rājan*—O King; *bṛhat-śravāḥ*—whose activities were great; *tasya*—his; *avijñāta*—the unknown one; *nāmā*—of the name; *āsīt*—there was; *sakhā*—friend; *avijñāta*—unknown; *ceṣṭitaḥ*—whose activities.

TRANSLATION

My dear King, once in the past lived a king named Purañjana, who was celebrated for his great activities. He had a friend named Avijñāta [the unknown one]. No one could understand the activities of Avijñāta.

PURPORT

Every living entity is *purañjana*. The word *puram* means within this body, within this form, and *jana* means living entity. Thus everyone is *purañjana*. Every living entity is supposed to be the king of his body because the living entity is given full freedom to use his body as he likes. He usually engages his body for sense gratification, because one who is in the bodily conception of life feels that the ultimate goal of life is to serve the senses. This is the process of *karma-kāṇḍa*. One who has no inner knowledge, who does not know that he is actually the spirit soul living within the body, who is simply enamored by the dictation of the senses, is called a materialist. A materialistic person interested in sense gratification can be called a *purañjana*. Because such a materialistic person utilizes his senses according to his whims, he may also be called a king. An irresponsible king takes the royal position to be his personal property and misuses his treasury for sense gratification.

The word *bṛhac-chravāḥ* is also significant. The word *śravaḥ* means fame. The living entity is famous from ancient times, for, as stated in *Bhagavad-gītā, na jāyate mriyate vā* (Bg. 2.20). "The living entity is never born and never dies." Because he is eternal, his activities are eternal, although they are performed in different types of bodies. *Na hanyate hanyamāne śarīre*

(Bg. 2.20). "He does not die, even after the annihilation of the body." Thus the living entity transmigrates from one body to another and performs various activities. In each body the living entity performs so many acts. Sometimes he becomes a great hero—just like Hiraṇyakaśipu and Kaṁsa, or in the modern age Napoleon or Hitler. The activities of such men are certainly very great, but as soon as their bodies are finished, everything else is finished. Then they remain in name only. Therefore a living entity may be called *bṛhac-chravāḥ;* he may have a great reputation for various types of activities. Nonetheless, he has a friend whom he does not know. Materialistic persons do not understand that God is present as the Supersoul and situated within the heart of every living entity. Although the Paramātmā sits beside the *jīvātmā* as a friend, the *jīvātmā*, or living entity, does not know it. Consequently he is described as *avijñāta-sakhā,* meaning "one who has an unknown friend." The word *avijñāta-ceṣṭitaḥ* is also significant because a living entity works hard under the direction of the Paramātmā and is carried away by the laws of nature. Nonetheless, he thinks himself independent of God and independent of the stringent laws of material nature. It is stated in *Bhagavad-gītā:*

acchedyo 'yam adāhyo 'yam
akledyo 'śoṣya eva ca
nityaḥ sarva-gataḥ sthāṇur
acalo 'yaṁ sanātanaḥ

"This individual soul is unbreakable and insoluble and can be neither burned nor dried. He is everlasting, all-pervading, unchangeable, immovable and eternally the same." (Bg. 2.24)

The living entity is *sanātana,* eternal. Because he cannot be killed by any weapon, burnt into ashes by fire, soaked or moistened by water, nor dried up by air, he is considered to be immune to material reactions. Although he is changing bodies, he is not affected by the material conditions. He is placed under the material conditions, and he acts according to the directions of his friend, the Supersoul. As stated in *Bhagavad-gītā:*

sarvasya cāhaṁ hṛdi sanniviṣṭo
mattaḥ smṛtir jñānam apohanaṁ ca
vedaiś ca sarvair aham eva vedyo
vedānta-kṛd veda-vid eva cāham

"I am seated in everyone's heart, and from Me come remembrance, knowledge and forgetfulness. By all the *Vedas* am I to be known; indeed I am the compiler of *Vedānta,* and I am the knower of the *Vedas.* (Bg. 15.15)

Thus the Lord as Paramātmā is situated in everyone's heart, and He gives directions to the living entity to act in whatever way the living entity desires. In this life and in his previous lives the living entity does not know that the Lord is giving him a chance to fulfill all kinds of desires. No one can fulfill any desire without the sanction of the Lord. All the facilities given by the Lord are unknown to the conditioned soul.

TEXT 11

सोऽन्वेषमाणः शरणं बभ्राम पृथिवीं प्रभुः ।
नानुरूपं यदाविन्दद्भूत्स विमना इव ॥११॥

so 'nveṣamāṇaḥ śaraṇaṁ
babhrāma pṛthivīṁ prabhuḥ
nānurūpaṁ yadāvindad
abhūt sa vimanā iva

saḥ—that King Purañjana; *anveṣamāṇaḥ*—searching after; *śaraṇam*—shelter; *babhrāma*—traveled over; *pṛthivīm*—the whole planet earth; *prabhuḥ*—to become an independent master; *na*—never; *anurūpam*—to his liking; *yadā*—when; *avindat*—he could find; *abhūt*—became; *saḥ*—he; *vimanāḥ*—morose; *iva*—like.

TRANSLATION

King Purañjana began to search for a suitable place to live, and thus he traveled all over the world. Even after a great deal of traveling, he could not find a place just to his liking. Finally he became morose and disappointed.

PURPORT

The travelings of Purañjana are similar to the travelings of the modern hippies. Generally hippies are sons of great fathers and great families. It is not that they are always poor. But some way or another they abandon the shelter of their rich fathers and travel all over the world. As stated in this verse, the living entity wants to become a *prabhu*, or master. The word *prabhu* means master, but actually the living entity is not a master; he is the eternal servant of God. When the living entity abandons the shelter of God, Kṛṣṇa, and tries to become a *prabhu* independently, he travels all over the creation. There are 8,400,000 species of life and millions and millions and trillions of planets within the creation. The living entity wanders throughout these various types of bodies and throughout different planets, and thus he is like King Purañjana, who travels all over the world looking for a suitable place to live.

Śrī Narottama dāsa Ṭhākura has sung: *karma-kāṇḍa, jñāna-kāṇḍa, kevala viṣera bhāṇḍa.* "The path of *karma-kāṇḍa* [fruitive activities] and the path of *jñāna-kāṇḍa* [speculation] are just like strong pots of poison." *Amṛta baliyā yebā khāya, nānā yoni sadā phire:* "A person who mistakes this poison to be nectar and drinks it travels in different species of life." *Kadarya bhakṣaṇa kare:* "And, according to his body, he eats all types of abominable things." For instance, when the living entity is in the body of a hog, he eats stool. When the living entity is in the body of a crow, he eats all kinds of refuse, even pus and mucus, and enjoys it. Thus Narottama dāsa Ṭhākura points out that the living entity travels in different types of bodies and eats all kinds of abominable things. When he does not become ultimately happy, he becomes morose or takes to the ways of hippies.

Thus in this verse it is said (*na anurūpam*) that the King could never find a place suitable for his purposes. This is because in any form of life and on any planet in the material world, a living entity cannot be happy because everything in the material world is unsuitable for the spirit soul. As stated in this verse, the living entity independently wants to become a *prabhu,* but as soon as he gives up this idea and becomes a servant of God, Kṛṣṇa, his happiness immediately begins. Therefore Śrīla Bhaktivinoda Ṭhākura sings: *(miche) māyāra vaśe, yāccha bhese', khāccha hābuḍubu, bhāi.* "My dear living entity, why are you being carried away by the waves of *māyā*?" As stated in the *Bhagavad-gītā:*

īśvaraḥ sarva-bhūtānāṁ
hṛd-deśe 'rjuna tiṣṭhati
bhrāmayan sarva-bhūtāni
yantrārūḍhāni māyayā

"The Supreme Lord is situated in everyone's heart, O Arjuna, and is directing the wanderings of all living entities, who are seated as on a machine, made of the material energy." (Bg. 18.61)

The living entity is carried in the machine of the body through so many species of life on so many planets. Therefore Bhaktivinoda Ṭhākura asks the living entity why he is being carried away in these bodily machines to be placed in so many different circumstances. He advises that one surmount the waves of *māyā* by surrendering unto Kṛṣṇa. *(Jīva) kṛṣṇa-dāsa, e viśvāsa, karle ta' āra duḥkha nāi.* As soon as we confront Kṛṣṇa, Kṛṣṇa advises:

sarva-dharmān parityajya
mām ekaṁ śaraṇaṁ vraja
ahaṁ tvāṁ sarva-pāpebhyo
mokṣayiṣyāmi mā śucaḥ

"Abandon all varieties of religion and just surrender unto Me. I shall deliver you from all sinful reaction. Do not fear." (Bg. 18.66)

Thus we are immediately relieved from traveling from one body to another and from one planet to another. Śrī Caitanya Mahāprabhu says: *brahmāṇḍa bhramite kona bhāgyavān jīva* (Cc. *Madhya* 19.151). If, while traveling, a living entity becomes fortunate enough to become blessed by the association of devotees and to come to Kṛṣṇa consciousness, his real life actually begins. This Kṛṣṇa consciousness movement is giving all wandering living entities a chance to take to the shelter of Kṛṣṇa and thus become happy.

In this verse the words *vimanā iva* are very significant. In this material world even the great King of heaven is also full of anxiety. If even Lord Brahmā is full of anxiety, what of these ordinary living entities who are working within this planet? *Bhagavad-gītā* confirms:

ābrahma-bhuvanāl lokāḥ
punar āvartino 'rjuna

"From the highest planet in the material world down to the lowest, all are places of misery wherein repeated birth and death take place." (Bg. 8.16) In the material world a living entity is never satisfied. Even in the position of Brahmā or in the position of Indra or Candra, one is full of anxiety simply because he has accepted this material world as a place of happiness.

TEXT 12

न साधु मेने ताः सर्वा भूतले यावतीः पुरः ।
कामान् कामयमानोऽसौ तस्य तस्योपपत्तये ।।१२।।

na sādhu mene tāḥ sarvā
bhūtale yāvatīḥ puraḥ
kāmān kāmayamāno 'sau
tasya tasyopapattaye

na—never; *sādhu*—good; *mene*—thought; *tāḥ*—them; *sarvāḥ*—all; *bhūtale*—on this earth; *yāvatīḥ*—all kinds of; *puraḥ*—residential houses; *kāmān*—

objects for sense enjoyment; *kāmayamānaḥ*—desiring; *asau*—that King; *tasya*—his; *tasya*—his; *upapattaye*—for obtaining.

TRANSLATION

King Purañjana had unlimited desires for sense enjoyment; consequently he traveled all over the world to find a place where all his desires could be fulfilled. Unfortunately he found a feeling of insufficiency everywhere.

PURPORT

Śrīla Vidyāpati, a great Vaiṣṇava poet, has sung:

tātala saikate, vāribindu-sama,
suta-mita-ramaṇī-samāje

Material sense gratification, with society, friendship and love, is herein compared to a drop of water falling on a desert. A desert requires oceans of water to satisfy it, and if only a drop of water is supplied, what is its use? Similarly, the living entity is part and parcel of the Supreme Personality of Godhead, who, as stated in the *Vedānta-sūtra,* is *ānandamayo 'bhyāsāt,* full of enjoyment. Being part and parcel of the Supreme Personality of Godhead, the living entity is also seeking complete enjoyment. However, complete enjoyment cannot be achieved separate from the Supreme Personality of Godhead. In his wanderings in the different species of life, the living entity may taste some type of enjoyment in one body or another, but full enjoyment of the senses cannot be obtained in any material body. Thus Purañjana, the living entity, wanders in different types of bodies but everywhere meets frustration in his attempt to enjoy. In other words, the spiritual spark covered by matter cannot fully enjoy the senses in any circumstance in material life. A deer may become absorbed in the musical sounds vibrated by the hunter, but the result is that it loses its life. Similarly, a fish is very expert in gratifying its tongue, but when it eats the bait offered by the fisherman, it loses its life. Even the elephant, who is so strong, is captured and loses its independence while satisfying its genitals with a female elephant. In each and every species of life, the living entity gets a body to satisfy various senses, but he cannot enjoy all his senses at one time. In the human form of life he gets an opportunity to enjoy all his senses pervertedly, but the result is that he becomes so harassed in his attempted sense gratification that he ultimately becomes morose. As he tries to satisfy his senses more and more, he becomes more and more entangled.

TEXT 13

स एकदा हिमवतो दक्षिणेष्वथ सानुषु ।
ददर्श नवभिर्द्वार्भिः पुरं लक्षितलक्षणाम् ॥१३॥

sa ekadā himavato
dakṣiṇeṣv atha sānuṣu
dadarśa navabhir dvārbhiḥ
puraṁ lakṣita-lakṣaṇām

saḥ—that King Purañjana; *ekadā*—once upon a time; *himavataḥ*—of the Himalayan Mountains; *dakṣiṇeṣu*—southern; *atha*—after this; *sānuṣu*—on the ridges; *dadarśa*—found; *navabhiḥ*—with nine; *dvārbhiḥ*—gates; *puram*—a city; *lakṣita*—visible; *lakṣaṇām*—having all auspicious facilities.

TRANSLATION

Once while wandering in this way, he saw on the southern side of the Himalayas, in a place named Bhārata-varṣa [India], a city that had nine gates all about and was characterized by all auspicious facilities.

PURPORT

The tract of land south of the Himalayan Mountains is the land of India, which was known as Bhārata-varṣa. When a living entity takes birth in Bhārata-varṣa he is considered to be most fortunate. Indeed, Caitanya Mahāprabhu has stated:

bhārata-bhūmite haila manuṣya-janma yāra
janma sārthaka kari' kara para-upakāra
(Cc. *Ādi* 9.41)

Thus whoever takes birth in the land of Bhārata-varṣa attains all the facilities of life. He may take advantage of all these facilities for both material and spiritual advancement and thus make his life successful. After attaining the goal of life, one may distribute his knowledge and experience all over the world for humanitarian purposes. In other words, one who takes birth in the land of Bhārata-varṣa by virtue of his past pious activities gets full facility to develop the human form of life. In India, the climatic condition is such that one can live very peacefully without being disturbed by material conditions. Indeed, during the time of Mahārāja Yudhiṣṭhira or Lord Rāmacandra, people were free from all anxieties. There was not even extreme cold or extreme heat. The three kinds of miserable conditions—*adhyātmika, adhibhautika, adhidaivika* (miseries inflicted by the body and mind itself, those inflicted by other living entities, and natural disturbances)—were all absent during the reign of Lord Rāmacandra or Mahārāja Yudhiṣṭhira. But at present, compared to other countries on earth, India is artificially disturbed. Despite these material disturbances, however, the country's culture is such that one can easily attain the goal of life—namely salvation, or liberation from material bondage. Thus in order to take birth in India one must perform many pious activities in a past life.

In this verse the word *lakṣita-lakṣaṇām* indicates that the human body attained in Bhārata-varṣa is very auspicious. Vedic culture is full of knowledge, and a person born in India can fully take advantage of Vedic cultural knowledge and the cultural system known as *varṇāśrama-dharma.* Even at the present time, as we travel all over the world, we see that in some countries human beings have many material facilities but no facilities for spiritual advancement. We find everywhere the defects of one-sided facilities and a lack of full facilities. A blind man can walk but not see, and a lame man cannot walk but can see. *Andha-paṅgu-nyāya.* The blind man may take the lame man over his shoulder, and as he walks the lame man may give him directions. Thus combined they may work, but individually neither the blind man nor the lame man can walk successfully. Similarly, this human form of life is meant for the advancement of spiritual life and for keeping the material necessities in order. Especially in the Western countries there are ample facilities for material comforts, but no one has any idea of spiritual advancement. Many are hankering after spiritual advancement, but many cheaters come, take advantage of their money, bluff them and go away. Fortunately the Kṛṣṇa consciousness movement is there to give all facilities for both material and spiritual advancement. In this way people in the Western countries may take advantage of this movement, and in India any man in the villages, unaffected by the industrial cities of India, can still live in any condition and make spiritual advancement.

The body has been called the city of nine gates, and these nine gates include two eyes, two ears, two nostrils, one mouth, a genital and a rectum. When the nine gates are clean and working properly, it is to be understood that the body is healthy. In India these nine gates are kept clean by the villagers who rise early in the morning, bathe in the well or rivers, go to the temples to attend *maṅgalārati,* chant the Hare Kṛṣṇa *mahā-mantra* and take *prasāda.* In this way one can take advantage of all the facilities of human life. We are gradually introducing this system in different centers in our society in the Western countries. One who takes advantage of it becomes more and more enlightened in spiritual life. At the present moment, India may be compared to the lame man and the Western countries to the blind man. For the past two thousand years India has been subjugated to the rule of foreigners, and the legs of progress have been broken. In the Western countries the eyes of the people have become blind due to the dazzling glitter of material opulence. The blind man of the Western countries and the lame man of India should combine together in this Kṛṣṇa consciousness movement. Then the lame man of India can walk with the help of the Westerner, and the blind Westerner can see with the help of the lame man. In short, the material advancement of the Western countries and the spiritual assets of India should combine for the elevation of all human society.

TEXT 14

प्राकारोपवनाट्टालपरिखैरक्षतोरणैः ।
स्वर्णरौप्यायसैः शृङ्गैः संकुलां सर्वतो गृहैः ॥१४॥

prākāropavanāṭṭāla-
parikhair akṣa-toraṇaiḥ
svarṇa-raupyāyasaiḥ śṛṅgaiḥ
saṅkulāṁ sarvato gṛhaiḥ

prākāra—walls; *upavana*—parks; *aṭṭāla*—towers; *parikhaiḥ*—with trenches; *akṣa*—windows; *toraṇaiḥ*—with gates; *svarṇa*—gold; *raupya*—silver; *ayasaiḥ*—made of iron; *śṛṅgaiḥ*—with domes; *saṅkulām*—congested; *sarvataḥ*—everywhere; *gṛhaiḥ*—with houses.

TRANSLATION

That city was surrounded by walls and parks, and within it were towers, canals, windows and outlets. The houses there were decorated with domes made of gold, silver and iron.

PURPORT

The body is protected by walls of skin. The hairs on the body are compared to parks, and the highest parts of the body, like the nose and head, are compared to towers. The wrinkles and depressions on different parts of the body are compared to trenches or canals, the eyes are compared to windows, and the eyelids are compared to protective gates. The three types of metal—gold, silver and iron—represent the three modes of material nature. Gold represents goodness, silver passion, and iron ignorance. The body is also sometimes considered to be a bag containing three elements (*tri-dhātu*): mucus, bile and air (*kapha, pitta* and *vāyu*). *Yasyātma-buddhiḥ kuṇape tri-dhātuke* (*Bhāg.* 10.84.13). According to *Bhāgavatam,* one who considers this bag of mucus, bile and air to be the self is considered no better than a cow or an ass.

TEXT 15

नीलस्फटिकवैदूर्यमुक्तामरकतारुणैः ।
क्लृप्तहर्म्यस्थलीं दीप्तां श्रिया भोगवतीमिव ॥१५॥

nīla-sphaṭika-vaidūrya-
muktā-marakatāruṇaiḥ
kḷpta-harmya-sthalīṁ dīptāṁ
śriyā bhogavatīm iva

nīla—sapphires; *sphaṭika*—crystal; *vaidūrya*—diamonds; *muktā*—pearls; *marakata*—emeralds; *aruṇaiḥ*—with rubies; *kḷpta*—bedecked; *harmya-sthalīm*—the floors of the palaces; *dīptām*—lustrous; *śriyā*—with beauty; *bhogavatīm*—the celestial town named Bhogavatī; *iva*—like.

TRANSLATION

The floors of the houses in that city were made of sapphire, crystal, diamonds, pearls, emeralds and rubies. Because of the luster of the houses in the capital, the city was compared to the celestial town named Bhogavatī.

PURPORT

In the city of the body, the heart is considered to be the capital. Just as the capital of a state is especially gorgeously filled with various high buildings and lustrous palaces, the heart of the body is filled with various desires and plans for material enjoyment. Such plans are sometimes compared to valuable jewels such as sapphires, rubies, pearls and emeralds. The heart becomes the center for all planning for material enjoyment.

TEXT 16

सभाचत्वररथ्याभिराक्रीडायतनापणैः ।
चैत्यध्वजपताकाभिर्युक्तां विद्रुमवेदिभिः ॥१६॥

sabhā-catvara-rathyābhir
ākrīḍāyatanāpaṇaiḥ
caitya-dhvaja-patākābhir
yuktāṁ vidruma-vedibhiḥ

sabhā—assembly houses; *catvara*—squares; *rathyābhiḥ*—by streets; *ākrīḍa-āyatana*—gambling houses; *āpaṇaiḥ*—by shops; *caitya*—resting places; *dhvaja-patākābhiḥ*—with flags and festoons; *yuktām*—decorated; *vidruma*—without trees; *vedibhiḥ*—with platforms.

TRANSLATION

In that city there were many assembly houses, street crossings, streets, restaurants, gambling houses, markets, resting places, flags, festoons and beautiful parks. All these surrounded the city.

PURPORT

In this way the capital is described. In the capital there are assembly houses and many squares, many street crossings, avenues and streets, many gambling places, markets and places of rest, all decorated with flags and festoons. The squares are surrounded with railings and are devoid of trees. The heart of the body can be compared to the assembly house, for the living entity is within the heart along with the Paramātmā, as stated in *Bhagavad-gītā:*

sarvasya cāhaṁ hṛdi sanniviṣṭo
mattaḥ smṛtir jñānam apohanaṁ ca
vedaiś ca sarvair aham eva vedyo
vedānta-kṛd veda-vid eva cāham

"I am seated in everyone's heart, and from Me come remembrance, knowledge and forgetfulness. By all the *Vedas* am I to be known; indeed I am the compiler of *Vedānta,* and I am the knower of the *Vedas.*" (Bg. 15.15)

The heart is the center of all remembrance, forgetfulness and deliberation. In the body the eyes, ears and nose are different places of attraction for sense enjoyment, and the streets for going hither and thither may be compared to different types of air blowing within the body. The yogic process for controlling the air within the body and the different nerves is called *suṣumnā,* the path of liberation. The body is also a resting place because when the living entity becomes fatigued he takes rest within the body. The palms and soles of the feet are compared to flags and festoons.

TEXT 17

पुर्यास्तु बाह्योपवने दिव्यद्रुमलताकुले ।
नदद्विहङ्गालिकुलकोलाहलजलाशये ॥१७॥

puryās tu bāhyopavane
divya-druma-latākule
nadad-vihaṅgāli-kula-
kolāhala-jalāśaye

puryāḥ—of that town; *tu*—then; *bāhya-upavane*—in an outside garden; *divya*—very nice; *druma*—trees; *latā*—creepers; *ākule*—filled with; *nadat*—vibrating; *vihaṅga*—birds; *ali*—bees; *kula*—groups of; *kolāhala*—humming; *jala-āśaye*—with a lake.

TRANSLATION

On the outskirts of that city were many beautiful trees and creepers encircling a nice lake. Also surrounding that lake were many groups of birds and bees that were always chanting and humming.

PURPORT

Since the body is a great city, there must be various arrangements such as lakes and gardens for sense enjoyment. Of the various parts of the body, those which incite sexual impulses are referred to here indirectly. Because the body has genitals, when the living entity attains the right age—be he man or woman—he becomes agitated by the sex impulse. As long as one remains a child, he is not agitated by seeing a beautiful woman. Although the sense organs are present, unless the age is ripe there is no sex impulse. The favorable conditions surrounding the sex impulse are compared here to a garden or a nice solitary park. When one sees the opposite sex, naturally the sex impulse increases. It is said that if a man in a solitary place does not become agitated upon seeing a woman, he is to be considered a *brahmacārī*. But this practice is almost impossible. The sex impulse is so strong that even by seeing, touching or talking, coming into contact with, or even thinking of the opposite sex—even in so many subtle ways—one becomes sexually impelled. Consequently a *brahmacārī* or *sannyāsī* is prohibited to associate with women, especially in a secret place. The *śāstras* enjoin that one should not even talk to a woman in a secret place, even if she happens to be one's own daughter, sister or mother. The sex impulse is so strong that even if one is very learned, he becomes agitated in such circumstances. If this is the case, how can a young man in a nice park remain calm and quiet after seeing a beautiful young woman?

TEXT 18

हिमनिर्झरविप्रुष्मत्कुसुमाकरवायुना ।
चलत्प्रवालविटपनलिनीतटसम्पदि ॥१८॥

hima-nirjhara-vipruṣmat-
kusumākara-vāyunā
calat-pravāla-viṭapa-
nalinī-taṭa-sampadi

hima-nirjhara—from the icy mountain waterfall; *vipruṣ-mat*—carrying particles of water; *kusumākara*—springtime; *vāyunā*—by the air; *calat*—moving; *pravāla*—branches; *viṭapa*—trees; *nalinī-taṭa*—on the bank of the lake with lotus flowers; *sampadi*—opulent.

TRANSLATION

The branches of the trees standing on the bank of the lake received particles of water carried by the spring air from the falls coming down from the icy mountain.

PURPORT

In this verse the word *hima-nirjhara* is particularly significant. The waterfall represents a kind of liquid humor or *rasa* (relationship). In the body there are different types of humor, *rasa* or mellow. The supreme mellow (relationship) is called the sexual mellow (*ādi-rasa*). When this *ādi-rasa* or sex desire comes in contact with the spring air moved by Cupid, it becomes agitated. In other words, all these are representations of *rūpa, rasa, gandha, śabda* and *sparśa.* The wind is *sparśa,* or touch. The waterfall is *rasa,* or taste. The spring air (*kusumākara*) is smell. All these varieties of enjoyment make life very pleasing, and thus we become captivated by material existence.

TEXT 19

नानारण्यमृगव्रातैरनाबाधे मुनिव्रतैः ।
आहूतं मन्यते पान्थो यत्र कोकिलकूजितैः ॥१९॥

nānāraṇya-mṛga-vrātair
anābādhe muni-vrataiḥ
āhūtaṁ manyate pāntho
yatra kokila-kūjitaiḥ

nānā—various; *araṇya*—forest; *mṛga*—animals; *vrātaiḥ*—with groups; *anābādhe*—in the matter of nonviolence; *muni-vrataiḥ*—like the great sages; *āhūtam*—as if invited; *manyate*—thinks; *pānthaḥ*—passenger; *yatra*—where; *kokila*—of cuckoos; *kūjitaiḥ*—by the cooing.

TRANSLATION

In such an atmosphere even the animals of the forest became nonviolent and nonenvious like great sages. Consequently the animals did not attack anyone. Over and above everything was the cooing of the cuckoos. Any passenger passing along that path was invited by that atmosphere to take rest in that nice garden.

PURPORT

A peaceful family with wife and children is compared to the peaceful atmosphere of the forest. Children are compared to nonviolent animals. Sometimes, however, wives and children are called *svajanākhya-dasyu,* burglars in the name of kinsmen. A man earns his livelihood with hard labor, but the result is that he is plundered by his wife and children exactly as a person in a forest is attacked by some thieves and burglars who take his money. Nonetheless in family life the turmoil of wife and children appears to be like the cooing of the cuckoos in the garden of family life. Being invited by such an atmosphere, the person who is passing through such a blissful family life desires to have his family with him at all costs.

TEXT 20

यदृच्छयाऽऽगतां तत्र ददर्श प्रमदोत्तमाम् ।
भृत्यैर्दशभिरायान्तीमेकैकशतनायकैः ॥२०॥

yadṛcchayāgatāṁ tatra
dadarśa pramadottamām
bhṛtyair daśabhir āyāntīm
ekaika-śata-nāyakaiḥ

yadṛcchayā—all of a sudden, without engagement; *āgatām*—arrived; *tatra*—there; *dadarśa*—he saw; *pramadā*—one woman; *uttamām*—very beautiful;

bhṛtyaiḥ—surrounded by servants; *daśabhiḥ*—ten in number; *āyāntīm*—coming forward; *eka-eka*—each one of them; *śata*—of hundreds; *nāyakaiḥ*—the leaders.

TRANSLATION

While wandering here and there in that wonderful garden, King Purañjana suddenly came in contact with a very beautiful woman who was walking there without any engagement. She had ten servants with her, and each servant had hundreds of wives accompanying him.

PURPORT

The body has already been compared to a beautiful garden. During youth the sex impulse is awakened, and the intelligence, according to one's imagination, is prone to contact the opposite sex. In youth a man or woman is in search of the opposite sex by intelligence or imagination, if not directly. The intelligence influences the mind, and the mind controls the ten senses. Five of these senses gather knowledge, and five work directly. Each sense has many desires to be fulfilled. This is the position of the body and the owner of the body, *purañjana,* who is within the body.

TEXT 21

पञ्चशीर्षाहिना गुप्तां प्रतीहारेण सर्वतः ।
अन्वेषमाणामृषभमप्रौढां कामरूपिणीम् ॥२१॥

pañca-śīrṣāhinā guptāṁ
pratīhāreṇa sarvataḥ
anveṣamāṇām ṛṣabham
aprauḍhāṁ kāma-rūpiṇīm

pañca—five; *śīrṣa*—heads; *ahinā*—by a snake; *guptām*—protected; *pratīhāreṇa*—by a bodyguard; *sarvataḥ*—all around; *anveṣamāṇām*—one who is searching after; *ṛṣabham*—a husband; *aprauḍhām*—not very old; *kāma-rūpiṇīm*—very attractive to fulfill lusty desires.

TRANSLATION

The woman was protected on all sides by a five-hooded snake. She was very beautiful and young, and she appeared very anxious to find a suitable husband.

PURPORT

The vital force of a living entity includes the five kinds of air working within the body, which are known as *prāṇa, apāna, vyāna, samāna,* and *udāna.* The vital force is compared to a serpent because a serpent can live by simply drinking air. The vital force carried by the air is described as the *pratīhāra,* or the bodyguard. Without the vital force one cannot live for a moment. Indeed, all the senses are working under the protection of the vital force.

The woman, who represents intelligence, was searching after a husband. This indicates that intelligence cannot act without consciousness. A beautiful woman is useless unless protected by the proper husband. Intelligence must always be very fresh; therefore the word *apraudha* (very young) is used here. Material enjoyment means utilizing the intelligence for the sake of *rūpa, rasa, gandha, śabda* and *sparśa,* or form, taste, smell, sound and touch.

TEXT 22

सुनासां सुदतीं बालां सुकपोलां वराननाम् ।
समविन्यस्तकर्णाभ्यां बिभ्रतीं कुण्डलश्रियम् ॥२२॥

sunāsāṁ sudatīṁ bālāṁ
sukapolāṁ varānanām
sama-vinyasta-karṇābhyāṁ
bibhratīṁ kuṇḍala-śriyam

su-nāsām—very beautiful nose; *su-datīm*—very beautiful teeth; *bālām*—the young woman; *su-kapolām*—nice forehead; *vara-ānanām*—beautiful face; *sama*—equally; *vinyasta*—arranged; *karṇābhyām*—both ears; *bibhratīm*—dazzling; *kuṇḍala-śriyam*—having beautiful earrings.

TRANSLATION

The woman's nose, teeth and forehead were all very beautiful. Her ears were equally very beautiful and were bedecked with dazzling earrings.

PURPORT

The body of intelligence enjoys the objects of sense gratification that cover it, such as smell, vision and hearing. The word *sunāsām* (beautiful nose) indicates the organ for acquiring knowledge by smell. Similarly, the mouth is the instrument for acquiring knowledge by taste, for by chewing an object and touching it with the tongue we can understand its taste. The word *sukapolām* (nice forehead) indicates a clear brain capable of understanding things as they are. By intelligence one can set things in order. The earrings set upon the two ears are placed there by the work of the intelligence. Thus the ways of acquiring knowledge are described metaphorically.

TEXT 23

पिशङ्गनीवीं सुश्रोणीं श्यामां कनकमेखलाम् ।
पद्भ्यां क्वणद्भ्यां चलन्तीं नूपुरैर्देवतामिव ॥२३॥

piśaṅga-nīvīṁ suśroṇīṁ
śyāmāṁ kanaka-mekhalām
padbhyāṁ kvaṇadbhyāṁ calantīṁ
nūpurair devatām iva

piśaṅga—yellow; *nīvīm*—garment; *su-śroṇīm*—beautiful waist; *śyāmām*—blackish; *kanaka*—golden; *mekhalām*—belt; *padbhyām*—with the feet; *kvaṇadbhyām*—tinkling; *calantīm*—walking; *nūpuraiḥ*—with ankle bells; *devatām*—a denizen of the heavens; *iva*—like.

TRANSLATION

The waist and hips of the woman were very beautiful. She was dressed in a yellow sari with a golden belt. While she walked, her ankle bells rang. She appeared exactly like a denizen of the heavens.

PURPORT

This verse expresses the joyfulness of the mind upon seeing a woman with raised hips and breasts dressed in an attractive sari and bedecked with ornaments.

TEXT 24

स्तनौ व्यञ्जितकैशोरौ समवृत्तौ निरन्तरौ ।
वस्त्रान्तेन निगूहन्तीं व्रीडया गजगामिनीम् ॥२४॥

stanau vyañjita-kaiśorau
sama-vṛttau nirantarau

vastrāntena nigūhantīṁ
vrīḍayā gaja-gāminīm

stanau—breasts; *vyañjita*—indicating; *kaiśorau*—new youth; *sama-vṛttau*—equally round; *nirantarau*—fixed close, side by side; *vastra-antena*—by the end of the sari; *nigūhantīm*—trying to cover; *vrīḍayā*—out of shyness; *gaja-gāminīm*—walking just like a great elephant.

TRANSLATION

With the end of her sari the woman was trying to cover her breasts, which were equally round and well-placed side by side. She again and again tried to cover them out of shyness while she walked exactly like a great elephant.

PURPORT

The two breasts represent attachment and envy. The symptoms of *rāga* and *dveṣa* (attachment and envy) are described in *Bhagavad-gītā:*

indriyasyendriyasyārthe
rāga-dveṣau vyavasthitau
tayor na vaśam āgacchet
tau hy asya paripanthinau

"Attraction and repulsion for sense objects are felt by embodied beings, but one should not fall under the control of senses and sense objects because they are stumbling blocks on the path of self-realization." (Bg. 3.34)

These representatives of attachment and envy are very much unfavorable for advancement in spiritual life. One should not be attracted by the breasts of young women. The great saint Śaṅkarācārya has described the breasts of women, especially young women, as nothing but a combination of muscles and blood, so one should not be attracted by the illusory energy of raised breasts with nipples. They are agents of *māyā* meant to victimize the opposite sex. Because the breasts are equally attractive, they are described as *sama-vṛttau.* The sex impulse remains in an old man's heart also, even up to the point of death. To be rid of such agitation, one must be very much advanced in spiritual consciousness, like Yāmunācārya, who said:

yadavadhi mama cetaḥ kṛṣṇa-pādāravinde
nava-nava-rasa-dhāmany udyataṁ rantum āsīt
tadavadhi bata nārī-saṅgame smaryamāṇe
bhavati mukha-vikāraḥ suṣṭhu niṣṭhīvanaṁ ca

"Since I have been engaged in the transcendental loving service of Kṛṣṇa, realizing ever new pleasure in Him, whenever I think of sex pleasure, I spit at the thought, and my lips curl with distaste."

When one is spiritually advanced he can no longer be attracted by the lumps of flesh and blood which are the breasts of young women. The word *nirantarau* is significant because although the breasts are situated in different locations, the action is the same. We should not make any distinction between attachment and envy. As described in *Bhagavad-gītā*, they are both products of *rajo-guṇa:*

śrī bhagavān uvāca
kāma eṣa krodha eṣa
rajoguṇa-samudbhavaḥ
mahāśano mahā-pāpmā
viddhy enam iha vairiṇam

"The Blessed Lord said: It is lust only, Arjuna, which is born of contact with the material modes of passion and later transformed into wrath, and which is the all-devouring, sinful enemy of this world." (Bg. 3.37)

The word *nigūhantīm* (trying to cover) indicates that even if one is tainted by *kāma, lobha, krodha,* etc., they can be transfigured by Kṛṣṇa consciousness. In other words, one can utilize *kāma* (lust) for serving Kṛṣṇa. Being impelled by lust, an ordinary worker will work hard day and night; similarly a devotee can work hard day and night to satisfy Kṛṣṇa. Just as *karmīs* are working hard to satisfy *kāma-krodha,* a devotee should work in the same way to satisfy Kṛṣṇa. Similarly, *krodha* (anger) can also be used in the service of Kṛṣṇa when it is applied to the nondevotee demons. Hanumānjī applied his anger in this way. He was a great devotee of Lord Rāmacandra, and he utilized his anger to set fire to the kingdom of Rāvaṇa, a nondevotee demon. Thus *kāma* (lust) can be utilized to satisfy Kṛṣṇa, and *krodha* (anger) can be utilized to punish the demons. When both are used for Kṛṣṇa's service, they lose their material significance and become spiritually important.

TEXT 25

तामाह ललितं वीरः सव्रीडस्मितशोभनाम् ।
स्निग्धेनापाङ्गपुङ्खेन स्पृष्टः प्रेमोद्भ्रमद्भ्रुवा ॥२५॥

tām āha lalitaṁ vīraḥ
savrīḍa-smita-śobhanām

snigdhenāpāṅga-puṅkhena
spṛṣṭaḥ premodbhramad-bhruvā

tām—unto her; *āha*—addressed; *lalitam*—very gently; *vīraḥ*—the hero; *sa-vrīḍa*—with shyness; *smita*—smiling; *śobhanām*—very beautiful; *snigdhena*—by sex desire; *apāṅga-puṅkhena*—by the arrow of glancing; *spṛṣṭaḥ*—thus pierced; *prema-udbhramat*—exciting love; *bhruvā*—by the eyebrows.

TRANSLATION

Purañjana, the hero, became attracted by the eyebrows and smiling face of the very beautiful girl and was immediately pierced by the arrows of her lusty desires. When she smiled shyly, she looked very beautiful to Purañjana, who, although a hero, could not refrain from addressing her.

PURPORT

Every living entity is a hero in two ways. When he is a victim of the illusory energy, he works as a great hero in the material world, as a great leader, politician, businessman, industrialist, etc., and his heroic activities contribute to the material advancement of civilization. One can also become a hero by being master of the senses, a *gosvāmī*. Material activities are false heroic activities, whereas restraining the senses from material engagement is great heroism. However great a hero one may be in the material world, he can be immediately conquered by the lumps of flesh and blood known as the breasts of women. In the history of material activities there are many examples, like the Roman hero Antony, who became captivated by the beauty of Cleopatra. Similarly, a great hero in India named Bajirao became a victim of a woman during the time of Mahārāṣṭrian politics, and he was defeated. From his story we understand that formerly politicians used to employ beautiful girls who were trained as *viṣa-kanyā*. These girls had poison injected into their bodies from the beginning of their lives so that in due course of time they would become so immune to the poison and so poisonous themselves that simply by kissing a person they could kill him. Thus these poisonous girls were engaged to see an enemy and kill him with a kiss. Thus there are many instances in human history of heros who have been curbed simply by women. Being part and parcel of Kṛṣṇa, the living entity is certainly a great hero, but due to his own weakness he becomes attracted to the material features.

kṛṣṇa-bahirmukha hañā bhoga-vāñchā kare
nikaṭa-stha māyā tāre jāpaṭiyā dhare

It is said in the *Prema-vivarta* that when a living entity wants to enjoy material nature, he is immediately victimized by the material energy. A living entity is not forced to come into the material world. He makes his own choice, being attracted by beautiful women. Every living entity has the freedom to be attracted by material nature or to stand as a hero and resist that attraction. It is simply a question of the living entity's being attracted or not being attracted. There is no question of his being forced to come into contact with material energy. One who can keep himself steady and resist the attraction of material nature is certainly a hero and deserves to be called a *gosvāmī.* Unless one is master of the senses, he cannot become a *gosvāmī.* The living entity can take one of two positions in this world. He may become a servant of his senses or he may become master of them. By becoming a servant of the senses, one becomes a great material hero, and by becoming master of the senses, he becomes a *gosvāmī,* or spiritual hero.

TEXT 26

का त्वं कञ्जपलाशाक्षि कस्यासीह कुतः सति ।
इमामुप पुरीं भीरु किं चिकीर्षसि शंस मे ॥२६॥

kā tvaṁ kañja-palāśākṣi
kasyāsīha kutaḥ sati
imām upa purīṁ bhīru
kiṁ cikīrṣasi śaṁsa me

kā—who; *tvam*—you; *kañja-palāśa*—like the petals of the lotus; *akṣi*—eyes; *kasya*—whose; *asi*—you are; *iha*—here; *kutaḥ*—wherefrom; *sati*—O chaste one; *imām*—this; *upa*—near; *purīm*—city; *bhīru*—O timid one; *kim*—what; *cikīrṣasi*—you are trying to do; *śaṁsa*—kindly explain; *me*—unto me.

TRANSLATION

My dear lotus-eyed, kindly explain to me where you are coming from, who you are, and whose daughter you are. You appear very chaste. What is the purpose of your coming here? What are you trying to do? Please explain all these things to me.

PURPORT

The first aphorism in the *Vedānta-sūtra* is *athāto brahma-jijñāsā.* In the human form of life one should put many questions to himself and to his intelligence. In the various forms of life lower than human life the intelligence does not go beyond the range of life's primary necessities—namely, eating, sleeping, mating and defending. Dogs, cats and tigers are always busy trying to find something to eat or a place to sleep, trying to defend and have sexual intercourse successfully. In the human form of life, however, one should be intelligent enough to ask what he is, why he has come into the world, what his duty is, who is the supreme controller, what is the difference between dull matter and the living entity, etc. There are so many questions, and the person who is actually intelligent should simply inquire about the supreme source of everything: *athāto brahma-jijñāsā.* A living entity is always connected with a certain amount of intelligence, but in the human form of life the living entity must inquire about his spiritual identity. This is real human intelligence. It is said that one who is simply conscious of the body is no better than an animal, even though he be in the human form. In *Bhagavad-gītā* Śrī Kṛṣṇa says:

sarvasya cāhaṁ hṛdi sanniviṣṭo
mattaḥ smṛtir jñānam apohanaṁ ca
vedaiś ca sarvair aham eva vedyo
vedānta-kṛd veda-vid eva cāham

"I am seated in everyone's heart, and from Me come remembrance, knowledge and forgetfulness. By all the *Vedas* am I to be known; indeed I am the compiler of *Vedānta* and I am the knower of the *Vedas.*" (Bg. 15.15)

In the animal form the living entity is completely forgetful of his relationship with God. This is called *apohanam,* or forgetfulness. In the human form of life, however, consciousness is more greatly developed, and consequently the human being has a chance to understand his relationship with God. In the human form one should utilize his intelligence by asking all these questions, just as Purañjana, the living entity, is asking the unknown girl where she has come from, what her business is, why she is present, etc. These are inquiries about *ātma-tattva*—self-realization. The conclusion is that unless a living entity is inquisitive about self-realization he is nothing but an animal.

TEXT 27

क एतेऽनुपथा ये त एकादश महाभटाः ।
एता वा ललनाः सुभ्रु कोऽयं तेऽहिः पुरःसरः ॥२७॥

ka ete 'nupathā ye ta
ekādaśa mahā-bhaṭāḥ

etā vā lalanāḥ subhru
ko 'yaṁ te 'hiḥ puraḥ-saraḥ

ke—who; *ete*—all these; *anupathāḥ*—followers; *ye*—they who; *te*—your; *ekādaśa*—eleven; *mahā-bhaṭāḥ*—very powerful bodyguards; *etāḥ*—all of these; *vā*—also; *lalanāḥ*—women; *su-bhru*—O beautiful-eyed one; *kaḥ*—who; *ayam*—this; *te*—your; *ahiḥ*—the snake; *puraḥ*—in front; *saraḥ*—going.

TRANSLATION

My dear lotus-eyed, who are those eleven strong bodyguards with you, and who are those ten specific servants? Who are those women following the ten servants, and who is the snake that is preceding you?

PURPORT

The ten strong servants of the mind are the five working senses and the five knowledge-gathering senses. All these ten senses work under the aegis of the mind. The mind and the ten senses combine to become eleven strong bodyguards. The hundreds of women under the jurisdiction of the senses are addressed here as *lalanāḥ*. The mind works under the intelligence, and under the mind are the ten senses, and under the ten senses are innumerable desires to be fulfilled. All these, however, depend on the vital life force, which is here represented by the snake. As long as the vital life force is there, the mind works, and under the mind the senses work, and the senses give rise to so many material desires. Actually the living entity, known as *purañjana,* is embarrassed by so much paraphernalia. All this paraphernalia simply constitutes different sources of anxiety, but one who is surrendered unto the Supreme Personality of Godhead, who leaves all business to Him, is freed from such anxieties. Therefore Prahlāda Mahārāja advises a person who has taken to the materialistic way of life, which is never permanent but always temporary, to take shelter of the Supreme Personality of Godhead and leave aside all his so-called responsibilities in order to get free from all anxieties.

TEXT 28

त्वं ह्रीर्भवान्यस्यथ वाग्रमा पतिं
विचिन्वती किं मुनिवद्रहो वने ।
त्वदङ्घ्रिकामाप्तसमस्तकामं
क्व पद्मकोशः पतितः कराग्रात् ॥२८॥

tvaṁ hrīr bhavāny asy atha vāg ramā patiṁ
vicinvatī kiṁ munivad raho vane
tvad-aṅghri-kāmāpta-samasta-kāmaṁ
kva padma-kośaḥ patitaḥ karāgrāt

tvam—you; *hrīḥ*—shyness; *bhavānī*—the wife of Lord Śiva; *asi*—are; *atha*—rather; *vāk*—Sarasvatī, the goddess of learning; *ramā*—the goddess of fortune; *patim*—husband; *vicinvatī*—searching after, thinking of; *kim*—are you; *muni-vat*—like a sage; *rahaḥ*—in this lonely place; *vane*—in the forest; *tvat-aṅghri*—your feet; *kāma*—desiring; *āpta*—achieved; *samasta*—all; *kāmam*—desirable things; *kva*—where is; *padma-kośaḥ*—the lotus flower; *patitaḥ*—fallen; *kara*—of the hand; *agrāt*—from the front portion, or palm.

TRANSLATION

My dear beautiful girl, you are exactly like the goddess of fortune, or the wife of Lord Śiva, or the goddess of learning, the wife of Lord Brahmā. Although you must be one of them, I see that you are loitering in this forest. Indeed, you are as silent as the great sages. Is it that you are searching after your own husband? Whoever your husband may be, simply by understanding that you are so faithful to him, he will come to possess all opulences. I think you must be the goddess of fortune, but I do not see the lotus flower in your hand. Therefore I am asking you where you have thrown that lotus.

PURPORT

Everyone thinks that his intelligence is perfect. Sometimes one employs his intelligence in the worship of Umā, the wife of Lord Śiva, in order to obtain a beautiful wife. Sometimes, when one wants to become as learned as Lord Brahmā, he employs his intelligence in the worship of the goddess of learning, Sarasvatī. Sometimes, when one wishes to become as opulent as Lord Viṣṇu, he worships the goddess of fortune, Lakṣmī. In this verse all these inquiries are made by King Purañjana, the living entity who is bewildered and does not know how to employ his intelligence. Intelligence should be employed in the service of the Supreme Personality of Godhead. As soon as one uses his intelligence in this way, the goddess of fortune automatically becomes favorable to him. The goddess of fortune, Lakṣmī, never remains without her husband, Lord Viṣṇu. Consequently, when one worships Lord Viṣṇu he automatically obtains the favor of the goddess of fortune. One should not, like Rāvaṇa, worship the goddess of fortune alone, for she cannot remain long without her husband. Thus her other name is

Cañcalā, or restless. In this verse it is clear that Purañjana is representing our intelligence while he is talking with the girl. He not only appreciated the shyness of the girl, but he actually became more and more attracted by that shyness. He was actually thinking of becoming her husband and consequently was asking her whether she was thinking of her prospective husband or whether she was married. This is an example of *bhoga-icchā*—the desire for enjoyment. One who is attracted by such desires becomes conditioned in this material world, and one who is not so attracted attains liberation. King Purañjana was appreciating the beauty of the girl as if she were the goddess of fortune, but at the same time he was careful to understand that the goddess of fortune cannot be enjoyed by anyone except Lord Viṣṇu. Since he doubted whether the girl was the goddess of fortune, he inquired about the lotus flower she was not holding. The material world is also the goddess of fortune because the material energy works under the direction of Lord Viṣṇu. As stated in *Bhagavad-gītā:*

mayādhyakṣeṇa prakṛtiḥ
sūyate sa-carācaram
hetunānena kaunteya
jagad viparivartate

"This material nature is working under My direction, O son of Kuntī, and it is producing all moving and unmoving beings. By its rule this manifestation is created and annihilated again and again." (Bg. 9.10)

The material world cannot be enjoyed by any living entity. If one so desires to enjoy it, he immediately becomes a demon like Rāvaṇa, Hiraṇyakaśipu or Kaṁsa. Because Rāvaṇa wanted to enjoy the goddess of fortune, Sītādevī, he was vanquished with all his family, wealth and opulence. One can, however, enjoy that *māyā* bestowed upon the living entity by Lord Viṣṇu. The satisfaction of one's senses and desires means enjoying *māyā,* not the goddess of fortune.

TEXT 29

नासां वरोर्वन्यतमा भुविस्पृक्
पुरीमिमां वीरवरेण साकम् ।
अर्हस्यलङ्कर्तुमदभ्रकर्मणा
लोकं परं श्रीरिव यज्ञपुंसा ॥२९॥

nāsāṁ varorv anyatamā bhuvi-spṛk
purīm imāṁ vīra-vareṇa sākam
arhasy alaṅkartum adabhra-karmaṇā
lokaṁ paraṁ śrīr iva yajña-puṁsā

na—not; *āsām*—of these; *varoru*—O most fortunate one; *anyatamā*—anyone; *bhuvi-spṛk*—touching the ground; *purīm*—city; *imām*—this; *vīra-vareṇa*—the great hero; *sākam*—along with; *arhasi*—you deserve; *alaṅkartum*—to decorate; *adabhra*—glorious; *karmaṇā*—whose activities; *lokam*—world; *param*—transcendental; *śrīḥ*—the goddess of fortune; *iva*—like; *yajña-puṁsā*—with the enjoyer of all *yajñas.*

TRANSLATION

O greatly fortunate one, it appears that you are none of the women I have mentioned because I see that your feet are touching the ground. But if you are some woman of this planet, you can, like the goddess of fortune who, accompanied by Lord Viṣṇu, increases the beauty of the Vaikuṇṭha planets, also increase the beauty of this city by associating with me. You should understand that I am a great hero and a very powerful king on this planet.

PURPORT

There is a difference between demoniac mentality and devotional mentality. Devotees know perfectly well that the goddess of fortune, who is the constant companion of Viṣṇu or Nārāyaṇa, cannot be enjoyed by a living entity. This higher sense of understanding is called Kṛṣṇa consciousness. Nonetheless, everyone wants to become happy by imitating the prosperity of Nārāyaṇa. In this verse Purañjana states that the girl appears to be an ordinary woman. However, since he is attracted by her, he requests that she become as happy as the goddess of fortune by associating with him. Thus he introduces himself as a great king with great influence so that she might accept him as her husband and be as happy as the goddess of fortune. To desire to enjoy this material world as a subordinate of the Supreme Personality of Godhead is godly. The demons, however, want to enjoy this material world without considering the Supreme Personality of Godhead. This is the difference between a demon and a demigod.

The word *bhuvi-spṛk* mentioned in this verse is very significant. When the demigods sometimes come to this planet, they do not touch the ground. Purañjana could understand that this girl did not belong to the transcendental world or the higher planetary system because her feet were touching the ground. Since every woman in this world wants her husband to be very influential, rich and powerful, Purañjana, to seduce the girl, introduced himself as such a personality. In the material world, whether one be a man or a woman, one wants to enjoy. A man wants to enjoy a beautiful woman, and a woman wants to enjoy a powerful, opulent man. Every living entity who possesses such material desires is called *puruṣa,* an enjoyer. Superficially it appears that the woman is the enjoyed and the man is the enjoyer, but internally everyone is an enjoyer. Consequently everything in this material world is called *māyā.*

TEXT 30

यदेष मापाङ्गविखण्डितेन्द्रियं
सव्रीडभावस्मितविभ्रमद्भ्रुवा ।
त्वयोपसृष्टो भगवान्मनोभवः
प्रबाधतेऽथानुगृहाण शोभने ॥३०॥

yad eṣa māpāṅga-vikhaṇḍitendriyaṁ
savrīḍa-bhāva-smita-vibhramad-bhruvā
tvayopasṛṣṭo bhagavān mano-bhavaḥ
prabādhate 'thānugṛhāṇa śobhane

yat—because; *eṣaḥ*—this; *mā*—me; *apāṅga*—by your glances; *vikhaṇḍita*—agitated; *indriyam*—whose senses or mind; *sa-vrīḍa*—with shyness; *bhāva*—affection; *smita*—smiling; *vibhramat*—bewildering; *bhruvā*—with eyebrows; *tvayā*—by you; *upasṛṣṭaḥ*—being influenced; *bhagavān*—the most powerful; *manaḥ-bhavaḥ*—Cupid; *prabādhate*—is harassing; *atha*—therefore; *anugṛhāṇa*—be merciful; *śobhane*—O very beautiful one.

TRANSLATION

Certainly your glancing upon me today has very much agitated my mind. Your smile, which is full of shyness but at the same time lusty, is agitating the most powerful cupid within me. Therefore, O most beautiful, I ask you to be merciful upon me.

PURPORT

Everyone has lusty desires within, and as soon as one is agitated by the movement of a beautiful woman's eyebrows, the cupid within immediately throws his arrow at the heart. Thus one is quickly conquered by the eyebrows of a beautiful woman. When one is agitated by lusty desires, his senses are attracted by all kinds of *viṣaya* (enjoyable things like sound, touch, form, smell and taste). These attractive sense objects oblige one to come under the control of a woman. In this way the conditional life of a living entity begins. Conditional life means being under the control of a woman, and certainly the living entity is always at the mercy of a woman or a man. Thus living entities live in bondage to one another, and thus they continue this conditional material life illusioned by *māyā*.

TEXT 31

त्वदाननं सुभ्रु सुतारलोचनं
व्यालम्बिनीलालकवृन्दसंवृतम् ।
उन्नीय मे दर्शय वल्गुवाचकं
यद्व्रीडया नाभिमुखं शुचिस्मिते ॥३१॥

tvad-ānanaṁ subhru sutāra-locanaṁ
vyālambi-nīlālaka-vṛnda-saṁvṛtam
unnīya me darśaya valgu-vācakaṁ
yad vrīḍayā nābhimukhaṁ śuci-smite

tvat—your; *ānanam*—face; *su-bhru*—having nice eyebrows; *su-tāra*—with nice pupils; *locanam*—eyes; *vyālambi*—scattered; *nīla*—bluish; *alaka-vṛnda*—by locks of hair; *saṁvṛtam*—surrounded; *unnīya*—having raised; *me*—unto me; *darśaya*—show; *valgu-vācakam*—having words very sweet to hear; *yat*—which face; *vrīḍayā*—by shyness; *na*—not; *abhimukham*—face to face; *śuci-smite*—O woman with lovely smiles.

TRANSLATION

My dear girl, your face is so beautiful with your nice eyebrows and eyes and with your bluish hair scattered about. In addition, very sweet sounds are coming from your mouth. Nonetheless you are so covered with shyness that you do not see me face to face. I therefore request you, my dear girl, to smile and kindly raise your head to see me.

PURPORT

Such a speech is typical of a living entity attracted by the opposite sex. This is called bewilderment occasioned by becoming conditioned by material nature. When thus attracted by the beauty of the material energy, one becomes very eager to enjoy. This is elaborately described in this instance of Purañjana's becoming attracted by the beautiful woman. In conditional life the living entity is attracted by a face, eyebrows, or eyes, a voice or anything. In short, everything becomes attractive. When a man or a woman is attracted by the opposite sex, it doesn't matter whether the opposite sex is beautiful or not. The lover sees everything beautiful in the face of the beloved and thus becomes attracted. This attraction causes the living entity to fall down in this material world. This is described in *Bhagavad-gītā:*

icchā-dveṣa-samutthena
dvandva-mohena bhārata
sarva-bhūtāni sammohaṁ
sarge yānti parantapa

"O scion of Bharata [Arjuna], O conquerer of the foe, all living entities are born into delusion, overcome by the dualities of desire and hate." (Bg. 7.27)

This condition of life is called *avidyā.* Opposed to this *avidyā* is real knowledge. *Śrī Īśopaniṣad* distinguishes between *vidyā* and *avidyā,* knowledge and ignorance. By *avidyā* (ignorance) one becomes conditioned, and by *vidyā* (knowledge) one becomes liberated. Purañjana admits herein that he is attracted by *avidyā.* Now he wishes to see the complete feature of *avidyā* and so requests the girl to raise her head so that he can see her face to face. He thus wishes to see the various features that make *avidyā* attractive.

TEXT 32

नारद उवाच

इत्थं पुरञ्जनं नारी याचमानमधीरवत् ।
अभ्यनन्दत तं वीरं हसन्ती वीर मोहिता ॥३२॥

nārada uvāca
itthaṁ purañjanaṁ nārī
yācamānam adhīravat
abhyanandata taṁ vīraṁ
hasantī vīra mohitā

nāradaḥ uvāca—the great sage Nārada continued to speak; *ittham*—upon this; *purañjanam*—unto Purañjana; *nārī*—the woman; *yācamānam*—begging; *adhīra-vat*—being too impatient; *abhyanandata*—she addressed; *tam*—him; *vīram*—the hero; *hasantī*—smiling; *vīra*—O hero; *mohitā*—being attracted by him.

TRANSLATION

Nārada continued: My dear King, when Purañjana became so attracted and impatient to touch the girl and enjoy her, the girl also became attracted by his words and accepted his request by smiling. By this time she was certainly attracted by the King.

PURPORT

By this incident we can understand that when a man is aggressive and begins to woo a woman, the woman becomes attracted to the man. This process is described in the *Bhāgavatam* as *puṁsaḥ striyā mithunī-bhāvam etam* (*Bhāg.* 5.5.8). This attraction is enacted on the platform of sexual life. Thus the sex impulse is the platform of material engagement. This conditional life, the platform of material sense enjoyment, is the cause of forgetfulness of spiritual life. In this way a living entity's original Kṛṣṇa consciousness becomes covered or converted into material consciousness. Thus one engages in the business of sense gratification.

TEXT 33

न विदाम वयं सम्यक्कर्तारं पुरुषर्षभ ।
आत्मनश्च परस्यापि गोत्रं नाम च यत्कृतम् ॥३३॥

na vidāma vayaṁ samyak
kartāraṁ puruṣarṣabha
ātmanaś ca parasyāpi
gotraṁ nāma ca yat-kṛtam

na—do not; *vidāma*—know; *vayam*—I; *samyak*—perfectly; *kartāram*—maker; *puruṣa-ṛṣabha*—O best of human beings; *ātmanaḥ*—of myself; *ca*—and; *parasya*—of others; *api*—also; *gotram*—family history; *nāma*—name; *ca*—and; *yat-kṛtam*—which has been made by whom.

TRANSLATION

The girl said: O best of human beings, I do not know who has begotten me. I cannot speak to you perfectly about this. Nor do I know the names or the origin of the associates with me.

PURPORT

The living entity is ignorant of his origin. He does not know why this material world was created, why others are working in this material world, and what the ultimate source of this manifestation is. No one knows the answers to these questions, and this is called ignorance. By researching into the origin of life, important scientists are finding some chemical compositions or cellular combinations, but actually no one knows the original source of life within this material world. The phrase *brahma-jijñāsā* is used to indicate an inquisitiveness to know the original source of our existence in this material world. No philosopher, scientist or politician actually knows wherefrom we have come, why we are here struggling so hard for existence and where we will go. Generally people are of the opinion that we are all here accidently and that as soon as these bodies are finished all our dramatic activities will be finished and we will become zero. Such scientists and philosophers are impersonalists and voidists. In this verse the girl is expressing the actual position of the living entity. She cannot tell Purañjana her father's name because she does not know from where she has come. Nor does she know why she is present in that place. She frankly said that she did not know anything about all this. This is the position of the living entity in the material world. There are so many scientists, philosophers and big leaders, but they do not know wherefrom they have come, nor do they know why they are busy within this material world to obtain a position of so-called happiness. In this material world we have many nice facilities for living, but we are so foolish that we do not ask who has made this world habitable for us and has arranged it so nicely. Everything is functioning in order, but people foolishly think that they are produced by chance in this material world and that after death they will become zero. They think that this beautiful place of habitation will automatically remain.

TEXT 34

इहाद्य सन्तमात्मानं विदाम न ततः परम् ।
येनेयं निर्मिता वीर पुरी शरणमात्मनः ॥३४॥

ihādya santam ātmānaṁ
vidāma na tataḥ param
yeneyaṁ nirmitā vīra
purī śaraṇam ātmanaḥ

iha—here; *adya*—today; *santam*—existing; *ātmānam*—living entities; *vidāma*—that much we know; *na*—not; *tataḥ param*—beyond that; *yena*—

by whom; *iyam*—this; *nirmitā*—created; *vīra*—O great hero; *purī*—city; *śaraṇam*—resting place; *ātmanaḥ*—of all living entities.

TRANSLATION

O great hero, we only know that we are existing in this place. We do not know what will come after. Indeed, we are so foolish that we do not care to understand who has created this beautiful place for our residence.

PURPORT

This lack of Kṛṣṇa consciousness is called ignorance. In *Śrīmad-Bhāgavatam* it is called *parābhavas tāvad abodha-jātaḥ* (*Bhāg.* 5.5.5.). Everyone is born ignorant. The *Bhāgavatam* therefore says that we are all born ignorant within this material world. In our ignorance we may create nationalism, philanthropy, internationalism, science, philosophy and so many other things. The basic principle behind all these is ignorance. What then is the value of all this advancement of knowledge if the basic principle is ignorance? Unless a person comes to Kṛṣṇa consciousness, all of his activities are defeated. This human form of life is especially meant to dissipate ignorance, but without understanding how to dissipate ignorance people are planning and building many things. After death, however, all of this is finished.

TEXT 35

एते सखायः सख्यो मे नरा नार्यश्च मानद ।
सुप्तायां मयि जागर्ति नागोऽयं पालयन् पुरीम् ।।३५।।

ete sakhāyaḥ sakhyo me
narā nāryaś ca mānada
suptāyāṁ mayi jāgarti
nāgo 'yaṁ pālayan purīm

ete—all these; *sakhāyaḥ*—male friends; *sakhyaḥ*—female associates; *me*—my; *narāḥ*—men; *nāryaḥ*—women; *ca*—and; *māna-da*—O very respectful one; *suptāyām*—while sleeping; *mayi*—I am; *jāgarti*—keeps awake; *nāgaḥ*—snake; *ayam*—this; *pālayan*—protecting; *purīm*—this city.

TRANSLATION

My dear gentleman, all these men and women with me are known as my friends, and the snake, who always remains awake, protects this city even during my sleeping hours. So much I know. I do not know anything beyond this.

PURPORT

Purañjana inquired from the woman about those eleven men and their wives as well as the snake. The woman gave a brief description of them. She was obviously without full knowledge of her surrounding men and women and the snake. As stated before, the snake is the vital force of the living being. This vital force always remains awake even when the body and the senses become fatigued and do no work. Even in the state of unconsciousness, when we sleep, the snake or the life force remains intact and awake. Consequently we dream when we sleep. When the living entity gives up this material body, the vital force still remains intact and is carried to another material body. That is called transmigration, or change of the body, and we have come to know this process as death. Actually, there is no death. The vital force always exists with the soul, and when the soul is awakened from so-called sleep, he can see his eleven friends, or the active senses and the mind with their various desires (wives). The vital life force remains. Even during our sleeping hours we can understand by virtue of our breathing process that the snake lives by eating the air that passes within this body. Air is exhibited in the form of breathing, and as long as breath is there, one can understand that a sleeping man is alive. Thus even when the gross body is asleep the vital force remains active and alive to protect the body. Thus the snake is described as living and eating air to keep the body fit for life.

TEXT 36

दिष्टयाऽऽगतोऽसि भद्रं ते ग्राम्यान् कामानभीप्ससे
उद्वहिष्यामि तांस्तेऽहं स्वबन्धुभिररिन्दम ॥३६॥

diṣṭyāgato 'si bhadraṁ te
grāmyān kāmān abhīpsase
udvahiṣyāmi tāṁs te 'haṁ
sva-bandhubhir arindama

diṣṭyā—fortunately for me; *āgataḥ asi*—you have come here; *bhadram*—all auspiciousness; *te*—unto you; *grāmyān*—sensual; *kāmān*—desired enjoyable objects; *abhīpsase*—you want to enjoy; *udvahiṣyāmi*—I shall supply; *tān*—all of them; *te*—unto you; *aham*—I; *sva-bandhubhiḥ*—with all my friends; *arindama*—O killer of the enemy.

TRANSLATION

O killer of the enemy, you have somehow or other come here. This is certainly great fortune for me. I wish all auspicious things for you. You

have a great desire to satisfy your senses, and all my friends and I shall try our best in all respects to fulfill your desires.

PURPORT

The living entity comes down into this material world for sense gratification, and his intelligence, represented by the woman, gives him the proper direction by which he can satisfy his senses to their best capacity. In actuality, however, intelligence comes from the Supersoul, or the Supreme Personality of Godhead, and He gives full facility to the living entity who has come down to this material world. As stated in *Bhagavad-gītā:*

vyavasāyātmikā buddhir
ekeha kuru-nandana
bahu-śākhā hy anantāś ca
buddhayo 'vyavasāyinām

"Those who are on this path are resolute in purpose, and their aim is one. O beloved child of the Kurus, the intelligence of those who are irresolute is many-branched." (Bg. 2.41)

When a devotee is advancing toward spiritual realization, his only aim is the service of the Supreme Personality of Godhead. He doesn't care for any other material or spiritual activity. King Purañjana represents the ordinary living entity, and the woman represents the ordinary living entity's intelligence. Combined, the living entity enjoys his material senses, and the intelligence supplies all paraphernalia for his enjoyment. As soon as he enters the human form, the living entity is entrapped by a family tradition, nationality, customs, etc. These are all supplied by the *māyā* of the Supreme Personality of Godhead. Thus the living entity, under the bodily conception of life, utilizes his intelligence to his best capacity in order to satisfy his senses.

TEXT 37

इमां त्वमधितिष्ठस्व पुरीं नवमुखीं विभो ।
मयोपनीतान् गृह्णानः कामभोगान् शतं समाः ॥३७॥

imāṁ tvam adhitiṣṭhasva
purīṁ nava-mukhīṁ vibho
mayopanītān gṛhṇānaḥ
kāma-bhogān śataṁ samāḥ

imām—this; *tvam*—your good self; *adhitiṣṭhasva*—just remain; *purīm*—in the city; *nava-mukhīm*—with nine gates; *vibho*—O my lord; *mayā*—by me; *upanītān*—arranged; *gṛhṇānaḥ*—taking; *kāma-bhogān*—the materials for sense gratification; *śatam*—a hundred; *samāḥ*—years.

TRANSLATION

My dear lord, I have just arranged this city of nine gates for you so that you can have all kinds of sense gratification. You may live here for one hundred years, and everything for your sense gratification will be supplied.

PURPORT

Dharmārtha-kāma-mokṣānāṁ dhārāḥ samprāpti-hetavaḥ. The wife is the cause of all kinds of success in religion, economic development, sense gratification, and ultimately salvation. When one accepts a wife, it is to be understood that he is being helped in his progressive march toward liberation. In the beginning of life a person is trained as a *brahmacārī* and is then allowed to marry a suitable girl and become a householder. If one is thoroughly trained in household life, he finds all facilities for human life—eating, sleeping, mating and defending. Everything is there if it is executed according to regulative principles.

TEXT 38

कं नु त्वदन्यं रमये ह्यरतिज्ञमकोविदम् ।
असम्परायाभिमुखमश्वस्तनविदं पशुम् ॥३८॥

kaṁ nu tvad-anyaṁ ramaye
hy arati-jñam akovidam
asamparāyābhimukham
aśvastana-vidaṁ paśum

kam—unto whom; *nu*—then; *tvat*—than yourself; *anyam*—other; *ramaye*—I shall allow to enjoy; *hi*—certainly; *arati-jñam*—without knowledge of sex enjoyment; *akovidam*—therefore almost foolish; *asamparāya*—without knowledge of the next life; *abhimukham*—looking forward; *aśvastana-vidam*—one who does not know what is happening next; *paśum*—like animals.

TRANSLATION

How can I expect to unite with others who are neither conversant about sex nor capable of knowing how to enjoy life while living or after death?

Such foolish persons are like animals because they do not know the process of sense enjoyment in this life and after death.

PURPORT

Since there are 8,400,000 species of life, there are also many different living conditions. In the lower grades of life (in plant and tree life) there is no system for sexual intercourse. In the upper grades (in the life of birds and bees) there is sex, but the insects and animals do not know how to actually enjoy sex life. In the human form of life, however, there is full knowledge of how to enjoy sex. Indeed, there are many so-called philosophers who give directions on how to enjoy sex life. There is even a science called *kāma-śāstra,* which is the science of sex. In human life there are also such divisions as *brahmacarya, gṛhastha, vānaprastha,* and *sannyāsa.* There is no sex life except in the *gṛhastha* or householder *āśrama.* The *brahmacārī* is not allowed any sex, a *vānaprastha* voluntarily refrains from sex, and the *sannyāsī* is completely renounced. The *karmīs* do not practice *brahmacarya, vānaprastha* or *sannyāsa* life, for they are very much interested in *gṛhastha* life. In other words, a human being is very much materially inclined. Indeed, all living entities are materially inclined. They prefer *gṛhastha* life because there is concession for sex. The *karmīs* think the other statuses of life are worse than animal life, for animals also have sex, whereas the *brahmacārī, vānaprastha* and *sannyāsī* completely give up sex. The *karmīs,* therefore, abhor these orders of spiritual life.

TEXT 39

धर्मो ह्यत्रार्थकामौ च प्रजानन्दोऽमृतं यशः ।
लोका विशोका विरजा यान् न केवलिनो विदुः ॥३९॥

dharmo hy atrārtha-kāmau ca
prajānando 'mṛtaṁ yaśaḥ
lokā viśokā virajā
yān na kevalino viduḥ

dharmaḥ—religious ritual; *hi*—certainly; *atra*—here in this *gṛhastha-āśrama,* or householder life; *artha*—economic development; *kāmau*—sense gratification; *ca*—and; *prajā-ānandaḥ*—the pleasure of generations; *amṛtam*—the results of sacrifice; *yaśaḥ*—reputation; *lokāḥ*—planetary systems; *viśokāḥ*—without lamentation; *virajāḥ*—without disease; *yān*—which; *na*—never; *kevalinaḥ*—the transcendentalists; *viduḥ*—know.

TRANSLATION

The woman continued: In this material world, a householder's life brings all kinds of happiness in religion, economic development, sense gratification and in the begetting of children, sons and grandsons. After that, one may desire liberation as well as material reputation. The householder can appreciate the results of sacrifices, which enable him to gain promotion to superior planetary systems. All this material happiness is practically unknown to the transcendentalists. They cannot even imagine such happiness.

PURPORT

According to Vedic instructions, there are two paths for human activities. One is called *pravṛtti-mārga,* and the other is called *nivṛtti-mārga.* The basic principle for either of these paths is religious life. In animal life there is only *pravṛtti-mārga. Pravṛtti-mārga* means sense enjoyment, and *nivṛtti-mārga* means spiritual advancement. In the life of animals and demons, there is no conception of *nivṛtti-mārga,* nor is there any actual conception of *pravṛtti-mārga. Pravṛtti-mārga* maintains that even though one has the propensity for sense gratification, he can gratify his senses according to the directions of the Vedic injunctions. For example, everyone has the propensity for sex life, but in demoniac civilization sex is enjoyed without restriction. According to Vedic culture, sex is enjoyed under Vedic instructions. Thus the *Vedas* give direction to civilized human beings to enable them to satisfy their propensities for sense gratification.

In the *nivṛtti-mārga,* however, on the path of transcendental realization, sex is completely forbidden. The social orders are divided into four parts—*brahmacarya, gṛhastha, vānaprastha* and *sannyāsa*—and only in the householder life can the *pravṛtti-mārga* be encouraged or accepted according to Vedic instructions. In the orders of *brahmacarya, vānaprastha* and *sannyāsa,* there are no facilities for sex.

In this verse the woman is advocating *pravṛtti-mārga* only and is discouraging the path of *nivṛtti-mārga.* She clearly says that the *yatis,* the transcendentalists who are concerned only with spiritual life (*kaivalya*), cannot imagine the happiness of *pravṛtti-mārga.* In other words, the man who follows the Vedic principles enjoys the materialistic way of life not only by becoming happy in this life, but also in the next life by being promoted to the heavenly planets. In this life such a person gets all kinds of material opulences, such as sons and grandsons, because he is always engaged in various religious functions. The material distresses are birth, old age, disease and death, but those who are interested in *pravṛtti-mārga* hold various religious functions at the time of birth, old age, disease and death. Without caring for the distresses of birth, old age, disease and death, they are addicted to performing the special functions according to the Vedic ritualistic ceremonies.

Factually, however, *pravṛtti-mārga* is based on sex life. As stated in *Śrīmad-Bhāgavatam, yan maithunādi-gṛhamedhi-sukhaṁ hi tuccham* (*Bhāg.* 7.9.45). A householder who is too much addicted to *pravṛtti-mārga* is actually called a *gṛhamedhī,* not a *gṛhastha.* Although the *gṛhastha* desires sense gratification, he acts according to Vedic instructions. The *gṛhamedhī,* however, who is interested only in sense gratification, does not follow any Vedic instruction. The *gṛhamedhī* engages himself as an advocate of sex life and also allows his sons and daughters to engage in sex and to be deprived of any glorious end in life. A *gṛhastha* enjoys sex life in this life as well as in the next, but a *gṛhamedhī* does not know what the next life is about because he is simply interested in sex in this life. On the whole, when one is too much inclined towards sex, he does not care for the transcendental spiritual life. In this age of Kali especially, no one is interested in spiritual advancement. Even though it is sometimes found that one may be interested in spiritual advancement, he is most likely to accept a bogus method of spiritual life, being misguided by so many pretenders.

TEXT 40

पितृदेवर्षिमर्त्यानां भूतानामात्मनश्च ह ।
क्षेम्यं वदन्ति शरणं भवेऽस्मिन् यद् गृहाश्रमः ॥४०॥

pitṛ-devarṣi-martyānāṁ
bhūtānām ātmanaś ca ha
kṣemyaṁ vadanti śaraṇaṁ
bhave 'smin yad gṛhāśramaḥ

pitṛ—forefathers; *deva*—demigods; *ṛṣi*—sages; *martyānām*—of humanity in general; *bhūtānām*—of the infinite living entities; *ātmanaḥ*—of oneself; *ca*—also; *ha*—certainly; *kṣemyam*—beneficial; *vadanti*—they say; *śaraṇam*—shelter; *bhave*—in the material world; *asmin*—this; *yat*—that which; *gṛha-āśramaḥ*—householder life.

TRANSLATION

The woman continued: According to authorities, the householder life is pleasing not only to oneself but to all the forefathers, demigods, great

sages, saintly persons and everyone else. A householder life is thus beneficial.

PURPORT

According to the Vedic system, when one is born in this material world he has many obligations. He has obligations to the demigods—the demigods of the sun and moon, King Indra, Varuṇa, etc.—because they are supplying the necessities of life. We receive heat, light, water and all other natural amenities through the mercy of the demigods. We are also indebted to our forefathers who have given us these bodies, paternal property, intelligence, society, friendship and love. Similarly, we are indebted to the general public for politics and sociology, and we are also indebted to lower animals such as horses, cows, asses, dogs and cats. In this way, as soon as one is born in this material world as a human being, he has so many obligations and is bound to repay all these obligations. If he does not repay them, he is further entangled in the process of birth and death. The *gṛhamedhī*, however, who is overly addicted to material things, does not know that if he simply takes shelter at the lotus feet of Mukunda, he is immediately freed from all obligations to others. Unfortunately a *gṛhamedhī* does not have any interest in Kṛṣṇa consciousness. Prahlāda Mahārāja says: *matir na kṛṣṇe parataḥ svato vā mitho 'bhipadyeta gṛha-vratānām* (*Bhāg.* 7.5.30). A *gṛhavrata* is the same as a *gṛhamedhī*. One who takes sex life to be supreme finds action in Kṛṣṇa consciousness confusing. Either due to his own personal consideration, or due to his having taken instructions from others or conferring with them, he becomes addicted to sexual indulgence and cannot act in Kṛṣṇa consciousness.

TEXT 41

का नाम वीर विख्यातं वदान्यं प्रियदर्शनम् ।
न वृणीत प्रियं प्राप्तं मादृशी त्वादृशं पतिम् ॥४१॥

kā nāma vīra vikhyātaṁ
vadānyaṁ priya-darśanam
na vṛṇīta priyaṁ prāptaṁ
mādṛśī tvādṛśaṁ patim

kā—who; *nāma*—indeed; *vīra*—my dear hero; *vikhyātam*—famous; *vadānyam*—magnanimous; *priya-darśanam*—beautiful; *na*—not; *vṛṇīta*—would accept; *priyam*—easily; *prāptam*—gotten; *mā-dṛśī*—like me; *tvā-dṛśam*—like you; *patim*—husband.

TRANSLATION

O my dear hero, who in this world will not accept a husband like you? You are so famous, so magnanimous, so beautiful and so easily gotten.

PURPORT

Every husband is certainly a great hero to his wife. In other words, if a woman loves a man, that man appears very beautiful and magnanimous. Unless one becomes beautiful in the eyes of another, one cannot dedicate his whole life to another. The husband is considered very magnanimous because he gives as many children to the wife as she likes. Every woman is fond of children; therefore any husband who can please his wife by sex and give her children is considered very magnanimous. Not only does the husband become magnanimous by begetting children, but by giving his wife ornaments, nice food and dresses, he keeps her completely under submission. Such a satisfied wife will never give up the company of her husband. *Manu-saṁhitā* recommends that to keep a wife satisfied a husband should give her some ornaments because women are generally fond of home, ornaments, dresses, children, etc. In this way the woman is the center of all material enjoyment.

In this regard, the word *vikhyātam* is very significant. A man is always famous for his aggression toward a beautiful woman, and such aggression is sometimes considered rape. Although rape is not legally allowed, it is a fact that a woman likes a man who is very expert at rape.

TEXT 42

कस्या मनस्ते भुवि भोगिभोगयोः
स्त्रिया न सज्जेद्भुजयोर्महाभुज ।
योऽनाथवर्गाधिमलं घृणोद्धत-
स्मितावलोकेन चरत्यपोहितुम् ॥४२॥

kasyā manas te bhuvi bhogi-bhogayoḥ
striyā na sajjed bhujayor mahā-bhuja
yo 'nātha-vargādhim alaṁ ghṛṇoddhata-
smitāvalokena caraty apohitum

kasyāḥ—whose; *manaḥ*—mind; *te*—your; *bhuvi*—in this world; *bhogi-bhogayoḥ*—like the body of a serpent; *striyāḥ*—of a woman; *na*—not; *sajjet*

—becomes attracted; *bhujayoḥ*—by the arms; *mahā-bhuja*—O mighty-armed; *yaḥ*—one who; *anātha-vargā*—of poor women like me; *adhim*—distresses of the mind; *alam*—able; *ghṛṇā-uddhata*—by aggressive mercy; *smita-avalokena*—by attractive smiling; *carati*—travels; *apohitum*—to dissipate.

TRANSLATION

O mighty-armed, who in this world will not be attracted by your arms, which are just like the bodies of serpents? Actually you relieve the distress of husbandless women like us by your attractive smile and your aggressive mercy. We think that you are traveling on the surface of the earth just to benefit us only.

PURPORT

When a husbandless woman is attacked by an aggressive man, she takes his action to be mercy. A woman is generally very much attracted by a man's long arms. A serpent's body is round, and it becomes narrower and thinner at the end. The beautiful arms of a man appear to a woman just like serpents, and they very much desire to be embraced by such arms.

The word *anātha-vargā* is very significant in this verse. *Nātha* means husband, and *a* means without. A young woman who has no husband is called *anātha,* meaning one who is not protected. As soon as a woman attains the age of puberty, she immediately becomes very much agitated by sexual desire. It is therefore the duty of the father to get his daughter married before she attains puberty. Otherwise she will be very much mortified by not having a husband. Anyone who satisfies her desire for sex at that age becomes a great object of satisfaction. It is a psychological fact that when a woman at the age of puberty meets a man and the man satisfies her sexually, she will love that man for the rest of her life, regardless who he is. Thus so-called love within this material world is nothing but sexual satisfaction.

TEXT 43

नारद उवाच

इति तौ दम्पती तत्र समुद्य समयं मिथः ।
तां प्रविश्य पुरीं राजन्मुमुदाते शतं समाः ॥४३॥

nārada uvāca
iti tau dam-patī tatra
samudya samayaṁ mithaḥ

tāṁ praviśya purīṁ rājan
mumudāte śataṁ samāḥ

nāradaḥ uvāca—the great sage Nārada spoke; *iti*—thus; *tau*—they; *dampatī*—husband and wife; *tatra*—there; *samudya*—being equally enthusiastic; *samayam*—accepting one another; *mithaḥ*—mutually; *tām*—in that place; *praviśya*—entering; *purīm*—in that city; *rājan*—O King; *mumudāte*—they enjoyed life; *śatam*—one hundred; *samāḥ*—years.

TRANSLATION

The great sage Nārada continued: My dear King, those two—the man and the woman—supporting one another through mutual understanding, entered that city and enjoyed life for one hundred years.

PURPORT

One hundred years is significant in this connection because every human being is given the concession to live up to a hundred years. The span of life is different on different planets, according to the planet's distance from the sun. In other words, one hundred years on this planet is different from one hundred years on another planet. Lord Brahmā lives for one hundred years according to time on the Brahmaloka planet, but one day of Brahmā is equal to millions of years on this planet. Similarly, the days on the heavenly planets are equal to six months on this planet. On every planet, however, the span of life for a human being is roughly one hundred years. According to the life spans on different planets, the standards of living also differ.

TEXT 44

उपगीयमानो ललितं तत्र तत्र च गायकैः ।
क्रीडन् परिवृतः स्त्रीभिर्ह्रदिनीमाविशच्छुचौ ॥४४॥

upagīyamāno lalitaṁ
tatra tatra ca gāyakaiḥ
krīḍan parivṛtaḥ strībhir
hradinīm āviśac chucau

upagīyamānaḥ—being sung about; *lalitam*—very nicely; *tatra tatra*—here and there; *ca*—also; *gāyakaiḥ*—by the singers; *krīḍan*—playing; *parivṛtaḥ*—surrounded; *strībhiḥ*—by women; *hradinīm*—in the water of the river; *āviśat*—entered; *śucau*—when it was too hot.

TRANSLATION

Many professional singers used to sing about the glories of King Purañjana and his glorious activities. When it was too hot in the summer, he used to enter a reservoir of water. He would surround himself with many women and enjoy their company.

PURPORT

A living being has different activities in different stages of life. One stage is called *jāgrat,* or the life of awakening, and another is called *svapna,* or the life of dream. Another stage is called *suṣupti,* or life in an unconscious state, and still another stage occurs after death. In the previous verse the life of awakening was described; that is, the man and the woman were married and enjoyed life for one hundred years. In this verse life in the dream state is described, for the activities Purañjana accomplished during the day were also reflected at night in the dream state. Purañjana used to live with his wife for sense enjoyment, and at night this very sense enjoyment was appreciated in different ways. A man sleeps very soundly when he is greatly fatigued, and when a rich man is greatly fatigued he goes to his garden house with many female friends and there enters the water and enjoys their company. Such is the tendency of the living entity within this material world. A living entity is never satisfied with a woman unless he is trained in the system of *brahmacarya.* Generally a man's tendency is to enjoy many women, and even at the very end of life the sex impulse is so strong that even though one is very old he still wants to enjoy the company of young girls. Thus because of the strong sex impulse the living entity becomes more and more involved in this material world.

TEXT 45

सप्तोपरि कृता द्वारः पुरस्तस्यास्तु द्वे अधः ।
पृथग्विषयगत्यर्थं तस्यां यः कश्चनेश्वरः ॥४५॥

saptopari kṛtā dvāraḥ
puras tasyās tu dve adhaḥ
pṛthag-viṣaya-gaty-arthaṁ
tasyāṁ yaḥ kaścaneśvaraḥ

sapta—seven; *upari*—up; *kṛtāḥ*—made; *dvāraḥ*—gates; *puraḥ*—of the city; *tasyāḥ*—that; *tu*—then; *dve*—two; *adhaḥ*—down; *pṛthak*—different; *viṣaya*—to places; *gati-artham*—for going; *tasyām*—in that city; *yaḥ*—one who; *kaścana*—whoever; *īśvaraḥ*—governor.

TRANSLATION

Of the nine gates in that city, seven were on the surface and two were subterranean. A total of nine doors were constructed, and these led to different places. All the gates were used by the city's governor.

PURPORT

The seven gates of the body that are situated upward are the two eyes, two nostrils, two ears and one mouth. The two subterranean gates are the rectum and the genitals. The king, or the ruler of the body, who is the living entity, uses all these doors to enjoy different types of material pleasures. The system of opening different gates to different places is still evident in old Indian cities. Formerly a capital was surrounded by walls, and one passed through various gates to go to various cities or towards specific directions. In old Delhi there are still remnants of surrounding walls and various gates known as the Kaśmiri Gate, the Lahori Gate, etc. Similarly, in Ahmedabad there is a Delhi Gate. The point of this simile is that the living entity wants to enjoy different types of material opulences, and to this end nature has given him various holes in his body that he can utilize for sense enjoyment.

TEXT 46

पञ्च द्वारस्तु पौरस्त्या दक्षिणैका तथोत्तरा ।
पश्चिमे द्वे अमूषां ते नामानि नृप वर्णये ॥४६॥

pañca dvāras tu paurastyā
dakṣiṇaikā tathottarā
paścime dve amūṣāṁ te
nāmāni nṛpa varṇaye

pañca—five; *dvāraḥ*—doors; *tu*—then; *paurastyāḥ*—facing the eastern side; *dakṣiṇā*—southern; *ekā*—one; *tathā*—also; *uttarā*—one towards the north; *paścime*—similarly, on the western side; *dve*—two; *amūṣām*—of them; *te*—unto you; *nāmāni*—names; *nṛpa*—O King; *varṇaye*—I shall describe.

TRANSLATION

My dear King, of the nine doors, five led toward the eastern side, one led toward the northern side, one led toward the southern side, and two led toward the western side. I shall try to give the names of these different doors.

PURPORT

Of the seven doors on the surface—namely the two eyes, two ears, two nostrils and one mouth—five look forward, and these are described as the doors facing the eastern side. Since looking forward means seeing the sun, these are described as the eastern gates, for the sun rises in the east. The gate on the northern side and the gate on the southern side represent the two ears, and the two gates facing the western side represent the rectum and genitals. All the doors and gates are described below.

TEXT 47

खद्योताऽऽविर्मुखी च प्राग्द्वारावेकत्र निर्मिते ।
विभ्राजितं जनपदं याति ताभ्यां द्युमत्सखः ॥४७॥

khadyotāvirmukhī ca prāg
dvārāv ekatra nirmite
vibhrājitaṁ jana-padaṁ
yāti tābhyāṁ dyumat-sakhaḥ

khadyotā—of the name Khadyotā; *āvirmukhī*—of the name Āvirmukhī; *ca*—also; *prāk*—toward the eastern side; *dvārau*—two gates; *ekatra*—in one place; *nirmite*—were constructed; *vibhrājitam*—of the name Vibhrājita; *jana-padam*—city; *yāti*—used to go; *tābhyām*—by them; *dyumat*—of the name Dyumān; *sakhaḥ*—with his friend.

TRANSLATION

The two gates named Khadyotā and Āvirmukhī were situated facing the eastern side, but they were constructed in one place. Through those two gates the King used to go to the city of Vibhrājita accompanied by a friend whose name was Dyumān.

PURPORT

The two names Khadyotā and Āvirmukhī mean "glowworm" and "torchlight." This indicates that of the two eyes, the left eye is less powerful in its ability to see. Although both eyes are constructed in one place, one is stronger than the other in the power to see. The king, or the living entity, uses these two gates to see things properly, but he cannot see unless accompanied by a friend whose name is Dyumān. This friend is the sun. Although the two eyes are situated in one place, they have no power to see without the sunlight. *Vibhrājitaṁ jana-padam.* If one wants to see something very clearly (*vibhrājitam*), he must see it with two eyes and the assistance of his friend the sunlight. Within this body everyone is a king because he uses his different gates according to his own will. Although he is very much proud of his power to see or hear, he is nonetheless dependent on the assistance of nature.

TEXT 48

नलिनी नालिनी च प्रागृद्वारावेकत्र निर्मिते ।
अवधूतसखस्ताभ्यां विषयं याति सौरभम् ।।४८।।

nalinī nālinī ca prāg
dvārāv ekatra nirmite
avadhūta-sakhas tābhyāṁ
viṣayaṁ yāti saurabham

nalinī—of the name Nalinī; *nālinī*—of the name Nālinī; *ca*—also; *prāk*—eastern; *dvārau*—two gates; *ekatra*—in one place; *nirmite*—constructed; *avadhūta*—of the name Avadhūta; *sakhaḥ*—with his friend; *tābhyām*—by those two gates; *viṣayam*—place; *yāti*—used to go; *saurabham*—of the name Saurabha.

TRANSLATION

Similarly in the east there were two sets of gates named Nalinī and Nālinī, and these were also constructed in one place. Through these gates the King, accompanied by a friend named Avadhūta, used to go to the city of Saurabha.

PURPORT

The two gates named Nalinī and Nālinī are the two nostrils. The living entity enjoys these two gates with the help of different *avadhūtas,* or airs, which constitute the breathing process. Through these gates the living entity goes to the town of Saurabha, or aroma. In other words, the nostrils, with the help of their friend the air, enjoy various aromas in the material world. Nalinī and Nālinī are the pipes of the nostrils through which one inhales and exhales, enjoying the aroma of sense pleasure.

TEXT 49

मुख्या नाम पुरस्ताद्द्वास्तयाऽऽपणबहूदनौ ।
विषयौ याति पुरराड्रसज्ञविपणान्वितः ।।४९।।

mukhyā nāma purastād dvās
tayāpaṇa-bahūdanau
viṣayau yāti pura-rāḍ
rasajña-vipaṇānvitaḥ

mukhyā—the chief; *nāma*—called; *purastāt*—on the eastern side; *dvāḥ*—gate; *tayā*—by that; *āpaṇa*—of the name Āpaṇa; *bahūdanau*—of the name Bahūdana; *viṣayau*—two places; *yāti*—used to go; *pura-rāṭ*—the King of the city (Purañjana); *rasa-jña*—of the name Rasajña; *vipaṇa*—of the name Vipaṇa; *anvitaḥ*—along with.

TRANSLATION

The fifth gate situated on the eastern side was named Mukhyā, or the chief. Through this gate, accompanied by his friends named Rasajña and Vipaṇa, he used to visit two places named Bahūdana and Āpaṇa.

PURPORT

The mouth is here described as the chief or the most important gate. The mouth is a very important entrance because one has two functions to conduct with the mouth. One function is eating, and the other is speaking. Our eating is done with the friend Rasajña, by whom the tongue can taste so many different types of foods. The tongue is also used for speaking, and it can speak of either material sense enjoyment or Vedic knowledge. Of course, here material sense enjoyment is stressed. Therefore the word Rasajña is used.

TEXT 50

पितृहूर्नृप पुर्या द्वार्दक्षिणेन पुरञ्जनः ।
राष्ट्रं दक्षिणपञ्चालं याति श्रुतधरान्वितः ॥५०॥

pitṛhūr nṛpa puryā dvār
dakṣiṇena purañjanaḥ
rāṣṭraṁ dakṣiṇa-pañcālaṁ
yāti śruta-dharānvitaḥ

pitṛhūḥ—of the name Pitṛhū; *nṛpa*—O King; *puryāḥ*—of the city; *dvāḥ*—gate; *dakṣiṇena*—on the southern side; *purañjanaḥ*—King Purañjana; *rāṣṭram*—country; *dakṣiṇa*—southern; *pañcālam*—of the name Pañcāla; *yāti*—used to go; *śruta-dhara-anvitaḥ*—along with his friend Śrutadhara.

TRANSLATION

The southern gate of the city was known as Pitṛhū, and through that gate King Purañjana used to visit the city named Dakṣiṇa-pañcāla accompanied by his friend Śrutadhara.

PURPORT

The right ear is used for *karma-kāṇḍīya,* or fruitive activities. As long as one is attached to the enjoyment of material resources, he hears from the right ear and uses the five senses to elevate himself to the higher planetary systems like Pitṛloka. Consequently the right ear is here described as the Pitṛhū gate.

TEXT 51

देवहूर्नाम पुर्या द्वा उत्तरेण पुरञ्जनः ।
राष्ट्रमुत्तरपञ्चालं याति श्रुतधरान्वितः ॥५१॥

devahūr nāma puryā dvā
uttareṇa purañjanaḥ
rāṣṭram uttara-pañcālaṁ
yāti śruta-dharānvitaḥ

devahūḥ—of the name Devahū; *nāma*—as it was called; *puryāḥ*—of the city; *dvāḥ*—gate; *uttareṇa*—on the northern side; *purañjanaḥ*—King Purañjana; *rāṣṭram*—country; *uttara*—northern; *pañcālam*—of the name Pañcāla; *yāti*—used to go; *śruta-dhara-anvitaḥ*—with his friend Śrutadhara.

TRANSLATION

On the northern side was the gate named Devahū. Through that gate, King Purañjana used to go with his friend Śrutadhara to the place known as Uttara-pañcāla.

PURPORT

The two ears are situated on the northern side and the southern side. The ear on the southern side is very strong and is always anxious to hear about sense enjoyment. The ear on the northern side, however, is used for taking initiation from the spiritual master and for gaining promotion to the spiritual sky. The right ear, or the ear on the southern side, is called Pitṛhū, which indicates that it is used for attaining the higher planetary systems known as Pitṛloka, but the left ear, which is known as Devahū, is utilized for hearing about even higher planetary systems such as Maharloka, Tapoloka and Brahmaloka—or yet even higher planets situated in the spiritual universe, where one becomes more inclined to be permanently situated. This is explained in *Bhagavad-gītā:*

yānti deva-vratā devān
pitṝn yānti pitṛ-vratāḥ
bhūtāni yānti bhūtejyā
yānti mad-yājino 'pi mām

"Those who worship the demigods will take birth among the demigods; those who worship ghosts and spirits will take birth among such beings; those who worship ancestors go to the ancestors; and those who worship Me will live with Me." (Bg. 9.25)

One who is interested in being happy on this planet as well as after death generally wants to be elevated to the Pitṛlokas. Such a person can use the right ear for hearing Vedic instructions. However, one who is interested in going to Tapoloka, Brahmaloka, the Vaikuṇṭha planets or Kṛṣṇaloka may take initiation from the spiritual master in order to be elevated to such *lokas.*

TEXT 52

आसुरी नाम पश्चाद्‌ द्वास्तया याति पुरञ्जनः ।
ग्रामकं नाम विषयं दुर्मदेन समन्वितः ॥५२॥

āsurī nāma paścād dvās
tayā yāti purañjanaḥ
grāmakaṁ nāma viṣayaṁ
durmadena samanvitaḥ

āsurī—of the name Āsurī; *nāma*—called; *paścāt*—on the western side; *dvāḥ*—gate; *tayā*—by which; *yāti*—used to go; *purañjanaḥ*—King Purañjana; *grāmakam*—of the name Grāmaka; *nāma*—called; *viṣayam*—the city of sense enjoyment; *durmadena*—by Durmada; *samanvitaḥ*—accompanied.

TRANSLATION

On the western side was a gate named Āsurī. Through that gate King Purañjana used to go to the city of Grāmaka, accompanied by his friend Durmada.

PURPORT

The gate on the western side of the city was known as Āsurī because it was especially meant for the *asuras.* The word *asura* refers to those who are interested in sense gratification, specifically in sex life, to which they are overly attracted. Thus Purañjana, the living entity, enjoys himself to his greatest satisfaction by means of the genitals. Consequently he used to go to the place known as Grāmaka. Material sense gratification is also called *grāmya,* and the place where sex life is indulged in to a great extent is called Grāmaka. When going to Grāmaka, Purañjana used to be accompanied by his friend Durmada. The word *viṣaya* refers to the four bodily necessities of life—eating, sleeping, mating and defending. The word *durmadena* may be analyzed in this way: *dur* means *duṣṭa,* or sinful, and *mada* means madness. Every living entity who is in contact with material nature is called *mada,* or mad. It is said: *piśācī pāile yena mati-cchanna haya/ māyā-grasta jīvera haya se-bhāva udaya.* When a person is haunted, he becomes practically insane. When one is in an insane condition, he speaks all kinds of nonsense. Thus to become engaged in sense gratification, one has to accept a friend who is *durmada,* or badly affected by the material disease.

The words *āsurī nāma paścād dvāḥ* are significant in another sense. The sunrise is first visible from the eastern side—the Bay of Bengal—and gradually it progresses toward the west. It is practically experienced that people in the West are more addicted to sense gratification. Śrī Caitanya Mahāprabhu Himself has certified: *paścimera loka saba mūḍha anācāra* (Cc. *Ādi* 10.89). The more one goes to the western side, the more he will find people disinterested in spiritual life. He will find them behaving against the Vedic standards. Because of this, people living in the West are more addicted to sense gratification. In this *Bhāgavatam* it is confirmed: *āsurī nāma paścād dvāḥ.* In other words, the population on the western side is interested in an asuric civilization, that is, a materialistic way of life. Lord Caitanya consequently wanted this Kṛṣṇa consciousness movement to be preached on the western side of the world so that people addicted to sense gratification might be benefited by His teachings.

TEXT 53

निर्ऋतिर्नाम पश्चाद् द्वास्तया याति पुरञ्जनः ।
वैशसं नाम विषयं लुब्धकेन समन्वितः ॥५३॥

nirṛtir nāma paścād dvās
tayā yāti purañjanaḥ
vaiśasaṁ nāma viṣayaṁ
lubdhakena samanvitaḥ

nirṛtiḥ—of the name Nirṛti; *nāma*—called; *paścāt*—western; *dvāḥ*—gate; *tayā*—by which; *yāti*—used to go; *purañjanaḥ*—King Purañjana; *vaiśasam*—of the name Vaiśasa; *nāma*—called; *viṣayam*—to the place; *lubdhakena*—by the friend named Lubdhaka; *samanvitaḥ*—accompanied.

TRANSLATION

Another gate on the western side was known as Nirṛti. Purañjana used to go through this gate to the place known as Vaiśasa, accompanied by his friend Lubdhaka.

PURPORT

This is a reference to the rectum. The rectum is supposed to be situated on the western side of the eyes, nose and ears. This gate is especially meant for death. When an ordinary living entity abandons his present body, he passes through the rectum. It is therefore painful. When one is called by nature to evacuate, one also experiences pain. The friend of the living entity who accompanies him through this gate is named Lubdhaka, which means greed. Due to our greed, we eat unnecessarily, and such gluttony causes pain at the time of evacuation. The conclusion is that the living entity feels well if he evacuates properly. This gate is known as Nirṛti, or the painful gate.

TEXT 54

अन्धावमीषां पौराणां निर्वाक्पेशस्कृतावुभौ ।
अक्षण्वतामधिपतिस्ताभ्यां याति करोति च ॥५४॥

andhāv amīṣāṁ paurāṇāṁ
nirvāk-peśaskṛtāv ubhau
akṣaṇvatām adhipatis
tābhyāṁ yāti karoti ca

andhau—blind; *amīṣām*—among those; *paurāṇām*—of the inhabitants; *nirvāk*—of the name Nirvāk; *peśaskṛtau*—of the name Peśaskṛt; *ubhau*—both of them; *akṣaṇ-vatām*—of the people who possessed eyes; *adhipatiḥ*—

ruler; *tābhyām*—with both of them; *yāti*—used to go; *karoti*—used to act; *ca*—and.

TRANSLATION

Of the many inhabitants of this city, there are two persons named Nirvāk and Peśaskṛt. Although King Purañjana was the ruler of citizens who possessed eyes, he unfortunately used to associate with these blind men. Accompanied by them, he used to go here and there and perform various activities.

PURPORT

This is a reference to the arms and legs of the living entity. The two legs do not speak, and they are blind. If a person simply trusts his legs to take him walking, he is likely to fall into a hole or to bump into something. Thus led by the blind legs, one's life may be placed in jeopardy.

Of the senses that are working, the hands and legs are very important, but they have no eyes to see. This means that in the hands and legs there are no holes. In the head there are many holes—two eyes, two nostrils, two ears and one mouth—but lower down, in the arms and legs, there are no holes. Consequently the arms and legs have been described as *andha,* blind. Although the living entity has many holes in his body, he nonetheless has to work with his hands and arms. Although the living entity is the master of many other senses, when he has to go somewhere, do something or touch something, he has to use his blind legs and hands.

TEXT 55

स यर्ह्यन्तःपुरगतो विषूचीनसमन्वितः ।
मोहं प्रसादं हर्षं वा याति जायात्मजोद्भवम् ॥५५॥

sa yarhy antaḥpura-gato
viṣūcīna-samanvitaḥ
mohaṁ prasādaṁ harṣaṁ vā
yāti jāyātmajodbhavam

saḥ—he; *yarhi*—when; *antaḥ-pura*—to his private home; *gataḥ*—used to go; *viṣūcīna*—by the mind; *samanvitaḥ*—accompanied; *moham*—illusion; *prasādam*—satisfaction; *harṣam*—happiness; *vā*—or; *yāti*—used to enjoy; *jāyā*—wife; *ātma-ja*—children; *udbhavam*—produced by them.

TRANSLATION

Sometimes he used to go to his private home with one of his chief servants, the mind, who was named Viṣūcīna. At that time, illusion, satisfaction and happiness used to be produced from his wife and children.

PURPORT

According to the Vedic conclusion, one's self is situated within the heart. As stated in Vedic language, *hṛdy ayam ātmā pratiṣṭhitaḥ:* the self is situated within the heart. In the material condition, however, the spirit soul is covered by the material qualities—namely goodness, passion and darkness—and within the heart these three qualities react. For instance, when one is in goodness, he feels happiness; when one is in passion, he feels satisfaction through material enjoyment; and when one is in darkness, he feels bewilderment. All these activities are of the mind, and they function on the platform of thinking, feeling and willing.

When the living entity is encircled by wife, children and home, he acts on the mental plane. Sometimes he is very happy, sometimes he is very much satisfied, sometimes he is not satisfied, and sometimes he is bewildered. Bewilderment is called *moha,* illusion. Illusioned by society, friendship and love, the living entity thinks that his so-called society, friendship and love, nationality, community, society, etc., will give him protection. He does not know that after death he will be thrown into the hands of a very strong material nature that will force him to accept a certain type of body according to his present work. This body may not even be a human body. Thus the living entity's feeling of security in this life in the midst of society, wife and friendship is nothing but illusion. All living entities encaged in various material bodies are illusioned by the present activities of material enjoyment. They forget their real business, which is to go back home, back to Godhead.

Everyone who is not in Kṛṣṇa consciousness must be considered to be in illusion. One's so-called feelings of happiness and satisfaction resulting from material things are also illusions. Factually neither society, friendship, love nor anything else can save one from the onslaught of the external energy, which is symptomized by birth, death, old age and disease. To get even one living entity out of the illusory condition is very difficult; therefore Lord Kṛṣṇa says in *Bhagavad-gītā:*

daivī hy eṣā guṇamayī
mama māyā duratyayā

mām eva ye prapadyante
māyām etāṁ taranti te

"This divine energy of Mine, consisting of the three modes of material nature, is difficult to overcome. But those who have surrendered unto Me can easily cross beyond it." (Bg. 7.14)

Therefore, unless one surrenders completely at the lotus feet of Kṛṣṇa, he cannot get out of the entanglement of the three modes of material nature.

TEXT 56

एवं कर्मसु संसक्तः कामात्मा वञ्चितोऽबुधः ।
महिषी यद्यदीहेत तत्तदेवान्ववर्तत ॥५६॥

evaṁ karmasu saṁsaktaḥ
kāmātmā vañcito 'budhaḥ
mahiṣī yad yad īheta
tat tad evānvavartata

evam—thus; *karmasu*—in fruitive activities; *saṁsaktaḥ*—being too much attached; *kāma-ātmā*—lusty; *vañcitaḥ*—cheated; *abudhaḥ*—less intelligent; *mahiṣī*—the Queen; *yat yat*—whatsoever; *īheta*—she would desire; *tat tat*—all of that; *eva*—certainly; *anvavartata*—he followed.

TRANSLATION

Being thus entangled in different types of mental concoction and engaged in fruitive activities, King Purañjana came completely under the control of material intelligence and was thus cheated. Indeed, he used to fulfill all the desires of his wife, the Queen.

PURPORT

When a living entity is in such bewilderment that he is under the control of his wife, or material intelligence, he has to satisfy the intelligence of his so-called wife and act exactly according to her dictates. Various *śāstras* advise that for material convenience one should keep his wife always satisfied by giving her ornaments and by following her instructions. In this way there will be no trouble in family life. Therefore for one's own social benefit, one is advised to keep his wife satisfied. In this way, when one becomes the servant of his wife, he must act according to the desires of his wife. Thus one becomes more and more entangled. In Bengal it is said that if one becomes an obedient servant of his wife, he loses all reputation. However, the difficulty is that unless one becomes a most obedient servant of his wife, family life becomes disturbed. In the Western countries this disturbance gives rise to the divorce law, and in Eastern countries like India there is separation. Now this disturbance is confirmed by the new introduction of the divorce law in India. Within the heart, the mind is acting, thinking, feeling and willing, and falling under the control of one's wife is the same as falling under the control of material intelligence. Thus one begets children by his wife and becomes entangled in so many activities and mental concoctions.

TEXTS 57-61

क्वचित्पिबन्त्यां पिबति मदिरां मदविह्वलः ।
अश्नन्त्यां क्वचिदश्नाति जक्षत्यां सह जक्षिति ॥५७॥
क्वचिद्गायति गायन्त्यां रुदत्यां रुदति क्वचित् ।
क्वचिद्धसन्त्यां हसति जल्पन्त्यामनु जल्पति ॥५८॥
क्वचिद्धावति धावन्त्यां तिष्ठन्त्यामनु तिष्ठति ।
अनु शेते शयानायामन्वास्ते क्वचिदासतीम् ॥५९॥
क्वचिच्छृणोति शृण्वन्त्यां पश्यन्त्यामनु पश्यति ।
क्वचिज्जिघ्रति जिघ्रन्त्यां स्पृशन्त्यां स्पृशति क्वचित् ॥६०॥
क्वचिच्च शोचतीं जायामनुशोचति दीनवत् ।
अनु हृष्यति हृष्यन्त्यां मुदितामनु मोदते ॥६१॥

kvacit pibantyāṁ pibati
madirāṁ mada-vihvalaḥ
aśnantyāṁ kvacid aśnāti
jakṣatyāṁ saha jakṣiti

kvacid gāyati gāyantyāṁ
rudatyāṁ rudati kvacit
kvacid dhasantyāṁ hasati
jalpantyām anu jalpati

kvacid dhāvati dhāvantyāṁ
tiṣṭhantyām anu tiṣṭhati

anu śete śayānāyām
anvāste kvacid āsatīm

kvacic chṛṇoti śṛṇvantyāṁ
paśyantyām anu paśyati
kvacij jighrati jighrantyāṁ
spṛśantyāṁ spṛśati kvacit

kvacic ca śocatīṁ jāyām
anu śocati dīnavat
anu hṛṣyati hṛṣyantyāṁ
muditām anu modate

kvacit—sometimes; *pibantyām*—while drinking; *pibati*—he drank; *madirām*—liquor; *mada-vihvalaḥ*—being intoxicated; *aśnantyām*—while she was eating; *kvacit*—sometimes; *aśnāti*—he ate; *jakṣatyām*—while she was chewing; *saha*—with her; *jakṣiti*—he chewed; *kvacit*—sometimes; *gāyati*—he used to sing; *gāyantyām*—while his wife was singing; *rudatyām*—when the wife was crying; *rudati*—he also cried; *kvacit*—sometimes; *kvacit*—sometimes; *hasantyām*—while she was laughing; *hasati*—he also laughed; *jalpantyām*—while she was talking loosely; *anu*—following her; *jalpati*—he also talked loosely; *kvacit*—sometimes; *dhāvati*—he also used to walk; *dhāvantyām*—when she was walking; *tiṣṭhantyām*—while she was standing silently; *anu*—following her; *tiṣṭhati*—he used to stand; *anu*—following her; *śete*—he used to lie down; *śayānāyām*—while she was lying on the bed; *anu*—following her; *āste*—he also used to sit; *kvacit*—sometimes; *āsatīm*—while she was sitting; *kvacit*—sometimes; *śṛṇoti*—he used to hear; *śṛṇvantyām*—while she was engaged in hearing; *paśyantyām*—while she was seeing something; *anu*—following her; *paśyati*—he also used to see; *kvacit*—sometimes; *jighrati*—he used to smell; *jighrantyām*—while his wife was smelling; *spṛśantyām*—while the wife was touching; *spṛśati*—he was also touching; *kvacit*—at that time; *kvacit ca*—sometimes also; *śocatīm*—when she was lamenting; *jāyām*—his wife; *anu*—following her; *śocati*—he was also lamenting; *dīna-vat*—like a poor man; *anu*—following her; *hṛṣyati*—he used to enjoy; *hṛṣyantyām*—while she was feeling enjoyment; *muditām*—when she was satisfied; *anu*—following her; *modate*—he felt satisfaction.

TRANSLATION

When the Queen drank liquor, King Purañjana also engaged in drinking. When the Queen dined, he used to dine with her, and when she chewed,

King Purañjana used to chew along with her. When the Queen sang, he also sang. Similarly, when the Queen cried, he also cried, and when the Queen laughed, he also laughed. When the Queen talked loosely, he also talked loosely, and when the Queen walked, the King walked behind her. When the Queen would stand still, the King would also stand still, and when the Queen would lie down in bed, he would also follow and lie down with her. When the Queen sat, he would also sit, and when the Queen heard something, he would follow her to hear the same thing. When the Queen saw something, the King would also look at it, and when the Queen smelled something, the King would follow her to smell the same thing. When the Queen touched something, the King would also touch it, and when the dear Queen was lamenting, the poor King also had to follow her in lamentation. In the same way, when the Queen felt enjoyment, he also enjoyed, and when the Queen was satisfied, the King also felt satisfaction.

PURPORT

The mind is the place where the self is situated, and the mind is conducted by the intelligence. The living entity, situated within the heart, follows the intelligence. The intelligence is herein depicted as the Queen, and the soul, under mental control, follows the material intelligence just as the King follows his wife. The conclusion is that material intelligence is the cause of bondage for the living entity. The point is that one has to take to spiritual intelligence to come out of this entanglement.

In the life of Mahārāja Ambarīṣa, we find that the great Mahārāja first engaged his mind on the lotus feet of Kṛṣṇa. In this way his intelligence became purified. Mahārāja Ambarīṣa also used his other senses in the service of the Lord. He engaged his eyes in seeing the Deity in the temple nicely decorated with flowers. He engaged his sense of smell by smelling the flowers, and he engaged his legs by walking to the temple. His hands were engaged in cleansing the temple, and his ears were engaged in hearing about Kṛṣṇa. His tongue was engaged in two ways: in speaking about Kṛṣṇa and in tasting *prasāda* offered to the Deity. Materialistic persons, who are under the full control of material intelligence, cannot perform all these activities. Thus, consciously or unconsciously, they become entangled by the dictations of material intelligence. This fact is summarized in the following verse.

TEXT 62

विप्रलब्धो महिष्यैवं सर्वप्रकृतिवञ्चितः ।
नेच्छन्ननुकरोत्यज्ञः क्लैब्यात्क्रीडामृगो यथा ॥६२॥

vipralabdho mahiṣyaivaṁ
sarva-prakṛti-vañcitaḥ
necchann anukaroty ajñaḥ
klaibyāt krīḍā-mṛgo yathā

vipralabdhaḥ—captivated; *mahiṣyā*—by the Queen; *evam*—thus; *sarva*—all; *prakṛti*—existence; *vañcitaḥ*—being cheated; *na icchan*—without desiring; *anukaroti*—used to follow and imitate; *ajñaḥ*—the foolish King; *klaibyāt*—by force; *krīḍā-mṛgaḥ*—a pet animal; *yathā*—just like.

TRANSLATION

In this way, King Purañjana was captivated by his nice wife and was thus cheated. Indeed, he became cheated in his whole existence in the material world. Even against that poor foolish King's desire, he remained under the control of his wife, just like a pet animal that dances according to the order of its master.

PURPORT

The word *vipralabdhaḥ* is very significant in this verse. *Vi* means "specifically," and *pralabdha* means "obtained." Just to satisfy his desires, the King got the Queen, and thus he became cheated by material existence. Although he was not willing to do so, he remained as a pet animal under the control of material intelligence. Just as a pet monkey dances according to the desires of its master, the King danced according to the desires of the Queen. In *Śrīmad-Bhāgavatam* it is said: *mahat-sevāṁ dvāram āhur vimukteḥ* (5.5.2). If one associates with a saintly person, a devotee, his path of liberation becomes clear. But if one associates with a woman, or with a person who is too much addicted to a woman, his path of bondage becomes completely clear.

On the whole, for spiritual advancement, one must give up the company of women. This is what is meant by the order of *sannyāsa,* the renounced order. Before taking *sannyāsa,* or completely renouncing the material world, one has to practice avoiding illicit sex. Sex life, licit or illicit, is practically the same, but through illicit sex one becomes more and more captivated. By regulating one's sex life there is a chance that one may eventually be able to renounce sex or renounce the association of women. If this can be done, advancement in spiritual life comes very easily.

How one becomes captivated by the association of one's dear wife is explained in this chapter by Nārada Muni. Attraction for one's wife means attraction for the material qualities. One who is attracted by the material quality of darkness is in the lowest stage of life, whereas one who is attracted by the material quality of goodness is in a better position. Sometimes we see that when a person is on the platform of material goodness, he is attracted more or less by the cultivation of knowledge. This is, of course, a better position, for knowledge gives one the preference to accept devotional service. Unless one comes to the platform of knowledge, the *brahma-bhūta* stage, one cannot advance in devotional service. As Kṛṣṇa says in *Bhagavad-gītā:*

brahma-bhūtaḥ prasannātmā
na śocati na kāṅkṣati
samaḥ sarveṣu bhūteṣu
mad-bhaktiṁ labhate parām

"One who is thus transcendentally situated at once realizes the Supreme Brahman. He never laments nor desires to have anything; he is equally disposed to every living entity. In that state he attains pure devotional service unto Me." (Bg. 18.54)

The platform of knowledge is advantageous because it is a means by which one may come to the stage of devotional service. However, if one takes to devotional service directly, knowledge is revealed without separate endeavor. This is confirmed in *Śrīmad-Bhāgavatam: vāsudeve bhagavati bhakti-yogaḥ prayojitaḥ/ janayaty āśu vairāgyaṁ jñānaṁ ca yad ahaitukam* (1.2.7). Devotional service automatically reveals actual knowledge of our material existence. One who is sufficiently intelligent immediately attains the stage of renunciation of so-called society, family and love as well as other things. As long as we are attached to society, family and love of the material world, there is no question of knowledge. Nor is there a question of devotional service. By directly taking to devotional service, however, one becomes filled with knowledge and renunciation. In this way one's life becomes successful.

Thus end the Bhaktivedanta purports of the Fourth Canto, Twenty-fifth Chapter, of the Śrīmad-Bhāgavatam, *entitled "The Descriptions of the Characteristics of King Purañjana."*

CHAPTER TWENTY-SIX

King Purañjana Goes to the Forest to Hunt, and His Queen Becomes Angry

TEXTS 1-3

नारद उवाच
स एकदा महेष्वासो रथं पञ्चाश्वमाशुगम् ।
द्वीषं द्विचक्रमेकाक्षं त्रिवेणुं पञ्चबन्धुरम् ॥ १ ॥
एकरश्म्येकदमनमेकनीडं द्विकूबरम् ।
पञ्चप्रहरणं सप्तवरूथं पञ्चविक्रमम् ॥ २ ॥
हैमोपस्करमारुह्य स्वर्णवर्माक्षयेषुधिः ।
एकादशचमूनाथः पञ्चप्रस्थमगाद्वनम् ॥ ३ ॥

nārada uvāca
sa ekadā maheṣvāso
rathaṁ pañcāśvam āśugam
dvīṣaṁ dvi-cakram ekākṣaṁ
tri-veṇuṁ pañca-bandhuram

eka-raśmy eka-damanam
eka-nīḍaṁ dvi-kūbaram
pañca-praharaṇaṁ sapta-
varūthaṁ pañca-vikramam

haimopaskaram āruhya
svarṇa-varmākṣayeṣudhiḥ
ekādaśa-camūnāthaḥ
pañca-prastham agād vanam

nāradaḥ uvāca—Nārada said; *saḥ*—King Purañjana; *ekadā*—once upon a time; *maheṣvāsaḥ*—carrying his strong bow and arrows; *ratham*—chariot; *pañca-aśvam*—five horses; *āśu-gam*—going very swiftly; *dvi-īṣam*—two arrows; *dvi-cakram*—two wheels; *eka*—one; *akṣam*—axle; *tri*—three; *veṇum*—flags; *pañca*—five; *bandhuram*—obstacles; *eka*—one; *raśmi*—rope, rein; *eka*—one; *damanam*—chariot driver; *eka*—one; *nīḍam*—sitting place; *dvi*—two; *kūbaram*—posts to which the harnesses are fixed; *pañca*—five; *praharaṇam*—weapons; *sapta*—seven; *varūtham*—coverings or ingredients of the body; *pañca*—five; *vikramam*—processes; *haima*—golden; *upaskaram*—ornaments; *āruhya*—riding on; *svarṇa*—golden; *varmā*—armor; *akṣaya*—inexhaustible; *iṣudhiḥ*—quiver; *ekādaśa*—eleven; *camū-nāthaḥ*—commanders; *pañca*—five; *prastham*—destinations, objectives; *agāt*—went; *vanam*—to the forest.

TRANSLATION

The great sage Nārada continued: My dear King, once upon a time King Purañjana took up his great bow, and, equipped with golden armor and a quiver of unlimited arrows and accompanied by eleven commanders, he sat on his chariot driven by five swift horses and went to the forest named Pañca-prastha. He took with him in that chariot two explosive arrows. The chariot itself was situated on two wheels and one revolving axle. On the chariot were three flags, one rein, one chariot driver, one sitting place, two poles to which the harness was fixed, five weapons and seven coverings. The chariot moved in five different styles, and five obstacles lay before it. All the decorations of the chariot were made of gold.

PURPORT

These three verses explain how the material body of the living entity is under the control of the three qualities of the external energy. The body itself is the chariot, and the living entity is the owner of the body, as explained in *Bhagavad-gītā: dehino 'smin yathā dehe* (Bg. 2.13). The owner of the body is called the *dehī,* and he is situated within this body, specifically within the heart. The living entity is driven by one chariot driver. The chariot itself is made of three *guṇas,* three qualities of material nature, as confirmed in *Bhagavad-gītā: yantrārūḍhāni māyayā* (Bg. 18.61). The word *yantra* means carriage. The body is given by material nature, and the driver of that body is Paramātmā, the Supersoul. The living entity is seated within the chariot. This is the actual position.

The living entity is always being influenced by the three qualities—*sattva* (goodness), *rajaḥ* (passion) and *tamaḥ* (ignorance). This is also confirmed in *Bhagavad-gītā:*

tribhir guṇamayair bhāvair
ebhiḥ sarvam idaṁ jagat
mohitaṁ nābhijānāti
mām ebhyaḥ param avyayam

"Deluded by the three modes [goodness, passion and ignorance], the whole world does not know Me, who am above the modes and inexhaustible." (Bg. 7.13)

The living entity is thus bewildered by the three qualities of material nature. These three qualities are described in this verse as three flags. By a flag, one can come to know who the owner of the chariot is; similarly, by the influence of the three qualities of material nature, one can easily know the direction in which the chariot is moving. In other words, one who has eyes to see can understand how the body is being driven, influenced by the particular type or quality of material nature. In these three verses the activity of the living entity is described to prove how the body becomes influenced by the quality of ignorance, even when a person wants to be religious. Nārada Muni wanted to prove to King Prācīnabarhiṣat that the King was being influenced by the *tamo-guṇa,* the quality of ignorance, even though the King was supposed to be very religious.

According to *karma-kāṇḍīya,* the process of fruitive activities, a person performs various sacrifices directed by the *Vedas,* and in all those sacrifices animal killing, or experimenting on the life of animals to test the power of Vedic *mantras,* is enjoined. Animal killing is certainly conducted under the influence of the mode of ignorance. Even though one may be religiously inclined, animal sacrifice is nonetheless recommended in the *śāstras,* not only in the *Vedas* but even in the modern scriptures of other sects. These animal sacrifices are recommended in the name of religion, but actually animal sacrifice is meant for persons in the mode of ignorance. When such people kill animals, they can at least do so in the name of religion. However, when the religious system is transcendental, like the Vaiṣṇava religion, there is no place for animal sacrifice. Such a transcendental religious system is recommended by Kṛṣṇa in *Bhagavad-gītā:*

sarva-dharmān parityajya
mām ekaṁ śaraṇaṁ vraja
ahaṁ tvāṁ sarva-pāpebhyo
mokṣayiṣyāmi mā śucaḥ

"Abandon all varieties of religion and just surrender unto Me. I shall deliver you from all sinful reaction. Do not fear." (Bg. 18.66)

Because King Prācīnabarhiṣat was engaged in performing various sacrifices in which animals were killed, Nārada Muni pointed out that such sacrifices are influenced by the mode of ignorance. From the very beginning of *Śrīmad-Bhāgavatam* it is said: *dharmaḥ projjhita-kaitavo 'tra* (1.1.2). All kinds of religious systems that are involved in cheating are completely kicked out of *Śrīmad-Bhāgavatam.* In the *bhagavad-dharma,* the religion dealing with one's relationship with the Supreme Personality of Godhead, animal sacrifice is not recommended. In the performance of *saṅkīrtana-yajña*—Hare Kṛṣṇa, Hare Kṛṣṇa, Kṛṣṇa Kṛṣṇa, Hare Hare/ Hare Rāma, Hare Rāma, Rāma Rāma, Hare Hare—there is no recommendation for animal sacrifices.

In these three verses, King Purañjana's going to the forest to kill animals is symbolic of the living entity's being driven by the mode of ignorance and thus engaging in different activities for sense gratification. The material body itself indicates that the living entity is already influenced by the three modes of material nature and that he is driven to enjoy material resources. When the body is influenced by the mode of ignorance, its infection becomes very acute. When it is influenced by the mode of passion, the infection is at the symptomatic stage. However, when the body is influenced by the mode of goodness, the materialistic infection becomes purified. The ritualistic ceremonies recommended in religious systems are certainly on the platform of goodness, but because within this material world even the mode of goodness is sometimes polluted by the other qualities (namely passion and ignorance), a man in goodness is sometimes driven by the influence of ignorance.

It is herein described that King Purañjana once went to the forest to kill animals. This means that he, the living entity, came under the influence of the mode of ignorance. The forest in which King Purañjana engaged in hunting was named Pañca-prastha. The word *pañca* means five, and this indicates the objects of the five senses. The body has five working senses, namely, the hands, the legs, the tongue, the rectum and the genitals. By taking full advantage of these working senses, the body enjoys material life. The chariot is driven by five horses, which represent the five sense organs—namely, the eyes, ears, nose, skin and tongue. These sense organs are very easily attracted by the sense objects. Consequently the horses are described as moving swiftly. On the chariot King Purañjana kept two explosive weapons, which may be compared to *ahaṅkāra,* or false ego. This false ego is typified by two attitudes: "I am this body" (*ahantā*), and "Everything in my bodily relationships belongs to me" (*mamatā*).

The two wheels of the chariot may be compared to the two moving facilities—namely sinful life and religious life. The chariot is decorated with three flags, which represent the three modes of material nature. The five kinds of obstacles, or uneven roads, represent the five kinds of air passing within the body. These are *prāṇa, apāna, udāna, samāna* and *vyāna.* The body itself is covered by seven coverings, namely, skin, muscle, fat, blood, marrow, bone and semen. The living entity is covered by three subtle material elements and five gross material elements. These are actually obstacles placed before the living entity on the path of liberation from material bondage.

The word *raśmi* (rope) in this verse indicates the mind. The word *nīḍa* is also significant, for *nīḍa* indicates the nest where a bird takes rest. In this case *nīḍa* is the heart where the living entity is situated. The living entity sits in one place only. The causes of his bondage are two: namely lamentation and illusion. In material existence the living entity simply hankers to get something he can never get. Therefore he is in illusion. As a result of being in this illusory situation, the living entity is always lamenting. Thus lamentation and illusion are described herein as *dvi-kūbara,* the two posts of bondage.

The living entity carries out various desires through five different processes, which indicate the working of the five working senses. The golden ornaments and dress indicate that the living entity is influenced by the quality of *rajo-guṇa,* passion. One who has a good deal of money or riches is especially driven by the mode of passion. Being influenced by the mode of passion, one desires so many things for enjoyment in this material world. The eleven commanders represent the ten senses and the mind. The mind is always making plans with the ten commanders to enjoy the material world. The forest named Pañca-prastha, where the King went to hunt, is the forest of the five sense objects: form, taste, sound, smell and touch. Thus in these three verses Nārada Muni describes the position of the material body and the encagement of the living entity within it.

TEXT 4

चचार मृगयां तत्र दृप्त आत्तेषुकार्मुकः ।
विहाय जायामतदर्हां मृगव्यसनलालसः ॥ ४ ॥

cacāra mṛgayāṁ tatra
dṛpta ātteṣu-kārmukaḥ

vihāya jāyām atad-arhāṁ
mṛga-vyasana-lālasaḥ

cacāra—executed; *mṛgayām*—hunting; *tatra*—there; *dṛptaḥ*—being proud; *ātta*—having taken; *iṣu*—arrows; *kārmukaḥ*—bow; *vihāya*—giving up; *jāyām*—his wife; *a-tat-arhām*—although impossible; *mṛga*—hunting; *vyasana*—evil activities; *lālasaḥ*—being inspired by.

TRANSLATION

It was almost impossible for King Purañjana to give up the company of his Queen even for a moment. Nonetheless, on that day, being very much inspired by the desire to hunt, he took up his bow and arrow with great pride and went to the forest, not caring for his wife.

PURPORT

One form of hunting is known as woman-hunting. A conditioned soul is never satisfied with one wife. Those whose senses are very much uncontrolled especially try to hunt for many women. King Purañjana's abandoning the company of his religiously married wife is representative of the conditioned soul's attempt to hunt for many women for sense gratification. Wherever a king goes, he is supposed to be accompanied by his queen, but when the king, or conditioned soul, becomes greatly overpowered by the desire for sense gratification, he does not care for religious principles. Instead, with great pride, he accepts the bow and arrow of attachment and hatred. Our consciousness is always working in two ways—the right way and the wrong way. When one becomes too proud of his position, influenced by the mode of passion, he gives up the right path and accepts the wrong one. *Kṣatriya* kings are sometimes advised to go to the forest to hunt ferocious animals just to learn how to kill, but such forays are never meant for sense gratification. Killing animals to eat their flesh is forbidden for human beings.

TEXT 5

आसुरीं वृत्तिमाश्रित्य घोरात्मा निरनुग्रहः ।
न्यहनन्निशितैर्बाणैर्वनेषु वनगोचरान् ॥ ५ ॥

āsurīṁ vṛttim āśritya
ghorātmā niranugrahaḥ

nyahanan niśitair bāṇair
vaneṣu vana-gocarān

āsurīm—demoniac; *vṛttim*—occupation; *āśritya*—taken shelter of; *ghora*—horrible; *ātmā*—consciousness, heart; *niranugrahaḥ*—without mercy; *nyahanat*—killed; *niśitaiḥ*—by sharp; *bāṇaiḥ*—arrows; *vaneṣu*—in the forests; *vana-gocarān*—the forest animals.

TRANSLATION

At that time King Purañjana was very much influenced by demoniac propensities. Because of this, his heart became very hard and merciless, and with sharp arrows he killed many innocent animals in the forest, taking no consideration.

PURPORT

When a man becomes too proud of his material position, he tries to enjoy his senses in an unrestricted way, being influenced by the modes of passion and ignorance. He is thus described as asuric, or demoniac. When people are demoniac in spirit, they are not merciful toward the poor animals. Consequently they maintain various animal slaughterhouses. This is technically called *sūnā* or *hiṁsā*, which means the killing of living beings. In Kali-yuga, due to the increase of the modes of passion and ignorance, almost all men are asuric or demoniac; therefore they are very much fond of eating flesh, and for this end they maintain various kinds of animal slaughterhouses.

In this age of Kali the propensity for mercy is almost nil. Consequently there is always fighting and wars between men and nations. Men do not understand that because they unrestrictedly kill so many animals, they also must be slaughtered like animals in big wars. This is very much evident in the Western countries. In the West, slaughterhouses are maintained without restriction, and therefore every fifth or tenth year there is a big war in which countless people are slaughtered even more cruelly than the animals. Sometimes during war, soldiers keep their enemies in concentration camps and kill them in very cruel ways. These are reactions brought about by unrestricted animal killing in the slaughterhouse and by hunters in the forest. Proud, demoniac persons do not know the laws of nature, nor do they know the laws of God. Consequently they unrestrictedly kill poor animals, not caring for them at all. In this Kṛṣṇa consciousness movement animal killing is completely prohibited. One is not accepted as a bona fide student in this movement unless he promises to follow the four regulative principles:

no animal killing, no intoxication, no illicit sex, and no gambling. This Kṛṣṇa consciousness movement is the only means by which the sinful activities of men in this Kali-yuga can be counteracted.

TEXT 6

तीर्थेषु प्रतिदृष्टेषु राजा मेध्यान् पशून् वने ।
यावदर्थमलं लुब्धो हन्यादिति नियम्यते ॥ ६ ॥

tīrtheṣu pratidṛṣṭeṣu
rājā medhyān paśūn vane
yāvad-artham alaṁ lubdho
hanyād iti niyamyate

tīrtheṣu—in holy places; *pratidṛṣṭeṣu*—according to the direction of the *Vedas; rājā*—a king; *medhyān*—fit for sacrifice; *paśūn*—animals; *vane*—in the forest; *yāvat*—so much as; *artham*—required; *alam*—not more than that; *lubdhaḥ*—being greedy; *hanyāt*—one may kill; *iti*—thus; *niyamyate*—it is regulated.

TRANSLATION

If a king is too attracted to eating flesh, he may, according to the directions of the revealed scriptures on sacrificial performances, go to the forest and kill some animals that are recommended for killing. One is not allowed to kill animals unnecessarily or without restrictions. The Vedas regulate animal killing to stop the extravagance of foolish men influenced by the modes of passion and ignorance.

PURPORT

The question may be raised why a living being should be restricted in sense gratification. If a king, to learn how to kill, may go to the forest and kill animals, why should a living entity, who has been given senses, not be allowed unrestricted sense gratification? At the present moment this argument is put forward even by so-called *svāmīs* and *yogīs* who publicly say that because we have senses we must satisfy them by sense gratification. These foolish *svāmīs* and *yogīs*, however, do not know the injunctions of the *śāstras.* Indeed, sometimes these rascals come out to defy the *śāstras.* They even publicly announce that there should be no more *śāstras,* no more books. "Just come to me," they say, "and I shall touch you, and you will become immediately spiritually advanced."

Because demoniac people want to be cheated, so many cheaters are present to cheat them. At the present moment in this age of Kali-yuga, the entire human society has become an assembly of cheaters and cheated. For this reason the Vedic scriptures have given us the proper directions for sense gratification. Everyone is inclined in this age to eat meat and fish, drink liquor, and indulge in sex life, but according to the Vedic injunctions, sex is allowed only in marriage, meat-eating is allowed only when the animal is killed and offered before the goddess Kālī, and intoxication is allowed only in a restricted way. In this verse the word *niyamyate* indicates that all these things—namely, animal killing, intoxication and sex—should be regulated.

Regulations are meant for human beings, not for animals. The traffic regulations on the street, telling people to keep to the right or the left, are meant for human beings, not for animals. If an animal violates such a law, he is never punished, but a human being is punished. The *Vedas* are not meant for the animals but for the understanding of human society. A person who indiscriminately violates the rules and regulations given by the *Vedas* is liable to be punished. One should therefore not enjoy his senses according to his lusty desires but should restrict himself according to the regulative principles given in the *Vedas.* If a king is allowed to hunt in a forest, it is not for his sense gratification. We cannot simply experiment in the art of killing. If a king, being afraid to meet rogues and thieves, kills poor animals and eats their flesh comfortably at home, he may lose his position.

Because in this age kings have such demoniac propensities, monarchy is abolished by the laws of nature in every country. People have become so degraded in this age that on the one hand they restrict polygamy and on the other hand they hunt for women in so many ways. Many business concerns publicly advertise that topless girls are available in this club or in that shop. Thus women have become instruments of sense enjoyment in modern society. The *Vedas* enjoin, however, that if a man has the propensity to enjoy more than one wife—as is sometimes the propensity for men in the higher social order, such as the *brāhmaṇas, kṣatriyas* and the *vaiśyas,* and even sometimes the *śūdras*—he is allowed to marry more than one wife. Marriage means taking complete charge of a woman and living peacefully without debauchery. At the present moment, however, debauchery is unrestricted. Nonetheless, society makes a law that one should not marry more than one wife. This is typical of a demoniac society.

TEXT 7

य एवं कर्म नियतं विद्वान् कुर्वीत मानवः ।
कर्मणा तेन राजेन्द्र ज्ञानेन न स लिप्यते ॥ ७ ॥

ya evaṁ karma niyataṁ
vidvān kurvīta mānavaḥ
karmaṇā tena rājendra
jñānena na sa lipyate

yaḥ—anyone who; *evam*—thus; *karma*—activities; *niyatam*—regulated; *vidvān*—learned; *kurvīta*—should perform; *mānavaḥ*—a human being; *karmaṇā*—by such activities; *tena*—by this; *rāja-indra*—O King; *jñānena*—by advancement of knowledge; *na*—never; *saḥ*—he; *lipyate*—becomes involved.

TRANSLATION

Nārada Muni continued to speak to King Prācīnabarhiṣat: My dear King, any person who works according to the directions of the Vedic scriptures does not become involved in fruitive activities.

PURPORT

Just as a government may issue trade licenses in order for its citizens to act in a certain way, the *Vedas* contain injunctions that restrain and regulate all of our fruitive activities. All living entities have come into this material world to enjoy themselves. Consequently the *Vedas* are given to regulate sense enjoyment. One who enjoys his senses under the Vedic regulative principles does not become entangled in the actions and reactions of his activities. As stated in *Bhagavad-gītā:*

yajñārthāt karmaṇo 'nyatra
loko 'yaṁ karma-bandhanaḥ
tad-arthaṁ karma kaunteya
mukta-saṅgaḥ samācara

"Work done as a sacrifice for Viṣṇu has to be performed, otherwise work binds one to this material world. Therefore, O son of Kuntī, perform your prescribed duties for His satisfaction, and in that way you will always remain unattached and free from bondage." (Bg. 3.9)

A human being is especially meant to attain liberation from the bondage of birth, death, old age and disease. He is therefore directed by the Vedic regulative principles to work in such a way that he may fulfill his desires for sense gratification and at the same time gradually become freed from material bondage. Action according to such principles is called knowledge. Indeed, the word *veda* means knowledge. The words *jñānena na sa lipyate* indicate that by following the Vedic principles, one does not become involved in the actions and reactions of his fruitive activities.

Everyone is therefore advised to act in terms of the Vedic injunctions and not irresponsibly. When a person within a state acts according to the laws and licenses of the government, he does not become involved in criminal activities. Man-made laws, however, are always defective because they are made by men who are prone to committing mistakes, being illusioned, cheating and having imperfect senses. The Vedic instructions are different because they do not have these four defects. Vedic instructions are not subject to mistakes. The knowledge of the *Vedas* is knowledge received directly from God, and there is consequently no question of illusion, cheating, mistakes or imperfect senses. All Vedic knowledge is perfect because it is received directly from God by the *paramparā* disciplic succession. In *Śrīmad-Bhāgavatam* it is said: *tene brahma hṛdā ya ādi-kavaye* (*Bhāg.* 1.1.1). The original creature of this universe, known as the *ādi-kavi*, or Lord Brahmā, was instructed by Kṛṣṇa through the heart. After receiving these Vedic instructions from Lord Kṛṣṇa Himself, Brahmā distributed the knowledge by the *paramparā* system to Nārada, and Nārada in turn distributed the knowledge to Vyāsa. In this way Vedic knowledge is perfect. If we act according to Vedic knowledge, there is no question of being involved in sinful activities.

TEXT 8

अन्यथा कर्म कुर्वाणो मानारूढो निबध्यते ।
गुणप्रवाहपतितो नष्टप्रज्ञो व्रजत्यधः ॥ ८ ॥

anyathā karma kurvāṇo
mānārūḍho nibadhyate
guṇa-pravāha-patito
naṣṭa-prajño vrajaty adhaḥ

anyathā—otherwise; *karma*—fruitive activities; *kurvāṇaḥ*—while acting; *māna-ārūḍhaḥ*—being influenced by false prestige; *nibadhyate*—one becomes entangled; *guṇa-pravāha*—by the influence of the material qualities; *patitaḥ*—fallen; *naṣṭa-prajñaḥ*—bereft of all intelligence; *vrajati*—thus he goes; *adhaḥ*—down.

TRANSLATION

Otherwise a person who acts whimsically falls down due to false prestige. Thus he becomes involved in the laws of nature, which are composed of

the three qualities [goodness, passion and ignorance]. In this way a living entity becomes devoid of his real intelligence and becomes perpetually lost in the cycle of birth and death. Thus he goes up and down from a microbe in stool to a high position in the Brahmaloka planet.

PURPORT

There are many important words in this verse. The first is *anyathā*, "otherwise," which indicates one who does not care for the Vedic rules and regulations. The rules and regulations laid down in the *Vedas* are called *śāstra-vidhi. Bhagavad-gītā* clearly states that one who does not accept the *śāstra-vidhi,* or rules and regulations mentioned in the Vedic scriptures, and acts whimsically or puffed up with false pride, never attains perfection in this life, nor does he attain happiness or liberation from the material condition.

yaḥ śāstra-vidhim utsṛjya
vartate kāma-kārataḥ
na sa siddhim avāpnoti
na sukhaṁ na parāṁ gatim

"He who discards scriptural injunctions and acts according to his own whims attains neither perfection, nor happiness, nor the supreme destination." (Bg. 16.23)

Thus one who is deliberately transgressing the rules and regulations of the *śāstras* is simply involving himself more and more in material existence in the three modes of material nature. Human society should therefore follow the Vedic principles of life, which are summarized in *Bhagavad-gītā.* Otherwise life in material existence will continue. Foolish persons do not know that the soul is passing through 8,400,000 species of life. By the gradual process of evolution, when one comes to the human form of life, he is supposed to follow the rules and regulations laid down in the *Vedas.* Śrī Caitanya Mahāprabhu says that the living entity, since time immemorial, is suffering the threefold miseries of material nature due to his demoniac attitude, which is his spirit of revolt against the Supreme Personality of Godhead. Kṛṣṇa also confirms this in *Bhagavad-gītā:*

mamaivāṁśo jīva-loke
jīva-bhūtaḥ sanātanaḥ
manaḥ ṣaṣṭhānīndriyāṇi
prakṛti-sthāni karṣati

"The living entities in this conditioned world are My eternal, fragmental parts. Due to conditioned life, they are struggling very hard with the six senses, which include the mind." (Bg. 15.7)

Every living entity is part and parcel of God. There is no reason for the living entity's being put into the miserable threefold condition of material existence but that he voluntarily accepts material existence on the false pretext of becoming an enjoyer. To save him from this horrible condition, the Lord has given all the Vedic literatures in His incarnation of Vyāsadeva. It is therefore said:

kṛṣṇa bhuli' sei jīva anādi-bahirmukha
ataeva māyā tāre deya saṁsāra-duḥkha

"By forgetting Kṛṣṇa, the living entity has become materialistic since time immemorial. Therefore the illusory energy of Kṛṣṇa is giving him different types of miseries in material existence." (Cc. *Madhya* 20.117)

māyā-mugdha jīvera nāhi svataḥ kṛṣṇa-jñāna
jīvere kṛpāya kailā kṛṣṇa veda-purāṇa

"When a living entity is enchanted by the external energy, he cannot revive his original Kṛṣṇa consciousness independently. Due to such circumstances, Kṛṣṇa has kindly given him the Vedic literatures, such as the four *Vedas* and eighteen *Purāṇas.*" (Cc. *Madhya* 20.122)

Every human being should therefore take advantage of the Vedic instructions; otherwise one will be bound by his whimsical activities and will be without any guide.

The word *mānārūḍhaḥ* is also very significant in this verse. Under the pretext of becoming great philosophers and scientists, men throughout the whole world are working on the mental platform. Such men are generally nondevotees, due to not caring for the instructions given by the Lord to the first living creature, Lord Brahmā. The *Bhāgavatam* therefore says:

harāv abhaktasya kuto mahad-guṇā
mano-rathenāsati dhāvato bahiḥ (*Bhāg.* 5.18.12)

A person who is a nondevotee has no good qualifications because he acts on the mental platform. One who acts on the mental platform has to change his standard of knowledge periodically. We consequently see that one philosopher may disagree with another philosopher, and one scientist may put forward a theory contradicting the theory of another scientist. All of this is due to their working on the mental platform without a standard of knowledge. In the Vedic instructions, however, the standard of knowledge is accepted, even though it may sometimes appear that the statements are contradictory. Because the *Vedas* are the standard of knowledge, even though they may appear contradictory, they should be accepted. If one does not accept them, he will be bound by the material conditions.

The material conditions are described in this verse as *guṇa-pravāha,* the flowing of the three modes of material nature. Śrīla Bhaktivinoda Ṭhākura therefore says in a song, (*miche*) *māyāra vaśe, yāccha bhese', khāccha hābuḍubu, bhāi:* "Why are you suffering? Why are you sometimes being drowned in the waves of material nature and sometimes coming to the surface?" *(Jīva) kṛṣṇa-dāsa, e viśvāsa, karle ta' āra duḥkha nāi:* "Please therefore accept yourself as the servant of Kṛṣṇa. Then you will be freed from all miseries." As soon as one surrenders to Kṛṣṇa and accepts the perfect standard of knowledge, which is *Bhagavad-gītā* as it is, he then comes out of the material modes of nature and does not fall down and lose his knowledge.

Naṣṭa-prajñaḥ. The word *prajña* means "perfect knowledge," and *naṣṭa-prajña* means "one who has no perfect knowledge." One who does not have perfect knowledge has only mental speculation. By such mental speculation one falls down and down into a hellish condition of life. By transgressing the laws laid down in the *śāstras,* one cannot become pure in heart. When one's heart is not purified, one acts according to the three material modes of nature. These activities are very nicely explained in verses 1-6 of the Seventeenth Chapter of *Bhagavad-gītā. Bhagavad-gītā* further explains:

traiguṇya-viṣayā vedā
nistraiguṇyo bhavārjuna
nirdvandvo nitya-sattva-stho
niryoga-kṣema ātmavān

"The *Vedas* mainly deal with the subject of the three modes of material nature. Rise above these modes, O Arjuna. Be transcendental to all of them. Be free from all dualities and from all anxieties for gain and safety, and be established in the Self." (Bg. 2.45)

The entire world and all material knowledge is within the three modes of material nature. One has to transcend these modes, and to attain that platform of transcendence one must follow the instruction of the Supreme Personality of Godhead and thus become perfect in life. Otherwise one will be knocked down by the waves of the material nature's three modes. This is further explained in *Śrīmad-Bhāgavatam* in the words of Prahlāda Mahārāja:

matir na kṛṣṇe parataḥ svato vā
mitho 'bhipadyeta gṛha-vratānām
adānta-gobhir viśatāṁ tamisraṁ
punaḥ punaś carvita-carvaṇānām
(*Bhāg.* 7.5.30)

Materialistic persons who are too much engaged in material enjoyment and who do not know anything beyond their material experiences are carried by the whims of material nature. They live a life characterized by chewing the chewed, and they are controlled by their uncontrolled senses. Thus they go down to the darkest regions of hellish life.

TEXT 9

तत्र निर्भिन्नगात्राणां चित्रवाजैः शिलीमुखैः ।
विप्लवोऽभूद्दुःखितानां दुःसहः करुणात्मनाम् ॥ ९ ॥

tatra nirbhinna-gātrāṇāṁ
citra-vājaiḥ śilī-mukhaiḥ
viplavo 'bhūd duḥkhitānāṁ
duḥsahaḥ karuṇātmanām

tatra—there; *nirbhinna*—being pierced; *gātrāṇām*—whose bodies; *citra-vājaiḥ*—with variegated feathers; *śilī-mukhaiḥ*—by the arrows; *viplavaḥ*—destruction; *abhūt*—was done; *duḥkhitānām*—of the most aggrieved; *duḥsahaḥ*—unbearable; *karuṇā-ātmanām*—for persons who are very merciful.

TRANSLATION

When King Purañjana was hunting in this way, many animals within the forest lost their lives with great pain, being pierced by the sharp arrowheads. Upon seeing these devastating, ghastly activities performed by the King, all the people who were merciful by nature became very unhappy. Such merciful persons could not tolerate seeing all this killing.

PURPORT

When demoniac persons engage in animal killing, the demigods, or devotees of the Lord, are very much afflicted by this killing. Demoniac civilizations in this modern age maintain various types of slaughterhouses all over the world. Rascal *svāmīs* and *yogīs* encourage foolish persons to go on eating flesh and killing animals and at the same time continue their so-called meditation and mystical practices. All these affairs are ghastly, and a compassionate person, namely a devotee of the Lord, becomes very unhappy to see such a sight. The hunting process is also carried on in a different way, as we have already explained. Hunting women, drinking different types of liquor, becoming intoxicated, killing animals and enjoying sex all serve as the basis of modern civilization. Vaiṣṇavas are unhappy to see such a situation in the world, and therefore they are very busy spreading this Kṛṣṇa consciousness movement.

The devotees are pained to see the hunting and killing of animals in the forest, the wholesale slaughter of animals in the slaughterhouses, and the exploitation of young girls in brothels that function under different names as clubs and societies. Being very much compassionate upon the killing of animals in sacrifice, the great sage Nārada began his instructions to King Prācīnabarhiṣat. In these instructions, Nārada Muni explained that devotees like him are very much afflicted by all the killing that goes on in human society. Not only are saintly persons afflicted by this killing, but even God Himself is afflicted and therefore comes down in the incarnation of Lord Buddha. Jayadeva Gosvāmī therefore sings: *sadaya-hṛdaya-darśita-paśu-ghātam.* Simply to stop the killing of animals, Lord Buddha compassionately appeared. Some rascals put forward the theory that an animal has no soul or is something like dead stone. In this way they rationalize that there is no sin in animal killing. Actually animals are not dead stone, but the killers of animals are stone-hearted. Consequently no reason or philosophy appeals to them. They continue keeping slaughterhouses and killing animals in the forest. The conclusion is that one who does not care for the instructions of saintly persons like Nārada and his disciplic succession surely falls into the category of *naṣṭa-prajña* and thus goes to hell.

TEXT 10

शशान् वराहान् महिषान् गवयान् रुरुशल्यकान् ।
मेध्यानन्यांश्च विविधान् विनिघ्नन् श्रममध्यगात् ॥१०॥

śaśān varāhān mahiṣān
gavayān ruru-śalyakān
medhyān anyāṁś ca vividhān
vinighnan śramam adhyagāt

śaśān—rabbits; *varāhān*—boars; *mahiṣān*—buffaloes; *gavayān*—bisons; *ruru*—black deer; *śalyakān*—porcupines; *medhyān*—game animals; *anyān*—others; *ca*—and; *vividhān*—various; *vinighnan*—by killing; *śramam adhyagāt*—became very tired.

TRANSLATION

In this way King Purañjana killed many animals, including rabbits, boars, buffaloes, bisons, black deer, porcupines and other game animals. After killing and killing, the King became very tired.

PURPORT

A person in the mode of ignorance commits many sinful activities. In the *Bhakti-rasāmṛta-sindhu,* Śrīla Rūpa Gosvāmī explains that a man becomes sinful out of ignorance only. The resultant effect of sinful life is suffering. Those who are not in knowledge, who commit violations of the standard laws, are subject to be punished under criminal laws. Similarly, the laws of nature are very stringent. If a child touches fire without knowing the effect, he must be burned, even though he is only a child. If a child violates the law of nature, there is no compassion. Only through ignorance does a person violate the laws of nature, and when he comes to knowledge he does not commit any more sinful acts.

The King became tired after killing so many animals. When a man comes in contact with a saintly person, he becomes aware of the stringent laws of nature and thus becomes a religious person. Irreligious persons are like animals, but in this Kṛṣṇa consciousness movement such persons can come to a sense of understanding things as they are and abandon the four principles of prohibited activities—namely, illicit sex life, meat-eating, gambling and intoxication. This is the beginning of religious life. Those who are so-called religious and indulge in these four principles of prohibited activities are pseudo-religionists. Religious life and sinful activity cannot parallel one another. If one is serious in accepting a religious life, or the path of salvation, he must adhere to the four basic rules and regulations. However sinful a man may be, if he receives knowledge from the proper spiritual master and repents his past activities in his sinful life and stops them, he immediately becomes eligible to return home, back to Godhead. This is made possible just by following the rules and regulations given by the *śāstra* and following the bona fide spiritual master.

At present the whole world is on the verge of retiring from a blind materialistic civilization, which may be likened to hunting animals in the forest. People should take advantage of this Kṛṣṇa consciousness movement and leave their troublesome life of killing. It is said that the killers of animals should neither live nor die. If they live only to kill animals and enjoy women, life is not very prosperous. And as soon as a killer dies, he enters the cycle of birth and death in the lower species of life. That also is not desirable. The conclusion is that killers should retire from the killing business and take to this Kṛṣṇa consciousness movement to make life perfect. A confused, frustrated man cannot get relief by committing suicide because suicide will simply lead him to take birth in the lower species of life or to remain as a ghost, unable to attain a gross material body. Therefore the perfect course is to retire altogether from sinful activities and take up Kṛṣṇa consciousness. In this way one can become completely perfect and go back home, back to Godhead.

TEXT 11

ततः क्षुत्तृट्परिश्रान्तो निवृत्तो गृहमेयिवान् ।
कृतस्नानोचिताहारः संविवेश गतक्लमः ॥११॥

tataḥ kṣut-tṛṭ-pariśrānto
nivṛtto gṛham eyivān
kṛta-snānocitāhāraḥ
saṁviveśa gata-klamaḥ

tataḥ—thereafter; *kṣut*—by hunger; *tṛṭ*—thirst; *pariśrāntaḥ*—being too fatigued; *nivṛttaḥ*—having ceased; *gṛham eyivān*—came back to his home; *kṛta*—taken; *snāna*—bath; *ucita-āhāraḥ*—exactly required foodstuffs; *saṁviveśa*—took rest; *gata-klamaḥ*—freed from all fatigue.

TRANSLATION

After this, the King, very much fatigued, hungry and thirsty, returned to his royal palace. After returning, he took a bath and had dinner. Then he took rest and thus became freed from all restlessness.

PURPORT

A materialistic person works throughout the whole week very, very hard. He is always asking, "Where is money? Where is money?" Then, at the end of the week, he wants to retire from these activities and go to some secluded place to rest. King Purañjana returned to his home because he was very much fatigued from hunting animals in the forest. In this way his conscience came to stop him from committing further sinful activities and make him return home. In *Bhagavad-gītā* materialistic persons are described as *duṣkṛtinaḥ,* which indicates those who are always engaged in sinful activities. When a person comes to his senses and understands how he is engaging in sinful activities, he returns to his conscience, which is herein figuratively described as the palace. Generally a materialistic person is infected by the material modes of passion and ignorance. The results of passion and ignorance are lust and greed. In the life of a materialist, activity means working in lust and greed. However, when he comes to his senses, he wants to retire. According to Vedic civilization, such retirement is positively recommended, and this portion of life is called *vānaprastha.* Retirement is absolutely necessary for a materialist who wants to become free from the activities of a sinful life.

King Purañjana's coming home, taking bath and having an appropriate dinner indicate that a materialistic person must retire from sinful activities and become purified by accepting a spiritual master and hearing from him about the values of life. If one would do this, he would feel completely refreshed, just as one feels after taking a bath. After receiving initiation from a bona fide spiritual master, one must abandon all kinds of sinful activities, namely, illicit sex, intoxication, gambling and meat-eating.

The word *ucitāhāra* used in this verse is important. *Ucita* means appropriate. One must eat appropriately and not take after food like hogs take after stool. For a human being there are eatables described in *Bhagavad-gītā* (Bg. 17.8) as *sāttvika-āhāra,* or food in the mode of goodness. One should not indulge in eating food in the modes of passion and ignorance. This is called *ucitāhāra,* or appropriate eating. One who is always eating meat or drinking liquor, which is eating and drinking in passion and ignorance, must give these things up so that his real consciousness may be awakened. In this way one may become peaceful and refreshed. If one is restless or fatigued, one cannot understand the science of God. As stated in *Śrīmad-Bhāgavatam* (1.2.20):

evaṁ prasanna-manaso
bhagavad-bhakti-yogataḥ
bhagavat-tattva-vijñānaṁ
mukta-saṅgasya jāyate

Unless one can become free from the influence of passion and ignorance, he cannot be pacified, and without being pacified, one cannot understand the science of God. King Purañjana's returning home is indicative of man's returning to his original consciousness, known as Kṛṣṇa consciousness. Kṛṣṇa consciousness is absolutely necessary for one who has committed a lot of sinful activities, especially killing animals or hunting in the forest.

TEXT 12

आत्मानमर्हयाञ्चक्रे धूपालेपस्रगादिभिः ।
साध्वलङ्कृतसर्वाङ्गो महिष्यामादधे मनः ॥१२॥

ātmānam arhayāñ cakre
dhūpālepa-srag-ādibhiḥ
sādhv-alaṅkṛta-sarvāṅgo
mahiṣyām ādadhe manaḥ

ātmānam—himself; *arhayām*—as it ought to be done; *cakre*—did; *dhūpa*—incense; *ālepa*—smearing the body with sandalwood pulp; *srak*—garlands; *ādibhiḥ*—beginning with; *sādhu*—saintly, beautifully; *alaṅkṛta*—being decorated; *sarva-aṅgaḥ*—all over the body; *mahiṣyām*—unto the Queen; *ādadhe*—he gave; *manaḥ*—mind.

TRANSLATION

After this, King Purañjana decorated his body with suitable ornaments. He also smeared scented sandalwood pulp over his body and put on flower garlands. In this way he became completely refreshed. After this, he began to search out his Queen.

PURPORT

When a man comes into good consciousness and accepts a saintly person as a spiritual master, he hears many Vedic instructions in the form of philosophy, stories, narrations about great devotees and transactions between God and His devotees. In this way a man becomes refreshed in mind, exactly like a person who smears scented sandalwood pulp all over his body and decorates himself with ornaments. These decorations may be compared to knowledge of religion and the self. Through such knowledge one becomes detached from a materialistic way of life and engages himself in always hearing *Śrīmad-Bhāgavatam, Bhagavad-gītā* and other Vedic literatures. The word *sādhv-alaṅkṛta* used in this verse indicates that one must be absorbed in knowledge gathered from the instructions of saintly persons. Just as King Purañjana began to search out his better half, the Queen, one who is decorated with knowledge and instructions from saintly persons should try to search out his original consciousness, Kṛṣṇa consciousness. One cannot return to Kṛṣṇa consciousness unless he is favored by the instructions of a saintly person. Therefore Śrīla Narottama dāsa Ṭhākura sings: *sādhu-śāstra-guru-vākya, cittete kariyā aikya.* If we want to become saintly persons, or if we want to return to our original Kṛṣṇa consciousness, we must associate with *sādhu* (a saintly person), *śāstra* (authoritative Vedic literature), and *guru* (a bona fide spiritual master). This is the process.

TEXT 13

तृप्तो हृष्टः सुदृप्तश्च कन्दर्पाकृष्टमानसः ।
न व्यचष्ट वरारोहां गृहिणीं गृहमेधिनीम् ॥१३॥

tṛpto hṛṣṭaḥ sudṛptaś ca
kandarpākṛṣṭa-mānasaḥ
na vyacaṣṭa varārohāṁ
gṛhiṇīṁ gṛha-medhinīm

tṛptaḥ—satisfied; *hṛṣṭaḥ*—joyful; *su-dṛptaḥ*—being very proud; *ca*—also; *kandarpa*—by Cupid; *ākṛṣṭa*—attracted; *mānasaḥ*—his mind; *na*—did not; *vyacaṣṭa*—try; *varārohām*—higher consciousness; *gṛhiṇīm*—wife; *gṛha-medhinīm*—one who keeps her husband in material life.

TRANSLATION

After taking his dinner and having his thirst and hunger satisfied, King Purañjana felt some joy within his heart. Instead of being elevated to a higher consciousness, he became captivated by Cupid, and was moved by a desire to find his wife, who kept him satisfied in his household life.

PURPORT

This verse is very significant for those desiring to elevate themselves to a higher level of Kṛṣṇa consciousness. When a person is initiated by a spiritual master, he changes his habits and does not eat undesirable eatables or engage in the eating of meat, the drinking of liquor, illicit sex or gambling. *Sāttvika-āhāra,* foodstuffs in the mode of goodness, are described in the *śāstras* as wheat, rice, vegetables, fruits, milk, sugar, and milk products. Simple food like rice, dahl, chapatis, vegetables, milk and sugar constitute a balanced diet, but sometimes it is found that an initiated person, in the name of *prasāda,* eats very luxurious foodstuffs. Due to his past sinful life he becomes attracted by Cupid and eats good food voraciously. It is clearly visible that when a neophyte in Kṛṣṇa consciousness eats too much, he falls down. Instead of being elevated to pure Kṛṣṇa consciousness, he becomes attracted by Cupid. The so-called *brahmacārī* becomes agitated by women, and the *vānaprastha* may again become captivated into having sex with his wife. Or he may begin to search out another wife. Due to some sentiment, he may give up his own wife and come into the association of devotees and a spiritual master, but due to his past sinful life he cannot stay. Instead of being elevated to Kṛṣṇa consciousness, he falls down, being attracted by Cupid, and takes to another wife for sex enjoyment. The fall of the neophyte devotee from the path of Kṛṣṇa consciousness down to material life is described in *Śrīmad-Bhāgavatam* by Nārada Muni.

tyaktvā sva-dharmaṁ caraṇāmbujaṁ harer
bhajann apakvo 'tha patet tato yadi
yatra kva vābhadram abhūd amuṣya kiṁ
ko vārtha āpto 'bhajatāṁ sva-dharmataḥ
(*Bhāg.* 1.5.17)

This indicates that although a neophyte devotee may fall down from the path of Kṛṣṇa consciousness due to his immaturity, his service to Kṛṣṇa never goes in vain. However, a person who remains steadfast in his family duty or so-called social or family obligation but does not take to Kṛṣṇa consciousness receives no profit. One who comes to Kṛṣṇa consciousness must be very cautious and refrain from prohibited activities, as defined by Rūpa Gosvāmī in his *Upadeśāmṛta:*

atyāhāraḥ prayāsaś ca
prajalpo niyamāgrahaḥ
jana-saṅgaś ca laulyaṁ ca
ṣaḍbhir bhaktir vinaśyati

A neophyte devotee should neither eat too much nor collect more money than necessary. Eating too much or collecting too much is called *atyāhāra.* For such *atyāhāra* one must endeavor very much. This is called *prayāsa.* Superficially one may show himself to be very much faithful to the rules and regulations but at the same time not to be fixed in the regulative principles. This is called *niyamāgraha.* By mixing with undesirable persons or *jana-saṅga,* one becomes tainted with lust and greed and falls down from the path of devotional service.

TEXT 14

अन्तःपुरस्त्रियोऽपृच्छद्विमना इव वेदिषत् ।
अपि वः कुशलं रामाः सेश्वरीणां यथा पुरा ॥१४॥

antaḥpura-striyo 'pṛcchad
vimanā iva vediṣat
api vaḥ kuśalaṁ rāmāḥ
seśvarīṇāṁ yathā purā

antaḥpura—household; *striyaḥ*—women; *apṛcchat*—he asked; *vimanāḥ*—being too much anxious; *iva*—like; *vediṣat*—O King Prācīnabarhi; *api*—whether; *vaḥ*—your; *kuśalam*—good fortune; *rāmāḥ*—O you beautiful women; *sa-īśvarīṇām*—with your mistress; *yathā*—as; *purā*—before.

TRANSLATION

At that time King Purañjana was a little anxious, and he inquired from the household women: My dear beautiful women, are you and your mistress all very happy like before, or not?

PURPORT

In this verse the word *vediṣat* indicates King Prācīnabarhi. When a man becomes refreshed by association with devotees and awakes to Kṛṣṇa consciousness, he consults the activities of his mind—namely, thinking, feeling and willing—and decides whether he should again return to his material activities or stay steady in spiritual consciousness. The word *kuśalam* refers to that which is auspicious. One can make his home perfectly auspicious when he engages in devotional service to Lord Viṣṇu. When one is engaged in activities other than *viṣṇu-bhakti,* or in other words when one is engaged in material activities, he is always filled with anxieties. A sane man should consult his mind, its thinking, feeling and willing processes, and decide how these processes should be utilized. If one always thinks of Kṛṣṇa, feels how to serve Him and wills to execute the order of Kṛṣṇa, it should be known that he has taken good instruction from his intelligence, which is called the mother. Although the King was refreshed, he nonetheless inquired about his wife. Thus he was consulting, thinking and willing how he could again return to his steady good consciousness. The mind may suggest that by *viṣaya-bhoga,* or sense enjoyment, one can become happy, but when one becomes advanced in Kṛṣṇa consciousness, he does not derive happiness from material activities. This is explained in *Bhagavad-gītā:*

viṣayā vinivartante
nirāhārasya dehinaḥ
rasa-varjaṁ raso 'py asya
paraṁ dṛṣṭvā nivartate

"The embodied soul may be restricted from sense enjoyment, though the taste for sense objects remains. But, ceasing such engagements by experiencing a higher taste, he is fixed in consciousness." (Bg. 2.59)

One cannot be artificially unattached to the sense objects unless he finds better engagement in devotional service. *Paraṁ dṛṣṭvā nivartate.* One can cease from material activities only when one actually engages in devotional service.

TEXT 15

न तथैतर्हि रोचन्ते गृहेषु गृहसम्पदः ।
यदि न स्याद् गृहे माता पत्नी वा पतिदेवता ।
व्यङ्गे रथ इव प्राज्ञः को नामासीत दीनवत् ॥१५॥

na tathaitarhi rocante
gṛheṣu gṛha-sampadaḥ
yadi na syād gṛhe mātā
patnī vā pati-devatā
vyaṅge ratha iva prājñaḥ
ko nāmāsīta dīnavat

na—not; *tathā*—like before; *etarhi*—at this moment; *rocante*—become pleasing; *gṛheṣu*—at home; *gṛha-sampadaḥ*—all household paraphernalia; *yadi*—if; *na*—not; *syāt*—there is; *gṛhe*—at home; *mātā*—mother; *patnī*—wife; *vā*—or; *pati-devatā*—devoted to the husband; *vyaṅge*—without wheels; *rathe*—in a chariot; *iva*—like; *prājñaḥ*—learned man; *kaḥ*—who is that; *nāma*—indeed; *āsīta*—would sit; *dīna-vat*—like a poverty-stricken creature.

TRANSLATION

King Purañjana said: I do not understand why my household paraphernalia does not attract me as before. I think that if there is neither a mother nor devoted wife at home, the home is like a chariot without wheels. Where is the fool who will sit down on such an unworkable chariot?

PURPORT

The great politician Cāṇakya Paṇḍita said:

mātā yasya gṛhe nāsti bhāryā ca priya-vādinī
araṇyaṁ tena gantavyaṁ yathāraṇyaṁ tathā gṛham

"If a person has neither a mother nor a pleasing wife at home, he should leave home and go to the forest, because for him there is no difference between the forest and home." The real *mātā,* or mother, is devotional service to the Lord, and the real *patnī,* or devoted wife, is a wife who helps her husband execute religious principles in devotional service. These two things are required for a happy home.

Actually, a woman is supposed to be the energy of the man. Historically, in the background of every great man there is either a mother or a wife. One's household life is very successful if he has both a good wife and mother. In such a case, everything about household affairs and all the paraphernalia in the house become very pleasing. Lord Caitanya Mahāprabhu had both a good mother and pleasing wife, and He was very happy at home. Nonetheless, for the benefit of the whole human race, He took *sannyāsa* and left both His mother and wife. In other words, it is essential that one have both a good mother and wife in order to become perfectly happy at home. Otherwise home life has no meaning. Unless one is religiously guided by intelligence and renders devotional service unto the Supreme Personality of Godhead, his home can never become very pleasing to a saintly person. In other words, if a man has a good mother or a good wife, there is no need of his taking *sannyāsa*—that is, unless it is absolutely necessary, as it was for Lord Caitanya Mahāprabhu.

TEXT 16

क्व वर्तते सा ललना मज्जन्तं व्यसनार्णवे ।
या मामुद्धरते प्रज्ञां दीपयन्ती पदे पदे ॥१६॥

kva vartate sā lalanā
majjantaṁ vyasanārṇave
yā mām uddharate prajñāṁ
dīpayantī pade pade

kva—where; *vartate*—is now staying; *sā*—she; *lalanā*—woman; *majjantam*—while drowning; *vyasana-arṇave*—in the ocean of danger; *yā*—who; *mām*—me; *uddharate*—delivers; *prajñām*—good intelligence; *dīpayantī*—enlightening; *pade pade*—in every step.

TRANSLATION

Kindly let me know the whereabouts of that beautiful woman who always saves me when I am drowning in the ocean of danger. By giving me good intelligence at every step, she always saves me.

PURPORT

There is no difference between a good wife and good intelligence. One who possesses good intelligence can deliberate properly and save himself from many dangerous conditions. In material existence there is danger at every step. In *Śrīmad-Bhāgavatam* it is said: *padaṁ padaṁ yad vipadāṁ na teṣām* (*Bhāg.* 10.14.58). This material world is not actually a place of residence for an intelligent person or a devotee because here there is danger at every step. Vaikuṇṭha is the real home for the devotee, for there is no anxiety and no danger. Good intelligence means becoming Kṛṣṇa conscious. In the *Caitanya-caritāmṛta* it is said: *kṛṣṇa ye bhaje se baḍa catura.* Unless one is Kṛṣṇa conscious, he cannot be called an intelligent person.

Herein we see that King Purañjana was searching after his good wife, who always helped him out of the dangerous situations that always occur in material existence. As already explained, a real wife is *dharma-patnī.* That is, a woman accepted in marriage by ritualistic ceremony is called *dharma-patnī,* which signifies that she is accepted in terms of religious principles. Children born of *dharma-patnī,* or a woman married according to religious principles, inherit the property of the father, but children born of a woman who is not properly married do not inherit the father's property. The word *dharma-patnī* also refers to a chaste wife. A chaste wife is one who never had any connection with men before her marriage. Once a woman is given the freedom to mingle with all kinds of men in her youth, it is very difficult for her to keep chaste. She generally cannot remain chaste.

When butter is brought into the proximity of fire, it melts. The woman is like fire, and man is like the butter. But if one gets a chaste wife, accepted through a religious marriage ritual, she can be of great help when one is threatened by the many dangerous situations of life. Actually such a wife can become the source of all good intelligence. With such a good wife, the family's engagement in the devotional service of the Lord actually makes a home a *gṛhastha-āśrama,* or household dedicated to spiritual cultivation.

TEXT 17

रामा ऊचुः
नरनाथ न जानीमस्त्वत्प्रिया यद्व्यवस्यति ।
भूतले निरवस्तारे शयानां पश्य शत्रुहन् ॥१७॥

rāmā ūcuḥ
nara-nātha na jānīmas
tvat-priyā yad vyavasyati
bhūtale niravastāre
śayānāṁ paśya śatru-han

rāmāḥ ūcuḥ—the women thus spoke; *nara-nātha*—O King; *na jānīmaḥ*—we do not know; *tvat-priyā*—your beloved; *yad vyavasyati*—why she has taken to this sort of life; *bhū-tale*—on the ground; *niravastāre*—without bedding; *śayānām*—lying down; *paśya*—look; *śatru-han*—O killer of the enemies.

TRANSLATION

All the women addressed the King: O master of the citizens, we do not know why your dear wife has taken on this sort of existence. O killer of enemies, kindly look! She is lying on the ground without bedding. We cannot understand why she is acting this way.

PURPORT

When a person is devoid of devotional service, or *viṣṇu-bhakti,* he takes to many sinful activities. King Purañjana left home, neglected his own wife, and engaged himself in killing animals. This is the position of all materialistic men. They do not care for a married chaste wife. They take the wife only as an instrument for sense enjoyment, not as a means for devotional service. To have unrestricted sex life, the *karmīs* work very hard.

They have concluded that the best course is to have sex with any woman and simply pay the price for her, as though she were a mercantile commodity. Thus they engage their energy in working very hard for such material acquisitions. Such materialistic people have lost their good intelligence. They must search out their intelligence within the heart. A person who does not have a chaste wife accepted by religious principles always has a bewildered intelligence.

The wife of King Purañjana was lying on the ground because she was neglected by her husband. Actually the woman must always be protected by her husband. We always speak of the goddess of fortune as being placed on the chest of Nārāyaṇa. In other words, the wife must remain embraced by her husband. Thus she becomes beloved and well protected. Just as one saves his money and places it under his own personal protection, one should similarly protect his wife by his own personal supervision. Just as intelligence is always within the heart, so a beloved chaste wife should always have her place on the chest of a good husband. This is the proper relationship between husband and wife. A wife is therefore called *ardhāṅganī*, or half of the body. One cannot remain with only one leg, one hand or only one side of the body. He must have two sides. Similarly, according to nature's way, husband and wife should live together. In the lower species of life, among birds and animals, it is seen that by nature's arrangement the husband and wife live together. It is similarly ideal in human life for the husband and wife to live together. The home should be a place for devotional service, and the wife should be chaste and accepted by a ritualistic ceremony. In this way one can become happy at home.

TEXT 18

नारद उवाच
पुरञ्जनः स्वमहिषीं निरीक्ष्यावधुतां भुवि ।
तत्सङ्गोन्मथितज्ञानो वैक्लव्यं परमं ययौ ॥१८॥

nārada uvāca
purañjanaḥ sva-mahiṣīṁ
nirīkṣyāvadhutāṁ bhuvi
tat-saṅgonmathita-jñāno
vaiklavyaṁ paramaṁ yayau

nāradaḥ uvāca—the great sage Nārada spoke; *purañjanaḥ*—King Purañjana; *sva-mahiṣīm*—his own Queen; *nirīkṣya*—after seeing; *avadhutām*—appearing like a mendicant; *bhuvi*—on the ground; *tat*—her; *saṅga*—by association; *unmathita*—encouraged; *jñānaḥ*—whose knowledge; *vaiklavyam*—bewilderment; *paramam*—supreme; *yayau*—obtained.

TRANSLATION

The great sage Nārada continued: My dear King Prācīnabarhi, as soon as King Purañjana saw his Queen lying on the ground, appearing like a mendicant, he immediately became bewildered.

PURPORT

In this verse the word *avadhutām* is especially significant, for it refers to a mendicant who does not take care of his body. Since the Queen was lying on the ground without bedding and proper dress, King Purañjana became very much aggrieved. In other words, he repented that he had neglected his intelligence and had engaged himself in the forest in killing animals. In other words, when one's good intelligence is separated or neglected, he fully engages in sinful activities. Due to neglecting one's good intelligence, or Kṛṣṇa consciousness, one becomes bewildered and engages in sinful activities. Upon realizing this, a man becomes repentant. Such repentance is described by Narottama dāsa Ṭhākura: *hari hari viphale janama goṅāinu/ manuṣya-janama pāiyā, rādhā-kṛṣṇa nā bhajiyā, jāniyā śuniyā viṣa khāinu.* Narottama dāsa Ṭhākura herein says that he repents for having spoiled his human life and knowingly drunk poison. By not being Kṛṣṇa conscious, one willingly drinks the poison of material life. The purport is that one certainly becomes addicted to sinful activities when he becomes devoid of his good chaste wife, or when he has lost his good sense and does not take to Kṛṣṇa consciousness.

TEXT 19

सान्त्वयन् श्लक्ष्णया वाचा हृदयेन विदूयता ।
प्रेयस्याः स्नेहसंरम्भलिङ्गमात्मनि नाभ्यगात् ॥१९॥

sāntvayan ślakṣṇayā vācā
hṛdayena vidūyatā
preyasyāḥ sneha-saṁrambha-
liṅgam ātmani nābhyagāt

sāntvayan—pacifying; *ślakṣṇayā*—by sweet; *vācā*—words; *hṛdayena*—with a heart; *vidūyatā*—regretting very much; *preyasyāḥ*—of his beloved; *sneha*—

from affection; *saṁrambha*—of anger; *liṅgam*—symptom; *ātmani*—in her heart; *na*—did not; *abhyagāt*—arouse.

TRANSLATION

The King, with aggrieved mind, began to speak to his wife with very pleasing words. Although he was filled with regret and tried to pacify her, he could not see any symptom of anger caused by love within the heart of his beloved wife.

PURPORT

The King very much regretted having left his Queen and having gone to the forest to execute sinful activities. When a person regrets his sinful activities, the abandoning of Kṛṣṇa consciousness and good intelligence, his path of deliverance from the path of material clutches is opened. As stated in *Śrīmad-Bhāgavatam: parābhavas tāvad abodha-jāto yāvan na jijñāsata ātma-tattvam* (*Bhāg.* 5.5.5). When a person loses his Kṛṣṇa consciousness and loses interest in self-realization, he must engage in sinful activities. All one's activities in a life devoid of Kṛṣṇa consciousness simply lead to defeat and misuse of one's life. Naturally one who comes to Kṛṣṇa consciousness regrets his previous sinful activities in the human form. Only by this process can one be delivered from the clutches of nescience or ignorance in materialistic life.

TEXT 20

अनुनिन्येऽथ शनकैर्वीरोऽनुनयकोविदः ।
पस्पर्श पादयुगलमाह चोत्सङ्गलालिताम् ॥२०॥

anuninye 'tha śanakair
vīro 'nunaya-kovidaḥ
pasparśa pāda-yugalam
āha cotsaṅga-lālitām

anuninye—began to flatter; *atha*—thus; *śanakaiḥ*—gradually; *vīraḥ*—the hero; *anunaya-kovidaḥ*—one who is very expert in flattery; *pasparśa*—touched; *pāda-yugalam*—both the feet; *āha*—he said; *ca*—also; *utsaṅga*—on his lap; *lālitām*—thus being embraced.

TRANSLATION

Because the King was very expert in flattery, he began to pacify his Queen very slowly. First he touched her two feet, then embraced her nicely, seating her on his lap, and began to speak as follows.

PURPORT

One has to awaken his Kṛṣṇa consciousness by first regretting his past deeds. Just as King Purañjana began to flatter his Queen, one should, by deliberate consideration, raise himself to the platform of Kṛṣṇa consciousness. To attain such an end, one must touch the lotus feet of the spiritual master. Kṛṣṇa consciousness cannot be achieved by self-endeavor. One must therefore approach a self-realized Kṛṣṇa conscious person and touch his lotus feet. Prahlāda Mahārāja therefore said:

naiṣāṁ matis tāvad urukramāṅghriṁ
spṛśaty anarthāpagamo yad-arthaḥ
mahīyasāṁ pāda-rajo 'bhiṣekaṁ
niṣkiñcanānāṁ na vṛṇīta yāvat
(*Bhāg.* 7.5.32)

One cannot come to the precincts of Kṛṣṇa consciousness unless he touches the dust of the lotus feet of a person who has become a *mahātmā*, a great devotee. This is the beginning of the surrendering process. Lord Kṛṣṇa wants everyone to surrender unto Him, and this surrendering process begins when one touches the lotus feet of a bona fide spiritual master. By sincerely rendering service to a bona fide spiritual master, one begins his spiritual life in Kṛṣṇa consciousness. Touching the lotus feet of a spiritual master means giving up one's false prestige and unnecessarily puffed up position in the material world. Those who remain in the darkness of material existence due to their falsely prestigious positions—so-called scientists and philosophers—are actually atheists. They do not know the ultimate cause of everything. Although bewildered, they are not ready to surrender themselves to the lotus feet of a person who knows things in their proper perspective. In other words, one cannot arouse Kṛṣṇa consciousness simply by his own mental speculation. One must surrender to a bona fide spiritual master. Only this process will help him.

TEXT 21

पुरञ्जन उवाच
नूनं त्वकृतपुण्यास्ते भृत्या येष्वीश्वराः शुभे ।
कृतागःस्वात्मसात्कृत्वा शिक्षादण्डं न युञ्जते ॥२१॥

purañjana uvāca
nūnaṁ tv akṛta-puṇyās te
bhṛtyā yeṣv īśvarāḥ śubhe

kṛtāgaḥsv ātmasāt kṛtvā
śikṣā-daṇḍaṁ na yuñjate

purañjanaḥ uvāca—Purañjana said; *nūnam*—certainly; *tu*—then; *akṛta-puṇyāḥ*—those who are not pious; *te*—such; *bhṛtyāḥ*—servants; *yeṣu*—unto whom; *īśvarāḥ*—the masters; *śubhe*—O most auspicious one; *kṛta-āgaḥsu*—having committed an offense; *ātmasāt*—accepting as their own; *kṛtvā*—doing so; *śikṣā*—instructive; *daṇḍam*—punishment; *na yuñjate*—do not give.

TRANSLATION

King Purañjana said: My dear beautiful wife, when a master accepts a servant as his own man but does not punish him for his offenses, the servant must be considered unfortunate.

PURPORT

According to Vedic civilization, domestic animals and servants are treated exactly like one's own children. Animals and children are sometimes punished not out of vengeance but out of love. Similarly, a master sometimes punishes his servant, not out of vengeance but out of love, to correct him and bring him to the right point. Thus King Purañjana took his punishment dealt by his wife, the Queen, as mercy upon him. He considered himself the most obedient servant of the Queen. She was angry at him for his sinful activities—namely, hunting in the forest and leaving her at home. King Purañjana accepted the punishment as actual love and affection from his wife. In the same way, when a person is punished by the laws of nature, by the will of God, he should not be disturbed. A real devotee thinks in this way. When a devotee is put into an awkward position, he takes it as the mercy of the Supreme Lord.

tat te 'nukampāṁ su-samīkṣamāṇo
bhuñjāna evātma-kṛtaṁ vipākam
hṛd-vāg-vapurbhir vidadhan namas te
jīveta yo mukti-pade sa dāya-bhāk (*Bhāg.* 10.14.8)

This verse states that the devotee accepts a reversal of his position in life as a benediction by the Lord and consequently offers the Lord more obeisances and prayers, thinking that the punishment is due to his past misdeeds and that the Lord is punishing him very mildly. The punishment awarded by the state or by God for one's own faults is actually for one's benefit. In the *Manu-saṁhitā* it is said that the king should be considered merciful when he condemns a murderer to death because a murderer punished in this life becomes freed from his sinful activity and in the next life takes birth cleared of all sins. If one accepts punishment as a reward dealt by the master, he becomes intelligent enough not to commit the same mistake again.

TEXT 22

परमोऽनुग्रहो दण्डो भृत्येषु प्रभुणार्पितः ।
बालो न वेद तत्तन्वि बन्धुकृत्यममर्षणः ॥२२॥

paramo 'nugraho daṇḍo
bhṛtyeṣu prabhuṇārpitaḥ
bālo na veda tat tanvi
bandhu-kṛtyam amarṣaṇaḥ

paramaḥ—supreme; *anugrahaḥ*—mercy; *daṇḍaḥ*—punishment; *bhṛtyeṣu*—upon the servants; *prabhuṇā*—by the master; *arpitaḥ*—awarded; *bālaḥ*—foolish; *na*—does not; *veda*—know; *tat*—that; *tanvi*—O slender maiden; *bandhu-kṛtyam*—the duty of a friend; *amarṣaṇaḥ*—angry.

TRANSLATION

My dear slender maiden, when a master chastises his servant, the servant should accept this as great mercy. One who becomes angry must be very foolish not to know that such is the duty of his friend.

PURPORT

It is said that when a foolish man is instructed in something very nice, he generally cannot accept it. Indeed, he actually becomes angry. Such anger is compared to the poison of a serpent, for when a serpent is fed milk and bananas, its poison actually increases. Instead of becoming merciful or sober, the serpent increases its poisonous venom when fed nice foodstuffs. Similarly, when a fool is instructed, he does not rectify himself, but actually becomes angry.

TEXT 23

सा त्वं मुखं सुदति सुभ्र्वनुरागभार-
व्रीडाविलम्बविलसद्धसितावलोकम् ।
नीलालकालिभिरुपस्कृतमुन्नसं नः
स्वानां प्रदर्शय मनस्विनि वल्गुवाक्यम् ॥२३॥

sā tvaṁ mukhaṁ sudati subhrv anurāga-bhāra-
vrīḍā-vilamba-vilasad-dhasitāvalokam
nīlālakālibhir upaskṛtam unnasaṁ naḥ
svānāṁ pradarśaya manasvini valgu-vākyam

sā—that (you, my wife); *tvam*—you; *mukham*—your face; *su-dati*—with beautiful teeth; *su-bhru*—with beautiful eyebrows; *anurāga*—attachment; *bhāra*—loaded by; *vrīḍā*—feminine shyness; *vilamba*—hanging down; *vilasat*—shining; *hasita*—smiling; *avalokam*—with glances; *nīla*—bluish; *alaka*—with hair; *alibhiḥ*—bee-like; *upaskṛtam*—thus being beautiful; *unnasam*—with a raised nose; *naḥ*—to me; *svānām*—who am yours; *pradarśaya*—please show; *manasvini*—O most thoughtful lady; *valgu-vākyam*—with sweet words.

TRANSLATION

My dear wife, your teeth are very beautifully set, and your attractive features make you appear very thoughtful. Kindly give up your anger, be merciful upon me, and please smile upon me with loving attachment. When I see a smile on your beautiful face, and when I see your hair, which is as beautiful as the color blue, and see your raised nose and hear your sweet talk, you will become more beautiful to me and thus attract me and oblige me. You are my most respected mistress.

PURPORT

An effeminate husband, simply being attracted by the external beauty of his wife, tries to become her most obedient servant. Śrīpāda Śaṅkarācārya has therefore advised that we not become attracted by a lump of flesh and blood. The story is told that at one time a man, very much attracted to a beautiful woman, wooed the woman in such a way that she devised a plan to show him the ingredients of her beauty. The woman made a date to see him, and before seeing him she took a purgative, and that whole day and night she simply passed stool, and she preserved that stool in a pot. The next night, when the man came to see her, she appeared very ugly and emaciated. When the man inquired from her about the woman with whom he had an engagement, she replied, "I am that very woman." The man refused to believe her, not knowing that she had lost all her beauty due to the violent purgative that caused her to pass stool day and night. When the man began to argue with her, the woman said that she was not looking beautiful because she was separated from the ingredients of her beauty. When the man asked how she could be so separated, the woman said, "Come on, and I will show you." She then showed him the pot filled with liquid stool and vomit. Thus the man became aware that a beautiful woman is simply a lump of matter composed of blood, stool, urine and similar other disgusting ingredients. This is the actual fact, but in a state of illusion, man becomes attracted by illusory beauty and becomes a victim of *māyā*.

King Purañjana begged his Queen to return to her original beauty. He tried to revive her just as a living entity tries to revive his original consciousness, Kṛṣṇa consciousness, which is very beautiful. All the beautiful features of the Queen could be compared to the beautiful features of Kṛṣṇa consciousness. When one returns to his original Kṛṣṇa consciousness, he actually becomes steady, and his life becomes successful.

TEXT 24

तस्मिन्दधे दममहं तव वीरपत्नि
योऽन्यत्र भूसुरकुलात्कृतकिल्बिषस्तम् ।
पश्ये न वीतभयमुन्मुदितं त्रिलोक्या-
मन्यत्र वै मुररिपोरितरत्र दासात् ॥२४॥

tasmin dadhe damam ahaṁ tava vīra-patni
yo 'nyatra bhūsura-kulāt kṛta-kilbiṣas tam
paśye na vīta-bhayam unmuditaṁ tri-lokyām
anyatra vai mura-ripor itaratra dāsāt

tasmin—unto him; *dadhe*—shall give; *damam*—punishment; *aham*—I; *tava*—to you; *vīra-patni*—O wife of the hero; *yaḥ*—one who; *anyatra*—besides; *bhū-sura-kulāt*—from the group of demigods on this earth, (the *brāhmaṇas*); *kṛta*—done; *kilbiṣaḥ*—offense; *tam*—him; *paśye*—I see; *na*—not; *vīta*—without; *bhayam*—fear; *unmuditam*—without anxiety; *tri-lokyām*—within the three worlds; *anyatra*—elsewhere; *vai*—certainly; *mura-ripoḥ*—of the enemy of Mura (Kṛṣṇa); *itaratra*—on the other hand; *dāsāt*—than the servant.

TRANSLATION

O hero's wife, kindly tell me if someone has offended you. I am prepared to give such a person punishment as long as he does not belong to the brāhmaṇa caste. But for the servant of Muraripu [Kṛṣṇa], I excuse no one within or beyond these three worlds. No one can freely move after offending you, for I am prepared to punish him.

PURPORT

According to Vedic civilization, a *brāhmaṇa,* or one who is properly qualified to understand the Absolute Truth—that is, one belonging to the most intelligent social order—as well as the devotee of Lord Kṛṣṇa, who is known as Muradviṣa, enemy of a demon named Mura, is not subject to the rules and regulations of the state. In other words, upon breaking the laws of the state, everyone can be punished by the government except the *brāhmaṇas* and Vaiṣṇavas. *Brāhmaṇas* and Vaiṣṇavas never transgress the laws of the state or the laws of nature because they know perfectly well the resultant reactions caused by such law-breaking. Even though they may sometimes appear to violate the laws, they are not to be punished by the king. This instruction was given to King Prācīnabarhiṣat by Nārada Muni. King Purañjana was a representative of King Prācīnabarhiṣat, and Nārada Muni was reminding King Prācīnabarhiṣat of his forefather, Mahārāja Pṛthu, who never chastised a *brāhmaṇa* or a Vaiṣṇava.

One's pure intelligence, or pure Kṛṣṇa consciousness, becomes polluted by material activities. Pure consciousness can again be revived by the process of sacrifice, charity, pious activities, etc., but when one pollutes his Kṛṣṇa consciousness by offending a *brāhmaṇa* or a Vaiṣṇava, it is very difficult to revive. Śrī Caitanya Mahāprabhu has described the *vaiṣṇava-aparādha,* or offense to a Vaiṣṇava, as "the mad elephant offense." One should be very careful not to offend a Vaiṣṇava or a *brāhmaṇa.* Even the great *yogī* Durvāsā was harassed by the Sudarśana *cakra* when he offended the Vaiṣṇava Mahārāja Ambarīṣa, who was neither a *brāhmaṇa* nor a *sannyāsī* but an ordinary householder. Mahārāja Ambarīṣa was a Vaiṣṇava, and consequently Durvāsā Muni was chastised.

The conclusion is that if Kṛṣṇa consciousness is covered by material sins, one can eliminate the sins simply by chanting the Hare Kṛṣṇa *mantra,* but if one pollutes his Kṛṣṇa consciousness by offending a *brāhmaṇa* or a Vaiṣṇava, one cannot revive it until one properly atones for the sin by pleasing the offended Vaiṣṇava or *brāhmaṇa.* This was the course that Durvāsā Muni had to follow, for he surrendered unto Mahārāja Ambarīṣa. A *vaiṣṇava-aparādha* cannot be atoned for by any means other than by begging the pardon of the offended Vaiṣṇava.

TEXT 25

वक्त्रं न ते वितिलकं मलिनं विहर्षं
संरम्भभीममविमृष्टमपेतरागम् ।
पश्ये स्तनावपि शुचोपहतौ सुजातौ
बिम्बाधरं विगतकुङ्कुमपङ्करागम् ॥२५॥

vaktraṁ na te vitilakaṁ malinaṁ viharṣaṁ
saṁrambha-bhīmam avimṛṣṭam apeta-rāgam
paśye stanāv api śucopahatau sujātau
bimbādharaṁ vigata-kuṅkuma-paṅka-rāgam

vaktram—face; *na*—never; *te*—your; *vitilakam*—without being decorated; *malinam*—unclean; *viharṣam*—morose; *saṁrambha*—with anger; *bhīmam*—dangerous; *avimṛṣṭam*—without luster; *apeta-rāgam*—without affection; *paśye*—I have seen; *stanau*—your breasts; *api*—also; *śucā-upahatau*—wet because of your tears; *su-jātau*—so nice; *bimba-adharam*—red lips; *vigata*—without; *kuṅkuma-paṅka*—saffron; *rāgam*—color.

TRANSLATION

My dear wife, until this day I have never seen your face without tilaka decorations, nor have I seen you so morose and without luster or affection. Nor have I seen your two nice breasts wet with tears from your eyes. Nor have I ever before seen your lips, which are ordinarily as red as the bimba fruit, without their reddish hue.

PURPORT

Every woman looks very beautiful when decorated with *tilaka* and vermillion. A woman generally becomes very attractive when her lips are colored with reddish saffron or vermillion. But when one's consciousness and intelligence are without any brilliant thoughts about Kṛṣṇa, they become morose and lusterless, so much so that one cannot derive any benefit despite sharp intelligence.

TEXT 26

तन्मे प्रसीद सुहृदः कृतकिल्बिषस्य
स्वैरं गतस्य मृगयां व्यसनातुरस्य ।
का देवरं वशगतं कुसुमास्त्रवेग-
विस्रस्तपौंस्नमुशती न भजेत कृत्ये ॥२६॥

tan me prasīda suhṛdaḥ kṛta-kilbiṣasya
svairaṁ gatasya mṛgayāṁ vyasanāturasya
kā devaraṁ vaśa-gataṁ kusumāstra-vega-
visrasta-pauṁsnam uśatī na bhajeta kṛtye

tat—therefore; *me*—unto me; *prasīda*—be kind; *su-hṛdaḥ*—intimate friend; *kṛta-kilbiṣasya*—having committed sinful activities; *svairam*—independently; *gatasya*—who went; *mṛgayām*—hunting; *vyasana-āturasya*—being influenced by sinful desire; *kā*—what woman; *devaram*—the husband; *vaśa-gatam*—under her control; *kusumāstra-vega*—pierced by the arrow of Cupid; *visrasta*—scattered; *pauṁsnam*—his patience; *uśatī*—very beautiful; *na*—never; *bhajeta*—would embrace; *kṛtye*—in proper duty.

TRANSLATION

My dear Queen, due to my sinful desires I went to the forest to hunt without asking you. Therefore I must admit that I have offended you. Nonetheless, thinking of me as your most intimate subordinate, you should still be very much pleased with me. Factually I am very much bereaved, but being pierced by the arrow of Cupid, I am feeling lusty. But where is the beautiful woman who would give up her lusty husband and refuse to unite with him?

PURPORT

Both man and woman desire one another; that is the basic principle of material existence. Women in general always keep themselves beautiful so that they can be attractive to their lusty husbands. When a lusty husband comes before his wife, the wife takes advantage of his aggressive activities and enjoys life. Generally when a woman is attacked by a man—whether her husband or some other man—she enjoys the attack, being too lusty. In other words, when one's intelligence is properly utilized, both the intellect and the intelligent person enjoy one another with great satisfaction. As stated in *Śrīmad-Bhāgavatam: yan maithunādi gṛhamedhi-*

sukhaṁ hi tucchaṁ kaṇḍūyanena karayor iva duḥkha-duḥkham (*Bhāg.* 7.9.45). The actual happiness of the *karmīs* is sex life. They work very hard outside the home, and to satiate their hard labor, they come home to enjoy sex life. King Purañjana went to the forest to hunt, and after his hard labor he returned home to enjoy sex life. If a man lives outside the home and spends a week in a city or somewhere else, at the end of the week he becomes very anxious to return home and enjoy sex with his wife. This is confirmed in *Śrīmad-Bhāgavatam: yan maithunādi gṛhamedhi-sukhaṁ hi tuccham. Karmīs* work very hard simply to enjoy sex. Modern human society has improved the materialistic way of life simply by inducing unrestricted sex life in many different ways. This is most prominently visible in the Western world.

Thus end the Bhaktivedanta purports of the Fourth Canto, Twenty-sixth Chapter, of the Śrīmad-Bhāgavatam, *entitled "King Purañjana Goes to the Forest to Hunt, and His Queen Becomes Angry."*

CHAPTER TWENTY-SEVEN

Attack by Caṇḍavega on the City of King Purañjana; the Character of Kālakanyā

TEXT 1

नारद उवाच

इत्थं पुरञ्जनं सध्र्यग्वशमानीय विभ्रमैः ।
पुरञ्जनी महाराज रेमे रमयती पतिम् ॥ १ ॥

nārada uvāca
itthaṁ purañjanaṁ sadhryag
vaśamānīya vibhramaiḥ
purañjanī mahā-rāja
reme ramayatī patim

nāradaḥ uvāca—Nārada said; *ittham*—thus; *purañjanam*—King Purañjana; *sadhryak*—completely; *vaśamānīya*—bringing under her control; *vibhramaiḥ*—by her charms; *purañjanī*—the wife of King Purañjana; *mahā-rāja*—O King; *reme*—enjoyed; *ramayatī*—giving all satisfaction; *patim*—to her husband.

TRANSLATION

The great sage Nārada continued: My dear King, after bewildering her husband in different ways and bringing him under her control, the wife of King Purañjana gave him all satisfaction and enjoyed sex life with him.

PURPORT

After hunting in the forest, King Purañjana returned home, and after refreshing himself by taking a bath and eating nice food, he searched for his wife. When he saw her lying down on the ground without a bed, as if neglected, and devoid of any proper dress, he became very much aggrieved.

He then became attracted to her and began to enjoy her company. A living entity is similarly engaged in the material world in sinful activities. These sinful activities may be compared to King Purañjana's hunting in the forest.

A sinful life can be counteracted by various processes of religion such as *yajña, vrata* and *dāna*—that is, the performance of sacrifices, the taking of a vow for some religious ritual, and the giving of charity. In this way one may become free from the reactions of sinful life and at the same time awaken his original Kṛṣṇa consciousness. By coming home, taking his bath, eating nice foodstuffs, getting refreshed and searching out his wife, King Purañjana came to his good consciousness in his family life. In other words, a systematic family life as enjoined in the *Vedas* is better than an irresponsible sinful life. If a husband and wife combine together in Kṛṣṇa consciousness and live together peacefully, that is very nice. However, if a husband becomes too much attracted by his wife and forgets his duty in life, the implications of materialistic life will again resume. Śrīla Rūpa Gosvāmī has therefore recommended *anāsaktasya viṣayān* (Bh.r.s. 1.2.255). Without being attached by sex, the husband and wife may live together for the advancement of spiritual life. The husband should engage in devotional service, and the wife should be faithful and religious according to the Vedic injunctions. Such a combination is very good. However, if the husband becomes too much attracted to the wife due to sex, the position becomes very dangerous. Women in general are very much sexually inclined. Indeed, it is said that a woman's sex desire is nine times stronger than a man's. It is therefore a man's duty to keep a woman under his control by satisfying her, giving her ornaments, nice food and clothes, and engaging her in religious activities. Of course a woman should have a few children and in this way not be disturbing to the man. Unfortunately, if the man becomes attracted to the woman simply for sex enjoyment, then family life becomes abominable.

The great politician Cāṇakya Paṇḍita has said: *bhāryā rūpavatī śatruḥ*—a beautiful wife is an enemy. Of course every woman in the eyes of her husband is very beautiful. Others may see her as not very beautiful, but the husband, being very much attracted to her, sees her always as very beautiful. If the husband sees the wife as very beautiful, it is to be assumed that he is too much attracted to her. This attraction is the attraction of sex. The whole world is captivated by the two modes of material nature *rajo-guṇa* and *tamo-guṇa,* passion and ignorance. Generally women are very much passionate and are less intelligent; therefore somehow or other a man should not be under the control of their passion and ignorance. However, by performing *bhakti-yoga,* or devotional service, a man can be raised to the platform of goodness. If a husband situated in the mode of goodness can control his wife, who is in passion and ignorance, the woman is benefited. Forgetting her natural inclination for passion and ignorance, the woman becomes obedient and faithful to her husband, who is situated in goodness. Such a life becomes very welcome. The intelligence of the man and woman may then work very nicely together, and they can make a progressive march towards spiritual realization. Otherwise, the husband, coming under the control of the wife, sacrifices his quality of goodness and becomes subservient to the qualities of passion and ignorance. In this way the whole situation becomes polluted.

The conclusion is that a household life is better than a sinful life devoid of responsibility, but if in the household life the husband becomes subordinate to the wife, involvement in materialistic life again becomes prominent. In this way a man's material bondage becomes enhanced. Because of this, according to the Vedic system, after a certain age a man is recommended to abandon his family life for the stages of *vānaprastha* and *sannyāsa.*

TEXT 2

स राजा महिषीं राजन् सुस्नातां रुचिराननाम् ।
कृतस्वस्त्ययनां तृप्तामभ्यनन्ददुपागताम् ॥ २ ॥

sa rājā mahiṣīṁ rājan
susnātāṁ rucirānanām
kṛta-svasty-ayanāṁ tṛptām
abhyanandad upāgatām

saḥ—he; *rājā*—the King; *mahiṣīm*—the Queen; *rājan*—O King; *su-snātām*—nicely bathed; *rucira-ānanām*—attractive face; *kṛta-svasti-ayanām*—dressed with auspicious garments and ornaments; *tṛptām*—satisfied; *abhyanandat*—he welcomed; *upāgatām*—approached.

TRANSLATION

The Queen took her bath and dressed herself nicely with all auspicious garments and ornaments. After taking food and becoming completely satisfied, she returned to the King. Upon seeing her beautifully decorated attractive face, the King welcomed her with all devotion.

PURPORT

A woman is generally accustomed to dress herself nicely with fine garments and decorative ornaments. She may even sometimes wear flowers in her hair. Women especially dress themselves up in the evening because the husband comes home in the evening after working hard all day. It is the duty of the wife to dress herself up very nicely so that when her husband returns home he becomes attracted by her dress and cleanliness and thus becomes satisfied. In other words, the wife is the inspiration of all good intelligence. Upon seeing one's wife dressed nicely, one can think very soberly about family business. When a person is too anxious about family affairs, he cannot discharge his family duties nicely. A wife is therefore supposed to be an inspiration and should keep the husband's intelligence in good order so that they can combinedly prosecute the affairs of family life without impediment.

TEXT 3

तयोपगूढः परिरब्धकन्धरो
रहोऽनुमन्त्रैरपकृष्टचेतनः ।
न कालरंहो बुबुधे दुरत्ययं
दिवा निशेति प्रमदापरिग्रहः ॥ ३ ॥

tayopagūḍhaḥ parirabdha-kandharo
raho 'numantrair apakṛṣṭa-cetanaḥ
na kāla-raṁho bubudhe duratyayaṁ
divā niśeti pramadā-parigrahaḥ

tayā—by the Queen; *upagūḍhaḥ*—was embraced; *parirabdha*—embraced; *kandharaḥ*—shoulders; *rahaḥ*—in a solitary place; *anumantraiḥ*—by joking words; *apakṛṣṭa-cetanaḥ*—having degraded consciousness; *na*—not; *kāla-raṁhaḥ*—the passing of time; *bubudhe*—was aware of; *duratyayam*—impossible to overcome; *divā*—day; *niśā*—night; *iti*—thus; *pramadā*—by the woman; *parigrahaḥ*—captivated.

TRANSLATION

Queen Purañjanī embraced the King, and the King also responded by embracing her shoulders. In this way, in a solitary place, they enjoyed

joking words. Thus King Purañjana became very much captivated by his beautiful wife and deviated from his good sense. He forgot that the passing of days and nights meant that his span of life was being reduced without profit.

PURPORT

The word *pramadā* in this verse is very significant. A beautiful wife is certainly enlivening to her husband but at the same time is the cause of degradation. The word *pramadā* means enlivening as well as maddening. Generally a householder does not take the passing of days and nights very seriously. A person in ignorance takes it as the usual course that days come, and, after the days, the nights come. This is the law of material nature. But a man in ignorance does not know that when the sun rises early in the morning it begins to take away the balance of his life. Thus day after day the span of one's life is reduced, and, forgetting the duty of human life, the foolish man simply remains in the company of his wife and enjoys her in a secluded place. Such a condition is called *apakṛṣṭa-cetana,* or degraded consciousness. Human consciousness should be used for elevation to Kṛṣṇa consciousness. But when a person is too much attracted to his wife and family affairs, he does not take Kṛṣṇa consciousness very seriously. He thus becomes degraded, not knowing that he cannot buy back even a second of his life in return for millions of dollars. The greatest loss in life is passing time without understanding Kṛṣṇa. Every moment of our lives should be utilized properly, and the proper use of life is to increase devotional service to the Lord. Without devotional service to the Lord, the activities of life become simply a waste of time. *Śrama eva hi kevalam.* Simply by becoming "dutiful" we do not make any profit in life. As confirmed in *Śrīmad-Bhāgavatam:*

dharmaḥ svanuṣṭhitaḥ puṁsāṁ
viṣvaksena-kathāsu yaḥ
notpādayed yadi ratiṁ
śrama eva hi kevalam

"Duties [*dharma*] executed by men, regardless of occupation, are only so much useless labor if they do not provoke attraction for the message of the Supreme Lord." (*Bhāg.* 1.2.8)

If after performing one's occupational duty very perfectly, one does not make progress in Kṛṣṇa consciousness, it should be understood that he has simply wasted his time in valueless labor.

TEXT 4

शयान उन्नद्धमदो महामना
महार्हतल्पे महिषीभुजोपधिः ।
तामेव वीरो मनुते परं यत-
स्तमोऽभिभूतो न निजं परं च यत् ॥ ४ ॥

śayāna unnaddha-mado mahā-manā
mahārha-talpe mahiṣī-bhujopadhiḥ
tām eva vīro manute paraṁ yatas
tamo-'bhibhūto na nijaṁ paraṁ ca yat

śayānaḥ—lying down; *unnaddha-madaḥ*—increasingly illusioned; *mahā-manāḥ*—advanced in consciousness; *mahā-arha-talpe*—on a valuable bedstead; *mahiṣī*—of the Queen; *bhuja*—arms; *upadhiḥ*—pillow; *tām*—her; *eva*—certainly; *vīraḥ*—the hero; *manute*—he considered; *param*—the goal of life; *yataḥ*—from which; *tamaḥ*—by ignorance; *abhibhūtaḥ*—overwhelmed; *na*—not; *nijam*—his actual self; *param*—the Supreme Personality of Godhead; *ca*—and; *yat*—what.

TRANSLATION

In this way, increasingly overwhelmed by illusion, King Purañjana, although advanced in consciousness, remained always lying down with his head on the pillow of his wife's arms. In this way he considered woman to be his ultimate life and soul. Becoming thus overwhelmed by the mode of ignorance, he could not understand the meaning of self-realization, of his self, or of the Supreme Personality of Godhead.

PURPORT

Human life is meant for self-realization. First of all one has to realize his own self, which is described in this verse as *nijam*. Then he has to understand or realize the Supersoul or Paramātmā, the Supreme Personality of Godhead. However, when one becomes too much materially attached, he takes a woman to be everything. This is the basic principle of material attachment. In such a condition, one cannot realize his own self or the Supreme Personality of Godhead. In *Śrīmad-Bhāgavatam* it is therefore said: *mahat-sevāṁ dvāram āhur vimuktes tamo-dvāraṁ yoṣitāṁ saṅgi-saṅgam* (*Bhāg.* 5.5.2). If one associates with *mahātmās*, or devotees, his path of liberation is opened. But if one becomes too much attached to women or to persons who are also attached to women—that is, attached to women directly or indirectly—he opens the *tamo-dvāram*, the door to the darkest region of hellish life.

King Purañjana was a great soul, highly intellectual and possessed of advanced consciousness, but due to his being too much addicted to women, his whole consciousness was covered. In the modern age the consciousness of people is too much covered by wine, women and flesh. Consequently people are completely unable to make any progress in self-realization. The first step of self-realization is to know oneself as spirit soul apart from the body. In the second stage of self-realization one comes to know that every soul, every individual living entity, is part and parcel of the Supreme Soul, Paramātmā, or the Supreme Personality of Godhead. This is confirmed in *Bhagavad-gītā:*

mamaivāṁśo jīva-loke
jīva-bhūtaḥ sanātanaḥ
manaḥ ṣaṣṭhānīndriyāṇi
prakṛti-sthāni karṣati

"The living entities in this conditioned world are My eternal, fragmental parts. Due to conditioned life, they are struggling very hard with the six senses, which include the mind." (Bg. 15.7)

All living entities are part and parcel of the Supreme Lord. Unfortunately in this present civilization both men and women are allowed to be attracted to one another from the very beginning of life, and because of this they are completely unable to come to the platform of self-realization. They do not know that without self-realization they suffer the greatest loss in the human form of life. Thinking of a woman always within one's heart is tantamount to lying down with a woman on a valuable bedstead. The heart is the bedstead, and it is the most valuable bedstead. When a man thinks of women and money, he lies down and rests on the arms of his beloved woman or wife. In this way he overindulges in sex life and thus becomes unfit for self-realization.

TEXT 5

तयैवं रममाणस्य कामकश्मलचेतसः ।
क्षणार्धमिव राजेन्द्र व्यतिक्रान्तं नवं वयः ॥ ५ ॥

tayaivaṁ ramamāṇasya
kāma-kaśmala-cetasaḥ

kṣaṇārdham iva rājendra
vyatikrāntaṁ navaṁ vayaḥ

tayā—with her; *evam*—in this way; *ramamāṇasya*—enjoying; *kāma*—full of lust; *kaśmala*—sinful; *cetasaḥ*—his heart; *kṣaṇa-ardham*—in half a moment; *iva*—like; *rāja-indra*—O King; *vyatikrāntam*—expired; *navam*—new; *vayaḥ*—life.

TRANSLATION

My dear King Prācīnabarhiṣat, in this way King Purañjana, with his heart full of lust and sinful reactions, began to enjoy sex with his wife, and in this way his new life and youth expired in half a moment.

PURPORT

Śrīla Govinda dāsa Ṭhākura has sung:

e-dhana, yauvana, putra, parijana,
ithe ki āche paratīti re
kamala-dala-jala, jīvana ṭalamala,
bhaja huṅ hari-pada niti re

In this verse Śrīla Govinda dāsa actually says that there is no bliss in the enjoyment of youthful life. In youth a person becomes very lusty to enjoy all kinds of sense objects. The sense objects are form, taste, smell, touch and sound. The modern scientific method, or advancement of scientific civilization, encourages the enjoyment of these five senses. The younger generation is very pleased to see a beautiful form, to hear radio messages of material news and sense gratificatory songs, to smell nice scents, nice flowers, and to touch the soft body or breasts of a young woman and gradually touch the sex organs. All of this is also very pleasing to the animals; therefore in human society there are restrictions in the enjoyment of the five sense objects. If one does not follow, he becomes exactly like an animal.

Thus in this verse it is specifically stated, *kāma-kaśmala-cetasaḥ:* the consciousness of King Purañjana was polluted by lusty desires and sinful activities. In the previous verse it is stated that Purañjana, although advanced in consciousness, lay down on a very soft bed with his wife. This indicates that he indulged too much in sex. The words *navaṁ vayaḥ* are also significant in this verse. They indicate the period of youth from age sixteen to thirty. These thirteen or fifteen years of life are years in which one can very strongly enjoy the senses. When one comes to this age he thinks that life will go on and that he will simply continue enjoying his senses, but "time and tide wait for no man." The span of youth expires very quickly. One who wastes his life simply by committing sinful activities in youth immediately becomes disappointed and disillusioned when the brief period of youth is over. The material enjoyments of youth are especially pleasing to a person who has no spiritual training. If one is trained only according to the bodily conception of life, he simply leads a disappointed life because bodily sense enjoyment finishes within forty years or so. After forty years, one simply leads a disillusioned life because he has no spiritual knowledge. For such a person, the expiration of youth occurs in half a moment. Thus King Purañjana's pleasure, which he took in lying down with his wife, expired very quickly.

Kāma-kaśmala-cetasaḥ also indicates that unrestricted sense enjoyment is not allowed in the human form of life by the laws of nature. If one enjoys his senses unrestrictedly, he leads a sinful life. The animals do not violate the laws of nature. For example, the sex impulse in animals is very strong during certain months of the year. The lion is very powerful. He is a flesh-eater and is very strong, but he enjoys sex only once in a year. Similarly, according to religious injunctions a man is restricted to enjoy sex only once in a month, after the menstrual period of the wife, and if the wife is pregnant, he is not allowed sex life at all. That is the law for human beings. A man is allowed to keep more than one wife because he cannot enjoy sex when the wife is pregnant. If he wants to enjoy sex at such a time, he may go to another wife who is not pregnant. These are laws mentioned in the *Manu-saṁhitā* and other scriptures.

These laws and scriptures are meant for human beings. As such, if one violates these laws, he becomes sinful. The conclusion is that unrestricted sense enjoyment means sinful activities. Illicit sex is sex that violates the laws given in the scriptures. When one violates the laws of the scriptures, or the *Vedas,* he commits sinful activities. One who is engaged in sinful activities cannot change his consciousness. Our real function is to change our consciousness from *kaśmala,* sinful consciousness, to Kṛṣṇa, the supreme pure, as confirmed in *Bhagavad-gītā: paraṁ brahma paraṁ dhāma pavitraṁ paramaṁ bhavān:* "You are the Supreme Brahman, the ultimate, the supreme abode and purifier." (Bg. 10.12)

Kṛṣṇa is the supreme pure, and if we change our consciousness from material enjoyment to Kṛṣṇa, we become purified. This is the process recommended by Lord Caitanya Mahāprabhu as the process of *ceto-darpaṇa-mārjanam,* cleansing the mirror of the heart.

TEXT 6

तस्यामजनयत्पुत्रान् पुरञ्जन्यां पुरञ्जनः ।
शतान्येकादश विराडायुषोऽर्धमथात्यगात् ॥ ६ ॥

tasyām ajanayat putrān
purañjanyāṁ purañjanaḥ
śatāny ekādaśa virāḍ
āyuṣo 'rdham athātyagāt

tasyām—within her; *ajanayat*—he begot; *putrān*—sons; *purañjanyām*—in Purañjanī; *purañjanaḥ*—King Purañjana; *śatāni*—hundreds; *ekādaśa*—eleven; *virāṭ*—O King; *āyuṣaḥ*—of life; *ardham*—half; *atha*—in this way; *atyagāt*—he passed.

TRANSLATION

The great sage Nārada then addressed King Prācīnabarhiṣat: O one whose life span is great [virāṭ], in this way King Purañjana begot 1,100 sons within the womb of his wife Purañjanī. However, in this business he passed away half of his life span.

PURPORT

In this verse there are several significant words, the first of which is *ekādaśa śatāni.* Purañjana had begotten 1,100 sons within the womb of his wife, and thus passed away half of his life. Actually every man follows a similar process. If one lives for one hundred years at the utmost, in his family life he simply begets children up to the age of fifty. Unfortunately at the present moment people do not live even a hundred years; nonetheless they beget children up to the age of sixty. Another point is that formerly people used to beget one hundred to two hundred sons and daughters. As will be evident from the next verse, King Purañjana not only begot 1,100 sons but also 110 daughters. At the present moment no one can produce such huge quantities of children. Instead, mankind is very busy checking the increase of population by contraceptive methods.

We do not find in Vedic literatures that they ever used contraceptive methods, although they were begetting hundreds of children. Checking population by a contraceptive method is another sinful activity, but in this age of Kali people have become so sinful that they do not care for the resultant reactions of their sinful lives. King Purañjana lay down with his wife Purañjanī and begot a large number of children, and there is no mention in these verses that he used contraceptive methods. According to the Vedic scriptures the contraceptive method should be restraint in sex life. It is not that one should indulge in unrestricted sex life and avoid children by using some method to check pregnancy. If a man is in good consciousness, he consults with his religious wife, and as a result of this consultation, with intelligence, one advances in his ability to estimate the value of life. In other words, if one is fortunate enough to have a good conscientious wife, he can decide by mutual consultation that human life is meant for advancing in Kṛṣṇa consciousness and not for begetting a large number of children. Children are called *pariṇāma*, or by-products, and when one consults his good intelligence he can see that his by-products should be the expansion of his Kṛṣṇa consciousness.

TEXT 7

दुहितॄर्दशोत्तरशतं पितृमातृयशस्करीः ।
शीलौदार्यगुणोपेताः पौरञ्जन्यः प्रजापते ॥ ७ ॥

duhitṝr daśottara-śataṁ
pitṛ-mātṛ-yaśaskarīḥ
śīlaudārya-guṇopetāḥ
paurañjanyaḥ prajā-pate

duhitṝḥ—daughters; *daśa-uttara*—ten more than; *śatam*—one hundred; *pitṛ*—like the father; *mātṛ*—and mother; *yaśaskarīḥ*—glorified; *śīla*—good behavior; *audārya*—magnanimity; *guṇa*—good qualities; *upetāḥ*—possessed of; *paurañjanyaḥ*—daughters of Purañjana; *prajā-pate*—O Prajāpati.

TRANSLATION

O Prajāpati, King Prācīnabarhiṣat, in this way King Purañjana also begot 110 daughters. All of these were equally glorified like the father and mother. Their behavior was gentle, and they possessed magnanimity and other good qualities.

PURPORT

Children begotten under the rules and regulations of the scriptures generally become as good as the father and mother, but children born illegitimately mainly become *varṇa-saṅkara.* The *varṇa-saṅkara* population is irresponsible to the family, community and even to themselves. Formerly the *varṇa-saṅkara* population was checked by the observation of the reformatory method called *garbhādhāna-saṁskāra,* a child-begetting religious ceremony. In this verse we find that although King Purañjana had begotten so many children, they were not *varṇa-saṅkara.* All of them were good, well-behaved children, and they had good qualities like their father and mother.

Even though we may produce many good children, our desire for sex that is beyond the prescribed method is to be considered sinful. Too much enjoyment of any of the senses (not only sex) results in sinful activities. Therefore one has to become a *svāmī* or a *gosvāmī* at the end of his life. One may beget children up to the age of fifty, but after fifty, one must stop begetting children and should accept the *vānaprastha* order. In this way he must leave home and then become a *sannyāsī.* A *sannyāsī's* title is *svāmī* or *gosvāmī,* which means that he completely refrains from sense enjoyment. One should not accept the *sannyāsa* order whimsically; he must be fully confident that he can restrain his desires for sense gratification. King Purañjana's family life was, of course, very happy. As mentioned in these verses, he begot 1,100 sons and 110 daughters. Everyone desires to have more sons than daughters, and since the number of daughters was less than the number of sons, it appears that King Purañjana's family life was very comfortable and pleasing.

TEXT 8

स पञ्चालपतिः पुत्रान् पितृवंशविवर्धनान् ।
दारैः संयोजयामास दुहितॄः सदृशैर्वरैः ॥ ८ ॥

sa pañcāla-patiḥ putrān
pitṛ-vaṁśa-vivardhanān
dāraiḥ saṁyojayām āsa
duhitṝḥ sadṛśair varaiḥ

saḥ—he; *pañcāla-patiḥ*—King of Pañcāla; *putrān*—sons; *pitṛ-vaṁśa*—paternal family; *vivardhanān*—increasing; *dāraiḥ*—with wives; *saṁyojayām āsa*—married; *duhitṝḥ*—daughters; *sadṛśaiḥ*—qualified; *varaiḥ*—with husbands.

TRANSLATION

After this, King Purañjana, King of the Pañcāla country, in order to increase the descendants of his paternal family, married his sons with qualified wives and married his daughters with qualified husbands.

PURPORT

According to the Vedic system, everyone should marry. One has to accept a wife because a wife will produce children, and the children in their turn will offer foodstuffs and funeral ceremonies so that the forefathers, wherever they may live, will be made happy. The offering of oblations in the name of Lord Viṣṇu is called *piṇḍodaka,* and it is necessary that the descendants of a family offer *piṇḍa* to the forefathers.

Not only was Purañjana, the King of Pañcāla, satisfied in his own sex life, but he arranged for the sex life of his 1,100 sons and 110 daughters. In this way one can elevate an aristocratic family to the platform of a dynasty. It is significant in this verse that Purañjana got both sons and daughters married. It is the duty of a father and mother to arrange for the marriage of their sons and daughters. That is the obligation in Vedic society. Sons and daughters should not be allowed freedom to intermingle with the opposite sex unless they are married. This Vedic social organization is very good in that it stops the promulgation of illicit sex life, or *varṇa-saṅkara,* which appears under different names in this present day. Unfortunately in this age although the father and mother are anxious to get their children married, the children refuse to get married by the arrangement of the parents. Consequently the number of *varṇa-saṅkara* has increased throughout the world under different names.

TEXT 9

पुत्राणां चाभवन् पुत्रा एकैकस्य शतं शतम् ।
यैर्वै पौरञ्जनो वंशः पञ्चालेषु समेधितः ॥ ९ ॥

putrāṇāṁ cābhavan putrā
ekaikasya śataṁ śatam
yair vai paurañjano vaṁśaḥ
pañcāleṣu samedhitaḥ

putrāṇām—of the sons; *ca*—also; *abhavan*—were produced; *putrāḥ*—sons; *eka-ekasya*—of each one; *śatam*—hundred; *śatam*—hundred; *yaiḥ*—by whom; *vai*—certainly; *pauranjanaḥ*—of King Purañjana; *vaṁśaḥ*—family; *pañcāleṣu*—in the land of Pañcāla; *samedhitaḥ*—greatly increased.

TRANSLATION

Of these many sons, each produced hundreds and hundreds of grandsons. In this way the whole city of Pañcāla became overcrowded by these sons and grandsons of King Purañjana.

PURPORT

We must remember that Purañjana is the living entity, and the city Pañcāla is the body. The body is the field of activity for the living entity, as stated in *Bhagavad-gītā: kṣetra-kṣetrajña* (Bg. 13.27). There are two constituents: one is the living entity (*kṣetra-jña*), and the other is the body of the living entity (*kṣetra*). Any living entity can know that he is covered by the body if he only contemplates the body a little bit. Just with a little contemplation he can come to understand that the body is his possession. One can understand this by practical experience and by the authority of the *śāstras*. In *Bhagavad-gītā* it is said: *dehino 'smin yathā dehe* (Bg. 2.13). The proprietor of the body, the soul, is within the body. The body is taken as the *pañcāla-deśa,* or the field of activities wherein the living entity can enjoy the senses in their relationship to the five sense objects—namely, *gandha, rasa, rūpa, sparśa* and *śabda*—that is, sense objects made out of earth, water, fire, air and sky. Within this material world covered by the material body of subtle and gross matter, every living entity creates actions and reactions, which are herein known allegorically as sons and grandsons. There are two kinds of actions and reactions—namely, pious and impious. In this way our material existence becomes coated by different actions and reactions. In this regard, Śrīla Narottama dāsa Ṭhākura states:

karma-kāṇḍa, jñāna-kāṇḍa, kevala viṣera bhāṇḍa,
amṛta baliyā yebā khāya
nānā yoni sadā phire, kadarya bhakṣaṇa kare,
tāra janma adhaḥ-pāte yāya

"Fruitive activities and mental speculation are simply cups of poison. Whoever drinks of them, thinking them to be nectar, must struggle very hard life after life, in different types of bodies. Such a person eats all kinds of nonsense and becomes condemned by his activities of so-called sense enjoyment."

Thus the field of action and reactions, by which one's descendants are increased, begins with sex life. Purañjana increased his whole family by begetting sons who in their turn begot grandsons. Thus the living entity, being inclined toward sexual gratification, becomes involved in many hundreds and thousands of actions and reactions. In this way he remains within the material world simply for the purpose of sense gratification and transmigrates from one body to another. His process of reproducing so many sons and grandsons results in so-called societies, nations, communities and so on. All these communities, societies, dynasties and nations simply expand from sex life. As stated by Prahlāda Mahārāja: *yan maithunādi gṛhamedhi-sukhaṁ hi tuccham* (*Bhāg.* 7.9.45). A *gṛhamedhī* is one who wants to remain within this material existence. This means that he wants to remain within this body or society and enjoy friendship, love and community. His only enjoyment is in increasing the number of sex enjoyers. He enjoys sex and produces children, who in their turn marry and produce grandchildren. The grandchildren also marry and in their turn produce great-grandchildren. In this way the entire earth becomes overpopulated, and then suddenly there are reactions provoked by material nature in the form of war, famine, pestilence and earthquakes, etc. Thus the entire population is again extinguished simply to be recreated. This process is explained in *Bhagavad-gītā:*

bhūta-grāmaḥ sa evāyaṁ
bhūtvā bhūtvā pralīyate
rātry-āgame 'vaśaḥ pārtha
prabhavaty ahar-āgame

"Again and again the day comes, and this host of beings is active, and again the night falls, O Pārtha, and they are helplessly dissolved." (Bg. 8.19)

Due to a lack of Kṛṣṇa consciousness, all this creation and annihilation is going on under the name of human civilization. This cycle continues due to man's lack of knowledge of the soul and the Supreme Personality of Godhead.

TEXT 10

तेषु तद्रिक्थहारेषु गृहकोशानुजीविषु ।
निरूढेन ममत्वेन विषयेष्वन्वबध्यत ॥१०॥

teṣu tad-riktha-hāreṣu
gṛha-kośānujīviṣu
nirūḍhena mamatvena
viṣayeṣv anvabadhyata

teṣu—to them; *tat-riktha-hāreṣu*—the plunderers of his money; *gṛha*—home; *kośa*—treasury; *anujīviṣu*—to the followers; *nirūḍhena*—deep-rooted; *mamatvena*—by attachment; *viṣayeṣu*—to sense objects; *anvabadhyata*—became bound.

TRANSLATION

These sons and grandsons were virtually plunderers of King Purañjana's riches, including his home, treasury, servants, secretaries and all other paraphernalia. Purañjana's attachment for these things was very deep-rooted.

PURPORT

In this verse the word *riktha-hāreṣu,* meaning plunderers of wealth, is very significant. One's sons, grandsons and other descendants are ultimately plunderers of one's accumulated wealth. There are many celebrated businessmen and industrialists who produce great wealth and are highly praised by the public, but all their money is ultimately plundered by their sons and grandsons. In India we have actually seen one industrialist, who, like King Purañjana, was very much sexually inclined and had a half dozen wives. Each of these wives had a separate establishment that necessitated the expenditure of several thousands of rupees. When I was engaged in talking with him, I saw that he was very busy trying to secure money so that all his sons and daughters would get at least 500,000 rupees each. Thus such industrialists, businessmen or *karmīs* are called *mūḍhas* in the *śāstras.* They work very hard, accumulate money, and are satisfied to see that this money is plundered by their sons and grandsons. Such people do not want to return their wealth to its actual owner. As stated in *Bhagavad-gītā:*

bhoktāraṁ yajña-tapasāṁ
sarva-loka-maheśvaram
suhṛdaṁ sarva-bhūtānāṁ
jñātvā māṁ śāntim ṛcchati

"The sages, knowing Me as the ultimate purpose of all sacrifices and austerities, the Supreme Lord of all planets and demigods and the benefactor and well-wisher of all living entities, attain peace from the pangs of material miseries." (Bg. 5.29)

The real proprietor of all wealth is the Supreme Personality of Godhead. He is the actual enjoyer. So-called earners of money are those who simply know tricks by which they can take away God's money under the guise of business and industry. After accumulating this money, they enjoy seeing it plundered by their sons and grandsons. This is the materialistic way of life. In materialistic life one is encaged within the body and deluded by false egoism. Thus one thinks, "I am this body. I am a human being. I am an American. I am an Indian." This bodily conception is due to false ego. Being deluded by false ego, one identifies himself with a certain family, nation or community. In this way one's attachment for the material world grows deeper and deeper. Thus it becomes very difficult for the living entity to extricate himself from his entanglement. Such people are graphically described in the Sixteenth Chapter of *Bhagavad-gītā* in this way:

idam adya mayā labdham
imaṁ prāpsye manoratham
idam astīdam api me
bhaviṣyati punar dhanam

asau mayā hataḥ śatrur
haniṣye cāparān api
īśvaro 'ham ahaṁ bhogī
siddho 'haṁ balavān sukhī

āḍhyo 'bhijanavān asmi
ko 'nyo 'sti sadṛśo mayā
yakṣye dāsyāmi modiṣya
ity ajñāna-vimohitāḥ

"The demoniac person thinks: 'So much wealth do I have today, and I will gain more according to my schemes. So much is mine now, and it will increase in the future, more and more. He is my enemy, and I have killed him; and my other enemy will also be killed. I am the lord of everything, I am the enjoyer, I am perfect, powerful and happy. I am the richest man, surrounded by aristocratic relatives. There is none so powerful and happy as I am. I shall perform sacrifices, I shall give some charity, and thus I shall rejoice.' In this way, such persons are deluded by ignorance." (Bg. 16.13-15)

In this way people engage in various laborious activities, and their attachment for body, home, family, nation and community becomes more and more deep-rooted.

TEXT 11

ईजे च क्रतुभिर्घोरैर्दीक्षितः पशुमारकैः ।
देवान् पितॄन् भूतपतीन्नानाकामो यथा भवान् ॥११॥

īje ca kratubhir ghorair
dīkṣitaḥ paśu-mārakaiḥ
devān pitṝn bhūta-patīn
nānā-kāmo yathā bhavān

īje—he worshiped; *ca*—also; *kratubhiḥ*—by sacrifices; *ghoraiḥ*—ghastly; *dīkṣitaḥ*—inspired; *paśu-mārakaiḥ*—wherein poor animals are killed; *devān*—the demigods; *pitṝn*—forefathers; *bhūta-patīn*—great leaders of the human society; *nānā*—various; *kāmaḥ*—having desires; *yathā*—like; *bhavān*—you.

TRANSLATION

The great sage Nārada continued: My dear King Prācīnabarhiṣat, like you King Purañjana also became implicated in so many desires. Thus he worshiped demigods, forefathers and social leaders with various sacrifices, which were all very ghastly because they were inspired by the desire to kill animals.

PURPORT

In this verse the great sage Nārada discloses that the character of Purañjana was being described to give lessons to King Prācīnabarhiṣat. Actually the entire description was figuratively describing the activities of King Prācīnabarhiṣat. In this verse Nārada frankly says "like you" (*yathā bhavān*), which indicates that King Purañjana is none other than King Prācīnabarhiṣat himself. Being a great Vaiṣṇava, Nārada Muni wanted to stop animal killing in sacrifices. He knew that if he tried to stop the King from performing sacrifices, the King would not hear him. Therefore he is describing the life of Purañjana. But in this verse he first discloses the intention, although not fully, by saying "like you." Generally the *karmīs,* who are attached to increasing descendants, have to perform so many sacrifices and worship so many demigods for future generations, as well as to satisfy so many leaders, politicians, philosophers and scientists to make things go on properly for future generations. The so-called scientists are very eager to see that future generations will live very comfortably, and as such they are trying to find different means of generating energy to drive locomotives, cars, airplanes and so on. Now they are exhausting the petroleum supply. These activities are described in the *Bhagavad-gītā.*

vyavasāyātmikā buddhir
ekeha kuru-nandana
bahu-śākhā hy anantāś ca
buddhayo 'vyavasāyinām

"Those who are on this path are resolute in purpose, and their aim is one. O beloved child of the Kurus, the intelligence of those who are irresolute is many-branched." (Bg. 2.41)

Actually those who are in knowledge of everything are determined to execute Kṛṣṇa consciousness, but those who are rascals (*mūḍhāḥ*), sinners (*duṣkṛtinaḥ*) and the lowest of mankind (*narādhamāḥ*), who are bereft of all intelligence (*māyayāpahṛta-jñānāḥ*) and who take shelter of the demoniac way of life (*āsuraṁ bhāvam āśritāḥ*), are disinterested in Kṛṣṇa consciousness. As such they become implicated and take on so many activities. Most of these activities center around the killing of animals. Modern civilization is centered around animal killing. *Karmīs* are advertising that without eating meat, their vitamin value or vitality will be reduced; so to keep oneself fit to work hard, one must eat meat, and to digest meat, one must drink liquor, and to keep the balance of drinking wine and eating meat, one must have sufficient sexual intercourse to keep fit to work very hard like an ass.

There are two ways of animal killing. One way is in the name of religious sacrifices. All the religions of the world—except the Buddhists—have a program for killing animals in places of worship. According to Vedic civilization, the animal-eaters are recommended to sacrifice a goat in the temple of goddess Kālī under certain restrictive rules and regulations and eat the flesh. Similarly, they are recommended to drink wine by worshiping the goddess Caṇḍikā. The purpose is restriction. People have given up all this restriction. Now they are regularly opening wine distilleries and slaughterhouses and indulging in drinking alcohol and eating flesh. A Vaiṣṇava *ācārya* like Nārada Muni knows very well that persons engaged in such animal killing in the name of religion are certainly becoming involved in the cycle of birth and death, forgetting the real aim of life: to go home, back to Godhead.

Thus the great sage Nārada, while instructing *Śrīmad-Bhāgavatam* to Vyāsa Muni, condemned the *karma-kāṇḍa* (fruitive) activities mentioned in the *Vedas.* Nārada told Vyāsa:

jugupsitaṁ dharma-kṛte 'nuśāsataḥ
sva-bhāva-raktasya mahān vyatikramaḥ
yad-vākyato dharma itītaraḥ sthito
na manyate tasya nivāraṇaṁ janaḥ

"The people in general are naturally inclined to enjoy, and you have encouraged them in that way in the name of religion. This is verily condemned and is quite unreasonable. Because they are guided under your instructions, they will accept such activities in the name of religion and will hardly care for prohibitions." (*Bhāg.* 1.5.15)

Śrīla Nārada Muni chastised Vyāsadeva for compiling so many Vedic supplementary scriptures, which are all intended for guiding the people in general. Nārada Muni condemned these scriptures because they do not mention direct devotional service. Under Nārada's instructions, direct worship of the Supreme Personality of Godhead, as described in the *Śrīmad-Bhāgavatam,* was set forth by Vyāsadeva. The conclusion is that neither the Supreme Personality of Godhead Viṣṇu nor His devotee ever sanctions animal killing in the name of religion. Indeed, Kṛṣṇa incarnated Himself as Lord Buddha to put an end to animal killing in the name of religion. Animal sacrifice under the name of religion is conducted by the influence of *tamo-guṇa* (the mode of ignorance), as indicated in the Eighteenth Chapter of *Bhagavad-gītā.*

yayā dharmam adharmaṁ ca
kāryaṁ cākāryam eva ca
ayathāvat prajānāti
buddhiḥ sā pārtha rājasī

adharmaṁ dharmam iti yā
manyate tamasāvṛtā
sarvārthān viparītāṁś ca
buddhiḥ sā pārtha tāmasī

"And that understanding which cannot distinguish between the religious way of life and the irreligious, between action that should be done and action that should not be done—that imperfect understanding, O son of Pṛthā, is in the mode of passion. That understanding which considers irreligion to be religion and religion to be irreligion, under the spell of illusion and darkness, and strives always in the wrong direction, O Pārtha, is in the mode of ignorance." (Bg. 18.31-32)

Those who are involved in the mode of ignorance manufacture religious systems for killing animals. Actually *dharma* is transcendental. As Lord Śrī Kṛṣṇa teaches, we must give up all other systems of religion and simply surrender unto Him (*sarva-dharmān parityajya*). Thus the Lord and His devotees and representatives teach the transcendental *dharma*, which does not allow animal killing at all. At the present moment it is the greatest misfortune that in India many so-called missionary workers are spreading irreligion in the name of religion. They claim an ordinary human being to be God and recommend meat-eating for everyone, including so-called *sannyāsīs*.

TEXT 12

युक्तेष्वेवं प्रमत्तस्य कुटुम्बासक्तचेतसः ।
आससाद स वै कालो योऽप्रियः प्रिययोषिताम् ॥१२॥

yukteṣv evaṁ pramattasya
kuṭumbāsakta-cetasaḥ
āsasāda sa vai kālo
yo 'priyaḥ priya-yoṣitām

yukteṣu—to beneficial activities; *evam*—thus; *pramattasya*—being inattentive; *kuṭumba*—to kith and kin; *āsakta*—attached; *cetasaḥ*—consciousness; *āsasāda*—arrived; *saḥ*—that; *vai*—certainly; *kālaḥ*—time; *yaḥ*—which; *apriyaḥ*—not very pleasing; *priya-yoṣitām*—for persons attached to women.

TRANSLATION

Thus King Purañjana, being attached to fruitive activities [karma-kāṇḍīya] as well as kith and kin, and being obsessed with polluted consciousness, eventually arrived at that point not very much liked by those who are overly attached to material things.

PURPORT

In this verse the words *priya-yoṣitām* and *apriyaḥ* are very significant. The word *yoṣit* means woman, and *priya* means dear or pleasing. Death is not very much welcome for those who are too much attached to material enjoyment, which culminates in sex. There is an instructive story in this connection. Once when a saintly person was passing on his way, he met a prince, the son of a king, and he blessed him, saying, "My dear prince, may you live forever." The sage next met a saintly person, and he said to him, "You may either live or die." Eventually the sage met a *brahmacārī* devotee, and he blessed him, saying, "My dear devotee, you may die immediately." Finally the sage met a hunter, and he blessed him, saying, "Neither live nor die." The point is that those who are very sensual and are engaged in sense gratification do not wish to die. Generally a prince has enough money to enjoy his senses; therefore the great sage said that he should live forever, for as long as he lived he could enjoy life, but after his death he would go to hell. Since the *brahmacārī* devotee was leading a life of severe austerities and penances in order to be promoted back to Godhead, the sage said that he should die immediately so that he need not continue to labor hard and could instead go back home, back to Godhead. A saintly person may either live or die, for during his life he is engaged in serving the Lord, and after his death he also serves the Lord. Thus this life and the next are the same for a saintly devotee, for in both he serves the Lord. Since the hunter lives a very ghastly life due to killing animals, and since he will go to hell when he dies, he is advised to neither live nor die.

King Purañjana finally arrived at the point of old age. In old age the senses lose their strength, and although an old man desires to enjoy his senses and especially sex life, he is very miserable because his instruments of enjoyment no longer function. Such sensualists are never prepared for death. They simply want to live on and on and extend their life by so-called scientific advancement. Some foolish Russian scientists also claim that they are going to make man immortal through scientific advancement. Under the leadership of such crazy fellows, civilization is going on. Cruel death, however, comes and takes all of them away despite their desire to live forever. This type of mentality was exhibited by Hiraṇyakaśipu, but when the time was ripe, the Lord personally killed him within a second.

TEXT 13

चण्डवेग इति ख्यातो गन्धर्वाधिपतिर्नृप ।
गन्धर्वास्तस्य बलिनः षष्ट्युत्तरशतत्रयम् ॥१३॥

caṇḍa-vega iti khyāto
gandharvādhipatir nṛpa
gandharvās tasya balinaḥ
ṣaṣṭy-uttara-śata-trayam

caṇḍa-vegaḥ—Caṇḍavega; *iti*—thus; *khyātaḥ*—celebrated; *gandharva*—belonging to the Gandharvaloka; *adhipatiḥ*—king; *nṛpa*—O King; *gandharvāḥ*—other Gandharvas; *tasya*—his; *balinaḥ*—very powerful soldiers; *ṣaṣṭi*—sixty; *uttara*—surpassing; *śata*—hundred; *trayam*—three.

TRANSLATION

O King! In Gandharvaloka there is a king named Caṇḍavega. Under him there are 360 very powerful Gandharva soldiers.

PURPORT

Time is figuratively described here as Caṇḍavega. Since time and tide wait for no man, time is herein called Caṇḍavega, which means "very swiftly passing away." As time passes, it is calculated in terms of years. One year contains 360 days, and the soldiers of Caṇḍavega herein mentioned represent these days. Time passes swiftly; Caṇḍavega's powerful soldiers of Gandharvaloka very swiftly carry away all the days of our life. As the sun rises and sets, it snatches away the balance of our life span. Thus as each day passes, each one of us loses some of life's duration. It is therefore said that the duration of one's life cannot be saved. But if one is engaged in devotional service, his time cannot be taken away by the sun. As stated in *Śrīmad-Bhāgavatam: āyur harati vai puṁsām udyann astaṁ ca yann asau* (*Bhāg.* 2.3.17). The conclusion is that if one wants to make himself immortal, he should give up sense gratification. By engaging oneself in devotional service, one can gradually enter into the eternal kingdom of God.

Mirages and other illusory things are sometimes called Gandharvas. Our losing our life span is taken as advancement of age. This imperceptible passing away of the days of life is figuratively referred to in this verse as Gandharvas. As explained in later verses, such Gandharvas are both male and female. This indicates that both men and women lose their life span imperceptibly by the force of time, which is herein described as Caṇḍavega.

TEXT 14

गन्धर्व्यस्तादृशीरस्य मैथुन्यश्च सितासिताः ।
परिवृत्त्या विलुम्पन्ति सर्वकामविनिर्मिताम् ॥१४॥

gandharvyas tādṛśīr asya
maithunyaś ca sitāsitāḥ

parivṛttyā vilumpanti
sarva-kāma-vinirmitām

gandharvyaḥ—Gandharvīs; *tādṛśīḥ*—similarly; *asya*—of Caṇḍavega; *maithunyaḥ*—companions for sexual intercourse; *ca*—also; *sita*—white; *asitāḥ*—black; *parivṛttyā*—by surrounding; *vilumpanti*—they plundered; *sarva-kāma*—all kinds of desirable objects; *vinirmitām*—manufactured.

TRANSLATION

Along with Caṇḍavega were as many female Gandharvīs as there were soldiers, and all of them repetitively plundered all the paraphernalia for sense enjoyment.

PURPORT

The days have been compared to the soldiers of Caṇḍavega. Night is generally a time for sex enjoyment. Days are considered to be white, and nights are considered to be black, or, from another point of view, there are two kinds of nights—black nights and white nights. All these days and nights combine to pass away our span of life and everything we manufacture for sense gratification. Material activity means manufacturing things for sense gratification. Scientists are conducting research to find out how we can satisfy our senses more and more elaborately. In this Kali-yuga, the demoniac mentality is employed in manufacturing various machines to facilitate the process of sense gratification. There are so many machines for ordinary household activities. There are machines for washing dishes, cleansing the floor, shaving, clipping hair—today everything is done by machine. All these facilities for sense gratification are described in this verse as *sarva-kāma-vinirmitām.* The time factor, however, is so strong that not only is our span of life being expended, but all the machines and facilities for sense gratification are deteriorating. Therefore in this verse the word *vilumpanti* (plundering) is used. Everything is being plundered from the very beginning of our lives.

This plundering of our possessions and life span begins with the day of our birth. One day will come when death will finish everything, and the living entity will have to enter another body to begin another chapter of life and again begin the cycle of material sense gratification. Prahlāda Mahārāja describes this process as *punaḥ punaś carvita-carvaṇānām* (*Bhāg.* 7.5.30). Materialistic life means chewing the chewed again and again. The central point of material life is sense gratification. In different types of bodies, the living entity enjoys various senses, and through creating various types of facilities, he chews the chewed. Whether we squeeze sugar out of the sugar cane with our teeth or a machine, the result is the same—sugar cane juice. We may discover many ways to squeeze the juice out of the sugar cane, but the result is the same.

TEXT 15

ते चण्डवेगानुचराः पुरञ्जनपुरं यदा ।
हर्तुमारेभिरे तत्र प्रत्यषेधत्प्रजागरः ॥१५॥

te caṇḍa-vegānucarāḥ
purañjana-puraṁ yadā
hartum ārebhire tatra
pratyaṣedhat prajāgaraḥ

te—all of them; *caṇḍa-vega*—of Caṇḍavega; *anucarāḥ*—followers; *purañjana*—of King Purañjana; *puram*—city; *yadā*—when; *hartum*—to plunder; *ārebhire*—began; *tatra*—there; *pratyaṣedhat*—defended; *prajāgaraḥ*—the big serpent.

TRANSLATION

When King Gandharva-rāja [Caṇḍavega] and his followers began to plunder the city of Purañjana, a snake with five hoods began to defend the city.

PURPORT

When one is sleeping, the life air remains active in different dreams. The five hoods of the snake indicate that the life air is surrounded by five kinds of air known as *prāṇa, apāna, vyāna, udāna* and *samāna.* When the body is inactive, the *prāṇa,* or the life air, is active. Up to the age of fifty one can actively work for sense gratification, but after the fiftieth year one's energy decreases, although one can with great strain work for two or three more years—perhaps up to the fifty-fifth year. Thus the fifty-fifth year is generally taken by government regulations as the final year for retirement. The energy, which is fatigued after fifty years, is figuratively described herein as a serpent with five hoods.

TEXT 16

स सप्तभिः शतैरेको विंशत्या च शतं समाः ।
पुरञ्जनपुराध्यक्षो गन्धर्वैर्युयुधे बली ॥१६॥

sa saptabhiḥ śatair eko
viṁśatyā ca śataṁ samāḥ
purañjana-purādhyakṣo
gandharvair yuyudhe balī

saḥ—he; *saptabhiḥ*—with seven; *śataiḥ*—hundred; *ekaḥ*—alone; *viṁśatyā*—with twenty; *ca*—also; *śatam*—hundred; *samāḥ*—years; *purañjana*—of King Purañjana; *pura-adhyakṣaḥ*—superintendent of the city; *gandharvaiḥ*—with the Gandharvas; *yuyudhe*—fought; *balī*—very valiant.

TRANSLATION

The five-hooded serpent, the superintendent and protector of the city of King Purañjana, fought with the Gandharvas for one hundred years. He fought alone, with all of them, although they numbered 720.

PURPORT

The 360 days and 360 nights combine to become the 720 soldiers of Caṇḍavega (time). One has to fight these soldiers throughout one's lifespan, beginning with birth and ending with death. This fight is called the struggle for existence. Despite this struggle, however, the living entity does not die. As confirmed in *Bhagavad-gītā*, the living entity is eternal:

na jāyate mriyate vā kadācin
nāyaṁ bhūtvā bhavitā vā na bhūyaḥ
ajo nityaḥ śāśvato 'yaṁ purāṇo
na hanyate hanyamāne śarīre

"For the soul there is never birth nor death. Nor, having once been, does he ever cease to be. He is unborn, eternal, ever-existing, undying and primeval. He is not slain when the body is slain." (Bg. 2.20) Actually the living entity does not take birth nor does he die, but he has to fight with the stringent laws of material nature throughout the entire span of his lifetime. He must also face different kinds of miserable conditions. Despite all this, the living entity, due to illusion, thinks that he is well situated in sense gratification.

TEXT 17

क्षीयमाणे स्वसम्बन्धे एकस्मिन् बहुभिर्युधा ।
चिन्तां परां जगामार्तः सराष्ट्रपुरबान्धवः ॥१७॥

kṣīyamāṇe sva-sambandhe
ekasmin bahubhir yudhā
cintāṁ parāṁ jagāmārtaḥ
sa-rāṣṭra-pura-bāndhavaḥ

kṣīyamāṇe—when he became weak; *sva-sambandhe*—his intimate friend; *ekasmin*—alone; *bahubhiḥ*—with many warriors; *yudhā*—by battle; *cintām*—anxiety; *parām*—very great; *jagāma*—obtained; *ārtaḥ*—being aggrieved; *sa*—along with; *rāṣṭra*—of the kingdom; *pura*—of the city; *bāndhavaḥ*—friends and relatives.

TRANSLATION

Because he had to fight alone with so many soldiers, all of whom were great warriors, the serpent with five hoods became very weak. Seeing that his most intimate friend was weakening, King Purañjana and his friends and citizens living within the city all became very anxious.

PURPORT

The living entity resides within the body and struggles for existence with the limbs of the body, which are referred to here as citizens and friends. One can struggle alone with many soldiers for some time, but not for all time. The living entity within the body can struggle up to the limit of a hundred years with good luck, but after that it is not possible to prolong the struggle. Thus the living entity submits and falls victim. In this regard, Śrīla Bhaktivinoda Ṭhākura has sung: *vṛddha kāla āola saba sukha bhāgala.* When one becomes old, it becomes impossible to enjoy material happiness. Generally people think that religion and piety come at the end of life, and at this time one generally becomes meditative and takes to some so-called yogic process to relax in the name of meditation. Meditation, however, is simply a farce for those who have enjoyed life in sense gratification. As described in the Sixth Chapter of *Bhagavad-gītā,* meditation (*dhyāna, dhāraṇā*) is a difficult subject matter that one has to learn from his very youth. To meditate, one must restrain himself from all kinds of sense gratification. Unfortunately, meditation has now become a fashion for those who are overly addicted to sensual things. Such meditation is defeated by the struggle for existence. Sometimes such meditative processes pass for transcendental meditation. King Purañjana, the living entity, being thus victimized by the hard struggle for existence, took to transcendental meditation with his friends and relatives.

TEXT 18

स एव पुर्यां मधुभुक्पञ्चालेषु स्वपार्षदैः ।
उपनीतं बलिं गृह्णन् स्त्रीजितो नाविदद्भयम् ॥१८॥

sa eva puryāṁ madhu-bhuk
pañcāleṣu sva-pārṣadaiḥ
upanītaṁ baliṁ gṛhṇan
strī-jito nāvidad bhayam

saḥ—he; *eva*—certainly; *puryām*—within the city; *madhu-bhuk*—enjoying sex life; *pañcāleṣu*—in the kingdom of Pañcāla (five sense objects); *sva-pārṣadaiḥ*—along with his followers; *upanītam*—brought; *balim*—taxes; *gṛhṇan*—accepting; *strī-jitaḥ*—conquered by women; *na*—did not; *avidat*—understand; *bhayam*—fear of death.

TRANSLATION

King Purañjana collected taxes in the city known as Pañcāla and thus was able to engage in sexual indulgence. Being completely under the control of women, he could not understand that his life was passing away and that he was reaching the point of death.

PURPORT

Government men—including kings, presidents, secretaries and ministers—are in a position to utilize taxes collected from the citizens for sense gratification. It is stated in *Śrīmad-Bhāgavatam* that in this Kali-yuga government men (*rājanyas*) and those connected with the government, as well as exalted government ministers, secretaries and presidents, will all simply collect taxes for sense gratification. The government is top-heavy, and without increasing taxes the government cannot maintain itself. When taxes are collected, they are utilized for the sense gratification of the governmental officials. Such irresponsible politicians forget that there is a time when death will come to take away all their sense gratification. Some of them are convinced that after life everything is finished. This atheistic theory was conceived long ago by a philosopher called Cārvāka. Cārvāka recommended that man should live very opulently by either begging, borrowing or stealing. He also maintained that one should not be afraid of death, the next life, the past life, or an impious life because after the body is burned to ashes, everything is finished. This is the philosophy of those who are too much materially addicted. Such philosophizing will not save one from the danger of death, nor will it save one from an abominable afterlife.

TEXT 19

कालस्य दुहिता काचित्त्रिलोकीं वरमिच्छती ।
पर्यटन्ती न बर्हिष्मन् प्रत्यनन्दत कश्चन ॥१९॥

kālasya duhitā kācit
tri-lokīṁ varam icchatī
paryaṭantī na barhiṣman
pratyanandata kaścana

kālasya—of the formidable Time; *duhitā*—the daughter; *kācit*—someone; *tri-lokīm*—within the three worlds; *varam*—husband; *icchatī*—desiring; *paryaṭantī*—traveling all over the universe; *na*—never; *barhiṣman*—O King Prācīnabarhiṣat; *pratyanandata*—accepted her proposal; *kaścana*—anyone.

TRANSLATION

My dear King Prācīnabarhiṣat, at this time the daughter of formidable Time was seeking her husband throughout the three worlds. Although no one agreed to accept her, she came.

PURPORT

In due course of time, when the body becomes old and practically invalid, it is called *jarā*, subject to the sufferings of old age. There are four basic kinds of suffering—birth, old age, disease and death. No scientist or philosopher has ever been able to make a solution of these four miserable conditions. The invalidity of old age known as *jarā* is figuratively explained here as the daughter of Time. No one likes her, but she is very much anxious to accept anyone as her husband. No one likes to become old and invalid, but this is inevitable for everyone.

TEXT 20

दौर्भाग्येनात्मनो लोके विश्रुता दुर्भगेति सा ।
या तुष्टा राजर्षये तु वृतादात्पूरवे वरम् ॥२०॥

daurbhāgyenātmano loke
viśrutā durbhageti sā
yā tuṣṭā rājarṣaye tu
vṛtādāt pūrave varam

daurbhāgyena—on account of misfortune; *ātmanaḥ*—of herself; *loke*—in the world; *viśrutā*—celebrated; *durbhagā*—most unfortunate; *iti*—thus; *sā*—she; *yā*—who; *tuṣṭā*—being satisfied; *rāja-ṛṣaye*—unto the great king; *tu*—but; *vṛtā*—being accepted; *adāt*—delivered; *pūrave*—unto King Pūru; *varam*—benediction.

TRANSLATION

The daughter of Time [jarā] was very unfortunate. Consequently she was known as durbhagā [ill-fated]. However, she was once pleased with a great king, and because the king accepted her, she granted him a great benediction.

PURPORT

As Bhaktivinoda Ṭhākura sings: *saba sukha bhāgala.* All kinds of happiness disappear in old age. Consequently no one likes old age, or *jarā.* Thus *jāra,* as the daughter of Time, is known as a most unfortunate daughter. She was, however, at one time accepted by a great king, Yayāti. Yayāti was cursed by his father-in-law Śukrācārya to accept her. When Śukrācārya's daughter was married to King Yayāti, one of her friends named Śarmiṣṭhā went with her. Later King Yayāti became very much attached to Śarmiṣṭhā, and Śukrācārya's daughter complained to her father. Consequently Śukrācārya cursed King Yayāti to become prematurely old. King Yayāti had five youthful sons, and he begged all his sons to exchange their youth for his old age. No one agreed except the youngest son, whose name was Pūru. Upon accepting Yayāti's old age, Pūru was given the kingdom. It is said that two of Yayāti's other sons, being disobedient to their father, were given kingdoms outside of India, most probably Turkey and Greece. The purport is that one can accumulate wealth and all kinds of material opulences, but during old age one cannot enjoy them. Although Pūru attained his father's kingdom, he could not enjoy all the opulence because he had sacrificed his youth. One should not wait for old age in order to become Kṛṣṇa conscious. Due to the invalidity of old age, one cannot make progress in Kṛṣṇa consciousness, however opulent he may be materially.

TEXT 21

कदाचिदटमाना सा ब्रह्मलोकान्महीं गतम् ।
वव्रे बृहद्व्रतं मां तु जानती काममोहिता ॥२१॥

kadācid aṭamānā sā
brahma-lokān mahīṁ gatam
vavre bṛhad-vrataṁ māṁ tu
jānatī kāma-mohitā

kadācit—once upon a time; *aṭamānā*—traveling; *sā*—she; *brahma-lokāt*—from the Brahmaloka, the highest planet; *mahīm*—on the earth; *gatam*—having come; *vavre*—she proposed; *bṛhat-vratam*—avowed *brahmacārī; mām*—unto me; *tu*—then; *jānatī*—knowing; *kāma-mohitā*—being illusioned by lust.

TRANSLATION

When I once came to this earth from Brahmaloka, the highest planetary system, the daughter of Time, wandering over the universe, met me. Knowing me to be an avowed brahmacārī, she became lusty and proposed that I accept her.

PURPORT

The great sage Nārada Muni was a *naiṣṭhika-brahmacārī*—that is, he never had sex life. He was consequently an ever-green youth. Old age, *jarā,* could not attack him. The invalidity of old age can overcome an ordinary man, but Nārada Muni was different. Taking Nārada Muni to be an ordinary man, the daughter of Time confronted him with her lusty desire. It requires great strength to resist a woman's attraction. It is difficult for old men, and what to speak of young. Those who live as *brahmacārīs* must follow in the footsteps of the great sage Nārada Muni, who never accepted the proposals of *jarā.* Those who are too much sexually addicted become victims of *jarā,* and very soon their life span is shortened. Without utilizing the human form of life for Kṛṣṇa consciousness the victims of *jarā* die very soon in this world.

TEXT 22

मयि संरभ्य विपुलमदाच्छापं सुदुःसहम् ।
स्थातुमर्हसि नैकत्र मद्याच्ञाविमुखो मुने ॥२२॥

mayi saṁrabhya vipula-
madāc chāpaṁ suduḥsaham
sthātum arhasi naikatra
mad-yācñā-vimukho mune

mayi—unto me; *saṁrabhya*—having become angry; *vipula*—unlimited; *madāt*—out of illusion; *śāpam*—curse; *su-duḥsaham*—unbearable; *sthātum arhasi*—you may remain; *na*—never; *ekatra*—in one place; *mat*—my; *yācñā*—request; *vimukhaḥ*—having refused; *mune*—O great sage.

TRANSLATION

The great sage Nārada continued: When I refused to accept her request, she became very angry at me and cursed me severely. Because I refused her request, she said that I would not be able to stay in one place for a long time.

PURPORT

The great sage Nārada Muni has a spiritual body; therefore old age, disease, birth and death do not affect him. Nārada is the most kind devotee of the Supreme Lord, and his only business is to travel all over the universe and preach God consciousness. In other words, his business is to make everyone a Vaiṣṇava. Under the circumstances, there is ordinarily no need for him to stay in one place for more than the time he requires to preach. Since by his own free will he is already traveling all over the universe, the curse of the Kālakanyā is described as fortunate. Like Nārada Muni, many other devotees of the Lord are engaged in preaching the glories of the Lord in different places and in different universes. Such personalities are beyond the jurisdiction of material laws.

TEXT 23

ततो विहतसङ्कल्पा कन्यका यवनेश्वरम् ।
मयोपदिष्टमासाद्य वव्रे नाम्ना भयं पतिम् ॥२३॥

tato vihata-saṅkalpā
kanyakā yavaneśvaram
mayopadiṣṭam āsādya
vavre nāmnā bhayaṁ patim

tataḥ—thereafter; *vihata-saṅkalpā*—being disappointed in her determination; *kanyakā*—the daughter of Time; *yavana-īśvaram*—unto the king of the untouchables; *mayā upadiṣṭam*—indicated by me; *āsādya*—having approached; *vavre*—accepted; *nāmnā*—of the name; *bhayam*—fear; *patim*—as her husband.

TRANSLATION

After she was thus disappointed by me, with my permission she approached the King of the Yavanas, whose name was Bhaya, or fear, and she accepted him as her husband.

PURPORT

Being the most perfect Vaiṣṇava, Śrī Nārada Muni is always willing to do good to others, even to one who curses him. Although Kālakanyā, the daughter of Time, was refused by Nārada Muni, she was given a shelter. Of course no one could give her shelter, but a Vaiṣṇava gives shelter somewhere to such an unfortunate girl. When *jarā*, or old age, attacks, everyone dwindles and deteriorates. In one stroke Nārada Muni gave shelter to Kālakanyā and counterattacked the ordinary *karmīs*. If one accepts the instructions of Nārada Muni, the ocean of fear (*bhaya*) can be very quickly removed by the grace of that great Vaiṣṇava.

TEXT 24

ऋषभं यवनानां त्वां वृणे वीरेप्सितं पतिम् ।
सङ्कल्पस्त्वयि भूतानां कृतः किल न रिष्यति ॥२४॥

ṛṣabhaṁ yavanānāṁ tvāṁ
vṛṇe vīrepsitaṁ patim
saṅkalpas tvayi bhūtānāṁ
kṛtaḥ kila na riṣyati

ṛṣabham—the best; *yavanānām*—of the untouchables; *tvām*—you; *vṛṇe*—I accept; *vīra*—O great hero; *īpsitam*—desired; *patim*—husband; *saṅkalpaḥ*—the determination; *tvayi*—unto you; *bhūtānām*—of all living entities; *kṛtaḥ*—if done; *kila*—certainly; *na*—never; *riṣyati*—becomes baffled.

TRANSLATION

Approaching the King of the Yavanas, Kālakanyā addressed him as a great hero, saying: My dear sir, you are the best of the untouchables. I am in love with you, and I want you as my husband. I know that no one is baffled if he makes friends with you.

PURPORT

The words *yavanānām ṛṣabham* refer to the King of the Yavanas. The Sanskrit words *yavana* and *mleccha* apply to those who do not follow the Vedic principles. According to the Vedic principles, one should rise early in the morning, take bath, chant Hare Kṛṣṇa, offer *maṅgala-ārati* to the Deities, study Vedic literature, take *prasāda,* and engage in dressing and decorating the Deities. One must also collect money for the temple expenditures, or if one is a householder he must go to work in accordance with the prescribed duties of a *brāhmaṇa, kṣatriya, vaiśya* or *śūdra.* In this way one should live a life of spiritual understanding, and this is the Vedic way of civilization. One who does not follow all these rules and regulations is called a *yavana* or *mleccha.* One should not mistakenly think that these words refer to certain classes of men in other countries. There is no question of limitation according to nationalism. Whether one lives in India or outside of India, he is called a *yavana* or *mleccha* if he does not follow the Vedic principles. One who does not actually follow the hygienic principles prescribed in the Vedic rules and regulations will be subjected to many contagious diseases. Because the students in this Kṛṣṇa consciousness movement are advised to follow the Vedic principles, they naturally become hygienic.

If a person is Kṛṣṇa conscious, he can work like a young man even if he is seventy-five or eighty years old. Thus the daughter of Kāla (time) cannot overcome a Vaiṣṇava. Śrīla Kṛṣṇadāsa Kavirāja Gosvāmī engaged in writing *Caitanya-caritāmṛta* when he was very old, yet he presented the most wonderful literature of the activities of Lord Caitanya. Śrīla Rūpa Gosvāmī and Sanātana Gosvāmī began their spiritual lives at a very old age, that is, after they retired from their occupations and family lives. Yet they presented many valuable literatures for the advancement of spiritual life. This is confirmed by Śrīla Śrīnivāsa Ācārya, who praised the Gosvāmīs in this way:

nānā-śāstra-vicāraṇaika-nipuṇau sad-dharma-saṁsthāpakau
lokānāṁ hita-kāriṇau tri-bhuvane mānyau śaraṇyākarau

rādhā-kṛṣṇa-padāravinda-bhajanānandena mattālikau
vande rūpa-sanātanau raghu-yugau śrī-jīva-gopālakau

"I offer my respectful obeisances unto the six Gosvāmīs, namely Śrī Sanātana Gosvāmī, Śrī Rūpa Gosvāmī, Śrī Raghunātha Bhaṭṭa Gosvāmī, Śrī Raghunātha dāsa Gosvāmī, Śrī Jīva Gosvāmī and Śrī Gopāla Bhaṭṭa Gosvāmī, who are very expert in scrutinizingly studying all the revealed scriptures with the aim of establishing eternal religious principles for the benefit of all human beings. Thus they are honored all over the three worlds, and they are worth taking shelter of because they are absorbed in the mood of the *gopīs* and are engaged in the transcendental loving service of Rādhā and Kṛṣṇa."

Thus *jarā,* the effect of old age, does not harass a devotee. This is because a devotee follows the instructions and the determination of Nārada Muni. All devotees are in the disciplic succession stemming from Nārada Muni because they worship the Deity according to Nārada Muni's direction, namely the *Nārada-pañcarātra* or the *pāñcarātrika-vidhi.* A devotee follows the principles of *pāñcarātrika-vidhi* as well as *bhāgavata-vidhi. Bhāgavata-vidhi* includes preaching work—*śravaṇaṁ kīrtanaṁ viṣṇoḥ*—the hearing and chanting of the glories of Lord Viṣṇu, the Supreme Personality of Godhead. The *pāñcarātrika-vidhi* includes *arcanaṁ vandanaṁ dāsyaṁ sakhyam ātma-nivedanam.* Because a devotee rigidly follows the instructions of Nārada Muni, he has no fear of old age, disease or death. Apparently a devotee may grow old, but he is not subjected to the symptoms of defeat experienced by a common man in old age. Consequently old age does not make a devotee fearful of death, as a common man is fearful of death. When *jarā,* or old age, takes shelter of a devotee, Kālakanyā diminishes the devotee's fear. A devotee knows that after death he is going back home, back to Godhead; therefore he has no fear of death. Thus instead of depressing a devotee, advanced age helps him become fearless and thus happy.

TEXT 25

द्वाविमावनुशोचन्ति बालावसदवग्रहौ ।
यल्लोकशास्त्रोपनतं न राति न तदिच्छति ॥२५॥

dvāv imāv anuśocanti
bālāv asad-avagrahau
yal loka-śāstropanataṁ
na rāti na tad icchati

dvau—two kinds; *imau*—these; *anuśocanti*—they lament; *bālau*—ignorant; *asat*—the foolish; *avagrahau*—taking the path of; *yat*—that which; *loka*—by custom; *śāstra*—by scripture; *upanatam*—presented; *na*—never; *rāti*—follows; *na*—neither; *tat*—that; *icchati*—desires.

TRANSLATION

One who does not give charity according to the customs or injunctions of the scriptures and one who does not accept charity in that way are considered to be in the mode of ignorance. Such persons follow the path of the foolish. Surely they must lament at the end.

PURPORT

It is herein stated that one should strictly follow the scriptures if one actually wants an auspicious life. The same is explained in *Bhagavad-gītā*.

yaḥ śāstra-vidhim utsṛjya
vartate kāma-kārataḥ
na sa siddhim avāpnoti
na sukhaṁ na parāṁ gatim

"But he who discards scriptural injunctions and acts according to his own whims attains neither perfection, nor happiness, nor the supreme destination." (Bg. 16.23)

One who does not strictly follow the terms of the Vedic injunctions never attains success in life or happiness. And what to speak of going home, back to Godhead.

One śāstric injunction holds that a householder, a *kṣatriya*, or an administrative head should not refuse to accept a woman if she voluntarily requests to become a wife. Since Kālakanyā, the daughter of Time, was deputed by Nārada Muni to offer herself to Yavana-rāja, the King of the Yavanas could not refuse her. All transactions must be performed in light of the śāstric injunctions. The śāstric injunctions are confirmed by great sages like Nārada Muni. As stated by Narottama dāsa Ṭhākura: *sādhu-śāstra-guru-vākya, cittete kariyā aikya.* One should follow the principles of saintly persons, scriptures and the spiritual master. In this way one is sure to attain success in life. Kālakanyā, the daughter of Time, presented herself before the King of the Yavanas precisely in terms of *sādhu, śāstra* and *guru.* Thus there was no reason for not accepting her.

TEXT 26

अथो भजस्व मां भद्र भजन्तीं मे दयां कुरु ।
एतावान् पौरुषो धर्मो यदार्ताननुकम्पते ॥२६॥

atho bhajasva māṁ bhadra
bhajantīṁ me dayāṁ kuru
etāvān pauruṣo dharmo
yad ārtān anukampate

atho—therefore; *bhajasva*—accept; *mām*—me; *bhadra*—O gentle one; *bhajantīm*—willing to serve; *me*—to me; *dayām*—mercy; *kuru*—do; *etāvān*—such a measure; *pauruṣaḥ*—for any gentleman; *dharmaḥ*—religious principle; *yat*—that; *ārtān*—to the distressed; *anukampate*—is compassionate.

TRANSLATION

Kālakanyā continued: O gentle one, I am now present before you to serve you. Please accept me and thus show me mercy. It is a gentleman's greatest duty to be compassionate upon a person who is distressed.

PURPORT

Yavana-rāja, the King of the Yavanas, could also refuse to accept Kālakanyā, daughter of Time, but he considered the request due to the order of Nārada Muni. Thus he accepted Kālakanyā in a different way. In other words, the injunctions of Nārada Muni, or the path of devotional service, can be accepted by anyone within the three worlds, and certainly by the King of the Yavanas. Lord Caitanya Himself requested everyone to preach the cult of *bhakti-yoga* all over the world, in every village and town. Preachers in the Kṛṣṇa consciousness movement have actually experienced that even the *yavanas* and *mlecchas* have taken to spiritual life on the strength of Nārada Muni's *pāñcarātrika-vidhi.* When mankind follows the disciplic succession, as recommended by Caitanya Mahāprabhu, everyone throughout the world will benefit.

TEXT 27

कालकन्योदितवचो निशम्य यवनेश्वरः ।
चिकीर्षुर्देवगुह्यं स सस्मितं तामभाषत ॥२७॥

kāla-kanyodita-vaco
niśamya yavaneśvaraḥ
cikīrṣur deva-guhyaṁ sa
sasmitaṁ tām abhāṣata

kāla-kanyā—by the daughter of Time; *udita*—expressed; *vacaḥ*—words; *niśamya*—hearing; *yavana-īśvaraḥ*—the King of the Yavanas; *cikīrṣuḥ*—desiring to execute; *deva*—of providence; *guhyam*—confidential duty; *saḥ*—he; *sa-smitam*—smilingly; *tām*—her; *abhāṣata*—addressed.

TRANSLATION

After hearing the statement of Kālakanyā, daughter of Time, the King of the Yavanas began to smile and devise a means for executing his confidential duty on behalf of providence. He then addressed Kālakanyā as follows.

PURPORT

In *Caitanya-caritāmṛta* it is said:

ekale īśvara kṛṣṇa, āra saba bhṛtya
yāre yaiche nācāya, se taiche kare nṛtya
(Cc. *Ādi* 5.142)

Actually the supreme controller is the Personality of Godhead, Kṛṣṇa, and everyone is His servant. Yavana-rāja, the King of the Yavanas, was also a servant of Kṛṣṇa. Consequently he wanted to execute the purpose of Kṛṣṇa through the agency of Kālakanyā. Although Kālakanyā means invalidity or old age, Yavana-rāja wanted to serve Kṛṣṇa by introducing Kālakanyā everywhere. Thus a sane person, by attaining old age, will become fearful of death. Foolish people engage in material activities as if they will live forever and enjoy material advancement, but actually there is no material advancement. Under illusion people think that material opulence will save them, but although there has been much advancement in material science, the problems of human society—birth, death, old age and disease—are still unsolved. Nonetheless foolish scientists are thinking that they have advanced materially. When Kālakanyā, the invalidity of old age, attacks them, they become fearful of death, if they are sane. Those who are insane simply don't care for death, nor do they know what is going to happen after death. They are under the wrong impression that after death there is no life, and consequently they act very irresponsibly in this life and enjoy unrestricted sense gratification. For an intelligent person, the appearance of old age is an impetus to spiritual life. People naturally fear impending death. The King of the Yavanas tried to utilize Kālakanyā for this purpose.

TEXT 28

मया निरूपितस्तुभ्यं पतिरात्मसमाधिना ।
नाभिनन्दति लोकोऽयं त्वामभद्रामसम्मताम् ॥२८॥

mayā nirūpitas tubhyaṁ
patir ātma-samādhinā
nābhinandati loko 'yaṁ
tvām abhadrām asammatām

mayā—by me; *nirūpitaḥ*—settled; *tubhyam*—for you; *patiḥ*—husband; *ātma*—of the mind; *samādhinā*—by meditation; *na*—never; *abhinandati*—welcome; *lokaḥ*—the people; *ayam*—these; *tvām*—you; *abhadrām*—inauspicious; *asammatām*—unacceptable.

TRANSLATION

The King of the Yavanas replied: After much consideration, I have arrived at a husband for you. Actually, as far as everyone is concerned, you are inauspicious and mischievous. Since no one likes you, how can anyone accept you as his wife?

PURPORT

After much consideration, the King of the Yavanas decided to make the best use of a bad bargain. Kālakanyā was a bad bargain, and no one liked her, but everything can be used for the service of the Lord. Thus the King of the Yavanas tried to utilize her for some purpose. The purpose has already been explained—that is, Kālakanyā as *jarā,* the invalidity of old age, can be used to arouse a sense of fear in people so that they will prepare for the next life by engaging in Kṛṣṇa consciousness.

TEXT 29

त्वमव्यक्तगतिर्भुङ्क्ष्व लोकं कर्मविनिर्मितम् ।
याहि मे पृतनायुक्ता प्रजानाशं प्रणेष्यसि ॥२९॥

tvam avyakta-gatir bhuṅkṣva
lokaṁ karma-vinirmitam
yā hi me pṛtanā-yuktā
prajā-nāśaṁ praṇeṣyasi

tvam—you; *avyakta-gatiḥ*—whose movement is imperceptible; *bhuṅkṣva*—enjoy; *lokam*—this world; *karma-vinirmitam*—manufactured by fruitive activities; *yā*—one who; *hi*—certainly; *me*—my; *pṛtanā*—soldiers; *yuktā*—helped by; *prajā-nāśam*—annihilation of the living entities; *praṇeṣyasi*—you shall carry out without any hindrance.

TRANSLATION

This world is a product of fruitive activities. Therefore you may imperceptibly attack people in general. Helped by my soldiers, you can kill them without opposition.

PURPORT

The word *karma-vinirmitam* means "manufactured by fruitive activities." This entire material world, especially in these days, is the result of fruitive activities. Everyone is fully engaged in decorating the world by highways, motor cars, electricity, skyscrapers, industries, businesses, etc. All this appears very nice for those who are simply engaged in sense gratification and who are ignorant of spiritual identity. As described in *Śrīmad-Bhāgavatam:*

nūnaṁ pramattaḥ kurute vikarma
yad indriya-prītaya āpṛnoti
na sādhu manye yata ātmano 'yam
asann api kleśada āsa dehaḥ (*Bhāg.* 5.5.4)

Those without knowledge of the spirit soul are mad after materialistic activities, and they perform all kinds of sinful activities simply for sense gratification. According to Ṛṣabhadeva, such activities are inauspicious because they force one to accept an abominable body in the next life. Everyone can experience that although we try to keep the body in a comfortable position, it is always giving pain and is subjected to the threefold miseries. Otherwise, why are there so many hospitals, welfare boards and insurance establishments? Actually in this world there is no happiness. People are simply engaged trying to counteract unhappiness. Foolish people accept unhappiness as happiness; therefore the King of the Yavanas decided to attack such foolish people imperceptibly by old age, disease, and ultimately death. Of course, after death there must be birth; therefore Yavana-rāja thought it wise to kill all the *karmīs* through the agency of Kālakanyā and thus try to make them aware that materialistic advancement is not actually advancement. Every living entity is a spiritual being, and consequently without spiritual advancement the human form of life is ruined.

TEXT 30

प्रज्वारोऽयं मम भ्राता त्वं च मे भगिनी भव ।
चराम्युभाभ्यां लोकेऽस्मिन्नव्यक्तो भीमसैनिकः ।३०।

prajvāro 'yaṁ mama bhrātā
tvaṁ ca me bhaginī bhava
carāmy ubhābhyāṁ loke 'sminn
avyakto bhīma-sainikaḥ

prajvāraḥ—named Prajvāra; *ayam*—this; *mama*—my; *bhrātā*—brother; *tvam*—you; *ca*—also; *me*—my; *bhaginī*—sister; *bhava*—become; *carāmi*—I shall go about; *ubhābhyām*—by both of you; *loke*—in the world; *asmin*—this; *avyaktaḥ*—without being manifest; *bhīma*—dangerous; *sainikaḥ*—with soldiers.

TRANSLATION

The King of the Yavanas continued: Here is my brother Prajvāra. I now accept you as my sister. I shall employ both of you, as well as my dangerous soldiers, to act imperceptibly within this world.

PURPORT

Kālakanyā was sent by Nārada Muni to Yavana-rāja so that she might become his wife, but instead of accepting her as his wife, Yavana-rāja accepted her as his sister. Those who do not follow the Vedic principles are unrestricted as far as sex life is concerned. Consequently they sometimes do not hesitate to have sex with their sisters. In this age of Kali there are many instances of such incest. Although Yavana-rāja accepted the request of Nārada Muni to show respect to him, he was nonetheless thinking of illicit sex. This was due to his being the King of the *yavanas* and *mlecchas*.

The word *prajvāraḥ* is very significant, for it means "the fever sent by Lord Viṣṇu." Such a fever is always set at 107 degrees, the temperature at which a man dies. Thus the King of the *mlecchas* and *yavanas* requested the daughter of Time, Kālakanyā, to become his sister. There was no need to ask her to become his wife because the *yavanas* and *mlecchas* do not make distinctions as far as sex life is concerned. Thus one may outwardly be a sister, mother or daughter and still have sex. Yavana-rāja's brother was Prajvāra, and Kālakanyā was invalidity itself. Combined and strengthened by the soldiers of Yavana-rāja—namely non-hygienic conditions, illicit sex and ultimately a high degree of temperature to bring on death—they would be able to smash the materialistic way of life. In this connection it is significant that just as Nārada was immune to the attack of *jarā,* or invalidity, similarly, *jarā,* or the destructive force, cannot attack any follower of Nārada Muni or a pure Vaiṣṇava.

Thus end the Bhaktivedanta purports of the Fourth Canto, Twenty-seventh Chapter, of the Śrīmad-Bhāgavatam, *entitled "Attack by Caṇḍavega on the City of King Purañjana; the Character of Kālakanyā."*

CHAPTER TWENTY-EIGHT

Purañjana Becomes a Woman in the Next Life

TEXT 1

नारद उवाच
सैनिका भयनाम्नो ये बर्हिष्मन् दिष्टकारिणः ।
प्रज्वारकालकन्याभ्यां विचेरुरवनीमिमाम् ॥ १ ॥

nārada uvāca
sainikā bhaya-nāmno ye
barhiṣman diṣṭa-kāriṇaḥ
prajvāra-kāla-kanyābhyāṁ
vicerur avanīm imām

nāradaḥ uvāca—the great sage Nārada continued to speak; *sainikāḥ*—the soldiers; *bhaya-nāmnaḥ*—of Bhaya (fearfulness); *ye*—all of them who; *barhiṣman*—O King Prācīnabarhiṣat; *diṣṭa-kāriṇaḥ*—the order carriers of death; *prajvāra*—with Prajvāra; *kāla-kanyābhyām*—and with Kālakanyā; *viceruḥ*—traveled; *avanīm*—on earth; *imām*— this.

TRANSLATION

The great sage Nārada continued: My dear King Prācīnabarhiṣat, afterwards, the King of the Yavanas, whose name is fear itself, as well as his soldiers, Prajvāra and Kālakanyā, began to travel all over the world.

PURPORT

The period of life just prior to death is certainly very dangerous because usually at this time people are attacked by the weakness of old age as well as many kinds of disease. The diseases that attack the body are compared here to soldiers. These soldiers are not ordinary soldiers, for they are guided by the King of the Yavanas, who acts as their commander-in-chief. The word *diṣṭa-kāriṇaḥ* indicates that he is their commander. When a man is young, he does not care for old age but enjoys sex to the best of his satisfaction, not knowing that at the end of life his sexual indulgence will bring on various diseases, which so much disturb the body that one will pray for immediate death. The more one enjoys sex during youth, the more he suffers in old age.

TEXT 2

त एकदा तु रभसा पुरञ्जनपुरीं नृप ।
रुरुधुर्भौमभोगाढ्यां जरत्पन्नगपालिताम् ॥ २ ॥

ta ekadā tu rabhasā
purañjana-purīṁ nṛpa
rurudhur bhauma-bhogāḍhyāṁ
jarat-pannaga-pālitām

te—they; *ekadā*—once upon a time; *tu*—then; *rabhasā*—with great force; *purañjana-purīm*—the city of Purañjana; *nṛpa*—O King; *rurudhuḥ*—encircled; *bhauma-bhoga-āḍhyām*—full of sense enjoyments; *jarat*—old; *pannaga*—by the serpent; *pālitām*—protected.

TRANSLATION

Once the dangerous soldiers attacked the city of Purañjana with great force. Although the city was full of paraphernalia for sense gratification, it was being protected by the old serpent.

PURPORT

As one's body engages in sense gratification, it becomes weaker and weaker daily. Finally the vital force becomes so weak that it is herein compared to a weak serpent. The life air has already been compared to the serpent. When the vital force within the body becomes weak, the body itself also becomes weak. At such a time the death symptoms—that is, the dangerous soldiers of death's superintendent, Yamarāja—begin to attack very severely. According to the Vedic system, before coming to such a stage one should leave home and take *sannyāsa* to preach the message of God for the duration of life. However, if one sits at home and is served by his beloved wife and children, he certainly becomes weaker and weaker due to sense gratification. When death finally comes, one leaves the body devoid of spiritual assets. At the present time, even the oldest man in the family does not leave home, being attracted by wife, children, money, opulence, dwelling, etc. Thus at the end of life one worries about how his wife will be protected and how she will manage the great family responsibilities. In this way a man usually thinks of his wife before death. According to *Bhagavad-gītā:*

yaṁ yaṁ vāpi smaran bhāvaṁ
tyajaty ante kalevaram
taṁ tam evaiti kaunteya
sadā tad-bhāva-bhāvitaḥ

"Whatever state of being one remembers when he quits his body, that state he will attain without fail." (Bg. 8.6)

At the end of life, a person thinks of what he has done throughout his whole life; thus he gets another body (*dehāntara*) according to his thoughts and desires at the end of life. One overly addicted to life at home naturally thinks of his beloved wife at the end of life. Consequently in the next life he gets the body of a woman, and he also acquires the results of his pious or impious activities. In this chapter the acceptance of a woman's body by King Purañjana will be thoroughly explained.

TEXT 3

कालकन्यापि बुभुजे पुरञ्जनपुरं बलात् ।
ययाभिभूतः पुरुषः सद्यो निःसारतामियात् ॥ ३ ॥

kāla-kanyāpi bubhuje
purañjana-puraṁ balāt
yayābhibhūtaḥ puruṣaḥ
sadyo niḥsāratām iyāt

kāla-kanyā—the daughter of Kāla; *api*—also; *bubhuje*—took possession of; *purañjana-puram*—the city of Purañjana; *balāt*—by force; *yayā*—by whom; *abhibhūtaḥ*—being overwhelmed; *puruṣaḥ*—a person; *sadyaḥ*—immediately; *niḥsāratām*—uselessness; *iyāt*—gets.

TRANSLATION

Gradually Kālakanyā, with the help of dangerous soldiers, attacked all the inhabitants of Purañjana's city and thus rendered them useless for all purposes.

PURPORT

At the fag end of life, when the invalidity of old age attacks a man, his body becomes useless for all purposes. Therefore Vedic training dictates that when a man is in his boyhood he should be trained in the process of *brahmacarya,* that is, he should be completely engaged in the service of the Lord and should not in any way associate with women. When the boy becomes a young man, he marries between the ages of twenty and twenty-five. When he is married at the right age, he can immediately beget strong healthy sons. Now female descendants are increasing because young men are very weak sexually. A male child will be born if the husband is sexually stronger than the wife, but if the female is stronger, a female child will be born. Thus it is essential to practice the system of *brahmacarya* if one wishes to beget a male child when one is married. When one reaches the age of fifty, he should give up family life. At that time one's child should be grown up so that the father can leave the family responsibilities to him. The husband and wife may then go abroad to live a retired life and travel to different places of pilgrimage. When both the husband and wife lose their attachment for family and home, the wife returns home to live under the care of her grown-up children and to remain aloof from family affairs. The husband then takes *sannyāsa* to render some service to the Supreme Personality of Godhead.

This is the perfect system of civilization. The human form of life is especially meant for God realization. If one is unable to take to the process of Kṛṣṇa consciousness from the very beginning of life, he must be trained to accept these principles at the fag end of life. Unfortunately, there is no training even in childhood, nor can one give up his family life even at the end. This is the situation with the city of Purañjana, figuratively described in these verses.

TEXT 4

तयोपभुज्यमानां वै यवनाः सर्वतोदिशम् ।
द्वार्भिः प्रविश्य सुभृशं प्रार्दयन् सकलां पुरीम्॥ ४ ॥

tayopabhujyamānāṁ vai
yavanāḥ sarvato-diśam
dvārbhiḥ praviśya subhṛśaṁ
prārdayan sakalāṁ purīm

tayā—by Kālakanyā; *upabhujyamānām*—being taken possession of; *vai*—certainly; *yavanāḥ*—the Yavanas; *sarvataḥ-diśam*—from all sides; *dvārbhiḥ*—

through the gates; *praviśya*—having entered; *su-bhṛśam*—greatly; *prārdayan* —giving trouble; *sakalām*—all over; *purīm*—the city.

TRANSLATION

When Kālakanyā, daughter of Time, attacked the body, the dangerous soldiers of the King of the Yavanas entered the city through different gates. They then began to give severe trouble to all the citizens.

PURPORT

The body has nine gates—the two eyes, two nostrils, two ears, mouth, rectum and genitals. When one is harassed by the invalidity of old age, various diseases manifest at the gates of the body. For example, the eyes become so dim that one requires spectacles, and the ears become too weak to hear directly, and therefore one requires hearing aids. The nostrils are blocked by mucus, and one has to always sniff a medicinal bottle containing ammonia. Similarly, the mouth, too weak to chew, requires false teeth. The rectum also gives one trouble, and the evacuation process becomes difficult. Sometimes one has to take enemas and sometimes use a surgical nozzle to accelerate the passing of urine. In this way the city of Purañjana was attacked at various gates by the soldiers. Thus in old age all the gates of the body are blocked by so many diseases, and one has to take help from so many medicines.

TEXT 5

तस्यां प्रपीड्यमानायामभिमानी पुरञ्जनः ।
अवापोरुविधांस्तापान् कुटुम्बी ममताकुलः ॥ ५ ॥

tasyāṁ prapīḍyamānāyām
abhimānī purañjanaḥ
avāporu-vidhāṁs tāpān
kuṭumbī mamatākulaḥ

tasyām—when the city; *prapīḍyamānāyām*—was put into different difficulties; *abhimānī*—too much absorbed; *purañjanaḥ*—King Purañjana; *avāpa*—achieved; *uru*—many; *vidhān*—varieties; *tāpān*—pains; *kuṭumbī*—family man; *mamatā-ākulaḥ*—too much affected with attachment to family.

TRANSLATION

When the city was thus endangered by the soldiers and Kālakanyā, King Purañjana, being overly absorbed in affection for his family, was placed in difficulty by the attack of Yavana-rāja and Kālakanyā.

PURPORT

When we refer to the body, we include the external gross body with its various limbs, as well as the mind, intelligence and ego. In old age these all become weak when they are attacked by different diseases. The proprietor of the body, the living soul, becomes very sad at not being able to use the field of activities properly. In *Bhagavad-gītā* it is clearly explained that the living entity is the proprietor of this body (*kṣetra-jña*) and that the body is the field of activities (*kṣetra*). When a field is overgrown with thorns and weeds, it becomes very difficult for the owner to work it. That is the position of the spirit soul when the body itself becomes a burden due to disease. Extra burdens are placed on the body in the form of anxiety and general deterioration of the bodily functions.

TEXT 6

कन्योपगूढो नष्टश्रीः कृपणो विषयात्मकः ।
नष्टप्रज्ञो हृतैश्वर्यो गन्धर्वयवनैर्बलात् ॥ ६ ॥

kanyopagūḍho naṣṭa-śrīḥ
kṛpaṇo viṣayātmakaḥ
naṣṭa-prajño hṛtaiśvaryo
gandharva-yavanair balāt

kanyā—by the daughter of Time; *upagūḍhaḥ*—being embraced; *naṣṭa-śrīḥ*—bereft of all beauty; *kṛpaṇaḥ*—miser; *viṣaya-ātmakaḥ*—addicted to sense gratification; *naṣṭa-prajñaḥ*—bereft of intelligence; *hṛta-aiśvaryaḥ*—bereft of opulence; *gandharva*—by the Gandharvas; *yavanaiḥ*—and by the Yavanas; *balāt*—by force.

TRANSLATION

When King Purañjana was embraced by Kālakanyā, he gradually lost all his beauty. Having been too much addicted to sex, he became very poor in intelligence and lost all his opulence. Being bereft of all possessions, he was conquered forcibly by the Gandharvas and the Yavanas.

PURPORT

When a person is attacked by the invalidity of old age and is still addicted to sense gratification, he gradually loses all his personal beauty, intelligence and good possessions. He thus cannot resist the forceful attack of the daughter of Time.

TEXT 7

विशीर्णां स्वपुरीं वीक्ष्य प्रतिकूलाननादृतान् ।
पुत्रान् पौत्रानुगामात्याञ्जायां च गतसौहृदाम् ॥ ७ ॥

viśīrṇāṁ sva-purīṁ vīkṣya
pratikūlān anādṛtān
putrān pautrānugāmātyāñ
jāyāṁ ca gata-sauhṛdām

viśīrṇām—scattered; *sva-purīm*—his own town; *vīkṣya*—seeing; *pratikūlān*—opposing elements; *anādṛtān*—being disrespectful; *putrān*—sons; *pautra*—grandsons; *anuga*—servants; *amātyān*—ministers; *jāyām*—wife; *ca*—and; *gata-sauhṛdām*—indifferent.

TRANSLATION

King Purañjana then saw that everything in his town was scattered and that his sons, grandsons, servants and ministers were all gradually opposing him. He also noted that his wife was becoming cold and indifferent.

PURPORT

When one becomes an invalid, his senses and organs are weakened. In other words, they are no longer under one's control. The senses and sense objects then begin to oppose him. When a person is in a distressed condition, even his family members—his sons, grandsons and wife—become disrespectful. They no longer are under the command of the master of the house. Just as we wish to use our senses for sense gratification, the senses also require strength from the body in reciprocation. A man keeps a family for enjoyment, and similarly family members demand enjoyment from the head of the family. When they do not receive sufficient money from him, they grow disinterested and ignore his commands or desires. This is all due to one's being a *kṛpaṇa* (miser). This word *kṛpaṇa,* used in the sixth verse, is in opposition to the word *brāhmaṇa.* In the human form of life one should become a *brāhmaṇa,* which means that one should understand the constitutional position of the Absolute Truth, Brahman, and then engage in His service as a Vaiṣṇava. We get this facility in the human form of life, but if we do not properly utilize this opportunity, we become a *kṛpaṇa,* miser. A miser is one who gets money but does not spend it properly. This human form of life is especially meant for understanding Brahman, for becoming a *brāhmaṇa,* and if we do not utilize it properly, we remain a *kṛpaṇa.* We can actually see that when one has money but does not spend it, he remains a miser and is never happy. Similarly, when one's intelligence is spoiled due to sense gratification, he remains a miser throughout his life.

TEXT 8

आत्मानं कन्यया ग्रस्तं पञ्चालानरिदूषितान् ।
दुरन्तचिन्तामापन्नो न लेभे तत्प्रतिक्रियाम् ॥ ८ ॥

ātmānaṁ kanyayā grastaṁ
pañcālān ari-dūṣitān
duranta-cintām āpanno
na lebhe tat-pratikriyām

ātmānam—himself; *kanyayā*—by Kālakanyā; *grastam*—being embraced; *pañcālān*—Pañcāla; *ari-dūṣitān*—infected by the enemies; *duranta*— insurmountable; *cintām*—anxiety; *āpannaḥ*—having obtained; *na*—not; *lebhe*—achieved; *tat*—of that; *pratikriyām*—counteraction.

TRANSLATION

When King Purañjana saw that all his family members, relatives, followers, servants, secretaries and everyone else had turned against him, he certainly became very anxious. But, he could not counteract the situation because he was thoroughly overwhelmed by Kālakanyā.

PURPORT

When a person becomes weak from the attack of old age, the family members, servants and secretaries do not care for him. He is then unable to counteract this. Thus he becomes more and more anxious and laments his frightful condition.

TEXT 9

कामानभिलषन्दीनो यातयामांश्च कन्यया ।
विगतात्मगतिस्नेहः पुत्रदारांश्च लालयन् ॥ ९ ॥

kāmān abhilaṣan dīno
yāta-yāmāṁś ca kanyayā
vigatātma-gati-snehaḥ
putra-dārāṁś ca lālayan

kāmān—objects of enjoyment; *abhilaṣan*—always lusting after; *dīnaḥ*—the poor man; *yāta-yāmān*—stale; *ca*—also; *kanyayā*—by the influence of Kālakanyā; *vigata*—lost; *ātma-gati*—real purpose of life; *snehaḥ*—attachment to; *putra*—sons; *dārān*—wife; *ca*—and; *lālayan*—affectionately maintaining.

TRANSLATION

The objects of enjoyment became stale by the influence of Kālakanyā. Due to the continuance of his lusty desires, King Purañjana became very poor in everything. Thus he did not understand the aim of life. He was still very affectionate toward his wife and children, and he worried about maintaining them.

PURPORT

This is exactly the position of present civilization. Everyone is engaged in maintaining the body, home and family. Consequently everyone becomes confused at the end of life, not knowing what spiritual life and the goal of human life are. In a civilization of sense gratification, there cannot be spiritual life because a person only thinks of this life. Although the next life is a fact, no information is given about it.

TEXT 10

गन्धर्वयवनाक्रान्तां कालकन्योपमर्दिताम् ।
हातुं प्रचक्रमे राजा तां पुरीमनिकामतः ॥१०॥

gandharva-yavanākrāntāṁ
kāla-kanyopamarditām
hātuṁ pracakrame rājā
tāṁ purīm anikāmataḥ

gandharva—by the Gandharva soldiers; *yavana*—and by the Yavana soldiers; *ākrāntām*—overcome; *kāla-kanyā*—by Kālakanyā (the daughter of Time); *upamarditām*—being smashed; *hātum*—to give up; *pracakrame*—proceeded; *rājā*—King Purañjana; *tām*—that; *purīm*—the city; *anikāmataḥ*—unwilling.

TRANSLATION

The city of King Purañjana was overcome by the Gandharva and Yavana soldiers, and although the King had no desire to leave the city, he was circumstantially forced to do so, for it was smashed by Kālakanyā.

PURPORT

The living entity, separated from the association of the Supreme Personality of Godhead, tries to enjoy this material world. He is given a chance to enjoy it in a particular type of body, beginning with the body of a Brahmā down to that of the microbe. From the Vedic history of creation we can understand that the first living creature was Lord Brahmā, who created the seven great sages and other *prajāpatis* to increase the universal population. Thus every living entity, according to *karma,* his past desires and activities, gets a particular type of body, from that of Brahmā to that of a microbe or germ in stool. Due to long association with a particular type of material body and also due to the grace of Kālakanyā and her *māyā,* one becomes overly attached to a material body, although it is the abode of pain. Even if one tries to separate a worm from stool, the worm will be unwilling to leave. It will again return to the stool. Similarly, a hog generally lives in a very filthy state, eating stool, but if one tries to separate it from its condition and give it a nice place, the hog will be unwilling. In this way if we study each and every living entity, we will find that he will defy offers of a more comfortable position. Although King Purañjana was attacked from all sides, he was nonetheless unwilling to leave the city. In other words, the living entity—whatever his condition—does not want to give up the body. But he will be forced to give it up because, after all, this material body cannot exist forever.

The living entity wishes to enjoy the material world in different ways, and therefore by nature's law he is allowed to transmigrate from one body to another, exactly as a person transmigrates from the body of an infant, to a child, to a boy, to a youth, to a man. This process is constantly going on. At the last stage, when the gross body becomes old and invalid, the living entity is reluctant to give it up, despite the fact that it is no longer usable. Although material existence and the material body are not comfortable, why does the living entity not want to leave? As soon as one gets a material body, he has to work very hard to maintain it. He may engage in different fields of activity, but whatever the case, everyone has to work very hard to maintain the material body. Unfortunately, society has no information of the soul's transmigration. Because the living entity does not hope to enter the spiritual kingdom of eternal life, bliss and knowledge, he wants to stick to his present body, even though it may be useless. Consequently the greatest welfare activity in this material world is the furthering of this Kṛṣṇa consciousness movement.

This movement is giving human society information about the kingdom of God. There is God, there is Kṛṣṇa, and everyone can return to God and live eternally in bliss and knowledge. A Kṛṣṇa conscious person is not afraid of giving up the body because his position is always eternal. A Kṛṣṇa conscious person engages in the transcendental loving service of the Lord eternally; therefore as long as he lives within the body, he is happy to engage in the loving service of the Lord, and when he gives up the body, he is also permanently situated in the service of the Lord. The saintly devotees are always free and liberated, whereas the *karmīs,* who have no knowledge of spiritual life or the transcendental loving service of the Lord, are very much afraid of giving up the rotten material body.

TEXT 11

भयनाम्नोऽग्रजो भ्राता प्रज्वारः प्रत्युपस्थितः ।
ददाह तां पुरीं कृत्स्नां भ्रातुः प्रियचिकीर्षया ॥११॥

bhaya-nāmno 'grajo bhrātā
prajvāraḥ pratyupasthitaḥ
dadāha tāṁ purīṁ kṛtsnāṁ
bhrātuḥ priya-cikīrṣayā

bhaya-nāmnaḥ—of Bhaya (fearfulness); *agra-jaḥ*—elder; *bhrātā*—brother; *prajvāraḥ*—named Prajvāra; *pratyupasthitaḥ*—being present there; *dadāha*—set fire; *tām*—to that; *purīm*—city; *kṛtsnām*—wholesale; *bhrātuḥ*—his brother; *priya-cikīrṣayā*—in order to please.

TRANSLATION

Under the circumstances the elder brother of Yavana-rāja, known as Prajvāra, set fire to the city to please his younger brother, whose other name is fear itself.

PURPORT

According to the Vedic system, a dead body is set on fire, but before death there is another fire or fever, which is called *prajvāra,* or *viṣṇu-jvāra.* Medical science verifies that when one's temperature is raised to 107 degrees, a man immediately dies. This *prajvāra,* or high fever, at the last stage of life places the living entity in the midst of a blazing fire.

TEXT 12

तस्यां सन्दह्यमानायां सपौरः सपरिच्छदः ।
कौटुम्बिकः कुटुम्बिन्या उपातप्यत सान्वयः ॥१२॥

tasyāṁ sandahyamānāyāṁ
sapauraḥ saparicchadaḥ
kauṭumbikaḥ kuṭumbinyā
upātapyata sānvayaḥ

tasyām—when that city; *sandahyamānāyām*—was ablaze; *sa-pauraḥ*—along with all the citizens; *sa-paricchadaḥ*—along with all servants and followers; *kauṭumbikaḥ*—the King, having so many relatives; *kuṭumbinyā*—along with his wife; *upātapyata*—began to suffer the temperature of the fire; *sa-anvayaḥ*—along with descendants.

TRANSLATION

When the city was set ablaze, all the citizens and servants of the King, as well as all family members, sons, grandsons, wives and other relatives, were within the fire. King Purañjana thus became very unhappy.

PURPORT

There are many parts of the body—the senses, the limbs, the skin, the muscles, blood, marrow, etc.—and all these are considered here figuratively as sons, grandsons, citizens and dependents. When the body is attacked by the *viṣṇu-jvāra,* the fiery condition becomes so acute that sometimes one remains in a coma. This means that the body is in such severe pain that one becomes unconscious and cannot feel the miseries taking place within the body. Indeed, the living entity becomes so helpless at the time of death, that, although unwilling, he is forced to give up the body and enter another. In *Bhagavad-gītā* it is stated that man may, by scientific advancement, improve the temporary living conditions but that he cannot avoid the pangs of birth, old age, disease and death. These are under the control of the Supreme Personality of Godhead through the agency of material nature. A foolish person cannot understand this simple fact. Now people are very busy trying to find petroleum in the midst of the ocean. They are very anxious to make provisions for the future petroleum supply, but they do not make any attempts to ameliorate the conditions of birth, old age, disease and death. Thus not knowing anything about his own future life, a person in ignorance is certainly defeated in all his activities.

TEXT 13

यवनोपरुद्धायतनो ग्रस्तायां कालकन्यया ।
पुर्यां प्रज्वारसंसृष्टः पुरपालोऽन्वतप्यत ॥१३॥

yavanoparuddhāyatano
grastāyāṁ kāla-kanyayā
puryāṁ prajvāra-saṁsṛṣṭaḥ
pura-pālo 'nvatapyata

yavana—by the Yavanas; *uparuddha*—attacked; *āyatanaḥ*—his abode; *grastāyām*—when seized; *kāla-kanyayā*—by the daughter of Time; *puryām*—the city; *prajvāra-saṁsṛṣṭaḥ*—being approached by Prajvāra; *pura-pālaḥ*—the city superintendent; *anvatapyata*—become also very much aggrieved.

TRANSLATION

The city's superintendent of police, the serpent, saw that the citizens were being attacked by Kālakanyā, and he became very aggrieved to see his own residence set ablaze after being attacked by the Yavanas.

PURPORT

The living entity is covered by two different types of bodies—the gross body and the subtle body. At death we can see that the gross body is finished, but actually the living entity is carried by the subtle body to another gross body. The so-called scientists of the modern age cannot see how the subtle body is working in carrying the soul from one body to another. This subtle body has been figuratively described as a serpent, or the city's police superintendent. When there is fire everywhere, the police superintendent cannot escape either. When there is security and an absence of fire in the city, the police superintendent can impose his authority upon the citizens, but when there is an all-out attack on the city, he is rendered useless. As the life air was ready to leave the gross body, the subtle body also began to experience pain.

TEXT 14

न शेके सोऽवितुं तत्र पुरुकृच्छ्रोरुवेपथुः ।
गन्तुमैच्छत्ततो वृक्षकोटरादिव सानलात् ॥१४॥

na śeke so 'vituṁ tatra
puru-kṛcchroru-vepathuḥ
gantum aicchat tato vṛkṣa-
koṭarād iva sānalāt

na—not; *śeke*—was able; *saḥ*—he; *avitum*—to protect; *tatra*—there; *puru*—very much; *kṛcchra*—difficulty; *uru*—great; *vepathuḥ*—suffering; *gantum*—to go out; *aicchat*—desired; *tataḥ*—from there; *vṛkṣa*—of a tree; *koṭarāt*—from the hollow; *iva*—like; *sa-analāt*—on fire.

TRANSLATION

As a serpent living within the cavity of a tree wishes to leave when there is a forest fire, so the city's police superintendent, the snake, wished to leave the city due to the fire's severe heat.

PURPORT

It becomes very difficult for snakes to leave a forest when there is a fire. Other animals may flee due to their long legs, but serpents, only being able to crawl, are generally burned in the fire. At the last stage, the limbs of the body are not as much affected as the life air.

TEXT 15

शिथिलावयवो यर्हि गन्धर्वैर्हृतपौरुषः ।
यवनैररिभी राजन्नुपरुद्धो रुरोद ह ॥१५॥

śithilāvayavo yarhi
gandharvair hṛta-pauruṣaḥ

yavanair aribhī rājann
uparuddho ruroda ha

śithila—slackened; *avayavaḥ*—his limbs; *yarhi*—when; *gandharvaiḥ*—by the Gandharvas; *hṛta*—defeated; *pauruṣaḥ*—his bodily strength; *yavanaiḥ*—by the Yavanas; *aribhiḥ*—by the enemies; *rājan*—O King Prācīnabarhiṣat; *uparuddhaḥ*—being checked; *ruroda*—cried loudly; *ha*—indeed.

TRANSLATION

The limbs of the serpent's body were slackened by the Gandharvas and Yavana soldiers, who had thoroughly defeated his bodily strength. When he attempted to leave the body, he was checked by his enemies. Being thus baffled in his attempt, he began to cry loudly.

PURPORT

At the last stage of life, the different gates of the body are choked by the effects of disease, which are caused by an imbalance of bile, mucus and air. Thus the living entity cannot clearly express his difficulties, and surrounding relatives hear the sound "*ghura ghura*" from a dying man. In his *Mukunda-mālā-stotra,* King Kulaśekhara states:

kṛṣṇa tvadīya-pada-paṅkaja-pañjarāntam
adyaiva me viśatu mānasa-rāja-haṁsaḥ
prāṇa-prayāṇa-samaye kapha-vāta-pittaiḥ
kaṇṭhāvarodhana-vidhau smaraṇaṁ kutas te

"My dear Kṛṣṇa, please help me die immediately so that the swan of my mind may be encircled by the stem of Your lotus feet. Otherwise at the time of my final breath, when my throat is choked up, how will it be possible for me to think of You?" The swan takes great pleasure in diving within water and being encircled by the stem of the lotus flower. This entanglement is sporting joy. If, in our healthy condition, we think of the lotus feet of the Lord and die, it is most fortunate. In old age, at the time of death, the throat sometimes becomes choked with mucus or blocked by air. At such a time the sound vibration of Hare Kṛṣṇa, the *mahā-mantra,* may not come out. Thus one may forget Kṛṣṇa. Of course those who are strong in Kṛṣṇa consciousness cannot possibly forget Kṛṣṇa at any stage because they are accustomed to chanting the Hare Kṛṣṇa *mantra,* especially when there is a signal from death.

TEXT 16

दुहितॄः पुत्रपौत्रांश्च जामिजामातृपार्षदान् ।
स्वत्वावशिष्टं यत्किञ्चिद् गृहकोशपरिच्छदम् ॥१६॥

duhitṝḥ putra-pautrāṁś ca
jāmi-jāmātṛ-pārṣadān
svatvāvaśiṣṭaṁ yat kiñcid
gṛha-kośa-paricchadam

duhitṝḥ—daughters; *putra*—sons; *pautrān*—grandsons; *ca*—and; *jāmi*—daughters-in-law; *jāmātṛ*—sons-in-law; *pārṣadān*—associates; *svatva*—property; *avaśiṣṭam*—remaining; *yat kiñcit*—whatever; *gṛha*—home; *kośa*—accumulation of wealth; *paricchadam*—household paraphernalia.

TRANSLATION

King Purañjana then began to think of his daughters, sons, grandsons, daughters-in-law, sons-in-law, servants and other associates as well as his house, his household paraphernalia and his little accumulation of wealth.

PURPORT

It is not infrequent for a person overly attached to the material body to request a physician to prolong his life at least for some time. If the so-called scientific physician is able to prolong one's life for a few minutes through the use of oxygen or other medicines, he thinks that he is very successful in his attempts, although ultimately the patient will die. This is called the struggle for existence. At the time of death both patient and physician still think of prolonging life, although all the constituents of the body are practically dead and gone.

TEXT 17

अहं ममेति स्वीकृत्य गृहेषु कुमतिर्गृही ।
दध्यौ प्रमदया दीनो विप्रयोग उपस्थिते ॥१७॥

ahaṁ mameti svīkṛtya
gṛheṣu kumatir gṛhī
dadhyau pramadayā dīno
viprayoga upasthite

aham—I; *mama*—mine; *iti*—thus; *svī-kṛtya*—accepting; *gṛheṣu*—in the home; *ku-matiḥ*—whose mind is full of obnoxious thoughts; *gṛhī*—the householder; *dadhyau*—turn his attention to; *pramadayā*—with his wife; *dīnaḥ*—very poor; *viprayoge*—when separation; *upasthite*—occurred.

TRANSLATION

King Purañjana was overly attached to his family and conceptions of "I" and "mine." Because he was overly attracted to his wife, he was already quite poverty-stricken. At the time of separation, he became very sorry.

PURPORT

It is clear in this verse that at the time of death thoughts of material enjoyment do not go away. This indicates that the living entity, the soul, is carried by the subtle body—mind, intelligence and ego. Due to false ego, the living entity still wants to enjoy the material world, and for want of material enjoyment he becomes sorry or sad. He still makes intellectual plans to further his existence, and therefore, although he gives up the gross body, he is carried by the subtle body to another gross body. The transmigration of the subtle body is never visible to material eyes; therefore when one gives up the gross body, we think that he is finished. Plans for material enjoyment are made by the subtle body, and the gross body is the instrument for enjoying these plans. Thus the gross body can be compared to the wife, for the wife is the agent for all kinds of sense gratification. Because of long association with the gross body, the living entity becomes very sad to be separated from it. The mental activity of the living entity obliges him to accept another gross body and continue his material existence.

The Sanskrit word *strī* means "expansion." Through the wife one expands his various objects of attraction—sons, daughters, grandsons, and so on. Attachment to family members becomes very prominent at the time of death. One often sees that just before leaving his body a man may call for his beloved son to give him charge of his wife and other paraphernalia. He may say, "My dear boy, I am being forced to leave. Please take charge of the family affairs." He speaks in this way, not even knowing his destination.

TEXT 18

लोकान्तरं गतवति मय्यनाथा कुटुम्बिनी ।
वर्तिष्यते कथं त्वेषा बालकाननुशोचती ॥१८॥

lokāntaraṁ gatavati
mayy anāthā kuṭumbinī
vartiṣyate kathaṁ tv eṣā
bālakān anuśocatī

loka-antaram—into a different life; *gatavati mayi*—when I am gone; *anāthā*—bereft of husband; *kuṭumbinī*—surrounded by all family members; *vartiṣyate*—will exist; *katham*—how; *tu*—then; *eṣā*—this woman; *bālakān*—children; *anuśocatī*—lamenting about.

TRANSLATION

King Purañjana was anxiously thinking, "Alas, my wife is encumbered by so many children. When I pass from this body, how will she be able to maintain all these family members? Alas, she will be greatly harassed by thoughts of family maintenance."

PURPORT

All these thoughts of one's wife indicate that the King was overly engrossed with the thoughts of woman. Generally a chaste woman becomes a very obedient wife. This causes a husband to become attached to his wife, and consequently he thinks of his wife very much at the time of death. This is a very dangerous situation, as is evident from the life of King Purañjana. If one thinks of his wife instead of Kṛṣṇa at the time of death, he will certainly not return home, back to Godhead, but will be forced to accept the body of a woman and thus begin another chapter of material existence.

TEXT 19

न मय्यनाश्रिते भुङ्क्ते नास्नाते स्नाति मत्परा ।
मयि रुष्टे सुसंत्रस्ता भर्त्सिते यतवाग्भयात् ॥१९॥

na mayy anāśite bhuṅkte
nāsnāte snāti mat-parā
mayi ruṣṭe susantrastā
bhartsite yata-vāg bhayāt

na—never; *mayi*—when I; *anāśite*—had not eaten; *bhuṅkte*—she would eat; *na*—never; *asnāte*—had not taken bath; *snāti*—she would take her bath; *mat-parā*—always devoted to me; *mayi*—when I; *ruṣṭe*—was angry; *su-*

santrastā—very much frightened; *bhartsite*—when I chastised; *yata-vāk*—fully controlled of words; *bhayāt*—out of fear.

TRANSLATION

King Purañjana then began to think of his past dealings with his wife. He recalled that his wife would not take her dinner until he had finished his, that she would not take her bath until he had finished his, and that she was always very much attached to him, so much so that if he would sometimes become angry and chastise her, she would simply remain silent and tolerate his misbehavior.

PURPORT

A wife is always supposed to be submissive to her husband. Submission, mild behavior and subservience are qualities in a wife which make a husband very thoughtful of her. For family life it is very good for a husband to be attached to his wife, but it is not very good for spiritual advancement. Thus Kṛṣṇa consciousness must be established in every home. If a husband and wife are very much attached to one another in Kṛṣṇa consciousness, they will both benefit because Kṛṣṇa is the center of their existence. Otherwise, if the husband is too much attached to his wife, he becomes a woman in his next life. The woman, being overly attached to her husband, becomes a man in her next life. Of course, it is an advantage for a woman to become a man, but it is not at all advantageous for the man to become a woman.

TEXT 20

प्रबोधयति माविज्ञं व्युषिते शोककर्शिता ।
वर्त्मैतद् गृहमेधीयं वीरसूरपि नेष्यति ॥२०॥

prabodhayati māvijñaṁ
vyuṣite śoka-karśitā
vartmaitad gṛha-medhīyaṁ
vīra-sūr api neṣyati

prabodhayati—gives good counsel; *mā*—unto me; *avijñam*—foolish; *vyuṣite*—at the time of my being away; *śoka*—by aggrievement; *karśitā*—being aggrieved and thus dried up; *vartma*—path; *etat*—this; *gṛha-medhīyam*—of household responsibilities; *vīra-sūḥ*—the mother of great heroes; *api*—although; *neṣyati*—will she be able to execute.

TRANSLATION

King Purañjana continued thinking how, when he was in a state of bewilderment, his wife would give him good counsel and how she would become aggrieved when he was away from home. Although she was the mother of so many sons and heroes, the King still feared that she would not be able to maintain the responsibility of household affairs.

PURPORT

At the time of death King Purañjana was thinking of his wife, and this is called polluted consciousness. As Lord Kṛṣṇa explains in *Bhagavad-gītā:*

mamaivāṁśo jīva-loke
jīva-bhūtaḥ sanātanaḥ
manaḥ ṣaṣṭhānīndriyāṇi
prakṛti-sthāni karṣati

"The living entities in this conditioned world are My eternal, fragmental parts. Due to conditioned life, they are struggling very hard with the six senses, which include the mind." (Bg. 15.7)

The living entity is, after all, part and parcel of the Supreme Spirit, Kṛṣṇa. In other words, Kṛṣṇa's constitutional position and the living entity's constitutional position are the same qualitatively. The only difference is that the living entity is eternally an atomic particle of the Supreme Spirit. *Mamaivāṁśo jīva-loke jīva-bhūtaḥ sanātanaḥ.* In this material world of conditional life, the fragmental portion of the Supreme Lord, the individual soul, is struggling due to his contaminated mind and consciousness. As part and parcel of the Supreme Lord, a living entity is supposed to think of Kṛṣṇa, but here we see that King Purañjana (the living entity) is thinking of a woman. Such mental absorption with some sense object brings about the living entity's struggle for existence in this material world. Since King Purañjana is thinking of his wife, his struggle for existence in the material world will not be ended by death. As revealed in the following verses, King Purañjana had to accept the body of a woman in his next life due to his being overly absorbed in thoughts of his wife. Thus mental absorption in social, political, pseudo-religious, national and communal consciousness is cause for bondage. During one's lifetime one has to change his activities in order to attain release from bondage. This is confirmed in *Bhagavad-gītā:*

yajñārthāt karmaṇo 'nyatra
loko 'yaṁ karma-bandhanaḥ

tad-arthaṁ karma kaunteya
mukta-saṅgaḥ samācara

"Work done as a sacrifice for Viṣṇu has to be performed, otherwise work binds one to this material world. Therefore, O son of Kuntī, perform your prescribed duties for His satisfaction, and in that way you will always remain unattached and free from bondage." (Bg. 3.9) If we do not change our consciousness in this life, whatever we do in the name of social, political, religious or communal and national welfare will be the cause of our bondage. This means we have to continue in material conditional life. When the mind and senses are engaged in material activities, one has to continue his material existence and struggle to attain happiness. In each and every life, one is engaged in the struggle to become happy. Actually no one in this material world is happy, but the struggle gives a false sense of happiness. A person must work very hard, and when he attains the result of his hard work, he thinks himself happy. In the material world people do not know what real happiness is. Real happiness is to be attained by transcendental senses.

yatroparamate cittaṁ
niruddhaṁ yoga-sevayā
yatra caivātmanātmānaṁ
paśyann ātmani tuṣyati

sukham ātyantikaṁ yat tad
buddhi-grāhyam atīndriyam
vetti yatra na caivāyaṁ
sthitaś calati tattvataḥ

yaṁ labdhvā cāparaṁ lābhaṁ
manyate nādhikaṁ tataḥ
yasmin sthito na duḥkhena
guruṇāpi vicālyate
taṁ vidyād duḥkha-saṁyoga-
viyogaṁ yoga-saṁjñitam

"In the stage of perfection called trance, or *samādhi,* one's mind is completely restrained from material mental activities by practice of *yoga.* This is characterized by one's ability to see the self by the pure mind and to relish and rejoice in the self. In that joyous state, one is situated in boundless transcendental happiness and enjoys himself through transcendental senses. Established thus, one never departs from the truth, and upon gaining this he thinks there is no greater gain. Being situated in such a position, one is never shaken, even in the midst of greatest difficulty. This indeed is actual freedom from all miseries arising from material contact." (Bg. 6.20-23)

Thus real happiness must be appreciated by one's transcendental senses. Unless one is purified, the transcendental senses are not manifest; therefore to purify the senses one must take to Kṛṣṇa consciousness and engage the senses in the service of the Lord. Then there will be real happiness and liberation.

It is stated in *Bhagavad-gītā:*

śarīraṁ yad avāpnoti
yac cāpy utkrāmatīśvaraḥ
gṛhītvaitāni saṁyāti
vāyur gandhān ivāśayāt

"The living entity in the material world carries his different conceptions of life from one body to another as the air carries aromas." (Bg. 15.8)

If the wind passes over a garden of roses, it will carry the aroma of roses, and if it passes over a filthy place, it will carry the stench of obnoxious things. Similarly, King Purañjana, the living entity, now passes the air of his life over his wife, a woman; therefore he has to accept the body of a woman in his next life.

TEXT 21

कथं नु दारका दीना दारकीर्वापरायणाः ।
वर्तिष्यन्ते मयि गते भिन्ननाव इवोदधौ ॥२१॥

kathaṁ nu dārakā dīnā
dārakīr vāparāyaṇāḥ
vartiṣyante mayi gate
bhinna-nāva ivodadhau

katham—how; *nu*—indeed; *dārakāḥ*—sons; *dīnāḥ*—poor; *dārakīḥ*—daughters; *vā*—or; *aparāyaṇāḥ*—having no one else to depend on; *vartiṣyante*—will live; *mayi*—when I; *gate*—gone from this world; *bhinna*—broken; *nāvaḥ*—boat; *iva*—like; *udadhau*—in the ocean.

TRANSLATION

King Purañjana continued worrying: "After I pass from this world, how will my sons and daughters, who are now fully dependent on me, live and

continue their lives? Their position will be similar to that of passengers aboard a ship wrecked in the midst of the ocean."

PURPORT

At the time of death every living entity worries about what will happen to his wife and children. Similarly, a politician also worries about what will happen to his country or his political party. Unless one is fully Kṛṣṇa conscious, he has to accept a body in the next life according to his particular state of consciousness. Since Purañjana is thinking of his wife and children and is overly engrossed in thoughts of his wife, he will accept the body of a woman. Similarly, a politician or so-called nationalist who is inordinately attached to the land of his birth will certainly be reborn in the same land after ending his political career. One's next life will also be affected by the acts one performs during this life. Sometimes politicians act most sinfully for their own sense gratification. It is not unusual for a politician to kill the opposing party. Even though a politician may be allowed to take birth in his so-called homeland, he still has to undergo suffering due to his sinful activities in his previous life.

This science of transmigration is completely unknown to modern scientists. So-called scientists do not like to bother with these things because if they would at all consider this subtle subject matter and the problems of life, they would see that their future is very dark. Thus they try to avoid considering the future and continue committing all kinds of sinful activities in the name of social, political and national necessity.

TEXT 22

एवं कृपणया बुद्ध्या शोचन्तमतदर्हणम् ।
ग्रहीतुं कृतधीरेनं भयनामाभ्यपद्यत ॥२२॥

evaṁ kṛpaṇayā buddhyā
śocantam atad-arhaṇam
grahītuṁ kṛta-dhīr enaṁ
bhaya-nāmābhyapadyata

evam—thus; *kṛpaṇayā*—by miserly; *buddhyā*—intelligence; *śocantam*—lamenting; *a-tat-arhaṇam*—on which he should not have lamented; *grahītum*—in order to arrest; *kṛta-dhīḥ*—the determined King of the Yavanas; *enam*—him; *bhaya-nāmā*—whose name was fear; *abhyapadyata*—came there immediately.

TRANSLATION

Although King Purañjana should not have lamented over the fate of his wife and children, he nonetheless did so due to his miserly intelligence. In the meantime, Yavana-rāja, whose name was fear itself, immediately drew near to arrest him.

PURPORT

Foolish people do not know that every individual soul is responsible for his own actions and reactions in life. As long as a living entity in the form of a child or boy is innocent, it is the duty of the father and mother to lead him into a proper understanding of the values of life. When a child is grown, it should be left up to him to execute the duties of life properly. The parent, after his death, cannot help his child. A father may leave some estate for his children's immediate help, but he should not be overly absorbed in thoughts of how his family will survive after his death. This is the disease of the conditioned soul. Not only does he commit sinful activities for his own sense gratification, but he accumulates great wealth to leave behind so that his children may also gorgeously arrange for sense gratification.

In any case, everyone is afraid of death, and therefore death is called *bhaya,* or fear. Although King Purañjana was engaged in thinking of his wife and children, death did not wait for him. Death does not wait for any man; it will immediately carry out its duty. Since death must take away the living entity without hesitation, it is the ultimate God realization of the atheists, who spoil their lives thinking of country, society and relatives, to the neglect of God consciousness. In this verse the word *atad-arhaṇam* is very significant, for it means that one should not be overly engaged in welfare activities for one's family members, countrymen, society and community. None of these will help a person to advance spiritually. Unfortunately, in present day society so-called educated men have no idea what spiritual progress is. Although they have the opportunity in the human form of life to make spiritual progress, they remain misers. They use their lives improperly and simply waste them thinking about the material welfare of their relatives, countrymen, society and so on. One's actual duty is to learn how to conquer death. Lord Kṛṣṇa states the process of conquering death in *Bhagavad-gītā*:

janma karma ca me divyam
evaṁ yo vetti tattvataḥ
tyaktvā dehaṁ punar janma
naiti mām eti so 'rjuna

"One who knows the transcendental nature of My appearance and activities does not, upon leaving the body, take his birth again in this material world, but attains My eternal abode, O Arjuna." (Bg. 4.9)

After giving up this body, one who is fully Kṛṣṇa conscious does not accept another material body but returns home, back to Godhead. Everyone should try to attain this perfection. Unfortunately, instead of doing so, people are absorbed in thoughts of society, friendship, love and relatives. This Kṛṣṇa consciousness movement, however, is educating people throughout the world and informing them how to conquer death. *Hariṁ vinā na sṛtiṁ taranti.* One cannot conquer death without taking shelter of the Supreme Personality of Godhead.

TEXT 23

पशुवद्यवनैरेष नीयमानः स्वकं क्षयम् ।
अन्वद्रवन्ननुपथाः शोचन्तो भृशमातुराः ॥२३॥

paśuvad yavanair eṣa
nīyamānaḥ svakaṁ kṣayam
anvadravann anupathāḥ
śocanto bhṛśam āturāḥ

paśu-vat—like an animal; *yavanaiḥ*—by the Yavanas; *eṣaḥ*—Purañjana; *nīyamānaḥ*—being arrested and taken away; *svakam*—to their own; *kṣayam*—abode; *anvadravan*—followed; *anupathāḥ*—his attendants; *śocantaḥ*—lamenting; *bhṛśam*—greatly; *āturāḥ*—being distressed.

TRANSLATION

When the Yavanas were taking King Purañjana away to their place, binding him like an animal, the King's followers became greatly aggrieved. While they lamented, they were forced to go along with him.

PURPORT

When Yamarāja and his assistants take a living entity away to the place of judgment, the life, life air and desires, being followers of the living entity, also go with him. This is confirmed in the *Vedas.* When the living entity is taken away or arrested by Yamarāja (*tam utkrāmantam*), the life air also goes with him (*prāṇo 'nūtkrāmati*), and when the life air is gone (*prāṇam anūtkrāmantam*), all the senses (*sarve prāṇāḥ*) also go along (*anūtkrāmanti*). When the living entity and the life air are gone, the lump of matter produced of five elements—earth, water, air, fire and ether—is rejected and left behind. The living entity then goes to the court of judgment, and Yamarāja decides what kind of body he is going to get next. This process is unknown to modern scientists. Every living entity is responsible for his activities in this life, and after death he is taken to the court of Yamarāja, where it is decided what kind of body he will take next. Although the gross material body is left, the living entity and his desires, as well as the resultant reactions of his past activities, go on. It is Yamarāja who decides what kind of body one gets next in accordance with one's past actions.

TEXT 24

पुरीं विहायोपगत उपरुद्धो भुजङ्गमः ।
यदा तमेवानु पुरी विशीर्णा प्रकृतिं गता ॥२४॥

purīṁ vihāyopagata
uparuddho bhujaṅgamaḥ
yadā tam evānu purī
viśīrṇā prakṛtiṁ gatā

purīm—the city; *vihāya*—having given up; *upagataḥ*—gone out; *uparuddhaḥ*—arrested; *bhujaṅgamaḥ*—the serpent; *yadā*—when; *tam*—him; *eva*—certainly; *anu*—after; *purī*—the city; *viśīrṇā*—scattered; *prakṛtim*—matter; *gatā*—turned into.

TRANSLATION

The serpent, who had already been arrested by the soldiers of Yavanarāja and was out of the city, began to follow his master along with the others. As soon as they all left the city, it was immediately dismantled and smashed to dust.

PURPORT

When the living entity is arrested, all his followers—namely the life air, the senses and sense objects—immediately leave the lump of matter, the body. When the living entity and his companions leave, the body no longer works but turns into basic material elements—earth, water, fire, air and ether. When a city attacked by enemies is vacated by its inhabitants, the enemy immediately takes advantage of that city and bombards it to smash the whole thing to dust. When we say, "Dust thou art, and unto dust thou shall return," we refer to the body. When a city is attacked and bombarded by enemies, the citizens generally leave, and the city ceases to exist.

It is a foolish person who engages in improving the condition of a city without caring for the citizens or inhabitants. Similarly, a living entity who is not properly enlightened in spiritual knowledge simply takes care of the external body, not knowing that the spirit soul is the principal factor within the body. When one is advanced in spiritual knowledge, the spirit soul is saved from eternal transmigration. The *Bhāgavatam* considers those who are attached to their bodies to be like cows and asses (*sa eva go-kharaḥ*). The cow is a very innocent animal, and the ass is a beast of burden. One who labors under the bodily conception simply works like an ass and does not know his self-interest. It is therefore said:

yasyātma-buddhiḥ kuṇape tri-dhātuke
sva-dhīḥ kalatrādiṣu bhauma ijya-dhīḥ
yat-tīrtha-buddhiḥ salile na karhicij
janeṣv abhijñeṣu sa eva go-kharaḥ

"A human being who identifies this body made of three elements with his self, who considers the by-products of the body to be his kinsmen, who considers the land of birth as worshipable, and who goes to the place of pilgrimage simply to take a bath rather than meet men of transcendental knowledge there, is to be considered like an ass or a cow." (*Bhāg.* 10.84.13)

Human civilization devoid of Kṛṣṇa consciousness is simply a civilization of lower animals. Sometimes such a civilization may study the dead body and consider the brain or the heart. However, no part of the body is important unless the spirit soul is present. In a modern civilization of cows and asses, scientists try to search out some value in the brain or heart of a dead man.

TEXT 25

विकृष्यमाणः प्रसभं यवनेन बलीयसा ।
नाविन्दत्तमसाऽऽविष्टः सखायं सुहृदं पुरः ॥२५॥

vikṛṣyamāṇaḥ prasabhaṁ
yavanena balīyasā
nāvindat tamasāviṣṭaḥ
sakhāyaṁ suhṛdaṁ puraḥ

vikṛṣyamāṇaḥ—being dragged; *prasabham*—forcibly; *yavanena*—by the Yavana; *balīyasā*—who was very powerful; *na avindat*—could not remember; *tamasā*—by darkness of ignorance; *āviṣṭaḥ*—being covered; *sakhāyam*—his friend; *suhṛdam*—always a well-wisher; *puraḥ*—from the very beginning.

TRANSLATION

When King Purañjana was being dragged with great force by the powerful Yavana, out of his gross ignorance he still could not remember his friend and well-wisher, the Supersoul.

PURPORT

In *Bhagavad-gītā* Lord Kṛṣṇa says:

bhoktāraṁ yajña-tapasāṁ
sarva-loka-maheśvaram
suhṛdaṁ sarva-bhūtānāṁ
jñātvā māṁ śāntim ṛcchati

"The sages, knowing Me as the ultimate purpose of all sacrifices and austerities, the Supreme Lord of all planets and demigods and the benefactor and well-wisher of all living entities, attain peace from the pangs of material miseries." (Bg. 5.29)

A person can be in full Kṛṣṇa consciousness and become happy and satisfied if he knows but three things—namely, that the Supreme Lord Kṛṣṇa is the enjoyer of all benefits, that He is the proprietor of everything, and that He is the supreme friend of all living entities. If one does not know this and functions instead under the bodily conception, he is always harassed by the tribulations offered by material nature. In actuality, the Supreme Lord is sitting by the side of everyone.

īśvaraḥ sarva-bhūtānāṁ
hṛd-deśe 'rjuna tiṣṭhati
bhrāmayan sarva-bhūtāni
yantrārūḍhāni māyayā

"The Supreme Lord is situated in everyone's heart, O Arjuna, and is directing the wanderings of all living entities, who are seated as on a machine, made of the material energy." (Bg. 18.61)

The living entity and the Supersoul are sitting side by side in the same tree, but despite being harassed by the laws of material nature, the foolish living entity does not turn toward the Supreme Personality of Godhead for protection. However, he thinks that he is able to protect himself from the stringent laws of material nature. This, however, is not possible. The living entity must turn toward the Supreme Personality of Godhead and surrender unto Him. Only then will he be saved from the onslaught of the powerful Yavana, or Yamarāja.

The word *sakhāyam* (friend) is very significant in this verse because God is eternally present beside the living entity. The Supreme Lord is also described as *suhṛdam* (ever well-wisher). The Supreme Lord is always a well-wisher, just like a father or mother. Despite all the offenses of a son, the father and mother are always the son's well-wisher. Similarly, despite all our offenses and defiance of the desires of the Supreme Personality of Godhead, the Lord will give us immediate relief from all the hardships offered by material nature if we simply surrender unto Him. Lord Kṛṣṇa also confirms this in *Bhagavad-gītā:*

daivī hy eṣā guṇamayī
mama māyā duratyayā
mām eva ye prapadyante
māyām etāṁ taranti te

"This divine energy of Mine, consisting of the three modes of material nature, is difficult to overcome. But those who have surrendered unto Me can easily cross beyond it." (Bg. 7.14)

Unfortunately, due to our bad association and great attachment for sense gratification, we do not remember our best friend, the Supreme Personality of Godhead.

TEXT 26

तं यज्ञपशवोऽनेन संज्ञप्ता येऽदयालुना ।
कुठारैश्चिच्छिदुः क्रुद्धाः स्मरन्तोऽमीवमस्य तत् ॥२६॥

taṁ yajña-paśavo 'nena
saṁjñaptā ye 'dayālunā
kuṭhāraiś cicchiduḥ kruddhāḥ
smaranto 'mīvam asya tat

tam—him; *yajña-paśavaḥ*—the sacrificial animals; *anena*—by him; *saṁjñaptāḥ*—killed; *ye*—all of them who; *adayālunā*—by the most unkind; *kuṭhāraiḥ*—by axes; *cicchiduḥ*—pierced to pieces; *kruddhāḥ*—being very angry; *smarantaḥ*—remembering; *amīvam*—sinful activity; *asya*—of him; *tat*—that.

TRANSLATION

That most unkind king, Purañjana, killed many animals in various sacrifices. Now, taking advantage of this opportunity, all these animals began to pierce him with their horns. It was as though he were being cut to pieces by axes.

PURPORT

Those who are very enthusiastic about killing animals in the name of religion or for food must await similar punishment after death. The word *māṁsa* (meat) indicates that those animals whom we kill will be given an opportunity to kill us. Although in actuality no living entity is killed, the pains of being pierced by the horns of animals will be experienced after death. Not knowing this, rascals unhesitatingly go on killing poor animals. So-called human civilization has opened many slaughterhouses for animals in the name of religion or food. Those who are a little religious kill animals in temples, mosques or synagogues, and those who are more fallen maintain various slaughterhouses. Just as in civilized human society the law is a life for a life, similarly, no living entity can encroach upon another living entity as far as the Supreme Lord is concerned. Everyone should be given freedom to live at the cost of the Supreme Father, and animal killing—either for religion or for food—is always condemned by the Supreme Personality of Godhead. In *Bhagavad-gītā* Lord Kṛṣṇa says:

tān ahaṁ dviṣataḥ krūrān
saṁsāreṣu narādhamān
kṣipāmy ajasram aśubhān
āsurīṣv eva yoniṣu

"Those who are envious and mischievous, who are the lowest among men, are cast by Me into the ocean of material existence, into various demoniac species of life." (Bg. 16.19)

The animal killers (*dviṣataḥ*), envying other living entities and the Supreme Personality of Godhead, are placed in darkness and cannot understand the theme and objective of life. This is further explained in the following verses.

TEXT 27

अनन्तपारे तमसि मग्नो नष्टस्मृतिः समाः ।
शाश्वतीरनुभूयार्तिं प्रमदासङ्गदूषितः ॥२७॥

ananta-pāre tamasi
magno naṣṭa-smṛtiḥ samāḥ
śāśvatīr anubhūyārtiṁ
pramadā-saṅga-dūṣitaḥ

ananta-pāre—unlimitedly expanded; *tamasi*—in the material existence of darkness; *magnaḥ*—being merged; *naṣṭa-smṛtiḥ*—bereft of all intelligence; *samāḥ*—for many years; *śāśvatīḥ*—practically eternally; *anubhūya*—experiencing; *ārtim*—the threefold miseries; *pramadā*—of women; *saṅga*—by association; *dūṣitaḥ*—being contaminated.

TRANSLATION

Due to his contaminated association with women, a living entity like King Purañjana eternally suffers all the pangs of material existence and remains in the dark region of material life bereft of all remembrance for many, many years.

PURPORT

This is a description of material existence. Material existence is experienced when one becomes attached to a woman and forgets his real identity as the eternal servant of Kṛṣṇa (*naṣṭa-smṛtiḥ*). In this way, in one body after another, the living entity perpetually suffers the threefold miseries of material existence. To save human civilization from the darkness of ignorance, this movement was started. The main purpose of the Kṛṣṇa consciousness movement is to enlighten the forgetful living entity and remind him of his original Kṛṣṇa consciousness. In this way the living entity can be saved from the catastrophe of ignorance as well as bodily transmigration. As Śrīla Bhaktivinoda Ṭhākura has sung:

anādi karama-phale, paḍi' bhavārṇava-jale,
taribāre nā dekhi upāya
e viṣaya-halāhale, divā-niśi hiyā jvale,
mana kabhu sukha nāhi pāya

"Because of my past fruitive activities, I have now fallen into an ocean of nescience. I cannot find any means to get out of this great ocean, which is indeed like an ocean of poison. We are trying to be happy through sense enjoyment, but actually that so-called enjoyment is like food that is too hot and causes burning in the heart. I feel a burning sensation constantly, day and night, and thus my mind cannot find satisfaction."

Material existence is always full of anxiety. People are always trying to find many ways to mitigate anxiety, but because they are not guided by a real leader, they try to forget material anxiety through drink and sex indulgence. Foolish people do not know that by attempting to escape anxiety by drink and sex, they simply increase their duration of material life. It is not possible to escape material anxiety in this way.

The word *pramadā-saṅga-dūṣitaḥ* indicates that apart from all other contamination, if one simply remains attached to a woman, that single contamination will be sufficient to prolong one's miserable material existence. Consequently, in Vedic civilization one is trained from the beginning to give up attachment for women. The first stage of life is *brahmacārī,* the second stage *gṛhastha,* the third stage *vānaprastha,* and the fourth stage *sannyāsa.* All these stages are devised to enable one to detach himself from the association of women.

TEXT 28

तामेव मनसा गृह्णन् बभूव प्रमदोत्तमा ।
अनन्तरं विदर्भस्य राजसिंहस्य वेश्मनि ॥२८॥

tām eva manasā gṛhṇan
babhūva pramadottamā
anantaraṁ vidarbhasya
rāja-siṁhasya veśmani

tām—her; *eva*—certainly; *manasā*—by the mind; *gṛhṇan*—accepting; *babhūva*—became; *pramadā*—woman; *uttamā*—highly situated; *anantaram*—after death; *vidarbhasya*—of Vidarbha; *rāja-siṁhasya*—of the most powerful king; *veśmani*—at the house.

TRANSLATION

King Purañjana gave up his body while remembering his wife, and consequently in his next life he became a very beautiful and well-situated woman. He took his next birth as the daughter of King Vidarbha in the very house of the King.

PURPORT

Since King Purañjana thought of his wife at the time of death, he attained the body of a woman in his next birth. This verifies the following verse in *Bhagavad-gītā:*

yaṁ yaṁ vāpi smaran bhāvaṁ
tyajaty ante kalevaram
taṁ tam evaiti kaunteya
sadā tad-bhāva-bhāvitaḥ

"Whatever state of being one remembers when he quits his body, that state he will attain without fail." (Bg. 8.6)

When a living entity is accustomed to think of a particular subject matter or become absorbed in a certain type of thought, he will think of that subject at the time of death. At the time of death, one will think of the subject that has occupied his life while he was awake, lightly sleeping or dreaming, or while he was deeply sleeping. After falling from the association of the Supreme Lord, the living entity thus transmigrates from one bodily form to another according to nature's course, until he finally attains the human form. If he is absorbed in material thoughts and ignorant of spiritual life, and if he does not take shelter under the lotus feet of the Supreme Personality of Godhead, Govinda, who solves all questions of birth and death, he will become a woman in the next life, especially if he thinks of his wife. As stated in *Śrīmad-Bhāgavatam: karmaṇā daiva-netreṇa.* A living entity acts piously and impiously, and sometimes in both ways. All actions are taken into account, and the living entity is offered a new body by his superiors. Although King Purañjana was overly attached to his wife, he nonetheless performed many pious fruitive activities. Consequently, although he took the form of a woman, he was given a chance to be the daughter of a powerful king. As confirmed in *Bhagavad-gītā:*

prāpya puṇya-kṛtāṁ lokān
uṣitvā śāśvatīḥ samāḥ
śucīnāṁ śrīmatāṁ gehe
yoga-bhraṣṭo 'bhijāyate

"The unsuccessful *yogī,* after many, many years of enjoyment on the planets of the pious living entities, is born into a family of righteous people, or into a family of rich aristocracy." (Bg. 6.41)

If a person falls from the path of *bhakti-yoga,* God realization, due to attachment to fruitive activity, philosophical speculation or mystic *yoga,* he is given a chance to take birth in a high and rich family. The higher authorities appointed by the Supreme Personality of Godhead thus render justice to the living entity according to the living entity's desires. Although King Purañjana was overly absorbed in thoughts of his wife and thus became a woman, he nonetheless took birth in the family of a king due to his previous pious activities. The conclusion is that all our activities are taken into consideration before we are awarded another body. Nārada Muni therefore advised Vyāsadeva to take to Kṛṣṇa consciousness, devotional service, and abandon all ordinary occupational duties. This advice was also given by Lord Kṛṣṇa Himself. Although a devotee may fall from the path of spiritual consciousness, he will nonetheless attain a human body in the home of a devotee or a rich man. In this way one can resume his devotional service.

TEXT 29

उपयेमे वीर्यपणां वैदर्भीं मलयध्वजः ।
युधि निर्जित्य राजन्यान् पाण्ड्यः परपुरञ्जयः ॥२९॥

upayeme vīrya-paṇāṁ
vaidarbhīṁ malaya-dhvajaḥ
yudhi nirjitya rājanyān
pāṇḍyaḥ para-purañjayaḥ

upayeme—married; *vīrya*—of valor or prowess; *paṇām*—the prize; *vaidarbhīm*—daughter of Vidarbha; *malaya-dhvajaḥ*—Malayadhvaja; *yudhi*—in the fight; *nirjitya*—after conquering; *rājanyān*—other princes; *pāṇḍyaḥ*—best of the learned, or born in the country known as Pāṇḍu; *para*—transcendental; *puram*—city; *jayaḥ*—conqueror.

TRANSLATION

It was fixed that Vaidarbhī, daughter of King Vidarbha, was to be married to a very powerful man, Malayadhvaja, an inhabitant of the Pāṇḍu country. After conquering other princes, he married the daughter of King Vidarbha.

PURPORT

It is customary among *kṣatriyas* for a princess to be offered under certain conditions. For instance, Draupadī was offered in marriage to one who could pierce a fish with an arrow simply by seeing the reflection of that fish. Kṛṣṇa married one of His queens after conquering seven strong bulls. The Vedic system is for a daughter of a king to be offered under certain conditions. Vaidarbhī, the daughter of Vidarbha, was offered to a great devotee and powerful king. Since King Malayadhvaja was both a powerful king and great devotee, he fulfilled all the requirements. The name Malayadhvaja signifies a great devotee who stands as firm as Malaya Hill, and, through his propaganda, makes other devotees similarly as firm. Such a *mahā-bhāgavata* can prevail over the opinions of all others. A strong devotee makes propaganda against all other spiritual conceptions—namely *jñāna, karma* and *yoga.* With his devotional flag unfurled, he always stands fast to conquer other conceptions of transcendental realization. Whenever there is an argument between a devotee and a nondevotee, the pure, strong devotee comes out victorious.

The word *pāṇḍya* comes from the word *paṇḍā* meaning knowledge. Unless one is highly learned, he cannot conquer nondevotional conceptions. The word *para* means transcendental, and *pura* means city. The *para-pura* is Vaikuṇṭha, the kingdom of God, and the word *jaya* refers to one who can conquer. This means that a pure devotee, who is strong in devotional service and who has conquered all nondevotional conceptions, can also conquer the kingdom of God. In other words, one can conquer the kingdom of God, Vaikuṇṭha, only by rendering devotional service. The Supreme Personality of Godhead is called *ajita,* meaning that no one can conquer Him, but a devotee, by strong devotional service and sincere attachment to the Supreme Personality of Godhead, can easily conquer Him. Lord Kṛṣṇa is fear personified for everyone, but He voluntarily agreed to fear the stick of mother Yaśodā. Kṛṣṇa, God, cannot be conquered by anyone but His devotee. Such a devotee kindly married the daughter of King Vidarbha.

TEXT 30

तस्यां स जनयाञ्चक्र आत्मजामसितेक्षणाम् ।
यवीयसः सप्त सुतान् सप्त द्रविडभूभृतः ॥३०॥

tasyāṁ sa janayāñ cakra
ātmajām asitekṣaṇām
yavīyasaḥ sapta sutān
sapta draviḍa-bhūbhṛtaḥ

tasyām—through her; *saḥ*—the King; *janayām cakre*—begot; *ātma-jām*—daughter; *asita*—blue or black; *īkṣaṇām*—whose eyes; *yavīyasaḥ*—younger, very powerful; *sapta*—seven; *sutān*—sons; *sapta*—seven; *draviḍa*—province of Draviḍa or south India; *bhū*—of the land; *bhṛtaḥ*—kings.

TRANSLATION

King Malayadhvaja fathered one daughter, who had very black eyes. He also had seven sons, who later became rulers of that tract of land known as Draviḍa. Thus there were seven kings in that land.

PURPORT

King Malayadhvaja was a great devotee, and after he married the daughter of King Vidarbha, he gave her one nice daughter, whose eyes were black. Figuratively this means that the daughter of King Malayadhvaja was bestowed also with devotional service, for her eyes were always fixed on Kṛṣṇa. A devotee has no vision in his life other than Kṛṣṇa. The seven sons are the seven processes of devotional service—hearing, chanting, remembering, offering worship, offering prayers, rendering transcendental loving service and serving the lotus feet of the Lord. Of the nine types of devotional service, only seven were immediately given. The balance—friendship and surrendering everything—were to be developed later. In other words, devotional service is divided into two categories—namely *vidhi-mārga* and *rāga-mārga.* The process of becoming friends with the Lord and sacrificing everything for Him belong to the category of *rāga-mārga,* the stage of developed devotional service. For the neophyte, the important processes are those of hearing and chanting (*śravaṇaṁ kīrtanam*), remembering Kṛṣṇa, worshiping the Deity in the temple, offering prayers and always engaging in the service of the Lord, and worshiping the lotus feet of the Lord.

The word *yavīyasaḥ* indicates that these processes are very powerful. After a devotee engages in the processes of *śravaṇaṁ kīrtanaṁ viṣṇoḥ smaraṇaṁ pāda-sevanam arcanaṁ vandanaṁ dāsyam,* and is able to secure these processes, he can later become a devotee capable of rendering spontaneous devotional service—namely *sakhyam* and *ātma-nivedanam.* Generally the great *ācāryas* who preach devotional service all over the world belong to the category of *sakhyam ātma-nivedanam.* A neophyte devotee cannot actually become a preacher. The neophyte is advised to execute devotional service in the seven other fields (*śravaṇaṁ kīrtanam,* etc.). If one can successfully execute the preliminary seven items, he can in the future be situated on the platform of *sakhyam ātma-nivedanam.*

The specific mention of Draviḍa-deśa refers to the five Draviḍa-deśas in south India. All are very strong in rendering the preliminary devotional processes (*śravaṇaṁ kīrtanam*). Some great *ācāryas,* like Rāmānujācārya and Madhvācārya, also came from Draviḍa-deśa and became great preachers. These were all situated on the platform of *sakhyam ātma-nivedanam.*

TEXT 31

एकैकस्याभवत्तेषां राजन्नर्बुदमर्बुदम् ।
भोक्ष्यते यद्वंशधरैर्मही मन्वन्तरं परम् ॥३१॥

ekaikasyābhavat teṣāṁ
rājann arbudam arbudam
bhokṣyate yad-vaṁśa-dharair
mahī manv-antaraṁ param

eka-ekasya—of each one; *abhavat*—there became; *teṣām*—of them; *rājan*—O King; *arbudam*—ten million; *arbudam*—ten million; *bhokṣyate*—is ruled; *yat*—whose; *vaṁśa-dharaiḥ*—by descendants; *mahī*—the whole world; *manu-antaram*—up to the end of one Manu; *param*—and afterwards.

TRANSLATION

My dear King Prācīnabarhiṣat, the sons of Malayadhvaja gave birth to many thousands and thousands of sons, and all of these have been protecting the entire world up to the end of one Manu's life span and even afterwards.

PURPORT

There are fourteen Manus in one day of Brahmā. A *manvantara*, the life span of one Manu, is given as 71 multiplied by 4,320,000 years. After one such Manu passes on, another Manu begins his life span. In this way the life cycle of the universe is going on. As one Manu follows another, the cult of Kṛṣṇa consciousness is being imparted, as confirmed in *Bhagavad-gītā:*

śrī bhagavān uvāca
imaṁ vivasvate yogaṁ
proktavān aham avyayam
vivasvān manave prāha
manur ikṣvākave 'bravīt

"The Blessed Lord said: I instructed this imperishable science of *yoga* to the sun-god, Vivasvān, and Vivasvān instructed it to Manu, the father of mankind, and Manu in turn instructed it to Ikṣvāku." (Bg. 4.1)

Vivasvān, the sun-god, imparted *Bhagavad-gītā* to one Manu, and this Manu imparted it to his son, who imparted it to yet another Manu. In this way the propagation of Kṛṣṇa consciousness is never stopped. No one should think that this Kṛṣṇa consciousness movement is a new movement. As confirmed by *Bhagavad-gītā* and *Śrīmad-Bhāgavatam,* it is a very, very old movement, for it has been passing down from one Manu to another.

Among Vaiṣṇavas there may be some difference of opinion due to everyone's personal identity, but despite all personal differences, the cult of Kṛṣṇa consciousness must go on. We can see that under the instructions of Śrīla Bhaktivinoda Ṭhākura, Śrīla Bhaktisiddhānta Sarasvatī Gosvāmī Mahārāja began preaching the Kṛṣṇa consciousness movement in an organized way within the past hundred years. The disciples of Śrīla Bhaktisiddhānta Sarasvatī Gosvāmī Mahārāja are all Godbrothers, and although there are some differences of opinion, and although we are not acting conjointly, still every one of us is spreading this Kṛṣṇa consciousness movement according to his own capacity and producing many disciples to spread it all over the world. As far as we are concerned, we have already started the International Society for Krishna Consciousness, and many thousands of Europeans and Americans have joined this movement. Indeed, it is spreading like wildfire. This cult of Kṛṣṇa consciousness, based on the nine principles of devotional service (*śravaṇaṁ kīrtanaṁ viṣṇoḥ smaraṇaṁ pāda-sevanam/ arcanaṁ vandanaṁ dāsyaṁ sakhyam ātma-nivedanam*), will never be stopped. It will go on without distinction of caste, creed, color or country. No one can check it.

The word *bhokṣyate* is very important in this verse. Just as a king gives protection to his citizens, these devotees, following the principles of devotional service, will give protection to all the people of the world. The people of the world are very much harassed by so-called religious principled *svāmīs, yogīs, karmīs* and *jñānīs,* but none of these can show the right way to become elevated to the spiritual platform. There are primarily four parties spreading devotional service all over the universe. These are the Rāmānuja-sampradāya, the Madhva-sampradāya, the Viṣṇusvāmi-sampradāya and the Nimbārka-sampradāya. The Mādhva-Gauḍīya-sampradāya in particular comes from Lord Caitanya Mahāprabhu. All these devotees are spreading this Kṛṣṇa consciousness movement very widely and giving protection to innocent people who are being so much embarrassed by pseudo-*avatāras, svāmīs, yogīs* and others.

TEXT 32

अगस्त्यः प्राग्दुहितरमुपयेमे धृतव्रताम् ।
यस्यां दृढच्युतो जात इध्मवाहात्मजो मुनिः ॥३२॥

agastyaḥ prāg duhitaram
upayeme dhṛta-vratām
yasyāṁ dṛḍha-cyuto jāta
idhma-vāhātmajo muniḥ

agastyaḥ—the great sage Agastya Muni; *prāk*—first; *duhitaram*—daughter; *upayeme*—married; *dhṛta-vratām*—taken to vows; *yasyām*—through whom; *dṛḍha-cyutaḥ*—named Dṛḍhacyuta; *jātaḥ*—was born; *idhma-vāha*—named Idhmavāha; *ātma-jaḥ*—son; *muniḥ*—the great sage.

TRANSLATION

The great sage named Agastya married the first-born daughter of Malayadhvaja, the avowed devotee of Lord Kṛṣṇa. From her one son was born, whose name was Dṛḍhacyuta, and from him another son was born, whose name was Idhmavāha.

PURPORT

The name of Agastya Muni is very significant. The word *agastya* indicates that his senses do not act independently, and the word *muni* means "mind." The mind is the center of all the senses, and in the case of Agastya Muni, the senses could not work independent of the mind. When the mind takes to the cult of *bhakti,* it engages in devotional service. The cult of *bhakti* (*bhakti-latā*) is the first daughter of Malayadhvaja, and, as previously described, her eyes are always upon Kṛṣṇa (*asitekṣaṇām*). One cannot render *bhakti* to any demigod. *Bhakti* can be rendered only to Viṣṇu (*śravaṇaṁ kīrtanaṁ viṣṇoḥ*). Thinking the Absolute Truth to be without form, the Māyāvādīs say that the word *bhakti* can apply to any form of worship. If this were the case, a devotee could imagine any demigod or any godly form and worship it. This, however, is not the real fact. The real fact is that *bhakti* can only be applied to Lord Viṣṇu and His expansions. Therefore *bhakti-latā* is *dṛḍha-vrata,* the great vow, for when the mind is completely engaged in devotional service, the mind does not fall down. If one tries to advance by other means—by *karma-yoga* or *jñāna-yoga*—one will fall down, but if one is fixed in *bhakti,* he never falls down.

Thus from *bhakti-latā* the son Dṛḍhacyuta is born, and from Dṛḍhacyuta the next son, Idhmavāha, is born. The word *idhma-vāha* refers to one who carries wood for burning in a sacrifice when approaching a spiritual master. The point is that *bhakti-latā*, the cult of devotion, fixes one in his spiritual position. One so fixed never comes down, and he begets children who are strict followers of the śāstric injunctions. As said in the *Vedas:*

tad vijñānārthaṁ sa gurum evābhigacchet
samit-pāṇiḥ śrotriyaṁ brahma-niṣṭham

In the line of devotional service, those who are initiated are strict followers of the Vedic scriptural injunctions.

TEXT 33

विभज्य तनयेभ्यः क्ष्मां राजर्षिर्मलयध्वजः ।
आरिराधयिषुः कृष्णं स जगाम कुलाचलम् ॥३३॥

vibhajya tanayebhyaḥ kṣmāṁ
rājarṣir malaya-dhvajaḥ
ārirādhayiṣuḥ kṛṣṇaṁ
sa jagāma kulācalam

vibhajya—having divided; *tanayebhyaḥ*—amongst his sons; *kṣmām*—the whole world; *rāja-ṛṣiḥ*—great saintly king; *malaya-dhvajaḥ*—named Malayadhvaja; *ārirādhayiṣuḥ*—desiring to worship; *kṛṣṇam*—Lord Kṛṣṇa; *saḥ*—he; *jagāma*—went; *kulācalam*—unto Kulācala.

TRANSLATION

After this, the great saintly king Malayadhvaja divided his entire kingdom amongst his sons. Then, in order to worship Lord Kṛṣṇa with full attention, he went to a solitary place known as Kulācala.

PURPORT

Malayadhvaja, the great king, was certainly a *mahā-bhāgavata,* topmost devotee. By executing devotional service, he begot many sons and disciples for propagating the *bhakti* cult (*śravaṇaṁ kīrtanaṁ viṣṇoḥ*). Actually, the entire world should be divided amongst such disciples. Everyone should be engaged in preaching the cult of Kṛṣṇa consciousness. In other words, when disciples are grown up and are able to preach, the spiritual master should retire and sit down in a solitary place to write and execute *nirjana-bhajana.* This means sitting silently in a solitary place and executing devotional service. This *nirjana-bhajana,* which is the silent worship of the Supreme Lord, is not possible for a neophyte devotee. Śrīla Bhaktisiddhānta Sarasvatī Ṭhākura never advised a neophyte devotee to go to a solitary place to engage in devotional service. Indeed, he has written a song in this connection:

duṣṭa mana, tumi kisera vaiṣṇava?
pratiṣṭhāra tare, nirjanera ghare,
tava hari-nāma kevala kaitava

"My dear mind, what kind of devotee are you? Simply for cheap adoration you sit in a solitary place and pretend to chant the Hare Kṛṣṇa *mahā-mantra,* but this is all cheating." Thus Bhaktisiddhānta Sarasvatī Ṭhākura advocated that every devotee, under the guidance of an expert spiritual master, preach the *bhakti* cult, Kṛṣṇa consciousness, all over the world. Only when one is mature can he sit in a solitary place and retire from preaching all over the world. Following this example, the devotees of the International Society for Krishna Consciousness now render service as preachers in various parts of the world. Now they can allow the spiritual master to retire from active preaching work. In the last stage of the spiritual master's life, the devotees of the spiritual master should take preaching activities into their own hands. In this way the spiritual master can sit down in a solitary place and render *nirjana-bhajana.*

TEXT 34

हित्वा गृहान् सुतान् भोगान् वैदर्भी मदिरेक्षणा ।
अन्वधावत पाण्ड्येशं ज्योत्स्नेव रजनीकरम् ॥३४॥

hitvā gṛhān sutān bhogān
vaidarbhī madirekṣaṇā
anvadhāvata pāṇḍyeśaṁ
jyotsneva rajanī-karam

hitvā—giving up; *gṛhān*—home; *sutān*—children; *bhogān*—material happiness; *vaidarbhī*—the daughter of King Vidarbha; *madira-īkṣaṇā*—with enchanting eyes; *anvadhāvata*—followed; *pāṇḍya-īśam*—King Malayadhvaja; *jyotsnā iva*—like the moonshine; *rajanī-karam*—the moon.

TRANSLATION

Just as the moonshine follows the moon at night, immediately after King Malayadhvaja departed for Kulācala, his devoted wife, whose eyes

were very enchanting, followed him, giving up all homely happiness, despite family and children.

PURPORT

Just as in the *vānaprastha* stage the wife follows the husband, similarly when the spiritual master retires for *nirjana-bhajana,* some of his advanced devotees follow him and engage in his personal service. In other words, those who are very fond of family life should come forward in the service of the spiritual master and abandon so-called happiness afforded by society, friendship and love. A verse by Śrīla Viśvanātha Cakravartī Ṭhākura in his *Gurv-aṣṭaka* is significant in this regard. *Yasya prasādād bhagavat-prasādaḥ.* A disciple should always remember that by serving the spiritual master he can easily advance in Kṛṣṇa consciousness. All the scriptures recommend that it is by pleasing the spiritual master and serving him directly that one can attain the highest perfectional stage of devotional service.

The word *madirekṣaṇā* is also significant in this verse. Śrīla Jīva Gosvāmī has explained in his *Sandarbha* that the word *madira* means intoxicating. If one's eyes become intoxicated upon seeing the Deity, he may be called *madirekṣaṇa.* Queen Vaidarbhī's eyes were very enchanting, just as one's eyes are *madirekṣaṇa* when engaged in seeing the temple Deity. Unless one is an advanced devotee, he cannot fix his eyes on the Deity in the temple.

TEXTS 35-36

तत्र चन्द्रवसा नाम ताम्रपर्णी वटोदका ।
तत्पुण्यसलिलैर्नित्यमुभयत्रात्मनो मृजन् ॥३५॥
कन्दाष्टिभिर्मूलफलैः पुष्पपर्णैस्तृणोदकैः ।
वर्तमानः शनैर्गात्रकर्शनं तप आस्थितः ॥३६॥

tatra candra-vasā nāma
tāmra-parṇī vaṭodakā
tat-puṇya-salilair nityam
ubhayatrātmano mṛjan

kandāṣṭibhir mūla-phalaiḥ
puṣpa-parṇais tṛṇodakaiḥ
vartamānaḥ śanair gātra-
karśanaṁ tapa āsthitaḥ

tatra—there; *candra-vasā*—the Candravasā River; *nāma*—named; *tāmra-parṇī*—the Tāmraparṇī River; *vaṭodakā*—the Vaṭodakā River; *tat*—of those rivers; *puṇya*—pious; *salilaiḥ*—with the waters; *nityam*—daily; *ubhayatra*—in both ways; *ātmanaḥ*—of himself; *mṛjan*—washing; *kanda*—bulbs; *aṣṭibhiḥ*—and by seeds; *mūla*—roots; *phalaiḥ*—and by fruits; *puṣpa*—flowers; *parṇaiḥ*—and by leaves; *tṛṇā*—grass; *udakaiḥ*—and by water; *vartamānaḥ*—subsisting; *śanaiḥ*—gradually; *gātra*—his body; *karśanam*—rendering thin; *tapaḥ*—austerity; *āsthitaḥ*—he underwent.

TRANSLATION

In the province of Kulācala, there were rivers named Candravasā, Tāmraparṇī and Vaṭodakā. King Malayadhvaja used to go to those pious rivers regularly and take his bath there. Thus he purified himself externally and internally. He took his bath and ate bulbs, seeds, leaves, flowers, roots, fruits and grasses and drank water. In this way he underwent severe austerities. Eventually he became very skinny.

PURPORT

We can definitely see that to advance in Kṛṣṇa consciousness one must control his bodily weight. If one becomes too fat, it is to be assumed that he is not advancing spiritually. Śrīla Bhaktisiddhānta Sarasvatī Ṭhākura severely criticized his fat disciples. The idea is that one who intends to advance in Kṛṣṇa consciousness must not eat very much. Devotees used to go to forests, high hills or mountains on pilgrimages, but such severe austerities are not possible in these days. One should instead eat only *prasāda* and no more than required. According to the Vaiṣṇava calendar, there are many fasts, such as Ekādaśī and the appearance and disappearance days of God and His devotees. All of these are meant to decrease the fat within the body so that one will not sleep more than desired and will not become inactive and lazy. Overindulgence in food will cause a man to sleep more than required. This human form of life is meant for austerity, and austerity means controlling sex, food intake, etc. In this way time can be saved for spiritual activity, and one can purify himself both externally and internally. Thus both body and mind can be cleansed.

TEXT 37

शीतोष्णवातवर्षाणि क्षुत्पिपासे प्रियाप्रिये ।
सुखदुःखे इति द्वन्द्वान्यजयत्समदर्शनः ॥३७॥

śītoṣṇa-vāta-varṣāṇi
kṣut-pipāse priyāpriye
sukha-duḥkhe iti dvandvāny
ajayat sama-darśanaḥ

śīta—cold; *uṣṇa*—heat; *vāta*—wind; *varṣāṇi*—and rainy seasons; *kṣut*—hunger; *pipāse*—and thirst; *priya*—pleasant; *apriye*—and unpleasant; *sukha*—happiness; *duḥkhe*—and distress; *iti*—thus; *dvandvāni*—dualities; *ajayat*—he conquered; *sama-darśanaḥ*—equipoised.

TRANSLATION

Through austerity, King Malayadhvaja in body and mind gradually became equal to the dualities of cold and heat, happiness and distress, wind and rain, hunger and thirst, the pleasant and the unpleasant. In this way he conquered all relativities.

PURPORT

Liberation means becoming free from the relativities of the world. Unless one is self-realized, he has to undergo the dual struggle of the relative world. In *Bhagavad-gītā* Lord Kṛṣṇa advises Arjuna to conquer all relativities through tolerance. Lord Kṛṣṇa points out that it is the relativities like winter and summer that give us trouble in the material world. In the winter we do not like taking a bath, but in the summer we wish to take a bath twice, thrice or more a day. Thus Kṛṣṇa advises us not to be disturbed by such relativities and dualities when they come and go.

The common man has to undergo much austerity to become equipoised before dualities. One who becomes agitated by the relativities of life has accepted a relative position and must therefore undergo the austerities prescribed in the *śāstras* to transcend the material body and put an end to material existence. King Malayadhvaja underwent severe austerities by leaving his home, going to Kulācala, taking his bath in the sacred rivers and eating only vegetables like stems, roots, seeds, flowers and leaves, avoiding any cooked food or grains. These are very, very austere practices. In this age it is very difficult to leave home and go to the forest or the Himalayas to adopt the processes of austerity. Indeed, it is almost impossible. If one is even advised to give up meat-eating, drinking, gambling and illicit sex, one will fail to do so. What, then, would a person do if he went to the Himalayas or Kulācala? Such acts of renunciation are not possible in this age; therefore Lord Kṛṣṇa has advised us to accept the *bhakti-yoga* process.

Bhakti-yoga will automatically liberate a person from the dualities of life. In *bhakti-yoga,* Kṛṣṇa is the center, and Kṛṣṇa is always transcendental. Thus in order to transcend dualities, one must always engage in the service of the Lord, as confirmed by *Bhagavad-gītā:*

māṁ ca yo 'vyabhicāreṇa
bhakti-yogena sevate
sa guṇān samatītyaitān
brahma-bhūyāya kalpate

"One who engages in full devotional service, who does not fall down in any circumstance, at once transcends the modes of material nature and thus comes to the level of Brahman." (Bg. 14.26)

If one is factually engaged in the service of the Lord, *bhakti-yoga,* he will automatically control his senses, his tongue and so many other things. Once engaged in the *bhakti-yoga* process with all sincerity, one will have no chance of falling down. Even if one falls down, there is no loss. One's devotional activities may be stunned or choked for the time being, but as soon as there is another chance, the practitioner begins from the point where he left off.

TEXT 38

तपसा विद्यया पक्ककषायो नियमैर्यमैः ।
युयुजे ब्रह्मण्यात्मानं विजिताक्षानिलाशयः ॥३८॥

tapasā vidyayā pakva-
kaṣāyo niyamair yamaiḥ
yuyuje brahmaṇy ātmānaṁ
vijitākṣānilāśayaḥ

tapasā—by austerity; *vidyayā*—by education; *pakva*—burned up; *kaṣāyaḥ*—all dirty things; *niyamaiḥ*—by regulative principles; *yamaiḥ*—by self-control; *yuyuje*—he fixed up; *brahmaṇi*—in spiritual realization; *ātmānam*—his self; *vijita*—completely controlled; *akṣa*—senses; *anila*—life; *āśayaḥ*—consciousness.

TRANSLATION

By worshiping, executing austerities and following the regulative principles, King Malayadhvaja conquered his senses, his life and his con-

sciousness. Thus he fixed everything on the central point of the Supreme Brahman [Kṛṣṇa].

PURPORT

Whenever the word *brahman* appears, the impersonalists take this to mean the impersonal effulgence, the *brahmajyoti.* Actually, however, Parabrahman, the Supreme Brahman, is Kṛṣṇa, Vāsudeva. As stated in *Bhagavad-gītā, vāsudevaḥ sarvam iti:* Vāsudeva extends everywhere as the impersonal Brahman. One cannot fix one's mind upon an impersonal "something." *Bhagavad-gītā* therefore says, *kleśo 'dhikataras teṣām avyaktāsakta-cetasām:* "For those whose minds are attached to the unmanifested, impersonal feature of the Supreme, advancement is very troublesome." (Bg. 12.5) Consequently when it is said herein that King Malayadhvaja fixed his mind on *brahman, "brahman"* means the Supreme Personality of Godhead, Vāsudeva.

TEXT 39

आस्ते स्थाणुरिवैकत्र दिव्यं वर्षशतं स्थिरः ।
वासुदेवे भगवति नान्यद्वेदोद्वहन् रतिम् ॥३९॥

āste sthāṇur ivaikatra
divyaṁ varṣa-śataṁ sthiraḥ
vāsudeve bhagavati
nānyad vedodvahan ratim

āste—remains; *sthāṇuḥ*—immovable; *iva*—like; *ekatra*—in one place; *divyam*—of the demigods; *varṣa*—years; *śatam*—one hundred; *sthiraḥ*—steady; *vāsudeve*—unto Lord Kṛṣṇa; *bhagavati*—the Supreme Personality of Godhead; *na*—not; *anyat*—anything else; *veda*—did know; *udvahan*—possessing; *ratim*—attraction.

TRANSLATION

In this way he stayed immovable in one place for one hundred years by the calculations of the demigods. After this time, he developed pure devotional attraction for Kṛṣṇa, the Supreme Personality of Godhead, and remained fixed in that position.

PURPORT

bahūnāṁ janmanāṁ ante
jñānavān māṁ prapadyate

vāsudevaḥ sarvam iti
sa mahātmā sudurlabhaḥ

"After many births and deaths, he who is actually in knowledge surrenders unto Me, knowing Me to be the cause of all causes and all that is. Such a great soul is very rare." (Bg. 7.19)

Vāsudeva, the Supreme Personality of Godhead, Kṛṣṇa, is everything, and one who knows this is the greatest of all transcendentalists. It is stated in *Bhagavad-gītā* that one realizes this after many, many births. This is also confirmed in this verse with the words *divyaṁ varṣa-śatam* (one hundred years according to the calculations of the demigods). According to the calculations of the demigods, one day (twelve hours) is equal to six months on earth. A hundred years of the demigods would equal 36,000 earth years. Thus King Malayadhvaja executed austerities and penances for 36,000 years. After this time, he became fixed in the devotional service of the Lord. To live on earth for so many years, one has to take birth many times. This confirms the conclusion of Kṛṣṇa. To come to the conclusion of Kṛṣṇa consciousness and remain fixed in the realization that Kṛṣṇa is everything, as well as render service unto Kṛṣṇa, are characteristics of the perfectional stage. As said in *Caitanya-caritāmṛta: kṛṣṇe bhakti kaile sarva-karma kṛta haya* (Cc. *Madhya* 22.62). When one comes to the conclusion that Kṛṣṇa is everything by worshiping or by rendering devotional service unto Kṛṣṇa, one actually becomes perfect in all respects. Not only must one come to the conclusion that Kṛṣṇa is everything, but he must remain fixed in this realization. This is the highest perfection of life, and it is this perfection that King Malayadhvaja attained at the end.

TEXT 40

स व्यापकतयाऽऽत्मानं व्यतिरिक्ततयाऽऽत्मनि ।
विद्वान् स्वप्न इवामर्शसाक्षिणं विरराम ह ॥४०॥

sa vyāpakatayātmānaṁ
vyatiriktatayātmani
vidvān svapna ivāmarśa-
sākṣiṇaṁ virarāma ha

saḥ—King Malayadhvaja; *vyāpakatayā*—by all-pervasiveness; *ātmānam*—the Supersoul; *vyatiriktatayā*—by differentiation; *ātmani*—in his own self; *vidvān*—perfectly educated; *svapne*—in a dream; *iva*—like; *amarśa*—of deliberation; *sākṣiṇam*—the witness; *virarāma*—became indifferent; *ha*—certainly.

TRANSLATION

King Malayadhvaja attained perfect knowledge by being able to distinguish the Supersoul from the individual soul. The individual soul is localized, whereas the Supersoul is all-pervasive. He became perfect in knowledge that the material body is not the soul but that the soul is the witness of the material body.

PURPORT

The conditioned soul is often frustrated in trying to understand the distinctions between the material body, the Supersoul and the individual soul. There are two types of Māyāvādī philosophers—the followers of the Buddhist philosophy and the followers of the Śaṅkara philosophy. The followers of Buddha do not recognize that there is anything beyond the body; the followers of Śaṅkara conclude that there is no separate existence of the Paramātmā, the Supersoul. The Śaṅkarites believe that the individual soul is identical with the Paramātmā in the ultimate analysis. But the Vaiṣṇava philosopher, who is perfect in knowledge, knows that the body is made of the external energy and that the Supersoul, the Paramātmā, the Supreme Personality of Godhead, is sitting with the individual soul and is distinct from him. As Lord Kṛṣṇa states in *Bhagavad-gītā:*

kṣetrajñaṁ cāpi māṁ viddhi
sarva-kṣetreṣu bhārata
kṣetra-kṣetrajñayor jñānaṁ
yat taj jñānaṁ mataṁ mama

"O scion of Bharata, you should understand that I am also the knower in all bodies, and to understand this body and its owner is called knowledge. That is My opinion." (Bg. 13.3)

The body is taken to be the field, and the individual soul is taken to be the worker in that field. Yet there is another, who is known as the Supersoul, who, along with the individual soul, simply witnesses. The individual soul works and enjoys the fruits of the body, whereas the Supersoul simply witnesses the activities of the individual soul but does not enjoy the fruits of those activities. The Supersoul is present in every field of activity, whereas the individual soul is present in his one localized body. King Malayadhvaja attained this perfection of knowledge and was able to distinguish between the soul and the Supersoul and the soul and the material body.

TEXT 41

साक्षाद्भगवतोक्तेन गुरुणा हरिणा नृप ।
विशुद्धज्ञानदीपेन स्फुरता विश्वतोमुखम् ॥४१॥

sākṣād bhagavatoktena
guruṇā hariṇā nṛpa
viśuddha-jñāna-dīpena
sphuratā viśvato-mukham

sākṣāt—directly; *bhagavatā*—by the Supreme Personality of Godhead; *uktena*—instructed; *guruṇā*—the spiritual master; *hariṇā*—by Lord Hari; *nṛpa*—O King; *viśuddha*—pure; *jñāna*—knowledge; *dīpena*—by the light of; *sphuratā*—enlightening; *viśvataḥ-mukham*—all angles of vision.

TRANSLATION

In this way King Malayadhvaja attained perfect knowledge because in his pure state he was directly instructed by the Supreme Personality of Godhead. By means of such enlightening transcendental knowledge, he could understand everything from all angles of vision.

PURPORT

In this verse the words *sākṣād bhagavatoktena guruṇā hariṇā* are very significant. The Supreme Personality of Godhead speaks directly to the individual soul when the devotee has completely purified himself by rendering devotional service to the Lord. Lord Kṛṣṇa confirms this also in *Bhagavad-gītā:*

teṣāṁ satata-yuktānāṁ
bhajatāṁ prīti-pūrvakam
dadāmi buddhi-yogaṁ taṁ
yena mām upayānti te

"To those who are constantly devoted and worship Me with love, I give the understanding by which they can come to Me." (Bg. 10.10)

The Lord is the Supersoul seated in everyone's heart, and He acts as the *caitya-guru,* the spiritual master within. However, He gives direct instructions only to the advanced pure devotees. In the beginning, when a devotee is serious and sincere, the Lord gives him directions from within to approach a bona fide spiritual master. When one is trained by the spiritual master according to the regulative principles of devotional service and is situated on the platform of spontaneous attachment for the Lord (*rāga-bhakti*), the Lord also gives instructions from within. *Teṣāṁ satata-yuktānāṁ bhajatāṁ prīti-pūrvakam.* This distinct advantage is obtained by a liberated soul. Having attained this stage, King Malayadhvaja was directly in touch with the Supreme Lord and was receiving instructions from Him directly.

TEXT 42

परे ब्रह्मणि चात्मानं परं ब्रह्म तथाऽऽत्मनि ।
वीक्षमाणो विहायेक्षामस्मादुपरराम ह ॥४२॥

pare brahmaṇi cātmānaṁ
paraṁ brahma tathātmani
vīkṣamāṇo vihāyekṣām
asmād upararāma ha

pare—transcendental; *brahmaṇi*—in the Absolute; *ca*—and; *ātmānam*—the self; *param*—the supreme; *brahma*—Absolute; *tathā*—also; *ātmani*—in himself; *vīkṣamāṇaḥ*—thus observing; *vihāya*—giving up; *īkṣām*—reservation; *asmāt*—from this process; *upararāma*—retired; *ha*—certainly.

TRANSLATION

King Malayadhvaja could thus observe that the Supersoul was sitting by his side, and that he, as the individual soul, was sitting by the side of the Supersoul. Since both were together, there was no need for separate interests; thus he ceased from such activities.

PURPORT

In the advanced stage of devotional service, the devotee does not see anything separate between his own interests and those of the Supreme Personality of Godhead. Both interests become one, for the devotee does not act for a separate interest. Whatever he does, he does in the interest of the Supreme Personality of Godhead. At that time he sees everything in the Supreme Personality of Godhead and the Supreme Personality of Godhead in everything. Having attained this stage of understanding, he sees no distinction between the spiritual and material worlds. In perfect vision, the material world becomes the spiritual world due to its being the external energy of the Supreme Lord. For the perfect devotee, the energy and the energetic are nondifferent. Thus the so-called material world becomes spiritual (*sarvaṁ khalv idaṁ brahma*). Everything is intended for the service of the Supreme Lord, and the expert devotee can utilize any so-called material thing for the Lord's service. One cannot serve the Lord without being situated on the spiritual platform. Thus if a so-called material thing is dovetailed in the service of the Lord, it is no longer to be considered material. Thus the pure devotee, in his perfect vision, sees from all angles.

TEXT 43

पतिं परमधर्मज्ञं वैदर्भी मलयध्वजम् ।
प्रेम्णा पर्यचरद्धित्वा भोगान् सा पतिदेवता ॥४३॥

patiṁ parama-dharma-jñaṁ
vaidarbhī malaya-dhvajam
premṇā paryacarad dhitvā
bhogān sā pati-devatā

patim—her husband; *parama*—supreme; *dharma-jñam*—knower of religious principles; *vaidarbhī*—the daughter of Vidarbha; *malaya-dhvajam*—named Malayadhvaja; *premṇā*—with love and affection; *paryacarat*—served in devotion; *hitvā*—giving up; *bhogān*—sense enjoyments; *sā*—she; *pati-devatā*—accepting her husband as the Supreme Lord.

TRANSLATION

The daughter of King Vidarbha accepted her husband all in all as the Supreme. She gave up all sensual enjoyment and in complete renunciation followed the principles of her husband, who was so advanced. Thus she remained engaged in his service.

PURPORT

Figuratively, King Malayadhvaja is the spiritual master, and his wife, Vaidarbhī, is the disciple. The disciple accepts the spiritual master as the Supreme Personality of Godhead. As stated by Viśvanātha Cakravartī Ṭhākura in *Gurv-aṣṭaka, sākṣād-dharitvena:* "One directly accepts the *guru,* the spiritual master, as the Supreme Personality of Godhead." One should accept the spiritual master not in the sense that the Māyāvādī philosophers do but in the way recommended here. Since the spiritual master is the most confidential servant of the Lord, he should be treated exactly like the Supreme Personality of Godhead. The spiritual master should never be neglected or disobeyed, like an ordinary person.

If a woman is fortunate enough to be the wife of a pure devotee, she can serve her husband without any desire for sense gratification. If she remains engaged in the service of her exalted husband, she will automatically attain the spiritual perfections of her husband. If a disciple gets a bona fide spiritual master, simply by satisfying him, he can attain a similar opportunity to serve the Supreme Personality of Godhead.

TEXT 44

चीरवासा व्रतक्षामा वेणीभूतशिरोरुहा ।
बभावुप पतिं शान्ता शिखा शान्तमिवानलम् ॥४४॥

cīra-vāsā vrata-kṣāmā
veṇībhūta-śiroruhā
babhāv upa patiṁ śāntā
śikhā śāntam ivānalam

cīra-vāsā—wearing old garments; *vrata-kṣāmā*—lean and thin on account of austerities; *veṇībhūta*—entangled; *śiroruhā*—her hair; *babhau*—she shone; *upa patim*—near the husband; *śāntā*—peaceful; *śikhā*—flames; *śāntam*—without being agitated; *iva*—like; *analam*—fire.

TRANSLATION

The daughter of King Vidarbha wore old garments, and she was lean and thin because of her vows of austerity. Since she did not arrange her hair, it became entangled and twisted in locks. Although she remained always near her husband, she was as silent and unagitated as the flame of an undisturbed fire.

PURPORT

When one begins to burn firewood, there is smoke and agitation in the beginning. Although there are so many disturbances in the beginning, once the fire is completely set, the firewood burns steadily. Similarly, when both husband and wife follow the regulative principles of austerity, they remain silent and are not agitated by sex impulses. At such a time both husband and wife are benefited spiritually. One can attain this stage of life by completely giving up a luxurious mode of life.

In this verse the word *cīra-vāsā* refers to very old torn garments. The wife especially should remain austere, not desiring luxurious dresses and living standards. She should accept only the bare necessities of life and minimize her eating and sleeping. There should be no question of mating. Simply by engaging in the service of her exalted husband, who must be a pure devotee, the wife will never be agitated by sex impulses. The *vānaprastha* stage is exactly like this. Although the wife remains with the husband, she undergoes severe austerities and penances so that although both husband and wife live together, there is no question of sex. In this way both husband and wife can live together perpetually. Since the wife is weaker than the husband, this weakness is expressed in this verse with the words *upa patim. Upa* means "near to," or "almost equal to." Being a man, the husband is generally more advanced than his wife. Nonetheless, the wife is expected to give up all luxurious habits. She should not even dress nicely or comb her hair. Hair combing is one of the main businesses of women. In the *vānaprastha* stage the wife should not take care of her hair. Thus her hair will become tangled in knots. Consequently the wife herself will no longer be agitated by sex impulses. In this way both husband and wife can advance in spiritual consciousness. This advanced stage is called the *paramahaṁsa* stage, and once it is obtained, both husband and wife can be actually liberated from bodily consciousness. If the disciple remains steady in the service of the spiritual master, he need no longer fear falling down into the clutches of *māyā.*

TEXT 45

अजानती प्रियतमं यदोपरतमङ्गना ।
सुस्थिरासनमासाद्य यथापूर्वमुपाचरत् ॥४५॥

ajānatī priyatamaṁ
yadoparatam aṅganā
susthirāsanam āsādya
yathā-pūrvam upācarat

ajānatī—without any knowledge; *priya-tamam*—her dearmost husband; *yadā*—when; *uparatam*—passed away; *aṅganā*—the woman; *su-sthira*—fixed up; *āsanam*—on the seat; *āsādya*—going up to; *yathā*—as; *pūrvam*—before; *upācarat*—went on serving him.

TRANSLATION

The daughter of King Vidarbha continued as usual to serve her husband, who was seated in a steady posture, until she could ascertain that he had passed away from the body.

PURPORT

It appears that the Queen did not even talk to her husband while serving. She would simply perform her prescribed duties without talk. Thus she did not stop rendering service until she could ascertain that her husband had passed from the body.

TEXT 46

यदा नोपलभेताङ्घ्रावूष्माणं पत्युरर्चती ।
आसीत्संविग्नहृदया यूथभ्रष्टा मृगी यथा ॥४६॥

yadā nopalabhetāṅghrāv
ūṣmāṇaṁ patyur arcatī
āsīt saṁvigna-hṛdayā
yūtha-bhraṣṭā mṛgī yathā

yadā—when; *na*—not; *upalabheta*—could feel; *aṅghrau*—in the feet; *ūṣmāṇam*—heat; *patyuḥ*—of her husband; *arcatī*—while serving; *āsīt*—she became; *saṁvigna*—anxious; *hṛdayā*—at heart; *yūtha-bhraṣṭā*—bereft of her husband; *mṛgī*—the she deer; *yathā*—as.

TRANSLATION

While she was serving her husband by massaging his legs, she could feel that his feet were no longer warm and could thus understand that he had already passed from the body. She felt great anxiety upon being left alone. Bereft of her husband's company, she felt exactly as the deer feels upon being separated from its mate.

PURPORT

As soon as the circulation of blood and air within the body stops, it is to be understood that the soul within the body has left. The stoppage of the blood's circulation is perceived when the hands and feet lose heat. One tests whether a body is alive or not by feeling the heart's palpitations and the coldness of the feet and hands.

TEXT 47

आत्मानं शोचती दीनमबन्धुं विक्लवाश्रुभिः ।
स्तनावासिच्य विपिने सुस्वरं प्ररुरोद सा ॥४७॥

ātmānaṁ śocatī dīnam
abandhuṁ viklavāśrubhiḥ
stanāv āsicya vipine
susvaraṁ praruroda sā

ātmānam—about herself; *śocatī*—lamenting; *dīnam*—wretched; *abandhum*—without a friend; *viklava*—brokenhearted; *aśrubhiḥ*—by tears; *stanau*—her breasts; *āsicya*—wetting; *vipine*—in the forest; *su-svaram*—loudly; *praruroda*—began to cry; *sā*—she.

TRANSLATION

Being now alone and a widow in that forest, the daughter of Vidarbha began to lament, incessantly shedding tears, which soaked her breasts, and crying very loudly.

PURPORT

Figuratively the Queen is supposed to be the disciple of the King; thus when the mortal body of the spiritual master expires, his disciples should cry exactly as the Queen cries when the King leaves his body. However, the disciple and spiritual master are never separated because the spiritual master always keeps company with the disciple as long as the disciple follows strictly the instructions of the spiritual master. This is called the association of *vāṇī* (words). Physical presence is called *vapuḥ*. As long as the spiritual master is physically present, the disciple should serve the physical body of the spiritual master, and when the spiritual master is no longer physically existing, the disciple should serve the instructions of the spiritual master.

TEXT 48

उत्तिष्ठोत्तिष्ठ राजर्षे इमामुदधिमेखलाम् ।
दस्युभ्यः क्षत्रबन्धुभ्यो बिभ्यतीं पातुमर्हसि ॥४८॥

uttiṣṭhottiṣṭha rājarṣe
imām udadhi-mekhalām
dasyubhyaḥ kṣatra-bandhubhyo
bibhyatīṁ pātum arhasi

uttiṣṭha—please get up; *uttiṣṭha*—please get up; *rāja-ṛṣe*—O saintly king; *imām*—this earth; *udadhi*—by the ocean; *mekhalām*—surrounded; *dasyu-*

bhyaḥ—from the rogues; *kṣatra-bandhubhyaḥ*—from the unclean kings; *bibhyatīm*—very much afraid; *pātum*—to protect; *arhasi*—you ought.

TRANSLATION

O best of kings, please get up! Get up! Just see this world surrounded by water and infested with rogues and so-called kings. This world is very much afraid, and it is your duty to protect her.

PURPORT

Whenever an *ācārya* comes, following the superior orders of the Supreme Personality of Godhead or His representative, he establishes the principles of religion, as enunciated in *Bhagavad-gītā.* Religion means abiding by the orders of the Supreme Personality of Godhead. Religious principles begin from the time one surrenders to the Supreme Personality of Godhead. It is the *ācārya's* duty to spread a bona fide religious system and induce everyone to bow down before the Supreme Lord. One executes the religious principles by rendering devotional service, specifically the nine items like hearing, chanting and remembering. Unfortunately, when the *ācārya* disappears, rogues and nondevotees take advantage and immediately begin to introduce unauthorized principles in the name of so-called *svāmīs, yogīs,* philanthropists, welfare workers and so on. Actually human life is meant for executing the orders of the Supreme Lord, and this is stated in *Bhagavad-gītā:*

man-manā bhava mad-bhakto
mad-yājī māṁ namaskuru
mām evaiṣyasi yuktvaivam
ātmānaṁ mat-parāyaṇaḥ

"Engage your mind always in thinking of Me and become My devotee. Offer obeisances and worship Me. Being completely absorbed in Me, surely you will come to Me." (Bg. 9.34)

The main business of human society is to think of the Supreme Personality of Godhead at all times, to become His devotees, to worship the Supreme Lord and to bow down before Him. The *ācārya,* the authorized representative of the Supreme Lord, establishes these principles, but when he disappears, things once again become disordered. The perfect disciples of the *ācārya* try to relieve the situation by sincerely following the instructions of the spiritual master. At the present moment practically the entire world is afraid of rogues and nondevotees; therefore this Kṛṣṇa consciousness movement is started to save the world from irreligious principles. Everyone should cooperate with this movement in order to bring about actual peace and happiness in the world.

TEXT 49

एवं विलपन्ती बाला विपिनेऽनुगता पतिम् ।
पतिता पादयोर्भर्तू रुदत्यश्रूण्यवर्तयत् ॥४९॥

evaṁ vilapantī bālā
vipine 'nugatā patim
patitā pādayor bhartū
rudaty aśrūṇy avartayat

evam—thus; *vilapantī*—lamenting; *bālā*—the innocent woman; *vipine*—in the solitary forest; *anugatā*—strictly adherent; *patim*—unto her husband; *patitā*—fallen down; *pādayoḥ*—at the feet; *bhartuḥ*—of her husband; *rudatī*—while crying; *aśrūṇi*—tears; *avartayat*—she shed.

TRANSLATION

That most obedient wife thus fell down at the feet of her dead husband and began to cry pitifully in that solitary forest. Thus the tears rolled down from her eyes.

PURPORT

Just as a devoted wife becomes afflicted at the passing away of her husband, when a spiritual master passes away, the disciple becomes similarly bereaved.

TEXT 50

चितिं दारुमयीं चित्वा तस्यां पत्युः कलेवरम् ।
आदीप्य चानुमरणे विलपन्ती मनो दधे ॥५०॥

citiṁ dārumayīṁ citvā
tasyāṁ patyuḥ kalevaram
ādīpya cānumaraṇe
vilapantī mano dadhe

citim—funeral pyre; *dāru-mayīm*—made with wood; *citvā*—having piled up; *tasyām*—on that; *patyuḥ*—of the husband; *kalevaram*—body; *ādīpya*—

after igniting; *ca*—also; *anumaraṇe*—to die along with him; *vilapantī*—lamenting; *manaḥ*—her mind; *dadhe*—fixed.

TRANSLATION

She then prepared a blazing fire with firewood and placed the dead body of her husband upon it. When this was finished, she lamented severely and prepared herself to perish in the fire with her husband.

PURPORT

It is the long-standing tradition of the Vedic system that a faithful wife dies along with her husband. This is called *saha-maraṇa*. In India this system was prevalent even to the date of British occupation. At that time, however, a wife who did not wish to die with her husband was sometimes forced to do so by her relatives. Formerly that was not the case. The wife used to enter the fire voluntarily. The British government stopped this practice, considering it inhuman. However, from the early history of India we find that when Mahārāja Pāṇḍu died, he was survived by two wives—Mādrī and Kuntī. The question was whether both should die or one should die. After the death of Mahārāja Pāṇḍu, his wives settled that one should remain and the other should go. Mādrī would perish with her husband in the fire, and Kuntī would remain to take charge of the five Pāṇḍava children. Even as late as 1936 we saw a devoted wife voluntarily enter the fire of her husband.

This indicates that a devotee's wife must be prepared to act in such a way. Similarly, a devoted disciple of the spiritual master would rather die with the spiritual master than fail to execute the spiritual master's mission. As the Supreme Personality of Godhead comes down upon this earth to reestablish the principles of religion, so his representative, the spiritual master, also comes to reestablish religious principles. It is the duty of the disciples to take charge of the mission of the spiritual master and execute it properly. Otherwise the disciple should decide to die along with the spiritual master. In other words, to execute the will of the spiritual master, the disciple should be prepared to lay down his life and abandon all personal considerations.

TEXT 51

तत्र पूर्वतरः कश्चित्सखा ब्राह्मण आत्मवान् ।
सान्त्वयन् वल्गुना साम्ना तामाह रुदतीं प्रभो ॥५१॥

tatra pūrvataraḥ kaścit
sakhā brāhmaṇa ātmavān
sāntvayan valgunā sāmnā
tām āha rudatīṁ prabho

tatra—in that place; *pūrvataraḥ*—previous; *kaścit*—someone; *sakhā*—friend; *brāhmaṇaḥ*—a *brāhmaṇa; ātmavān*—very learned scholar; *sāntvayan*—pacifying; *valgunā*—by very nice; *sāmnā*—mitigating words; *tām*—unto her; *āha*—he said; *rudatīm*—while she was crying; *prabho*—my dear King.

TRANSLATION

My dear King, one brāhmaṇa, who was an old friend of King Purañjana, came to that place and began to pacify the Queen with sweet words.

PURPORT

The appearance of an old friend in the form of a *brāhmaṇa* is very significant. In His Paramātmā feature, Kṛṣṇa is the old friend of everyone. According to Vedic injunction, Kṛṣṇa is sitting with the living entity side by side. According to the *śruti-mantra* (*dvā suparṇā sayujā sakhāyā*),the Lord is sitting within the heart of every living entity as *suhṛt,* the best friend. The Lord is always eager to have the living entity come home, back to Godhead. Sitting with the living entity as witness, the Lord gives him all chances to enjoy himself materially, but whenever there is an opportunity, the Lord gives good counsel and advises the living entity to abandon trying to become happy through material adjustment and instead turn his face toward the Supreme Personality of Godhead and surrender unto Him. When one becomes serious to follow the mission of the spiritual master, his resolution is tantamount to seeing the Supreme Personality of Godhead. As explained before, this means meeting the Supreme Personality of Godhead in the instruction of the spiritual master. This is technically called *vāṇī-sevā.* Śrīla Viśvanātha Cakravartī Ṭhākura states in his *Bhagavad-gītā* commentary on the verse *vyavasāyātmikā buddhir ekeha kuru-nandana* (Bg. 2.41) that one should serve the words of the spiritual master. The disciple must stick to whatever the spiritual master orders. Simply by following on that line, one sees the Supreme Personality of Godhead.

The Supreme Personality of Godhead, Paramātmā, appeared before the Queen as a *brāhmaṇa,* but why didn't He appear in His original form as Śrī Kṛṣṇa? Śrīla Viśvanātha Cakravartī Ṭhākura remarks that unless one is very highly elevated in loving the Supreme Personality of Godhead, one cannot see Him as He is. Nonetheless, if one sticks to the principles enunciated by the spiritual master, somehow or other he is in association with the Supreme Personality of Godhead. Since the Lord is in the heart, He can advise a sincere disciple from within. This is also confirmed in *Bhagavad-gītā:*

teṣāṁ satata-yuktānāṁ
bhajatāṁ prīti-pūrvakam
dadāmi buddhi-yogaṁ taṁ
yena mām upayānti te

"To those who are constantly devoted and worship Me with love, I give the understanding by which they can come to Me." (Bg. 10.10)

In conclusion, if a disciple is very serious to execute the mission of the spiritual master, he immediately associates with the Supreme Personality of Godhead by *vāṇī* or *vapuḥ*. This is the only secret of success in seeing the Supreme Personality of Godhead. Instead of being eager to see the Lord in some bush of Vṛndāvana while at the same time engaging in sense gratification, if one instead sticks to the principle of following the words of the spiritual master, he will see the Supreme Lord without difficulty. Śrīla Bilvamaṅgala Ṭhākura has therefore said:

bhaktis tvayi sthiratarā bhagavan yadi syād
daivena naḥ phalati divya-kiśora-mūrtiḥ
muktiḥ svayaṁ mukulitāñjali sevate 'smān
dharmārtha-kāma-gatayaḥ samaya-pratīkṣāḥ

"If I am engaged in devotional service unto You, my dear Lord, then very easily can I perceive Your presence everywhere. And as far as liberation is concerned, I think that liberation stands at my door with folded hands, waiting to serve me—and all material conveniences of *dharma* [religiosity], *artha* [economic development] and *kāma* [sense gratification] stand with her." (*Kṛṣṇa-karṇāmṛta* 107) If one is very highly advanced in devotional service, he will have no difficulty in seeing the Supreme Personality of Godhead. If one engages in the service of the spiritual master, he not only sees the Supreme Personality of Godhead but attains liberation. As far as material conveniences are concerned, they automatically come, just as the maidservants of a queen follow the queen wherever she goes. Liberation is no problem for the pure devotee, and all material conveniences are simply awaiting him at all stages of life.

TEXT 52

ब्राह्मण उवाच
का त्वं कस्यासि को वायं शयानो यस्य शोचसि ।
जानासि किं सखायं मां येनाग्रे विचचर्थ ह ॥५२॥

brāhmaṇa uvāca
kā tvaṁ kasyāsi ko vāyaṁ
śayāno yasya śocasi
jānāsi kiṁ sakhāyaṁ māṁ
yenāgre vicacartha ha

brāhmaṇaḥ uvāca—the learned *brāhmaṇa* said; *kā*—who; *tvam*—you; *kasya*—whose; *asi*—are you; *kaḥ*—who; *vā*—or; *ayam*—this man; *śayānaḥ*—lying down; *yasya*—for whom; *śocasi*—you are lamenting; *jānāsi kim*—do you know; *sakhāyam*—friend; *mām*—Me; *yena*—with whom; *agre*—formerly; *vicacartha*—you consulted; *ha*—certainly.

TRANSLATION

The brāhmaṇa inquired as follows: Who are you? Whose wife or daughter are you? Who is the man lying here? It appears you are lamenting for this dead body. Don't you recognize Me? I am your eternal friend. You may remember that many times in the past you have consulted Me.

PURPORT

When a person's relative dies, renunciation is automatically visible. Consultation with the Supersoul seated within everyone's heart is possible only when one is completely free from the contamination of material attachment. One who is sincere and pure gets an opportunity to consult with the Supreme Personality of Godhead in His Paramātmā feature sitting within everyone's heart. The Paramātmā is always the *caitya-guru,* the spiritual master within, and He comes before one externally as the instructor and initiator spiritual master. The Lord can reside within the heart, and He can also come out before a person and give him instructions. Thus the spiritual master is not different from the Supersoul sitting within the heart. An uncontaminated soul or living entity can get a chance to meet the Paramātmā face to face. Just as one gets a chance to consult with the Paramātmā within his heart, he also gets a chance to see Him actually situated before him.

Then one can take instructions from the Supersoul directly. This is the duty of the pure devotee: to see the bona fide spiritual master and consult with the Supersoul within the heart.

When the *brāhmaṇa* asked the woman who the man lying on the floor was, she answered that he was her spiritual master and that she was perplexed about what to do in his absence. At such a time the Supersoul immediately appears, provided the devotee is purified in heart by following the directions of the spiritual master. A sincere devotee who follows the instructions of the spiritual master certainly gets direct instructions from his heart from the Supersoul. Thus a sincere devotee is always helped directly or indirectly by the spiritual master and the Supersoul. This is confirmed in *Caitanya-caritāmṛta: guru-kṛṣṇa-prasāde pāya bhakti-latā-bīja.* If the devotee serves his spiritual master sincerely, Kṛṣṇa automatically becomes pleased. *Yasya prasādād bhagavad-prasādaḥ.* By satisfying the spiritual master, one automatically satisfies Kṛṣṇa. Thus the devotee becomes enriched by both the spiritual master and Kṛṣṇa. The Supersoul is eternally the friend of the living entity and always remains with him. The Supersoul has always been ready to help the living entity, even before the creation of this material world. It is therefore stated here: *yenāgre vicacartha.* The word *agre* means "before the creation." Thus the Supersoul has been accompanying the living entity since before the creation.

TEXT 53

अपि स्मरसि चात्मानमविज्ञातसखं सखे ।
हित्वा मां पदमन्विच्छन् भौमभोगरतो गतः ॥५३॥

api smarasi cātmānam
avijñāta-sakhaṁ sakhe
hitvā māṁ padam anvicchan
bhauma-bhoga-rato gataḥ

api smarasi—do you remember; *ca*—also; *ātmānam*—the Supersoul; *avijñāta*—unknown; *sakham*—friend; *sakhe*—O friend; *hitvā*—giving up; *mām*—Me; *padam*—position; *anvicchan*—desiring; *bhauma*—material; *bhoga*—enjoyment; *rataḥ*—attached to; *gataḥ*—you became.

TRANSLATION

The brāhmaṇa continued: My dear friend, even though you cannot immediately recognize Me, can't you remember that in the past you had a

very intimate friend? Unfortunately, you gave up My company and accepted a position as enjoyer of this material world.

PURPORT

As stated in *Bhagavad-gītā:*

icchā-dveṣa-samutthena
dvandva-mohena bhārata
sarva-bhūtāni saṁmohaṁ
sarge yānti parantapa

"O scion of Bharata [Arjuna], O conquerer of the foe, all living entities are born into delusion, overcome by the dualities of desire and hate." (Bg. 7.27)

This is an explanation of how the living entity falls down into this material world. In the spiritual world there is no duality, nor is there hate. The Supreme Personality of Godhead expands Himself into many. In order to enjoy bliss more and more, the Supreme Lord expands Himself in different categories. As mentioned in the *Varāha Purāṇa,* He expands Himself in *viṣṇu-tattva* (the *svāṁśa* expansion) and in His marginal potency (the *vibhinnāṁśa,* or the living entity). These expanded living entities are innumerable, just as the minute molecules of sunshine are innumerable expansions of the sun. The *vibhinnāṁśa* expansions, the marginal potencies of the Lord, are the living entities. When the living entities desire to enjoy themselves, they develop a consciousness of duality and come to hate the service of the Lord. In this way the living entities fall into the material world. In the *Prema-vivarta* it is said:

kṛṣṇa-bahirmukha hañā bhoga-vāñcā kare
nikaṭa-stha māyā tāre jāpaṭiyā dhare

The natural position of the living entity is to serve the Lord in a transcendental loving attitude. When the living entity wants to become Kṛṣṇa Himself or imitate Kṛṣṇa, he falls down into the material world. Since Kṛṣṇa is the Supreme Father, His affection for the living entity is eternal. When the living entity falls down into the material world, the Supreme Lord, through His *svāṁśa* expansion (Paramātmā), keeps company with the living entity. In this way the living entity may some day return home, back to Godhead.

By misusing his independence, the living entity falls down from the service of the Lord and takes a position in this material world as an enjoyer. That is to say, the living entity takes his position within a material body.

Wanting to take a very exalted position, the living entity instead becomes entangled in a repetition of birth and death. He selects his position as a human being, a demigod, a cat, a dog, a tree, etc. In this way the living entity selects a body out of the 8,400,000 forms and tries to satisfy himself by a variety of material enjoyment. The Supersoul, however, does not like him to do this. Consequently the Supersoul instructs him to surrender unto the Supreme Personality of Godhead. The Lord then takes charge of the living entity. But unless the living entity is uncontaminated by material desires, he cannot surrender to the Supreme Lord. In *Bhagavad-gītā* the Lord says:

bhoktāraṁ yajña-tapasāṁ
sarva-loka-maheśvaram
suhṛdaṁ sarva-bhūtānāṁ
jñātvā māṁ śāntim ṛcchati

"The sages, knowing Me as the ultimate purpose of all sacrifices and austerities, the Supreme Lord of all planets and demigods and the benefactor and well-wisher of all living entities, attain peace from the pangs of material miseries." (Bg. 5.29)

The Supreme Lord is the supreme friend of everyone; however, no one can take advantage of the supreme friend's instructions while making his own plans to become happy and entangling himself in the modes of material nature. When there is creation, the living entities take on different forms according to past desires. This means that all the species or forms of life are simultaneously created. Darwin's theory stating that no human being existed from the beginning but that humans evolved after many, many years is simply a nonsensical theory. From Vedic literature we find that the first creature within the universe is Lord Brahmā. Being the most intelligent personality, Lord Brahmā could take charge of creating all the variety found within this material world.

TEXT 54

हंसावहं च त्वं चार्य सखायौ मानसायनौ ।
अभूतामन्तरा वौकः सहस्रपरिवत्सरान् ॥५४॥

haṁsāv ahaṁ ca tvaṁ cārya
sakhāyau mānasāyanau
abhūtām antarā vaukaḥ
sahasra pari vatsarān

haṁsau—two swans; *aham*—I; *ca*—and; *tvam*—you; *ca*—also; *ārya*—O great soul; *sakhāyau*—friends; *mānasāyanau*—together in the Mānasa Lake; *abhūtām*—became; *antarā*—separated; *vā*—indeed; *okaḥ*—from the original home; *sahasra*—thousands; *pari*—successively; *vatsarān*—years.

TRANSLATION

My dear gentle friend, both you and I are exactly like two swans. We live together in the same heart, which is just like the Mānasa lake. Although we have been living together for many thousands of years, we are still far away from our original home.

PURPORT

The original home of the living entity and the Supreme Personality of Godhead is the spiritual world. In the spiritual world both the Lord and the living entities live together very peacefully. Since the living entity remains engaged in the service of the Lord, they both share a blissful life in the spiritual world. However, when the living entity wants to enjoy himself, he falls down into the material world. Even while he is in that position, the Lord remains with him as the Supersoul, his intimate friend. Because of his forgetfulness, the living entity does not know that the Supreme Lord is accompanying him as the Supersoul. In this way the living entity remains conditioned in each and every millennium. Although the Lord follows him as a friend, the living entity, because of forgetful material existence, does not recognize Him.

TEXT 55

स त्वं विहाय मां बन्धो गतो ग्राम्यमतिर्महीम् ।
विचरन् पदमद्राक्षीः कयाचिन्निर्मितं स्त्रिया ॥५५॥

sa tvaṁ vihāya māṁ bandho
gato grāmya-matir mahīm
vicaran padam adrākṣīḥ
kayācin nirmitaṁ striyā

saḥ—that swan; *tvam*—yourself; *vihāya*—leaving; *mām*—Me; *bandho*—O friend; *gataḥ*—went; *grāmya*—material; *matiḥ*—whose consciousness; *mahīm*—to earth; *vicaran*—traveling; *padam*—position; *adrākṣīḥ*—you saw; *kayācit*—by someone; *nirmitam*—manufactured; *striyā*—by a woman.

TRANSLATION

My dear friend, you are now My very same friend. Since you left Me, You have become more and more materialistic, and, not seeing Me, you have been traveling in different forms throughout this material world, which was created by some woman.

PURPORT

When the living entity falls down, he goes into the material world, which was created by the external energy of the Lord. This external energy is described herein as "some woman," or *prakṛti.* This material world is composed of material elements, ingredients supplied by the *mahat-tattva,* the total material energy. The material world, created by this external energy, becomes the so-called home of the conditioned soul. Within this material world the conditioned soul accepts different apartments or different bodily forms and then travels about. Sometimes he travels in the higher planetary systems and sometimes in the lower systems. Sometimes he travels in higher species of life and sometimes in lower species. He has been wandering within this material universe since time immemorial. As explained by Śrī Caitanya Mahāprabhu:

brahmāṇḍa bhramite kona bhāgyavān jīva
guru-kṛṣṇa-prasāde pāya bhakti-latā-bīja
(Cc. *Madhya* 19.151)

The living entity wanders into many species of life, but he is fortunate when he once again meets his friend, either in person or through His representative.

Actually, it is Kṛṣṇa who personally advises all living entities to return home, back to Godhead. Sometimes Kṛṣṇa sends His representative, who, delivering Kṛṣṇa's very message, canvasses all living entities to return home, back to Godhead. Unfortunately the living entity is so greatly attached to material enjoyment that he does not take the instructions of Kṛṣṇa or His representative very seriously. This material tendency is mentioned in this verse as *grāmya-matiḥ* (sense gratification). The word *mahīm* means "within this material world." All living entities within this material world are sensually inclined. Consequently they become entangled in different types of bodies and suffer the pangs of material existence.

TEXT 56

पञ्चारामं नवद्वारमेकपालं त्रिकोष्ठकम् ।
षट्कुलं पञ्चविपणं पञ्चप्रकृति स्त्रीधवम् ॥५६॥

pañcārāmaṁ nava-dvāram
eka-pālaṁ tri-koṣṭhakam
ṣaṭ-kulaṁ pañca-vipaṇaṁ
pañca-prakṛti strī-dhavam

pañca-ārāmam—five gardens; *nava-dvāram*—nine gates; *eka*—one; *pālam*—protector; *tri*—three; *koṣṭhakam*—apartments; *ṣaṭ*—six; *kulam*—families; *pañca*—five; *vipaṇam*—stores; *pañca*—five; *prakṛti*—material elements; *strī*—woman; *dhavam*—master.

TRANSLATION

In that city [the material body] there are five gardens, nine gates, one protector, three apartments, six families, five stores, five material elements, and one woman who is lord of the house.

TEXT 57

पञ्चेन्द्रियार्था आरामा द्वारः प्राणा नव प्रभो ।
तेजोऽबन्नानि कोष्ठानि कुलमिन्द्रियसंग्रहः ॥५७॥

pañcendriyārthā ārāmā
dvāraḥ prāṇā nava prabho
tejo-'bannāni koṣṭhāni
kulam indriya-saṅgrahaḥ

pañca—five; *indriya-arthāḥ*—sense objects; *ārāmāḥ*—the gardens; *dvāraḥ*—gates; *prāṇāḥ*—apertures of the senses; *nava*—nine; *prabho*—O King; *tejaḥ-ap*—fire, water; *annāni*—food grains or earth; *koṣṭhāni*—apartments; *kulam*—families; *indriya-saṅgrahaḥ*—five senses and the mind.

TRANSLATION

My dear friend, the five gardens are the five objects of sense enjoyment, and the protector is the life air, which passes through the nine gates. The three apartments are the chief ingredients—fire, water, and earth. The six families are the aggregate total of the mind and five senses.

PURPORT

The five senses that acquire knowledge are sight, taste, smell, sound and touch, and these act through the nine gates—the two eyes, two ears, one mouth, two nostrils, one genital and one rectum. These holes are compared to gates in the walls of the city. The principal ingredients are earth, water and fire, and the principal actor is the mind, which is controlled by the intelligence (*buddhi*).

TEXT 58

विपणस्तु क्रियाशक्तिर्भूतप्रकृतिरव्यया ।
शक्त्यधीशः पुमांस्त्वत्र प्रविष्टो नावबुध्यते ॥५८॥

vipaṇas tu kriyā-śaktir
bhūta-prakṛtir avyayā
śakty-adhīśaḥ pumāṁs tv atra
praviṣṭo nāvabudhyate

vipaṇaḥ—stores; *tu*—then; *kriyā-śaktiḥ*—the energy for activities, or the working senses; *bhūta*—the five gross elements; *prakṛtiḥ*—the material elements; *avyayā*—eternal; *śakti*—the energy; *adhīśaḥ*—controller; *pumān*—man; *tu*—then; *atra*—here; *praviṣṭaḥ*—entered; *na*—does not; *avabudhyate*—become subjected to knowledge.

TRANSLATION

The five stores are the five working sensory organs. They transact their business through the combined forces of the five elements, which are eternal. Behind all this activity is the soul. The soul is a person and an enjoyer in reality. However, because he is now hidden within the city of the body, he is devoid of knowledge.

PURPORT

The living entity enters the material creation with the aid of the five elements—earth, water, fire, air and ether—and thus his body is formed. Although the living entity is working from within, he is nonetheless unknown. The living entity enters the material creation, but because he is bewildered by the material energy, he appears to be hidden. The bodily conception of life is prominent because of ignorance (*nāvabudhyate*). Intelligence is described in the feminine gender, but owing to her prominence in all activities, she is described in this verse as *adhīśaḥ,* the controller. The living entity lives by means of fire, water and foodgrain. It is through the combination of these three that the body is maintained. Consequently the body is called *prakṛti,* material creation. All the elements gradually combine to form flesh, bone, blood and so on. All these appear as various apartments. It is said in the *Vedas* that the digested foods are ultimately divided into three. The solid portion becomes stool, and the semi-liquid portion turns into flesh. The liquid portion turns yellow and is again divided into three. One of these liquid portions is called urine. Similarly, the fiery portion is divided into three, and one is called bone. Out of the five elements, fire, water and foodgrains are very important. These three are mentioned in the previous verse, whereas sky (ether) and air are not mentioned. This is all explained in *Bhagavad-gītā:*

prakṛtiṁ puruṣaṁ caiva
viddhy anādī ubhāv api
vikārāṁś ca guṇāṁś caiva
viddhi prakṛti-sambhavān

"Material nature and the living entities should be understood to be beginningless. Their transformations and the modes of matter are products of material nature." (Bg. 13.20)

Prakṛti, material nature, and *puruṣa,* the living entity, are eternal. When they both come in contact, there are different reactions and manifestations. All of them should be considered the results of the interaction of the three modes of material nature.

TEXT 59

तस्मिंस्त्वं रामया स्पृष्टो रममाणोऽश्रुतस्मृतिः ।
तत्सङ्गादीदृशीं प्राप्तो दशां पापीयसीं प्रभो ॥५९॥

tasmiṁs tvaṁ rāmayā spṛṣṭo
ramamāṇo 'śruta-smṛtiḥ
tat-saṅgād īdṛśīṁ prāpto
daśāṁ pāpīyasīṁ prabho

tasmin—in that situation; *tvam*—you; *rāmayā*—with the woman; *spṛṣṭaḥ*—being in contact; *ramamāṇaḥ*—enjoying; *a-śruta-smṛtiḥ*—without remembrance of spiritual existence; *tat*—with her; *saṅgāt*—by association; *īdṛśīm*—like this; *prāptaḥ*—you have attained; *daśām*—a state; *pāpīyasīm*—full of sinful activities; *prabho*—my dear friend.

TRANSLATION

My dear friend, when you enter such a body along with the woman of material desires, you become overly absorbed in sense enjoyment. Because of this, you have forgotten your spiritual life. Due to your material conceptions, you are placed in various miserable conditions.

PURPORT

When a person becomes materially engrossed, he has no capacity to hear about spiritual existence. Forgetfulness of spiritual existence entangles a man more and more in material existence. Such is the result of sinful life. Various bodies are developed with the material ingredients because of different types of sinful activities. King Purañjana assumed the body of a woman, Vaidarbhī, as a result of his sinful activities. *Bhagavad-gītā* clearly says (*striyo vaiśyās tathā śūdrāḥ*) that such a body is lowborn. If one takes shelter of the Supreme Personality of Godhead, however, he can be elevated to the highest perfection, even though he be lowborn. One acquires lower births when one's spiritual intelligence is reduced.

TEXT 60

न त्वं विदर्भदुहिता नायं वीरः सुहृत्तव ।
न पतिस्त्वं पुरञ्जन्या रुद्धो नवमुखे यया ॥६०॥

na tvaṁ vidarbha-duhitā
nāyaṁ vīraḥ suhṛt tava
na patis tvaṁ purañjanyā
ruddho nava-mukhe yayā

na—not; *tvam*—you; *vidarbha-duhitā*—daughter of Vidarbha; *na*—not; *ayam*—this; *vīraḥ*—hero; *su-hṛt*—well-wishing husband; *tava*—your; *na*—not; *patiḥ*—husband; *tvam*—you; *purañjanyāḥ*—of Purañjanī; *ruddhaḥ*—captured; *nava-mukhe*—in the body having nine gates; *yayā*—by the material energy.

TRANSLATION

Actually, you are not the daughter of Vidarbha, nor is this man, Malayadhvaja, your well-wishing husband. Nor were you the actual husband of Purañjanī. You were simply captivated in this body of nine gates.

PURPORT

In the material world many living entities come into contact with one another, and, increasing their attachment to a particular type of body, become related as father, husband, mother, wife, etc. Actually every living entity is a separate individual being, and it is because of his contact with matter that he comes together with other bodies and becomes falsely related. False bodies create various associations in the name of family, community, society and nationality. Actually every living entity is part and parcel of the Supreme Personality of Godhead, but the living entities are overly engrossed in the material body. The Supreme Personality of Godhead, Kṛṣṇa, appears and gives instructions in the form of *Bhagavad-gītā* and Vedic literatures. The Supreme Lord gives these instructions because He is the eternal friend of the living entities. His instructions are important because by them the living entity can obtain liberation from bodily engagement. As water passes down a river, many straws and grasses are carried from the shore. These straws and grasses come together in the river's current, but when the waves toss this way and that, they are separated and carried somewhere else. Similarly, the innumerable living entities within this material world are being carried by the waves of material nature. Sometimes the waves bring them together, and they form friendships and relate to one another on a bodily basis of family, community or nationality. Eventually they are thrown out of association by the waves of material nature. This process has been going on since the creation of material nature. In this regard, Śrīla Bhaktivinoda Ṭhākura sings,

(miche) māyāra vaśe, yāccha bhese',
khāccha hābuḍubu, bhāi
(jīva) kṛṣṇa-dāsa, e viśvāsa,
karle ta' āra duḥkha nāi

"My dear living entities, you are being carried away by the waves of material nature. Sometimes you are on the surface, sometimes you are being drowned. In this way your eternal life is being spoiled. If you simply catch hold of Kṛṣṇa and take shelter of His lotus feet, you will once again get free from all the miserable material conditions."

In this verse the words *suhṛt* (well-wisher) and *tava* (your) are very significant. One's so-called husband, relative, son, father, or whatever can not actually be a well-wisher. The only actual well-wisher is Kṛṣṇa Himself, as Kṛṣṇa confirms in *Bhagavad-gītā: suhṛdaṁ sarva-bhūtānām* (Bg. 5.29).

Society, friendship, love and well-wishers are all simply results of being packed in different bodies. One should know this well and try to get out of this bodily encagement into which one is thrown birth after birth. One should take shelter of the Supreme Personality of Godhead, Kṛṣṇa, and return home, back to Godhead.

TEXT 61

माया ह्येषा मया सृष्टा यत्पुमांसं स्त्रियं सतीम् ।
मन्यसे नोभयं यद्वै हंसौ पश्यावयोर्गतिम् ॥६१॥

māyā hy eṣā mayā sṛṣṭā
yat pumāṁsaṁ striyaṁ satīm
manyase nobhayaṁ yad vai
haṁsau paśyāvayor gatim

māyā—illusory energy; *hi*—certainly; *eṣā*—this; *mayā*—by Me; *sṛṣṭā*—created; *yat*—from which; *pumāṁsam*—a male; *striyam*—a female; *satīm*—chaste; *manyase*—you think; *na*—not; *ubhayam*—both; *yat*—because; *vai*—certainly; *haṁsau*—freed from material contamination; *paśya*—just see; *āvayoḥ*—our; *gatim*—factual position.

TRANSLATION

Sometimes you think yourself a man, sometimes a chaste woman, and sometimes a neutral eunuch. This is all because of the body, which is created by the illusory energy. This illusory energy is My potency, and actually both of us—you and I—are pure spiritual identities. Now just try to understand this. I am trying to explain our factual position.

PURPORT

The factual position of both the Supreme Personality of Godhead and the living entity is qualitatively one. The Supreme Lord is the Supreme Spirit, the Supersoul, and the living entity is the individual spiritual soul. Even though both of them are original spiritual identities, the living entity forgets his identity when he comes in contact with material nature and becomes conditioned. At such a time he identifies himself as a product of the material nature. Because of the material body, he forgets that he is the eternal (*sanātana*) part and parcel of the Supreme Personality of Godhead.

This is confirmed in this way: *mamaivāṁśo jīva-loke jīva-bhūtaḥ sanātanaḥ*. The word *sanātana* is found in several places in *Bhagavad-gītā.* Both the Lord and the living entity are *sanātana* (eternal), and there is also a place known as *sanātana* beyond this material nature. The real residence of both the living entity and God is the domain of *sanātana,* not this material world. The material world is the temporary external energy of the Lord, and the living entity is placed in this material world because he wanted to imitate the position of the Supreme Personality of Godhead. In this material world he tries to enjoy his senses to his best capacity. All the activities of the conditioned soul within this material world are perpetually taking place in different types of bodies, but when the living entity acquires developed consciousness, he should try to rectify his situation and again become a member of the spiritual world. The process by which one can return home, back to Godhead, is *bhakti-yoga,* sometimes called *sanātana-dharma.* Instead of accepting a temporary occupational duty based on the material body, one should take to the process of *sanātana-dharma,* or *bhakti-yoga,* so that he can put an end to this perpetual bondage in material bodies and once again return home, back to Godhead. As long as human society works on the basis of false material identification, all the so-called advancements of science and philosophy are simply useless. They only serve to mislead human society. *Andhā yathāndhair upanīyamānāḥ.* In the material world, the blind simply lead the blind.

TEXT 62

अहं भवान्न चान्यस्त्वं त्वमेवाहं विचक्ष्व भोः ।
न नौ पश्यन्ति कवयश्छिद्रं जातु मनागपि ॥६२॥

ahaṁ bhavān na cānyas tvaṁ
tvam evāhaṁ vicakṣva bhoḥ
na nau paśyanti kavayaś
chidraṁ jātu manāg api

aham—I; *bhavān*—you; *na*—not; *ca*—also; *anyaḥ*—different; *tvam*—you; *tvam*—you; *eva*—certainly; *aham*—as I am; *vicakṣva*—just observe; *bhoḥ*—My dear friend; *na*—not; *nau*—of us; *paśyanti*—do observe; *kavayaḥ*—learned scholars; *chidram*—faulty differentiation; *jātu*—at any time; *manāk*—in a small degree; *api*—even.

TRANSLATION

My dear friend, I, the Supersoul, and you, the individual soul, are not different in quality, for we are both spiritual. In fact, My dear friend, you are qualitatively not different from Me in your constitutional position. Just try to consider this subject. Those who are actually advanced scholars, who are in knowledge, do not find any qualitative difference between you and Me.

PURPORT

Both the Supreme Personality of Godhead and the living entity are qualitatively one. There is no factual difference between the two. The Māyāvādī philosophers are again and again defeated by the illusory energy because they think that there is no separation between the Supersoul and the individual soul or that there is no Supersoul. They are also misled in thinking that everything is the Supersoul. However, those who are *kavayaḥ*, learned scholars, actually know the facts. They do not commit such mistakes. They know that God and the individual soul are one in quality, but that the individual soul falls under the clutches of *māyā*, whereas the Supersoul, the Supreme Personality of Godhead, is the controller of *māyā*. *Māyā* is the creation of the Supreme Lord (*mayā sṛṣṭā*); therefore the Supreme Lord is the controller of *māyā*. Although one in quality with the Supreme Lord, the individual soul is under the control of *māyā*. Māyāvādī philosophers cannot distinguish between the controller and the controlled.

TEXT 63

यथा पुरुष आत्मानमेकमादर्शचक्षुषोः ।
द्विधाभूतमवेक्षेत तथैवान्तरमावयोः ॥६३॥

yathā puruṣa ātmānam
ekam ādarśa-cakṣuṣoḥ
dvidhābhūtam avekṣeta
tathaivāntaram āvayoḥ

yathā—as; *puruṣaḥ*—the living entity; *ātmānam*—his body; *ekam*—one; *ādarśa*—in a mirror; *cakṣuṣoḥ*—by the eyes; *dvidhā-ābhūtam*—existing as two; *avekṣeta*—sees; *tathā*—similarly; *eva*—certainly; *antaram*—difference; *āvayoḥ*—between ourselves.

TRANSLATION

As a person sees the reflection of his body in a mirror to be one with himself and not different, whereas others actually see two bodies, so in our material condition, in which the living being is affected and yet not affected, there is a difference between God and the living entity.

PURPORT

Being affected by the conditioning of matter, Māyāvādī philosophers cannot see the difference between the Supreme Lord and the living entity. When the sun is reflected in a pot of water, the sun knows that there is no difference between him and the reflected sun in the water. Those in ignorance, however, perceive that there are many small suns reflected in each and every pot. As far as the brilliance is concerned, there is brilliance both in the original sun and in the reflections, but the reflections are small, whereas the original sun is very large. Vaiṣṇava philosophers conclude that the living entity is simply a small sample of the original Supreme Personality of Godhead. Qualitatively, God and the living entities are one, but quantitatively the living entities are small fragments of the Supreme Personality of Godhead. The Supreme Lord is full, powerful and opulent. In the previous verse, the Lord says, "My dear friend, you and I are not different." This nondifference refers to qualitative oneness, for it was not necessary for the Paramātmā, the Supreme Personality, to remind the conditioned soul that he is not one in quantity. The self-realized soul never thinks that he and the Supreme Personality of Godhead are one in every respect. Although he and the Supreme Personality of Godhead are one in quality, the living entity is prone to forget his spiritual identity, whereas the Supreme Personality never forgets. This is the difference between *lipta* and *alipta.* The Supreme Personality of Godhead is eternally *alipta,* uncontaminated by the external energy. The conditioned soul, however, being in contact with material nature, forgets his real identity; therefore when he sees himself in the conditioned state, he identifies himself with the body. For the Supreme Personality of Godhead, however, there is no difference between the body and the soul. He is completely soul; He has no material body. Although the Supersoul, Paramātmā, and the individual soul are both within the body, the Supersoul is devoid of designation, whereas the conditioned soul is designated by his particular type of body. The Supersoul is called *antaryāmī,* and He is extensive. This is confirmed in *Bhagavad-gītā:*

kṣetrajñaṁ cāpi māṁ viddhi
sarva-kṣetreṣu bhārata
kṣetra-kṣetrajñayor jñānaṁ
yat taj jñānaṁ mataṁ mama

"O scion of Bharata, you should understand that I am also the knower in all bodies, and to understand this body and its owner is called knowledge. That is My opinion." (Bg. 13.3)

The Supersoul is present in everyone's body, whereas the individual soul is conditioned in one particular type of body. The individual soul cannot understand what is taking place in another's body, but the Supersoul knows very well what is happening in all bodies. In other words, the Supersoul is always present in His full spiritual position, whereas the individual soul is prone to forget himself. Nor is the individual soul present everywhere. Generally in his conditioned state the individual soul cannot understand his relationship with the Supersoul, but sometimes, when he is free from all conditional existence, he can see the real difference between the Supersoul and himself. When the Supersoul tells the conditioned soul, "You and I are one and the same," it is to remind the conditioned soul of his spiritual identity as being qualitatively one. In the Third Canto of *Śrīmad-Bhāgavatam,* it is said:

yatholmukād visphuliṅgād
dhūmād vāpi sva-sambhavāt
apy ātmatvenābhimatād
yathāgniḥ pṛthag ulmukāt
(*Bhāg.* 3.28.40)

Fire has different features. There is flame, the sparks and the smoke. Although these are one in quality, there is still a difference between the fire, the flame, the spark and the smoke. The living entity becomes conditioned, but the Supreme Personality of Godhead is different because He does not become conditioned at any point. In the *Vedas* it is stated: *ātmā tathā pṛthag draṣṭā bhagavān brahma-saṁjñitaḥ. Ātmā* is the individual soul as well as the Supreme Personality of Godhead, who is the seer of everything. Although both are spirit, still there is always a difference. In the *smṛti* it is also said: *yathāgneḥ kṣudrā visphuliṅgā vyuccaranti.* Just as sparks manifest in a large fire, similarly the small individual souls are present in the big spiritual flame. In *Bhagavad-gītā* Lord Kṛṣṇa says:

mayā tatam idaṁ sarvaṁ
jagad avyakta-mūrtinā
mat-sthāni sarva-bhūtāni
na cāhaṁ teṣv avasthitaḥ

"By Me, in My unmanifested form, this entire universe is pervaded. All beings are in Me, but I am not in them." (Bg. 9.4)

Although all living entities are resting in Him, as small fiery sparks rest on a large flame, both are differently situated. Similarly, in the *Viṣṇu Purāṇa* it is said:

eka-deśa-sthitasyāgner
jyotsnā vistāriṇī yathā
parasya brahmaṇaḥ śaktis
tathedam akhilaṁ jagat

"Fire is situated in one place, but it distributes heat and light. Similarly, the Supreme Personality of Godhead is distributing His energies in different ways." The living entity is but one of these energies (marginal energy). The energy and the energetic are one in one sense, but they are differently situated as energy and the energetic. Similarly, the *sac-cid-ānanda* form confirmed in *Brahma-saṁhitā* (*īśvaraḥ paramaḥ kṛṣṇaḥ sac-cid-ānanda-vigrahaḥ*) is different from that of the living entity in both his conditioned and liberated states. Only atheists consider the living entity and the Personality of Godhead equal in all respects. Caitanya Mahāprabhu therefore says, *māyāvādi-bhāṣya śunile haya sarva-nāśa.* "If one follows the instructions of Māyāvādī philosophers and believes that the Supreme Personality of Godhead and the individual soul are one, his understanding of real philosophy is forever doomed."

TEXT 64

एवं स मानसो हंसो हंसेन प्रतिबोधितः ।
स्वस्थस्तद्व्यभिचारेण नष्टामाप पुनः स्मृतिम् ॥६४॥

evaṁ sa mānaso haṁso
haṁsena pratibodhitaḥ
sva-sthas tad-vyabhicāreṇa
naṣṭām āpa punaḥ smṛtim

evam—thus; *saḥ*—he (the individual soul); *mānasaḥ*—living together within the heart; *haṁsaḥ*—like the swan; *haṁsena*—by the other swan; *pratibodhitaḥ*—being instructed; *sva-sthaḥ*—situated in self-realization; *tat-vyabhicāreṇa*—by being separated from the Supersoul; *naṣṭām*—which was lost; *āpa*—gained; *punaḥ*—again; *smṛtim*—real memory.

TRANSLATION

In this way both swans live together in the heart. When the one swan is instructed by the other, he is situated in his constitutional position. This means he regains his original Kṛṣṇa consciousness, which was lost because of his material attraction.

PURPORT

Here it is clearly stated: *haṁso haṁsena pratibodhitaḥ*. The individual soul and the Supersoul are both compared to swans (*haṁsa*) because they are white or uncontaminated. One swan, however, is superior and is the instructor of the other. When the inferior swan is separated from the other swan, he is attracted to material enjoyment. This is the cause of his fall-down. When he hears the instructions of the other swan, he understands his real position and is again revived to his original consciousness. The Supreme Personality of Godhead, Kṛṣṇa, comes down (*avatāra*) to deliver His devotees and kill the demons. He also gives His sublime instructions in the form of *Bhagavad-gītā*. The individual soul has to understand his position by the grace of the Lord and the spiritual master because the text of *Bhagavad-gītā* cannot be understood simply by academic qualifications. One has to learn *Bhagavad-gītā* from a realized soul.

tad viddhi praṇipātena
paripraśnena sevayā
upadekṣyanti te jñānaṁ
jñāninas tattva-darśinaḥ

"Just try to learn the truth by approaching a spiritual master. Inquire from him submissively and render service unto him. The self-realized soul can impart knowledge unto you because he has seen the truth." (Bg. 4.34)

Thus one has to select a bona fide spiritual master and become enlightened to his original consciousness. In this way the individual soul can understand that he is always subordinate to the Supersoul. As soon as he declines to remain subordinate and tries to become an enjoyer, he begins his material conditioning. When he abandons this spirit of being an individual owner or enjoyer, he becomes situated in his liberated state. The word *sva-sthaḥ,* meaning "situated in one's original position," is very significant in this verse. When one gives up his unwanted attitude of superiority, he becomes situated in his original position. The word *tad-vyabhicāreṇa* is also significant, for it indicates that when one is separated from God due to disobedience, his real sense is lost. Again, by the grace of Kṛṣṇa and *guru,* he can be properly situated in his liberated position. These verses are spoken by Śrīla Nārada Muni, and his purpose in speaking them is to revive our consciousness. Although the living entity and the Supersoul are one in quality, the individual soul has to pursue the instruction of the Supersoul. That is the state of liberation.

TEXT 65

बर्हिष्मन्नेतदध्यात्मं पारोक्ष्येण प्रदर्शितम् ।
यत्परोक्षप्रियो देवो भगवान् विश्वभावनः ॥६५॥

barhiṣmann etad adhyātmaṁ
pārokṣyeṇa pradarśitam
yat parokṣa-priyo devo
bhagavān viśva-bhāvanaḥ

barhiṣman—O King Prācīnabarhi; *etat*—this; *adhyātmam*—narration of self-realization; *pārokṣyeṇa*—indirectly; *pradarśitam*—instructed; *yat*—because; *parokṣa-priyaḥ*—interesting by indirect description; *devaḥ*—the Supreme Lord; *bhagavān*—Personality of Godhead; *viśva-bhāvanaḥ*—the cause of all causes.

TRANSLATION

My dear King Prācīnabarhi, the Supreme Personality of Godhead, the cause of all causes, is celebrated to be known indirectly. Thus I have described the story of Purañjana to you. Actually it is an instruction for self-realization.

PURPORT

There are many similar stories in the *Purāṇas* for self-realization. As stated in the *Vedas: parokṣa-priyā iva hi devāḥ.* There are many stories in the *Purāṇas* that are intended to interest ordinary men in transcendental subjects, but actually these refer to real facts. They are not to be considered stories without a transcendental purpose. Some of them refer to real historical facts. One should be interested, however, in the real purport of the story. Indirect instruction is quickly understandable for a common man. Factually the path of *bhakti-yoga* is the path of hearing directly about the pastimes of the Supreme Personality of Godhead (*śravaṇaṁ kīrtanaṁ viṣṇoḥ*), but those who are not interested in hearing directly about the activities of the Lord, or who cannot understand them, can very effectively hear such stories and fables like this one narrated by Nārada Muni.

The following is a glossary of some of the important words in this chapter.

Ādeśakārī. The actions resulting from sinful activities.
Agastya. The mind.
Amātya. The governor of the senses, the mind.
Arbuda-arbuda. Various types of *śravaṇa* and *kīrtana* of the Supreme Lord's name, quality, form and so on.
Ari. Impediments like disease.

Bhoga. Enjoyment. Herein this word refers to real enjoyment in spiritual life.
Bhṛtya. The servants of the body, namely the senses.

Draviḍa-rāja. Devotional service or a person eligible to act in devotional service.
Dvāra. The doors of the body, such as the eyes and ears.

Gṛha. Home. For spiritual cultivation one requires an undisturbed place or the good association of devotees.

Idhmavāha. The devotee who approaches the spiritual master. *Idhma* refers to wood that is taken to burn as fuel for a fire. A *brahmacārī* is supposed to take this *idhma* to ignite the fire used in performing sacrifices. By spiritual instruction a *brahmacārī* is trained to ignite a fire and offer oblations in the morning. He is supposed to go to the spiritual master to take lessons on transcendental subject matter, and the Vedic injunction is that when approaching the spiritual master one must carry with him fuel to perform *yajñas,* or sacrifices. The exact Vedic injunction is as follows:

tad-vijñānārthaṁ sa gurum evābhigacchet
samit-pāṇiḥ śrotriyaṁ brahma-niṣṭham

"To learn transcendental subject matter, one must approach the spiritual master. In doing so, he should carry fuel to burn in sacrifice. The symptom of such a spiritual master is that he is expert in understanding the Vedic conclusion and therefore he constantly engages in the service of the Supreme Personality of Godhead." (*Muṇḍaka Upaniṣad* 1.2.12) By serving such a bona fide spiritual master, gradually a conditioned soul becomes detached from material enjoyment and invariably makes progress in spiritual realization under the direction of the spiritual master. Those who are misled by the illusory energy are never interested in approaching a spiritual master to make life successful.

Jāyā. Intelligence.
Jīrṇa-sarpa. The fatigued air of life.

Kālakanyā. The invalidity of old age.
Kāma. A high fever.
Kulācala. The place where there is no disturbance.
Kuṭumbinī. Intelligence.

Madirekṣaṇā. Madirekṣaṇā refers to one whose eyes are so attractive that one who observes them becomes maddened by her. In other words, *madirekṣaṇā* means a very beautiful young girl. According to Jīva Gosvāmī, *madirekṣaṇā* means the personified deity of *bhakti.* If one is attracted by the *bhakti* cult, he becomes engaged in the service of the Lord and the spiritual master, and thus his life becomes successful. Vaidarbhī, the woman, became a follower of her husband. As she left her comfortable home for the service of her husband, so a serious student of spiritual understanding must give up everything for the service of the spiritual master. As stated by Viśvanātha Cakravartī Ṭhākura, *yasya prasādād bhagavat-prasādaḥ:* if one wants actual success in life, he must strictly follow the instructions of the spiritual master. By following such instructions, one is sure to make rapid progress in spiritual life. This statement by Viśvanātha Cakravartī is in pursuance of the following injunction from the *Śvetāśvatara Upaniṣad:*

yasya deve parā bhaktir
yathā deve tathā gurau
tasyaite kathitā hy arthāḥ
prakāśante mahātmanaḥ

"Only unto those great souls who have implicit faith in both the Lord and the spiritual master are all the imports of Vedic knowledge automatically revealed." (*Śvet. Up.* 6.23) In the *Chāndogya Upaniṣad* it is said, *ācāryavān puruṣo veda:* "One who approaches a bona fide spiritual master can understand everything about spiritual realization."

Malayadhvaja. A nice devotee who is like sandalwood.

Pañcāla. The five sense objects.

Paricchada. The total aggregate of the senses.

Paura-jana. The seven elements that constitute the body.

Pautra. Patience and gravity.

Prajvāra. A kind of fever called *viṣṇu-jvāra.*

Pratikriyā. Counteracting agents such as *mantras* and medicines.

Pura-pālaka. The life air.

Putra. Consciousness.

Sainika. The condition of threefold miseries.

Sapta-suta. The seven sons, namely hearing, chanting, remembering, offering prayers, serving the lotus feet of the Lord, worshiping the Deity, and becoming a servant of the Lord.

Sauhṛdya. Endeavor.

Suta. The son of Vaidarbhī, or, in other words, one who is somewhat advanced in fruitive activities and who comes in contact with a devotee spiritual master. Such a person becomes interested in the subject matter of devotional service.

Vaidarbhī. The woman who was formerly a man but took birth as a woman in his next life because of too much attachment to woman. *Darbha* means *kuśa* grass. In fruitive activities, or *karma-kāṇḍīya* ceremonies, one requires *kuśa* grass. Thus *vaidarbhī* refers to one who takes birth in a family of *karma-kāṇḍīya* understanding. However, if by *karma-kāṇḍa* activities one by chance comes in contact with a devotee, as Vaidarbhī did when she married Malayadhvaja, his life becomes successful. He then pursues the devotional service of the Lord. The conditioned soul becomes liberated simply by following the instructions of the bona fide spiritual master.

Vidarbha-rājasiṁha. The best of persons who are expert in fruitive activities.

Vīrya. One who has mercy.

Yavana. The servant of Yamarāja.

Thus end the Bhaktivedanta purports of the Fourth Canto, Twenty-eighth Chapter, of the Śrīmad-Bhāgavatam, *entitled "Purañjana Becomes a Woman in the Next Life."*

CHAPTER TWENTY-NINE

Talks Between Nārada and King Prācīnabarhi

TEXT 1

प्राचीनबर्हिरुवाच

भगवंस्ते वचोऽस्माभिर्न सम्यगवगम्यते ।
कवयस्तद्विजानन्ति न वयं कर्ममोहिताः ॥ १ ॥

prācīnabarhir uvāca
bhagavaṁs te vaco 'smābhir
na samyag avagamyate
kavayas tad vijānanti
na vayaṁ karma-mohitāḥ

prācīnabarhiḥ uvāca—King Prācīnabarhi said; *bhagavan*—O my lord; *te*—your; *vacaḥ*—words; *asmābhiḥ*—by us; *na*—never; *samyak*—perfectly; *avagamyate*—are understood; *kavayaḥ*—those who are expert; *tat*—that; *vijānanti*—can understand; *na*—never; *vayam*—we; *karma*—by fruitive activities; *mohitāḥ*—enchanted.

TRANSLATION

King Prācīnabarhi replied: My dear lord, we could not appreciate completely the purport of your allegorical story of King Purañjana. Actually those who are perfect in spiritual knowledge can understand, but for us, who are overly attached to fruitive activities, to realize the purpose of your story is very difficult.

PURPORT

In *Bhagavad-gītā* Lord Kṛṣṇa says:

tribhir guṇamayair bhāvair
ebhiḥ sarvam idaṁ jagat

mohitaṁ nābhijānāti
mām ebhyaḥ param avyayam

"Deluded by the three modes [goodness, passion and ignorance], the whole world does not know Me, who am above the modes and inexhaustible." (Bg. 7.13)

Generally people are enchanted by the three modes of material nature and therefore practically unable to understand that behind all materialistic activities in the cosmic manifestation is the Supreme Personality of Godhead, Kṛṣṇa. Generally when people are engaged in sinful or pious activities, they are not perfect in knowledge of devotional service. The allegorical story narrated by Nārada Muni to King Barhiṣmān is especially meant to engage conditioned souls in devotional service. The entire story, narrated allegorically, is easily understood by a person in devotional service, but those who are engaged not in devotional service but in sense gratification cannot perfectly understand it. That is admitted by King Barhiṣmān.

This Twenty-ninth Chapter describes that by too much attachment for women one becomes a woman in the next life, but a person who associates with the Supreme Personality of Godhead or His representative becomes free from all material attachments and is thus liberated.

TEXT 2

नारद उवाच
पुरुषं पुरञ्जनं विद्याद्यद् व्यनक्त्यात्मनः पुरम्।
एकद्वित्रिचतुष्पादं बहुपादमपादकम् ॥ २ ॥

nārada uvāca
puruṣaṁ purañjanaṁ vidyād
yad vyanakty ātmanaḥ puram
eka-dvi-tri-catuṣ-pādaṁ
bahu-pādam apādakam

nāradaḥ uvāca—Nārada said; *puruṣam*—the living entity, the enjoyer; *purañjanam*—King Purañjana; *vidyāt*—one should know; *yat*—inasmuch as; *vyanakti*—he produces; *ātmanaḥ*—of himself; *puram*—dwelling place; *eka*—one; *dvi*—two; *tri*—three; *catuḥ-pādam*—with four legs; *bahu-pādam*—with many legs; *apādakam*—without legs.

TRANSLATION

The great sage Nārada Muni continued: You must understand that Purañjana, the living entity, transmigrates according to his own work into different types of bodies, which may be one-legged, two-legged, three-legged, four-legged, many-legged or simply legless. Transmigrating into these various types of bodies, the living entity, as the so-called enjoyer, is known as Purañjana.

PURPORT

How the spirit soul transmigrates from one type of body to another is nicely described here. The word *eka-pāda,* one-legged, refers to ghosts, for it is said that ghosts walk on one leg. The word *dvi-pāda,* meaning biped, refers to human beings. When he is old and invalid, the human being is supposed to be a triped, or three-legged, because he walks with the help of a stick or some kind of cane. Of course the word *catuṣ-pāda* refers to quadrupeds or animals. The word *bahu-pāda* refers to those creatures who have more than four legs. There are many insects, such as the centipede, and also many aquatic animals that have many legs. The word *apādaka,* meaning without legs, refers to serpents. The name Purañjana indicates one who enjoys possessing different types of bodies. His mentality for enjoyment in the material world is accommodated by different types of bodies.

TEXT 3

योऽविज्ञाताहृतस्तस्य पुरुषस्य सखेश्वरः ।
यन्न विज्ञायते पुम्भिर्नामभिर्वा क्रियागुणैः ॥ ३ ॥

yo 'vijñātāhṛtas tasya
puruṣasya sakheśvaraḥ
yan na vijñāyate pumbhir
nāmabhir vā kriyā-guṇaiḥ

yaḥ—he who; *avijñāta*—unknown; *āhṛtaḥ*—described; *tasya*—of him; *puruṣasya*—of the living entity; *sakhā*—eternal friend; *īśvaraḥ*—the master; *yat*—because; *na*—never; *vijñāyate*—is understood; *pumbhiḥ*—by the living entities; *nāmabhiḥ*—by names; *vā*—or; *kriyā-guṇaiḥ*—by activities or qualities.

TRANSLATION

The person I have described as unknown is the Supreme Personality of Godhead, the master and eternal friend of the living entity. Since the

living entities cannot realize the Supreme Personality of Godhead by material names, activities or qualities, He remains everlastingly unknown to the conditioned soul.

PURPORT

Because the Supreme Personality of Godhead is unknown to the conditioned soul, He is sometimes described in Vedic literatures as *nirākāra, avijñāta,* or *avāṅmanasa-gocara.* Actually it is a fact that the Supreme Personality of Godhead cannot be perceived by material senses as far as His form, name, quality, pastimes or paraphernalia are concerned. However, when one is spiritually advanced, one can understand the name, form, qualities, pastimes and paraphernalia of the Supreme Lord. This is confirmed in *Bhagavad-gītā:*

bhaktyā mām abhijānāti
yāvān yaś cāsmi tattvataḥ
tato māṁ tattvato jñātvā
viśate tad-anantaram

"One can understand the Supreme Personality as He is only by devotional service. And when one is in full consciousness of the Supreme Lord by such devotion, he can enter into the kingdom of God." (Bg. 18.55)

One can understand in truth the Supreme Personality of Godhead only when one is engaged in devotional service. Ordinary persons engaged in pious and impious activities cannot understand the form, name and activities of the Lord. The devotee, however, can know the Personality of Godhead in many respects. He can understand that Kṛṣṇa is the Supreme Personality of Godhead, that His address is Goloka Vṛndāvana and that His activities are all spiritual. Because the Lord's form and activities cannot be understood by materialistic people, He is described by the *śāstras* as *nirākāra,* that is, one whose form cannot be ascertained by a materialistic person. This does not mean that the Supreme Personality of Godhead has no form; it means that it is not understood by the *karmīs* or fruitive actors. His form is described in *Brahma-saṁhitā* as *sac-cid-ānanda vigraha.* As confirmed by the *Padma Purāṇa:*

ataḥ śrī-kṛṣṇa-nāmādi
na bhaved grāhyam indriyaiḥ
sevonmukhe hi jihvādau
svayam eva sphuraty adaḥ

"No one can understand Kṛṣṇa as He is by utilizing the blunt material senses. However, the Lord reveals Himself to His devotees, being pleased with them because of their transcendental loving service rendered unto Him."

Since the name, form, qualities and activities of the Supreme Personality of Godhead Kṛṣṇa cannot be understood by the material senses, He is also called *adhokṣaja,* meaning beyond sense perception. When the senses are purified by devotional activity, the devotee understands everything about the Lord by the Lord's grace. In this verse the words *pumbhir nāmabhir vā kriyā-guṇaiḥ* are especially significant because God, Kṛṣṇa, the Supreme Personality of Godhead, has many names, activities and qualities, although none of them are material. Despite the fact that all these names, activities and pastimes are mentioned in the *śāstras* and understood by the devotees, the *karmīs* (fruitive laborers) cannot understand them. Nor can the *jñānīs* (mental speculators) understand them. Although there are thousands of names of Lord Viṣṇu, the *karmīs* and *jñānīs* intermingle the names of the Supreme Godhead with the names of demigods and human beings. Because they cannot understand the actual name of the Supreme Personality of Godhead, they take for granted that any name can be accepted. They believe that since the Absolute Truth is impersonal, they can call Him by any name. Otherwise, they maintain, He has no name. This is not a fact. Here it is clearly stated: *nāmabhir vā kriyā-guṇaiḥ.* The Lord has specific names such as Rāma, Kṛṣṇa, Govinda, Nārāyaṇa, Viṣṇu and Adhokṣaja. There are indeed many names, but the conditioned soul cannot understand them.

TEXT 4

यदा जिघृक्षन् पुरुषः कार्त्स्न्येन प्रकृतेर्गुणान् ।
नवद्वारं द्विहस्ताङ्घ्रि तत्रामनुत साध्विति ॥ ४ ॥

yadā jighṛkṣan puruṣaḥ
kārtsnyena prakṛter guṇān
nava-dvāraṁ dvi-hastāṅghri
tatrāmanuta sādhv iti

yadā—when; *jighṛkṣan*—desiring to enjoy; *puruṣaḥ*—the living entity; *kārtsnyena*—in total; *prakṛteḥ*—of material nature; *guṇān*—the modes; *nava-dvāram*—having nine gates; *dvi*—two; *hasta*—hands; *aṅghri*—legs; *tatra*—there; *amanuta*—he thought; *sādhu*—very good; *iti*—thus.

TRANSLATION

When the living entity wants to enjoy the modes of material nature in their totality, he prefers, out of many bodily forms, to accept that body which has nine gates, two hands and two legs. Thus he prefers to become a human being or a demigod.

PURPORT

This is a very nice explanation of how the spiritual being, the part and parcel of Kṛṣṇa, God, accepts a material body by virtue of his own desires. Accepting two hands, two legs, and so on, the living entity fully enjoys the modes of material nature. Lord Kṛṣṇa says in *Bhagavad-gītā:*

icchā-dveṣa samutthena
dvandva-mohena bhārata
sarva-bhūtāni sammohaṁ
sarge yānti parantapa

"O scion of Bharata [Arjuna], O conquerer of the foe, all living entities are born into delusion, overcome by the dualities of desire and hate." (Bg. 7.27)

Originally the living entity is a spiritual being, but when he actually desires to enjoy this material world, he comes down. From this verse we can understand that the living entity first accepts a body that is human in form, but gradually, due to his degraded activities, he falls into lower forms of life—into the animal, plant and aquatic forms. By the gradual process of evolution, the living entity again attains the body of a human being and is given another chance to get out of the process of transmigration. If he again misses his chance in the human form to understand his position, he is again placed in the cycle of birth and death in various types of bodies.

The desire of the living entity to come into the material world is not very difficult to understand. Although one may be born in a family of Āryans, where there are restrictions against meat-eating, intoxication, gambling and illicit sex, still one may want to enjoy these forbidden things. There is always someone who wants to go to a prostitute for illicit sex or to a hotel to eat meat and drink wine. There is always someone who wants to gamble at nightclubs or enjoy so-called sports. All these propensities are already within the hearts of the living entities, but some living entities stop to enjoy these abominable activities and consequently fall down to a degraded platform. The more one desires a degraded life within his heart, the more he falls down to occupy different forms of abominable existence. This is the process of transmigration and evolution. A particular type of animal may have a strong tendency to enjoy one kind of sense enjoyment, but in the human form one can enjoy all the senses. The human form has the facility to utilize all the senses for gratification. Unless one is properly trained, he becomes a victim of the modes of material nature, as confirmed by *Bhagavad-gītā:*

prakṛteḥ kriyamāṇāni
guṇaiḥ karmāṇi sarvaśaḥ
ahaṅkāra-vimūḍhātmā
kartāham iti manyate

"The bewildered spirit soul, under the influence of the three modes of material nature, thinks himself the doer of activities that are in actuality carried out by nature." (Bg. 3.27)

As soon as one desires to enjoy his senses, he puts himself under the control of material energy and automatically or mechanically is placed into the cycle of birth and death in various life forms.

TEXT 5

बुद्धिं तु प्रमदां विद्यान्ममाहमिति यत्कृतम् ।
यामधिष्ठाय देहेऽस्मिन् पुमान् भुङ्क्तेऽक्षभिर्गुणान् ॥५॥

buddhiṁ tu pramadāṁ vidyān
mamāham iti yat-kṛtam
yām adhiṣṭhāya dehe 'smin
pumān bhuṅkte 'kṣabhir guṇān

buddhim—intelligence; *tu*—then; *pramadām*—the young woman (Purañjanī); *vidyāt*—one should know; *mama*—my; *aham*—I; *iti*—thus; *yat-kṛtam*—done by intelligence; *yām*—which intelligence; *adhiṣṭhāya*—taking shelter of; *dehe*—in the body; *asmin*—this; *pumān*—the living entity; *bhuṅkte*—suffers and enjoys; *akṣabhiḥ*—by the senses; *guṇān*—the modes of material nature.

TRANSLATION

The great sage Nārada continued: The word pramadā mentioned in this regard refers to material intelligence, or ignorance. It is to be understood

as such. When one takes shelter of this kind of intelligence, he identifies himself with the material body. Influenced by the material consciousness of "I" and "mine," he begins to enjoy and suffer through his senses. Thus the living entity is entrapped.

PURPORT

In material existence so-called intelligence is actually ignorance. When intelligence is cleared up, it is called *buddhi-yoga.* In other words, when intelligence is dovetailed with the desires of Kṛṣṇa, it is called *buddhi-yoga* or *bhakti-yoga.* Therefore in *Bhagavad-gītā* Kṛṣṇa says:

teṣāṁ satata-yuktānāṁ
bhajatāṁ prīti-pūrvakam
dadāmi buddhi-yogaṁ taṁ
yena mām upayānti te

"To those who are constantly devoted and worship Me with love, I give the understanding by which they can come to Me." (Bg. 10.10)

Real intelligence means linking with the Supreme Personality of Godhead. When this is done, the Supreme Personality of Godhead from within gives one the real intelligence by which one can return home, back to Godhead. Intelligence in the material world is described in this verse as *pramadā* because in material existence the living entity falsely claims things to be his. He thinks, "I am the monarch of all I survey." This is ignorance. Actually nothing belongs to him. Even the body and the senses do not belong to him, for they are given to him by the grace of the Lord to satisfy his different propensities through the material energy. Nothing actually belongs to the living entity, but he becomes mad after everything, claiming, "This is mine. This is mine. This is mine." *Janasya moho 'yam ahaṁ mameti.* This is called illusion. Nothing belongs to the living entity, but he claims that everything belongs to him. Lord Caitanya Mahāprabhu recommends that this false intelligence be purified (*ceto-darpaṇa-mārjanam*). When the mirror of intelligence is polished, the real activities of the living entity begin. This means that when a person comes to the platform of Kṛṣṇa consciousness, his real intelligence acts. At that time he knows that everything belongs to Kṛṣṇa and nothing belongs to him. As long as one thinks that everything belongs to him, he is in material consciousness, and when he knows perfectly that everything belongs to Kṛṣṇa, he is in Kṛṣṇa consciousness.

TEXT 6

सखाय इन्द्रियगणा ज्ञानं कर्म च यत्कृतम् ।
सख्यस्तद्वृत्तयः प्राणः पञ्चवृत्तिर्यथोरगः ॥ ६ ॥

sakhāya indriya-gaṇā
jñānaṁ karma ca yat-kṛtam
sakhyas tad-vṛttayaḥ prāṇaḥ
pañca-vṛttir yathoragaḥ

sakhāyaḥ—the male friends; *indriya-gaṇāḥ*—the senses; *jñānam*—knowledge; *karma*—activity; *ca*—also; *yat-kṛtam*—done by the senses; *sakhyaḥ*—female friends; *tat*—of the senses; *vṛttayaḥ*—engagements; *prāṇaḥ*—life air; *pañca-vṛttiḥ*—having five processes; *yathā*—like; *uragaḥ*—the serpent.

TRANSLATION

The five working senses and the five senses that acquire knowledge are all male friends of Purañjanī. The living entity is assisted by these senses in acquiring knowledge and engaging in activity. The engagements of the senses are known as girl friends, and the serpent, which was described as having five heads, is the life air acting within the five circulatory processes.

PURPORT

kṛṣṇa-bahirmukha hañā bhoga-vāñchā kare
nikaṭa-stha māyā tāre jāpaṭiyā dhare
(*Prema-vivarta* 6.2)

Because of his desire to enjoy the material world, the living entity is dressed with the material gross and subtle bodies. Thus he is given a chance to enjoy the senses. The senses are therefore the instruments for enjoying the material world; consequently the senses have been described as friends. Sometimes, because of too much sinful activity, the living entity does not get a material gross body, but hovers on the subtle platform. This is called ghostly life. Because of his not possessing a gross body, he creates a great deal of trouble in his subtle body. Thus the presence of a ghost is horrible for those who are living in the gross body. As stated in *Bhagavad-gītā:*

utkrāmantaṁ sthitaṁ vāpi
bhuñjānaṁ vā guṇānvitam

vimūḍhā nānupaśyanti
paśyanti jñāna-cakṣuṣaḥ

"The foolish cannot understand how a living entity can quit his body, nor can they understand what sort of body he enjoys under the spell of the modes of nature. But one whose eyes are trained in knowledge can see all this." (Bg. 15.10)

The living entities are merged into the air of life, which acts in different ways for circulation. There is *prāṇa, apāna, udāna, vyāna,* and *samāna,* and because the life air functions in this fivefold way, it is compared to the five-hooded serpent. The soul passes through the *kuṇḍalinī-cakra* like a serpent crawling on the ground. The life air is compared to *uraga,* the serpent. *Pañca-vṛtti* is the desire to satisfy the senses, attracted by five sense objects—namely, form, taste, sound, smell and touch.

TEXT 7

बृहद्बलं मनो विद्यादुभयेन्द्रियनायकम् ।
पञ्चालाः पञ्च विषया यन्मध्ये नवखं पुरम् ॥ ७ ॥

bṛhad-balaṁ mano vidyād
ubhayendriya-nāyakam
pañcālāḥ pañca viṣayā
yan-madhye nava-khaṁ puram

bṛhat-balam—very powerful; *manaḥ*—the mind; *vidyāt*—one should know; *ubhaya-indriya*—of both groups of senses; *nāyakam*—the leader; *pañcālāḥ*—the kingdom named Pañcāla; *pañca*—five; *viṣayāḥ*—sense objects; *yat*—of which; *madhye*—in the midst; *nava-kham*—having nine apertures; *puram*—the city.

TRANSLATION

The eleventh attendant, who is the commander of the others, is known as the mind. He is the leader of the senses both in the acquisition of knowledge and in the performance of work. The Pañcāla kingdom is that atmosphere in which the five sense objects are enjoyed. Within that Pañcāla kingdom is the city of the body, which has nine gates.

PURPORT

The mind is the center of all activities and is described here as *bṛhad-bala,* very powerful. To get out of the clutches of *māyā,* material existence, one has to control his mind. According to training, the mind is the friend and the enemy of the living entity. If one gets a good manager, his estate is very nicely managed, but if the manager is a thief, his estate is spoiled. Similarly, in his material conditional existence, the living entity gives power of attorney to his mind. As such, he is liable to be misdirected by his mind into enjoying sense objects. Śrīla Ambarīṣa Mahārāja therefore first engaged his mind upon the lotus feet of the Lord. *Sa vai manaḥ kṛṣṇa-padāravindayoḥ.* When the mind is engaged in meditation on the lotus feet of the Lord, the senses are controlled. This system of control is called *yama,* and this means subduing the senses. One who can subdue the senses is called a *gosvāmī,* but one who cannot control the mind is called *go-dāsa.* The mind directs the activities of the senses, which are expressed through different outlets, as described in the next verse.

TEXT 8

अक्षिणी नासिके कर्णौ मुखं शिश्नगुदाविति ।
द्वे द्वे द्वारौ बहिर्याति यस्तदिन्द्रियसंयुतः ॥ ८ ॥

akṣiṇī nāsike karṇau
mukhaṁ śiśna-gudāv iti
dve dve dvārau bahir yāti
yas tad-indriya-saṁyutaḥ

akṣiṇī—two eyes; *nāsike*—two nostrils; *karṇau*—two ears; *mukham*—mouth; *śiśna*—genitals; *gudau*—and rectum; *iti*—thus; *dve*—two; *dve*—two; *dvārau*—gates; *bahiḥ*—outside; *yāti*—goes; *yaḥ*—one who; *tat*—through the gates; *indriya*—by the senses; *saṁyutaḥ*—accompanied.

TRANSLATION

The eyes, nostrils and ears are pairs of gates situated in one place. The mouth, genital and rectum are also different gates. Being placed into a body having these nine gates, the living entity acts externally in the material world and enjoys sense objects like form and taste.

PURPORT

Not being aware of his spiritual position, the living entity, directed by the mind, goes out through the nine gates to enjoy material objects. Because of long association with material objects, he forgets his real spiritual activities and is thus misled. The entire world is going on being misled by so-called leaders like scientists and philosophers who have no knowledge of the spirit soul. Thus the conditioned soul becomes more and more entangled.

TEXT 9

अक्षिणी नासिके आस्यमिति पञ्चपुरः कृताः ।
दक्षिणा दक्षिणः कर्ण उत्तरा चोत्तरः स्मृतः ।
पश्चिमे इत्यधोद्वारौ गुदं शिश्नमिहोच्यते ॥ ९ ॥

akṣiṇī nāsike āsyam
iti pañca puraḥ kṛtāḥ
dakṣiṇā dakṣiṇaḥ karṇa
uttarā cottaraḥ smṛtaḥ
paścime ity adho dvārau
gudaṁ śiśnam ihocyate

akṣiṇī—two eyes; *nāsike*—two nostrils; *āsyam*—the mouth; *iti*—thus; *pañca*—five; *puraḥ*—on the front; *kṛtāḥ*—made; *dakṣiṇā*—southern gate; *dakṣiṇaḥ*—right; *karṇaḥ*—ear; *uttarā*—northern gate; *ca*—also; *uttaraḥ*—left ear; *smṛtaḥ*—understood; *paścime*—on the west; *iti*—thus; *adhaḥ*—downwards; *dvārau*—two gates; *gudam*—rectum; *śiśnam*—genital; *iha*—here; *ucyate*—is said.

TRANSLATION

Two eyes, two nostrils and a mouth—all together five—are situated in the front. The right ear is accepted as the southern gate, and the left ear as the northern gate. The two holes or gates situated in the west are known as the rectum and genital.

PURPORT

Of all the sides, the eastern is considered most important, primarily because the sun rises from that direction. The gates on the eastern side—the eyes, nose and mouth—are thus very important gates in the body.

TEXT 10

खद्योताऽऽविर्मुखी चात्र नेत्रे एकत्र निर्मिते ।
रूपं विभ्राजितं ताभ्यां विचष्टे चक्षुषेश्वरः ॥१०॥

khadyotāvirmukhī cātra
netre ekatra nirmite
rūpaṁ vibhrājitaṁ tābhyāṁ
vicaṣṭe cakṣuṣeśvaraḥ

khadyotā—named Khadyotā; *āvirmukhī*—named Āvirmukhī; *ca*—also; *atra*—here; *netre*—the two eyes; *ekatra*—in one place; *nirmite*—created; *rūpam*—form; *vibhrājitam*—named Vibhrājita (brilliant); *tābhyām*—through the eyes; *vicaṣṭe*—perceives; *cakṣuṣā*—with the sense of sight; *īśvaraḥ*—the master.

TRANSLATION

The two gates named Khadyotā and Āvirmukhī, which have been spoken of, are the two eyes side by side in one place. The town named Vibhrājita should be understood as form. In this way the two eyes are always engaged in seeing different kinds of forms.

PURPORT

The two eyes are attracted by brilliant things like light. Sometimes we find that little insects are attracted by the brightness of fire and thus enter into it. Similarly, the two eyes of the living entity are attracted by bright and beautiful forms. They are entangled in these forms, exactly as the insect becomes attracted to fire.

TEXT 11

नलिनी नालिनी नासे गन्धः सौरभ उच्यते ।
घ्राणोऽवधूतो मुख्यास्यं विपणो वाग्रसविद्रसः ॥११॥

nalinī nālinī nāse
gandhaḥ saurabha ucyate
ghrāṇo 'vadhūto mukhyāsyaṁ
vipaṇo vāg rasavid rasaḥ

nalinī—named Nalinī; *nālinī*—named Nālinī; *nāse*—the two nostrils; *gandhaḥ*—aroma; *saurabhaḥ*—Saurabha (fragrance); *ucyate*—is called; *ghrāṇaḥ*—the sense of smell; *avadhūtaḥ*—called Avadhūta; *mukhyā*—called Mukhyā (principal); *āsyam*—the mouth; *vipaṇaḥ*—named Vipaṇa; *vāk*—the faculty of speech; *rasa-vit*—named Rasajña (expert in tasting); *rasaḥ*—the sense of taste.

TRANSLATION

The two doors named Nalinī and Nālinī should be known as the two nostrils, and the city named Saurabha represents aroma. The companion spoken of as Avadhūta is the sense of smell. The door called Mukhyā is the mouth, and Vipaṇa is the faculty of speech. Rasajña is the sense of taste.

PURPORT

The word *avadhūta* means "most free." A person is not under the rules and regulations of any injunction when he has attained the stage of *avadhūta.* In other words, he can act as he likes. This *avadhūta* is exactly like air, which does not care for any obstruction. In *Bhagavad-gītā* it is said:

cañcalaṁ hi manaḥ kṛṣṇa
pramāthi balavad dṛḍham
tasyāhaṁ nigrahaṁ manye
vāyor iva suduṣkaram

"For the mind is restless, turbulent, obstinate and very strong, O Kṛṣṇa, and to subdue it is, it seems to me, more difficult than controlling the wind." (Bg. 6.34)

Just as the air or wind cannot be checked by anyone, the two nostrils, situated in one place, enjoy the sense of smell without impediment. When the tongue is present, the mouth continually tastes all kinds of relishable foodstuffs.

TEXT 12

आपणो व्यवहारोऽत्र चित्रमन्धो बहूदनम् ।
पितृहूर्दक्षिणः कर्ण उत्तरो देवहूः स्मृतः ॥१२॥

āpaṇo vyavahāro 'tra
citram andho bahūdanam
pitṛhūr dakṣiṇaḥ karṇa
uttaro devahūḥ smṛtaḥ

āpaṇaḥ—named Āpaṇa; *vyavahāraḥ*—business of the tongue; *atra*—here; *citram*—of all varieties; *andhaḥ*—eatables; *bahūdanam*—named Bahūdana; *pitṛ-hūḥ*—named Pitṛhū; *dakṣiṇaḥ*—right; *karṇaḥ*—ear; *uttaraḥ*—left; *deva-hūḥ*—Devahū; *smṛtaḥ*—is called.

TRANSLATION

The city called Āpaṇa represents engagement of the tongue in speech, and Bahūdana is the variety of foodstuffs. The right ear is called the gate of Pitṛhū, and the left ear is called the gate of Devahū.

TEXT 13

प्रवृत्तं च निवृत्तं च शास्त्रं पञ्चालसंज्ञितम् ।
पितृयानं देवयानं श्रोत्राच्छ्रुतधराद्व्रजेत् ॥१३॥

pravṛttaṁ ca nivṛttaṁ ca
śāstraṁ pañcāla-saṁjñitam
pitṛ-yānaṁ deva-yānaṁ
śrotrāc chruta-dharād vrajet

pravṛttam—the process of sense enjoyment; *ca*—also; *nivṛttam*—the process of detachment; *ca*—also; *śāstram*—scripture; *pañcāla*—Pañcāla; *saṁjñitam*—is described as; *pitṛ-yānam*—going to Pitṛloka; *deva-yānam*—going to Devaloka; *śrotrāt*—by hearing; *śruta-dharāt*—by the companion named Śrutadhara; *vrajet*—one can be elevated.

TRANSLATION

Nārada Muni continued: The city spoken of as Dakṣiṇa-pañcāla represents the scriptures meant for directing pravṛtti, the process of sense enjoyment in fruitive activities. The other city, named Uttara-pañcāla, represents the scriptures meant for decreasing fruitive activities and increasing knowledge. The living entity receives different kinds of knowledge by means of two ears, and some living entities are promoted to Pitṛloka and some to Devaloka. All this is made possible by the two ears.

PURPORT

The *Vedas* are known as *śruti,* and the knowledge received from them through aural reception is called *śrutadhara.* As stated in *Bhagavad-gītā,* one can be promoted to the planets of the demigods or to the planets of the *pitās* (forefathers), or even to the Vaikuṇṭha planets, simply through the process of hearing. These things have already been explained in previous chapters.

TEXT 14

आसुरी मेढ्रमर्वाग्द्वार्व्यवायो ग्रामिणां रतिः ।
उपस्थो दुर्मदः प्रोक्तो निर्ऋतिर्गुद उच्यते ॥१४॥

āsurī meḍhram arvāg-dvār
vyavāyo grāmiṇāṁ ratiḥ
upastho durmadaḥ prokto
nirṛtir guda ucyate

āsurī—called Āsurī; *meḍhram*—the genital; *arvāk*—of the fools and rascals; *dvāḥ*—gate; *vyavāyaḥ*—performing sexual affairs; *grāmiṇām*—of common men; *ratiḥ*—attraction; *upasthaḥ*—the faculty of procreation; *durmadaḥ*—Durmada; *proktaḥ*—is called; *nirṛtiḥ*—Nirṛti; *gudaḥ*—rectum; *ucyate*—is called.

TRANSLATION

The city called Grāmaka, which is approached through the lower gate of Āsurī [the genital], is meant for sex, which is very pleasing to common men who are simply fools and rascals. The faculty of procreation is called Durmada, and the rectum is called Nirṛti.

PURPORT

When the world becomes degraded, civilization becomes demoniac, and for the common man the rectum and the genital are taken very seriously as the centers of all activity. Even in such a sacred place as Vṛndāvana, India, unintelligent men pass off this rectal and genital business as spiritual activity. Such people are called *sahajiyā.* According to their philosophy, through sexual indulgence one can elevate oneself to the spiritual platform. From these verses of *Śrīmad-Bhāgavatam,* however, we understand that the desires for sexual satisfaction are meant for the *arvāk,* the lowest among men. To rectify these rascals and fools is very difficult. After all, the sex desires of the common man are condemned in these verses. The word *durmada* means "wrongly directed," and *nirṛti* means "sinful activity." Although this clearly indicates that sex indulgence is abominable and misdirected even from the ordinary point of view, the *sahajiyās* nonetheless pass themselves off as devotees conducting spiritual activities. For this reason, Vṛndāvana is no longer visited by intelligent men. Sometimes we are often asked why we have made our center in Vṛndāvana.

From the external point of view, it can be concluded that Vṛndāvana has become degenerate due to these *sahajiyā* activities, yet from the spiritual point of view, Vṛndāvana is the only place where all these sinful persons can be rectified by means of taking birth in the forms of dogs, hogs and monkeys. By living in Vṛndāvana as a dog, hog or monkey, the living entity can be elevated to the spiritual platform in the next life.

TEXT 15

वैशसं नरकं पायुर्लुब्धकोऽन्धौ तु मे शृणु ।
हस्तपादौ पुमांस्ताभ्यां युक्तो याति करोति च ॥१५॥

vaiśasaṁ narakaṁ pāyur
lubdhako 'ndhau tu me śṛṇu
hasta-pādau pumāṁs tābhyāṁ
yukto yāti karoti ca

vaiśasam—named Vaiśasa; *narakam*—hell; *pāyuḥ*—the working sense in the rectum; *lubdhakaḥ*—named Lubdhaka (very greedy); *andhau*—blind; *tu*—then; *me*—to me; *śṛṇu*—listen; *hasta-pādau*—hands and legs; *pumān*—the living entity; *tābhyām*—with them; *yuktaḥ*—being engaged; *yāti*—goes; *karoti*—works; *ca*—and.

TRANSLATION

When it is said that Purañjana goes to Vaiśasa, it is meant that he goes to hell. He is accompanied by Lubdhaka, which is the working sense in the rectum. Formerly I have also spoken of two blind associates. These associates should be understood to be the hands and legs. Being helped by the hands and legs, the living entity performs all kinds of work and moves hither and thither.

TEXT 16

अन्तःपुरं च हृदयं विषूचिर्मन उच्यते ।
तत्र मोहं प्रसादं वा हर्षं प्राप्नोति तद्गुणैः ॥१६॥

antaḥ-puraṁ ca hṛdayaṁ
viṣūcir mana ucyate
tatra mohaṁ prasādaṁ vā
harṣaṁ prāpnoti tad-guṇaiḥ

antaḥ-puram—private residence; *ca*—and; *hṛdayam*—the heart; *viśūciḥ*—the servant named Viṣūcīna; *manaḥ*—the mind; *ucyate*—is said; *tatra*—there; *moham*—illusion; *prasādam*—satisfaction; *vā*—or; *harṣam*—jubilation; *prāpnoti*—obtains; *tat*—of the mind; *guṇaiḥ*—by the modes of nature.

TRANSLATION

The word antaḥpura refers to the heart. The word viṣūcīna, meaning "going everywhere," indicates the mind. Within the mind the living entity enjoys the effects of the modes of material nature. These effects sometimes cause illusion, sometimes satisfaction and sometimes jubilation.

PURPORT

The mind and intelligence of the living entity in material existence are affected by the modes of material nature, and according to the association of the material modes, the mind is habituated to go here and there. The heart feels satisfaction, jubilation or illusion according to the effects of the modes of material nature. Actually the living entity in his material condition remains inert. It is the modes of material nature that act on the mind and heart. The results are enjoyed or suffered by the living entity. This is clearly stated in *Bhagavad-gītā:*

prakṛteḥ kriyamāṇāni
guṇaiḥ karmāṇi sarvaśaḥ
ahaṅkāra-vimūḍhātmā
kartāham iti manyate

"The bewildered spirit soul, under the influence of the three modes of material nature, thinks himself the doer of activities that are in actuality carried out by nature." (Bg. 3.27)

TEXT 17

यथा यथा विक्रियते गुणाक्तो विकरोति वा ।
तथा तथोपद्रष्टाऽऽत्मा तद्वृत्तीरनुकार्यते ॥१७॥

yathā yathā vikriyate
guṇākto vikaroti vā
tathā tathopadraṣṭātmā
tad-vṛttīr anukāryate

yathā yathā—just as; *vikriyate*—is agitated; *guṇa-aktaḥ*—associated with the modes of nature; *vikaroti*—as it does; *vā*—or; *tathā tathā*—similarly; *upadraṣṭā*—observer; *ātmā*—the soul; *tat*—of the intelligence; *vṛttīḥ*—occupations; *anukāryate*—imitates.

TRANSLATION

Formerly it was explained that the Queen is one's intelligence. While one is awake or asleep, that intelligence creates different situations. Being influenced by contaminated intelligence, the living entity envisions something and simply imitates the actions and reactions of his intelligence.

PURPORT

The Queen of Purañjana is described herein as intelligence itself. Intelligence acts both in the dream state and in the waking state, but it is contaminated by the three modes of material nature. Since the intelligence is contaminated, the living entity is also contaminated. In the conditioned state, the living entity acts according to his contaminated intelligence. Although he simply remains an observer, he nonetheless acts, being forced by a contaminated intelligence, which in reality is a passive agent.

TEXTS 18-20

देहो रथस्त्विन्द्रियाश्वः संवत्सररयोऽगतिः ।
द्विकर्मचक्रस्त्रिगुणध्वजः पञ्चासुबन्धुरः ॥१८॥
मनोरश्मिर्बुद्धिसूतो हृन्नीडो द्वन्द्वकूबरः ।
पञ्चेन्द्रियार्थप्रक्षेपः सप्तधातुवरूथकः ॥१९॥
आकूतिर्विक्रमो बाह्यो मृगतृष्णां प्रधावति ।
एकादशेन्द्रियचमूः पञ्चसूनाविनोदकृत् ॥२०॥

deho rathas tv indriyāśvaḥ
saṁvatsara-rayo 'gatiḥ
dvi-karma-cakras tri-guṇa-
dhvajaḥ pañcāsu-bandhuraḥ

mano raśmir buddhi-sūto
hṛn nīḍo dvandva-kūbaraḥ

pañcendriyārtha-prakṣepaḥ
sapta-dhātu-varūthakaḥ

ākūtir vikramo bāhyo
mṛga-tṛṣṇāṁ pradhāvati
ekādaśendriya-camūḥ
pañca-sūnā vinoda-kṛt

dehaḥ—body; *rathaḥ*—chariot; *tu*—but; *indriya*—the knowledge-acquiring senses; *aśvaḥ*—the horses; *saṁvatsara*—total years; *rayaḥ*—duration of life; *agatiḥ*—without advancing; *dvi*—two; *karma*—activities; *cakraḥ*—wheels; *tri*—three; *guṇa*—modes of nature; *dhvajaḥ*—flags; *pañca*—five; *asu*—life airs; *bandhuraḥ*—bondage; *manaḥ*—the mind; *raśmiḥ*—rope; *buddhi*—intelligence; *sūtaḥ*—chariot driver; *hṛt*—heart; *nīḍaḥ*—sitting place; *dvandva*—duality; *kūbaraḥ*—the posts for the harness; *pañca*—five; *indriya-artha*—sense objects; *prakṣepaḥ*—weapons; *sapta*—seven; *dhātu*—elements; *varūthakaḥ*—coverings; *ākūtiḥ*—attempts of the five working senses; *vikramaḥ*—prowess or processes; *bāhyaḥ*—external; *mṛga-tṛṣṇām*—false aspiration; *pradhāvati*—runs after; *ekādaśa*—eleven; *indriya*—senses; *camūḥ*—soldiers; *pañca*—five; *sūnā*—enviousness; *vinoda*—pleasure; *kṛt*—doing.

TRANSLATION

Narada Muni continued: What I referred to as the chariot was in actuality the body. The senses are the horses that pull that chariot. As time passes, year after year, these horses run without obstruction, but in fact they make no progress. Pious and impious activities are the two wheels of the chariot. The three modes of material nature are the chariot's flags. The five types of life air constitute the living entity's bondage, and the mind is considered to be the rope. Intelligence is the chariot driver. The heart is the sitting place in the chariot, and the dualities of life, such as pleasure and pain, are the knotting place. The seven elements are the coverings of the chariot, and the working senses are the five external processes. The eleven senses are the soldiers. Being engrossed in sense enjoyment, the living entity, seated on the chariot, hankers after fulfillment of his false desires and runs after sense enjoyment life after life.

PURPORT

The entanglement of the living entity in sense enjoyment is very nicely explained in these verses. The word *saṁvatsara,* meaning the progress of time, is significant. Day after day, week after week, fortnight after fortnight, month after month, year after year, the living entity becomes entangled in the chariot's progress. The chariot rests on two wheels, which are pious and impious activities. The living entity attains a certain position in life in a particular type of body according to his pious and impious activities, but his transmigration into different bodies should not be taken as progress. Real progress is explained in *Bhagavad-gītā.*

janma karma ca me divyam
evaṁ yo vetti tattvataḥ
tyaktvā dehaṁ punar janma
naiti mām eti so 'rjuna

"One who knows the transcendental nature of My appearance and activities does not, upon leaving the body, take his birth again in this material world, but attains My eternal abode, O Arjuna." (Bg. 4.9)

One makes real progress when he does not have to take on another material body. As stated in *Caitanya-caritāmṛta:*

eita brahmāṇḍa bhari' ananta jīva-gaṇa
caurāśī-lakṣa yonite karaye bhramaṇa
(Cc. *Madhya* 19.138)

The living entity is wandering throughout the entire universe and taking birth in different species on different planets. Thus he moves up and down, but that is not real progress. Real progress is getting out of this material world altogether. As stated in *Bhagavad-gītā:*

ābrahma-bhuvanāl lokāḥ
punar āvartino 'rjuna
mām upetya tu kaunteya
punar janma na vidyate

"From the highest planet in the material world down to the lowest, all are places of misery wherein repeated birth and death take place. But one who attains to My abode, O son of Kuntī, never takes birth again." (Bg. 8.16)

Even if one is promoted to Brahmaloka, the highest planet in the universe, he has to come down again to the lower planetary systems. Thus he is wandering up and down perpetually under the influence of the three modes of material nature. Being illusioned, he thinks he is making progress. He is like an airplane encircling the earth day and night, incapable of leaving the earth's gravitational field. Factually there is no progress because the airplane is conditioned by the earth's gravity.

Just as a king is seated on a chariot, the living entity is seated in the body. The sitting place is the heart, and the living entity sits there and engages in the struggle for existence, which goes on without progress perpetually. In the words of Narottama dāsa Ṭhākura:

karma-kāṇḍa, jñāna-kāṇḍa, kevala viṣera bhāṇḍa,
amṛta baliyā yebā khāya
nānā yoni sadā phire, kadarya bhakṣaṇa kare,
tāra janma adhaḥ-pāte yāya

The living entity struggles very hard due to the influence of fruitive activity and mental speculation and simply gets a different type of body life after life. He eats all kinds of nonsense and is condemned by his activities of sense enjoyment. If one really wants to progress in life, he must give up the ways of *karma-kāṇḍa* and *jñāna-kāṇḍa,* fruitive activities and mental speculation. Being fixed in Kṛṣṇa consciousness, one can become free from the entanglement of birth and death and the vain struggle for existence. In these verses the words *mṛga-tṛṣṇāṁ pradhāvati* are very significant because the living entity is influenced by a thirst for sense enjoyment. He is like a deer that goes to the desert to search out water. In a desert an animal simply searches in vain for water. Of course there is no water in the desert, and the animal simply sacrifices his life in an attempt to find it. Everyone is planning for future happiness, thinking that somehow or other, if he can reach a certain point, he will be happy. In actuality, however, when he comes to that point, he sees that there is no happiness. He then plans to go further and further to another point. This is called *mṛga-tṛṣṇā,* and its basis is sense enjoyment in this material world.

TEXT 21

संवत्सरश्चण्डवेगः कालो येनोपलक्षितः ।
तस्याहानीह गन्धर्वा गन्धर्व्यो रात्रयः स्मृताः ।
हरन्त्यायुः परिक्रान्त्या षष्ट्युत्तरशतत्रयम् ॥२१॥

saṁvatsaraś caṇḍa-vegaḥ
kālo yenopalakṣitaḥ
tasyāhānīha gandharvā
gandharvyo rātrayaḥ smṛtāḥ
haranty āyuḥ parikrāntyā
ṣaṣṭhy-uttara-śata-trayam

saṁvatsaraḥ—year; *caṇḍa-vegaḥ*—called Caṇḍavega; *kālaḥ*—time; *yena*—by which; *upalakṣitaḥ*—symbolized; *tasya*—of the duration of life; *ahāni*—days; *iha*—in this life; *gandharvāḥ*—Gandharvas; *gandharvyaḥ*—Gandharvīs; *rātrayaḥ*—nights; *smṛtāḥ*—are understood; *haranti*—they take away; *āyuḥ*—duration of life; *parikrāntyā*—by traveling; *ṣaṣṭhi*—sixty; *uttara*—above; *śata*—hundred; *trayam*—three.

TRANSLATION

What was previously explained as Caṇḍavega, powerful time, is covered by days and nights, named Gandharvas and Gandharvīs. The body's life span is gradually reduced by the passage of days and nights, which number 360.

PURPORT

The word *parikrāntyā* means "by traveling." The living entity travels on his chariot day and night during a year consisting of 360 (or more) days and nights. Life's progress is taken for the unnecessary labor required to cover these 360 days and nights of life.

TEXT 22

कालकन्या जरा साक्षाल्लोकस्तां नाभिनन्दति ।
स्वसारं जगृहे मृत्युः क्षयाय यवनेश्वरः ॥२२॥

kāla-kanyā jarā sākṣāl
lokas tāṁ nābhinandati
svasāraṁ jagṛhe mṛtyuḥ
kṣayāya yavaneśvaraḥ

kāla-kanyā—the daughter of Time; *jarā*—old age; *sākṣāt*—directly; *lokaḥ*—all living entities; *tām*—her; *na*—never; *abhinandati*—welcome; *svasāram*—as his sister; *jagṛhe*—accepted; *mṛtyuḥ*—death; *kṣayāya*—for destruction; *yavana-īśvaraḥ*—the King of the Yavanas.

TRANSLATION

What was described as Kālakanyā should be understood as old age. No one wants to accept old age, but Yavaneśvara [Yavana-rāja], who is death, accepts jarā [old age] as his sister.

PURPORT

Encaged within the body, the living being accepts Kālakanyā, old age, just before death. Yavaneśvara is the emblem of death, Yamarāja. Before going to the place of Yamarāja, the living entity accepts *jarā,* old age, the sister of Yamarāja. One is subjected to the influence of Yavana-rāja and his sister due to impious activity. Those who are in Kṛṣṇa consciousness and are engaged in devotional service under the instructions of Nārada Muni are not subjected to the influence of Yamarāja and his sister *jarā.* If one is Kṛṣṇa conscious, he conquers death. After leaving the material body, he does not accept another body that is material but returns home, back to Godhead. This is verified by *Bhagavad-gītā* (4.9).

TEXTS 23-25

आधयो व्याधयस्तस्य सैनिका यवनाश्चराः ।
भूतोपसर्गाशुरयः प्रज्वारो द्विविधो ज्वरः ॥२३॥
एवं बहुविधैर्दुःखैर्दैवभूतात्मसम्भवैः ।
क्लिश्यमानः शतं वर्षं देहे देही तमोवृतः ॥२४॥
प्राणेन्द्रियमनोधर्मानात्मन्यध्यस्य निर्गुणः ।
शेते कामलवान्ध्यायन्ममाहमिति कर्मकृत् ॥२५॥

ādhayo vyādhayas tasya
sainikā yavanāś carāḥ
bhūtopasargāśu-rayaḥ
prajvāro dvi-vidho jvaraḥ

evaṁ bahu-vidhair duḥkhair
daiva-bhūtātma-sambhavaiḥ
kliśyamānaḥ śataṁ varṣaṁ
dehe dehī tamo-vṛtaḥ

prāṇendriya-mano-dharmān
ātmany adhyasya nirguṇaḥ
śete kāma-lavān dhyāyan
mamāham iti karma-kṛt

ādhayaḥ—disturbances of the mind; *vyādhayaḥ*—disturbances of the body or diseases; *tasya*—of Yavaneśvara; *sainikāḥ*—soldiers; *yavanāḥ*—Yavanas;

carāḥ—followers; *bhūta*—of living entities; *upasarga*—at the time of distress; *āśu*—very soon; *rayaḥ*—very powerful; *prajvāraḥ*—named Prajvāra; *dvi-vidhaḥ*—two kinds; *jvaraḥ*—fever; *evam*—thus; *bahu-vidhaiḥ*—of different varieties; *duḥkhaiḥ*—by tribulations; *daiva*—by providence; *bhūta*—by other living entities; *ātma*—by the body and mind; *sambhavaiḥ*—produced; *kliśyamānaḥ*—subjected to sufferings; *śatam*—hundred; *varṣam*—years; *dehe*—in the body; *dehī*—the living entity; *tamaḥ-vṛtaḥ*—covered by material existence; *prāṇa*—of life; *indriya*—of the senses; *manaḥ*—of the mind; *dharmān*—characteristics; *ātmani*—unto the soul; *adhyasya*—wrongly attributing; *nirguṇaḥ*—although transcendental; *śete*—lies down; *kāma*—of sense enjoyment; *lavān*—on fragments; *dhyāyan*—meditating; *mama*—mine; *aham*—I; *iti*—thus; *karma-kṛt*—the actor.

TRANSLATION

The followers of Yavaneśvara [Yamarāja] are called the soldiers of death, and they are known as the various types of disturbances that pertain to the body and mind. Prajvāra represents the two types of fever: extreme heat and extreme cold—typhoid and pneumonia. The living entity lying down within the body is disturbed by many tribulations pertaining to providence, to other living entities and to his own body and mind. Despite all kinds of tribulations, the living entity, subjected to the necessities of the body, mind and senses and suffering from various types of disease, is carried away by many plans due to his lust to enjoy the world. Although transcendental to this material existence, the living entity, out of ignorance, accepts all these material miseries under the pretext of false egoism (I and mine). In this way he lives for a hundred years within this body.

PURPORT

In the *Vedas* it is stated: *asaṅgo 'yaṁ puruṣaḥ.* The living entity is actually separate from material existence, for the soul is not material. In *Bhagavad-gītā* it is also said that the living entity is the superior energy, and the material elements—earth, water, fire, air and so on—are the inferior energy. The material elements are also described as *bhinna,* or separated energy. When the internal or superior energy comes in contact with the external energy, it is subjected to so many tribulations. In *Bhagavad-gītā* the Lord also says:

mātrā-sparśās tu kaunteya
śītoṣṇa-sukha-duḥkha-dāḥ
āgamāpāyino 'nityās
tāṁs titikṣasva bhārata

"O son of Kuntī, the nonpermanent appearance of happiness and distress, and their disappearance in due course, are like the appearance and disappearance of winter and summer seasons. They arise from sense perception, O scion of Bharata, and one must learn to tolerate them without being disturbed." (Bg. 2.14)

Because of the material body, the living entity is subjected to many tribulations brought about by air, water, fire, extreme heat, extreme cold, sunshine, excessive eating, unhealthy food, maladjustments of the three elements of the body (*kapha, pitta* and *vāyu*), and so on. The intestines, the throat, the brain and the other parts of the body are affected by all kinds of diseases that are so powerful that they become sources of extreme suffering for the living entity. The living entity, however, is different from all these material elements. The two types of fever described in this verse can be explained in contemporary language as pneumonia and typhoid. When there is an extreme fever in the body, there is typhoid and pneumonia, and they are described as Prajvāra. There are also other miseries created by other living entities. The state exacts taxes, and there are also many thieves, rogues and cheaters. Miseries brought about by other living entities are called *adhibhautika.* There are also miseries in the form of famine, pestilence, scarcity, war, earthquakes and so on. These are caused by the demigods or other sources beyond our control. Actually there are many enemies of the living entities, and these are all described to point out how miserable this material existence is.

Knowing the basic misery of material existence, one should be induced to get out of the material clutches and return home, back to Godhead. Actually the living entity is not at all happy in this material body. Because of the body, he suffers thirst and hunger and is influenced by the mind, by words, by anger, by the belly, by the genitals, by the rectum, and so on. Manifold miseries encircle the transcendental living entity simply because he desires to satisfy his senses in this material world. If he simply withdraws from activities of sense gratification and applies his senses in the service of the Lord, all the problems of material existence will immediately diminish, and, with the advancement of Kṛṣṇa consciousness, he will be freed from all tribulation and, after giving up the body, will return home, back to Godhead.

TEXTS 26-27

यदाऽऽत्मानमविज्ञाय भगवन्तं परं गुरुम् ।
पुरुषस्तु विषज्जेत गुणेषु प्रकृतेः स्वदृक् ॥२६॥

गुणाभिमानी स तदा कर्माणि कुरुतेऽवशः ।
शुक्लं कृष्णं लोहितं वा यथाकर्माभिजायते ॥२७॥

yadātmānam avijñāya
bhagavantaṁ paraṁ gurum
puruṣas tu viṣajjeta
guṇeṣu prakṛteḥ sva-dṛk

guṇābhimānī sa tadā
karmāṇi kurute 'vaśaḥ
śuklaṁ kṛṣṇaṁ lohitaṁ vā
yathā-karmābhijāyate

yadā—when; *ātmānam*—the Supreme Soul; *avijñāya*—forgetting; *bhagavantam*—the Supreme Personality of Godhead; *param*—supreme; *gurum*—the instructor; *puruṣaḥ*—the living entity; *tu*—then; *viṣajjeta*—gives himself up; *guṇeṣu*—to the modes; *prakṛteḥ*—of material nature; *sva-dṛk*—one who can see his own welfare; *guṇa-abhimānī*—identified with the modes of nature; *saḥ*—he; *tadā*—at that time; *karmāṇi*—fruitive activities; *kurute*—performs; *avaśaḥ*—spontaneously; *śuklam*—white; *kṛṣṇam*—black; *lohitam*—red; *vā*—or; *yathā*—according to; *karma*—work; *abhijāyate*—takes birth.

TRANSLATION

The living entity by nature has minute independence to choose his own good or bad fortune, but when he forgets his supreme master, the Personality of Godhead, he gives himself up unto the modes of material nature. Being influenced by the modes of material nature, he identifies himself with the body and, for the interest of the body, becomes attached to various activities. Sometimes he is under the influence of the mode of ignorance, sometimes the mode of passion, and sometimes the mode of goodness. The living entity thus gets different types of bodies under the modes of material nature.

PURPORT

These different types of bodies are explained in *Bhagavad-gītā:*

puruṣaḥ prakṛti-stho hi
bhuṅkte prakṛti-jān guṇān
kāraṇaṁ guṇa-saṅgo 'sya
sad-asad-yoni-janmasu

"The living entity in material nature thus follows the ways of life, enjoying the three modes of nature. This is due to his association with that material nature. Thus he meets with good and evil amongst various species." (Bg. 13.22)

Because of associating with the modes of nature, the living entity gets a variety of bodies from the 8,400,000 forms. It is clearly explained herein that the living entity has a little independence, indicated by the word *sva-dṛk,* meaning "one who can see his own welfare." The living entity's constitutional position is very minute, and he can be misled in his choice. He may choose to imitate the Supreme Personality of Godhead. A servant may desire to start his own business and imitate his master, and when he chooses to do so, he may leave the protection of his master. Sometimes he is a failure, and sometimes he is successful. Similarly, the living entity, part and parcel of Kṛṣṇa, starts his own business to compete with the Lord. There are many competitors out to attain the Lord's position, but to become like the Lord is not at all possible. Thus there is a great struggle for existence within the material world as different parties try to imitate the Lord. Material bondage is caused by deviation from the service of the Lord and attempts to imitate Him. The Lord is imitated by Māyāvādī philosophers who try to become one with the Lord in an artificial way. When the Māyāvādī philosophers think of themselves as liberated, they are under the delusion of mental concoction. No one can become one with or equal to God. To imagine this is to continue one's bondage in material existence.

TEXT 28

शुक्लात्प्रकाशभूयिष्ठाँल्लोकानाप्नोति कर्हिचित् ।
दुःखोदर्कान् क्रियायासांस्तमःशोकोत्कटान् क्वचित् ॥२८॥

śuklāt prakāśa-bhūyiṣṭhāṁl
lokān āpnoti karhicit
duḥkhodarkān kriyāyāsāṁs
tamaḥ śokotkaṭān kvacit

śuklāt—by goodness; *prakāśa*—by illumination; *bhūyiṣṭhān*—characterized; *lokān*—planets; *āpnoti*—achieves; *karhicit*—sometimes; *duḥkha*—distress; *udarkān*—having as the end result; *kriyā-āyāsān*—full of laborious activities; *tamaḥ*—darkness; *śoka*—in lamentation; *utkaṭān*—abounding; *kvacit*—sometimes.

TRANSLATION

Those who are situated in the mode of goodness act piously according to Vedic injunctions. Thus they are elevated to the higher planetary systems where the demigods live. Those who are influenced by the mode of passion engage in various types of productive activities in the planetary systems where human beings live. Similarly, those influenced by the mode of darkness are subjected to various types of misery and live in the animal kingdom.

PURPORT

There are three planetary systems—upper, middle and lower. Those influenced by the mode of goodness are given places in the upper planetary systems—Brahmaloka (Satyaloka), Tapoloka, Janaloka and Maharloka. Those influenced by the mode of passion are given places in the Bhūrloka and Bhuvarloka. Those influenced by the mode of ignorance are given places in Atala, Vitala, Sutala, Talātala, Mahātala, Rasātala, Pātāla or the animal kingdom. Qualitatively the living entity is the same as the Supreme Personality of Godhead, but because of his forgetfulness he gets different bodies in different planetary systems. At the present moment human society is overly influenced by the mode of passion, and consequently people are engaged in working in big factories. They forget how distressful it is to live in such places. In *Bhagavad-gītā* such activities are described as *ugra-karma,* that is, distressful activities. Those who utilize the energies of the worker are called capitalists, and those who actually perform the work are called laborers. In actuality they are both capitalists, and the workers are in the modes of passion and ignorance. The result is that there is always a distressful situation. In contrast to these men are those influenced by the mode of goodness—the *karmīs* and *jñānīs.* The *karmīs,* under the direction of Vedic instructions, try to elevate themselves to higher planetary systems. The *jñānīs* try to merge into the existence of Brahman, the impersonal feature of the Lord. In this way all classes of living entities in various species of life are existing within this material world. This explains superior and inferior life forms within the material world.

TEXT 29

क्वचित्पुमान् क्वचिच्च स्त्री क्वचिन्नोभयमन्धधीः ।
देवो मनुष्यस्तिर्यग्वा यथाकर्मगुणं भवः ॥२९॥

kvacit pumān kvacic ca strī
kvacin nobhayam andha-dhīḥ
devo manuṣyas tiryag vā
yathā-karma-guṇaṁ bhavaḥ

kvacit—sometimes; *pumān*—male; *kvacit*—sometimes; *ca*—also; *strī*—female; *kvacit*—sometimes; *na*—not; *ubhayam*—both; *andha*—blind; *dhīḥ*—he whose intelligence; *devaḥ*—demigod; *manuṣyaḥ*—human being; *tiryak*—animal, bird, beast; *vā*—or; *yathā*—according to; *karma*—of activities; *guṇam*—the qualities; *bhavaḥ*—birth.

TRANSLATION

Covered by the mode of ignorance in material nature, the living entity is sometimes a male, sometimes a female, sometimes a eunuch, sometimes a human being, sometimes a demigod, sometimes a bird, an animal, and so on. In this way he is wandering within the material world. His acceptance of different types of bodies is brought about by his activities under the influence of the modes of nature.

PURPORT

Actually the living entity is part and parcel of the Lord; therefore he is spiritual in quality. The living entity is never material, and his material conception is simply a mistake due to forgetfulness. He is as brilliant as the Supreme Personality of Godhead. Both the sun and the sunshine are very brilliant. The Lord is like the full shining sun, and the living entities are like the small particles of that sun which constitute the all-pervasive sunshine. When these small particles are covered by the cloud of *māyā*, they lose their shining capacity. When the cloud of *māyā* is gone, the particles again become brilliant and shining. As soon as the living entity is covered by the ignorance of *māyā* or darkness, he cannot understand his relationship with the Supreme God. Somehow or other, if he comes before the Lord, he can see himself as shining as the Supreme Lord, although he is not as extensive as the Lord. Because the living entity desires to imitate the Supreme Lord, he is covered by *māyā*. We cannot imitate the Lord, nor can we become the supreme enjoyer. This is not possible, and when we think it is, we become conditioned by *māyā*. Thus the encagement of the living entity under the clutches of *māyā* is brought about by forgetfulness of his relationship with the Supreme Lord.

Under the influence of *māyā*, the living entity becomes exactly like a person haunted by a ghost. Such a person speaks all kinds of nonsense.

When the living entity is covered by the influence of *māyā,* he becomes a so-called scientist, philosopher, politician or socialist, and at every moment presents different plans for the benefit of human society. All these plans are ultimately failures because they are illusory. In this way the living entity forgets his position as an eternal servant of the Lord. He instead becomes a servant of *māyā.* In any case he remains a servant. It is his misfortune that by forgetting his real contact with the Supreme Lord, he becomes a servant of *māyā.* As servant of *māyā,* he sometimes becomes a king, sometimes an ordinary citizen, sometimes a *brāhmaṇa,* a *śūdra,* and so on. Sometimes he is a happy man, sometimes a prosperous man, sometimes a small insect. Sometimes he is in heaven, and sometimes in hell. Sometimes he is a demigod, and sometimes he is a demon. Sometimes he is a servant, and sometimes he is a master. In this way the living entity wanders all over the universe. Only when he comes in contact with the bona fide spiritual master can he understand his real constitutional position. He then becomes disgusted with material existence. At that time, in full Kṛṣṇa consciousness, he regrets his past experiences in material existence. This regret is very beneficial because it purifies the living entity of material conditional life. He then prays to the Lord to engage in His service, and, at that time, Kṛṣṇa grants liberation from the clutches of *māyā.* Lord Kṛṣṇa explains this in *Bhagavad-gītā:*

daivī hy eṣā guṇamayī
mama māyā duratyayā
mām eva ye prapadyante
māyām etāṁ taranti te

"This divine energy of Mine, consisting of the three modes of material nature, is difficult to overcome. But those who have surrendered unto Me can easily cross beyond it." (Bg. 7.14)

Only by the grace of Kṛṣṇa can one get out of the clutches of *māyā.* It is not possible to get out by mental speculation or other activities. When the living entity understands his real position by the grace of Kṛṣṇa, he keeps himself always fit in Kṛṣṇa consciousness and acts accordingly. Thus he gradually becomes completely free from the clutches of *māyā.* When he is strong in Kṛṣṇa consciousness, *māyā* cannot touch him. In this way, in the association of Kṛṣṇa conscious devotees, the living entity can get free from the contamination of material existence. In this connection, Śrīla Kṛṣṇadāsa Kavirāja Gosvāmī says:

tāte kṛṣṇa bhaje, kare gurura sevana
māyā-jāla chuṭe, pāya kṛṣṇera caraṇa

"In the Kṛṣṇa conscious state, the living entity engages in devotional service under the direction of the spiritual master. In this way he gets out of the clutches of *māyā* and takes shelter under the lotus feet of Lord Kṛṣṇa." (Cc. *Madhya* 22.25)

TEXTS 30-31

क्षुत्परीतो यथा दीनः सारमेयो गृहं गृहम् ।
चरन् विन्दति यद्दिष्टं दण्डमोदनमेव वा ॥३०॥
तथा कामाशयो जीव उच्चावचपथा भ्रमन् ।
उपर्यधो वा मध्ये वा याति दिष्टं प्रियाप्रियम् ॥३१॥

kṣut-parīto yathā dīnaḥ
sārameyo gṛhaṁ gṛham
caran vindati yad-diṣṭaṁ
daṇḍam odanam eva vā

tathā kāmāśayo jīva
uccāvaca-pathā bhraman
upary adho vā madhye vā
yāti diṣṭaṁ priyāpriyam

kṣut-parītaḥ—overcome by hunger; *yathā*—as; *dīnaḥ*—poor; *sārameyaḥ*—a dog; *gṛham*—from one house; *gṛham*—to another house; *caran*—wandering; *vindati*—receives; *yat*—whose; *diṣṭam*—according to destiny; *daṇḍam*—punishment; *odanam*—food; *eva*—certainly; *vā*—or; *tathā*—similarly; *kāma-āśayaḥ*—pursuing different types of desires; *jīvaḥ*—the living entity; *ucca*—high; *avaca*—low; *pathā*—on a path; *bhraman*—wandering; *upari*—high; *adhaḥ*—low; *vā*—or; *madhye*—in the middle; *vā*—or; *yāti*—goes towards; *diṣṭam*—according to destiny; *priya*—pleasing; *apriyam*—not pleasing.

TRANSLATION

The living entity is exactly like a dog, who, overcome with hunger, goes from door to door for some food. According to his destiny, he sometimes receives punishment and is driven out and at other times receives a little food to eat. Similarly, the living entity, being influenced by so many desires, wanders in different species of life according to destiny. Some-

times he is high, and sometimes he is low. Sometimes he goes to the heavenly planets, sometimes to hell, sometimes to the middle planets and so on.

PURPORT

The living entity's position is herein likened to a dog's. By chance a dog may have a very rich owner, and by chance he may become a street dog. As the dog of a rich man, he will live very opulently. Sometimes in Western countries we hear of a master leaving millions of dollars to a dog in his will. Of course there are many dogs loitering in the street without food. Therefore, to liken the conditional existence of the living entity to that of a dog is very appropriate. An intelligent human being, however, can understand that if he has to live the life of a dog, he had best become Kṛṣṇa's dog. In the material world a dog is sometimes elevated and is sometimes on the street, but in the spiritual world, Kṛṣṇa's dog is perpetually, eternally happy. Śrīla Bhaktivinoda Ṭhākura has therefore sung: *vaiṣṇava ṭhākura tomāra kukura baliyā jānaha more.* In this way Bhaktivinoda Ṭhākura offers to become a Vaiṣṇava's dog. A dog always keeps himself at his master's door and does not allow any person unfavorable to the master to enter. Similarly, one should engage in the service of a Vaiṣṇava and try to please him in every respect. Unless one does so, he does not make spiritual advancement. Apart from spiritual advancement, in the material world if one does not develop his qualities in goodness, he cannot be promoted to the higher planetary system. As confirmed by *Bhagavad-gītā:*

ūrdhvaṁ gacchanti sattva-sthā
madhye tiṣṭhanti rājasāḥ
jaghanya-guṇa-vṛtti-sthā
adho gacchanti tāmasāḥ

"Those situated in the mode of goodness gradually go upward to the higher planets; those in the mode of passion live on the earthly planets; and those in the mode of ignorance go down to the hellish worlds."(Bg. 14.18)

There are many varieties of life in the different planetary systems, and these come about due to the living entity's developing his qualities in goodness, passion and ignorance. If one is in goodness, he is promoted to the higher systems; if in passion, he remains in the middle systems; and, if in ignorance, he is pushed down to the lower species of life.

TEXT 32

दुःखेष्वेकतरेणापि दैवभूतात्महेतुषु ।
जीवस्य न व्यवच्छेदः स्याच्चेत्तत्तत्प्रतिक्रिया ॥३२॥

duḥkheṣv ekatareṇāpi
daiva-bhūtātma-hetuṣu
jīvasya na vyavacchedaḥ
syāc cet tat-tat-pratikriyā

duḥkheṣu—in the matter of distresses; *ekatareṇa*—from one kind; *api*—even; *daiva*—providence; *bhūta*—other living entities; *ātma*—the body and mind; *hetuṣu*—on account of; *jīvasya*—of the living entity; *na*—never; *vyavacchedaḥ*—stopping; *syāt*—is possible; *cet*—although; *tat-tat*—of those miseries; *pratikriyā*—counteraction.

TRANSLATION

The living entities are trying to counteract different miserable conditions pertaining to providence, other living entities, or the body and mind. Still, they must remain conditioned by the laws of nature, despite all attempts to counter these laws.

PURPORT

Just as a dog wanders here and there for a piece of bread or punishment, the living entity perpetually wanders about trying to be happy and planning in so many ways to counteract material misery. This is called the struggle for existence. We can actually see in our daily lives how we are forced to make plans to drive away miserable conditions. To get rid of one miserable condition, we have to put ourselves in another kind of miserable condition. A poor man suffers for want of money, but if he wants to become rich, he has to struggle in so many ways. Actually that is not a valid counteracting process but a snare of the illusory energy. If one does not endeavor to counteract his situation but is satisfied with his position, knowing that he has obtained his position through past activities, he can instead engage his energy to develop Kṛṣṇa consciousness. This is recommended in all Vedic literature.

tasyaiva hetoḥ prayateta kovido
na labhyate yad-bhramatām upary adhaḥ
tal-labhyate duḥkhavad anyataḥ sukhaṁ
kālena sarvatra gabhīra-raṁhasā

"Persons who are actually intelligent and philosophically inclined should endeavor only for that purposeful end which is not obtainable even by wandering from the topmost planet [Brahmaloka] down to the lowest planet [Pātāla]. As far as happiness derived from sense enjoyment is concerned, it can be obtained automatically in course of time, just as in course of time we obtain miseries even though we do not desire them." (*Bhāg.* 1.5.18) One should simply try to develop his Kṛṣṇa consciousness and not waste his time trying to improve his material condition. Actually the material condition cannot be improved. The process of improvement means accepting another miserable condition. However, if we endeavor to improve our Kṛṣṇa consciousness, the distresses of material life will disappear without extraneous endeavor. Kṛṣṇa therefore promises:

kṣipraṁ bhavati dharmātmā
śaśvac-chāntiṁ nigacchati
kaunteya pratijānīhi
na me bhaktaḥ praṇaśyati

"He quickly becomes righteous and attains lasting peace. O son of Kuntī, declare it boldly that My devotee never perishes." (Bg. 9.31)

One who takes to the path of devotional service will never be vanquished, despite all miseries of the body and mind and despite all misery brought about by other living entities and providence, miseries which are beyond our control.

TEXT 33

यथा हि पुरुषो भारं शिरसा गुरुमुद्वहन् ।
तं स्कन्धेन स आधत्ते तथा सर्वाः प्रतिक्रियाः ॥३३॥

yathā hi puruṣo bhāraṁ
śirasā gurum udvahan
taṁ skandhena sa ādhatte
tathā sarvāḥ pratikriyāḥ

yathā—as; *hi*—certainly; *puruṣaḥ*—a man; *bhāram*—a burden; *śirasā*—on the head; *gurum*—heavy; *udvahan*—carrying; *tam*—that; *skandhena*—on the shoulder; *saḥ*—he; *ādhatte*—puts; *tathā*—similarly; *sarvāḥ*—all; *pratikriyāḥ*—counteractions.

TRANSLATION

A man may carry a burden on his head, and when he feels it to be too heavy, he sometimes gives relief to his head by putting the burden on his

shoulder. In this way he tries to relieve himself of the burden. However, whatever process he devises to counteract the burden does nothing more than put the same burden from one place to another.

PURPORT

This is a good description of an attempt to transfer a burden from one place to another. When one gets tired of keeping a burden on his head, he will place it on his shoulder. This does not mean that he has become freed from the strains of carrying the burden. Similarly, human society in the name of civilization is creating one kind of trouble to avoid another kind of trouble. In contemporary civilization we see that there are many automobiles manufactured to carry us swiftly from one place to another, but at the same time we have created other problems. We have to construct so many roads, and yet these roads are insufficient to cope with automobile congestion and traffic jams. There are also the problems of air pollution and fuel shortage. The conclusion is that the processes we manufacture to counteract or minimize our distresses do not actually put an end to our pains. It is all simply illusion. We simply place the burden from the head to the shoulder. The only real way we can minimize our problems is to surrender unto the Supreme Personality of Godhead and give ourselves up to His protection. The Lord, being all-powerful, can make arrangements to mitigate our painful life in material existence.

TEXT 34

नैकान्ततः प्रतीकारः कर्मणां कर्म केवलम् ।
द्वयं ह्यविद्योपसृतं स्वप्ने स्वप्न इवानघ ॥३४॥

naikāntataḥ pratīkāraḥ
karmaṇāṁ karma kevalam
dvayaṁ hy avidyopasṛtaṁ
svapne svapna ivānagha

na—never; *ekāntataḥ*—ultimately; *pratīkāraḥ*—counteraction; *karmaṇām*—of different activities; *karma*—another activity; *kevalam*—only; *dvayam*—both; *hi*—because; *avidyā*—due to illusion; *upasṛtam*—accepted; *svapne*—in a dream; *svapnaḥ*—a dream; *iva*—like; *anagha*—O you who are free from sinful activities.

TRANSLATION

Nārada continued: O you who are free from all sinful activity! No one can counteract the effects of fruitive activity simply by manufacturing a different activity devoid of Kṛṣṇa consciousness. All such activity is due to our ignorance. When we have a troublesome dream, we cannot relieve it with a troublesome hallucination. One can counteract a dream only by awaking. Similarly, our material existence is due to ignorance and illusion. Unless we awaken to Kṛṣṇa consciousness, we cannot be relieved of such dreams. For the ultimate solution to all problems, we must awaken to Kṛṣṇa consciousness.

PURPORT

There are two kinds of fruitive activity. We can place the burden on the head, or we can place it on the shoulder. Actually, keeping the burden in either place is the same. The transferral, however, is taking place under the name of counteraction. In this connection Prahlāda Mahārāja said that fools and rascals in the material world plan so gorgeously for bodily comfort without knowing that such arrangements, even if successful, are only *māyā*. People are working hard day and night for the illusory happiness of the body. This is not a way to achieve happiness. One has to get out of this material entanglement and return home, back to Godhead. That is real happiness. The *Vedas* therefore enjoin: "Don't remain in the darkness of this material world. Go to the light of the spiritual world." To counteract the distress of this material body, one has to take on another distressed condition. Both situations are only illusion. There is no gain in taking on one trouble to counteract another trouble. The conclusion is that one cannot be perpetually happy as long as one exists in this material world. The only remedy is to get out of this material world altogether and return home, back to Godhead.

TEXT 35

अर्थे ह्यविद्यमानेऽपि संसृतिर्न निवर्तते ।
मनसा लिङ्गरूपेण स्वप्ने विचरतो यथा ॥३५॥

arthe hy avidyamāne 'pi
saṁsṛtir na nivartate
manasā liṅga-rūpeṇa
svapne vicarato yathā

arthe—factual cause; *hi*—certainly; *avidyamāne*—not existing; *api*—although; *saṁsṛtiḥ*—material existence; *na*—not; *nivartate*—ceases; *manasā*—by the mind; *liṅga-rūpeṇa*—by subtle form; *svapne*—in a dream; *vicarataḥ*—acting; *yathā*—as.

TRANSLATION

Sometimes we suffer because we see a tiger in a dream or a snake in a vision, but actually there is neither a tiger nor a snake. Thus we create some situation in a subtle form and suffer the consequences. These sufferings cannot be mitigated unless we are awakened from our dream.

PURPORT

As stated in the *Vedas,* the living entity is always separate from two kinds of material bodies—the subtle and the gross. All our sufferings are due to these material bodies. This is explained in *Bhagavad-gītā:*

mātrā-sparśās tu kaunteya
śītoṣṇa-sukha-duḥkha-dāḥ
āgamāpāyino 'nityās
tāṁs titikṣasva bhārata

"O son of Kuntī, the nonpermanent appearance of happiness and distress, and their disappearance in due course, are like the appearance and disappearance of winter and summer seasons. They arise from sense perception, O scion of Bharata, and one must learn to tolerate them without being disturbed." (Bg. 2.14)

Lord Kṛṣṇa thus informed Arjuna that all the distresses brought about by the body come and go. One has to learn how to tolerate them. Material existence is the cause of all our sufferings, for we do not suffer once we are out of the material condition. The *Vedas* therefore enjoin that one should factually understand that he is not material but is actually Brahman, (*ahaṁ brahmāsmi*). This understanding cannot be fully realized unless one is engaged in Brahman activities, namely devotional service. To get free from the material conditions, one has to take to Kṛṣṇa consciousness. That is the only remedy.

TEXTS 36-37

अथात्मनोऽर्थभूतस्य यतोऽनर्थपरम्परा ।
संसृतिस्तद्व्यवच्छेदो भक्त्या परमया गुरौ ॥३६॥

वासुदेवे भगवति भक्तियोगः समाहितः ।
सध्रीचीनेन वैराग्यं ज्ञानं च जनयिष्यति ॥३७॥

athātmano 'rtha-bhūtasya
yato 'nartha-paramparā
saṁsṛtis tad-vyavacchedo
bhaktyā paramayā gurau

vāsudeve bhagavati
bhakti-yogaḥ samāhitaḥ
sadhrīcīnena vairāgyaṁ
jñānaṁ ca janayiṣyati

atha—therefore; *ātmanaḥ*—of the living entity; *artha-bhūtasya*—having his real interest; *yataḥ*—from which; *anartha*—of all unwanted things; *paramparā*—a series one after another; *saṁsṛtiḥ*—material existence; *tat*—of that; *vyavacchedaḥ*—stopping; *bhaktyā*—by devotional service; *paramayā*—unalloyed; *gurau*—unto the Supreme Lord or His representative; *vāsudeve*—Vāsudeva; *bhagavati*—the Supreme Personality of Godhead; *bhakti-yogaḥ*—devotional service; *samāhitaḥ*—applied; *sadhrīcīnena*—completely; *vairāgyam*—detachment; *jñānam*—full knowledge; *ca*—and; *janayiṣyati*—will cause to become manifest.

TRANSLATION

The real interest of the living entity is to get out of the nescience that causes him to endure repeated birth and death. The only remedy is to surrender unto the Supreme Personality of Godhead through His representative. Unless one renders devotional service unto the Supreme Personality of Godhead, Vāsudeva, he cannot possibly become completely detached from this material world, nor can he possibly manifest real knowledge.

PURPORT

This is the way to become detached from the artificial material condition. The only remedy is to take to Kṛṣṇa consciousness and constantly engage in the devotional service of Lord Vāsudeva, the Supreme Personality of Godhead. Everyone is trying to be happy, and the process adopted to achieve that happiness is called self-interest. Unfortunately the conditioned soul hovering within this material world does not know that his ultimate goal of self-interest is Vāsudeva. *Saṁsṛti*, or material existence, begins with the illusioned bodily conception of life, and on the basis of this conception there ensues a series of unwanted things (*anarthas*). These unwanted things are actually mental desires for various types of sense gratification. In this way one accepts different types of bodies within this material world. One first has to control the mind so that the desires of the mind can be purified. This process is described in the *Nārada-pañcarātra* as *sarvopādhi-vinirmuktaṁ tat-paratvena nirmalam.* Unless one purifies his mind, there is no question of getting free from the material condition. As stated in *Śrīmad-Bhāgavatam:*

anarthopaśamaṁ sākṣād
bhakti-yogam adhokṣaje
lokasyājānato vidvāṁś
cakre sātvata-saṁhitām

"The material miseries of the living entity, which are superfluous to him, can be directly mitigated by the linking process of devotional service. But the mass of people do not know this, and therefore the learned Vyāsadeva compiled this Vedic literature, which is in relation to the Supreme Truth." (*Bhāg.* 1.7.6) *Anarthas,* unwanted things, come down from one bodily life to another. To get out of this entanglement, one has to take to the devotional service of Lord Vāsudeva, Kṛṣṇa, the Supreme Personality of Godhead. The word *guru* is significant in this connection. The word *guru* may be translated as "heavy," or "the supreme." In other words, the *guru* is the spiritual master. Śrīla Ṛṣabhadeva advised his sons: *gurur na sa syāt... na mocayed yaḥ samupeta-mṛtyum.* "One should not take up the post of spiritual master unless is able to lead his disciple from the cycle of birth and death." (*Bhāg.* 5.5.18) Material existence is actually a chain of action and reaction brought about by different types of fruitive activities. This is the cause of birth and death. One can stop this process only by engaging oneself in the service of Vāsudeva.

Bhakti refers to those activities performed in the service of Lord Vāsudeva. Because Lord Vāsudeva is the Supreme, one should engage himself in His service, not in the service of the demigods. Devotional service begins from the neophyte stage—the stage of observing the rules and regulations—and extends to the point of spontaneous loving service to the Lord. The purpose of all stages is to satisfy Lord Vāsudeva. When one is perfectly advanced in the devotional service of Vāsudeva, he becomes completely detached from the service of the body, that is, his designated position in material existence. After becoming so detached, one becomes actually perfect in knowledge and engages perfectly in the service of Lord Vāsudeva. Śrī Caitanya Mahāprabhu says: *jīvera 'svarūpa' haya——kṛṣṇera 'nitya-dāsa'.* "Every living entity is by constitutional position an eternal servant of Kṛṣṇa." As soon as one engages in the service of Lord Vāsudeva, he attains his normal constitutional position. This position is called the liberated stage. *Muktir hitvānyathā rūpaṁ svarūpeṇa vyavasthitiḥ:* in the liberated stage one is situated in his original Kṛṣṇa conscious position. He gives up all engagement in the service of matter, engagements concocted under the names of social service, national service, community service, dog service, automobile service, and so many other services conducted under the illusion of "I" and "mine."

As explained in the Second Chapter of the First Canto:

vāsudeve bhagavati
bhakti-yogaḥ prayojitaḥ
janayaty āśu vairāgyaṁ
jñānaṁ ca yad ahaitukam

"By rendering devotional service unto the Personality of Godhead, Śrī Kṛṣṇa, one immediately acquires causeless knowledge and detachment from the world." (*Bhāg.* 1.2.7) Thus one must engage in the service of Vāsudeva without material desire, mental speculation or fruitive activity.

TEXT 38

सोऽचिरादेव राजर्षे स्यादच्युतकथाश्रयः ।
शृण्वतः श्रद्दधानस्य नित्यदा स्यादधीयतः ॥३८॥

so 'cirād eva rājarṣe
syād acyuta-kathāśrayaḥ
śṛṇvataḥ śraddadhānasya
nityadā syād adhīyataḥ

saḥ—that; *acirāt*—very soon; *eva*—certainly; *rāja-ṛṣe*—O best of kings; *syāt*—becomes; *acyuta*—of the Supreme Personality of Godhead; *kathā*—narrations; *āśrayaḥ*—depending on; *śṛṇvataḥ*—of one who is hearing; *śraddadhānasya*—faithful; *nityadā*—always; *syāt*—becomes; *adhīyataḥ*—by cultivation.

TRANSLATION

O best of kings, one who is faithful, who is always hearing the glories of the Supreme Personality of Godhead, who is always engaged in the culture of Kṛṣṇa consciousness and in hearing of the Lord's activities, very soon becomes eligible to see the Supreme Personality of Godhead face to face.

PURPORT

Constant engagement in the transcendental loving service of Vāsudeva means constantly hearing the glories of the Lord. The principles of *bhakti-yoga—śravaṇaṁ kīrtanaṁ viṣṇoḥ smaraṇaṁ pāda-sevanam/ arcanaṁ vandanaṁ dāsyaṁ sakhyam ātma-nivedanam*—are the only means by which perfection can be attained. Simply by hearing of the glories of the Lord, one is elevated to the transcendental position.

TEXTS 39-40

यत्र भागवता राजन् साधवो विशदाशयाः ।
भगवद्गुणानुकथनश्रवणव्यग्रचेतसः ॥३९॥
तस्मिन्महन्मुखरिता मधुभिच्चरित्र-
पीयूषशेषसरितः परितः स्रवन्ति ।
ता ये पिबन्त्यवितृषो नृप गाढकर्णै-
स्तान्न स्पृशन्त्यशनतृड्भयशोकमोहाः ॥४०॥

yatra bhāgavatā rājan
sādhavo viśadāśayāḥ
bhagavad-guṇānukathana-
śravaṇa-vyagra-cetasaḥ

tasmin mahan-mukharitā madhubhic-caritra-
pīyūṣaśeṣa-saritaḥ paritaḥ sravanti
tā ye pibanty avitṛṣo nṛpa gāḍha-karṇais
tān na spṛśanty aśana-tṛḍ-bhaya-śoka-mohāḥ

yatra—where; *bhāgavatāḥ*—great devotees; *rājan*—O King; *sādhavaḥ*—saintly persons; *viśada-āśayāḥ*—broad-minded; *bhagavat*—of the Supreme Personality of Godhead; *guṇa*—the qualities; *anukathana*—to regularly recite; *śravaṇa*—to hear; *vyagra*—eager; *cetasaḥ*—whose consciousness; *tasmin*—there; *mahat*—of great saintly persons; *mukharitāḥ*—emanating from the mouths; *madhu-bhit*—of the killer of the Madhu demon; *caritra* —the activities or the character; *pīyūṣa*—of nectar; *śeṣa*—surplus; *saritaḥ*—rivers; *paritaḥ*—all around; *sravanti*—flow; *tāḥ*—all of them; *ye*—they who; *pibanti*—drink; *avitṛṣaḥ*—without being satisfied; *nṛpa*—O King; *gāḍha*—attentive; *karṇaiḥ*—with their ears; *tān*—them; *na*—never; *spṛśanti*—touch; *aśana*—hunger; *tṛṭ*—thirst; *bhaya*—fear; *śoka*—lamentation; *mohāḥ*—illusion.

TRANSLATION

My dear king, in the place where pure devotees live, following the rules and regulations and thus purely conscious and engaged with great eagerness in hearing and chanting the glories of the Supreme Personality of Godhead, in that place if one gets a chance to hear their constant flow of nectar, which is exactly like the waves of a river, one will forget the necessities of life—namely hunger and thirst—and become immune to all kinds of fear, lamentation and illusion.

PURPORT

The cultivation of Kṛṣṇa consciousness is possible where great devotees live together and constantly engage in hearing and chanting the glories of the Lord. In a holy place like Vṛndāvana, there are many devotees constantly engaged in chanting and hearing the glories of the Lord. If one gets the chance to hear from pure devotees in such a place, allowing the constant flow of the river of nectar to come from the mouth of pure devotees, then the cultivation of Kṛṣṇa consciousness becomes very easy. When one is engaged in constantly hearing the glories of the Lord, he certainly rises above the bodily conception. When one is in the bodily conception, he feels the pangs of hunger and thirst, fear, lamentation and illusion. But when one is engaged in hearing and chanting the glories of the Lord, he transcends the bodily conception.

The word *bhagavad-guṇānukathana-śravaṇa-vyagra-cetasaḥ,* meaning "always eager to find the place where the glories of the Lord are being heard and chanted," is significant in this verse. A businessman is always very eager to go to a place where business is transacted. Similarly, a devotee is very eager to hear from the lips of liberated devotees. As soon as one hears the glories of the Lord from the liberated devotees, he immediately becomes impregnated with Kṛṣṇa consciousness. This is also confirmed in another verse:

satāṁ prasaṅgān mama vīrya-saṁvido
bhavanti hṛt-karṇa-rasāyanāḥ kathāḥ
taj-joṣaṇād āśv apavarga-vartmani
śraddhā ratir bhaktir anukramiṣyati

"In the association of pure devotees, discussion of the pastimes and activities of the Supreme Personality of Godhead is very pleasing and satisfying to the ear and to the heart. By cultivating such knowledge one gradually becomes advanced on the path of liberation, and thereafter he is freed, and his attraction becomes fixed. Then real devotion and devotional service begin." (*Bhāg.* 3.25.25) In the association of pure devotees, one becomes attached to hearing and chanting the glories of the Lord. In this way one can cultivate Kṛṣṇa consciousness, and as soon as this cultivation is advanced, one can become faithful to the Lord, devoted to the Lord and attached to the Lord, and thus one can very quickly attain full Kṛṣṇa consciousness. The secret of success in the cultivation of Kṛṣṇa consciousness is hearing from the right person. A Kṛṣṇa conscious person is never disturbed by the bodily necessities—namely, eating, sleeping, mating and defending.

TEXT 41

एतैरुपद्रुतो नित्यं जीवलोकः स्वभावजैः ।
न करोति हरेर्नूनं कथामृतनिधौ रतिम् ॥४१॥

etair upadruto nityaṁ
jīva-lokaḥ svabhāvajaiḥ
na karoti harer nūnaṁ
kathāmṛta-nidhau ratim

etaiḥ—by these; *upadrutaḥ*—disturbed; *nityam*—always; *jīva-lokaḥ*—the conditioned soul in the material world; *sva-bhāva-jaiḥ*—natural; *na karoti*—does not do; *hareḥ*—of the Supreme Personality of Godhead; *nūnam*—certainly; *kathā*—of the words; *amṛta*—of nectar; *nidhau*—in the ocean; *ratim*—attachment.

TRANSLATION

Because the conditioned soul is always disturbed by the bodily necessities such as hunger and thirst, he has very little time to cultivate attachment to hearing the nectarean words of the Supreme Personality of Godhead.

PURPORT

Unless one is associated with devotees, he cannot cultivate Kṛṣṇa consciousness. *Nirjana-bhajana*—cultivating Kṛṣṇa consciousness in a solitary place—is not possible for the neophyte, for he will be disturbed by the bodily necessities (eating, sleeping, mating and defending). Being so disturbed, one cannot cultivate Kṛṣṇa consciousness. We therefore see that devotees known as *sahajiyā,* who make everything very easy, do not associate with advanced devotees. Such persons, in the name of devotional activities, are addicted to all kinds of sinful acts—illicit sex, intoxication, gambling, and meat-eating. There are also many so-called devotees passing themselves off as devotees while engaging in these sinful activities. In other words, one who is influenced by sinful activity cannot be accepted as a person in Kṛṣṇa consciousness. A person addicted to sinful life cannot develop Kṛṣṇa consciousness, as indicated in this verse.

TEXTS 42-44

प्रजापतिपतिः साक्षाद्भगवान् गिरिशो मनुः ।
दक्षादयः प्रजाध्यक्षा नैष्ठिकाः सनकादयः ॥४२॥
मरीचिरत्र्यङ्गिरसौ पुलस्त्यः पुलहः क्रतुः ।
भृगुर्वसिष्ठ इत्येते मदन्ता ब्रह्मवादिनः ॥४३॥
अद्यापि वाचस्पतयस्तपोविद्यासमाधिभिः ।
पश्यन्तोऽपि न पश्यन्ति पश्यन्तं परमेश्वरम् ॥४४॥

prajāpati-patiḥ sākṣād
bhagavān giriśo manuḥ
dakṣādayaḥ prajādhyakṣā
naiṣṭhikāḥ sanakādayaḥ

marīcir atry-aṅgirasau
pulastyaḥ pulahaḥ kratuḥ
bhṛgur vasiṣṭha ity ete
mad-antā brahma-vādinaḥ

adyāpi vācas-patayas
tapo-vidyā-samādhibhiḥ
paśyanto 'pi na paśyanti
paśyantaṁ parameśvaram

prajāpati-patiḥ—Brahmā, the father of all progenitors; *sākṣāt*—directly; *bhagavān*—the most powerful; *giriśaḥ*—Lord Śiva; *manuḥ*—Manu; *dakṣa-ādayaḥ*—headed by King Dakṣa; *prajā-adhyakṣāḥ*—the rulers of humankind; *naiṣṭhikāḥ*—the strong *brahmacārīs; sanaka-ādayaḥ*—headed by Sanaka; *marīciḥ*—Marīci; *atri-aṅgirasau*—Atri and Aṅgirā; *pulastyaḥ*—Pulastya; *pulahaḥ*—Pulaha; *kratuḥ*—Kratu; *bhṛguḥ*—Bhṛgu; *vasiṣṭhaḥ*—Vasiṣṭha; *iti*—thus; *ete*—all of them; *mat-antāḥ*—ending with me; *brahma-vādinaḥ*—*brāhmaṇas,* speakers on Vedic literature; *adya api*—up to date; *vācaḥ-patayaḥ*—masters of speaking; *tapaḥ*—austerities; *vidyā*—knowledge; *samādhibhiḥ*—and by meditation; *paśyantaḥ*—observing; *api*—although; *na paśyanti*—do not observe; *paśyantam*—the one who sees; *parama-īśvaram*—the Supreme Personality of Godhead.

TRANSLATION

The most powerful Lord Brahmā, the father of all progenitors; Lord Śiva, Manu, Dakṣa and the other rulers of humankind; the four saintly first-class brahmacārīs headed by Sanaka and Sanātana; the great sages Marīci, Atri, Aṅgirā, Pulastya, Pulaha, Kratu, Bhṛgu and Vasiṣṭha; and my humble self [Nārada] are all stalwart brāhmaṇas who can speak authoritatively on Vedic literature. We are very powerful because of austerities, meditation and education. Nonetheless, even after inquiring about the Supreme Personality of Godhead, whom we always see, we do not know perfectly about Him.

PURPORT

According to the foolish Darwinian theory of the anthropologists, it is said that 40,000 years ago Homo sapiens had not appeared on this planet because the process of evolution had not reached that point. However, the Vedic histories—the *Purāṇas* and *Mahābhārata*—relate human histories that extend millions and millions of years into the past. In the beginning of creation, there was a very intelligent personality, Lord Brahmā, and from him emanated all the Manus, the *brahmacārīs* like Sanaka and Sanātana, as well as Lord Śiva, the great sages and Nārada. All these personalities underwent great austerities and penances and thus became authorities in Vedic knowledge. Perfect knowledge for human beings, as well as all living entities, is contained in the *Vedas.* All the above-mentioned great personalities are not only powerful—being cognizant of past, present and future—but are also devotees. Still, in spite of their great education in knowledge, and despite their meeting the Supreme Personality of Godhead, Lord Viṣṇu, they cannot actually understand the perfection of the living entity's relationship with Lord Viṣṇu. This means that these personalities are still limited as far as their knowledge of the unlimited is concerned. The conclusion is that simply by advancing one's knowledge, one cannot be accepted as an expert in understanding the Supreme Personality of Godhead. The Supreme Personality of Godhead can be understood not by advanced knowledge but by pure devotional service, as confirmed in *Bhagavad-gītā:*

bhaktyā mām abhijānāti
yāvān yaś cāsmi tattvataḥ
tato māṁ tattvato jñātvā
viśate tad-anantaram

"One can understand the Supreme Personality as He is only by devotional service. And when one is in full consciousness of the Supreme Lord by such devotion, he can enter into the kingdom of God." (Bg. 18.55)

Unless one takes to pure transcendental devotional service, he cannot understand the Supreme Personality of Godhead in truth. Everyone has some imperfect ideas about the Lord. So-called scientists and philosophical speculators are unable to understand the Supreme Lord by virtue of their knowledge. Knowledge is not perfect unless one comes to the platform of devotional service. This is confirmed by the Vedic version:

athāpi te deva padāmbuja-dvaya-
prasāda-leśānugṛhīta eva hi
jānāti tattvaṁ bhagavan mahimno
na cānya eko 'pi ciraṁ vicinvan
(*Bhāg.* 10.14.29)

The speculators, the *jñānīs,* go on speculating about the Supreme Personality of Godhead for many many hundreds of thousands of years, but unless one is favored by the Supreme Personality of Godhead, one cannot understand His supreme glories. All the great sages mentioned in this verse have their planets near Brahmaloka, the planet where Lord Brahmā resides along with four great sages—Sanaka, Sanātana, Sanandana and Sanat-kumāra. These sages reside in different stars known as the southern stars, which circle the pole star. The pole star, called Dhruvaloka, is the pivot of this universe, and all planets move around this pole star. All the stars are planets, as far as we can see, within this one universe. According to Western theory, all the stars are different suns, but according to Vedic information, there is only one sun within this universe. All the so-called stars are but different planets. Besides this universe, there are many millions of other universes, and each of them contains similar innumerable stars and planets.

TEXT 45

शब्दब्रह्मणि दुष्पारे चरन्त उरुविस्तरे ।
मन्त्रलिङ्गैर्व्यवच्छिन्नं भजन्तो न विदुः परम् ॥४५॥

śabda-brahmaṇi duṣpāre
caranta uru-vistare
mantra-liṅgair vyavacchinnaṁ
bhajanto na viduḥ param

śabda-brahmaṇi—in the Vedic literature; *duṣpāre*—unlimited; *carantaḥ*—being engaged; *uru*—greatly; *vistare*—expansive; *mantra*—of Vedic hymns; *liṅgaiḥ*—by the symptoms; *vyavacchinnam*—partially powerful (the demigods); *bhajantaḥ*—worshiping; *na viduḥ*—they do not know; *param*—the Supreme.

TRANSLATION

Despite the cultivation of Vedic knowledge, which is unlimited, and the worship of different demigods by the symptoms of Vedic mantras, demigod worship does not help one to understand the Supreme Powerful Personality of Godhead.

PURPORT

As stated in *Bhagavad-gītā:*

kāmais tais tair hṛta-jñānāḥ
prapadyante 'nya-devatāḥ
taṁ taṁ niyamam āsthāya
prakṛtyā niyatāḥ svayā

"Those whose minds are distorted by material desires surrender unto demigods and follow the particular rules and regulations of worship according to their own natures." (Bg. 7.20)

Most people are interested in worshiping demigods to acquire powers. Each demigod has a particular power. For instance, the demigod Indra, the King of heaven, has power to shower rain on the surface of the globe to give sufficient vegetation to the earth. This demigod is described in the *Vedas: vajra-hastaḥ purandaraḥ.* Indra rules the water supply with a thunderbolt in his hand. The thunderbolt itself is controlled by Indra. Similarly, other demigods—Agni, Varuṇa, Candra, Sūrya—have particular powers. All these demigods are worshiped in the Vedic hymns through a symbolic weapon. Therefore it is said here: *mantra-liṅgair vyavacchinnam.* By such worship, *karmīs* may obtain the benediction of material opulence in the form of animals, riches, beautiful wives, many followers, and so on. By such material opulence, however, one cannot understand the Supreme Personality of Godhead.

TEXT 46

यदा यस्यानुगृह्णाति भगवानात्मभावितः ।
स जहाति मतिं लोके वेदे च परिनिष्ठिताम् ॥४६॥

yadā yasyānugṛhṇāti
bhagavān ātma-bhāvitaḥ
sa jahāti matiṁ loke
vede ca pariniṣṭhitām

yadā—when; *yasya*—whom; *anugṛhṇāti*—favors by causeless mercy; *bhagavān*—the Supreme Personality of Godhead; *ātma-bhāvitaḥ*—realized by a devotee; *saḥ*—such a devotee; *jahāti*—gives up; *matim*—consciousness; *loke*—in the material world; *vede*—in the Vedic functions; *ca*—also; *pariniṣṭhitām*—fixed.

TRANSLATION

When a person is fully engaged in devotional service, he is favored by the Lord, who bestows His causeless mercy. At such a time, the awakened devotee gives up all material activities and ritualistic performances mentioned in the Vedas.

PURPORT

In the previous verse, those who are in knowledge have been described as unable to appreciate the Supreme Personality of Godhead. Similarly, this verse indicates that those who are followers of the Vedic rituals, as well as those who are followers of fruitive activities, are unable to see the Supreme Personality of Godhead. In these two verses both the *karmīs* and *jñānīs* are described as unfit to understand Him. As described by Śrīla Rūpa Gosvāmī, only when one is completely free from mental speculation and fruitive activity (*anyābhilāṣitā-śūnyaṁ jñāna-karmādy-anāvṛtam*) can one engage in pure devotional service without being polluted by material desires. The significant word *ātma-bhāvitaḥ* indicates that the Lord is awakened in one's mind if one constantly thinks of Him. A pure devotee is always thinking of the lotus feet of the Lord (*sa vai manaḥ kṛṣṇa-padāravindayoḥ*). A pure devotee cannot remain a moment without being absorbed in thoughts of the Supreme Personality of Godhead. This constant thinking of the Lord is described in *Bhagavad-gītā* as *satata-yuktānām,* always engaging in the Lord's service. *Bhajatāṁ prīti-pūrvakam:* this is devotional service in love and affection. Because the Supreme Personality of Godhead dictates to the pure devotee from within, the devotee is saved from all material activities. Even the Vedic ritualistic ceremonies are considered material activities because by such activities one is simply elevated to other planetary systems, the residential abodes of the demigods. Lord Kṛṣṇa says in *Bhagavad-gītā:*

yānti deva-vratā devān
pitṝn yānti pitṛ-vratāḥ
bhūtāni yānti bhūtejyā
yānti mad-yājino 'pi mām

"Those who worship the demigods will take birth among the demigods; those who worship ghosts and spirits will take birth among such beings; those who worship ancestors go to the ancestors; and those who worship Me will live with Me." (Bg. 9.25)

The word *ātma-bhāvitaḥ* also indicates that a devotee is always engaged in preaching to deliver conditioned souls. It is said of the six Gosvāmīs: *nānā-śāstra-vicāraṇaika-nipuṇau sad-dharma-saṁsthāpakau lokānāṁ hita-kāriṇau.* A pure devotee of the Supreme Personality of Godhead is always thinking of how fallen conditioned souls can be delivered. The Supreme Personality of Godhead, influenced by the merciful devotees' attempt to deliver fallen souls, enlightens the people in general from within by His causeless mercy. If a devotee is benedicted by another devotee, he becomes free from *karma-kāṇḍa* and *jñāna-kāṇḍa* activities. As confirmed in *Brahma-saṁhitā, vedeṣu durlabham:* the Supreme Personality of Godhead cannot be realized through *karma-kāṇḍa* and *jñāna-kāṇḍa. Adurlabham ātma-bhaktau:* the Lord is realized only by a sincere devotee.

This material world, the cosmic manifestation, is created by the Supreme Personality of Godhead, and the living entities have come here to enjoy themselves. The Vedic instructions guide them according to different regulative principles, and intelligent people take advantage of these instructions. They thus enjoy material life without being disturbed. This is actually illusion, and to get out of this illusion by one's own endeavor is very difficult. The general populace is engaged in material activities, and when people are a little advanced, they become attracted by the ritualistic ceremonies mentioned in the *Vedas.* However, when one is frustrated in the performance of these ritualistic ceremonies, he again comes to material activities. In this way both the followers of the Vedic rituals and the followers of material activities are entangled in conditional life. These people get the seed of devotional service only by the good will of the *guru* and Kṛṣṇa. This is confirmed in *Caitanya-caritāmṛta: guru-kṛṣṇa-prasāde pāya bhakti-latā-bīja.*

When one is engaged in devotional service, he is no longer attracted to material activities. When a man is covered by different designations, he cannot engage in devotional service. One has to become freed from such designative activities (*sarvopādhi-vinirmuktam*) and become pure in order to serve the Supreme Personality of Godhead through purified senses. *Hṛṣīkeṇa hṛṣīkeśa-sevanaṁ bhaktir ucyate:* the service of the Lord through purified senses is called *bhakti-yoga* or devotional service. The sincere devotee is always helped by the Supersoul, who resides within the heart of every living entity, as Lord Kṛṣṇa confirms in *Bhagavad-gītā:*

teṣāṁ satata-yuktānāṁ
bhajatāṁ prīti-pūrvakam
dadāmi buddhi-yogaṁ taṁ
yena mām upayānti te

"To those who are constantly devoted and worship Me with love, I give the understanding by which they can come to Me." (Bg. 10.10)

This is the stage of becoming free from the contamination of the material world. At such a time a devotee makes friends with another devotee, and his engagement in material activities ceases completely. At that time,he attains the favor of the Lord and loses his faith in material civilization, which begins with *varṇāśrama-dharma.* Śrī Caitanya Mahāprabhu speaks clearly of one's becoming liberated from the *varṇāśrama-dharma,* the most exalted system of human civilization. At such a time one feels himself to be perpetually the servant of Lord Kṛṣṇa, a position taken by Śrī Caitanya Mahāprabhu Himself.

nāhaṁ vipro na ca nara-patir nāpi vaiśyo na śūdro
nāhaṁ varṇī na ca gṛha-patir no vana-stho yatir vā
kintu prodyan nikhila-paramānanda-pūrṇāmṛtābdher
gopī-bhartuḥ pada-kamalayor dāsa-dāsānudāsaḥ
(*Padyāvalī* 63)

"I am not a *brāhmaṇa, kṣatriya, vaiśya* or *śūdra.* I am not a *brahmacārī, gṛhastha, vānaprastha* or *sannyāsī.* What am I? I am the eternal servant of the servant of the servant of Lord Kṛṣṇa." Through the disciplic succession, one can attain this conclusion, which is perfect elevation to the transcendental platform.

TEXT 47

तस्मात्कर्मसु बर्हिष्मन्नज्ञानादर्थकाशिषु ।
मार्थदृष्टिं कृथाः श्रोत्रस्पर्शिष्वस्पृष्टवस्तुषु ॥४७॥

tasmāt karmasu barhiṣmann
ajñānād artha-kāśiṣu
mārtha-dṛṣṭiṁ kṛthāḥ śrotra-
sparśiṣv aspṛṣṭa-vastuṣu

tasmāt—therefore; *karmasu*—in fruitive activities; *barhiṣman*—O King Prācīnabarhiṣat; *ajñānāt*—out of ignorance; *artha-kāśiṣu*—in the matter of glittering fruitive result; *mā*—never; *artha-dṛṣṭim*—considering as the aim of life; *kṛthāḥ*—do; *śrotra-sparśiṣu*—pleasing to the ear; *aspṛṣṭa*—without touching; *vastuṣu*—real interest.

TRANSLATION

My dear King Barhiṣmān, you should never out of ignorance take to the Vedic rituals or to fruitive activity, which may be pleasing to hear about or which may appear to be the goal of self-interest. You should never take these to be the ultimate goal of life.

PURPORT

In *Bhagavad-gītā* it is said:

yām imāṁ puṣpitāṁ vācaṁ
pravadanty avipaścitaḥ
veda-vāda-ratāḥ pārtha
nānyad astīti vādinaḥ

kāmātmānaḥ svarga-parā
janma-karma-phala-pradām
kriyā-viśeṣa-bahulāṁ
bhogaiśvarya-gatiṁ prati

"Men of small knowledge are very much attached to the flowery words of the *Vedas,* which recommend various fruitive activities for elevation to heavenly planets, resultant good birth, power, and so forth. Being desirous of sense gratification and opulent life, they say that there is nothing more than this." (Bg. 2.42-43)

Generally people are very much attracted to the fruitive activities sanctioned in the Vedic rituals. One may be very much attracted to becoming elevated to heavenly planets by performing great sacrifices, like those of King Barhiṣmān. Śrī Nārada Muni wanted to stop King Barhiṣmān from engaging in such fruitive activities. Therefore he is now directly telling him, "Don't be interested in such temporary benefits." In modern civilization people are very much interested in exploiting the resources of material nature through the methods of science. Indeed, this is considered advancement. This is not actually advancement, however, but is simply pleasing to hear. Although we are advancing according to such concocted methods, we are nonetheless forgetting our real purpose. Bhaktivinoda Ṭhākura therefore says: *jaḍa-vidyā yata māyāra vaibhava tomāra bhajane bādhā.* "Materialistic studies are the glare of *māyā* only, for they are an obstacle to spiritual progress."

The temporary comforts of life experienced either on this planet or on other planets are all to be taken as illusory because they do not touch the real purpose of life. The real purpose of life is to go back home, back to Godhead. Ignorant of the real purpose of life, people take to either gross materialistic activities or ritualistic activities. King Barhiṣmān is herein requested not to be attached to such activities. In the *Vedas* it is stated that the performance of sacrifice is the actual purpose of life. A section of the Indian population known as the Ārya Samājists lay too much stress on the sacrificial portion of the *Vedas.* This verse indicates, however, that such sacrifices are to be taken as illusory. Actually the aim of human life should be God realization, or Kṛṣṇa consciousness. The Vedic performances are, of course, very glittering and pleasing to hear about, but they do not serve the real purpose of life.

TEXT 48

स्वं लोकं न विदुस्ते वै यत्र देवो जनार्दनः ।
आहुर्धूम्रधियो वेदं सकर्मकमतद्विदः ॥४८॥

svaṁ lokaṁ na vidus te vai
yatra devo janārdanaḥ

āhur dhūmra-dhiyo vedaṁ
sakarmakam atad-vidaḥ

svam—own; *lokam*—abode; *na*—never; *viduḥ*—know; *te*—such persons; *vai*—certainly; *yatra*—where; *devaḥ*—the Supreme Personality of Godhead; *janārdanaḥ*—Kṛṣṇa or Viṣṇu; *āhuḥ*—speak; *dhūmra-dhiyaḥ*—the less intelligent class of men; *vedam*—the four *Vedas; sa-karmakam*—full of ritualistic ceremonies; *a-tat-vidaḥ*—persons who are not in knowledge.

TRANSLATION

Those who are less intelligent accept the Vedic ritualistic ceremonies as all in all. They do not know that the purpose of the Vedas is to understand one's own home, where the Supreme Personality of Godhead lives. Not being interested in their real home, they are illusioned and search after other homes.

PURPORT

Generally people are not aware of their interest in life—to return home, back to Godhead. People do not know about their real home in the spiritual world. In the spiritual world there are many Vaikuṇṭha planets, and the topmost planet is Kṛṣṇaloka, Goloka Vṛndāvana. Despite the so-called advancement of civilization, there is no information of the Vaikuṇṭhalokas, the spiritual planets. At the present moment so-called advanced civilized men are trying to go to other planets, but they do not know that even if they go to the highest planetary system, Brahmaloka, they have to come back again to this planet. This is confirmed in *Bhagavad-gītā:*

ābrahma-bhuvanāl lokāḥ
punar āvartino 'rjuna
mām upetya tu kaunteya
punar janma na vidyate

"From the highest planet in the material world down to the lowest, all are places of misery wherein repeated birth and death take place. But one who attains to My abode, O son of Kuntī, never takes birth again." (Bg. 8.16)

If one goes to the highest planetary system within this universe he still has to return after the effects of pious activities are finished. Space vehicles may go very high in the sky, but as soon as their fuel is finished, they have to return to this earthly planet. All these activities are performed in illusion. The real attempt should now be to return home, back to Godhead. The process is mentioned in *Bhagavad-gītā. Yānti mad-yājino 'pi mām:* those who engage in the devotional service of the Supreme Personality of Godhead return home, back to Godhead. Human life is very valuable, and one should not waste it in vain exploration of other planets. One should be intelligent enough to return to Godhead. One should be interested in information about the spiritual Vaikuṇṭha planets, and in particular the planet known as Goloka Vṛndāvana, and should learn the art of going there by the simple method of devotional service, beginning with hearing (*śravaṇaṁ kīrtanaṁ viṣṇoḥ*). This is also confirmed in *Śrīmad-Bhāgavatam:*

kaler doṣa-nidhe rājann
asti hy eko mahān guṇaḥ
kīrtanād eva kṛṣṇasya
mukta-saṅgaḥ paraṁ vrajet (*Bhāg.* 12.3.51)

One can go to the supreme planet (*paraṁ vrajet*) simply by chanting the Hare Kṛṣṇa *mantra.* This is especially meant for the people of this age (*kaler doṣa-nidhe*). It is the special advantage of this age that simply by chanting the Hare Kṛṣṇa *mahā-mantra* one can become purified of all material contamination and return home, back to Godhead. There is no doubt about this.

TEXT 49

आस्तीर्य दर्भैः प्रागग्रैः कार्त्स्न्येन क्षितिमण्डलम् ।
स्तब्धो बृहद्वधान्मानी कर्म नावैषि यत्परम् ।
तत्कर्म हरितोषं यत्सा विद्या तन्मतिर्यया ॥४९॥

āstīrya darbhaiḥ prāg-agraiḥ
kārtsnyena kṣiti-maṇḍalam
stabdho bṛhad-vadhān mānī
karma nāvaiṣi yat param
tat karma hari-toṣaṁ yat
sā vidyā tan-matir yayā

āstīrya—having covered; *darbhaiḥ*—by *kuśa* grass; *prāk-agraiḥ*—with the points facing east; *kārtsnyena*—altogether; *kṣiti-maṇḍalam*—the surface of the world; *stabdhaḥ*—proud upstart; *bṛhat*—great; *vadhāt*—by killing; *mānī*—thinking yourself very important; *karma*—activity; *na avaiṣi*—you do not know; *yat*—which; *param*—supreme; *tat*—that; *karma*—activity; *hari-*

toṣam—satisfying the Supreme Lord; *yat*—which; *sā*—that; *vidyā*—education; *tat*—unto the Lord; *matiḥ*—consciousness; *yayā*—by which.

TRANSLATION

My dear King, the entire world is covered with the sharp points of kuśa grass, and on the strength of this you have become proud because you have killed various types of animals in sacrifices. Because of your foolishness, you do not know that devotional service is the only way one can please the Supreme Personality of Godhead. You cannot understand this fact. Your only activities should be those that can please the Personality of Godhead. Our education should be such that we can become elevated to Kṛṣṇa consciousness.

PURPORT

In this verse the great sage Nārada Muni directly insults the King because he was engaged in performing sacrifices that entail the killing of a great number of animals. The King was thinking that he was great for having performed so many sacrifices, but the great sage Nārada directly chastises him, informing him that his animal killing only leads to his being puffed up with false prestige. Actually anything that is done which does not lead to Kṛṣṇa consciousness is a sinful activity, and any education that does not lead one to understand Kṛṣṇa is false education. If Kṛṣṇa consciousness is missing, one is simply engaged in false activities and false educational pursuits.

TEXT 50

हरिर्देहभृतामात्मा स्वयं प्रकृतिरीश्वरः ।
तत्पादमूलं शरणं यतः क्षेमो नृणामिह ॥५०॥

harir deha-bhṛtām ātmā
svayaṁ prakṛtir īśvaraḥ
tat-pāda-mūlaṁ śaraṇaṁ
yataḥ kṣemo nṛṇām iha

hariḥ—Śrī Hari; *deha-bhṛtām*—of living entities who have accepted material bodies; *ātmā*—the Supersoul; *svayam*—Himself; *prakṛtiḥ*—material nature; *īśvaraḥ*—the controller; *tat*—His; *pāda-mūlam*—feet; *śaraṇam*—shelter; *yataḥ*—from which; *kṣemaḥ*—good fortune; *nṛṇām*—of men; *iha*—in this world.

TRANSLATION

Śrī Hari, the Supreme Personality of Godhead, is the Supersoul and guide of all living entities who have accepted material bodies within this world. He is the supreme controller of all material activities in material nature. He is also our best friend, and everyone should take shelter at His lotus feet. In doing so, one's life will be auspicious.

PURPORT

In *Bhagavad-gītā* it is said:

īśvaraḥ sarva-bhūtānāṁ
hṛd-deśe 'rjuna tiṣṭhati
bhrāmayan sarva-bhūtāni
yantrārūḍhāni māyayā

"The Supreme Lord is situated in everyone's heart, O Arjuna, and is directing the wanderings of all living entities, who are seated as on a machine, made of the material energy." (Bg. 18.61)

The living entity is within the body, and the Supersoul, the Supreme Personality of Godhead, is also there. He is called *antaryāmī* and *caitya-guru.* As Lord Kṛṣṇa states in *Bhagavad-gītā,* He is controlling everything.

sarvasya cāhaṁ hṛdi sanniviṣṭo
mattaḥ smṛtir jñānam apohanaṁ ca
vedaiś ca sarvair aham eva vedyo
vedānta-kṛd veda-vid eva cāham

"I am seated in everyone's heart, and from Me come remembrance, knowledge and forgetfulness. By all the *Vedas,* I am to be known; indeed I am the compiler of Vedānta, and I am the knower of the *Vedas.*" (Bg. 15.15)

Everything is being directed by the Supersoul within the body; therefore the better part of valor is to take His direction and be happy. To take His directions, one needs to be a devotee, and this is also confirmed in *Bhagavad-gītā.*

teṣāṁ satata-yuktānāṁ
bhajatāṁ prīti-pūrvakam
dadāmi buddhi-yogaṁ taṁ
yena mām upayānti te

"To those who are constantly devoted and worship Me with love, I give the understanding by which they can come to Me." (Bg. 10.10)

Although the Supersoul is in everyone's heart (*īśvaraḥ sarva-bhūtānāṁ hṛd-deśe 'rjuna tiṣṭhati*), He talks only to the pure devotees who constantly engage in His service. In *Caitanya-bhāgavata* it is said:

tāhāre se bali vidyā, mantra, adhyayana
kṛṣṇa-pāda-padme ye karaye sthira mana

"One who has fixed his mind on the lotus feet of Kṛṣṇa is to be understood as having the best education and as having studied all the *Vedas*." (Cb. *Antya* 3.45) There are also other appropriate quotes in *Caitanya-bhāgavata:*

sei se vidyāra phala jāniha niścaya
kṛṣṇa-pāda-padme yadi citta-vṛtti raya

"The perfect result of an education is the fixing of one's mind on the lotus feet of Kṛṣṇa." (Cb. *Ādi* 13.178)

'dig-vijaya kariba,'— vidyāra kārya nahe
īśvare bhajile, sei vidyā 'satya' kahe

"Conquering the world by means of material education is not desirable. If one engages himself in devotional service, his education is perfected." (Cb. *Ādi* 13.173)

paḍe kene loka—kṛṣṇa-bhakti jānibāre
se yadi nahila, tabe vidyāya ki kare

"The purpose of education is to understand Kṛṣṇa and His devotional service. If one does not do so, then education is false." (Cb. *Ādi* 12.49)

tāhāre se bali dharma, karma sadācāra
īśvare se prīti janme sammata sabāra

"Being cultured, educated, very active and religious means developing natural love for Kṛṣṇa." (Cb. *Antya* 3.44) Everyone has dormant love for Kṛṣṇa, and by culture and education that has to be awakened. That is the purpose of this Kṛṣṇa consciousness movement. Once Lord Caitanya asked Śrī Rāmānanda Rāya what the best part of education was, and Rāmānanda

Rāya replied that the best part of education is advancement in Kṛṣṇa consciousness.

TEXT 51

स वै प्रियतमश्चात्मा यतो न भयमण्वपि ।
इति वेद स वै विद्वान्यो विद्वान् स गुरुर्हरिः ॥५१॥

sa vai priyatamaś cātmā
yato na bhayam aṇv api
iti veda sa vai vidvān
yo vidvān sa gurur hariḥ

saḥ—He; *vai*—certainly; *priya-tamaḥ*—the most dear; *ca*—also; *ātmā*—Supersoul; *yataḥ*—from whom; *na*—never; *bhayam*—fear; *aṇu*—little; *api*—even; *iti*—thus; *veda*—(one who) knows; *saḥ*—he; *vai*—certainly; *vidvān*—educated; *yaḥ*—he who; *vidvān*—educated; *saḥ*—he; *guruḥ*—spiritual master; *hariḥ*—not different from the Lord.

TRANSLATION

One who is engaged in devotional service has not the least fear in material existence. This is because the Supreme Personality of Godhead is the Supersoul and friend of everyone. One who knows this secret is actually educated, and one thus educated can become the spiritual master of the world. One who is an actually bona fide spiritual master, representative of Kṛṣṇa, is not different from Kṛṣṇa.

PURPORT

Śrīla Viśvanātha Cakravartī Ṭhākura says: *sākṣād-dharitvena samasta-śāstrair uktas tathā bhāvyata eva sadbhiḥ.* The spiritual master is described in every scripture as the representative of the Supreme Personality of Godhead. The spiritual master is accepted as identical with the Supreme Personality of Godhead because he is the most confidential servant of the Lord (*kintu prabhor yaḥ priya eva tasya*). The purport is that both the Supersoul and the individual soul are very dear to everyone. Everyone loves himself, and when he becomes more advanced, he loves the Supersoul also. A person who is self-realized does not recommend the worship of anyone but the Supersoul. He knows that to worship the

Supreme Personality of Godhead is easier than to worship various demigods under the influence of lust and the desire for material enjoyment. The devotee is therefore always engaged in the loving devotional service of the Lord. Such a person is a true *guru.* In *Padma Purāṇa* it is said:

ṣaṭ-karma-nipuṇo vipro
mantra-tantra-viśāradaḥ
avaiṣṇavo gurur na syād
vaiṣṇavaḥ śva-paco guruḥ

"Even if a *brāhmaṇa* is very learned in Vedic scriptures and knows the six occupational duties of a *brāhmaṇa,* he cannot become a *guru* or spiritual master unless he is a devotee of the Supreme Personality of Godhead. However, if one is born in a family of dog-eaters but is a pure devotee of the Lord, he can become a spiritual master." The conclusion is that one cannot become a spiritual master unless he is a pure devotee of the Lord. One who is a spiritual master in accordance with the above descriptions of devotional service is to be understood as the Supreme Personality of Godhead personally present. According to the words mentioned here (*gurur hariḥ*), consulting a bona fide spiritual master means consulting the Supreme Personality of Godhead personally. One should therefore take shelter of such a bona fide spiritual master. Success in life means accepting a spiritual master who knows Kṛṣṇa as the only supreme beloved personality. One should worship such a confidential devotee of the Lord.

TEXT 52

नारद उवाच
प्रश्न एवं हि संछिन्नो भवतः पुरुषर्षभ ।
अत्र मे वदतो गुह्यं निशामय सुनिश्चितम् ॥५२॥

nārada uvāca
praśna evaṁ hi sañchinno
bhavataḥ puruṣarṣabha
atra me vadato guhyaṁ
niśāmaya suniścitam

nāradaḥ uvāca—Nārada said; *praśnaḥ*—question; *evam*—thus; *hi*—certainly; *sañchinnaḥ*—answered; *bhavataḥ*—your; *puruṣa-ṛṣabha*—O great personality; *atra*—here; *me vadataḥ*—as I am speaking; *guhyam*—confidential; *niśāmaya*—hear; *su-niścitam*—perfectly ascertained.

TRANSLATION

The great saint Nārada continued: O great personality, I have replied properly about all that you have asked me. Now hear another narration that is accepted by saintly persons and is very confidential.

PURPORT

Śrī Nārada Muni is personally acting as the spiritual master of King Barhiṣmān. It was Nārada Muni's intention that through his instructions the King would immediately give up all engagement in fruitive activity and take to devotional service. However, although the King understood everything, he was still not prepared to give up his engagements. As the following verses will show, the King was contemplating sending for his sons, who were away from home executing austerities and penances. After their return, he would entrust his kingdom to them and then leave home. This is the position of most people. They accept a bona fide spiritual master and listen to him, but when the spiritual master indicates that they should leave home and fully engage in devotional service, they hesitate. The duty of the spiritual master is to instruct the disciple as long as he does not come to the understanding that this materialistic way of life, fruitive activity, is not at all beneficial. Actually one should take to devotional service from the beginning of life, as Prahlāda Mahārāja advised: *kaumāra ācaret prājño dharmān bhāgavatān iha* (*Bhāg.* 7.6.1). According to all the instructions of the *Vedas,* we can understand that unless one takes to Kṛṣṇa consciousness and devotional service, he is simply wasting his time engaging in the fruitive activities of material existence. Nārada Muni therefore decided to relate another allegory to the King so that he might be induced to give up family life within material existence.

TEXT 53

क्षुद्रंश्चरं सुमनसां शरणे मिथित्वा
रक्तं षडङ्घ्रिगणसामसु लुब्धकर्णम् ।
अग्रे वृकानसुतृपोऽविगणय्य यान्तं
पृष्ठे मृगं मृगय लुब्धकबाणभिन्नम् ॥५३॥

kṣudrañ caraṁ sumanasāṁ śaraṇe mithitvā
raktaṁ ṣaḍ-aṅghri-gaṇa-sāmasu lubdha-karṇam

agre vṛkān asu-tṛpo 'vigaṇayya yāntaṁ
pṛṣṭhe mṛgaṁ mṛgaya lubdhaka-bāṇa-bhinnam

kṣudram—on grass; *caram*—grazing; *sumanasām*—of a beautiful flower garden; *śaraṇe*—under the protection; *mithitvā*—being united with a woman; *raktam*—attached; *ṣaṭ-aṅghri*—of bumblebees; *gaṇa*—of groups; *sāmasu*—to the singing; *lubdha-karṇam*—whose ear is attracted; *agre*—in front; *vṛkān*—tigers; *asu-tṛpaḥ*—who live at the cost of another's life; *avigaṇayya*—neglecting; *yāntam*—moving; *pṛṣṭhe*—behind; *mṛgam*—the deer; *mṛgaya*—search out; *lubdhaka*—of a hunter; *bāṇa*—by the arrows; *bhinnam*—liable to be pierced.

TRANSLATION

My dear King, please search out that deer who is engaged in eating grass in a very nice flower garden along with his wife. That deer is very much attached to his business, and he is enjoying the sweet singing of the bumblebees in his garden. Just try to understand his position. He is unaware that before him is a tiger which is accustomed to living at the cost of another's flesh. Behind the deer is a hunter, who is threatening to pierce him with sharp arrows. Thus the deer's death is imminent.

PURPORT

Here is an allegory in which the King is advised to find a deer that is always in a dangerous position. Although threatened from all sides, the deer simply eats grass in a nice flower garden, unaware of the danger all around him. All living entities, especially human beings, think themselves very happy in the midst of families. As if living in a flower garden and hearing the sweet humming of bumblebees, everyone is centered around his wife, who is the beauty of family life. The bumblebees' humming may be compared to the talk of children. The human being, just like the deer, enjoys his family without knowing that before him is the factor of time, which is represented by the tiger. The fruitive activities of a living entity simply create another dangerous position and oblige him to accept different types of bodies. For a deer to run after a mirage of water in the desert is not unusual. The deer is also very fond of sex. The conclusion is that one who lives like a deer will be killed in due course of time. Vedic literatures therefore advise that we should understand our constitutional position and take to devotional service before death comes. According to the *Bhāgavatam:*

labdhvā sudurlabham idaṁ bahu-sambhavānte
mānuṣyam arthadam anityam apīha dhīraḥ
tūrṇaṁ yateta na pated anumṛtyu yāvan
niḥśreyasāya viṣayaḥ khalu sarvataḥ syāt
(*Bhāg.* 11.9.29)

After many births we have attained this human form; therefore before death comes, we should engage ourselves in the transcendental loving service of the Lord. That is the fulfillment of human life.

TEXT 54

सुमनः समधर्मणां स्त्रीणां शरण आश्रमे
पुष्पमधुगन्धवत्क्षुद्रतमं काम्यकर्मविपाकजं काम-
सुखलवं जैह्वयौपस्थ्यादि विचिन्वन्तं मिथुनीभूय
तदभिनिवेशितमनसं षडङ्घ्रिगणसामगीतवदति-
मनोहरवनितादिजनालापेष्वतितरामतिप्रलोभितकर्ण-
मग्रे वृकयूथवदात्मन आयुर्हरतोऽहोरात्रान्तान् काल-
लवविशेषानविगणय्य गृहेषु विहरन्तं पृष्ठत एव
परोक्षमनुप्रवृत्तो लुब्धकः कृतान्तोऽन्तःशरेण यमिह
पराविध्यति तमिममात्मानमहो राजन् भिन्नहृदयं
द्रष्टुमर्हसीति ॥५४॥

sumanaḥ-sama-dharmaṇāṁ strīṇāṁ śaraṇa āśrame puṣpa-madhu-gandhavat kṣudratamaṁ kāmya-karma-vipākajaṁ kāma-sukha-lavaṁ jaihvyaupasthyādi vicinvantaṁ mithunī-bhūya tad-abhiniveśita-manasaṁ ṣaḍ-aṅghri-gaṇa-sāma-gīta-vad ati-manohara-vanitādi-janālāpeṣv atitarām ati-pralobhita-karṇam agre vṛka-yūthavad ātmana āyur harato 'ho-rātrān tān kāla-lava-viśeṣān avigaṇayya gṛheṣu viharantaṁ pṛṣṭhata eva parokṣam anupravṛtto lubdhakaḥ kṛtānto 'ntaḥ śareṇa yam iha parāvidhyati tam imam ātmānam aho rājan bhinna-hṛdayaṁ draṣṭum arhasīti.

sumanaḥ—flowers; *sama-dharmaṇām*—exactly like; *strīṇām*—of women; *śaraṇe*—in the shelter; *āśrame*—household life; *puṣpa*—in flowers; *madhu*—

of honey; *gandha*—the flavor; *vat*—like; *kṣudra-tamam*—most insignificant; *kāmya*—desired; *karma*—of activities; *vipāka-jam*—obtained as a result; *kāma-sukha*—of sense gratification; *lavam*—a fragment; *jaihvya*—enjoyment of the tongue; *aupasthya*—sex enjoyment; *ādi*—beginning with; *vicinvantam*—always thinking of; *mithunī-bhūya*—engaging in sex life; *tat*—in his wife; *abhiniveśita*—always absorbed; *manasam*—whose mind; *ṣaṭ-aṅghri*—of bumblebees; *gaṇa*—of crowds; *sāma*—gentle; *gīta*—the chanting; *vat*—like; *ati*—very; *manohara*—attractive; *vanitā-ādi*—beginning with the wife; *jana*—of people; *ālāpeṣu*—to the talks; *atitarām*—excessively; *ati*—very much; *pralobhita*—attracted; *karṇam*—whose ears; *agre*—in front; *vṛka-yūtha*—a group of tigers; *vat*—like; *ātmanaḥ*—of one's self; *āyuḥ*—span of life; *harataḥ*—taking away; *ahaḥ-rātrān*—days and nights; *tān*—all of them; *kāla-lava-viśeṣān*—the moments of time; *avigaṇayya*—without considering; *gṛheṣu*—in household life; *viharantam*—enjoying; *pṛṣṭhataḥ*—from the back; *eva*—certainly; *parokṣam*—without being seen; *anupravṛttaḥ*—following behind; *lubdhakaḥ*—the hunter; *kṛta-antaḥ*—the superintendent of death; *antaḥ*—in the heart; *śareṇa*—by an arrow; *yam*—whom; *iha*—in this world; *parāvidhyati*—pierces; *tam*—that; *imam*—this; *ātmānam*—yourself; *aho rājan*—O King; *bhinna-hṛdayam*—whose heart is pierced; *draṣṭum*—to see; *arhasi*—you ought; *iti*—thus.

TRANSLATION

My dear King, woman, who is very attractive in the beginning but in the end very disturbing, is exactly like the flower, which is attractive in the beginning and detestable at the end. With woman, the living entity is entangled with lusty desires and sex. He thus enjoys a life of sense gratification—from his tongue to his genitals—and in this way the living entity considers himself very happy in family life. United with his wife, he always remains absorbed in such thoughts. He feels great pleasure in hearing the talks of his wife and children, which are like the sweet humming of bumblebees that collect honey from flower to flower. He forgets that before him is time, which is taking away his life span with the passing of day and night. He does not see the gradual diminishing of his life, nor does he care about the superintendent of death, who is trying to kill him from behind. Just try to understand this. You are in a precarious position and are threatened from all sides.

PURPORT

Materialistic life means forgetting one's constitutional position as the eternal servant of Kṛṣṇa, and this forgetfulness is especially enhanced in the *gṛhastha-āśrama.* In the *gṛhastha-āśrama* a young man accepts a young wife who is very beautiful in the beginning, but in due course of time, after giving birth to many children and becoming older and older, she demands many things from the husband to maintain the entire family. At such a time the wife becomes detestable to the very man who accepted her in her younger days. One becomes attached to the *gṛhastha-āśrama* for two reasons only—the wife cooks palatable dishes for the satisfaction of her husband's tongue, and she gives him sexual pleasure at night. A person attached to the *gṛhastha-āśrama* is always thinking of these two things—palatable food and sex enjoyment. The talks of the wife, which are enjoyed as a family recreation, and the talks of the children both attract the living entity. He thus forgets that he has to die someday and has to prepare for the next life if he wants to be put into a congenial body.

The deer in the flower garden is an allegory used by the great sage Nārada to point out to the King that the King himself is similarly entrapped by such surroundings. Actually everyone is surrounded by such a family life, which misleads one. The living entity thus forgets that he has to return home, back to Godhead. He simply becomes entangled in family life. Prahlāda Mahārāja has therefore hinted: *hitvātma-pātaṁ gṛham andha-kūpaṁ vanaṁ gato yad dharim āśrayeta.* Family life is considered a blind well (*andha-kūpam*) into which a person falls and dies without help. Prahlāda Mahārāja recommends that while one's senses are there and one is strong enough, he should abandon the *gṛhastha-āśrama* and take shelter of the lotus feet of the Lord, going to the forest of Vṛndāvana. According to Vedic civilization, one has to give up family life at a certain age (the age of fifty), take *vānaprastha* and eventually remain alone as a *sannyāsī.* That is the prescribed method of Vedic civilization known as *varṇāśrama-dharma.* When one takes *sannyāsa* after enjoying family life, he pleases the Supreme Lord Viṣṇu.

One has to understand one's position in family or worldly life. That is called intelligence. One should not remain always trapped in family life to satisfy his tongue and genitals in association with a wife. In such a way, one simply spoils his life. According to Vedic civilization, it is imperative to give up the family at a certain stage, by force if necessary. Unfortunately, so-called followers of Vedic life do not give up their family even at the end of life, unless they are forced by death. There should be a thorough overhauling of the social system, and society should revert to the Vedic principles, that is, the four *varṇas* and the four *āśramas.*

TEXT 55

स त्वं विचक्ष्य मृगचेष्टितमात्मनोऽन्त-
श्चित्तं नियच्छ हृदि कर्णधुनीं च चित्ते ।

जह्यङ्गनाश्रममसत्तमयूथगाथं
प्रीणीहि हंसशरणं विरम क्रमेण ॥५५॥

sa tvaṁ vicakṣya mṛga-ceṣṭitam ātmano 'ntaś
cittaṁ niyaccha hṛdi karṇa-dhunīṁ ca citte
jahy aṅganāśramam asattama-yūtha-gāthaṁ
prīṇīhi haṁsa-śaraṇaṁ virama krameṇa

saḥ—that very person; *tvam*—you; *vicakṣya*—considering; *mṛga-ceṣṭitam*—the activities of the deer; *ātmanaḥ*—of the self; *antaḥ*—within; *cittam*—consciousness; *niyaccha*—fix; *hṛdi*—in the heart; *karṇa-dhunīm*—aural reception; *ca*—and; *citte*—unto the consciousness; *jahi*—give up; *aṅgana-āśramam*—household life; *asat-tama*—most abominable; *yūtha-gātham*—full of stories of man and woman; *prīṇīhi*—just accept; *haṁsa-śaraṇam*—the shelter of the liberated souls; *virama*—become detached; *krameṇa*—gradually.

TRANSLATION

My dear King, just try to understand the allegorical position of the deer. Be fully conscious of yourself and give up the pleasure of hearing about promotion to heavenly planets by fruitive activity. Give up household life, which is full of sex, as well as stories about such things, and take shelter of the Supreme Personality of Godhead through the mercy of the liberated souls. In this way, please give up your attraction for material existence.

PURPORT

In one of his songs, Śrīla Narottama dāsa Ṭhākura writes:

karma-kāṇḍa, jñāna-kāṇḍa, kevala viṣera bhāṇḍa,
amṛta baliyā yebā khāya
nānā yoni sadā phire, kadarya bhakṣaṇa kare,
tāra janma adhaḥ-pāte yāya

"Fruitive activities and mental speculation are simply cups of poison. Whoever drinks of them, thinking them to be nectar, must struggle very hard life after life, in different types of bodies. Such a person eats all kinds of nonsense and becomes condemned by his activities of so-called sense enjoyment."

People are generally enamored of the fruitive results of worldly activity and mental speculation. They generally desire to be promoted to heavenly planets, merge into the existence of Brahman, or keep themselves in the midst of family life, enchanted by the pleasures of the tongue and genitals. The great sage Nārada clearly instructs King Barhiṣmān not to remain his entire life in the *gṛhastha-āśrama.* Being in the *gṛhastha-āśrama* means being under the control of one's wife. One has to give up all this and put himself into the *āśrama* of the *paramahaṁsa,* that is, put himself under the control of the spiritual master. The *paramahaṁsa-āśrama* is the *āśrama* of the Supreme Personality of Godhead, under whom the spiritual master has taken shelter. The symptoms of the bona fide spiritual master are stated in *Śrīmad-Bhāgavatam:*

tasmād guruṁ prapadyeta
jijñāsuḥ śreya uttamam
śābde pare ca niṣṇātaṁ
brahmaṇy upaśamāśrayam

"Any person who is seriously desirous of achieving real happiness must seek out a bona fide spiritual master and take shelter of him by initiation. The qualification of a spiritual master is that he must have realized the conclusion of the scriptures by deliberation and arguments and thus be able to convince others of these conclusions. Such great personalities who have taken complete shelter of the Supreme Godhead, leaving aside all material considerations, are to be understood as bona fide spiritual masters." (*Bhāg.* 11.3.21)

A *paramahaṁsa* is one who has taken shelter of the Parabrahman, the Supreme Personality of Godhead. If one takes shelter of the *paramahaṁsa* spiritual master, gradually, through training and instruction, he will become detached from worldly life and ultimately return home, back to Godhead. The particular mention of *aṅganāśramam asattama-yūtha-gātham* is very interesting. The whole world is in the clutches of *māyā,* being controlled by woman. Not only is one controlled by the woman who is one's wife, but one is also controlled by so many sex literatures. That is the cause of one's being entangled in the material world. One cannot give up this abominable association through one's own effort, but if one takes shelter of a bona fide spiritual master who is a *paramahaṁsa,* he will gradually be elevated to the platform of spiritual life.

The pleasing words of the *Vedas* that inspire one to elevate oneself to the heavenly planets or merge into the existence of the Supreme are for the less intelligent who are described in *Bhagavad-gītā* as *māyayāpahṛta-jñānāḥ* (those whose knowledge is taken away by the illusory energy). Real knowledge means understanding the miserable condition of material life. One should take shelter of a bona fide liberated soul, the spiritual master, and gradually elevate himself to the spiritual platform and thus become detached from the material world. According to Śrīla Viśvanātha Cakravartī Ṭhākura, *haṁsa-śaraṇam* refers to the cottage in which saintly persons live. Generally a saintly person lives in a remote place in the forest or in a humble cottage. However, we should note that the times have changed. It may be beneficial for a saintly person's own interest to go to the forest and live in a cottage, but if one becomes a preacher, especially in Western countries, he has to invite many classes of men who are accustomed to living in comfortable apartments. Therefore in this age a saintly person has to make proper arrangements to receive people and attract them to the message of Kṛṣṇa consciousness. Śrīla Bhaktisiddhānta Sarasvatī Ṭhākura, perhaps for the first time, introduced palatial buildings and motor cars for the residence of saintly persons just to attract the general public in big cities. The main fact is that one has to associate with a saintly person. In this age people are not going to search out a saint in the forest, so the saints and sages have to come to the big cities to make arrangements to receive the people in general, who are accustomed to the modern amenities of material life. Gradually such persons will learn that palatial buildings or comfortable apartments are not at all necessary. The real necessity is to become free from material bondage in whatever way possible. According to the orders of Śrīla Rūpa Gosvāmī:

anāsaktasya viṣayān
yathārham upayuñjataḥ
nirbandhaḥ kṛṣṇa-sambandhe
yuktaṁ vairāgyam ucyate

"When one is not attached to anything, but at the same time accepts everything in relation to Kṛṣṇa, one is rightly situated above possessiveness." (Bh.r.s. 1.2.255)

One should not be attached to material opulence, but material opulence may be accepted in the Kṛṣṇa consciousness movement to facilitate the propagation of the movement. In other words, material opulence may be accepted as *yukta-vairāgya,* that is, for renunciation.

TEXT 56

राजोवाच

श्रुतमन्वीक्षितं ब्रह्मन् भगवान् यदभाषत ।
नैतज्जानन्त्युपाध्यायाः किं न ब्रूयुर्विदुर्यदि ॥५६॥

rājovāca
śrutam anvīkṣitaṁ brahman
bhagavān yad abhāṣata
naitaj jānanty upādhyāyāḥ
kiṁ na brūyur vidur yadi

rājā uvāca—the King said; *śrutam*—was heard; *anvīkṣitam*—was considered; *brahman*—O *brāhmaṇa; bhagavān*—the most powerful; *yat*—which; *abhāṣata*—you have spoken; *na*—not; *etat*—this; *jānanti*—do know; *upādhyāyāḥ*—the teachers of fruitive activities; *kim*—why; *na brūyuḥ*—they did not instruct; *viduḥ*—they understood; *yadi*—if.

TRANSLATION

The King replied: My dear brāhmaṇa, whatever you have said I have heard with great attention, and, considering all of it, have come to the conclusion that the ācāryas [teachers] who engaged me in fruitive activity did not know this confidential knowledge. If they were aware of it, why did they not explain it to me?

PURPORT

Actually the so-called teachers or leaders of material society do not really know the goal of life. They are described in *Bhagavad-gītā* as *māyayāpahṛta-jñānāḥ*. They appear to be very learned scholars, but actually the influence of the illusory energy has taken away their knowledge. Real knowledge means searching out Kṛṣṇa.

sarvasya cāhaṁ hṛdi sanniviṣṭo
mattaḥ smṛtir jñānam apohanaṁ ca
vedaiś ca sarvair aham eva vedyo
vedānta-kṛd veda-vid eva cāham

"I am seated in everyone's heart, and from Me come remembrance, knowledge and forgetfulness. By all the *Vedas,* I am to be known; indeed, I am the compiler of *Vedānta,* and I am the knower of the *Vedas.*" (Bg. 15.15)

All Vedic knowledge is meant for searching out Kṛṣṇa because Kṛṣṇa is the origin of everything. *Janmādy asya yataḥ.* In *Bhagavad-gītā* Kṛṣṇa says:

na me viduḥ sura-gaṇāḥ
prabhavaṁ na maharṣayaḥ
aham ādir hi devānāṁ
maharṣīṇāṁ ca sarvaśaḥ

"Neither the hosts of demigods nor the great sages know My origin, for, in every respect, I am the source of the demigods and the sages." (Bg. 10.2)

Kṛṣṇa is the origin and beginning of all demigods, including Lord Brahmā, Lord Śiva and all others. The Vedic ritualistic ceremonies are concerned with satisfying different demigods, but unless one is very advanced, he cannot understand that the original personality is Śrī Kṛṣṇa. *Govindam ādi-puruṣaṁ tam ahaṁ bhajāmi.* After hearing the instructions of Nārada, King Barhiṣmān came to his senses. The real goal of life is to attain devotional service to the Supreme Personality of Godhead. The King therefore decided to reject the so-called priestly orders that simply engage their followers in the ritualistic ceremonies without giving effective instructions about the goal of life. At the present moment the churches, temples and mosques all over the world are not attracting people because foolish priests cannot elevate their followers to the platform of knowledge. Not being aware of the real goal of life, they simply keep their congregation in ignorance. Consequently those who are well educated have become uninterested in the ritualistic ceremonies. At the same time, they are not benefited with real knowledge. This Kṛṣṇa consciousness movement is therefore very important for the enlightenment of all classes. Following in the footsteps of Mahārāja Barhiṣmān, everyone should take advantage of this Kṛṣṇa consciousness movement and abandon the stereotyped ritualistic ceremonies that go under the garb of so many religions. The Gosvāmīs from the very beginning differed from the priestly class that was engaged in ritualistic ceremonies. Indeed, Śrīla Sanātana Gosvāmī compiled his *Hari-bhakti-vilāsa* for the guidance of the Vaiṣṇavas. The Vaiṣṇavas, not caring for the lifeless activities of the priestly classes, take to full Kṛṣṇa consciousness and become perfect in this very life. That is described in the previous verse as *paramhaṁsa-śaraṇam,* taking shelter of the *paramhaṁsa,* the liberated soul, and becoming successful in this life.

TEXT 57

संशयोऽत्र तु मे विप्र संछिन्नस्तत्कृतो महान् ।
ऋषयोऽपि हि मुह्यन्ति यत्र नेन्द्रियवृत्तयः ॥५७॥

saṁśayo 'tra tu me vipra
sañchinnas tat-kṛto mahān
ṛṣayo 'pi hi muhyanti
yatra nendriya-vṛttayaḥ

saṁśayaḥ—doubt; *atra*—here; *tu*—but; *me*—my; *vipra*—O *brāhmaṇa; sañchinnaḥ*—cleared; *tat-kṛtaḥ*—done by that; *mahān*—very great; *ṛṣayaḥ*—the great sages; *api*—even; *hi*—certainly; *muhyanti*—are bewildered; *yatra*—where; *na*—not; *indriya*—of the senses; *vṛttayaḥ*—activities.

TRANSLATION

My dear brāhmaṇa, there are contradictions between your instructions and those of my spiritual teachers who engaged me in fruitive activities. I now can understand the distinction between devotional service, knowledge and renunciation. I had some doubts about them, but you have now very kindly dissipated all these doubts. I can now understand how even the great sages are bewildered by the real purpose of life. Of course, there is no question of sense gratification.

PURPORT

King Barhiṣmān was engaged in different types of sacrifice for elevation to the heavenly planets. People generally are attracted by these activities, and very rarely is a person attracted to devotional service, as Śrī Caitanya Mahāprabhu confirms. Unless one is very very fortunate, he does not take to devotional service. Even the so-called learned Vedic scholars are bewildered by devotional service. They are generally attracted to the rituals for sense gratification. In devotional service there is no sense gratification but only transcendental loving service to the Lord. Consequently the so-called priests engaged in sense gratification do not very much like devotional service. The *brāhmaṇas,* the priests, have been against this Kṛṣṇa consciousness movement since it began with Lord Caitanya Mahāprabhu. When Caitanya Mahāprabhu started this movement, the priestly class lodged complaints to the Kazi, the magistrate of the Mohammedan government. Caitanya Mahāprabhu had to lead a civil disobedience movement against the propaganda of the so-called followers of Vedic principles. These people are described as *karma-jaḍa-smārtas,* which indicates that they are priests engaged in ritualistic ceremonies. It is here stated that such people become bewildered (*ṛṣayo 'pi hi muhyanti*). To save oneself from the hands of these *karma-jaḍa-smārtas,* one should strictly follow the instructions of the Supreme Personality of Godhead.

sarva-dharmān parityajya
mām ekaṁ śaraṇaṁ vraja
ahaṁ tvāṁ sarva-pāpebhyo
mokṣayiṣyāmi mā śucaḥ

"Abandon all varieties of religion and just surrender unto Me. I shall deliver you from all sinful reaction. Do not fear." (Bg. 18.66)

TEXT 58

कर्माण्यारभते येन पुमानिह विहाय तम् ।
अमुत्रान्येन देहेन जुष्टानि स यदश्नुते ॥५८॥

karmāṇy ārabhate yena
pumān iha vihāya tam
amutrānyena dehena
juṣṭāni sa yad aśnute

karmāṇi—fruitive activities; *ārabhate*—begins to perform; *yena*—by which; *pumān*—a living entity; *iha*—in this life; *vihāya*—giving up; *tam*—that; *amutra*—in the next life; *anyena*—another; *dehena*—by a body; *juṣṭāni*—the results; *saḥ*—he; *yat*—that; *aśnute*—enjoys.

TRANSLATION

The results of whatever a living entity does in this life are enjoyed in the next life.

PURPORT

A person generally does not know how one body is linked with another body. How is it possible that one suffers or enjoys the results of activities in this body in yet another body in the next life. This is a question the King wants Nārada Muni to answer. How may one have a human body in this life and not have a human body in the next? Even great philosophers and scientists cannot account for the transferral of *karma* from one body to another. As we experience, every individual soul has an individual body, and one person's activities, or one body's activities, are not enjoyed or suffered by another body or another person. The question is how the activities of one body are suffered or enjoyed in the next.

TEXT 59

इति वेदविदां वादः श्रूयते तत्र तत्र ह ।
कर्म यत्क्रियते प्रोक्तं परोक्षं न प्रकाशते ॥५९॥

iti veda-vidāṁ vādaḥ
śrūyate tatra tatra ha
karma yat kriyate proktaṁ
parokṣaṁ na prakāśate

iti—thus; *veda-vidām*—of persons who know the Vedic conclusions; *vādaḥ*—the thesis; *śrūyate*—is heard; *tatra tatra*—here and there; *ha*—certainly; *karma*—the activity; *yat*—what; *kriyate*—is performed; *proktam*—as it was said; *parokṣam*—unknown; *na prakāśate*—is not directly manifested.

TRANSLATION

The expert knowers of the Vedic conclusions say that one enjoys or suffers the results of his past activities. But practically it is seen that the body that performed the work in the last birth is already lost. So how is it possible to enjoy or suffer the reactions of that work in a different body?

PURPORT

Atheists want evidence for the resultant actions of past activities. Therefore they ask, "Where is the proof that I am suffering and enjoying the resultant actions of past *karma*?" They have no idea how the subtle body carries the results of the present body's actions down to the next gross body. The present body may be finished grossly, but the subtle body is not finished; it carries the soul to the next body. Actually the gross body is dependent on the subtle body. Therefore the next gross body must suffer and enjoy according to the subtle body. The soul is carried by the subtle body continuously until liberated from gross material bondage.

TEXT 60

नारद उवाच
येनैवारभते कर्म तेनैवामुत्र तत्पुमान् ।
भुङ्क्ते ह्यव्यवधानेन लिङ्गेन मनसा स्वयम् ॥६०॥

nārada uvāca
yenaivārabhate karma
tenaivāmutra tat pumān
bhuṅkte hy avyavadhānena
liṅgena manasā svayam

nāradaḥ uvāca—Nārada said; *yena*—by which; *eva*—certainly; *ārabhate*—begins; *karma*—fruitive activities; *tena*—by that body; *eva*—certainly; *amutra*—in the next life; *tat*—that; *pumān*—the living entity; *bhuṅkte*—enjoys; *hi*—because; *avyavadhānena*—without any change; *liṅgena*—by the subtle body; *manasā*—by the mind; *svayam*—personally.

TRANSLATION

The great sage Nārada continued: The living entity acts in a gross body in this life. This body is forced to act by the subtle body, composed of mind, intelligence and ego. After the gross body is lost, the subtle body is still there to enjoy or suffer. Thus there is no change.

PURPORT

The living entity has two kinds of body—the subtle body and the gross body. Actually he enjoys through the subtle body, which is composed of mind, intelligence and ego. The gross body is the instrumental outer covering. When the gross body is lost, or when it dies, the root of the gross body—the mind, intelligence and ego—continue and bring about another gross body. Although the gross bodies apparently change, the real root of the gross body—the subtle body of mind, intelligence and ego—is always there. The subtle body's activities—be they pious or impious—create another situation for the living entity to enjoy or suffer in the next gross body. Thus the subtle body continues whereas the gross bodies change one after another.

Since modern scientists and philosophers are too materialistic, and since their knowledge is taken away by the illusory energy, they cannot explain how the gross body is changing. The materialistic philosopher Darwin has tried to study the changes of the gross body, but because he had no knowledge of either the subtle body or the soul, he could not clearly explain how the evolutionary process is going on. One may change the gross body, but he works in the subtle body. People cannot understand the activities of the subtle body, and consequently they are bewildered as to how the actions of one gross body affect another gross body. The activities of the subtle body are also guided by the Supersoul, as explained in *Bhagavad-gītā:*

sarvasya cāhaṁ hṛdi sanniviṣṭo
mattaḥ smṛtir jñānam apohanaṁ ca
vedaiś ca sarvair aham eva vedyo
vedānta-kṛd veda-vid eva cāham

"I am seated in everyone's heart, and from Me come remembrance, knowledge and forgetfulness. By all the *Vedas,* I am to be known; indeed I am the compiler of *Vedānta,* and I am the knower of the *Vedas.*" (Bg. 15.15)

Because the Supreme Personality of Godhead as Supersoul is always guiding the individual soul, the individual soul always knows how to act according to the reactions of his past *karma.* In other words, the Supersoul reminds him to act in such a way. Therefore although there is apparently a change in the gross body, there is a continuation between the lives of an individual soul.

TEXT 61

शयानमिममुत्सृज्य श्वसन्तं पुरुषो यथा ।
कर्मात्मन्याहितं भुङ्क्ते तादृशेनेतरेण वा ॥६१॥

śayānam imam utsṛjya
śvasantaṁ puruṣo yathā
karmātmany āhitaṁ bhuṅkte
tādṛśenetareṇa vā

śayānam—lying down on a bed; *imam*—this body; *utsṛjya*—after giving up; *śvasantam*—breathing; *puruṣaḥ*—the living entity; *yathā*—as; *karma*—activity; *ātmani*—in the mind; *āhitam*—executed; *bhuṅkte*—enjoys; *tādṛśena*—by a similar body; *itareṇa*—by a different body; *vā*—or.

TRANSLATION

The living entity, while dreaming, gives up the actual living body. Through the activities of his mind and intelligence, he acts in another body, either as a god or a dog. After giving up this gross body, the living entity enters either an animal body or a demigod's body on this planet or on another planet. He thus enjoys the results of the actions of his past life.

PURPORT

Although the root of distress and happiness is the mind, intelligence and ego, a gross body is still required as an instrument for enjoyment. The gross body may change, but the subtle body continues to act. Unless the living entity gets another gross body, he will have to continue in a subtle body, or a ghostly body. One becomes a ghost when the subtle body acts without the help of the instrumental gross body. As stated in this verse, *śayānam imam utsṛjya śvasantam.* The gross body may lie on a bed and rest, and even though the machinery of the gross body is working, the living entity may leave, go into a dream, and return to the gross body. When he returns to the body, he forgets his dream. Similarly, when the living entity takes on another gross body, he forgets the present gross body. The conclusion is that the subtle body—mind, intelligence and ego—creates an atmosphere with desires and ambitions that the living entity enjoys in the subtle body. Actually the living entity is in the subtle body, even though the gross body apparently changes and even though he inhabits the gross body on various planets. All the activities performed by the living entity in the subtle body are called illusory because they are not permanent. Liberation means getting out of the clutches of the subtle body. Liberation from the gross body simply involves the transmigration of the soul from one gross body to another. When the mind is educated in Kṛṣṇa consciousness, or higher consciousness in the mode of goodness, one is transferred either to the upper heavenly planets or to the spiritual world, the Vaikuṇṭha planets. One therefore has to change his consciousness by cultivating knowledge received from Vedic instructions from the Supreme Personality of Godhead through the disciplic succession. If we train the subtle body in this life by always thinking about Kṛṣṇa, we will transfer to Kṛṣṇaloka after leaving the gross body. This is confirmed by the Supreme Personality of Godhead.

janma karma ca me divyam
evaṁ yo vetti tattvataḥ
tyaktvā dehaṁ punar janma
naiti mām eti so 'rjuna

"One who knows the transcendental nature of My appearance and activities does not, upon leaving the body, take his birth again in this material world, but attains My eternal abode, O Arjuna." (Bg. 4.9)

Thus the change of the gross body is not very important, but the change of the subtle body is important. The Kṛṣṇa consciousness movement is educating people to enlighten the subtle body. The perfect example in this regard is Ambarīṣa Mahārāja, who always engaged his mind on the lotus feet of Lord Kṛṣṇa. *Sa vai manaḥ kṛṣṇa-padāravindayoḥ.* Similarly, in this life we should always fix our mind on the lotus feet of Kṛṣṇa, who is present in His *arcā-vigraha,* the incarnation of the Deity in the temple. We should also always engage in His worship. If we engage our speech in describing the activities of the Lord and our ears in hearing about His pastimes, and if we follow the regulative principles to keep the mind intact for advancing in Kṛṣṇa consciousness, we shall certainly be elevated to the spiritual platform. Then at the time of death the mind, intelligence and ego will no longer be materially contaminated. The living entity is present, and the mind, intelligence and ego are also present. When the mind, intelligence and ego are purified, all the active senses of the living entity become spiritual. Thus the living entity attains his *sac-cid-ānanda-vigraha* form. The Supreme Lord is always in His *sac-cid-ānanda-vigraha* form, but the living entity, although part and parcel of the Lord, becomes materially contaminated when he desires to come to the material world for material enjoyment. The prescription for returning home, back to Godhead, is given by the Lord Himself in *Bhagavad-gītā:*

man-manā bhava mad-bhakto
mad-yājī māṁ namaskuru
mām evaiṣyasi yuktvaivam
ātmānaṁ mat-parāyaṇaḥ

"Always think of Me and become My devotee. Worship Me and offer your homage unto Me. Being completely absorbed in Me, surely you will come to Me." (Bg. 9.34)

TEXT 62

ममैते मनसा यद्यदसावहमिति ब्रुवन् ।
गृह्णीयात्तत्पुमान् राद्धं कर्म येन पुनर्भवः ॥६२॥

mamaite manasā yad yad
asāv aham iti bruvan

gṛhṇīyāt tat pumān rāddhaṁ
karma yena punar bhavaḥ

mama—mine; *ete*—all these; *manasā*—by the mind; *yat yat*—whatever; *asau*—that; *aham*—I (am); *iti*—thus; *bruvan*—accepting; *gṛhṇīyāt*—takes with him; *tat*—that; *pumān*—the living entity; *rāddham*—perfected; *karma*—work; *yena*—by which; *punaḥ*—again; *bhavaḥ*—material existence.

TRANSLATION

The living entity labors under the bodily conception of "I am this, I am that. My duty is this, and therefore I shall do it." These are all mental impressions, and all these activities are temporary; nonetheless, by the grace of the Supreme Personality of Godhead, the living entity gets a chance to execute all his mental concoctions. Thus he gets another body.

PURPORT

As long as one is absorbed in the bodily conception, his activities are performed on that platform. This is not very difficult to understand. In the world, we see that every nation is trying to supersede every other nation and that every man is trying to advance beyond his fellow man. All these activities are going on under the name of advancement of civilization. There are many plans for making the body comfortable, and these plans are carried in the subtle body after the destruction of the gross body. It is not a fact that after the gross body is destroyed the living entity is finished. Although many great philosophers and teachers in this world are under the impression that after the body is finished everything is finished, this is not a fact. Nārada Muni says in this verse that at death one takes his plans with him (*gṛhṇīyāt*), and to execute these plans he gets another body. This is called *punar bhavaḥ*. When the gross body is finished, the plans of the living entity are taken by the mind, and, by the grace of the Lord, the living entity gets a chance to give these plans shape in the next life. This is known as the law of *karma*. As long as the mind is absorbed in the laws of *karma*, a certain type of body must be accepted in the next life.

Karma is the aggregate of fruitive activities conducted to make this body comfortable or uncomfortable. We have actually seen that when one man was about to die he requested his physician to give him a chance to live four more years so that he could finish his plans. This means that while dying he was thinking of his plans. After his body was destroyed, he doubtlessly carried his plans with him by means of the subtle body composed of mind, intelligence and ego. Thus he would get another chance by the grace of the Supreme Lord, the Supersoul, who is always within the heart.

sarvasya cāhaṁ hṛdi sanniviṣṭo
mattaḥ smṛtir jñānam apohanaṁ ca
vedaiś ca sarvair aham eva vedyo
vedānta-kṛd veda-vid eva cāham

"I am seated in everyone's heart, and from Me come remembrance, knowledge and forgetfulness. By all the *Vedas*, I am to be known; indeed I am the compiler of *Vedānta*, and I am the knower of the *Vedas*." (Bg. 15.15)

In the next birth, one acquires remembrance from the Supersoul and begins to execute the plans begun in the previous life. This is also explained in *Bhagavad-gītā* in another verse:

īśvaraḥ sarva-bhūtānāṁ
hṛd-deśe 'rjuna tiṣṭhati
bhrāmayan sarva-bhūtāni
yantrārūḍhāni māyayā

"The Supreme Lord is situated in everyone's heart, O Arjuna, and is directing the wanderings of all living entities, who are seated as on a machine, made of the material energy." (Bg. 18.61)

Situated on the vehicle given by material nature and reminded by the Supersoul within the heart, the living entity struggles all over the universe to fulfill his plans, thinking, "I am a *brāhmaṇa*, I am a *kṣatriya*. I am an American, I am an Indian," and so on. All these designations are of the same essence. There is no point in becoming a *brāhmaṇa* in preference to an American or becoming an American in preference to a Negro. After all, these are all bodily conceptions under the modes of material nature.

TEXT 63

यथानुमीयते चित्तमुभयैरिन्द्रियेहितैः ।
एवं प्राग्देहजं कर्म लक्ष्यते चित्तवृत्तिभिः ॥६३॥

yathānumīyate cittam
ubhayair indriyehitaiḥ
evaṁ prāg-dehajaṁ karma
lakṣyate citta-vṛttibhiḥ

yathā—as; *anumīyate*—can be imagined; *cittam*—one's consciousness or mental condition; *ubhayaiḥ*—both; *indriya*—of the senses; *īhitaiḥ*—by the activities; *evam*—similarly; *prāk*—previous; *deha-jam*—performed by the body; *karma*—activities; *lakṣyate*—can be perceived; *citta*—of consciousness; *vṛttibhiḥ*—by the occupations.

TRANSLATION

One can understand the mental or conscious position of a living entity by the activities of two kinds of senses—the knowledge-acquiring senses and the executive senses. Similarly, by the mental condition or consciousness of a person, one can understand his position in the previous life.

PURPORT

There is an English proverb that says, "The face is the index of the mind." If one is angry, his anger is immediately expressed in his face. Similarly, other mental states are reflected by the actions of the gross body. In other words, the activities of the gross body are reactions of the mental condition. The mind's activities are thinking, feeling and willing. The willing portion of the mind is manifest by the activities of the body. The conclusion is that by the activities of the body and senses, we can understand the condition of the mind. The condition of the mind is affected by past activities in the past body. When the mind is joined with a particular sense, it immediately becomes manifest in a certain way. For instance, when there is anger in the mind, the tongue vibrates so many maledictions. Similarly, when the mind's anger is expressed through the hand, there is fighting. When it is expressed through the leg, there is kicking. There are so many ways in which the subtle activities of the mind are expressed through the various senses. The mind of a person in Kṛṣṇa consciousness also acts in a similar way. The tongue chants Hare Kṛṣṇa, the *mahā-mantra,* the hands are raised in ecstasy, and the legs dance in Kṛṣṇa consciousness. These symptoms are technically called *aṣṭa-sāttvika-vikāra.* This is transformation of the mental condition in goodness or sometimes transcendental ecstasy.

TEXT 64

नानुभूतं क्व चानेन देहेनादृष्टमश्रुतम् ।
कदाचिदुपलभ्येत यद्रूपं यादृगात्मनि ॥६४॥

nānubhūtaṁ kva cānena
dehenādṛṣṭam aśrutam
kadācid upalabhyeta
yad rūpaṁ yādṛg ātmani

na—never; *anubhūtam*—experienced; *kva*—at any time; *ca*—also; *anena dehena*—by this body; *adṛṣṭam*—never seen; *aśrutam*—never heard; *kadācit*—sometimes; *upalabhyeta*—may be experienced; *yat*—which; *rūpam*—form; *yādṛk*—whatever kind; *ātmani*—in the mind.

TRANSLATION

Sometimes we suddenly experience something that was never experienced in the present body by sight or hearing. Sometimes we see such things suddenly in dreams.

PURPORT

We sometimes see things in dreams that we have never experienced in the present body. Sometimes in dreams we think that we are flying in the sky, although we have no experience of flying. This means that once in a previous life, either as a demigod or astronaut, we flew in the sky. The impression is there in the stockpile of the mind, and it suddenly expresses itself. It is like fermentation taking place in the depths of water, which sometimes manifests itself in bubbles on the water's surface. Sometimes we dream of coming to a place we have never known or experienced in this lifetime, but this is proof that in a past life we experienced this. The impression is kept within the mind and sometimes becomes manifest either in dream or in thought. The conclusion is that the mind is the storehouse of various thoughts and experiences undergone during our past lives. Thus there is a chain of continuation from one life to another, from previous lives to this life, and from this life to future lives. This is also sometimes proved by saying that a man is a born poet, a born scientist or a born devotee. If, like Mahārāja Ambarīṣa, we think of Kṛṣṇa constantly in this life (*sa vai manaḥ kṛṣṇa-padāravindayoḥ*), we will certainly be transferred to the kingdom of God at the time of death. Even if our attempt to be Kṛṣṇa conscious is not complete, our Kṛṣṇa consciousness will continue in the next life. This is confirmed in *Bhagavad-gītā:*

prāpya puṇya-kṛtāṁ lokān
uṣitvā śāśvatīḥ samāḥ

śucīnāṁ śrīmatāṁ gehe
yoga-bhraṣṭo 'bhijāyate

"The unsuccessful *yogī*, after many, many years of enjoyment on the planets of the pious living entities, is born into a family of righteous people, or into a family of rich aristocracy." (Bg. 6.41)

If we rigidly follow the principles of meditation on Kṛṣṇa, there is no doubt that in our next life we will be transferred to Kṛṣṇaloka, Goloka Vṛndāvana.

TEXT 65

तेनास्य तादृशं राजँल्लिङ्गिनो देहसम्भवम् ।
श्रद्धत्स्वाननुभूतोऽर्थो न मनः स्प्रष्टुमर्हति ॥६५॥

tenāsya tādṛśaṁ rājaḻ̃
liṅgino deha-sambhavam
śraddhatsvānanubhūto 'rtho
na manaḥ spraṣṭum arhati

tena—therefore; *asya*—of the living entity; *tādṛśam*—like that; *rājan*—O King; *liṅginaḥ*—who has a subtle mental covering; *deha-sambhavam*—produced in the previous body; *śraddhatsva*—accept it as fact; *ananubhūtaḥ*—not perceived; *arthaḥ*—a thing; *na*—never; *manaḥ*—in the mind; *spraṣṭum*—to manifest; *arhati*—is able.

TRANSLATION

My dear King, the living entity, who has a subtle mental covering, develops all kinds of thoughts and images because of his previous body. Take this from me as certain. There is no possibility of concocting anything mentally without having perceived it in the previous body.

PURPORT

kṛṣṇa-bahirmukha hañā bhoga-vāñchā kare
nikaṭa-stha māyā tāre jāpaṭiyā dhare
(*Prema-vivarta* 6.2)

Actually the Supreme Personality of Godhead, Kṛṣṇa, is the supreme enjoyer. When a living entity wants to imitate Him, he is given a chance to satisfy his false desire to lord it over material nature. That is the beginning of his downfall. As long as he is within this material atmosphere, he has a subtle vehicle in the form of the mind, which is the stockpile of all kinds of material desires. Such desires become manifest in different bodily forms. Śrīla Nārada Muni requests the King to accept this fact from him because he is an authority. The conclusion is that the mind is the storehouse of our past desires, and we have this present body due to our past desires. Similarly, whatever we desire in this present body will be expressed in a future body. Thus the mind is the source of different kinds of bodies.

If the mind is purified by Kṛṣṇa consciousness, one will naturally in the future get a body that is spiritual and full of Kṛṣṇa consciousness. Such a body is our original form, as Śrī Caitanya Mahāprabhu confirms: *jīvera 'svarūpa' haya——kṛṣṇera 'nitya-dāsa'.* "Every living entity is constitutionally an eternal servant of Kṛṣṇa." If a person is engaged in the devotional service of the Lord, he is to be considered a liberated soul even in this life. This is confirmed by Śrīla Rūpa Gosvāmī:

īhā yasya harer dāsye
karmaṇā manasā girā
nikhilāsv apy avasthāsu
jīvan-muktaḥ sa ucyate

"One who engages in the transcendental service of the Lord in body, mind, and word is to be considered liberated in all conditions of material existence." (Bh.r.s. 1.2.187) The Kṛṣṇa consciousness movement is based on this principle. We must teach people to absorb themselves always in the service of the Lord because that position is their natural position. One who is always serving the Lord is to be considered already liberated. This is also confirmed in *Bhagavad-gītā:*

māṁ ca yo 'vyabhicāreṇa
bhakti-yogena sevate
sa guṇān samatītyaitān
brahma-bhūyāya kalpate

"One who engages in full devotional service, who does not fall down in any circumstance, at once transcends the modes of material nature and thus comes to the level of Brahman." (Bg. 14.26)

The devotee is therefore above the three modes of material nature and is even transcendental to the *brāhmaṇa* platform. A *brāhmaṇa* may be infected by the two baser modes–namely *rajo-guṇa* and *tamo-guṇa.* A pure devotee, who is free from all material desires experienced on the mental platform and who is also free from empiric philosophical speculation or fruitive activity, is always above material conditioning and is always liberated.

TEXT 66

मन एव मनुष्यस्य पूर्वरूपाणि शंसति ।
भविष्यतश्च भद्रं ते तथैव न भविष्यतः ॥६६॥

mana eva manuṣyasya
pūrva-rūpāṇi śaṁsati
bhaviṣyataś ca bhadraṁ te
tathaiva na bhaviṣyataḥ

manaḥ—the mind; *eva*—certainly; *manuṣyasya*—of a man; *pūrva*—past; *rūpāṇi*—forms; *śaṁsati*—indicates; *bhaviṣyataḥ*—of one who will take birth; *ca*—also; *bhadram*—good fortune; *te*—unto you; *tathā*—thus; *eva*—certainly; *na*—not; *bhaviṣyataḥ*—of one who will take birth.

TRANSLATION

O King, all good fortune unto you! The mind is the cause of the living entity's attaining a certain type of body in accordance with his association with material nature. According to one's mental composition, one can understand what the living entity was in his past life as well as what kind of body he will have in the future. Thus the mind indicates the past and future bodies.

PURPORT

The mind is the index of information about one's past and future life. If a man is a devotee of the Lord, he cultivated devotional service in his previous life. Similarly, if one's mind is criminal, he was criminal in his last life. In the same way, according to the mind, we can understand what will happen in a future life. In *Bhagavad-gītā* it is said:

ūrdhvaṁ gacchanti sattva-sthā
madhye tiṣṭhanti rājasāḥ
jaghanya-guṇa-vṛtti-sthā
adho gacchanti tāmasāḥ

"Those situated in the mode of goodness gradually go upward to the higher planets; those in the mode of passion live on the earthly planets;

and those in the mode of ignorance go down to the hellish worlds." (Bg. 14.18)

If a person is in the mode of goodness, his mental activities will promote him to a higher planetary system. Similarly, if he has a low mentality, his future life will be most abominable. The lives of the living entity, in both the past and the future, are indicated by the mental condition. Nārada Muni is herein offering the King blessings of all good fortune so that the King will not desire anything or make plans for sense gratification. The King was engaged in fruitive ritualistic ceremonies because he hoped to get a better life in the future. Nārada Muni desired him to give up all mental concoctions. As explained before, all bodies in heavenly planets and hellish planets arise from mental concoctions, and the sufferings and enjoyments of material life are simply on the mental platform. They take place on the chariot of the mind (*mano-ratha*). It is therefore said:

yasyāsti bhaktir bhagavaty akiñcanā
sarvair guṇais tatra samāsate surāḥ
harāv abhaktasya kuto mahad-guṇā
mano-rathenāsati dhāvato bahiḥ

"One who has unflinching devotion for the Personality of Godhead has all the good qualities of the demigods. But one who is not a devotee of the Lord has only material qualifications that are of little value. This is because he is hovering on the mental plane and is certain to be attracted by the glaring material energy." (*Bhāg.* 5.18.12)

Unless one becomes a devotee of the Lord or becomes fully Kṛṣṇa conscious, he will certainly hover on the mental platform and be promoted and degraded in different types of bodies. All qualities that are considered good according to the material estimation actually have no value because these so-called good qualities will not save a person from the cycle of birth and death. The conclusion is that one should be without mental desire. *Anyābhilāṣitā-śūnyaṁ jñāna-karmādy-anāvṛtam:* one should be fully free from material desires, philosophical speculation and fruitive activity. The best course for a human being is to favorably accept the transcendental devotional service of the Lord. That is the highest perfection of human life.

TEXT 67

अदृष्टमश्रुतं चात्र क्वचिन्मनसि दृश्यते ।
यथा तथानुमन्तव्यं देशकालक्रियाश्रयम् ॥६७॥

adṛṣṭam aśrutaṁ cātra
kvacin manasi dṛśyate
yathā tathānumantavyaṁ
deśa-kāla-kriyāśrayam

adṛṣṭam—never experienced; *aśrutam*—never heard; *ca*—and; *atra*—in this life; *kvacit*—at some time; *manasi*—in the mind; *dṛśyate*—is visible; *yathā*—as; *tathā*—accordingly; *anumantavyam*—to be understood; *deśa*—place; *kāla*—time; *kriyā*—activity; *āśrayam*—depending on.

TRANSLATION

Sometimes in a dream we see something never experienced or heard of in this life, but all these incidents have been experienced at different times, in different places and in different conditions.

PURPORT

In the previous verse it was explained that in dreams we see that which was experienced during the day. But why is it that we sometimes in our dreams see what we have never heard of or seen at any time during this life? Here it is stated that even though such events may not be experienced in this life, they were experienced in previous lives. According to time and circumstance, they combine so that in dreams we see something wonderful that we have never experienced. For instance, we may see an ocean on the peak of a mountain. Or we may see that the ocean has dried up. These are simply combinations of different experiences in time and space. Sometimes we may see a golden mountain, and this is due to our having experienced gold and mountains separately. In the dream, under illusion, we combine these separate factors. In this way we are able to see golden mountains or stars during the day. The conclusion is that these are all mental concoctions, although they have actually been experienced in different circumstances. They have simply combined together in a dream. This fact is further explained in the following verse.

TEXT 68

सर्वे क्रमानुरोधेन मनसीन्द्रियगोचराः ।
आयान्ति बहुशो यान्ति सर्वे समनसो जनाः ॥६८॥

sarve kramānurodhena
manasīndriya-gocarāḥ
āyānti bahuśo yānti
sarve samanaso janāḥ

sarve—all; *krama-anurodhena*—in order of chronology; *manasi*—in the mind; *indriya*—by the senses; *gocarāḥ*—experienced; *āyānti*—come; *bahuśaḥ*—in many ways; *yānti*—go away; *sarve*—all; *sa-manasaḥ*—with a mind; *janāḥ*—living entities.

TRANSLATION

The mind of the living entity continues to exist in various gross bodies, and according to one's desires for sense gratification, the mind records different thoughts. In the mind these appear together in different combinations; therefore these images sometimes appear as things never seen or never heard.

PURPORT

The activities of the living entity in the body of a dog may be experienced in the mind of a different body; therefore those activities appear never to have been heard or seen. The mind continues, although the body changes. Even in this lifespan we can sometimes experience dreams of our childhood. Although such incidents now appear strange, it is to be understood that they are recorded in the mind. Because of this, they become visible in dreams. The transmigration of the soul is caused by the subtle body, which is the storehouse of all kinds of material desires. Unless one is fully absorbed in Kṛṣṇa consciousness, material desires will come and go. That is the nature of the mind—thinking, feeling and willing. As long as the mind is not engaged in meditation on the lotus feet of the Supreme Personality of Godhead, Kṛṣṇa, the mind will desire so many material enjoyments. Sensual images are recorded in the mind in chronological order, and they become manifest one after another; therefore the living entity has to accept one body after another. The mind plans material enjoyment, and the gross body serves as the instrument to realize such desires and plans. The mind is the platform onto which all desires come and go. Śrīla Narottama dāsa Ṭhākura therefore sings:

guru-mukha-padma-vākya, cittete kariyā aikya,
āra nā kariha mane āśā

Narottama dāsa Ṭhākura advises everyone to stick to the principle of carrying out the orders of the spiritual master. One should not desire anything else. If the regulative principles ordered by the spiritual master are followed rigidly, the mind will gradually be trained to desire nothing but the service of Kṛṣṇa. Such training is the perfection of life.

TEXT 69

सत्त्वैकनिष्ठे मनसि भगवत्पार्श्ववर्तिनि ।
तमश्चन्द्रमसीवेदमुपरज्यावभासते ॥ ६९॥

sattvaika-niṣṭhe manasi
bhagavat-pārśva-vartini
tamaś candramasīvedam
uparajyāvabhāsate

sattva-eka-niṣṭhe—in full Kṛṣṇa consciousness; *manasi*—in a mind; *bhagavat*—with the Supreme Personality of Godhead; *pārśva-vartini*—being constantly associated; *tamaḥ*—the dark planet; *candramasi*—in the moon; *iva*—like; *idam*—this cosmic manifestation; *uparajya*—being connected; *avabhāsate*—becomes manifest.

TRANSLATION

Kṛṣṇa consciousness means constantly associating with the Supreme Personality of Godhead in such a mental state that the devotee can observe the cosmic manifestation exactly as the Supreme Personality of Godhead does. Such observation is not always possible, but it becomes manifest exactly like the dark planet known as Rāhu, which is observed in the presence of the full moon.

PURPORT

It has been explained in the previous verse that all desires on the mental platform become visible one after another. Sometimes, however, by the supreme will of the Supreme Personality of Godhead, the whole stockpile can be visible all at one time. In *Brahma-saṁhitā* it is said, *karmāṇi nirdahati kintu ca bhakti-bhājām* (5.54). When a person is fully absorbed in Kṛṣṇa consciousness, his stockpile of material desires is minimized. Indeed, the desires no longer fructify in the form of gross bodies. Instead, the stockpile of desires becomes visible on the mental platform by the grace of the Supreme Personality of Godhead.

In this connection, the darkness occurring before the full moon, the lunar eclipse, can be explained as being another planet, known as Rāhu. According to Vedic astronomy, the Rāhu planet, which is not visible, is accepted. Sometimes the Rāhu planet is visible in the presence of full moonlight. It then appears that this Rāhu planet exists somewhere near the orbit of the moon. The failure of modern moon excursionists may be due to the Rāhu planet. In other words, those who are supposed to be going to the moon may actually be going to this invisible planet Rāhu. Actually they are not going to the moon but to the planet Rāhu, and after reaching this planet, they come back. Apart from this discussion, the point is that a living entity has immense and unlimited desires for material enjoyment, and he has to transmigrate from one gross body to another until these desires are exhausted.

No living entity is free from the cycle of birth and death unless he takes to Kṛṣṇa consciousness; therefore in this verse it is clearly stated (*sattvaika-niṣṭhe*) that when one is fully absorbed in Kṛṣṇa consciousness, in one stroke he is freed of past and future mental desires. Then, by the grace of the Supreme Lord, everything becomes simultaneously manifest within the mind. In this regard, Viśvanātha Cakravartī Ṭhākura cites the example of mother Yaśodā's seeing the whole cosmic manifestation within the mouth of Lord Kṛṣṇa. By the grace of Lord Kṛṣṇa, mother Yaśodā saw all the universes and planets within the mouth of Kṛṣṇa. Similarly, by the grace of the Supreme Personality of Godhead, Kṛṣṇa, a Kṛṣṇa conscious person can see all his dormant desires at one time and finish all his future transmigrations. This facility is especially given to the devotee to make his path clear for returning home, back to Godhead.

Why we see things not experienced in this life is explained herein. That which we see is the future expression of a gross body or is already stocked in our mental stockpile. Because a Kṛṣṇa conscious person does not have to accept a future gross body, his recorded desires are fulfilled in a dream. We therefore sometimes find things in a dream never experienced in our present life.

TEXT 70

नाहं ममेति भावोऽयं पुरुषे व्यवधीयते ।
यावद् बुद्धिमनोऽक्षार्थगुणव्यूहो ह्यनादिमान् ॥ ७० ॥

nāhaṁ mameti bhāvo 'yaṁ
puruṣe vyavadhīyate
yāvad buddhi-mano-'kṣārtha-
guṇa-vyūho hy anādimān

na—not; *aham*—I; *mama*—mine; *iti*—thus; *bhāvaḥ*—consciousness; *ayam*—this; *puruṣe*—in the living entity; *vyavadhīyate*—is separated; *yāvat*—so long; *buddhi*—intelligence; *manaḥ*—mind; *akṣa*—senses; *artha*—sense objects; *guṇa*—of the material qualities; *vyūhaḥ*—a manifestation; *hi*—certainly; *anādimān*—the subtle body (existing since time immemorial).

TRANSLATION

As long as there exists the subtle material body composed of intelligence, mind, senses, sense objects and the reactions of the material qualities, the consciousness of false identification and its relative objective, the gross body, exist as well.

PURPORT

The desires in the subtle body of mind, intelligence and ego cannot be fulfilled without a gross body composed of the material elements earth, water, air, fire and ether. When the gross material body is not manifest, the living entity cannot factually act in the modes of material nature. In this verse it is clearly explained that the subtle activities of the mind and intelligence continue due to the sufferings and enjoyments of the living entity's subtle body. The consciousness of material identification (such as "I and mine") still continues because such consciousness has been extant from time immemorial. However, when one transfers to the spiritual world by virtue of understanding Kṛṣṇa consciousness, the actions and reactions of both gross and subtle bodies no longer bother the spirit soul.

TEXT 71

सुप्तिमूर्च्छोपतापेषु प्राणायनविघाततः ।
नेहतेऽहमिति ज्ञानं मृत्युप्रज्वारयोरपि ॥७१॥

supti-mūrcchopatāpeṣu
prāṇāyana-vighātataḥ
nehate 'ham iti jñānaṁ
mṛtyu-prajvārayor api

supti—in deep sleep; *mūrccha*—fainting; *upatāpeṣu*—or in great shock; *prāṇāyana*—of the movement of the life air; *vighātataḥ*—from prevention; *na*—not; *īhate*—thinks of; *aham*—I; *iti*—thus; *jñānam*—knowledge; *mṛtyu*—while dying; *prajvārayoḥ*—or during high fever; *api*—also.

TRANSLATION

When the living entity is in deep sleep, when he faints, when there is some great shock on account of severe loss, at the time of death, or when the body temperature is very high, the movement of the life air is arrested. At that time the living entity loses knowledge of identifying the body with the self.

PURPORT

Foolish people deny the existence of the soul, but it is a fact that when we sleep we forget the identity of the material body and when we awake, we forget the identity of the subtle body. In other words, while sleeping we forget the activities of the gross body, and when active in the gross body we forget the activities of sleeping. Actually both states—sleeping and waking—are creations of the illusory energy. The living entity actually has no connection with either the activities of sleep or the activities of the so-called wakened state. When a person is in deep sleep or when he has fainted, he forgets his gross body. Similarly, under chloroform or some other anesthetic, the living entity forgets his gross body and does not feel pain or pleasure during a surgical operation. Similarly, when a man is suddenly shocked by some great loss, he forgets his identification with the gross body. At the time of death, when the temperature of the body rises to 107 degrees, the living entity falls into a coma and is unable to identify his gross body. In such cases, the life air that moves within the body is choked up, and the living entity forgets his identification with the gross body. Because of our ignorance of the spiritual body, of which we have no experience, we do not know of the activities of the spiritual body, and, in ignorance, we jump from one false platform to another. We act sometimes in relation to the gross body and sometimes in relation to the subtle body. If, by Kṛṣṇa's grace, we act in our spiritual body, we can transcend both the gross and subtle bodies. In other words, we can gradually train ourselves to act in terms of the spiritual body. As stated in the *Nārada-pañcarātra, hṛṣīkeṇa hṛṣīkeśa-sevanaṁ bhaktir ucyate:* devotional service means engaging the spiritual body and spiritual senses in the service of the Lord. When we are engaged in such activities, the actions and reactions of the gross and subtle bodies cease.

TEXT 72

गर्भे बाल्येऽप्यपौष्कल्यादेकादशविधं तदा ।
लिङ्गं न दृश्यते यूनः कुह्वां चन्द्रमसो यथा ।।७२।।

garbhe bālye 'py apauṣkalyād
ekādaśa-vidhaṁ tadā
liṅgaṁ na dṛśyate yūnaḥ
kuhvāṁ candramaso yathā

garbhe—in the womb; *bālye*—in boyhood; *api*—also; *apauṣkalyāt*—because of immaturity; *ekādaśa*—the ten senses and the mind; *vidham*—in the form of; *tadā*—at that time; *liṅgam*—the subtle body or false ego; *na*—not; *dṛśyate*—is visible; *yūnaḥ*—of a youth; *kuhvām*—during the dark-moon night; *candramasaḥ*—the moon; *yathā*—as.

TRANSLATION

When one is a youth, all the ten senses and the mind are completely visible. However, in the mother's womb or in the boyhood state, the sense organs and the mind remain covered, just as the full moon is covered by the darkness of the dark-moon night.

PURPORT

When a living entity is within the womb, his gross body, the ten sense organs and the mind are not fully developed. At such a time the objects of the senses do not disturb him. In a dream a young man may experience the presence of a young woman because at that time the senses are active. Because of undeveloped senses, a child or boy will not see a young woman in his dreams. The senses are active in youth even when one dreams, and although there may be no young woman present, the senses may act and there may be a seminal discharge (nocturnal emission). The activities of the subtle and gross bodies depend on how developed conditions are. The example of the moon is very appropriate. On a dark-moon night, the full shining moon is still present, but it appears not to be present due to conditions. Similarly, the senses of the living entity are there, but they only become active when the gross body and the subtle body are developed. Unless the senses of the gross body are developed, they will not act on the subtle body. Similarly, because of the absence of desires in the subtle body, there may be no development in the gross body.

TEXT 73

अर्थे ह्यविद्यमानेऽपि संसृतिर्न निवर्तते ।
ध्यायतो विषयानस्य स्वप्नेऽनर्थागमो यथा ॥७३॥

arthe hy avidyamāne 'pi
saṁsṛtir na nivartate
dhyāyato viṣayān asya
svapne 'narthāgamo yathā

arthe—sense objects; *hi*—certainly; *avidyamāne*—not being present; *api*—although; *saṁsṛtiḥ*—material existence; *na*—never; *nivartate*—ceases; *dhyāyataḥ*—meditating; *viṣayān*—on sense objects; *asya*—of the living being; *svapne*—in dream; *anartha*—of unwanted things; *āgamaḥ*—appearance; *yathā*—as.

TRANSLATION

When the living entity dreams, the sense objects are not actually present. However, because one has associated with the sense objects, they become manifest. Similarly, the living entity with undeveloped senses does not cease to exist materially, even though he may not be exactly in contact with the sense objects.

PURPORT

It is sometimes said that because a child is innocent he is completely pure. Actually this is not the fact. The effects of fruitive activities reserved in the subtle body appear in three concurrent stages. One is called *bīja* (the root), another is called *kūṭastha* (the desire), and another is called *phalonmukha* (about to fructify). The manifest stage is called *prārabdha* (already in action). In a conscious or unconscious state, the actions of the subtle or gross bodies may not be manifest, but such states cannot be called the liberated state. A child may be innocent, but this does not mean that he is a liberated soul. Everything is held in reservation, and everything will become manifest in due course of time. Even in the absence of certain manifestations in the subtle body, the objects of sense enjoyment may act. The example has been given of a nocturnal emission in which the physical senses act even when the physical objects are not manifest. The three modes of material nature may not be manifest in the subtle body, but the contamination of the three modes remains conserved, and, in due course of time, it becomes manifest. Even if the reactions of the subtle and gross bodies are not manifest, one does not become free from the material conditions. Therefore it is wrong to say that a child is as good as a liberated soul.

TEXT 74

एवं पञ्चविधं लिङ्गं त्रिवृत् षोडशविस्तृतम् ।
एष चेतनया युक्तो जीव इत्यभिधीयते ॥७४॥

evaṁ pañca-vidhaṁ liṅgaṁ
tri-vṛt ṣoḍaśa-vistṛtam
eṣa cetanayā yukto
jīva ity abhidhīyate

evam—thus; *pañca-vidham*—the five sense objects; *liṅgam*—the subtle body; *tri-vṛt*—influenced by the three modes; *ṣoḍaśa*—sixteen; *vistṛtam*—expanded; *eṣaḥ*—this; *cetanayā*—with the living entity; *yuktaḥ*—combined; *jīvaḥ*—the conditioned soul; *iti*—thus; *abhidhīyate*—is understood.

TRANSLATION

The five sense objects, the five sense organs, the five knowledge-acquiring senses, and the mind are the sixteen material expansions. These combine with the living entity and are influenced by the three modes of material nature. Thus the existence of the conditioned soul is understood.

PURPORT

Lord Kṛṣṇa says in *Bhagavad-gītā:*

mamaivāṁśo jīva-loke
jīva-bhūtaḥ sanātanaḥ
manaḥ ṣaṣṭhānīndriyāṇi
prakṛti-sthāni karṣati

"The living entities in this conditioned world are My eternal, fragmental parts. Due to conditioned life, they are struggling very hard with the six senses, which include the mind." (Bg. 15.7)

Here it is also explained that the living entity comes in contact with the sixteen material elements and is influenced by the three modes of material nature. The living entity and this combination of elements combine to form what is called *jīva-bhūta,* the conditioned soul that struggles hard within material nature. The total material existence is first agitated by the three modes of material nature, and these become the living conditions of the living entity. Thus the subtle and gross bodies develop, and the ingredients are earth, water, fire, air, sky, and so on. According to Śrī Madhvācārya, when consciousness, the living force in the heart, is agitated by the three modes of material nature, then the subtle body of the living entity, consisting of the mind, the sense objects, the five senses that acquire knowledge, and the five senses for acting in the material condition, becomes possible.

TEXT 75

अनेन पुरुषो देहानुपादत्ते विमुञ्चति ।
हर्षं शोकं भयं दुःखं सुखं चानेन विन्दति ॥७५॥

anena puruṣo dehān
upādatte vimuñcati
harṣaṁ śokaṁ bhayaṁ duḥkhaṁ
sukhaṁ cānena vindati

anena—by this process; *puruṣaḥ*—the living entity; *dehān*—gross bodies; *upādatte*—achieves; *vimuñcati*—gives up; *harṣam*—enjoyment; *śokam*—lamentation; *bhayam*—fear; *duḥkham*—unhappiness; *sukham*—happiness; *ca*—also; *anena*—by the gross body; *vindati*—enjoys.

TRANSLATION

By virtue of the processes of the subtle body, the living entity develops and gives up gross bodies. This is known as the transmigration of the soul. Thus the soul becomes subjected to different types of so-called enjoyment, lamentation, fear, happiness and unhappiness.

PURPORT

According to this explanation, one can clearly understand that originally the living entity was as good as the Supreme Personality of Godhead in his pure spiritual existence. However, when the mind becomes polluted by desires for sense gratification in the material world, the living entity drops into the material conditions, as explained in this verse. Thus he begins his material existence, which means that he transmigrates from one body to another and becomes more and more entangled in material existence. The process of Kṛṣṇa consciousness, by which one always thinks of

Kṛṣṇa, is the transcendental process by which one can revert to his original spiritual existence. Devotional service means always thinking of Kṛṣṇa.

man-manā bhava mad-bhakto
mad-yājī māṁ namaskuru
mām evaiṣyasi satyaṁ te
pratijāne priyo 'si me

"Always think of Me and become My devotee. Worship Me and offer your homage unto Me. Thus you will come to Me without fail. I promise you this because you are My very dear friend." (Bg. 18.65)

One should always engage in the Lord's devotional service. As recommended in the *arcana-mārga,* one should worship the Deity in the temple and constantly offer obeisances to the spiritual master and the Deity. These processes are recommended to one who actually wants to become free from material entanglement. Modern psychologists can study the actions of the mind—thinking, feeling and willing—but they are unable to go deep into the matter. This is due to their lack of knowledge and to their not being associated with a liberated *ācārya.*

As stated in *Bhagavad-gītā:*

evaṁ paramparā-prāptam
imaṁ rājarṣayo viduḥ
sa kāleneha mahatā
yogo naṣṭaḥ parantapa

"This supreme science was thus received through the chain of disciplic succession, and the saintly kings understood it in that way. But in course of time the succession was broken, and therefore the science as it is appears to be lost." (Bg. 4.2)

Guided by so-called psychologists and philosophers, people in the modern age do not know of the activities of the subtle body and thus cannot understand what is meant by the transmigration of the soul. In these matters we have to take the authorized statements of *Bhagavad-gītā:*

dehino 'smin yathā dehe
kaumāraṁ yauvanaṁ jarā
tathā dehāntara-prāptir
dhīras tatra na muhyati

"As the embodied soul continually passes, in this body, from boyhood to youth to old age, the soul similarly passes into another body at death. The self-realized soul is not bewildered by such a change." (Bg. 2.13)

Unless all human society understands this important verse in *Bhagavad-gītā*, civilization will advance in ignorance, not in knowledge.

TEXTS 76-77

यथा तृणजलूकेयं नापयात्यपयाति च ।
न त्यजेन्म्रियमाणोऽपि प्राग्देहाभिमतिं जनः ॥७६॥
यावदन्यं न विन्देत व्यवधानेन कर्मणाम् ।
मन एव मनुष्येन्द्र भूतानां भवभावनम् ॥७७॥

yathā tṛṇa-jalūkeyaṁ
nāpayāty apayāti ca
na tyajen mriyamāṇo 'pi
prāg-dehābhimatiṁ janaḥ

yāvad anyaṁ na vindeta
vyavadhānena karmaṇām
mana eva manuṣyendra
bhūtānāṁ bhava-bhāvanam

yathā—as; *tṛṇa-jalūkā*—caterpillar; *iyam*—this; *na apayāti*—does not go; *apayāti*—goes; *ca*—also; *na*—not; *tyajet*—gives up; *mriyamāṇaḥ*—at the point of death; *api*—even; *prāk*—former; *deha*—with the body; *abhimatim*—identification; *janaḥ*—a person; *yāvat*—so long as; *anyam*—another; *na*—not; *vindeta*—obtains; *vyavadhānena*—by the termination; *karmaṇām*—of fruitive activities; *manaḥ*—the mind; *eva*—certainly; *manuṣya-indra*—O ruler of men; *bhūtānām*—of all living entities; *bhava*—of material existence; *bhāvanam*—the cause.

TRANSLATION

The caterpillar transports itself from one leaf to another by capturing one leaf before giving up the other. Similarly, according to his previous work, the living entity must capture another body before giving up the one he has. This is because the mind is the reservoir of all kinds of desires.

PURPORT

A living entity too much absorbed in material activity becomes very much attracted to the material body. Even at the point of death, he thinks of his present body and the relatives connected to it. Thus he remains fully absorbed in the bodily conception of life, so much so that even at the point of death he abhors leaving his present body. Sometimes it is found that a person on the verge of death remains in a coma for many days before giving up the body. This is common among so-called leaders and politicians who think that without their presence the entire country and all society will be in chaos. This is called *māyā.* Political leaders do not like to leave their political posts, and they either have to be shot by an enemy or obliged to leave by the arrival of death. By superior arrangement a living entity is offered another body, but because of his attraction to the present body, he does not like to transfer himself to another body. Thus he is forced to accept another body by the laws of nature.

prakṛteḥ kriyamāṇāni
guṇaiḥ karmāṇi sarvaśaḥ
ahaṅkāra-vimūḍhātmā
kartāham iti manyate

"The bewildered spirit soul, under the influence of the three modes of material nature, thinks himself the doer of activities that are in actuality carried out by nature." (Bg. 3.27)

Material nature is very strong, and the material modes force one to accept another body. This force is visible when the living entity transmigrates from a superior body to an inferior one. One who acts like a dog or hog in the present body will certainly be forced to accept the body of a dog or hog in the next life. A person may be enjoying the body of a prime minister or a president, but when he understands that he will be forced to accept the body of a dog or hog, he chooses not to leave the present body. Therefore he lies in a coma many days before death. This has been experienced by many politicians at the time of death. The conclusion is that the next body is already determined by superior control. The living entity immediately gives up the present body and enters another. Sometimes in the present body the living entity feels that many of his desires and imaginations are not fulfilled. Those who are overly attracted to their life situation are forced to remain in a ghostly body and are not allowed to accept another gross body. Even in the body of a ghost, they create disturbances for neighbors and relatives. The mind is the prime cause of such a situation. According to one's mind, different types of bodies are generated, and one is forced to accept them. As confirmed in *Bhagavad-gītā:*

yaṁ yaṁ vāpi smaran bhāvaṁ
tyajaty ante kalevaram
taṁ tam evaiti kaunteya
sadā tad-bhāva-bhāvitaḥ

"Whatever state of being one remembers when he quits his body, that state he will attain without fail." (Bg. 8.6)

Within one's body and mind, one can think as either a dog or a god, and the next life is offered to him accordingly. This is explained in *Bhagavad-gītā:*

puruṣaḥ prakṛti-stho hi
bhuṅkte prakṛti-jān guṇān
kāraṇaṁ guṇa-saṅgo 'sya
sad-asad-yoni-janmasu

"The living entity in material nature thus follows the ways of life, enjoying the three modes of nature. This is due to his association with that material nature. Thus he meets with good and evil amongst various species." (Bg. 13.22)

The living entity may transmigrate to either a superior or inferior body according to his association with the modes of material nature. If he associates with the mode of ignorance, he gets the body of an animal or an inferior man, but if he associates with the mode of goodness or passion, he gets a body accordingly. This is also confirmed in *Bhagavad-gītā:*

ūrdhvaṁ gacchanti sattva-sthā
madhye tiṣṭhanti rājasāḥ
jaghanya-guṇa-vṛtti-sthā
adho gacchanti tāmasāḥ

"Those situated in the mode of goodness gradually go upward to the higher planets; those in the mode of passion live on the earthly planets; and those in the mode of ignorance go down to the hellish worlds." (Bg. 14.18)

The root cause of one's association is the mind. This great Kṛṣṇa consciousness movement is the greatest boon to human society because it is teaching everyone to think always of Kṛṣṇa by executing devotional service. In this way, at the end of life, one may be transferred to the association of Kṛṣṇa. This is technically called *nitya-līlā-praviṣṭa,* entering into the planet Goloka Vṛndāvana. *Bhagavad-gītā* explains:

bhaktyā mām abhijānāti
yāvān yaś cāsmi tattvataḥ
tato māṁ tattvato jñātvā
viśate tad-anantaram

"One can understand the Supreme Personality as He is only by devotional service. And when one is in full consciousness of the Supreme Lord by such devotion, he can enter into the kingdom of God." (Bg. 18.55)

After the mind is completely absorbed in Kṛṣṇa consciousness, one can enter the planet known as Goloka Vṛndāvana. To enter the association of the Supreme Personality of Godhead, one has to understand Kṛṣṇa. The process of understanding Kṛṣṇa is devotional service.

After understanding Kṛṣṇa as He is, one can become eligible to enter Kṛṣṇaloka and associate with Him. The mind is the cause of such an exalted position. The mind can also get one a body like dogs and hogs. To absorb the mind always in Kṛṣṇa consciousness is therefore the greatest perfection of human life.

TEXT 78

यदाक्षैश्चरितान् ध्यायन् कर्माण्याचिनुतेऽसकृत् ।
सति कर्मण्यविद्यायां बन्धः कर्मण्यनात्मनः ॥७८॥

yadākṣaiś caritān dhyāyan
karmāṇy ācinute 'sakṛt
sati karmaṇy avidyāyāṁ
bandhaḥ karmaṇy anātmanaḥ

yadā—when; *akṣaiḥ*—by the senses; *caritān*—pleasures enjoyed; *dhyāyan*—thinking of; *karmāṇi*—activities; *ācinute*—performs; *asakṛt*—always; *sati karmaṇi*—when material affairs continue; *avidyāyām*—under illusion; *bandhaḥ*—bondage; *karmaṇi*—in activity; *anātmanaḥ*—of the material body.

TRANSLATION

As long as we desire to enjoy sense gratification, we create material activities. When the living entity acts in the material field, he enjoys the

senses, and while enjoying the senses, he creates another series of material activities. In this way the living entity becomes entrapped as a conditioned soul.

PURPORT

While in the subtle body we create many plans to enjoy sense gratification. These plans are recorded in the spool of one's mind as *bīja,* the root of fruitive activities. In conditional life the living entity creates a series of bodies one after another, and this is called *karma-bandhana.* As explained in *Bhagavad-gītā:*

yajñārthāt karmaṇo 'nyatra
loko 'yaṁ karma-bandhanaḥ
tad-arthaṁ karma kaunteya
mukta-saṅgaḥ samācara

"Work done as a sacrifice for Viṣṇu has to be performed, otherwise work binds one to this material world. Therefore, O son of Kuntī, perform your prescribed duties for His satisfaction, and in that way you will always remain unattached and free from bondage." (Bg. 3.9)

If we act only for the satisfaction of Viṣṇu, there is no bondage due to material activity. If we act otherwise, we become entrapped by one material activity after another. Under these circumstances, it is to be supposed that by thinking, feeling and willing, we are creating a series of future material bodies. In the words of Bhaktivinoda Ṭhākura, *anādi karama-phale, paḍi' bhavārṇava-jale.* The living entity falls into the ocean of *karma-bandhana* as a result of past material activities. Instead of plunging oneself into the ocean of material activity, one should accept material activity only to maintain body and soul together. The rest of one's time should be devoted to engaging in the transcendental loving service of the Lord. In this way one can attain relief from the reactions of material activity.

TEXT 79

अतस्तदपवादार्थं भज सर्वात्मना हरिम् ।
पश्यंस्तदात्मकं विश्वं स्थित्युत्पत्त्यप्यया यतः ॥७९॥

atas tad apavādārthaṁ
bhaja sarvātmanā harim
paśyaṁs tad-ātmakaṁ viśvaṁ
sthity-utpatty-apyayā yataḥ

ataḥ—therefore; *tat*—that; *apavāda-artham*—to counteract; *bhaja*—engage in devotional service; *sarva-ātmanā*—with all your senses; *harim*—unto the Supreme Personality of Godhead; *paśyan*—seeing; *tat*—of the Lord; *ātmakam*—under the control; *viśvam*—the cosmic manifestation; *sthiti*—maintenance; *utpatti*—creation; *apyayāḥ*—and annihilation; *yataḥ*—from whom.

TRANSLATION

You should always know that this cosmic manifestation is created, maintained and annihilated by the will of the Supreme Personality of Godhead. Consequently everything within this cosmic manifestation is under the control of the Lord. To be enlightened by this perfect knowledge, one should always engage himself in the devotional service of the Lord.

PURPORT

Self-realization, understanding oneself as Brahman or spirit soul, is very difficult in the material condition. However, if we accept the devotional service of the Lord, the Lord will gradually reveal Himself. In this way the progressive devotee will gradually realize his spiritual position. We cannot see anything in the darkness of night, not even our own selves, but when there is sunshine we can see not only the sun but everything within the world as well. Lord Kṛṣṇa explains in the Seventh Chapter of the *Bhagavad-gītā:*

mayy āsakta-manāḥ pārtha
yogaṁ yuñjan mad-āśrayaḥ
asaṁśayaṁ samagraṁ māṁ
yathā jñāsyasi tac chṛṇu

"Now hear, O son of Pṛthā [Arjuna], how by practicing *yoga* in full consciousness of Me, with mind attached to Me, you can know Me in full, free from doubt." (Bg. 7.1)

When we engage ourselves in the devotional service of the Lord to become Kṛṣṇa conscious, we understand not only Kṛṣṇa but everything related to Kṛṣṇa. In other words, through Kṛṣṇa consciousness we can understand not only Kṛṣṇa and the cosmic manifestation but also our constitutional position. In Kṛṣṇa consciousness we can understand that the entire material creation is created by the Supreme Personality of Godhead, maintained by Him, annihilated by Him, and absorbed in Him. We are also part and parcel of the Lord. Everything is under the control of the

Lord, and therefore our only duty is to surrender unto the Supreme and engage in His transcendental loving service.

TEXT 80

मैत्रेय उवाच

भागवतमुख्यो भगवान्नारदो हंसयोर्गतिम् ।
प्रदर्श्य ह्यमुमामन्त्र्य सिद्धलोकं ततोऽगमत् ॥८०॥

maitreya uvāca
bhāgavata-mukhyo bhagavān
nārado haṁsayor gatim
pradarśya hy amum āmantrya
siddha-lokaṁ tato 'gamat

maitreyaḥ uvāca—Maitreya said; *bhāgavata*—of the devotees; *mukhyaḥ*—the chief; *bhagavān*—the most powerful; *nāradaḥ*—Nārada Muni; *haṁsayoḥ*—of the living entity and the Lord; *gatim*—constitutional position; *pradarśya*—having shown; *hi*—certainly; *amum*—him (the King); *āmantrya*—after inviting; *siddha-lokam*—to Siddhaloka; *tataḥ*—thereafter; *agamat*—departed.

TRANSLATION

The great sage Maitreya continued: The supreme devotee, the great saint Nārada, thus explained to King Prācīnabarhi the constitutional position of the Supreme Personality of Godhead and the living entity. After giving an invitation to the King, Nārada Muni left to return to Siddhaloka.

PURPORT

Siddhaloka and Brahmaloka are both within the same planetary system. Brahmaloka is understood to be the highest planet within this universe. Siddhaloka is considered to be one of the satellites of Brahmaloka. The inhabitants of Siddhaloka have all the powers of yogic mysticism. From this verse it appears that the great sage Nārada is an inhabitant of Siddhaloka, although he travels to all the planetary systems. All the residents of Siddhaloka are spacemen, and they can travel in space without mechanical help. The residents of Siddhaloka can go from one planet to another individually by virtue of their yogic perfection. After giving instructions to the great King Prācīnabarhi, Nārada Muni departed and also invited him to Siddhaloka.

TEXT 81

प्राचीनबर्हीं राजर्षिः प्रजासर्गाभिरक्षणे ।
आदिश्य पुत्रानगमत्तपसे कपिलाश्रमम् ॥८१॥

prācīnabarhī rājarṣiḥ
prajā-sargābhirakṣaṇe
ādiśya putrān agamat
tapase kapilāśramam

prācīnabarhiḥ—King Prācīnabarhi; *rāja-ṛṣiḥ*—the saintly king; *prajā-sarga*—the mass of citizens; *abhirakṣaṇe*—to protect; *ādiśya*—after ordering; *putrān*—his sons; *agamat*—departed; *tapase*—for undergoing austerities; *kapila-āśramam*—to the holy place known as Kapilāśrama.

TRANSLATION

In the presence of his ministers, the saintly King Prācīnabarhi left orders for his sons to protect the citizens. He then left home and went off to undergo austerities in a holy place known as Kapilāśrama.

PURPORT

The word *prajā-sarga* is very important in this verse. When the saintly King Prācīnabarhi was induced by the great sage Nārada to leave home and take to the devotional service of the Lord, his sons had not yet returned from their austerities in the water. However, he did not wait for their return but simply left messages to the effect that his sons were to protect the mass of citizens. According to Vīrarāghava Ācārya, such protection means organizing the citizens into the specific divisions of the four *varṇas* and four *āśramas.* It was the responsibility of the royal order to see that the citizens were following the regulative principles of the four *varṇas* (namely the *brāhmaṇas, kṣatriyas, vaiśyas* and *śūdras*) and the *āśramas* (*brahmacarya, gṛhastha, vānaprastha* and *sannyāsa*). It is very difficult to rule citizens in a kingdom without organizing this *varṇāśrama-dharma.* To rule the mass of citizens in a state and keep them in a complete progressive order is not possible simply by passing laws every year in a legislative assembly. The *varṇāśrama-dharma* is essential in a good government. One class of men (the *brāhmaṇas*) must be intelligent and brahminically qualified, another class must be trained in administrative work (*kṣatriya*), another in mercantile business (*vaiśya*) and another simply in labor (*śūdra*). These four classes of men are already there according to nature, but it is the government's duty to see that all four of these classes follow the principles of their *varṇas* methodically. This is called *abhirakṣaṇa*, or protection.

It is significant that when Mahārāja Prācīnabarhi was convinced of the goal of life through the instructions of Nārada, he did not wait even a moment to see his sons return, but left immediately. There were many things to be done upon the return of his sons, but he simply left them a message. He knew what his prime duty was. He simply left instructions for his sons and went off for the purpose of spiritual advancement. This is the system of Vedic civilization.

Śrīdhara Svāmī informs us that Kapilāśrama is located at the confluence of the Ganges and the Bay of Bengal, a place known now as Gaṅgā-sāgara. This place is still famous as a place of pilgrimage, and many millions of people gather there every year on the day of Makara-saṅkrānti and take bath. It is called Kapilāśrama because of Lord Kapila's living there to perform His austerities and penances. Lord Kapila propounded the Sāṅkhya system of philosophy.

TEXT 82

तत्रैकाग्रमना धीरो गोविन्दचरणाम्बुजम् ।
विमुक्तसङ्गोऽनुभजन् भक्त्या तत्साम्यतामगात् ॥८२॥

tatraikāgra-manā dhīro
govinda-caraṇāmbujam
vimukta-saṅgo 'nubhajan
bhaktyā tat-sāmyatām agāt

tatra—there; *eka-agra-manāḥ*—with full attention; *dhīraḥ*—sober; *govinda*—of Kṛṣṇa; *caraṇa-ambujam*—unto the lotus feet; *vimukta*—freed from; *saṅgaḥ*—material association; *anubhajan*—continuously engaging in devotional service; *bhaktyā*—by pure devotion; *tat*—with the Lord; *sāmyatām*—qualitative equality; *agāt*—achieved.

TRANSLATION

Having undergone austerities and penances at Kapilāśrama, King Prācīnabarhi attained full liberation from all material designations. He constantly engaged in the transcendental loving service of the Lord and

attained a spiritual position qualitatively equal to that of the Supreme Personality of Godhead.

PURPORT

There is special significance in the words *tat-sāmyatām agāt.* The King attained the position of possessing the same status or the same form as that of the Lord. This definitely proves that the Supreme Personality of Godhead is always a person. In His impersonal feature, He is the rays of His transcendental body. When a living entity attains spiritual perfection, he also attains the same type of body, known as *sac-cid-ānanda-vigraha.* This spiritual body never mixes with the material elements. Although in conditional life the living entity is surrounded by material elements (earth, water, fire, air, sky, mind, intelligence and ego), he remains always aloof from them. In other words, the living entity can be liberated from the material condition at any moment, provided that he wishes to do so. The material environment is called *māyā.* According to Kṛṣṇa:

daivī hy eṣā guṇamayī
mama māyā duratyayā
mām eva ye prapadyante
māyām etāṁ taranti te

"This divine energy of Mine, consisting of the three modes of material nature, is difficult to overcome. But those who have surrendered unto Me can easily cross beyond it." (Bg. 7.14)

As soon as the living entity engages in the transcendental loving service of the Lord, he immediately attains freedom from all material conditions.

māṁ ca yo 'vyabhicāreṇa
bhakti-yogena sevate
sa guṇān samatītyaitān
brahma-bhūyāya kalpate

"One who engages in full devotional service, who does not fall down in any circumstance, at once transcends the modes of material nature and thus comes to the level of Brahman." (Bg. 14.26)

In the material state the living entity is on the *jīva-bhūta* platform, but when he renders devotional service to the Lord, he is elevated to the *brahma-bhūta* platform. On the *brahma-bhūta* platform the living entity is liberated from material bondage, and he engages in the service of the

Lord. In this verse the word *dhīra* is sometimes read as *vīra*. Actually there is not very much difference. The word *dhīra* means "sober," and *vīra* means "hero." One who is struggling against *māyā* is a hero, and one who is sober enough to understand his position is a *dhīra*. Without becoming sober or heroic, one cannot attain spiritual salvation.

TEXT 83

एतदध्यात्मपारोक्ष्यं गीतं देवर्षिणानघ ।
यः श्रावयेद्यः शृणुयात्स लिङ्गेन विमुच्यते ॥८३॥

etad adhyātma-pārokṣyaṁ
gītaṁ devarṣiṇānagha
yaḥ śrāvayed yaḥ śṛṇuyāt
sa liṅgena vimucyate

etat—this; *adhyātma*—spiritual; *pārokṣyam*—authorized description; *gītam*—narrated; *deva-ṛṣiṇā*—by the great sage Nārada; *anagha*—O spotless Vidura; *yaḥ*—anyone who; *śrāvayet*—may describe; *yaḥ*—anyone who; *śṛṇuyāt*—may hear; *saḥ*—he; *liṅgena*—from the bodily concept of life; *vimucyate*—becomes delivered.

TRANSLATION

My dear Vidura, one who hears this narration concerning the understanding of the living entity's spiritual existence, as described by the great sage Nārada, or who relates it to others, will be liberated from the bodily conception of life.

PURPORT

This material creation is the spirit soul's dream. Actually all existence in the material world is a dream of Mahā-Viṣṇu, as the *Brahma-saṁhitā* describes: *yaḥ kāraṇārṇava-jale bhajati sma yoga-nidrām ananta-jagadaṇḍa-saroma-kūpaḥ.* This material world is created by the dreaming of Mahā-Viṣṇu. The real factual platform is the spiritual world, but when the spirit soul wants to imitate the Supreme Personality of Godhead, he is put into this dreamland of material creation. After being in contact with the material modes of nature, the living entity develops the subtle and gross bodies. When the living entity is fortunate enough to associate with Śrī Nārada Mahāmuni or his servants, he is liberated from this dreamland of material creation and the bodily conception of life.

TEXT 84

एतन्मुकुन्दयशसा भुवनं पुनानं
देवर्षिवर्यमुखनिःसृतमात्मशौचम् ।
यः कीर्त्यमानमधिगच्छति पारमेष्ठ्यं
नास्मिन् भवे भ्रमति मुक्तसमस्तबन्धः ॥८४॥

etan mukunda-yaśasā bhuvanaṁ punānaṁ
devarṣi-varya-mukha-niḥsṛtam ātma-śaucam
yaḥ kīrtyamānam adhigacchati pārameṣṭhyaṁ
nāsmin bhave bhramati mukta-samasta-bandhaḥ

etat—this narration; *mukunda-yaśasā*—with the fame of Lord Kṛṣṇa; *bhuvanam*—this material world; *punānam*—sanctifying; *deva-ṛṣi*—of the great sages; *varya*—of the chief; *mukha*—from the mouth; *niḥsṛtam*—uttered; *ātma-śaucam*—purifying the heart; *yaḥ*—anyone who; *kīrtyamānam*—being chanted; *adhigacchati*—goes back; *pārameṣṭhyam*—to the spiritual world; *na*—never; *asmin*—in this; *bhave*—material world; *bhramati*—wanders; *mukta*—being liberated; *samasta*—from all; *bandhaḥ*—bondage.

TRANSLATION

This narration spoken by the great sage Nārada is full of the transcendental fame of the Supreme Personality of Godhead. Consequently this narration, when described, certainly sanctifies this material world. It purifies the heart of the living entity and helps him attain his spiritual identity. One who relates this transcendental narration will be liberated from all material bondage and will no longer have to wander within this material world.

PURPORT

As indicated in verse 79, Nārada Muni advised King Prācīnabarhi to take to devotional service rather than waste time performing ritualistic ceremonies and fruitive activities. The vivid descriptions of the subtle and gross bodies in this chapter are most scientific, and because they are given by the great sage Nārada, they are authoritative. Because these narrations are full of the glory of the Supreme Personality of Godhead, they constitute the most effective process for the purification of the mind. As Śrī Caitanya Mahāprabhu confirmed: *ceto-darpaṇa-mārjanam.* The more we talk of Kṛṣṇa, think of Kṛṣṇa, and preach for Kṛṣṇa, the more we become purified. This means we no longer have to accept a hallucinatory gross and subtle body but instead attain our spiritual identity. One who tries to understand this instructive spiritual knowledge is delivered from this ocean of nescience. The word *pārameṣṭhyam* is very significant in this connection. *Pārameṣṭhyam* is also called Brahmaloka; it is the planet on which Lord Brahmā lives. The inhabitants of Brahmaloka always discuss such narrations so that after the annihilation of the material world, they can be directly transferred to the spiritual world. One who is transferred to the spiritual world does not have to go up and down within this material world. Sometimes spiritual activities are also called *pārameṣṭhyam.*

TEXT 85

अध्यात्मपारोक्ष्यमिदं मयाधिगतमद्भुतम् ।
एवं स्त्रियाऽऽश्रमः पुंसश्छिन्नोऽमुत्र च संशयः ॥८५॥

adhyātma-pārokṣyam idaṁ
mayādhigatam adbhutam
evaṁ striyā 'śramaḥ puṁsaś
chinno 'mutra ca saṁśayaḥ

adhyātma—spiritual; *pārokṣyam*—described by authority; *idam*—this; *mayā*—by me; *adhigatam*—heard; *adbhutam*—wonderful; *evam*—thus; *striyā*—with a wife; *āśramaḥ*—shelter; *puṁsaḥ*—of the living entity; *chinnaḥ*—finished; *amutra*—about life after death; *ca*—also; *saṁśayaḥ*—doubt.

TRANSLATION

The allegory of King Purañjana, described herein according to authority, was heard by me from my spiritual master, and it is full of spiritual knowledge. If one can understand the purport of this allegory, he will certainly be relieved from the bodily conception and will clearly understand life after death. Although one may not understand what transmigration of the soul actually is, one can fully understand it by studying this narration.

PURPORT

The word *striyā,* meaning "along with the wife," is significant. The male and female living together constitute the sum and substance of material existence. The attraction between male and female in this material world is very strong. In all species of life the attraction between male and female is the basic principle of existence. The same principle of intermingling is also in human society but is in a regulative form. Material existence means living together as male and female and being attracted by one another. However, when one fully understands spiritual life, his attraction for the opposite sex is completely vanquished. By such attraction, one becomes overly attached to this material world. It is a hard knot within the heart.

puṁsaḥ striyā mithunī-bhāvam etaṁ
tayor mitho hṛdaya-granthim āhuḥ
ato gṛha-kṣetra-sutāpta-vittair
janasya moho 'yam ahaṁ mameti (*Bhāg.* 5.5.8)

Everyone comes to this material world attracted to sense gratification, and the hard knot of sense gratification is the attraction between male and female. By this attraction, one becomes overly attached to the material world in terms of *gṛha-kṣetra-suta-āpta-vitta*—that is, home, land, children, friends, money, and so forth. Thus one becomes entangled in the bodily conception of "I and mine." However, if one understands the story of King Purañjana and understands how, by sexual attraction, Purañjana became a female in his next life, one will also understand the process of transmigration.

SPECIAL NOTE: According to Vijayadhvaja Tīrtha, who belongs to the Madhvācārya-sampradāya, the first two of the following verses appear after the forty-fifth verse of this chapter, and the remaining two verses appear after the seventy-ninth verse.

TEXTS 1a – 2a

sarveṣām eva jantūnāṁ
satataṁ deha-poṣaṇe
asti prajñā samāyattā
ko viśeṣas tadā nṛṇām

labdhvehānte manuṣyatvaṁ
hitvā dehādy-asad-graham
ātma-sṛtyā vihāyedaṁ
jīvātmā sa viśiṣyate

sarveṣām—all; *eva*—certainly; *jantūnām*—of animals; *satatam*—always; *deha-poṣaṇe*—to maintain the body; *asti*—there is; *prajñā*—intelligence; *samāyattā*—resting on; *kaḥ*—what; *viśeṣaḥ*—difference; *tadā*—then; *nṛṇām*—of the human beings; *labdhvā*—having attained; *iha*—here; *ante*—at the end of many births; *manuṣyatvam*—a human life; *hitvā*—after giving up; *deha-ādi*—in the gross and subtle body; *asat-graham*—an incorrect conception of life; *ātma*—of spiritual knowledge; *sṛtyā*—by the path; *vihāya*—having abandoned; *idam*—this body; *jīva-ātmā*—the individual spirit soul; *saḥ*—that; *viśiṣyate*—becomes prominent.

TRANSLATION

A desire to maintain body, wife and children is also observed in animal society. The animals have full intelligence to manage such affairs. If a human being is simply advanced in this respect, what is the difference between him and an animal? One should be very careful to understand that this human life is attained after many, many births in the evolutionary process. A learned man who gives up the bodily conception of life, both gross and subtle, will, by the enlightenment of spiritual knowledge, become a prominent individual spirit soul, as the Supreme Lord is also.

PURPORT

It is said that man is a rational animal, but from this verse we can also understand that rationality exists even in animal life. Unless there is rationality, how can an animal maintain its body by working so hard? That the animals are not rational is untrue; their rationality, however, is not very advanced. In any case, we cannot deny them rationality. The point is that one should use one's reason to understand the Supreme Personality of Godhead, for that is the perfection of human life.

TEXT 1b

bhaktiḥ kṛṣṇe dayā jīveṣv
akuṇṭha-jñānam ātmani
yadi syād ātmano bhūyād
apavargas tu saṁsṛteḥ

bhaktiḥ—devotional service; *kṛṣṇe*—unto Kṛṣṇa; *dayā*—mercy; *jīveṣu*—unto other living entities; *akuṇṭha-jñānam*—perfect knowledge; *ātmani*—of the self; *yadi*—if; *syāt*—it becomes; *ātmanaḥ*—of one's self; *bhūyāt*—there must be; *apavargaḥ*—liberation; *tu*—then; *saṁsṛteḥ*—from the bondage of material life.

TRANSLATION

If a living entity is developed in Kṛṣṇa consciousness and is merciful to others, and if his spiritual knowledge of self-realization is perfect, he will immediately attain liberation from the bondage of material existence.

PURPORT

In this verse the word *dayā jīveṣu,* meaning mercy to other living entities, indicates that a living entity must be merciful to other living entities if he wishes to make progress in self-realization. This means he must preach this knowledge after perfecting himself and understanding his own position as an eternal servant of Kṛṣṇa. Preaching this is showing real mercy to living entities. Other types of humanitarian work may be temporarily beneficial for the body, but because a living entity is spirit soul, ultimately one can show him real mercy only by revealing knowledge of his spiritual existence. As Caitanya Mahāprabhu says, *jīvera 'svarūpa' haya—kṛṣṇera 'nitya-dāsa'.* "Every living entity is constitutionally a servant of Kṛṣṇa." One should know this fact perfectly and should preach it to the mass of people. If one realizes that he is an eternal servant of Kṛṣṇa but does not preach it, his realization is imperfect. Śrīla Bhaktisiddhānta Sarasvatī Ṭhākura therefore sings, *duṣṭa mana, tumi kisera vaiṣṇava? pratiṣṭhāra tare, nirjanera ghare, tava hari-nāma kevala kaitava.* "My dear mind, what kind of Vaiṣṇava are you? Simply for false prestige and a material reputation you are chanting the Hare Kṛṣṇa *mantra* in a solitary place." In this way people who do not preach are criticized. There are many Vaiṣṇavas in Vṛndāvana who do not like preaching; they chiefly try to imitate Haridāsa Ṭhākura. The actual result of their so-called chanting in a secluded place, however, is that they sleep and think of women and money. Similarly, one who simply engages in temple worship but does not see to the interests of the mass of people, or cannot recognize devotees, is called a *kaniṣṭha-adhikārī:*

arcāyām eva haraye
pūjāṁ yaḥ śraddhayehate
na tad-bhakteṣu cānyeṣu
sa bhaktaḥ prākṛtaḥ smṛtaḥ
(*Bhāg.* 11.2.47).

TEXT 2b

adṛṣṭaṁ dṛṣṭavan naṅkṣed
bhūtaṁ svapnavad anyathā

bhūtaṁ bhavad bhaviṣyac ca
suptaṁ sarva-raho-rahaḥ

adṛṣṭam—future happiness; *dṛṣṭa-vat*—like direct experience; *naṅkṣet*—becomes vanquished; *bhūtam*—the material existence; *svapna-vat*—like a dream; *anyathā*—otherwise; *bhūtam*—which happened in the past; *bhavat*—present; *bhaviṣyat*—future; *ca*—also; *suptam*—a dream; *sarva*—of all; *rahaḥ-rahaḥ*—the secret conclusion.

TRANSLATION

Everything happening within time, which consists of past, present and future, is merely a dream. That is the secret understanding in all Vedic literature.

PURPORT

Factually all of material existence is only a dream. Thus there is no question of past, present or future. Persons who are addicted to *karma-kāṇḍa-vicāra,* which means "working for future happiness through fruitive activities," are also dreaming. Similarly, past happiness and present happiness are merely dreams. The actual reality is Kṛṣṇa and service to Kṛṣṇa, which can save us from the clutches of *māyā,* for the Lord says in *Bhagavad-gītā* (7.14), *mām eva ye prapadyante māyām etāṁ taranti te:* "Those who surrender unto Me can easily cross beyond My illusory energy."

Thus end the Bhaktivedanta purports of the Fourth Canto, Twenty-ninth Chapter, of the Śrīmad-Bhāgavatam, *entitled "Talks Between Nārada and King Prācīnabarhi."*

CHAPTER THIRTY

The Activities of the Pracetās

TEXT 1

विदुर उवाच
ये त्वयाभिहिता ब्रह्मन् सुताः प्राचीनबर्हिषः ।
ते रुद्रगीतेन हरिं सिद्धिमापुः प्रतोष्य काम् ॥ १ ॥

vidura uvāca
ye tvayābhihitā brahman
sutāḥ prācīnabarhiṣaḥ
te rudra-gītena hariṁ
siddhim āpuḥ pratoṣya kām

viduraḥ uvāca—Vidura said; *ye*—those who; *tvayā*—by you; *abhihitāḥ*—were spoken about; *brahman*—O *brāhmaṇa; sutāḥ*—sons; *prācīnabarhiṣaḥ*—of King Prācīnabarhi; *te*—all of them; *rudra-gītena*—by the song composed by Lord Śiva; *harim*—the Lord; *siddhim*—success; *āpuḥ*—achieved; *pratoṣya*—having satisfied; *kām*—what.

TRANSLATION

Vidura inquired from Maitreya: O brāhmaṇa, you formerly spoke about the sons of Prācīnabarhi and informed me that they satisfied the Supreme Personality of Godhead by chanting a song composed by Lord Śiva. What did they achieve in this way?

PURPORT

In the beginning, Maitreya Ṛṣi narrated the activities of the sons of Prācīnabarhi. These sons went beside a great lake, which was like an ocean, and, fortunately finding Lord Śiva, they learned how to satisfy the Supreme Personality of Godhead by chanting the songs composed by Lord

Śiva. Now their father's attachment for fruitive activities was disapproved by Nārada, who therefore kindly instructed Prācīnabarhi by telling him the allegorical story of Purañjana. Now Vidura again wanted to hear about his sons, and he was especially inquisitive to know what they achieved by satisfying the Supreme Personality of Godhead. Here the words *siddhim āpuḥ*, or "achieved perfection," are very important. Lord Kṛṣṇa says in *Bhagavad-gītā:*

manuṣyāṇāṁ sahasreṣu
kaścid yatati siddhaye
yatatām api siddhānāṁ
kaścin māṁ vetti tattvataḥ

"Out of many thousands among men, one may endeavor for perfection, and of those who have achieved perfection, hardly one knows Me in truth." (Bg. 7.3)

Out of many many millions of people, one may be interested in learning how to attain success in spiritual matters. The supreme success is mentioned also in *Bhagavad-gītā:*

mām upetya punar janma
duḥkhālayam aśāśvatam
nāpnuvanti mahātmānaḥ
saṁsiddhiṁ paramāṁ gatāḥ

"After attaining Me, the great souls, who are *yogīs* in devotion, never return to this temporary world, which is full of miseries, because they have attained the highest perfection." (Bg. 8.15)

And what is that highest perfection? That is also explained in that verse. The highest perfection is to return home, back to Godhead, so that one will not have to return again to this material world and transmigrate from one body to another in the dream of material existence. By the grace of Lord Śiva, the Pracetās actually attained perfection and returned home, back to Godhead, after enjoying material facilities to the highest extent. Maitreya will now narrate that to Vidura.

TEXT 2

किं बार्हस्पत्येह परत्र वाथ
कैवल्यनाथप्रियपार्श्ववर्तिनः ।
आसाद्य देवं गिरिशं यदृच्छया
प्रापुः परं नूनमथ प्रचेतसः ॥ २ ॥

kiṁ bārhaspatyeha paratra vātha
kaivalya-nātha-priya-pārśva-vartinaḥ
āsādya devaṁ giriśaṁ yadṛcchayā
prāpuḥ paraṁ nūnam atha pracetasaḥ

kim—what; *bārhaspatya*—O disciple of Bṛhaspati; *iha*—here; *paratra*—in different planets; *vā*—or; *atha*—as such; *kaivalya-nātha*—to the bestower of liberation; *priya*—dear; *pārśva-vartinaḥ*—being associated with; *āsādya*—after meeting; *devam*—the great demigod; *giriśam*—the lord of the Kailāsa Hill; *yadṛcchayā*—by providence; *prāpuḥ*—achieved; *param*—the Supreme; *nūnam*—certainly; *atha*—therefore; *pracetasaḥ*—the sons of Barhiṣat.

TRANSLATION

My dear Bārhaspatya, what did the sons of King Barhiṣat, known as the Pracetās, obtain after meeting Lord Śiva, who is very dear to the Supreme Personality of Godhead, the bestower of liberation? Certainly they were transferred to the spiritual world, but apart from that, what did they obtain within this material world, either in this life or in other lives?

PURPORT

All types of material happiness are obtained in this life or in the next life, on this planet or on another. The living entity wanders within this material universe in so many species of life and so many planetary systems. The distress and happiness obtained during the span of life are called *iha,* and the distress and happiness obtained in the next life are called *paratra.*

Actually Lord Mahādeva (Śiva) is one of the great demigods within this material world. Generally his blessings bestowed on ordinary people mean material happiness. The predominating deity of this material world, Durgā, is under the control of Lord Mahādeva, Giriśa. Thus Lord Mahādeva can offer anyone any kind of material happiness. Generally people prefer to become devotees of Lord Giriśa to obtain material happiness, but the Pracetās met Lord Mahādeva by providential arrangement. Lord Mahādeva instructed them to worship the Supreme Personality of Godhead, and he personally offered a prayer. As stated in the previous verse (*rudra-gītena*), simply by chanting the prayers offered by Lord Śiva to Viṣṇu, the Pracetās were transferred to the spiritual world. Sometimes devotees desire to enjoy material happiness also; therefore, by the arrangement of the Supreme Personality of Godhead, the devotee is given a chance to enjoy the material world before his final entrance into the spiritual world. Sometimes a devotee is transferred to a heavenly planet, to Janaloka, Maharloka, Tapoloka,

Siddhaloka, and so on. However, a pure devotee never aspires for any kind of material happiness. The pure devotee is consequently transferred directly to Vaikuṇṭhaloka, which is described here as *param*. In this verse Vidura asks Maitreya, the disciple of Bṛhaspati, about the different achievements of the Pracetās.

TEXT 3

मैत्रेय उवाच

प्रचेतसोऽन्तरुदधौ पितुरादेशकारिणः ।
जपयज्ञेन तपसा पुरञ्जनमतोषयन् ॥ ३ ॥

maitreya uvāca
pracetaso 'ntar udadhau
pitur ādeśa-kāriṇaḥ
japa-yajñena tapasā
purañjanam atoṣayan

maitreyaḥ uvāca—Maitreya said; *pracetasaḥ*—the Pracetās; *antaḥ*—within; *udadhau*—the sea; *pituḥ*—of their father; *ādeśa-kāriṇaḥ*—the order carriers; *japa-yajñena*—by chanting *mantras; tapasā*—under severe austerities; *puramjanam*—the Supreme Personality of Godhead; *atoṣayan*—satisfied.

TRANSLATION

The great sage Maitreya said: The sons of King Prācīnabarhi, known as the Pracetās, underwent severe austerities within the seawater to carry out the order of their father. By chanting and repeating the mantras given by Lord Śiva, they were able to satisfy Lord Viṣṇu, the Supreme Personality of Godhead.

PURPORT

One can offer prayers to the Supreme Personality of Godhead directly, but if one repeats the prayers offered by great devotees like Lord Śiva and Lord Brahmā, or if one follows in the footsteps of great personalities, one can please the Supreme Personality of Godhead very easily. For instance, we sometimes chant this *mantra* of *Brahma-saṁhitā:*

cintāmaṇi-prakara-sadmasu kalpa-vṛkṣa-
lakṣāvṛteṣu surabhīr abhipālayantam
lakṣmī-sahasra-śata-sambhrama-sevyamānaṁ
govindam ādi-puruṣaṁ tam ahaṁ bhajāmi

"I worship Govinda, the primeval Lord, the first progenitor, who is tending the cows, yielding all desires, in abodes built with spiritual gems and surrounded by millions of purpose-trees. He is always served with great reverence and affection by hundreds of thousands of *lakṣmīs,* or *gopīs.*" (Bs. 5.29) Because this prayer was offered by Lord Brahmā, we follow him by reciting this prayer. That is the easiest way to satisfy the Supreme Personality of Godhead. The pure devotee never attempts to reach the Supreme Lord directly. The most important way to worship the Lord is to go through the disciplic succession of devotees. The prayers offered by Lord Śiva to the Supreme Personality of Godhead were thus repeated by the Pracetās, who were thus very successful in pleasing the Supreme Lord.

Here the Supreme Personality of Godhead is described as *purañjana.* According to Madhvācārya, the living entity is called *purañjana* because he has become an inhabitant of this material world, and, under the influence of the three modes of material nature, he is forced to live within it. The Supreme Personality of Godhead creates this material world (*pura*), and He also enters within it. *Aṇḍāntara-stha-paramāṇu-cayāntara-stham.* The Lord enters within the heart of the living entity and within the atom; therefore both the living entity and the Lord are called *purañjana.* One *purañjana,* the living entity, is subordinate to the supreme *purañjana;* therefore the duty of the subordinate *purañjana* is to satisfy the supreme *purañjana.* That is devotional service. Lord Rudra, or Lord Śiva, is the original *ācārya* of the Vaiṣṇava *sampradāya* called the Rudra-sampradāya. *Rudra-gītena* indicates that under the disciplic succession of Lord Rudra, the Pracetās achieved spiritual success.

TEXT 4

दशवर्षसहस्रान्ते पुरुषस्तु सनातनः ।
तेषामाविरभूत्कृच्छ्रं शान्तेन शमयन् रुचा ॥ ४ ॥

daśa-varṣa-sahasrānte
puruṣas tu sanātanaḥ
teṣām āvirabhūt kṛcchraṁ
śāntena śamayan rucā

daśa-varṣa—ten years; *sahasra-ante*—at the end of a thousand; *puruṣaḥ*—the Supreme Person; *tu*—then; *sanātanaḥ*—eternal; *teṣām*—of the Pracetās; *āvirabhūt*—appeared; *kṛcchram*—the severe austerity; *śāntena*—satisfying; *śamayan*—mitigating; *rucā*—by His beauty.

TRANSLATION

At the end of ten thousand years of severe austerities performed by the Pracetās, the Supreme Personality of Godhead, to reward their austerities, appeared before them in His very pleasing form. This appealed to the Pracetās and satisfied the labor of their austerities.

PURPORT

Performing ten thousand years of severe austerities does not seem a happy endeavor. Yet the devotees, the serious students of spiritual life, undergo such austerities to attain the favor of the Supreme Personality of Godhead. At that time, when the duration of life was very long, people could undergo severe austerities for thousands of years. It is said that Vālmīki, the author of *Rāmāyaṇa,* underwent meditational austerities for 60,000 years. The Supreme Personality of Godhead appreciated the austerities undergone by the Pracetās, and He finally appeared before them in a pleasing form. Thus they all became satisfied and forgot the austerities they underwent. In the material world, if one is successful after hard labor, he is very pleased. Similarly, the devotee forgets all his labors and austerities as soon as he contacts the Supreme Personality of Godhead. Although Dhruva Mahārāja was only a five-year-old boy, he underwent severe austerities by eating simply dry foliage, drinking only water and taking no food. In this way, after six months, he was able to see the Supreme Personality of Godhead face to face. When he saw the Lord, he forgot all his austerities and said, *svāmin kṛtārtho 'smi:* "My dear Lord, I am very pleased."

Of course, these austerities were performed in the Satya-yuga, Dvāpara-yuga and Tretā-yuga, but not in this age of Kali. In this Kali-yuga, one can attain the same results simply by chanting the Hare Kṛṣṇa *mahā-mantra.* Because the people of this age are fallen, the Lord is kind enough to give them the easiest method. Simply by chanting the Hare Kṛṣṇa *mantra,* one can attain the same results. However, as Lord Caitanya Mahāprabhu points out, we are so unfortunate that we are not even attracted to chanting the *mahā-mantra*—Hare Kṛṣṇa, Hare Kṛṣṇa, Kṛṣṇa Kṛṣṇa, Hare Hare/ Hare Rāma, Hare Rāma, Rāma Rāma, Hare Hare.

TEXT 5

सुपर्णस्कन्धमारूढो मेरुशृङ्गमिवाम्बुदः ।
पीतवासा मणिग्रीवः कुर्वन् वितिमिरा दिशः ॥ ५ ॥

suparṇa-skandham ārūḍho
meru-śṛṅgam ivāmbudaḥ
pīta-vāsā maṇi-grīvaḥ
kurvan vitimirā diśaḥ

suparṇa—of Garuḍa, the carrier of Lord Viṣṇu; *skandham*—the shoulder; *ārūḍhaḥ*—sitting on; *meru*—of the mountain named Meru; *śṛṅgam*—on the summit; *iva*—like; *ambudaḥ*—a cloud; *pīta-vāsāḥ*—wearing yellow garments; *maṇi-grīvaḥ*—His neck decorated with the Kaustubha jewel; *kurvan*—making; *vitimirāḥ*—free from darkness; *diśaḥ*—all directions.

TRANSLATION

The Personality of Godhead, appearing on the shoulder of Garuḍa, seemed like a cloud resting on the summit of the mountain known as Meru. The transcendental body of the Personality of Godhead was covered by attractive yellow garments, and His neck was decorated with the jewel known as Kaustubha-maṇi. The bodily effulgence of the Lord dissipated all the darkness of the universe.

PURPORT

As stated in *Caitanya-caritāmṛta, kṛṣṇa——sūrya-sama; māyā haya andhakāra/ yāhāṅ kṛṣṇa, tāhāṅ nāhi māyāra adhikāra* (Cc. *Madhya* 22.31). The Lord is just like the effulgent sun. Consequently whenever the Supreme Personality of Godhead is present, there cannot be darkness or ignorance. Actually this dark universe is illuminated by the sun, but the sun and moon simply reflect the bodily effulgence of the Supreme Lord. In *Bhagavad-gītā* the Lord says:

yad āditya-gataṁ tejo
jagad bhāsayate 'khilam
yac candramasi yac cāgnau
tat tejo viddhi māmakam

"The splendor of the sun, which dissipates the darkness of this whole world, comes from Me. And the splendor of the moon and the splendor of fire are also from Me." (Bg. 15.12)

The conclusion is that the origin of all life is the bodily effulgence of the Supreme Personality of Godhead. This is also confirmed in *Brahma-saṁhitā: yasya prabhā prabhavato jagad-aṇḍa-koṭi.* Being illuminated by the bodily effulgence of the Supreme Personality of Godhead, everything is freed from all darkness.

TEXT 6

काशिष्णुना कनकवर्णविभूषणेन
भ्राजत्कपोलवदनो विलसत्किरीटः ।
अष्टायुधैरनुचरैर्मुनिभिः सुरेन्द्रै-
रासेवितो गरुडकिन्नरगीतकीर्तिः ॥ ६ ॥

kāśiṣṇunā kanaka-varṇa-vibhūṣaṇena
bhrājat-kapola-vadano vilasat-kirīṭaḥ
aṣṭāyudhair anucarair munibhiḥ surendrair
āsevito garuḍa-kinnara-gīta-kīrtiḥ

kāśiṣṇunā—shining; *kanaka*—gold; *varṇa*—colored; *vibhūṣaṇena*—with ornaments; *bhrājat*—shining; *kapola*—forehead; *vadanaḥ*—His face; *vilasat*—dazzling; *kirīṭaḥ*—His helmet; *aṣṭa*—eight; *āyudhaiḥ*—with weapons; *anucaraiḥ*—by followers; *munibhiḥ*—by great sages; *surendraiḥ*—by demigods; *āsevitaḥ*—served; *garuḍa*—by Garuḍa; *kinnara*—inhabitant of the Kinnara planet; *gīta*—sung; *kīrtiḥ*—His glories.

TRANSLATION

The Lord's face was very beautiful, and His head was decorated with a shining helmet and golden ornaments. The helmet was dazzling and was very beautifully situated on His head. The Lord had eight arms, which each held a particular weapon. The Lord was surrounded by demigods, great sages and other associates. These were all engaged in His service. Garuḍa, the carrier of the Lord, glorified the Lord with Vedic hymns by flapping his wings. Garuḍa appeared to be an inhabitant of the planet known as Kinnaraloka.

PURPORT

Generally the Viṣṇu form is manifested with four hands holding four objects (a conchshell, disc, club and lotus flower). However, here Lord Viṣṇu is described as possessing eight arms with eight kinds of weapons. According to Vīrarāghava Ācārya, the conchshell and lotus flower are also accepted as weapons. Since the Lord is the supreme controller, whatever is in His hand can be considered a weapon. Four hands hold four kinds of weapons, and the extra four hands hold an arrow, bow, trident and snake. Śrī Vīrarāghava Ācārya describes the eight weapons as *śaṅkha, cakra, gadā, padma, śārṅga, śara,* etc.

A king is always accompanied by his ministers, secretaries and commanders, and Lord Viṣṇu is also accompanied by His followers, the demigods, great sages, saintly persons, and so on. He is never alone. Consequently there is no question of the Lord's being impersonal. He is always Himself, the Supreme Personality of Godhead, and His associates are also persons. From the description given in this verse, Garuḍa appears to have belonged to the Kinnara planet. The inhabitants of the Kinnara planet have the same features as Garuḍa. Their bodily features are like those of a human being, but they have wings. The word *gīta-kīrtiḥ* indicates that the inhabitants of Kinnaraloka are very expert in singing the glories of the Lord. In *Brahma-saṁhitā* it is said: *jagad-aṇḍa-koṭi-koṭiṣv aśeṣa-vasudhādi-vibhūti-bhinnam.* In each and every universe there are different types of planets, and each planet has distinctive features. On the strength of this verse, we can understand that in Kinnaraloka the inhabitants can fly with their wings. There is also a planet, known as Siddhaloka, where the inhabitants can fly even without wings. Thus each and every planet has some distinctive facility. That is the beauty of the varied creation of the Supreme Personality of Godhead.

TEXT 7

पीनायताष्टभुजमण्डलमध्यलक्ष्म्या
स्पर्धच्छ्रिया परिवृतो वनमालयाऽऽद्यः ।
बर्हिष्मतः पुरुष आह सुतान् प्रपन्नान्
पर्जन्यनादरुतया सघृणावलोकः ॥ ७ ॥

pīnāyatāṣṭa-bhuja-maṇḍala-madhya-lakṣmyā
spardhac-chriyā parivṛto vana-mālayādyaḥ
barhiṣmataḥ puruṣa āha sutān prapannān
parjanya-nāda-rutayā saghṛṇāvalokaḥ

pīna—stout; *āyata*—long; *aṣṭa*—eight; *bhuja*—arms; *maṇḍala*—encirclement; *madhya*—in the midst of; *lakṣmyā*—with the goddess of fortune; *spardhat*—contending; *śriyā*—whose beauty; *parivṛtaḥ*—encircled; *vana-mālayā*—by a flower garland; *ādyaḥ*—the original Personality of Godhead; *barhiṣmataḥ*—of King Prācīnabarhi; *puruṣaḥ*—the Supreme Personality of Godhead; *āha*—addressed; *sutān*—the sons; *prapannān*—surrendered; *parjanya*—like a cloud; *nāda*—whose sound; *rutayā*—by a voice; *sa-ghṛṇa*—with mercy; *avalokaḥ*—His glancing.

TRANSLATION

Around the neck of the Personality of Godhead hung a flower garland that reached to His knees. His eight stout and elongated arms were decorated with that garland, which challenged the beauty of the goddess of fortune. With a merciful glance and a voice like thunder, the Lord addressed the sons of King Prācīnabarhiṣat, who were very much surrendered unto Him.

PURPORT

The word *ādyaḥ* in this verse is very significant. The Supreme Personality of Godhead is the origin even of Paramātmā and Brahman. As confirmed in *Bhagavad-gītā:*

brahmaṇo hi pratiṣṭhāham
amṛtasyāvyayasya ca
śāśvatasya ca dharmasya
sukhasyaikāntikasya ca

"And I am the basis of the impersonal Brahman, which is the constitutional position of ultimate happiness, and which is immortal, imperishable and eternal." (Bg. 14.27)

The Absolute Truth thus begins not with the impersonal Brahman but with the original Personality of Godhead, Kṛṣṇa. When Arjuna realized Kṛṣṇa's greatness, he addressed Him in this way:

arjuna uvāca
paraṁ brahma paraṁ dhāma
pavitraṁ paramaṁ bhavān
puruṣaṁ śāśvataṁ divyam
ādi-devam ajaṁ vibhum

āhus tvām ṛṣayaḥ sarve
devarṣir nāradas tathā
asito devalo vyāsaḥ
svayaṁ caiva bravīṣi me

"Arjuna said: You are the Supreme Brahman, the ultimate, the supreme abode and purifier, the Absolute Truth and the eternal divine person. You are the primal God, transcendental and original, and You are the unborn and all-pervading beauty. All the great sages such as Nārada, Asita, Devala, and Vyāsa proclaim this of You, and now You Yourself are declaring it to me." (Bg. 10.12-13)

The *Brahma-saṁhitā* also says, *anādir ādir govindaḥ sarva-kāraṇa-kāraṇam:* "The Supreme Lord is not caused by anything [*anādi*], but He is the cause of all causes." The *Vedānta-sūtra* says, *janmādy asya yataḥ:* "The Absolute Truth is that from which everything emanates." The Absolute Truth is described as *ādi-puruṣa.* The Absolute Truth is therefore a person and is not impersonal.

TEXT 8

श्रीभगवानुवाच
वरं वृणीध्वं भद्रं वो यूयं मे नृपनन्दनाः ।
सौहार्देनापृथग्धर्मास्तुष्टोऽहं सौहृदेन वः ॥ ८ ॥

śrī bhagavān uvāca
varaṁ vṛṇīdhvaṁ bhadraṁ vo
yūyaṁ me nṛpa-nandanāḥ
sauhārdenāpṛthag-dharmās
tuṣṭo 'haṁ sauhṛdena vaḥ

śrī bhagavān uvāca—the Supreme Personality of Godhead said; *varam*—benediction; *vṛṇīdhvam*—ask; *bhadram*—good fortune; *vaḥ*—of you; *yūyam*—you; *me*—from Me; *nṛpa-nandanāḥ*—O sons of the King; *sauhārdena*—by friendship; *apṛthak*—nondifferent; *dharmāḥ*—occupation; *tuṣṭaḥ*—pleased; *aham*—I; *sauhṛdena*—by friendship; *vaḥ*—of you.

TRANSLATION

The Supreme Personality of Godhead said: My dear sons of the King, I am very much pleased by the friendly relationships amongst you. All of you are engaged in one occupation—devotional service. I am so pleased with your mutual friendship that I wish you all good fortune. Now you may ask a benediction of Me.

PURPORT

Since the sons of King Prācīnabarhiṣat were all united in Kṛṣṇa consciousness, the Lord was very pleased with them. Each and every one of the sons of King Prācīnabarhiṣat was an individual soul, but they were united in offering transcendental service to the Lord. The unity of the individual souls attempting to satisfy the Supreme Lord or rendering service to the Lord is real unity. In the material world such unity is not possible. Even though people may officially unite, they all have different interests. In the United Nations, for instance, all the nations have their particular national ambitions, and consequently they cannot be united. Disunity between individual souls is so strong within this material world that even in a society of Kṛṣṇa consciousness, members sometimes appear disunited due to their having different opinions and leaning toward material things. Actually in Kṛṣṇa consciousness there cannot be two opinions. There is only one goal: to serve Kṛṣṇa to one's best ability. If there is some disagreement over service, such disagreement is to be taken as spiritual. Those who are actually engaged in the service of the Supreme Personality of Godhead cannot be disunited in any circumstance. This makes the Supreme Personality of Godhead very happy and willing to award all kinds of benediction to His devotees, as indicated in this verse. We can see that the Lord is immediately prepared to award all benedictions to the sons of King Prācīnabarhiṣat.

TEXT 9

योऽनुस्मरति सन्ध्यायां युष्माननुदिनं नरः ।
तस्य भ्रातृष्वात्मसाम्यं तथा भूतेषु सौहृदम् ॥ ९ ॥

yo 'nusmarati sandhyāyāṁ
yuṣmān anudinaṁ naraḥ
tasya bhrātṛṣv ātma-sāmyaṁ
tathā bhūteṣu sauhṛdam

yaḥ—one who; *anusmarati*—always remembers; *sandhyāyām*—in the evening; *yuṣmān*—you; *anudinam*—every day; *naraḥ*—human being; *tasya bhrātṛṣu*—with his brothers; *ātma-sāmyam*—personal equality; *tathā*—as also; *bhūteṣu*—with all living beings; *sauhṛdam*—friendship.

TRANSLATION

The Lord continued: Those who remember you every evening of every day will become friendly with their brothers and with all other living entities.

TEXT 10

ये तु मां रुद्रगीतेन सायं प्रातः समाहिताः ।
स्तुवन्त्यहं कामवरान्दास्ये प्रज्ञां च शोभनाम् ॥ १० ॥

ye tu māṁ rudra-gītena
sāyaṁ prātaḥ samāhitāḥ
stuvanty ahaṁ kāma-varān
dāsye prajñāṁ ca śobhanām

ye—those persons who; *tu*—but; *mām*—unto Me; *rudra-gītena*—by the song sung by Lord Śiva; *sāyam*—in the evening; *prātaḥ*—in the morning; *samāhitāḥ*—being attentive; *stuvanti*—offer prayers; *aham*—I; *kāma-varān*—all benedictions to fulfill desires; *dāsye*—shall award; *prajñām*—intelligence; *ca*—also; *śobhanām*—transcendental.

TRANSLATION

Those who will offer Me the prayers composed by Lord Śiva, both in the morning and in the evening, will be given benedictions by Me. In this way they can both fulfill their desires and attain good intelligence.

PURPORT

Good intelligence means going back home, back to Godhead. This is confirmed in *Bhagavad-gītā:*

teṣāṁ satata-yuktānāṁ
bhajatāṁ prīti-pūrvakam
dadāmi buddhi-yogaṁ taṁ
yena mām upayānti te

"To those who are constantly devoted and worship Me with love, I give the understanding by which they can come to Me." (Bg. 10.10)

One who offers prayers to the Lord to fulfill his different desires must know that the highest perfectional fulfillment of desire is to go back home, back to Godhead. In this verse it is indicated that those who remember the activities of the Pracetās, the sons of King Prācīnabarhiṣat, will be delivered and benedicted. So what to speak of the sons of King Prācīnabarhiṣat, who are directly connected with the Supreme Personality of Godhead? This is the way of the *paramparā* system. If we follow the *ācāryas,* we attain the same benefit as our predecessors. If one follows the decisions of Arjuna, he should be considered to be directly hearing *Bhagavad-gītā* from the Supreme Personality of Godhead. There is no difference between hearing *Bhagavad-gītā* directly from the Supreme Lord and following a personality like Arjuna, who formerly heard *Bhagavad-gītā* directly from the Lord. Sometimes foolish people argue that since Kṛṣṇa is not present at the moment, one cannot take direct instructions from Him. Such foolish people do not know that there is no difference between directly hearing *Bhagavad-gītā* and reading it, as long as one accepts *Bhagavad-gītā* as it is, spoken by the Lord. However, if one wants to understand *Bhagavad-gītā* by his imperfect interpretations, one cannot possibly understand the mysteries of *Bhagavad-gītā,* even though one may be a great scholar according to mundane estimation.

TEXT 11

यद्यूयं पितुरादेशमग्रहीष्ट मुदान्विताः ।
अथो व उशती कीर्तिर्लोकाननु भविष्यति ॥११॥

yad yūyaṁ pitur ādeśam
agrahīṣṭa mudānvitāḥ
atho va uśatī kīrtir
lokān anu bhaviṣyati

yat—because; *yūyam*—you; *pituḥ*—of your father; *ādeśam*—the order; *agrahīṣṭa*—accepted; *mudā-anvitāḥ*—in great happiness; *atho*—therefore; *vaḥ*—your; *uśatī*—attractive; *kīrtiḥ*—glories; *lokān anu*—throughout the universe; *bhaviṣyati*—will become possible.

TRANSLATION

Because you have with pleasure accepted within your hearts the orders of your father and have executed those orders very faithfully, your attractive qualities will be celebrated all over the world.

PURPORT

Since every living entity is part and parcel of the Supreme Personality of Godhead, he has small independence. Sometimes unintelligent men ask why one is put into a miserable condition, even though everyone is under the control of the Supreme Personality of Godhead. Because of his minute independence, the living entity can obey or disobey the orders of the Supreme Lord. If he obeys the Supreme Lord's orders, he becomes happy. If he does not, he becomes unhappy. Therefore the living entity creates his own happiness or unhappiness. The Supreme Lord does not enforce these on anyone. The Supreme Lord praised the Pracetās because they all faithfully obeyed the orders of their father. The Lord therefore blessed the sons of King Prācīnabarhiṣat because they obeyed their father's orders.

TEXT 12

भविता विश्रुतः पुत्रोऽनवमो ब्रह्मणो गुणैः ।
य एतामात्मवीर्येण त्रिलोकीं पूरयिष्यति ॥१२॥

bhavitā viśrutaḥ putro
'navamo brahmaṇo guṇaiḥ
ya etām ātma-vīryeṇa
tri-lokīṁ pūrayiṣyati

bhavitā—there will be; *viśrutaḥ*—very famous; *putraḥ*—son; *anavamaḥ*—not inferior; *brahmaṇaḥ*—to Lord Brahmā; *guṇaiḥ*—by qualifications; *yaḥ*—who; *etām*—all this; *ātma-vīryeṇa*—by his progeny; *tri-lokīm*—the three worlds; *pūrayiṣyati*—will fill.

TRANSLATION

You will have a nice son, who will be in no way inferior to Lord Brahmā. Consequently, he will be very famous all over the universe, and the sons and grandsons generated by him will fill the three worlds.

PURPORT

As explained in the next verse, the Pracetās will marry the daughter of the great sage Kaṇḍu. It is suggested that the son's name will be Viśruta and that he will glorify both his father and mother because of his good character. In fact, he would be greater than Lord Brahmā. The great politician Cāṇakya said that if there is a good tree within a garden or forest, its flowers will fill the forest with their fragrance. Similarly, a good son within a family makes the whole family famous all over the world. Kṛṣṇa took birth in the family of the Yadus, and consequently the Yadu dynasty is famous all over the world.

TEXT 13

कण्डोः प्रम्लोचया लब्धा कन्या कमललोचना ।
तां चापविद्धां जगृहुर्भूरुहा नृपनन्दनाः ॥१३॥

kaṇḍoḥ pramlocayā labdhā
kanyā kamala-locanā

tāṁ cāpaviddhāṁ jagṛhur
bhūruhā nṛpa-nandanāḥ

kaṇḍoḥ—of the sage Kaṇḍu; *pramlocayā*—by a heavenly society girl named Pramlocā; *labdhā*—obtained; *kanyā*—daughter; *kamala-locanā*—lotus-eyed; *tām*—her; *ca*—also; *apaviddhām*—given up; *jagṛhuḥ*—accepted; *bhūruhāḥ*—the trees; *nṛpa-nandanāḥ*—O sons of King Prācīnabarhiṣat.

TRANSLATION

O sons of King Prācīnabarhiṣat, the heavenly society girl named Pramlocā kept the lotus-eyed daughter of Kaṇḍu in the care of the forest trees. Then she went back to the heavenly planet. This daughter was born by the coupling of the Apsarā named Pramlocā with the sage Kaṇḍu.

PURPORT

Whenever a great sage undergoes severe austerities for material power, the King of heaven, Indra, becomes very envious. All the demigods have responsible posts for the management of universal affairs and are very highly qualified with pious activities. Although they are ordinary living entities, they are nonetheless able to attain responsible posts, like Lord Brahmā, Indra, Candra and Varuṇa. As is the nature of this material world, the King of heaven, Indra, is very anxious if a great sage undergoes severe austerities. The whole material world is filled with such envy that everyone becomes afraid of his neighbors. Every businessman is afraid of his associates because this material world is the field of activities for all kinds of envious people who have come here to compete with the opulence of the Supreme Personality of Godhead. Thus Indra was very much afraid of the severe austerities performed by the great sage Kaṇḍu, and he sent Pramlocā to break his vows and austerities. A similar incident took place in the case of Viśvāmitra. From other incidents in the *śāstras,* it appears that Indra has always been envious. When King Pṛthu was celebrating various sacrifices, outdoing Indra, Indra became very envious, and he disturbed King Pṛthu's sacrifice. This has already been discussed in previous chapters. King Indra became successful in breaking the vow of the great sage Kaṇḍu, who became attracted by the beauty of the heavenly society girl Pramlocā and begot a female child. This child is described herein as lotus-eyed and very beautiful. Being thus successful in her mission, Pramlocā returned to the heavenly planets, leaving the newborn child to the care of the trees. Fortunately the trees accepted the child and agreed to raise her.

TEXT 14

क्षुत्क्षामाया मुखे राजा सोमः पीयूषवर्षिणीम् ।
देशिनीं रोदमानाया निदधे स दयान्वितः ॥१४॥

kṣut-kṣāmāyā mukhe rājā
somaḥ pīyūṣa-varṣiṇīm
deśinīṁ rodamānāyā
nidadhe sa dayānvitaḥ

kṣut—by hunger; *kṣāmāyāḥ*—when she was distressed; *mukhe*—within the mouth; *rājā*—the King; *somaḥ*—the moon; *pīyūṣa*—nectar; *varṣiṇīm*—pouring; *deśinīm*—forefinger; *rodamānāyāḥ*—while she was crying; *nidadhe*—placed; *saḥ*—he; *dayā-anvitaḥ*—being compassionate.

TRANSLATION

Thereafter the child, who was left to the care of the trees, began to cry in hunger. At that time the King of the forest, namely the King of the moon planet, out of compassion placed his finger, which poured forth nectar, within the child's mouth. Thus the child was raised by the mercy of the King of the moon.

PURPORT

Although the Apsarā left her child to the care of the trees, the trees could not take care of the child properly; therefore the trees handed the child over to the King of the moon. Thus Candra, King of the moon, put his finger within the mouth of the child to satisfy her hunger.

TEXT 15

प्रजाविसर्ग आदिष्टाः पित्रा मामनुवर्तता ।
तत्र कन्यां वरारोहां तामुद्वहत माचिरम् ॥१५॥

prajā-visarga ādiṣṭāḥ
pitrā mām anuvartatā
tatra kanyāṁ varārohāṁ
tām udvahata mā ciram

prajā-visarge—to create progeny; *ādiṣṭāḥ*—being ordered; *pitrā*—by your father; *mām*—My direction; *anuvartatā*—following; *tatra*—there; *kanyām*—

the daughter; *varārohām*—highly qualified and exquisitely beautiful; *tām*—her; *udvahata*—marry; *mā*—without; *ciram*—wasting time.

TRANSLATION

Since all of you are very much obedient to My orders, I ask you to immediately marry that girl, who is so well qualified with beauty and good qualities. According to the order of your father, create progeny through her.

PURPORT

The Pracetās not only were great devotees of the Supreme Personality of Godhead but were very obedient to the orders of their father. Therefore the Lord asked them to marry the daughter of Pramlocā.

TEXT 16

अपृथग्धर्मशीलानां सर्वेषां वः सुमध्यमा ।
अपृथग्धर्मशीलेयं भूयात्पत्न्यर्पिताशया ॥१६॥

apṛthag-dharma-śīlānāṁ
sarveṣāṁ vaḥ sumadhyamā
apṛthag-dharma-śīleyaṁ
bhūyāt patny arpitāśayā

apṛthak—without differences; *dharma*—occupation; *śīlānām*—whose character; *sarveṣām*—all; *vaḥ*—of you; *su-madhyamā*—a girl whose waist is slender; *apṛthak*—without differences; *dharma*—occupation; *śīlā*—well-behaved; *iyam*—this; *bhūyāt*—may she become; *patnī*—wife; *arpita-āśayā*—fully surrendered.

TRANSLATION

You brothers are all of the same nature, being devotees and obedient sons of your father. Similarly, that girl is also of the same type and is dedicated to all of you. Thus both the girl and you, the sons of Prācīnabarhiṣat, are on the same platform, being united on a common principle.

PURPORT

According to Vedic principles, a woman cannot have many husbands, although a husband can have many wives. In special instances, however, it is found that a woman has more than one husband. Draupadī, for instance, was married to all of the five Pāṇḍava brothers. Similarly, the Supreme Personality of Godhead ordered all the sons of Prācīnabarhiṣat to marry the one girl born of the great sage Kaṇḍu and Pramlocā. In special cases, a girl is allowed to marry more than one man, provided she is able to treat her husbands equally. This is not possible for an ordinary woman. Only one who is especially qualified can be allowed to marry more than one husband. In this age of Kali, to find such an equipoised woman is very difficult. Thus according to scripture, *kalau pañca vivarjayet.* In this age a woman is forbidden to marry her husband's brother. This system is still practiced in some of the hilly tracts of India. The Lord says: *apṛthag-dharma-śīleyaṁ bhūyāt patny arpitāśayā.* With the blessings of the Lord, all things are possible. The Lord especially benedicted the girl to surrender equally to all brothers. *Apṛthag-dharma,* meaning occupational duty without difference of purpose, is taught in *Bhagavad-gītā. Bhagavad-gītā* is divided into three primary divisions—*karma-yoga, jñāna-yoga,* and *bhakti-yoga.* The word *yoga* means acting on behalf of the Supreme Personality of Godhead. As confirmed by *Bhagavad-gītā:*

yajñārthāt karmaṇo 'nyatra
loko 'yaṁ karma-bandhanaḥ
tad-arthaṁ karma kaunteya
mukta-saṅgaḥ samācara

"Work done as a sacrifice for Viṣṇu has to be performed, otherwise work binds one to this material world. Therefore, O son of Kuntī, perform your prescribed duties for His satisfaction, and in that way you will always remain unattached and free from bondage." (Bg. 3.9)

One may act according to his own occupational duty just to satisfy the *yajña-puruṣa,* the Supreme Personality of Godhead. That is called *apṛthag-dharma.* Different limbs of the body may act in different ways, but the ultimate objective is to maintain the entire body. Similarly, if we work for the satisfaction of the Supreme Personality of Godhead, we will find that we satisfy everything. We should follow in the footsteps of the Pracetās, whose only aim was to satisfy the Supreme Lord. This is called *apṛthag-dharma.* According to *Bhagavad-gītā:*

sarva-dharmān parityajya
māṁ ekaṁ śaraṇaṁ vraja
ahaṁ tvāṁ sarva-pāpebhyo
mokṣayiṣyāmi mā śucaḥ

"Abandon all varieties of religion and just surrender unto Me. I shall deliver you from all sinful reaction. Do not fear." (Bg. 18.66)

This is the advice of Lord Kṛṣṇa. Our only aim should be to act in Kṛṣṇa consciousness for the satisfaction of the Lord. This is oneness, or *apṛthag-dharma.*

TEXT 17

दिव्यवर्षसहस्राणां सहस्रमहतौजसः ।
भौमान् भोक्ष्यथ भोगान् वै दिव्यांश्चानुग्रहान्मम ॥१७॥

divya-varṣa-sahasrāṇāṁ
sahasram ahataujasaḥ
bhaumān bhokṣyatha bhogān vai
divyāṁś cānugrahān mama

divya—of the heavenly planets; *varṣa*—years; *sahasrāṇām*—of thousands; *sahasram*—a thousand; *ahata*—without being defeated; *ojasaḥ*—your power; *bhaumān*—of this world; *bhokṣyatha*—you will enjoy; *bhogān*—enjoyments; *vai*—certainly; *divyān*—of the heavenly world; *ca*—also; *anugrahāt*—by mercy; *mama*—My.

TRANSLATION

The Lord then blessed all the Pracetās, saying: My dear princes, by My mercy, you can enjoy all the facilities of this world as well as the heavenly world. Indeed, you can enjoy all of them without hindrance and with full strength for one million celestial years.

PURPORT

The duration of life prescribed for the Pracetās by the Supreme Personality of Godhead is calculated by the time measurements of higher planetary systems. Our six earth months are said to equal one day (12 hours) in the higher planetary systems. Thirty days equal one month, and twelve months equal one year. In this way, for one million years according to the calculations of the higher planetary system the Pracetās were allowed to enjoy all kinds of material facilities. Although this lifespan was so long, the Pracetās were given full bodily strength by the grace of the Lord. In the material world, if one wants to live for many years, he must endure the difficulties of old age, invalidity and many other miserable conditions. The Pracetās, however, were given full bodily strength to enjoy material facilities. This special facility was given to the Pracetās so that they could continue rendering full devotional service. This will be explained in the following verse.

TEXT 18

अथ मय्यनपायिन्या भक्त्या पक्वगुणाशयाः ।
उपयास्यथ मद्धाम निर्विद्य निरयादतः ॥१८॥

atha mayy anapāyinyā
bhaktyā pakva-guṇāśayāḥ
upayāsyatha mad-dhāma
nirvidya nirayād ataḥ

atha—therefore; *mayi*—unto Me; *anapāyinyā*—without any deviation; *bhaktyā*—by devotional service; *pakva-guṇa*—free from material contamination; *āśayāḥ*—your mind; *upayāsyatha*—you will attain; *mat-dhāma*—My abode; *nirvidya*—being completely detached; *nirayāt*—from material existence; *ataḥ*—thus.

TRANSLATION

Thereafter you will develop unadulterated devotional service unto Me and be freed from all material contamination. At that time, being completely unattached to material enjoyment in the so-called heavenly planets as well as in hellish planets, you will return home, back to Godhead.

PURPORT

By the grace of the Lord, the Pracetās were given special facilities. Although they could live millions of years to enjoy material facilities, they still would not be deviated from the transcendental loving service of the Lord. Being thus fully engaged, the Pracetās would be completely freed from all material attachment. Material attachment is very strong. During one lifetime, a materialist engages in acquiring land, money, friends, society, friendship, love, and so on. He also wants to enjoy the heavenly planets after the annihilation of the body. If one is engaged in devotional serivce, however, he becomes unattached to all kinds of material enjoyment and suffering. In the material world, those who are elevated to the higher planetary systems are supposed to enjoy all material facilities, whereas those degraded to lower planetary systems are supposed to live in a hellish condition. A devotee, however, is transcendental to both heavenly and hellish conditions. According to *Bhagavad-gītā,* a devotee's position is described in this way:

māṁ ca yo 'vyabhicāreṇa
bhakti-yogena sevate
sa guṇān samatītyaitān
brahma-bhūyāya kalpate

"One who engages in full devotional service, who does not fall down in any circumstance, at once transcends the modes of material nature and thus comes to the level of Brahman." (Bg. 14.26)

A devotee is always situated on the Brahman platform. He has nothing to do with material happiness or distress. When one is strongly fixed in devotional service and free from all material attachment, uncontaminated by the material modes of nature, he becomes fit to return home, back to Godhead. Although by special blessing the Pracetās would enjoy material facilities for millions of years, they would not be attached to them. Thus at the end of their material enjoyment they would be promoted to the spiritual world and return to Godhead.

The word *pakva-guṇāśayāḥ* has special significance, for it means that by devotional service one is able to give up the influence of the three modes of material nature. As long as one is influenced by the modes of material nature, he cannot return to Godhead. It is clearly explained that all planets in the material world—beginning from Brahmaloka down to the hellish planets—are unfit places for a devotee. *Padaṁ padaṁ yad vipadāṁ na teṣām.* A place where there is danger at every step is certainly not a comfortable place. The Lord therefore says in *Bhagavad-gītā:*

ābrahma-bhuvanāl lokāḥ
punar āvartino 'rjuna
mām upetya tu kaunteya
punar janma na vidyate

"From the highest planet in the material world down to the lowest, all are places of misery wherein repeated birth and death take place. But one who attains to My abode, O son of Kuntī, never take birth again." (Bg. 8.16)

Thus there is no profit, even if one is promoted to the highest planet in the material universe, Brahmaloka. However, if one is somehow or other promoted to the abode of the Lord, he never returns to the material world.

TEXT 19

गृहेष्वाविशतां चापि पुंसां कुशलकर्मणाम् ।
मद्वार्तायातयामानां न बन्धाय गृहा मताः ॥१९॥

gṛheṣv āviśatāṁ cāpi
puṁsāṁ kuśala-karmaṇām
mad-vārtā-yāta-yāmānāṁ
na bandhāya gṛhā matāḥ

gṛheṣu—in family life; *āviśatām*—who have entered; *ca*—also; *api*—even; *puṁsām*—of persons; *kuśala-karmaṇām*—engaged in auspicious activities; *mat-vārtā*—in topics about Me; *yāta*—is expended; *yāmānām*—whose every moment; *na*—not; *bandhāya*—for bondage; *gṛhāḥ*—household life; *matāḥ*—considered.

TRANSLATION

Those who are engaged in auspicious activities in devotional service certainly understand that the ultimate enjoyer or beneficiary of all activities is the Supreme Personality of Godhead. Thus when one acts, he offers the results to the Supreme Personality of Godhead and passes life always engaged in the topics of the Lord. Even though such a person may be participating in family life, he is not affected by the results of his actions.

PURPORT

Generally a person living in a family becomes overly attached to fruitive activity. In other words, he tries to enjoy the results of his activities. A devotee, however, knows that Kṛṣṇa is the supreme enjoyer.

bhoktāraṁ yajña-tapasāṁ
sarva-loka-maheśvaram
suhṛdaṁ sarva-bhūtānāṁ
jñātvā māṁ śāntim ṛcchati

"The sages, knowing Me as the ultimate purpose of all sacrifices and austerities, the Supreme Lord of all planets and demigods and the benefactor and well-wisher of all living entities, attain peace from the pangs of material miseries." (Bg. 5.29)

The Supreme Lord is the supreme proprietor; consequently the devotee does not consider himself the proprietor of any occupation. The devotee always thinks of the Supreme Personality of Godhead as the proprietor; therefore the results of his business are offered to the Supreme Lord. One who thus lives in the material world with his family and children never becomes affected by the contaminations of the material world. This is confirmed in *Bhagavad-gītā* (3.9):

yajñārthāt karmaṇo 'nyatra
loko 'yaṁ karma-bandhanaḥ
tad-arthaṁ karma kaunteya
mukta-saṅgaḥ samācara

One who tries to enjoy the results of his activities becomes bound by the results. One who offers the results or profits to the Supreme Personality of Godhead, however, does not become entangled in the results. This is the secret of success. Generally people take *sannyāsa* to become free from the reactions of fruitive activity. One who does not receive the results of his actions but offers them instead to the Supreme Personality of Godhead certainly remains in a liberated condition. In *Bhakti-rasāmṛta-sindhu,* Śrīla Rūpa Gosvāmī confirms this:

īhā yasya harer dāsye
karmaṇā manasā girā
nikhilāsv apy avasthāsu
jīvan-muktaḥ sa ucyate

If one engages himself in the service of the Lord through his life, wealth, words, intelligence, and everything he possesses, he will always be liberated in any condition. Such a person is called a *jīvan-mukta,* one who is liberated during this lifetime. Devoid of Kṛṣṇa consciousness, those who engage in material activities simply become more entangled in material bondage. They have to suffer and enjoy the actions and reactions of all activity. This Kṛṣṇa consciousness movement is therefore the greatest boon to humanity because it keeps one always engaged in Kṛṣṇa's service. The devotees think of Kṛṣṇa, act for Kṛṣṇa, eat for Kṛṣṇa, sleep for Kṛṣṇa and work for Kṛṣṇa. Thus everything is engaged in the service of Kṛṣṇa. A total life in Kṛṣṇa consciousness saves one from material contamination. As stated by Bhaktisiddhānta Sarasvatī Gosvāmī Mahārāja, *kṛṣṇa bhajane yāhā haya anukūla, viṣaya baliyā tyāge tāhā haya bhūla.* If one is so expert that he can engage everything or dovetail everything in the service of the Lord, to give up the material world would be a great blunder. One should learn how to dovetail everything in the service of the Lord, for everything is connected to Kṛṣṇa. That is the real purpose of life and secret of success. As reiterated later in the Third Chapter of *Bhagavad-gītā:*

tasmād asaktaḥ satataṁ
kāryaṁ karma samācara

asakto hy ācaran karma
param āpnoti pūruṣaḥ

"Therefore, without being attached to the fruits of activities, one should act as a matter of duty; for by working without attachment, one attains the Supreme." (3.19)

The Third Chapter of *Bhagavad-gītā* specifically considers material activities for the purpose of sense gratification and material activities for the purpose of satisfying the Supreme Lord. The conclusion is that these are not one and the same. Material activities for sense gratification are the cause of material bondage, whereas the very same activities for the satisfaction of Kṛṣṇa are the cause of liberation. How the same activity can be the cause of bondage and liberation can be explained as follows. One may get indigestion due to eating too many milk preparations—condensed milk, sweet rice, and so on. But even though there is indigestion or diarrhea, another milk preparation—yogurt mixed with black pepper and salt—will immediately cure these maladies. In other words, one milk preparation can cause indigestion and diarrhea, and another milk preparation can cure them.

If one is placed in material opulence due to the special mercy of the Supreme Personality of Godhead, he should not consider that opulence a cause for bondage. When a mature devotee is blessed with material opulence, he does not become affected adversely because he knows how to employ material opulence in the service of the Lord. There are many such examples in the history of the world. There were kings like Pṛthu Mahārāja, Prahlāda Mahārāja, Janaka, Dhruva, Vaivasvata Manu and Mahārāja Ikṣvāku. All of these were great kings and were especially favored by the Supreme Personality of Godhead. If a devotee is not mature, the Supreme Lord will take away all his opulence. This principle is stated by the Supreme Personality of Godhead: *yasyāham anugṛhṇāmi hariṣye tad-dhanaṁ śanaiḥ.* "My first mercy shown to My devotee is to take away all his material opulence." Material opulence detrimental to devotional service is taken away by the Supreme Lord, whereas a person who is mature in devotional service is given all material facilities.

TEXT 20

नव्यवदृधृदये यज्ज्ञो ब्रह्मैतद्ब्रह्मवादिभिः ।
न मुह्यन्ति न शोचन्ति न हृष्यन्ति यतो गताः॥२०॥

navyavad dhṛdaye yaj jño
brahmaitad brahma-vādibhiḥ
na muhyanti na śocanti
na hṛṣyanti yato gatāḥ

navya-vat—ever increasingly fresh; *hṛdaye*—in the heart; *yat*—as; *jñaḥ*—the supreme knower, Paramātmā; *brahma*—Brahman; *etat*—this; *brahma-vādibhiḥ*—by the advocates of Absolute Truth; *na*—never; *muhyanti*—are bewildered; *na*—never; *śocanti*—lament; *na*—never; *hṛṣyanti*—are jubilant; *yataḥ*—when; *gatāḥ*—have attained.

TRANSLATION

Always engaging in the activities of devotional service, devotees feel ever-increasingly fresh and new in all their activities. The all-knower, the Supersoul within the heart of the devotee, makes everything increasingly fresh. This is known as the Brahman position by the advocates of the Absolute Truth. In such a liberated stage [brahma-bhūta], one is never bewildered. Nor does one lament or become unnecessarily jubilant. This is due to the brahma-bhūta situation.

PURPORT

A devotee is inspired by the Supersoul within the heart to advance in devotional service in a variety of ways. The devotee does not feel hackneyed nor stereotyped, nor does he feel that he is in a stagnant position. In the material world, if one engages in chanting a material name, he will feel tired after chanting a few times. However, one can chant the Hare Kṛṣṇa *mahā-mantra* all day and night and never feel tired. As chanting is increased, it will come out new and fresh. Śrīla Rūpa Gosvāmī said if he could somehow get millions of ears and tongues, then he could relish spiritual bliss by chanting the Hare Kṛṣṇa *mahā-mantra.* There is really nothing uninspiring for a highly advanced devotee. In *Bhagavad-gītā* the Lord says that He is situated in everyone's heart and that He helps the living entity forget and remember. By the grace of the Lord, the devotee gets inspiration.

teṣāṁ satata-yuktānāṁ
bhajatāṁ prīti-pūrvakam
dadāmi buddhi-yogaṁ taṁ
yena mām upayānti te

"To those who are constantly devoted and worship Me with love, I give the understanding by which they can come to Me." (Bg. 10.10)

As stated (*kuśala-karmaṇām*), those engaged in auspicious activities in devotional service are guided by the Supersoul, described in this verse as *jña*, one who knows everything past, present and future. The Supersoul gives instructions to the sincere unalloyed devotee on how he can progress more and more in approaching the Supreme Personality of Godhead. Śrīla Jīva Gosvāmī in this connection says that the Supersoul, the plenary expansion of the Personality of Godhead, exists in everyone's heart, but in the heart of the devotee He reveals Himself as ever increasingly new. Being inspired by Him, the devotee experiences increased transcendental bliss in the execution of his devotional service.

TEXT 21

मैत्रेय उवाच
एवं ब्रुवाणं पुरुषार्थभाजनं
जनार्दनं प्राञ्जलयः प्रचेतसः ।
तद्दर्शनध्वस्ततमोरजोमला
गिरागृणन् गद्गदया सुहृत्तमम् ॥२१॥

maitreya uvāca
evaṁ bruvāṇaṁ puruṣārtha-bhājanaṁ
janārdanaṁ prāñjalayaḥ pracetasaḥ
tad-darśana-dhvasta-tamo-rajo-malā
girāgṛṇan gadgadayā suhṛt-tamam

maitreyaḥ uvāca—Maitreya said; *evam*—thus; *bruvāṇam*—speaking; *puruṣa-artha*—of the ultimate goal of life; *bhājanam*—the bestower; *janārdanam*—who takes away all the disadvantages of the devotee; *prāñjalayaḥ*—with folded hands; *pracetasaḥ*—the Pracetā brothers; *tat*—Him; *darśana*—by seeing; *dhvasta*—dissipated; *tamaḥ*—of darkness; *rajaḥ*—of passion; *malāḥ*—whose contamination; *girā*—with a voice; *agṛṇan*—offered prayers; *gadgadayā*—faltering; *suhṛt-tamam*—unto the greatest of all friends.

TRANSLATION

The great sage Maitreya said: After the Personality of Godhead spoke thus, the Pracetās began to offer Him prayers. The Lord is the bestower of

all success in life and is the supreme benefactor. He is also the supreme friend who takes away all miserable conditions experienced by a devotee. In a faltering voice, due to ecstasy, the Pracetās began to offer prayers. They were purified by the presence of the Lord, who was before them face to face.

PURPORT

The Lord is herein described as *puruṣārtha-bhājanam* (the bestower of the ultimate goal of life). Whatever success we want in life can be attained by the mercy of the Lord. Since the Pracetās had already attained the Lord's mercy, they were no longer subject to the contamination of the material modes. The material modes dissipated from them just as the darkness of night immediately dissipates when the sun rises. Because the Lord appeared before them, naturally all the contaminations of the material qualities of *rajas* and *tamas* completely disappeared. Similarly, when an unalloyed devotee chants the Hare Kṛṣṇa *mahā-mantra,* he is also purified of all material contamination because the name of the Lord and the Lord are identical. As stated in *Śrīmad-Bhāgavatam:*

śṛṇvatāṁ sva-kathāḥ kṛṣṇaḥ
puṇya-śravaṇa-kīrtanaḥ
hṛdy antaḥ-stho hy abhadrāṇi
vidhunoti suhṛt satām

"Śrī Kṛṣṇa, the Personality of Godhead, who is the Paramātmā [Supersoul] in everyone's heart and the benefactor of the truthful devotee, cleanses desire for material enjoyment from the heart of the devotee who relishes his messages, which are in themselves virtuous when properly heard and chanted." (*Bhāg.* 1.2.17)

The holy name of the Lord is the Lord Himself. If one chants and hears, he becomes purified. Gradually all material contamination disappears. The Pracetās were already purified due to the Lord's presence before them, and they could therefore offer the proper prayers with folded hands. In other words, as soon as devotees are engaged in devotional service, they become transcendental to all material contamination immediately. As confirmed in *Bhagavad-gītā:*

māṁ ca yo 'vyabhicāreṇa
bhakti-yogena sevate
sa guṇān samatītyaitān
brahma-bhūyāya kalpate

"One who engages in full devotional service, who does not fall down in any circumstance, at once transcends the modes of material nature and thus comes to the level of Brahman." (Bg. 14.26)

Sometimes the devotees are dissatisfied due to their not seeing the Supreme Personality of Godhead personally. When the Pracetās saw the Supreme Lord personally present, their unhappiness vanished.

TEXT 22

प्रचेतस ऊचुः
नमो नमः क्लेशविनाशनाय
निरूपितोदारगुणाह्वयाय ।
मनोवचोवेगपुरोजवाय
सर्वाक्षमार्गैरगताध्वने नमः ॥२२॥

pracetasa ūcuḥ
namo namaḥ kleśa-vināśanāya
nirūpitodāra-guṇāhvayāya
mano-vaco-vega-puro-javāya
sarvākṣa-mārgair agatādhvane namaḥ

pracetasaḥ ūcuḥ—the Pracetās said; *namaḥ*—obeisances; *namaḥ*—obeisances; *kleśa*—material distress; *vināśanāya*—unto one who destroys; *nirūpita*—settled; *udāra*—magnanimous; *guṇa*—qualities; *āhvayāya*—whose name; *manaḥ*—of the mind; *vacaḥ*—of speech; *vega*—the speed; *puraḥ*—before; *javāya*—whose speed; *sarva-akṣa*—of all material senses; *mārgaiḥ*—by the paths; *agata*—not perceivable; *adhvane*—whose course; *namaḥ*—we offer our respects.

TRANSLATION

The Pracetās spoke as follows: Dear Lord, You relieve all kinds of material distress. Your magnanimous transcendental qualities and holy name are all-auspicious. This conclusion is already settled. You can go faster than the speed of mind and words. You cannot be perceived by material senses. We therefore offer You respectful obeisances again and again.

PURPORT

The word *nirūpita,* meaning "concluded," is very significant in this verse. No one has to conduct research work to find God or make progress in spiritual knowledge. Everything is conclusively there in the *Vedas.* Therefore the Lord says in *Bhagavad-gītā:*

sarvasya cāhaṁ hṛdi sanniviṣṭo
mattaḥ smṛtir jñānam apohanaṁ ca
vedaiś ca sarvair aham eva vedyo
vedānta-kṛd veda-vid eva cāham

"I am seated in everyone's heart, and from Me come remembrance, knowledge and forgetfulness. By all the *Vedas,* I am to be known; indeed, I am the compiler of *Vedānta,* and I am the knower of the *Vedas.*" (Bg. 15.15)

Understanding the Supreme Personality of Godhead through the process of the *Vedas* is perfect and conclusive. The *Vedas* state, *ataḥ śrī-kṛṣṇa-nāmādi na bhaved grāhyam indriyaiḥ:* the transcendental names, forms, qualities, paraphernalia and pastimes of the Lord cannot be understood by our blunt material senses. *Sevonmukhe hi jihvādau svayam eva sphuraty adaḥ:* when a devotee engages his senses favorably in devotional service, the Lord, through His causeless mercy, reveals Himself to the devotee. This is the conclusive Vedic process. The *Vedas* also indicate that simply by chanting the holy names of the Lord one can without a doubt become spiritually advanced. We cannot approach the Supreme Personality of Godhead by the speed of mind or words, but if we stick to devotional service we can easily and quickly approach Him. In other words, the Supreme Lord is attracted by devotional service, and He can approach us more swiftly than we can approach Him with our mental speculation. The Lord has stated that He is beyond the range of mental speculation and the speed of thought, yet He can be approached easily by His causeless mercy. Thus only by His causeless mercy can He be attained. Other methods will not be effective.

TEXT 23

शुद्धाय शान्ताय नमः स्वनिष्ठया
मनस्यपार्थं विलसद्द्वयाय ।
नमो जगत्स्थानलयोदयेषु
गृहीतमायागुणविग्रहाय ॥२३॥

śuddhāya śāntāya namaḥ sva-niṣṭhayā
manasy apārthaṁ vilasad-dvayāya
namo jagat-sthāna-layodayeṣu
gṛhīta-māyā-guṇa-vigrahāya

śuddhāya—unto the unadulterated; *śāntāya*—unto the most peaceful; *namaḥ*—we offer our obeisances; *sva-niṣṭhayā*—by being situated in one's position; *manasi*—in the mind; *apārtham*—without any meaning; *vilasat*—appearing; *dvayāya*—in whom the dual world; *namaḥ*—obeisances; *jagat*—of the cosmic manifestation; *sthāna*—maintenance; *laya*—annihilation; *udayeṣu*—and for creation; *gṛhīta*—accepted; *māyā*—material; *guṇa*—of the modes of nature; *vigrahāya*—the forms.

TRANSLATION

Dear Lord, we beg to offer our obeisances unto You. When the mind is fixed upon You, the world of duality, although a place for material enjoyment, appears meaningless. Your transcendental form is full of transcendental bliss. We therefore offer our respects unto You. Your appearances as Lord Brahmā, Lord Viṣṇu and Lord Śiva are meant for the purpose of creating, maintaining and annihilating this cosmic manifestation.

PURPORT

A pure devotee whose mind is always engaged in the service of the Lord can certainly appreciate the impermanence of this material world. Although such a devotee may be engaged in executing material activities, this stage is called *anāsakti.* As explained by Śrīla Rūpa Gosvāmī, *anāsaktasya viṣayān yathārham upayuñjataḥ.* A devotee is always unattached to material activities because in the liberated stage his mind is always fixed on the lotus feet of the Lord.

This material world is called *dvaita*, the world of duality. A devotee knows very well that everything within this material world is but a manifestation of the Supreme Lord's energy. To maintain the three modes of material nature, the Supreme Lord takes on different forms as Lord Brahmā, Lord Viṣṇu and Lord Śiva. Unaffected by the modes of material nature, the Lord takes on different forms to create, maintain and annihilate this cosmic manifestation. The conclusion is that although the pure devotee appears to engage in material activities in the service of the Lord, he knows very well that material enjoyment for sense gratification has no use whatsoever.

TEXT 24

नमो विशुद्धसत्त्वाय हरये हरिमेधसे ।
वासुदेवाय कृष्णाय प्रभवे सर्वसात्वताम् ॥२४॥

namo viśuddha-sattvāya
haraye hari-medhase
vāsudevāya kṛṣṇāya
prabhave sarva-sātvatām

namaḥ—obeisances; *viśuddha-sattvāya*—unto You, whose existence is free from all material influence; *haraye*—who takes away all miserable conditions of devotees; *hari-medhase*—whose brain works only for the deliverance of the conditioned soul; *vāsudevāya*—the all-pervading Supreme Personality of Godhead; *kṛṣṇāya*—unto Kṛṣṇa; *prabhave*—who increases the influence; *sarva-sātvatām*—of all kinds of devotees.

TRANSLATION

Dear Lord, we offer our respectful obeisances unto You because Your existence is completely independent of all material influences. Your Lordship always takes away the devotee's miserable conditions, for Your brain plans how to do so. You live everywhere as Paramātmā; therefore You are known as Vāsudeva. You also accept Vasudeva as Your father, and You are celebrated by the name of Kṛṣṇa. You are so kind that You always increase the influence of all kinds of devotees.

PURPORT

In the previous verse it has been said (*gṛhīta-māyā-guṇa-vigrahāya*) that the Lord accepts three kinds of bodies (Viṣṇu, Brahmā and Śiva) for the purposes of creating, maintaining and annihilating the cosmic manifestation. The three predominating deities of the material universe (Brahmā, Viṣṇu and Śiva) are called *guṇa-avatāras.* There are many kinds of incarnations of the Supreme Personality of Godhead, and the first incarnations within this material world are Brahmā, Viṣṇu and Maheśvara (Śiva). Out of these three, Lord Brahmā and Lord Śiva accept material bodies, but Lord Viṣṇu does not accept a material body. Lord Viṣṇu is therefore known as *viśuddha-sattva.* His existence is completely free from the contamination of the material modes of nature. One should therefore not think that Lord Viṣṇu is in the same category with Lord Brahmā and Śiva. The *śāstras* forbid us to think in this way.

yas tu nārāyaṇaṁ devaṁ
brahma-rudrādi-daivataiḥ
samatvenaiva vīkṣeta
sa pāṣaṇḍī bhaved dhruvam

One who considers Lord Viṣṇu to be in the same category with *devas* like Lord Brahmā or Lord Śiva or who thinks Lord Brahmā and Śiva to be equal to Lord Viṣṇu is to be considered as *pāṣaṇḍī* (a faithless nonbeliever). Therefore in this verse Lord Viṣṇu is distinguished in the words *namo viśuddha-sattvāya.* Although a living entity like us, Lord Brahmā is exalted due to his pious activities; therefore he is given the high post of Brahmā. Lord Śiva is not actually like a living entity, but he is not the Surpeme Personality of Godhead. His position is somewhere between Viṣṇu, the Supreme Personality of Godhead, and Brahmā, the living entity. Lord Śiva is therefore explained in *Brahma-saṁhitā* in this way:

kṣīraṁ yathā dadhi vikāra-viśeṣa-yogāt
sañjāyate na hi tataḥ pṛthag asti hetoḥ
yaḥ śambhutām api tathā samupaiti kāryād
govindam ādi-puruṣaṁ tam ahaṁ bhajāmi

Lord Śiva is considered to be like yogurt (*dadhi*). Yogurt is nothing but transformed milk; nonetheless yogurt cannot be accepted as milk. Similarly, Lord Śiva holds almost all the powers of Lord Viṣṇu, and he is also above the qualities of the living entity, but he is not exactly like Viṣṇu, just as yogurt, although transformed milk, is not exactly like milk.

The Supreme Personality of Godhead is also described herein as *vāsudevāya kṛṣṇāya.* Kṛṣṇa is the original Supreme Personality of Godhead, and all Viṣṇu expansions are His plenary portions or portions of His plenary portions (known as *svāṁśa* and *kalā*). The *svāṁśa,* or direct expansion, is also called *aṁśa.* All *viṣṇu-tattvas* are *svāṁśa,* direct parts and parcels of the Supreme Personality of Godhead, Kṛṣṇa. Kṛṣṇa is known as Vāsudeva because He appeared in this material world as the son of Vasudeva. Similarly, He is known as Devakī-nandana, Yaśodā-nandana, Nanda-nandana, and so on.

Again and again the Lord is very much interested in increasing the influence of His devotees. Therefore He is described herein as *prabhave sarva-sātvatām.* The *sātvata* community is a community of Vaiṣṇavas, pure devotees of the Lord. The Supreme Personality of Godhead has unlimited powers, and He wants to see that His devotees are also entrusted with unlimited powers. A devotee of the Lord is always, therefore, distinguished from all other living entities.

The word *hari* means "One who takes away all miserable conditions," and *hari-medhase* means that the Lord is always planning ways to deliver the conditioned soul from the clutches of *māyā*. The Lord is so kind that He personally incarnates to deliver the conditioned souls, and whenever He comes, He makes His plans.

paritrāṇāya sādhūnāṁ
vināśāya ca duṣkṛtām
dharma-saṁsthāpanārthāya
sambhavāmi yuge yuge

"To deliver the pious and to annihilate the miscreants, as well as to reestablish the principles of religion, I advent Myself millennium after millennium." (Bg. 4.8)

Since the Lord delivers all conditioned souls from the clutches of *māyā*, He is known as *hari-medhaḥ*. In the list of incarnations, Kṛṣṇa is described as the supreme and original Personality of Godhead.

ete cāṁśa-kalāḥ puṁsaḥ
kṛṣṇas tu bhagavān svayam
indrāri-vyākulaṁ lokaṁ
mṛḍayanti yuge yuge (*Bhāg.* 1.3.28)

Kṛṣṇa, the original personality of Godhead, appears in this material world when the demigods, who are devotees of the Lord, are disturbed by the demons.

TEXT 25

नमः कमलनाभाय नमः कमलमालिने ।
नमः कमलपादाय नमस्ते कमलेक्षण ॥२५॥

namaḥ kamala-nābhāya
namaḥ kamala-māline
namaḥ kamala-pādāya
namas te kamalekṣaṇa

namaḥ—we offer our respectful obeisances; *kamala-nābhāya*—unto the Supreme Personality of Godhead, from whose abdomen the original lotus flower originated; *namaḥ*—obeisances; *kamala-māline*—who is always decorated with a garland of lotus flowers; *namaḥ*—obeisances; *kamala-pādāya*—

whose feet are as beautiful and fragrant as the lotus flower; *namaḥ te*—obeisances unto You; *kamala-īkṣaṇa*—whose eyes are exactly like the petals of the lotus flower.

TRANSLATION

Dear Lord, we offer our respectful obeisances unto You because from Your abdomen sprouts the lotus flower, the origin of all living entities. You are always decorated with a lotus garland, and Your feet resemble the lotus flower with all its fragrance. Your eyes are also like the petals of a lotus flower. Therefore we always offer our respectful obeisances unto You.

PURPORT

The word *kamala-nābhāya* indicates that Lord Viṣṇu is the origin of the material creation. From the abdomen of Garbhodakaśāyī Viṣṇu, a lotus flower sprouts. Lord Brahmā, the first creature of the universe, is born from this lotus flower, and, subsequently, Lord Brahmā creates the whole universe. The origin of all creation is therefore Lord Viṣṇu, and the origin of all the *viṣṇu-tattvas* is Lord Kṛṣṇa. Consequently Kṛṣṇa is the origin of everything. This is also confirmed in *Bhagavad-gītā:*

ahaṁ sarvasya prabhavo
mattaḥ sarvaṁ pravartate
iti matvā bhajante māṁ
budhā bhāva-samanvitāḥ

"I am the source of all spiritual and material worlds. Everything emanates from Me. The wise who perfectly know this engage in My devotional service and worship Me with all their hearts." (Bg. 10.8) Lord Kṛṣṇa says: "I am the origin of everything." Therefore whatever we see emanates from Him. This is also confirmed in the *Vedānta-sūtra*. *Janmādy asya yataḥ:* "The Absolute Truth is He from whom everything emanates."

TEXT 26

नमः कमलकिञ्जल्कपिशङ्गामलवाससे ।
सर्वभूतनिवासाय नमोऽयुङ्क्ष्महि साक्षिणे ॥२६॥

namaḥ kamala-kiñjalka-
piśaṅgāmala-vāsase
sarva-bhūta-nivāsāya
namo 'yuṅkṣmahi sākṣiṇe

namaḥ—obeisances; *kamala-kiñjalka*—like the saffron in a lotus flower; *piśaṅga*—yellowish; *amala*—spotless; *vāsase*—unto Him whose garment; *sarva-bhūta*—of all living entities; *nivāsāya*—the shelter; *namaḥ*—obeisances; *ayuṅkṣmahi*—let us offer; *sākṣiṇe*—unto the supreme witness.

TRANSLATION

Dear Lord, the garment You have put on is yellowish in color like the saffron of a lotus flower, but it is not made of anything material. Since You live in everyone's heart, You are the direct witness of all the activities of all living entities. We offer our respectful obeisances unto You again and again.

PURPORT

In this verse the dress of the Supreme Personality of Godhead and His all-pervasive nature are described. The Lord puts on a dress that is yellow, but such a garment is never to be considered material. The garments of the Lord are also the Lord. They are nondifferent from the Lord because they are spiritual in nature.

The word *sarva-bhūta-nivāsāya* further clarifies how Lord Viṣṇu lives in everyone's heart and acts as the direct witness of all the activities of the conditioned soul. Within this material world the conditioned soul has desires and acts in accordance with these desires. All these acts are observed by the Supreme Personality of Godhead. This is also confirmed in *Bhagavad-gītā:*

sarvasya cāhaṁ hṛdi sanniviṣṭo
mattaḥ smṛtir jñānam apohanaṁ ca

"I am seated in everyone's heart, and from Me come remembrance, knowledge and forgetfulness." (Bg. 15.15) The Lord is present in everyone's heart, and He gives the living entity intelligence. According to the desires of the living entity, the Lord makes him remember or forget. If the living entity is demoniac and wants to forget the Supreme Personality of Godhead, the Lord gives him the intelligence to be able to forget the Supreme Lord forever. Similarly, when a devotee wants to serve the Supreme Lord, the Lord, as Paramātmā, gives the devotee the intelligence to make progress in devotional service. The Lord directly witnesses our activities and experiences our desires. The Supreme Lord gives us the facilities to act in the way we wish.

TEXT 27

रूपं भगवता त्वेतदशेषक्लेशसंक्षयम् ।
आविष्कृतं नः क्लिष्टानां किमन्यदनुकम्पितम् ॥२७॥

rūpaṁ bhagavatā tv etad
aśeṣa-kleśa-saṅkṣayam
āviṣkṛtaṁ naḥ kliṣṭānāṁ
kim anyad anukampitam

rūpam—form; *bhagavatā*—by Your Lordship; *tu*—but; *etat*—this; *aśeṣa*—unlimited; *kleśa*—miseries; *saṅkṣayam*—which dissipates; *āviṣkṛtam*—revealed; *naḥ*—of us; *kliṣṭānām*—who are suffering from material conditions; *kim anyat*—what to speak of; *anukampitam*—those to whom You are always favorably disposed.

TRANSLATION

Dear Lord, we conditioned souls are always covered by ignorance in the bodily conception of life. We therefore always prefer the miserable conditions of material existence. To deliver us from these miserable conditions, You have advented Yourself in this transcendental form. This is evidence of Your unlimited causeless mercy upon those of us who are suffering in this way. What, then, to speak of the devotees to whom You are always so favorably disposed?

PURPORT

When the Lord appears in His original form, He acts to deliver the pious and annihilate the miscreants (Bg. 4.8). Although He annihilates the demons, He nonetheless benefits them. It is said that all the living entities who died on the Battlefield of Kurukṣetra attained their original constitutional position (*svarūpa*) because they had the chance to see Kṛṣṇa face to face riding in the chariot of Arjuna. On the Battlefield of Kurukṣetra, superficially two things were going on—the demons were being killed, and the devotee, Arjuna, was being protected. However, the results were the same for everyone. Thus it is said that the appearance of the Lord diminishes all kinds of miserable conditions caused by material existence.

It is clearly stated in this verse that this form (*aśeṣa-kleśa-saṅkṣayam*) is meant to diminish all the miserable conditions experienced in life not only by the devotees but by all others. *Āviṣkṛtaṁ naḥ kliṣṭānām.* The

Pracetās identified themselves as common men. *Kim anyad anukampitam.* The devotees are always favorably accepted by the Lord. The Lord shows all mercy not only to conditioned souls, but also to the devotees who are already liberated due to their devotional service.

The form of the Lord as worshiped in the temples is called *arcā-vigraha* or *arcāvatāra,* the worshipable form, the Deity incarnation. This facility is offered to neophyte devotees so that they can see the real form of the Lord face to face and offer their respectful obeisances and sacrifices in the form of *arcā.* Through such facilities the neophytes gradually invoke their original Kṛṣṇa consciousness. Deity worship in the form of temple worship is the most valuable benediction given by the Lord to beginners. All neophytes must therefore engage in the worship of the Lord by keeping the *arcā-vigraha* (*arcāvatāra*) at home or in the temple.

TEXT 28

एतावत्त्वं हि विभुभिर्भाव्यं दीनेषु वत्सलैः ।
यदनुस्मर्यते काले स्वबुद्ध्याभद्ररन्धन ॥२८॥

etāvat tvaṁ hi vibhubhir
bhāvyaṁ dīneṣu vatsalaiḥ
yad anusmaryate kāle
sva-buddhyābhadra-randhana

etāvat—thus; *tvam*—Your Lordship; *hi*—certainly; *vibhubhiḥ*—by expansions; *bhāvyam*—to be conceived; *dīneṣu*—unto the humble devotees; *vatsalaiḥ*—compassionate; *yat*—which; *anusmaryate*—is always remembered; *kāle*—in due course of time; *sva-buddhyā*—by one's devotional service; *abhadra-randhana*—O killer of all inauspiciousness.

TRANSLATION

Dear Lord, You are the killer of all inauspicious things. You are compassionate upon Your poor devotees through the expansion of Your arcā-vigraha. You should certainly think of us as Your eternal servants.

PURPORT

The form of the Lord known as *arcā-vigraha* is an expansion of His unlimited potencies. When the Lord is gradually satisfied with the service of a devotee, in due course of time He accepts the devotee as one of His many unalloyed servants. By nature, the Lord is very compassionate; therefore the service of neophyte devotees is accepted by the Lord. As confirmed in *Bhagavad-gītā:*

patraṁ puṣpaṁ phalaṁ toyaṁ
yo me bhaktyā prayacchati
tad ahaṁ bhakty-upahṛtam
aśnāmi prayatātmanaḥ

"If one offers Me with love and devotion a leaf, a flower, fruit or water, I will accept it." (Bg. 9.26)

The devotee offers eatables in the form of vegetables, fruits, leaves and water to the *arcā-vigraha.* The Lord, being *bhakta-vatsala,* compassionate upon His devotees, accepts these offerings. Atheists may think that the devotees are engaged in idol worship, but the fact is different. Janārdana, the Supreme Lord, accepts *bhāva,* the attitude of service. The neophyte devotee engaged in the worship of the Lord may not understand the value of such worship, but the Supreme Lord, being *bhakta-vatsala,* accepts His devotee and in due course of time takes him home.

In this connection there is a story about a *brāhmaṇa* who was offering sweet rice to the Lord within his mind. The *brāhmaṇa* had no money nor any means of worshiping the Deity, but within his mind he arranged everything nicely. He had gold pots to bring water from the sacred rivers to wash the Deity, and he offered the Deity very sumptuous food, including sweet rice. Once, before he offered the sweet rice, he thought that it was too hot, and he thought, "Oh, let me test it. My, it is very hot." When he put his finger in the sweet rice to test it, his finger was burned and his meditation broken. Although he was offering food to the Lord within his mind, the Lord accepted it nonetheless. Consequently the Lord in Vaikuṇṭha immediately sent a chariot to bring the *brāhmaṇa* back home, back to Godhead. Thus it is the duty of every sincere devotee to accept the *arcā-vigraha* at home or in the temple and worship the form of the Lord as advised in authorized scriptures and directed by the spiritual master.

TEXT 29

येनोपशान्तिर्भूतानां क्षुल्लकानामपीहताम् ।
अन्तर्हितोऽन्तर्हृदये कस्मान्नो वेद नाशिषः ॥२९॥

yenopaśāntir bhūtānāṁ
kṣullakānām apīhatām

antarhito 'ntar-hṛdaye
kasmān no veda nāśiṣaḥ

yena—by which process; *upaśāntiḥ*—satisfaction of all desires; *bhūtānām*—of the living entities; *kṣullakānām*—very much fallen; *api*—although; *īhatām*—desiring many things; *antarhitaḥ*—hidden; *antaḥ-hṛdaye*—in the core of the heart; *kasmāt*—why; *naḥ*—our; *veda*—He knows; *na*—not; *āśiṣaḥ*—desires.

TRANSLATION

When the Lord, out of His natural compassion, thinks of His devotee, by that process only are all desires of the neophyte devotee fulfilled. The Lord is situated in every living entity's heart, although the living entity may be very insignificant. The Lord knows everything about the living entity, including all his desires. Although we are very insignificant, why should the Lord not know our desires?

PURPORT

A very advanced devotee does not think himself advanced. He is always very humble. The Supreme Personality of Godhead in His plenary expansion as the Paramātmā, or Supersoul, sits in everyone's heart and can understand the attitudes and desires of His devotees. The Lord also gives opportunity to the nondevotees to fulfill their desires, as confirmed in *Bhagavad-gītā* (*mattaḥ smṛtir jñānam apohanaṁ ca*).

Whatever a living entity desires, however insignificant he may be, is noted by the Lord, who gives him a chance to fulfill his desires. If the desires of the nondevotees are fulfilled, why not those of the devotee? A pure devotee simply wants to engage in the service of the Lord without material desire, and if he wants this within the core of his heart, where the Lord is situated, and if he is without ulterior motive, why should the Lord not understand? If a sincere devotee renders service to the Lord or to the *arcā-vigraha*, the form of the Lord, all his activities prove successful because the Lord is present within his heart and understands his sincerity. Thus if a devotee, with all confidence, goes on discharging the prescribed duties of devotional service, he will ultimately attain success.

TEXT 30

असावेव वरोऽस्माकमीप्सितो जगतः पते ।
प्रसन्नो भगवान् येषामपवर्गगुरुर्गतिः ॥३०॥

asāv eva varo 'smākam
īpsito jagataḥ pate
prasanno bhagavān yeṣām
apavarga-gurur gatiḥ

asau—that; *eva*—certainly; *varaḥ*—benediction; *asmākam*—our; *īpsitaḥ*—desired; *jagataḥ*—of the universe; *pate*—O Lord; *prasannaḥ*—satisfied; *bhagavān*—the Supreme Personality of Godhead; *yeṣām*—with whom; *apavarga*—of transcendental loving service; *guruḥ*—the teacher; *gatiḥ*—the ultimate goal of life.

TRANSLATION

O Lord of the universe, You are the actual teacher of the science of devotional service. We are satisfied that Your Lordship is the ultimate goal of our lives, and we pray that You will be satisfied with us. That is our benediction. We do not desire anything other than Your full satisfaction.

PURPORT

In this verse the words *apavarga-gurur gatiḥ* are very significant. According to *Śrīmad-Bhāgavatam,* the Supreme Lord is the ultimate fact of the Absolute Truth. *Brahmeti paramātmeti bhagavān iti śabdyate* (*Bhāg.* 1.2.11). The Absolute Truth is realized in three features—impersonal Brahman, localized Paramātmā and ultimately the Supreme Personality of Godhead, Bhagavān. The word *apavarga* means liberation. *Pavarga* means material existence. In material existence, one always works very hard but is ultimately baffled. One then dies and has to accept another body to work very hard again. This is the cycle of material existence. *Apavarga* means just the opposite. Instead of working hard like cats and dogs, one returns home, back to Godhead. Liberation begins with merging into the Brahman effulgence of the Supreme Lord. This conception is held by the *jñāni-sampradāya,* philosophical speculators, but realization of the Supreme Personality of Godhead is higher. When a devotee understands that the Lord is satisfied, liberation, or merging into the effulgence of the Lord, is not very difficult. One has to approach the Supreme Personality of Godhead through the impersonal Brahman effulgence just as one has to approach the sun through the sunshine. It is not very difficult to merge into the impersonal effulgence of the Lord, Brahman, if one has satisfied the Supreme Personality of Godhead.

TEXT 31

वरं वृणीमहेऽथापि नाथ त्वत्परतः परात् ।
न ह्यन्तस्त्वद्विभूतीनां सोऽनन्त इति गीयसे ॥३१॥

varaṁ vṛṇīmahe 'thāpi
nātha tvat parataḥ parāt
na hy antas tvad-vibhūtīnāṁ
so 'nanta iti gīyase

varam—benediction; *vṛṇīmahe*—we shall pray for; *athāpi*—therefore; *nātha*—O Lord; *tvat*—from You; *parataḥ parāt*—beyond the transcendence; *na*—not; *hi*—certainly; *antaḥ*—end; *tvat*—Your; *vibhūtīnām*—of opulences; *saḥ*—You; *anantaḥ*—unlimited; *iti*—thus; *gīyase*—are celebrated.

TRANSLATION

Dear Lord, we shall therefore pray for Your benediction because You are the Supreme beyond all transcendence and because there is no end to Your opulences. Consequently You are celebrated by the name Ananta.

PURPORT

There was no need for the Pracetās to ask any benediction from the Supreme Lord because the devotees are simply satisfied by the presence of the Supreme Personality of Godhead. Dhruva Mahārāja practiced severe austerities and penances to see the Supreme Lord, and his intention was to receive benediction from the Lord. He wanted to acquire the throne of his father—or attain an even better position—but when he was actually in the presence of the Supreme Lord, he forgot everything. He said, "My dear Lord, I do not wish to ask any benediction." This is the actual position of the devotee. The devotee simply wants to be in the presence of the Supreme Lord—either in this world or in the next—and engage in His service. That is the ultimate goal and benediction for the devotees.

The Lord asked the Pracetās to pray for some benediction, and they said, "What kind of benediction should we pray for? The Lord is unlimited, and there are unlimited benedictions." The purport is that if one must ask for benediction, he must ask for unlimited benediction. The words *tvat parataḥ* are very significant in this verse. The Supreme Personality of Godhead is *parataḥ parāt.* The word *para* means transcendental, beyond this material world. The impersonal Brahman effulgence is beyond this material world, and this is called *paraṁ padam. Āruhya kṛcchreṇa paraṁ padam* (*Bhāg.* 10.2.32). Merging into the impersonal effulgence of the Lord is called *paraṁ padam,* but there is a higher transcendental position, which is the association of the Supreme Personality of Godhead. *Brahmeti paramātmeti bhagavān iti śabdyate* (*Bhāg.* 1.2.11). The Absolute Truth is realized first as impersonal Brahman, then as Paramātmā, and finally as Bhagavān. Thus the Personality of Godhead, Bhagavān, is *parataḥ parāt,* beyond Brahman and Paramātmā realization. In this connection, Śrīla Jīva Gosvāmī points out that *parataḥ parāt* means "better than the best." The best is the spiritual world, and it is known as Brahman. The Supreme Personality of Godhead, however, is known as Parabrahman. Therefore *parataḥ parāt* means "better than Brahman realization."

As will be explained in the next verse, the Pracetās planned to ask the Lord for something that has no limit. The Lord's pastimes, qualities, forms and names are all unlimited. There is no limit to His name, forms, pastimes, creation and paraphernalia. The living entity cannot conceive of the unlimitedness of the unlimited. However, if living entities are engaged in hearing about the unlimited potencies of the Supreme Lord, they are factually connected directly to the unlimited. Such understanding of the unlimited becomes unlimited by hearing and chanting.

TEXT 32

पारिजातेऽञ्जसा लब्धे सारङ्गोऽन्यन्न सेवते ।
त्वदङ्घ्रिमूलमासाद्य साक्षात्किं किं वृणीमहि ॥३२॥

pārijāte 'ñjasā labdhe
sāraṅgo 'nyan na sevate
tvad-aṅghri-mūlam āsādya
sākṣāt kiṁ kiṁ vṛṇīmahi

pārijāte—the celestial tree known as *pārijāta; añjasā*—completely; *labdhe*—having achieved; *sāraṅgaḥ*—a bee; *anyat*—other; *na sevate*—does not resort to; *tvat-aṅghri*—Your lotus feet; *mūlam*—the root of everything; *āsādya*—having approached; *sākṣāt*—directly; *kim*—what; *kim*—what; *vṛṇīmahi*—may we ask.

TRANSLATION

Dear Lord, when the bee approaches the celestial tree called the pārijāta, it certainly does not leave the tree, because there is no need for such

action. Similarly, when we have approached Your lotus feet and taken shelter of them, what further benediction may we ask of You?

PURPORT

When a devotee is actually engaged in the service of the lotus feet of the Lord, his engagement in itself is so perfect that there is no need to ask for further benediction. When a bee approaches the *pārijāta* tree, it gets unlimited supplies of honey. There is no need to go to another tree. If one is fixed in the service of the lotus feet of the Lord, there is unlimited transcendental bliss, and as such there is no need to ask for further benediction. The *pārijāta* tree is not commonly found within this material world. The *pārijāta* tree is also known as *kalpa-vṛkṣa,* or the wish-fulfilling tree. One can get anything he desires from such a tree. In the material world, one can get oranges from an orange tree or mangoes from a mango tree, but there is no possibility of getting oranges from a mango tree or vice versa. However, one can get whatever he wants from the *pārijāta* tree—oranges, mangoes, bananas, and so on. This tree is found in the spiritual world. *Cintāmaṇi-prakara-sadmasu kalpa-vṛkṣa-lakṣāvṛteṣu.* The spiritual world, *cintāmaṇi-dhāma,* is surrounded by these *kalpa-vṛkṣa* trees, but the *pārijāta* tree is also found in the kingdom of Indra, that is, on Indra's heavenly planet. This *pārijāta* tree was brought by Kṛṣṇa to please Satyabhāmā, one of His queens, and this tree was implanted in the Dvārakā mansions constructed for the queens. The lotus feet of the Lord are exactly like the *pārijāta* trees, or wish-fulfilling trees, and the devotees are like bumblebees. They are always attracted by the lotus feet of the Lord.

TEXT 33

यावत्ते मायया स्पृष्टा भ्रमाम इह कर्मभिः ।
तावद्भवत्प्रसङ्गानां सङ्गः स्यान्नो भवे भवे ॥३३॥

yāvat te māyayā spṛṣṭā
bhramāma iha karmabhiḥ
tāvad bhavat-prasaṅgānāṁ
saṅgaḥ syān no bhave bhave

yāvat—as long as; *te*—Your; *māyayā*—by the illusory energy; *spṛṣṭāḥ*—contaminated; *bhramāmaḥ*—we wander; *iha*—in this material world; *karmabhiḥ*—by the reaction of fruitive activities; *tāvat*—so long; *bhavat-prasaṅgānām*—

of Your loving devotees; *saṅgaḥ*—association; *syāt*—let there be; *naḥ*—our; *bhave bhave*—in every species of life.

TRANSLATION

Dear Lord, as long as we have to remain within this material world due to our material contamination and wander from one type of body to another and from one planet to another, we pray that we may associate with those who are engaged in discussing Your pastimes. We pray for this benediction life after life, in different bodily forms and on different planets.

PURPORT

This is the best benediction that a devotee can ask of the Supreme Lord. This is also confirmed by Śrī Caitanya Mahāprabhu: *sthāne sthitāḥ śruti-gatāṁ tanu-vāṅ-manobhiḥ* (*Bhāg.* 10.14.3). One may be in one position or another according to destiny, but in any case one must continue to hear about the activities and pastimes of the Supreme Lord, regardless of circumstances. A pure devotee does not pray for liberation or for cessation of the cycle of birth and death because he does not consider that important. The most important thing for a devotee is getting a chance to hear about the pastimes and glories of the Lord. The devotees who engage in the service of the Lord in this world will have the same opportunity in the spiritual world also. Thus for a devotee, everything is in the spiritual world, for as long as he can hear about the pastimes of the Lord, or wherever he can chant, the Lord is personally present. *Tatra tiṣṭhāmi nārada yatra gāyanti mad-bhaktāḥ.* When the pure devotees assemble to chant, hear and talk about the Supreme Personality of Godhead, the place where they assemble becomes Vaikuṇṭha. For the devotee there is no need to pray to the Lord for transferral to the Vaikuṇṭha world. A pure devotee can create Vaikuṇṭha or Vṛndāvana anywhere simply by chanting the glories of the Lord without offense.

The Pracetās pray for an opportunity to hear of the glories of the Lord in every form of life (*bhave bhave*). A living entity transmigrates from one body to another. The devotee is not particularly eager to stop this process. Caitanya Mahāprabhu prays, *mama janmani janmanīśvare bhavatād bhaktir ahaitukī tvayi:* "My dear Lord, life after life may I be fixed in Your pure devotional service." Out of humility, a devotee considers himself unfit to be transferred to the spiritual world. He always thinks himself contaminated by the modes of material nature. Nor is there any need for a devotee to ask to be freed from the modes of material nature. Devotional service itself is in the transcendental position; therefore there is no question of asking for this special facility. The conclusion is that a pure devotee is not anxious to stop the repetition of birth and death, but is always eager to associate with other devotees who are engaged in chanting and hearing about the glories of the Lord.

TEXT 34

तुलयाम लवेनापि न स्वर्गं नापुनर्भवम् ।
भगवत्सङ्गिसङ्गस्य मर्त्यानां किमुताशिषः ॥३४॥

tulayāma lavenāpi
na svargaṁ nāpunar-bhavam
bhagavat-saṅgi-saṅgasya
martyānāṁ kim utāśiṣaḥ

tulayāmaḥ—we compare; *lavena*—with a moment; *api*—even; *na*—not; *svargam*—attainment of the heavenly planets; *na*—not; *apunaḥ-bhavam*—merging into the Brahman effulgence; *bhagavat*—of the Supreme Personality of Godhead; *saṅgi*—with associates; *saṅgasya*—of association; *martyānām*—of persons who are destined to die; *kim uta*—how much less; *āśiṣaḥ*—benedictions.

TRANSLATION

Even a moment's association with a pure devotee cannot be compared to being transferred to heavenly planets or even merging into the Brahman effulgence in complete liberation. For living entities who are destined to give up the body and die, association with pure devotees is the highest benediction.

PURPORT

The great saint Prabodhānanda Sarasvatī, a devotee of Lord Caitanya, has stated: *kaivalyaṁ narakāyate tridaśa-pūr ākāśa-puṣpāyate.* For a pure devotee, *kaivalya,* merging into the existence of Brahman, the Brahman effulgence, is no better than living in hell. Similarly, he considers promotion to heavenly planets (*tridaśa-pūr*) just another kind of phantasmagoria. In other words, a pure devotee does not place much value in the destination of the *karmīs* (the heavenly planets), nor in the destination of the *jñānīs* (merging into the Brahman effulgence). A pure devotee considers a moment's association with another pure devotee to be far superior to residing in a heavenly planet or merging in the Brahman effulgence. The topmost benediction for those who are living in this material world and are subjected to the repetition of birth and death (transmigration) is association with pure devotees. One should search out such pure devotees and remain with them. That will make one completely happy, even though living within the material world. This Kṛṣṇa consciousness movement is started for that purpose. A person who is overly affected materially may take advantage of this movement and become intimately associated with it. In this way the confused and frustrated inhabitants of this material world may find the highest happiness in association with devotees.

TEXT 35

यत्रेड्यन्ते कथा मृष्टास्तृष्णायाः प्रशमो यतः ।
निर्वैरं यत्र भूतेषु नोद्वेगो यत्र कश्चन ॥३५॥

yatreḍyante kathā mṛṣṭās
tṛṣṇāyāḥ praśamo yataḥ
nirvairaṁ yatra bhūteṣu
nodvego yatra kaścana

yatra—where; *īḍyante*—are worshiped or discussed; *kathāḥ*—words; *mṛṣṭāḥ*—pure; *tṛṣṇāyāḥ*—of material hankerings; *praśamaḥ*—satisfaction; *yataḥ*—by which; *nirvairam*—nonenviousness; *yatra*—where; *bhūteṣu*—among living entities; *na*—not; *udvegaḥ*—fear; *yatra*—where; *kaścana*—any.

TRANSLATION

Whenever pure topics of the transcendental world are discussed, the members of the audience forget all kinds of material hankerings, at least for the time being. Not only that, but they are no longer envious of one another, nor do they suffer from anxiety or fear.

PURPORT

Vaikuṇṭha means "without anxiety," and the material world means full of anxiety. As stated by Prahlāda Mahārāja: *sadā samudvigna-dhiyām asad-grahāt* (*Bhāg.* 7.5.5). The living entities who have accepted this material world as a residence are full of anxiety. A place immediately becomes Vaikuṇṭha whenever the holy topics of the Personality of Godhead are discussed by pure devotees. This is the process of *śravaṇaṁ kīrtanaṁ viṣṇoḥ*, chanting and hearing about the Supreme Lord Viṣṇu. As the Supreme Lord Himself confirms:

nāhaṁ tiṣṭhāmi vaikuṇṭhe
yogināṁ hṛdayeṣu vā
tatra tiṣṭhāmi nārada
yatra gāyanti mad-bhaktāḥ

"My dear Nārada, actually I do not reside in My abode, Vaikuṇṭha, nor do I reside within the hearts of *yogīs*, but I reside in that place where My pure devotees chant My holy name and discuss My form, pastimes and qualities." Because of the presence of the Lord in the form of the transcendental vibration, the Vaikuṇṭha atmosphere is evoked. This atmosphere is without fear and anxiety. One living entity does not fear another. By hearing the holy names and glories of the Lord, a person executes pious activities. *Śṛṇvatāṁ sva-kathāḥ kṛṣṇaḥ puṇya-śravaṇa-kīrtanaḥ* (*Bhāg.* 1.2.17). Thus his material hankerings immediately stop. This *saṅkīrtana* movement started by the Society for Krishna Consciousness is meant for creating Vaikuṇṭha, the transcendental world that is without anxiety, even in this material world. The method is the propagation of the *śravaṇaṁ kīrtanam* process throughout the world. In the material world everyone is envious of his fellow man. Animalistic envy exists in human society as long as there is no performance of *saṅkīrtana-yajña,* the chanting of the holy names—Hare Kṛṣṇa, Hare Kṛṣṇa, Kṛṣṇa Kṛṣṇa, Hare Hare/ Hare Rāma, Hare Rāma, Rāma Rāma, Hare Hare. The Pracetās therefore decided to remain always in the society of devotees, and they considered that to be the highest benediction possible in human life.

TEXT 36

यत्र नारायणः साक्षाद्भगवान्न्यासिनां गतिः ।
संस्तूयते सत्कथासु मुक्तसङ्गैः पुनः पुनः ॥३६॥

yatra nārāyaṇaḥ sākṣād
bhagavān nyāsināṁ gatiḥ
saṁstūyate sat-kathāsu
mukta-saṅgaiḥ punaḥ punaḥ

yatra—where; *nārāyaṇaḥ*—Lord Nārāyaṇa; *sākṣāt*—directly; *bhagavān*—the Supreme Personality of Godhead; *nyāsinām*—of persons in the renounced order of life; *gatiḥ*—the ultimate goal; *saṁstūyate*—is worshiped; *sat-kathāsu*—by discussing the transcendental vibration; *mukta-saṅgaiḥ*—

by those who are liberated from material contamination; *punaḥ punaḥ*—again and again.

TRANSLATION

The Supreme Lord, Nārāyaṇa, is present amongst devotees who are engaged in hearing and chanting the holy name of the Supreme Personality of Godhead. Lord Nārāyaṇa is the ultimate goal of sannyāsīs, those in the renounced order of life, and Nārāyana is worshiped through this saṅkīrtana movement by those who are liberated from material contamination. Indeed, they recite the holy name again and again.

PURPORT

The Māyāvādī *sannyāsīs* are missing the real presence of Nārāyaṇa. This is because they falsely claim to be Nārāyaṇa Himself. According to the customary etiquette of Māyāvādī *sannyāsīs,* they address one another as Nārāyaṇa. To say that everyone is a temple of Nārāyaṇa is correct, but to accept another human being as Nārāyaṇa is a great offense. The conception of *daridra-nārāyaṇa* (poor Nārāyaṇa), an attempt to identify the poor with Nārāyaṇa, is also a great offense. Even to identify Nārāyaṇa with demigods like Lord Brahmā and Lord Śiva is an offense.

yas tu nārāyaṇaṁ devaṁ
brahma-rudrādi-daivataiḥ
samatvenaiva vīkṣeta
sa pāṣaṇḍī bhaved dhruvam

"One who considers Lord Nārāyaṇa on a level with great demigods like Lord Brahmā and Lord Śiva is immediately listed amongst nonbelievers." The fact is that by performing *saṅkīrtana-yajña* one can immediately please the Supreme Personality of Godhead. Then Nārāyaṇa Himself descends and immediately is present. In this age of Kali, Nārāyaṇa is immediately present in the form of Lord Caitanya. Concerning Lord Caitanya, *Śrīmad-Bhāgavatam* states:

kṛṣṇa-varṇaṁ tviṣākṛṣṇaṁ
sāṅgopāṅgāstra-pārṣadam
yajñaiḥ saṅkīrtana-prāyair
yajanti hi sumedhasaḥ

"In the age of Kali, intelligent persons perform congregational chanting to worship the incarnation of Godhead who constantly sings the name of

Kṛṣṇa. Although His complexion is not blackish, He is Kṛṣṇa Himself. He is accompanied by His associates, servants, weapons and confidential companions." (*Bhāg.* 11.5.32)

After all, human life is meant for pleasing Nārāyaṇa, and this can easily be done by performing *saṅkīrtana-yajña.* Whenever there is congregational chanting of the holy names of the Lord, Gaura Nārāyaṇa, the Supreme Personality of Godhead in His incarnation as Lord Caitanya, immediately appears and is worshiped by *saṅkīrtana-yajña.*

In this verse it is said that Nārāyaṇa is *nyāsināṁ gatiḥ,* the ultimate goal of the *sannyāsīs.* The goal of those who have renounced the material world is the attainment of Nārāyaṇa. A Vaiṣṇava *sannyāsī* therefore dedicates his life to serving Nārāyaṇa; he does not falsely claim to be Nārāyaṇa. Instead of becoming *nirvaira* (nonenvious of other living entities), one who tries to become Nārāyaṇa becomes envious of the Supreme Lord. Therefore the attempt to become Nārāyaṇa constitutes the greatest offense. Actually when one chants or discusses the transcendental activities of the Lord, he immediately becomes nonenvious. In this material world everyone is envious of everyone else, but by vibrating or discussing the holy name of the Lord, one becomes nonenvious and devoid of material hankering. Because of our envy of the Supreme Personality of Godhead, we have become envious of all other living entities. When we are no longer envious of the Supreme Personality of Godhead, there will be real peace, unity and fraternity in human society. Without Nārāyaṇa or *saṅkīrtana-yajña* there cannot be peace in this material world.

TEXT 37

तेषां विचरतां पद्भ्यां तीर्थानां पावनेच्छया ।
भीतस्य किं न रोचेत तावकानां समागमः ॥३७॥

teṣāṁ vicaratāṁ padbhyāṁ
tīrthānāṁ pāvanecchayā
bhītasya kiṁ na roceta
tāvakānāṁ samāgamaḥ

teṣām—of them; *vicaratām*—who travel; *padbhyām*—by their feet; *tīrthānām*—the holy places; *pāvana-icchayā*—with a desire to purify; *bhītasya*—to the materialistic person who is always fearful; *kim*—why; *na*—not; *roceta*—becomes pleasing; *tāvakānām*—of Your devotees; *samāgamaḥ*—meeting.

TRANSLATION

Dear Lord, Your personal associates, devotees, wander all over the world to purify even the holy places of pilgrimage. Is not such activity pleasing to those who are actually afraid of material existence?

PURPORT

There are two kinds of devotees. One is called *goṣṭhānandī* and the other *bhajanānandī*. The word *bhajanānandī* refers to the devotee who does not move but remains in one place. Such a devotee is always engaged in the devotional service of the Lord. He chants the *mahā-mantra* as taught by many *ācāryas* and sometimes goes out for preaching work. The *goṣṭhānandī* is one who desires to increase the number of devotees all over the world. He travels all over the world just to purify the world and the people residing in it. Caitanya Mahāprabhu advised: *pṛthivīte āche yata nagarādi grāma sarvatra pracāra haibe mora nāma*. Lord Caitanya Mahāprabhu wanted His followers to move all over the world and preach in every town and village. In the Caitanya-sampradāya those who strictly follow the principles of Lord Caitanya must travel all over the world to preach the message of Lord Caitanya, which is the same as preaching the words of Kṛṣṇa—*Bhagavad-gītā*—and *Śrīmad-Bhāgavatam*. The more the devotees preach the principles of *kṛṣṇa-kathā*, the more people throughout the world will benefit.

Devotees like the great sage Nārada who travel all over to preach are called *goṣṭhānandī*. Nārada Muni is always wandering throughout the universe just to create different types of devotees. Nārada even made a hunter a devotee. He also made Dhruva Mahārāja and Prahlāda devotees. Actually all devotees are indebted to the great sage Nārada, for he has wandered both in heaven and in hell. A devotee of the Lord is not even afraid of hell. He goes to preach the glories of the Lord everywhere—even in hell—because there is no distinction between heaven and hell for a devotee.

nārāyaṇa-parāḥ sarve
na kutaścana bibhyati
svargāpavarga-narakeṣv
api tulyārtha-darśinaḥ

"A pure devotee of Nārāyaṇa is never afraid of going anywhere and everywhere. For him heaven and hell are one and the same." (*Bhāg.* 6.17.28) Such devotees, wandering all over the world, deliver those who are actually afraid of this material existence. Some people are already disgusted with material existence, being confused and frustrated by material enjoyment, and some people, who are intelligent, are interested in understanding the Supreme Lord. Both may take advantage of the pure devotee who wanders throughout the world.

When a pure devotee goes to a place of pilgrimage, he desires to purify that holy place of pilgrimage. Many sinful men bathe in the holy waters of the places of pilgrimage. They take their baths in the waters of the Ganges and Yamunā at places such as Prayāg, Vṛndāvana and Mathurā. In this way the sinful men are purified, but their sinful actions and reactions remain at the holy places of pilgrimage. When a devotee comes to take his bath at those places of pilgrimage, the sinful reactions left by the sinful men are neutralized by the devotee. *Tīrthī-kurvanti tīrthāni svāntaḥ-sthena gadā-bhṛtā* (*Bhāg.* 1.13.10). Because the devotee always carries the Supreme Personality of Godhead within his heart, wherever he goes becomes a place of pilgrimage, a holy place for understanding the Supreme Personality of Godhead. It is therefore the duty of everyone to associate with a pure devotee and thus attain freedom from material contamination. Everyone should take advantage of the wandering devotees whose only business is to deliver conditioned souls from the clutches of *māyā*.

TEXT 38

वयं तु साक्षाद्भगवन् भवस्य
प्रियस्य सख्युः क्षणसङ्गमेन ।
सुदुश्चिकित्स्यस्य भवस्य मृत्यो-
र्भिषक्तमं त्वाद्य गतिं गताः स्म ॥३८॥

vayaṁ tu sākṣād bhagavan bhavasya
priyasya sakhyuḥ kṣaṇa-saṅgamena
suduścikitsyasya bhavasya mṛtyor
bhiṣaktamaṁ tvādya gatiṁ gatāḥ sma

vayam—we; *tu*—then; *sākṣāt*—directly; *bhagavan*—O Lord; *bhavasya*—of Lord Śiva; *priyasya*—very dear; *sakhyuḥ*—Your friend; *kṣaṇa*—for a moment; *saṅgamena*—by association; *suduścikitsyasya*—very difficult to cure; *bhavasya*—of material existence; *mṛtyoḥ*—of death; *bhiṣak-tamam*—the most expert physician; *tvā*—You; *adya*—today; *gatim*—destination; *gatāḥ*—have achieved; *sma*—certainly.

TRANSLATION

Dear Lord, by virtue of a moment's association with Lord Śiva, who is very dear to You and who is Your most intimate friend, we were fortunate to attain You. You are the most expert physician capable of treating the incurable disease of material existence. On account of our great fortune, we have been able to take shelter at Your lotus feet.

PURPORT

It has been said: *hariṁ vinā na sṛtiṁ taranti.* Without taking shelter of the lotus feet of the Personality of Godhead, one cannot attain relief from the clutches of *māyā,* the repetition of birth, old age, disease and death. The Pracetās received the shelter of the Supreme Personality of Godhead by the grace of Lord Śiva. Lord Śiva is the supreme devotee of Lord Viṣṇu, the Supreme Personality of Godhead. *Vaiṣṇavānāṁ yathā śambhuḥ:* The most exalted Vaiṣṇava is Lord Śiva, and those who are actually devotees of Lord Śiva follow Lord Śiva's advice and take shelter at the lotus feet of Lord Viṣṇu. The so-called devotees of Lord Śiva who are simply after material prosperity are in a way deceived by Lord Śiva. He does not actually deceive them, because Lord Śiva has no business deceiving people, but because the so-called devotees of Lord Śiva want to be deceived, Lord Śiva, who is very easily pleased, allows them all kinds of material benedictions. These benedictions might ironically result in the destruction of the so-called devotees. For instance, Rāvaṇa took all material benediction from Lord Śiva, but the result was that he was ultimately destroyed with his family, kingdom and everything else because he misused Lord Śiva's benediction. Because of his material power, he became very proud and puffed up so that he dared kidnap the wife of Lord Rāmacandra. In this way he was ruined. To get material benedictions from Lord Śiva is not difficult, but actually these are not benedictions. The Pracetās received benediction from Lord Śiva, and as a result they attained the shelter of the lotus feet of Lord Viṣṇu. This is real benediction. The *gopīs* also worshiped Lord Śiva in Vṛndāvana, and the Lord is still staying there as Gopīśvara. The *gopīs,* however, prayed that Lord Śiva bless them by giving them Lord Kṛṣṇa as their husband. There is no harm in worshiping the demigods, provided that one's aim is to return home, back to Godhead. Generally people go to the demigods for material benefit, as indicated in *Bhagavad-gītā:*

kāmais tais tair hṛta-jñānāḥ
prapadyante 'nya-devatāḥ

taṁ taṁ niyamam āsthāya
prakṛtyā niyatāḥ svayā

"Those whose minds are distorted by material desires surrender unto demigods and follow the particular rules and regulations of worship according to their own natures." (Bg. 7.20)

One enamored by material benefits is called *hṛta-jñāna* (one who has lost his intelligence). In this connection it is to be noted that sometimes in revealed scriptures Lord Śiva is described as being nondifferent from the Supreme Personality of Godhead. The point is that Lord Śiva and Lord Viṣṇu are so intimately connected that there is no difference in opinion. The actual fact is: *ekale īśvara kṛṣṇa, āra saba bhṛtya.* "The only supreme master is Kṛṣṇa, and all others are His devotees or servants." (Cc. *Ādi* 5.142) This is the real fact, and there is no difference of opinion between Lord Śiva and Lord Viṣṇu in this connection. Nowhere in revealed scripture does Lord Śiva claim to be equal to Lord Viṣṇu. This is simply the creation of the so-called devotees of Lord Śiva, who claim that Lord Śiva and Lord Viṣṇu are one. This is strictly forbidden in the *vaiṣṇava-tantra: yas tu nārāyaṇaṁ devam.* Lord Viṣṇu, Lord Śiva and Lord Brahmā are intimately connected as master and servants. *Śiva-viriñci-nutam.* Viṣṇu is honored and offered obeisances by Lord Śiva and Lord Brahmā. To consider that they are all equal is a great offense. They are all equal in the sense that Lord Viṣṇu is the Supreme Personality of Godhead and all others are His eternal servants.

TEXTS 39-40

यन्नः स्वधीतं गुरवः प्रसादिता
विप्राश्च वृद्धाश्च सदानुवृत्त्या ।
आर्या नताः सुहृदो भ्रातरश्च
सर्वाणि भूतान्यनसूययैव ॥३९॥

यन्नः सुतप्तं तप एतदीश
निरन्धसां कालमदभ्रमप्सु ।
सर्वं तदेतत्पुरुषस्य भूम्नो
वृणीमहे ते परितोषणाय ॥४०॥

yan naḥ svadhītaṁ guravaḥ prasāditā
viprāś ca vṛddhāś ca sad-ānuvṛttyā
āryā natāḥ suhṛdo bhrātaraś ca
sarvāṇi bhūtāny anasūyayaiva

yan naḥ sutaptaṁ tapa etad īśa
nirandhasāṁ kālam adabhram apsu
sarvaṁ tad etat puruṣasya bhūmno
vṛṇīmahe te paritoṣaṇāya

yat—what; *naḥ*—by us; *svadhītam*—studied; *guravaḥ*—superior persons, spiritual masters; *prasāditāḥ*—satisfied; *viprāḥ*—the *brāhmaṇas; ca*—and; *vṛddhāḥ*—those who are elderly; *ca*—and; *sat-ānuvṛttyā*—by our gentle behavior; *āryāḥ*—those who are advanced in spiritual knowledge; *natāḥ*—were offered obeisances; *su-hṛdaḥ*—friends; *bhrātaraḥ*—brothers; *ca*—and; *sarvāṇi*—all; *bhūtāni*—living entities; *anasūyayā*—without any enviousness; *eva*—certainly; *yat*—what; *naḥ*—of us; *su-taptam*—severe; *tapaḥ*—penance; *etat*—this; *īśa*—O Lord; *nirandhasām*—without taking any food; *kālam*—time; *adabhram*—for a long duration; *apsu*—within the water; *sarvam*—all; *tat*—that; *etat*—this; *puruṣasya*—of the Supreme Personality of Godhead; *bhūmnaḥ*—the most exalted; *vṛṇīmahe*—we want this benediction; *te*—of You; *paritoṣaṇāya*—for the satisfaction.

TRANSLATION

Dear Lord, we have studied the Vedas, accepted a spiritual master, and offered respect to brāhmaṇas, advanced devotees and aged personalities who are spiritually very advanced. We have offered our respects to them, and we have not been envious of any brother, friends or anyone else. We have also undergone severe austerities within the water and have not taken food for a long time. All these spiritual assets of ours are simply offered for Your satisfaction. We pray for this benediction only, and nothing more.

PURPORT

As stated in *Śrīmad-Bhāgavatam, saṁsiddhir hari-toṣaṇam:* the real perfection of life is pleasing the Supreme Personality of Godhead. *Vedaiś ca sarvair aham eva vedyaḥ:* In understanding the *Vedas,* one has to understand the Supreme Personality of Godhead. One who has actually understood Him surrenders unto Him after many, many births. We find all these qualifications in the Pracetās. They underwent severe austerities and penances within the water, and they did not take any food for a very long time. They practiced these austerities not for material benediction but for the satisfaction of the Supreme Lord. One may engage in any business—material or spiritual—but the purpose should be the satisfaction of the Supreme Personality of Godhead. This verse presents a perfect picture of Vedic civilization. People training to become devotees should be respectful not only to the Supreme Personality of Godhead but also to those who are elderly in knowledge, who are Āryans and actual devotees of the Lord. An Āryan is one who does not boast but is an actual devotee of the Lord. Āryan means advanced. Formerly, those who claimed to be Āryans had to be devotees of the Lord. For instance, in *Bhagavad-gītā* Kṛṣṇa chastised Arjuna by saying that he was speaking like a non-Āryan.

śrī bhagavān uvāca
kutas tvā kaśmalam idaṁ
viṣame samupasthitam
anārya-juṣṭam asvargyam
akīrti-karam arjuna

"The Supreme Person [Bhagavān] said: My dear Arjuna, how have these impurities come upon you? They are not at all befitting a man who knows the progressive values of life. They do not lead to higher planets, but to infamy." (Bg. 2.2)

Arjuna, the *kṣatriya,* was refusing to fight despite being directly ordered by the Supreme Lord. He was thus chastised by the Lord as belonging to a non-Āryan family. Anyone who is advanced in the devotional service of the Lord certainly knows his duty. It does not matter whether this duty is violent or nonviolent. If it is sanctioned and ordered by the Supreme Lord, it must be performed. An Āryan performs his duty. It is not that the Āryans are unnecessarily inimical to living entities. The Āryans never maintained slaughterhouses, and they are never enemies of poor animals. The Pracetās underwent severe austerities for many, many years, even within the water. Accepting austerities and penances is the avowed business of those interested in advanced civilization.

The word *nirandhasām* means without food. Eating voraciously and unnecessarily is not the business of an Āryan. Rather, the eating process should be restricted as far as possible. When Āryans eat, they eat only prescribed eatables. Regarding this, the Lord says in *Bhagavad-gītā:*

patraṁ puṣpaṁ phalaṁ toyaṁ
yo me bhaktyā prayacchati

tad ahaṁ bhakty-upahṛtam
aśnāmi prayatātmanaḥ

"If one offers Me with love and devotion a leaf, a flower, fruit or water, I will accept it." (Bg. 9.26)

Thus there are restrictions for the advanced Āryans. Although the Lord Himself can eat anything and everything, He nonetheless restricts Himself to vegetables, fruits, milk, and so on. This verse thus describes the activities of those who claim to be Āryans.

TEXT 41

मनुः स्वयम्भूर्भगवान् भवश्च
येऽन्ये तपोज्ञानविशुद्धसत्त्वाः ।
अदृष्टपारा अपि यन्महिम्नः
स्तुवन्त्यथो त्वाऽऽत्मसमं गृणीमः ॥४१॥

manuḥ svayambhūr bhagavān bhavaś ca
ye 'nye tapo-jñāna-viśuddha-sattvāḥ
adṛṣṭa-pārā api yan-mahimnaḥ
stuvanty atho tvātma-samaṁ gṛṇīmaḥ

manuḥ—Svāyambhuva Manu; *svayam-bhūḥ*—Lord Brahmā; *bhagavān*—the most powerful; *bhavaḥ*—Lord Śiva; *ca*—also; *ye*—who; *anye*—others; *tapaḥ*—by austerity; *jñāna*—by knowledge; *viśuddha*—pure; *sattvāḥ*—whose existence; *adṛṣṭa-pārāḥ*—who cannot see the end; *api*—although; *yat*—Your; *mahimnaḥ*—of glories; *stuvanti*—they offer prayers; *atho*—therefore; *tvā*—unto You; *ātma-samam*—according to capacity; *gṛṇīmaḥ*—we offered prayers.

TRANSLATION

Dear Lord, even great yogīs and mystics who are very much advanced by virtue of austerities and knowledge and who have completely situated themselves in pure existence, as well as great personalities like Manu, Lord Brahmā and Lord Śiva, cannot fully understand Your glories and potencies. Nonetheless they have offered their prayers according to their own capacities. In the same way, we, although much lower than these personalities, also offer our prayers according to our own capability.

PURPORT

Lord Brahmā, Lord Śiva, Manu (the father of mankind), great saintly persons and also great sages who have elevated themselves to the transcendental platform through austerities and penance, as well as devotional service, are imperfect in knowledge compared to the Supreme Personality of Godhead. This is the case with anyone within this material world. No one can be equal to the Supreme Lord in anything, certainly not in knowledge. Consequently anyone's prayer to the Supreme Personality of Godhead is never complete. It is not possible to measure the complete glories of the Supreme Lord, who is unlimited. Even the Lord Himself in His incarnation as Ananta or Śeṣa cannot describe His own glories. Although Ananta has many thousands of faces and has been glorifying the Lord for many, many years, He could not find the limit of the glories of the Lord. Thus it is not possible to estimate the complete potencies and glories of the Supreme Lord.

Nonetheless, everyone in devotional service can offer essential prayers to the Lord. Everyone is situated in a relative position, and no one is perfect in glorifying the Lord. Beginning with Lord Brahmā and Lord Śiva down to ourselves, everyone is the servant of the Supreme Lord. We are all situated in relative positions according to our own *karma.* Yet every one of us can offer prayers with heart and soul as far as we can appreciate the Lord's glories. That is our perfection. Even when one is in the darkest region of existence, he is allowed to offer prayers to the Lord according to his own capacity. The Lord therefore says in *Bhagavad-gītā:*

māṁ hi pārtha vyapāśritya
ye 'pi syuḥ pāpa-yonayaḥ
striyo vaiśyās tathā śūdrās
te 'pi yānti parāṁ gatim

"O son of Pṛthā, those who take shelter in Me, though they be of lower birth—woman, *vaiśyas* [merchants], as well as *śūdras* [workers]—can approach the supreme destination." (Bg. 9.32)

If one seriously accepts the lotus feet of the Lord, he is purified by the grace of the Lord and by the grace of the Lord's servant. This is confirmed by Śukadeva Gosvāmī: *ye 'nye ca pāpā yad apāśrayāśrayāḥ śudhyanti tasmai prabhaviṣṇave namaḥ* (*Bhāg.* 2.4.18). One who is brought under the lotus feet of the Lord by the endeavor of the Lord's servant, the spiritual master, is certainly immediately purified, however lowborn he may be. He becomes eligible to return home, back to Godhead.

TEXT 42

नमः समाय शुद्धाय पुरुषाय पराय च ।
वासुदेवाय सत्त्वाय तुभ्यं भगवते नमः ॥४२॥

namaḥ samāya śuddhāya
puruṣāya parāya ca
vāsudevāya sattvāya
tubhyaṁ bhagavate namaḥ

namaḥ—we offer our respectful obeisances; *samāya*—who is equal to everyone; *śuddhāya*—who is never contaminated by sinful activities; *puruṣāya*—unto the Supreme Person; *parāya*—transcendental; *ca*—also; *vāsudevāya*—living everywhere; *sattvāya*—who is in the transcendental position; *tubhyam*—unto You; *bhagavate*—the Supreme Personality of Godhead; *namaḥ*—obeisances.

TRANSLATION

Dear Lord, You have no enemies or friends. Therefore You are equal to everyone. You cannot be contaminated by sinful activities, and Your transcendental form is always beyond the material creation. You are the Supreme Personality of Godhead because You remain everywhere within all existence. You are consequently known as Vāsudeva. We offer You our respectful obeisances.

PURPORT

The Supreme Personality of Godhead is known as Vāsudeva because He lives everywhere. The word *vas* means "to live." As stated in *Brahma-saṁhitā, eko 'py asau racayituṁ jagad-aṇḍa-koṭim:* the Lord, through His plenary portion, enters into each and every universe to create the material manifestation. He also enters into each and every heart in all living entities and into each and every atom also (*paramāṇu-cayāntara-stham*). Because the Supreme Lord lives everywhere, He is known as Vāsudeva. Although He lives everywhere within the material world, He is not contaminated by the modes of nature. The Lord is therefore described in *Īśopaniṣad* as *apāpa-viddham.* He is never contaminated by the modes of material nature. When the Lord descends on this planet, He acts in many ways. He kills demons and performs acts not sanctioned by the Vedic principles, that is, acts considered sinful. Even though He acts in such a way, He is never contaminated by His action. He is therefore described herein as *śuddha,* meaning always free from contamination. The Lord is also *sama,* equal to everyone. In this regard, He states in *Bhagavad-gītā:*

samo 'haṁ sarva-bhūteṣu
na me dveṣyo 'sti na priyaḥ
ye bhajanti tu māṁ bhaktyā
mayi te teṣu cāpy aham

"I envy no one, nor am I partial to anyone. I am equal to all. But whoever renders service unto Me in devotion is a friend, is in Me, and I am also a friend to him." (Bg. 9.29) The Lord has no one as His friend or enemy, and He is equal to everyone.

The word *sattvāya* indicates that the form of the Lord is not material. It is *sac-cid-ānanda-vigraha. Īśvaraḥ paramaḥ kṛṣṇaḥ sac-cid-ānanda-vigrahaḥ.* His body is different from our material bodies. One should not think that the Supreme Personality of Godhead has a material body like ours.

TEXT 43

मैत्रेय उवाच
इति प्रचेतोभिरभिष्टुतो हरिः
प्रीतस्तथेत्याह शरण्यवत्सलः ।
अनिच्छतां यानमतृप्तचक्षुषां
ययौ स्वधामानपवर्गवीर्यः ॥४३॥

maitreya uvāca
iti pracetobhir abhiṣṭuto hariḥ
prītas tathety āha śaraṇya-vatsalaḥ
anicchatāṁ yānam atṛpta-cakṣuṣāṁ
yayau sva-dhāmānapavarga-vīryaḥ

maitreyaḥ uvāca—Maitreya said; *iti*—thus; *pracetobhiḥ*—by the Pracetās; *abhiṣṭutaḥ*—being praised; *hariḥ*—the Supreme Personality of Godhead; *prītaḥ*—being pleased; *tathā*—so; *iti*—thus; *āha*—said; *śaraṇya*—to the surrendered souls; *vatsalaḥ*—affectionate; *anicchatām*—not desiring; *yānam*—His departure; *atṛpta*—not satisfied; *cakṣuṣām*—their eyes; *yayau*—He left; *sva-dhāma*—to His own abode; *anapavarga-vīryaḥ*—whose prowess is never defeated.

TRANSLATION

The great sage Maitreya continued: My dear Vidura, the Supreme Personality of Godhead, who is the protector of surrendered souls, being thus addressed by the Pracetās and worshiped by them, replied, "May whatever You have prayed for be fulfilled." After saying this, the Supreme Personality of Godhead, whose prowess is never defeated, left. The Pracetās were unwilling to be separated from Him because they had not seen Him to their full satisfaction.

PURPORT

The word *anapavarga-vīrya* is significant in this verse. The word *ana* means "without," *pavarga* means "the materialistic way of life," and *vīrya* means "prowess." The prowess of the Supreme Personality of Godhead always contains six basic opulences, one of which is renunciation. Although the Pracetās desired to see the Lord to their full satisfaction, the Lord nonetheless left. According to Śrīla Jīva Gosvāmī, this is an exhibition of His kindness to innumerable other devotees. Although He was being attracted by the Pracetās, He left. This is an example of His renunciation. This renunciation was also exhibited by Lord Caitanya Mahāprabhu when He stayed with Advaita Prabhu after taking *sannyāsa.* All the devotees there wanted Him to stay a few days longer, but Lord Caitanya left without hesitation. The conclusion is that although the Supreme Lord has unlimited kindness for His devotees, He is not attached to anyone. He is equally kind to His innumerable devotees all over the creation.

TEXT 44

अथ निर्याय सलिलात्प्रचेतस उदन्वतः ।
वीक्ष्याकुप्यन्द्रुमैश्छन्नां गां गां रोद्धुमिवोच्छ्रितैः ॥४४॥

atha niryāya salilāt
pracetasa udanvataḥ
vīkṣyākupyan drumaiś channāṁ
gāṁ gāṁ roddhum ivocchritaiḥ

atha—thereafter; *niryāya*—after coming out; *salilāt*—from the water; *pracetasaḥ*—all the Pracetās; *udanvataḥ*—of the sea; *vīkṣya*—having observed; *akupyan*—became very angry; *drumaiḥ*—by trees; *channām*—covered; *gām*—

the world; *gām*—the heavenly planets; *roddhum*—to obstruct; *iva*—as if; *ucchritaiḥ*—very tall.

TRANSLATION

Thereafter all the Pracetās emerged from the waters of the sea. They then saw that all the trees on land had grown very tall as if to obstruct the path of the heavenly planets. These trees had covered the entire surface of the world. At this time the Pracetās became very angry.

PURPORT

King Prācīnabarhiṣat left his kingdom before his sons arrived after their execution of penance and austerity. The sons, the Pracetās, were ordered by the Supreme Personality of Godhead to come out of the water and go to the kingdom of their father in order to take care of that kingdom. However, when they came out, they saw that everything had been neglected due to the King's absence. They first observed that foodgrains were not being produced and that there were no agricultural activities. Indeed, the surface of the world was practically covered by very tall trees. It seemed as though the trees were determined to stop people from going into outer space to reach the heavenly kingdoms. The Pracetās became very angry when they saw the surface of the globe covered in this way. They desired that the land be cleared for crops.

It is not a fact that jungles and trees attract clouds and rain, because we find rainfall over the sea. Human beings can inhabit any place on the surface of the earth by clearing jungles and converting land for agricultural purposes. People can keep cows, and all economic problems can be solved in that way. One need only work to produce grains and take care of the cows. The wood found in the jungles may be used for constructing cottages. In this way the economic problem of humanity can be solved. At the present moment there are many vacant lands throughout the world, and if they are properly utilized, there will be no scarcity of food. As far as rain is concerned, it is the performance of *yajña* that attracts rain. As stated in *Bhagavad-gītā:*

annād bhavanti bhūtāni
parjanyād anna-sambhavaḥ
yajñād bhavati parjanyo
yajñaḥ karma-samudbhavaḥ

"All living bodies subsist on food grains, which are produced from rains. Rains are produced by performance of *yajña* [sacrifice], and *yajña* is born of prescribed duties." (Bg. 3.14)

By performing sacrifice, man will have sufficient rainfall and crops.

TEXT 45

ततोऽग्निमारुतौ राजन्नमुञ्चन्मुखतो रुषा ।
महीं निर्वीरुधं कर्तुं संवर्तक इवात्यये ॥४५॥

tato 'gni-mārutau rājann
amuñcan mukhato ruṣā
mahīṁ nirvīrudhaṁ kartuṁ
saṁvartaka ivātyaye

tataḥ—thereafter; *agni*—fire; *mārutau*—and air; *rājan*—O King; *amuñcan*—they emitted; *mukhataḥ*—from their mouths; *ruṣā*—out of anger; *mahīm*—the earth; *nirvīrudham*—treeless; *kartum*—to make; *saṁvartakaḥ*—the fire of devastation; *iva*—like; *atyaye*—at the time of devastation.

TRANSLATION

My dear King, at the time of devastation, Lord Śiva emits fire and air from his mouth out of anger. To make the surface of the earth completely treeless, the Pracetās also emitted fire and air from their mouths.

PURPORT

In this verse Vidura is addressed as *rājan,* which means "O King." In this regard, Śrīla Viśvanātha Cakravartī Ṭhākura comments that a *dhīra* never becomes angry because he is always situated in devotional service. Advanced devotees can control their senses; therefore a devotee can be addressed as *rājan.* A king controls and rules in various ways amongst citizens; similarly, one who can control his senses is the king of his senses. He is a *svāmī* or *gosvāmī.* The *svāmīs* and *gosvāmīs* are therefore sometimes addressed as *mahārāja,* or king.

TEXT 46

भस्मसात्क्रियमाणांस्तान्द्रुमान् वीक्ष्य पितामहः ।
आगतः शमयामास पुत्रान् बर्हिष्मतो नयैः ॥४६॥

bhasmasāt kriyamāṇāṁs tān
drumān vīkṣya pitā-mahaḥ
āgataḥ śamayām āsa
putrān barhiṣmato nayaiḥ

bhasmasāt—into ashes; *kriyamāṇān*—being made; *tān*—all of them; *drumān*—the trees; *vīkṣya*—seeing; *pitā-mahaḥ*—Lord Brahmā; *āgataḥ*—came there; *śamayām āsa*—pacified; *putrān*—the sons; *barhiṣmataḥ*—of King Barhiṣmān; *nayaiḥ*—by logic.

TRANSLATION

After seeing that all the trees on the surface of the earth were being turned to ashes, Lord Brahmā immediately came to the sons of King Barhiṣmān and pacified them with words and logic.

PURPORT

Whenever there is some uncommon occurrence on any planet, Lord Brahmā, being in charge of the whole universe, immediately comes to control the situation. Lord Brahmā also came when Hiraṇyakaśipu underwent severe penances and austerities and made the whole universe tremble. A responsible man in any establishment is always alert to keep peace and harmony within the establishment. Similarly, Lord Brahmā is also allowed to keep peace and harmony within this universe. He consequently pacified the sons of King Barhiṣmān with good logic.

TEXT 47

तत्रावशिष्टा ये वृक्षा भीता दुहितरं तदा ।
उज्जहुस्ते प्रचेतोभ्य उपदिष्टाः स्वयम्भुवा ॥४७॥

tatrāvaśiṣṭā ye vṛkṣā
bhītā duhitaraṁ tadā
ujjahrus te pracetobhya
upadiṣṭāḥ svayambhuvā

tatra—there; *avaśiṣṭāḥ*—remaining; *ye*—which; *vṛkṣāḥ*—trees; *bhītāḥ*—being afraid; *duhitaram*—their daughter; *tadā*—at that time; *ujjahruḥ*—delivered; *te*—they; *pracetobhyaḥ*—unto the Pracetās; *upadiṣṭāḥ*—being advised; *svayam-bhuvā*—by Lord Brahmā.

TRANSLATION

The remaining trees, being very much afraid of the Pracetās, immediately delivered their daughter at the advice of Lord Brahmā.

PURPORT

The daughter of the trees is referred to in text thirteen of this chapter. This daughter was born of Kaṇḍu and Pramlocā. The society girl Pramlocā, after giving birth to the child, immediately left for the heavenly kingdom. While the child was crying, the King of the moon took compassion upon her and saved her by putting his finger into her mouth. This child was cared for by the trees, and when she grew up, by the order of Lord Brahmā, she was delivered to the Pracetās as their wife. The name of the girl was Māriṣā, as the next verse will explain. It was the predominating deity of the trees that delivered the daughter. In this connection Śrīla Jīva Gosvāmī Prabhupāda states, *vṛkṣāḥ tad-adhiṣṭhātṛ-devatāḥ:* "The 'trees' means the controlling deity of those trees." In Vedic literatures we find that there is a controlling deity of the water; similarly, there is a controlling deity of the trees. The Pracetās were engaged in burning all the trees to ashes, and they considered the trees their enemies. To pacify the Pracetās, the predominating deity of the trees, under the advice of Lord Brahmā, delivered the daughter Māriṣā.

TEXT 48

ते च ब्रह्मण आदेशान्मारिषामुपयेमिरे ।
यस्यां महदवज्ञानादजन्यजनयोनिजः ॥४८॥

te ca brahmaṇa ādeśān
māriṣām upayemire
yasyāṁ mahad-avajñānād
ajany ajana-yonijaḥ

te—all the Pracetās; *ca*—also; *brahmaṇaḥ*—of Lord Brahmā; *ādeśāt*—by the order; *māriṣām*—Māriṣā; *upayemire*—married; *yasyām*—in whom; *mahat*—to a great personality; *avajñānāt*—on account of disrespect; *ajani*—took birth; *ajana-yoni-jaḥ*—the son of Lord Brahmā, Dakṣa.

TRANSLATION

Following the order of Lord Brahmā, all the Pracetās accepted the girl as their wife. From the womb of this girl, the son of Lord Brahmā named Dakṣa took birth. Dakṣa had to take birth in the womb of Māriṣā due to his disobeying and disrespecting Lord Mahādeva [Śiva]. Consequently he had to give up his body twice.

PURPORT

In this connection the word *mahad-avajñānāt* is significant. King Dakṣa was the son of Lord Brahmā; therefore in a previous birth he was a *brāhmaṇa,* but because of his behaving like a non-*brāhmaṇa* (*abrāhmaṇa*) by insulting or disrespecting Lord Mahādeva, he had to take birth within the semen of a *kṣatriya.* That is to say, he became the son of the Pracetās. Not only that, but because of his disrespecting Lord Śiva, he had to undergo the tribulation of taking birth within the womb of a woman. In the Dakṣa-yajña arena, he was once killed by Lord Śiva's servant, Vīrabhadra. Because that was not sufficient, he again took birth in the womb of Māriṣā. At the end of the Dakṣa-yajña and the disastrous incidents there, Dakṣa offered his prayer to Lord Śiva. Although he had to give up his body and take birth in the womb of a woman impregnated by the semen of a *kṣatriya,* he nonetheless received all opulence by the grace of Lord Śiva. These are the subtle laws of material nature. Unfortunately, people in this modern age do not know how these laws are working. Having no knowledge of the eternity of the spirit soul and its transmigration, the population of the present age is in the greatest ignorance. Because of this, it is said in *Bhāgavatam: mandāḥ sumanda-matayo manda-bhāgyā hy upadrutāḥ* (*Bhāg.* 1.1.10). The total population in this age of Kali-yuga is very bad, lazy, unfortunate and disturbed by material conditions.

TEXT 49

चाक्षुषे त्वन्तरे प्राप्ते प्राक्सर्गे कालविद्रुते ।
यः ससर्ज प्रजा इष्टाः स दक्षो दैवचोदितः ॥४९॥

cākṣuṣe tv antare prāpte
prāk-sarge kāla-vidrute
yaḥ sasarja prajā iṣṭāḥ
sa dakṣo daiva-coditaḥ

cākṣuṣe—named Cākṣuṣa; *tu*—but; *antare*—the *manvantara; prāpte*—when it happened; *prāk*—previous; *sarge*—creation; *kāla-vidrute*—destroyed in due course of time; *yaḥ*—one who; *sasarja*—created; *prajāḥ*—living entities; *iṣṭāḥ*—desirable; *saḥ*—he; *dakṣaḥ*—Dakṣa; *daiva*—by the Supreme Personality of Godhead; *coditaḥ*—inspired.

TRANSLATION

His previous body had been destroyed, but he, the same Dakṣa, inspired by the supreme will, created all the desired living entities in the Cākṣuṣa manvantara.

PURPORT

As stated in *Bhagavad-gītā:*

sahasra-yuga-paryantam
ahar yad brahmaṇo viduḥ
rātriṁ yuga-sahasrāntāṁ
te 'ho-rātra-vido janāḥ

"By human calculation, a thousand ages taken together is the duration of Brahmā's one day. And such also is the duration of his night." (Bg. 8.17)

Brahmā's one day consists of one thousand cycles of the four *yugas*—Satya, Tretā, Dvāpara and Kali. In that one day there are fourteen *manvantaras,* and out of these *manvantaras* this Cākṣuṣa *manvantara* is the sixth. The various Manus existing in one day of Lord Brahmā are as follows: (1) Svāyambhuva (2) Svārociṣa (3) Uttama (4) Tāmasa (5) Raivata (6) Cākṣuṣa (7) Vaivasvata (8) Sāvarṇi (9) Dakṣa-sāvarṇi (10) Brahma-sāvarṇi (11) Dharma-sāvarṇi (12) Rudra-sāvarṇi (13) Deva-sāvarṇi and (14) Indra-sāvarṇi.

Thus there are fourteen Manus in one day of Brahmā. In a year there are 5,040 Manus. Brahmā has to live for one hundred years; consequently the total of Manus appearing and disappearing during the life of one Brahmā is 504,000. This is the calculation for one universe, and there are innumerable universes. All these Manus come and go simply by the breathing process of Mahā-Viṣṇu. As stated in the *Brahma-saṁhitā:*

yasyaika-niśvasita-kālam athāvalambya
jīvanti loma-vilajā jagad-aṇḍa-nāthāḥ
viṣṇur mahān sa iha yasya kalā-viśeṣo
govindam ādi-puruṣaṁ tam ahaṁ bhajāmi

The word *jagad-aṇḍa-nātha* means Lord Brahmā. There are innumerable *jagad-aṇḍa-nātha* Brahmās, and thus we can calculate the many Manus. The present age is under the control of Vaivasvata Manu. Each Manu lives 4,320,000 years multiplied by 71. The present Manu has already lived for 4,320,000 years multiplied by 28. All these long lifespans are ultimately ended by the laws of material nature. The controversy of Dakṣa-yajña took place in the Svāyambhuva *manvantara* period. As a result, Dakṣa was punished by Lord Śiva, but by virtue of his prayers to Lord Śiva he became eligible to regain his former opulence. According to Viśvanātha Cakravartī Ṭhākura, Dakṣa underwent severe penances up to the fifth *manvantara.* Thus at the beginning of the sixth *manvantara,* known as the Cākṣuṣa *manvantara,* Dakṣa regained his former opulence by the blessings of Lord Śiva.

TEXTS 50-51

यो जायमानः सर्वेषां तेजस्तेजस्विनां रुचा ।
स्वयोपादत्त दाक्ष्याच्च कर्मणां दक्षमब्रुवन् ॥५०॥

तं प्रजासर्गरक्षायामनादिरभिषिच्य च ।
युयोज युयुजेऽन्यांश्च स वै सर्वप्रजापतीन् ॥५१॥

yo jāyamānaḥ sarveṣāṁ
tejas tejasvināṁ rucā
svayopādatta dākṣyāc ca
karmaṇāṁ dakṣam abruvan

taṁ prajā-sarga-rakṣāyām
anādir abhiṣicya ca
yuyoja yuyuje 'nyāṁś ca
sa vai sarva-prajā-patīn

yaḥ—one who; *jāyamānaḥ*—just after his birth; *sarveṣām*—of all; *tejaḥ*—the brilliance; *tejasvinām*—brilliant; *rucā*—by effulgence; *svayā*—his; *upādatta*—covered; *dākṣyāt*—from being expert; *ca*—and; *karmaṇām*—in fruitive activities; *dakṣam*—Dakṣa; *abruvan*—was called; *tam*—him; *prajā*—living beings; *sarga*—generating; *rakṣāyām*—in the matter of maintaining; *anādiḥ*—the firstborn, Lord Brahmā; *abhiṣicya*—having appointed; *ca*—also; *yuyoja*—engaged; *yuyuje*—engaged; *anyān*—others; *ca*—and; *saḥ*—he; *vai*—certainly; *sarva*—all; *prajā-patīn*—progenitors of living entities.

TRANSLATION

After being born, Dakṣa, by the superexcellence of his bodily luster, covered all others' bodily opulence. Because he was very expert in performing fruitive activity, he was called by the name Dakṣa, meaning "the

very expert." Lord Brahmā therefore engaged Dakṣa in the work of generating living entities and maintaining them. In due course of time, Dakṣa also engaged other prajāpatis [progenitors] in the process of generation and maintenance.

PURPORT

Dakṣa became almost as powerful as Lord Brahmā. Consequently Lord Brahmā engaged him in generating population. Dakṣa was very influential and opulent. In his own turn, Dakṣa engaged other *prajāpatis,* headed by Marīci. In this way the population of the universe increased.

Thus end the Bhaktivedanta purports of the Fourth Canto, Thirtieth Chapter of the Śrīmad-Bhāgavatam, *entitled "The Activities of the Pracetās."*

CHAPTER THIRTY-ONE

Nārada Instructs the Pracetās

TEXT 1

मैत्रेय उवाच

तत उत्पन्नविज्ञाना आश्वधोक्षजभाषितम् ।
स्मरन्त आत्मजे भार्यां विसृज्य प्राव्रजन् गृहात् ॥ १ ॥

maitreya uvāca
tata utpanna-vijñānā
āśv adhokṣaja-bhāṣitam
smaranta ātmaje bhāryāṁ
visṛjya prāvrajan gṛhāt

maitreyaḥ uvāca—Maitreya said; *tataḥ*—thereafter; *utpanna*—developed; *vijñānāḥ*—possessing perfect knowledge; *āśu*—very soon; *adhokṣaja*—by the Supreme Personality of Godhead; *bhāṣitam*—what was enunciated; *smarantaḥ*—remembering; *ātma-je*—unto their son; *bhāryām*—their wife; *visṛjya*—after giving; *prāvrajan*—left; *gṛhāt*—from home.

TRANSLATION

The great saint Maitreya continued: After that, the Pracetās lived at home for thousands of years and developed perfect knowledge in spiritual consciousness. At last they remembered the blessings of the Supreme Personality of Godhead and left home, putting their wife in charge of a perfect son.

PURPORT

After the Pracetās had finished their penances, they were blessed by the Supreme Personality of Godhead. The Lord blessed them by telling them that after finishing their family life they would return home, back to Godhead, in due course of time. After finishing their family life, which lasted thousands of years according to the calculations of the demigods, the Pracetās decided to leave home, putting their wife in the charge of a son named Dakṣa. This is the process of Vedic civilization. In the beginning of life, as a *brahmacārī,* one has to undergo severe penances and austerities in order to be educated in spiritual values. The *brahmacārī* is never allowed to mingle with women and is thus kept from learning about sex enjoyment. The basic flaw in modern civilization is that boys and girls are given freedom during school and college to enjoy sex life. Most of the children are *varṇa-saṅkara,* meaning born of undesirable fathers and mothers. Consequently the whole world is in chaos. Actually human civilization should be based on the Vedic principles. This means that in the beginning of life boys and girls should undergo penances and austerities. When they are grown, they should get married, live for some time at home and beget children. When the children are grown up, the man should leave home and search for Kṛṣṇa consciousness. In this way one can make one's life perfect by going home to the kingdom of God.

Unless one practices penances and austerities in his student life, he cannot understand the existence of God. Without realizing Kṛṣṇa, one cannot make his life perfect. The conclusion is that when the children are grown, the wife should be put in the children's charge. The husband may then leave home to develop Kṛṣṇa consciousness. Everything depends on the development of mature knowledge. King Prācīnabarhiṣat, the father of the Pracetās, left home before the arrival of his sons, who were engaged in austerity within the water. As soon as the time is ripe, or as soon as one has developed perfect Kṛṣṇa consciousness, he should leave home, even though all his duties may not be fulfilled. Prācīnabarhiṣat was waiting for the arrival of his sons, but, following the instructions of Nārada, as soon as his intelligence was properly developed, he simply left instructions for his ministers to impart to his sons. Thus without waiting for their arrival, he left home.

Giving up a comfortable home life is absolutely necessary for human beings and is advised by Prahlāda Mahārāja. *Hitvātma-pātaṁ gṛham andha-kūpam:* To finish the materialistic way of life, one should leave his so-called comfortable home life, which is simply a means for killing the soul (*ātma-pātam*). The home is considered to be a dark well covered by grass, and if one falls within this well, he simply dies without anyone's caring. One should therefore not be too much attached to family life, for it will spoil one's development of Kṛṣṇa consciousness.

TEXT 2

दीक्षिता ब्रह्मसत्रेण सर्वभूतात्ममेधसा ।
प्रतीच्यां दिशि वेलायां सिद्धोऽभूद्यत्र जाजलिः ॥२॥

dīkṣitā brahma-satreṇa
sarva-bhūtātma-medhasā
pratīcyāṁ diśi velāyāṁ
siddho 'bhūd yatra jājaliḥ

dīkṣitāḥ—being determined; *brahma-satreṇa*—by understanding of the Supreme Spirit; *sarva*—all; *bhūta*—living entities; *ātma-medhasā*—considering as one's self; *pratīcyām*—in the western; *diśi*—direction; *velāyām*—on the seashore; *siddhaḥ*—perfect; *abhūt*—became; *yatra*—where; *jājaliḥ*—the great sage Jājali.

TRANSLATION

The Pracetās went to the seashore in the west where the great liberated sage Jājali was residing. After perfecting the spiritual knowledge by which one becomes equal to all living entities, the Pracetās became perfect in Kṛṣṇa consciousness.

PURPORT

The word *brahma-satra* means cultivation of spiritual knowledge. Actually both the *Vedas* and severe austerity are known as *brahma. Vedas tattvaṁ tapo brahma. Brahma* also means the Absolute Truth. One has to cultivate knowledge of the Absolute Truth by pursuing studies in the *Vedas* and undergoing severe austerities and penances. The Pracetās properly executed this function and consequently became equal to all other living entities. As *Bhagavad-gītā* confirms:

brahma-bhūtaḥ prasannātmā
na śocati na kāṅkṣati
samaḥ sarveṣu bhūteṣu
mad-bhaktiṁ labhate parām

"One who is thus transcendentally situated at once realizes the Supreme Brahman. He never laments nor desires to have anything; he is equally disposed to every living entity. In that state he attains pure devotional service unto Me." (Bg. 18.54)

When one actually becomes spiritually advanced, he does not see the difference between one living entity and another. This platform is attained by determination. When perfect knowledge is expanded, one ceases to see the outward covering of the living entity. He sees, rather, the spirit soul within the body. Thus he does not make distinctions between a human being and an animal, a learned *brāhmaṇa* and a *caṇḍāla.*

vidyā-vinaya-sampanne
brāhmaṇe gavi hastini
śuni caiva śvapāke ca
paṇḍitāḥ sama-darśinaḥ

"The humble sage, by virtue of true knowledge, sees with equal vision a learned and gentle *brāhmaṇa,* a cow, an elephant, a dog and a dog-eater [outcaste]." (Bg. 5.18)

A learned person sees everyone equally on a spiritual basis, and a learned person, a devotee, wants to see everyone developed in Kṛṣṇa consciousness. The place where the Pracetās were residing was perfect for executing spiritual activities, for it is indicated that the great sage Jājali attained *mukti* (liberation) there. One desiring perfection or liberation should associate with a person who is already liberated. This is called *sādhu-saṅga,* associating with a perfect devotee.

TEXT 3

तान्निर्जितप्राणमनोवचोदृशो
जितासनान् शान्तसमानविग्रहान् ।
परेऽमले ब्रह्मणि योजितात्मनः
सुरासुरेड्यो ददृशे स नारदः ॥ ३ ॥

tān nirjita-prāṇa-mano-vaco-dṛśo
jitāsanān śānta-samāna-vigrahān
pare 'male brahmaṇi yojitātmanaḥ
surāsureḍyo dadṛśe sma nāradaḥ

tān—all of them; *nirjita*—completely controlled; *prāṇa*—the life air (by the *prāṇāyāma* process); *manaḥ*—mind; *vacaḥ*—words; *dṛśaḥ*—and vision; *jita-āsanān*—who conquered the yogic *āsana,* or sitting posture; *śānta*—pacified; *samāna*—straight; *vigrahān*—whose bodies; *pare*—transcendental; *amale*—free from all material contamination; *brahmaṇi*—in the Supreme; *yojita*—engaged; *ātmanaḥ*—whose minds; *sura-asura-īḍyaḥ*—worshiped by the demons and by the demigods; *dadṛśe*—saw; *sma*—in the past; *nāradaḥ*—the great sage Nārada.

TRANSLATION

After practicing the yogāsana for mystic yoga, the Pracetās managed to control their life air, mind, words and external vision. Thus by the prāṇāyāma process they were completely relieved of material attachment. By remaining perpendicular, they could concentrate their minds on the uppermost Brahman. While they were practicing this prāṇāyāma, the great sage Nārada, who is worshiped both by demons and by demigods, came to see them.

PURPORT

In this verse the words *pare amale* are significant. The realization of Brahman is explained in *Śrīmad-Bhāgavatam.* The Absolute Truth is realized in three phases—impersonal effulgence (Brahman), localized Paramātmā and the Supreme Personality of Godhead, Bhagavān. In his prayers, Lord Śiva concentrated upon the personal features of Parabrahman, described in personal terms as *snigdha-prāvṛḍ-ghana-śyāmam* (*Bhāg.* 4.24.45). Following the instructions of Lord Śiva, the Pracetās also concentrated their minds on the Śyāmasundara form of the Supreme Brahman. Although impersonal Brahman, Paramātmā Brahman and Brahman as the Supreme Person are all on the same transcendental platform, the personal feature of the Supreme Brahman is the ultimate goal and last word in transcendence.

The great sage Nārada travels everywhere. He goes to the demons and the demigods and is equally respected. He is consequently described herein as *surāsureḍya,* worshiped both by demons and by demigods. For Nārada Muni, the door of every house is open. Although there is perpetual animosity between the demons and demigods, Nārada Muni is welcomed everywhere. Nārada is considered one of the demigods, of course, and the word *devarṣi* means "the saintly person among the demigods." Not even the demons envy Nārada Muni; therefore he is equally worshiped both by demons and by demigods. A perfect Vaiṣṇava's position should be just like Nārada Muni's, completely independent and unbiased.

TEXT 4

तमागतं त उत्थाय प्रणिपत्याभिनन्द्य च ।
पूजयित्वा यथादेशं सुखासीनमथाब्रुवन् ॥ ४ ॥

tam āgataṁ ta utthāya
praṇipatyābhinandya ca
pūjayitvā yathādeśaṁ
sukhāsīnam athābruvan

tam—to him; *āgatam*—appeared; *te*—all the Pracetās; *utthāya*—after getting up; *praṇipatya*—offering obeisances; *abhinandya*—offering welcome; *ca*—also; *pūjayitvā*—worshiping; *yathā ādeśam*—according to regulative principles; *sukha-āsīnam*—comfortably situated; *atha*—thus; *abruvan*—they said.

TRANSLATION

As soon as the Pracetās saw that the great sage Nārada had appeared, they immediately got up even from their āsanas. As required, they immediately offered obeisances and worshiped him, and when they saw that Nārada Muni was properly seated, they began to ask him questions.

PURPORT

It is significant that all the Pracetās were engaged in practicing *yoga* to concentrate their minds on the Supreme Personality of Godhead.

TEXT 5

प्रचेतस ऊचुः
स्वागतं ते सुरर्षेऽद्य दिष्टया नो दर्शनं गतः ।
तव चङ्क्रमणं ब्रह्मन्नभयाय यथा रवेः ॥ ५ ॥

pracetasa ūcuḥ
svāgataṁ te surarṣe 'dya
diṣṭyā no darśanaṁ gataḥ
tava caṅkramaṇaṁ brahmann
abhayāya yathā raveḥ

pracetasaḥ ūcuḥ—the Pracetās said; *su-āgatam*—welcome; *te*—unto you; *sura-ṛṣe*—O sage among the demigods; *adya*—today; *diṣṭyā*—by good fortune; *naḥ*—of us; *darśanam*—audience; *gataḥ*—you have come; *tava*—your; *caṅkramaṇam*—movements; *brahman*—O great *brāhmaṇa; abhayāya*—for fearlessness; *yathā*—as; *raveḥ*—of the sun.

TRANSLATION

All the Pracetās began to address the great sage Nārada: O great sage, O brāhmaṇa, we hope you met with no disturbances while coming here. It is due to our great fortune that we are now able to see you. By the traveling of the sun, people are relieved from the fear of the darkness of night—a fear brought about by thieves and rogues. Similarly, your traveling is like the sun's, for you drive away all kinds of fear.

PURPORT

Because of the night's darkness, everyone is afraid of rogues and thieves, especially in great cities. People are often afraid to go out on the streets, and we understand that even in a great city like New York people do not like to go out at night. More or less, when it is night, everyone is afraid, either in the city or in the village. However, as soon as the sun rises, everyone is relieved. Similarly, this material world is dark by nature. Everyone is afraid of danger at every moment, but when one sees a devotee like Nārada, all fear is relieved. Just as the sun disperses darkness, the appearance of a great sage like Nārada disperses ignorance. When one meets Nārada or his representative, a spiritual master, he is freed from all anxiety brought about by ignorance.

TEXT 6

यदादिष्टं भगवता शिवेनाधोक्षजेन च ।
तद् गृहेषु प्रसक्तानां प्रायशः क्षपितं प्रभो ॥ ६ ॥

yad ādiṣṭaṁ bhagavatā
śivenādhokṣajena ca
tad gṛheṣu prasaktānāṁ
prāyaśaḥ kṣapitaṁ prabho

yat—what; *ādiṣṭam*—was instructed; *bhagavatā*—by the exalted personality; *śivena*—Lord Śiva; *adhokṣajena*—by Lord Viṣṇu; *ca*—also; *tat*—that; *gṛheṣu*—to family affairs; *prasaktānām*—by us who were too much attached; *prāyaśaḥ*—almost; *kṣapitam*—forgotten; *prabho*—O master.

TRANSLATION

O master, may we inform you that because of our being overly attached to family affairs, we almost forgot the instructions we received from Lord Śiva and Lord Viṣṇu.

PURPORT

Remaining in family life is a kind of concession for sense enjoyment. One should know that sense enjoyment is not required, but one has to accept sense enjoyment inasmuch as one has to live. As confirmed in *Śrīmad-Bhāgavatam* (1.2.10): *kāmasya nendriya-prītiḥ*. One has to become a *gosvāmī* and control his senses. One should not simply use his senses for sense gratification; rather, the senses should be employed just as much as required for maintaining body and soul together. Śrīla Rūpa Gosvāmī recommends: *anāsaktasya viṣayān yathārham upayuñjataḥ*. One should not be attached to sense objects but should accept sense enjoyment as much as required, no more. If one wishes to enjoy the senses more than required, he becomes attached to family life, which means bondage. All the Pracetās admitted their fault in remaining in household life.

TEXT 7

तन्नः प्रद्योतयाध्यात्मज्ञानं तत्त्वार्थदर्शनम् ।
येनाञ्जसा तरिष्यामो दुस्तरं भवसागरम् ॥ ७ ॥

tan naḥ pradyotayādhyātma-
jñānaṁ tattvārtha-darśanam
yenāñjasā tariṣyāmo
dustaraṁ bhava-sāgaram

tat—therefore; *naḥ*—for us; *pradyotaya*—kindly awaken; *adhyātma*—transcendental; *jñānam*—knowledge; *tattva*—Absolute Truth; *artha*—for the purpose of; *darśanam*—philosophy; *yena*—by which; *añjasā*—easily; *tariṣyāmaḥ*—we can cross over; *dustaram*—formidable; *bhava-sāgaram*—the ocean of nescience.

TRANSLATION

Dear master, kindly enlighten us in transcendental knowledge, which may act as a torchlight by which we may cross the dark nescience of material existence.

PURPORT

The Pracetās requested Nārada to enlighten them in transcendental knowledge. Generally when a common man meets a saintly person, he wishes to get some material benediction. However, the Pracetās were not interested in material benefit, for they had enjoyed all this sufficiently.

Nor did they want the fulfillment of their material desires. They were simply interested in crossing the ocean of nescience. Everyone should be interested in getting out of these material clutches. Everyone should approach a saintly person in order to be enlightened in this connection. One should not bother a saintly person to get blessings for material enjoyment. Generally householders receive saintly persons to get their blessings, but their real aim is to become happy in the material world. Asking such material benedictions is not recommended in the *śāstras.*

TEXT 8

मैत्रेय उवाच

इति प्रचेतसां पृष्टो भगवान्नारदो मुनिः ।
भगवत्युत्तमश्लोक आविष्टात्माब्रवीन्नृपान् ॥ ८ ॥

maitreya uvāca
iti pracetasāṁ pṛṣṭo
bhagavān nārado muniḥ
bhagavaty uttama-śloka
āviṣṭātmābravīn nṛpān

maitreyaḥ uvāca—Maitreya said; *iti*—thus; *pracetasām*—by the Pracetās; *pṛṣṭaḥ*—being asked; *bhagavān*—the great devotee of the Supreme Personality of Godhead; *nāradaḥ*—Nārada; *muniḥ*—very thoughtful; *bhagavati*—in the Supreme Personality of Godhead; *uttama-śloke*—possessing excellent renown; *āviṣṭa*—absorbed; *ātmā*—whose mind; *abravīt*—replied; *nṛpān*—to the Kings.

TRANSLATION

The great sage Maitreya continued: My dear Vidura, being thus petitioned by the Pracetās, the supreme devotee, Nārada, who is always absorbed in thoughts of the Supreme Personality of Godhead, began to reply.

PURPORT

In this verse *bhagavān nāradaḥ* indicates that Nārada is always absorbed in thoughts of the Supreme Personality of Godhead. *Bhagavaty uttama-śloka āviṣṭātmā.* Nārada has no other business than thinking of Kṛṣṇa, talking of Kṛṣṇa and preaching about Kṛṣṇa; therefore he is sometimes called *bhagavān. Bhagavān* means "one who possesses all opulences." When a person possesses Bhagavān within his heart, he is also sometimes called *bhagavān.* Śrīla Viśvanātha Cakravartī Ṭhākura said, *sākṣād-dharitvena samasta-śāstraiḥ:* in every *śāstra* the spiritual master is accepted directly as the Supreme Personality of Godhead. This does not mean that the spiritual master or a saintly person like Nārada has actually become the Supreme Personality of Godhead, but he is accepted in this way because he possesses the Supreme Personality of Godhead within his heart constantly. As described here (*āviṣṭātmā*), when one is simply absorbed in the thought of Kṛṣṇa, he is also called *bhagavān.* Bhagavān possesses all opulence. If one possesses Bhagavān within his heart always, does he not automatically possess all opulence also? In that sense a great devotee like Nārada can be called *bhagavān.* However, we cannot tolerate when a rascal or imposter is called *bhagavān.* One must possess either all opulences or the Supreme Personality of Godhead, Bhagavān, who possesses all opulences.

TEXT 9

नारद उवाच
तज्जन्म तानि कर्माणि तदायुस्तन्मनो वचः ।
नृणां येन हि विश्वात्मा सेव्यते हरिरीश्वरः ॥ ९ ॥

nārada uvāca
taj janma tāni karmāṇi
tad āyus tan mano vacaḥ
nṛṇāṁ yena hi viśvātmā
sevyate harir īśvaraḥ

nāradaḥ uvāca—Nārada said; *tat janma*—that birth; *tāni*—those; *karmāṇi*—fruitive activities; *tat*—that; *āyuḥ*—span of life; *tat*—that; *manaḥ*—mind; *vacaḥ*—words; *nṛṇām*—of human beings; *yena*—by which; *hi*—certainly; *viśva-ātmā*—the Supersoul; *sevyate*—is served; *hariḥ*—the Supreme Personality of Godhead; *īśvaraḥ*—the supreme controller.

TRANSLATION

The great sage Nārada said: When a living entity is born to engage in the devotional service of the Supreme Personality of Godhead, who is the supreme controller, his birth, all his fruitive activities, his lifespan, his mind and his words are all factually perfect.

PURPORT

In this verse the word *nṛṇām* is very important. There are many other births besides human birth, but Nārada Muni is herein especially speaking of human birth. Amongst human beings there are different types of men. Of these, those who are advanced in spiritual consciousness or Kṛṣṇa consciousness are called Āryans. Amongst Āryans, one who engages in the devotional service of the Lord is most successful in life. The word *nṛṇām* indicates that lower animals do not engage in the devotional service of the Lord. In perfect human society everyone should engage in the devotional service of the Lord. It does not matter whether one is born poor or rich, black or white. There may be so many material distinctions for one who takes birth in human society, but everyone should engage in the Lord's devotional service. At the present moment civilized nations have given up God consciousness for economic development. They are actually no longer interested in advancing in God consciousness. Formerly their forefathers were engaged in executing religious principles. Whether one is Hindu, Moslem, Buddhist, Jewish or whatever, everyone has some religious institution. Real religion, however, means becoming God conscious. It is particularly mentioned herein that birth is successful if an interest in Kṛṣṇa consciousness is taken. Activity is successful if it results in serving the Lord. Philosophical speculation or mental speculation is successful when engaged in understanding the Supreme Personality of Godhead. The senses are worth possessing when engaged in the service of the Lord. Actually, devotional service means engaging the senses in the service of the Lord. At the present moment our senses are not purified; therefore our senses are engaged in the service of society, friendship, love, politics, sociology, and so on. However, when the senses are engaged in the service of the Lord, one attains *bhakti,* or devotional service. In the next verse these matters will be more clearly explained.

When one great devotee of Lord Caitanya Mahāprabhu saw the Lord, he said that all his desires were fulfilled. He said, "Today everything is auspicious. Today my birthplace and neighborhood are completely glorified. Today my senses, from my eyes down to my toes, are fortunate. Today my life is successful because I have been able to see the lotus feet that are worshiped by the goddess of fortune."

TEXT 10

किं जन्मभिस्त्रिभिर्वेह शौक्रसावित्रयाज्ञिकैः ।
कर्मभिर्वा त्रयीप्रोक्तैः पुंसोऽपि विबुधायुषा ॥१०॥

kiṁ janmabhis tribhir veha
śaukra-sāvitra-yājñikaiḥ

karmabhir vā trayī-proktaiḥ
puṁso 'pi vibudhāyuṣā

kim—what is the use; *janmabhiḥ*—of births; *tribhiḥ*—three; *vā*—or; *iha*—in this world; *śaukra*—by semina; *sāvitra*—by initiation; *yājñikaiḥ*—by becoming a perfect *brāhmaṇa; karmabhiḥ*—by activities; *vā*—or; *trayī*—in the *Vedas; proktaiḥ*—instructed; *puṁsaḥ*—of a human being; *api*—even; *vibudha*—of the demigods; *āyuṣā*—with a duration of life.

TRANSLATION

A civilized human being has three kinds of births. The first birth is by a pure father and mother, and this birth is called birth by semina. The next birth takes place when one is initiated by the spiritual master, and this birth is called sāvitra. The third birth, called yājñika, takes place when one is given the opportunity to worship Lord Viṣṇu. Despite the opportunities for attaining such births, even if one gets the lifespan of a demigod, if one does not actually engage in the service of the Lord, everything is useless. Similarly, one's activities may be mundane or spiritual, but they are useless if they are not meant for satisfying the Lord.

PURPORT

The word *śaukra-janma* means taking birth by seminal discharge. Animals can take their birth in this way too. However, a human being can be reformed from the *śaukra-janma,* as recommended in the Vedic civilization. Before the birth takes place, or before father and mother unite, there is a ceremony called *garbhādhāna-saṁskāra,* which must be adopted. This *garbhādhāna-saṁskāra* is especially recommended for higher castes, especially the *brāhmaṇa* caste. It is said in the *śāstras* that if the *garbhādhāna-saṁskāra* is not practiced amongst the higher castes, the entire family becomes *śūdra.* It is also stated that in this age of Kali, everyone is *śūdra* due to the absence of the *garbhādhāna-saṁskāra.* This is the Vedic system. According to the *pāñcarātrika* system, however, even though everyone is a *śūdra* due to the absence of the *garbhādhāna-saṁskāra,* if a person has but a little tendency to become Kṛṣṇa conscious, he should be given the chance to elevate himself to the transcendental platform of devotional service. Our Kṛṣṇa consciousness movement adopts this *pāñcarātrika-vidhi,* as advised by Śrīla Sanātana Gosvāmī, who says:

yathā kāñcanatāṁ yāti
kāṁsyaṁ rasa-vidhānataḥ

tathā dīkṣā-vidhānena
dvijatvaṁ jāyate nṛṇām

"As bell-metal, when mixed with mercury, is transformed to gold, a person, even though not golden pure, can be transformed into a *brāhmaṇa* or *dvija* simply by the initiation process." Thus if one is initiated by a proper person, he can be accepted as twice-born immediately. In our Kṛṣṇa consciousness movement, we therefore offer the student his first initiation and allow him to chant the Hare Kṛṣṇa *mahā-mantra*. By chanting the Hare Kṛṣṇa *mahā-mantra* regularly and following the regulative principles, one becomes qualified to be initiated as a *brāhmaṇa* because unless one is a qualified *brāhmaṇa* he cannot be allowed to worship Lord Viṣṇu. This is called *yājñika-janma*. In our Kṛṣṇa consciousness society, unless one is twice initiated—first by chanting Hare Kṛṣṇa and second by the Gāyatrī *mantra*—he is not allowed to enter the kitchen or Deity room to execute duties. However, when one is elevated to the platform on which he can worship the Deity, his previous birth does not matter.

caṇḍālo 'pi dvija-śreṣṭho
hari-bhakti-parāyaṇaḥ
hari-bhakti-vihīnaś ca
dvijo 'pi śvapacādhamaḥ

"Even if one is born in the family of a *caṇḍāla*, if one engages in the devotional service of the Lord, he becomes the best of *brāhmaṇas*. But even a *brāhmaṇa* who is devoid of devotional service is on the level of the lowest dog-eater."

If a person is advanced in devotional service, it does not matter whether he was born in a *caṇḍāla* family. He becomes purified. As Śrī Prahlāda Mahārāja said:

viprād dviṣaḍ-guṇa-yutād aravinda-nābha-
pādāravinda-vimukhāc chvapacaṁ variṣṭham
(*Bhāg.* 7.9.10)

Even if one is a *brāhmaṇa* and is qualified with all the brahminical qualifications, he is considered degraded if he is averse to worshiping the Supreme Personality of Godhead. But if a person is attached to the service of the Lord, he becomes glorified even if he is born in a *caṇḍāla* family. Indeed, such a *caṇḍāla* can deliver not only himself but all his family predecessors. Without devotional service, even a proud *brāhmaṇa* cannot deliver himself, and what to speak of his family. In many instances in the *śāstras* it is seen that even a *brāhmaṇa* has become a *kṣatriya*, *vaiśya*, *śūdra*, *mleccha* or non-*brāhmaṇa*. And there are many instances of one's being born a *kṣatriya* or *vaiśya* or even lower, and, in the eighteenth year, attaining elevation to the brahminical platform by the process of initiation. Therefore Nārada Muni says:

yasya yal lakṣaṇaṁ proktaṁ
puṁso varṇābhivyañjakam
yad anyatrāpi dṛśyeta
tat tenaiva vinirdiśet (*Bhāg.* 7.11.35)

It is not a fact that because one is born in a *brāhmaṇa* family he is automatically a *brāhmaṇa.* He has a better chance to become a *brāhmaṇa,* but unless he meets all the brahminical qualifications, he cannot be accepted as such. On the other hand, if the brahminical qualifications are found in the person of a *śūdra,* he should immediately be accepted as a *brāhmaṇa.* To substantiate this there are many quotations from *Bhāgavatam, Mahābhārata, Bharadvāja-saṁhitā* and the *Pañcarātra,* as well as many other scriptures.

As far as the duration of life of the demigods, concerning Lord Brahmā it is said:

sahasra-yuga-paryantam
ahar yad brahmaṇo viduḥ
rātriṁ yuga-sahasrāntāṁ
te 'ho-rātra-vido janāḥ (Bg. 8.17)

The duration of one day of Brahmā is one thousand times greater than the four *yugas* aggregating to 4,300,000 years. Similarly, Brahmā's one night. Brahmā lives for one hundred years of such days and nights. The word *vibudhāyuṣā* indicates that even if one gets a long life span, his life span is useless if he is not a devotee. A living entity is the eternal servitor of the Supreme Lord, and unless he comes to the platform of devotional service, his life span, good birth, glorious activities and everything else are null and void.

TEXT 11

श्रुतेन तपसा वा किं वचोभिश्चित्तवृत्तिभिः ।
बुद्ध्या वा किं निपुणया बलेनेन्द्रियराधसा ॥११॥

śrutena tapasā vā kiṁ
vacobhiś citta-vṛttibhiḥ
buddhyā vā kiṁ nipuṇayā
balenendriya-rādhasā

śrutena—by Vedic education; *tapasā*—by austerities; *vā*—or; *kim*—what is the meaning; *vacobhiḥ*—by words; *citta*—of consciousness; *vṛttibhiḥ*—by the occupations; *buddhyā*—by intelligence; *vā*—or; *kim*—what is the use; *nipuṇayā*—expert; *balena*—by bodily strength; *indriya-rādhasā*—by power of the senses.

TRANSLATION

Without devotional service, what is the meaning of severe austerities, the process of hearing, the power of speech, the power of mental speculation, elevated intelligence, strength and the power of the senses?

PURPORT

From the Upaniṣads we learn:

nāyam ātmā pravacanena labhyo
na medhayā na bahunā śrutena
yam evaiṣa vṛṇute tena labhyas
tasyaiṣa ātmā vivṛṇute tanūṁ svām
(*Muṇḍaka Upaniṣad* 3.2.3)

Our relationship with the Supreme Lord is never advanced by simple study of the *Vedas*. There are many Māyāvādī *sannyāsīs* fully engaged in studying the *Vedas, Vedānta-sūtra* and *Upaniṣads*, but unfortunately they cannot grasp the real essence of knowledge. In other words, they do not know the Supreme Personality of Godhead. What, then, is the use in studying all the *Vedas*, if one cannot grasp the essence of the *Vedas*, Kṛṣṇa? The Lord confirms in *Bhagavad-gītā, vedaiś ca sarvair aham eva vedyaḥ:* "By all the *Vedas*, I am to be known." (Bg. 15.15)

There are many religious systems wherein penances and austerities are greatly stressed, but at the end no one understands Kṛṣṇa, the Supreme Personality of Godhead. There is therefore no point in such penance (*tapasya*). If one has actually approached the Supreme Personality of Godhead, he does not need to undergo severe austerities. The Supreme Personality of Godhead is understood through the process of devotional service. In the Ninth Chapter of *Bhagavad-gītā* devotional service is explained as *rāja-guhyam*, the king of all confidential knowledge. There are many good reciters of Vedic literatures, and they recite works such as the *Rāmāyaṇa, Śrīmad-Bhāgavatam* and *Bhagavad-gītā*. Sometimes these professional readers manifest very good scholarship and exhibit word jugglery. Unfortunately they are never devotees of the Supreme Lord. Consequently they cannot impress upon the audience the real essence of knowledge, Kṛṣṇa. There are also many thoughtful writers and creative philosophers, but despite all their learning, if they cannot approach the Supreme Personality of Godhead, they are simply useless mental speculators. There are many sharply intelligent people in this material world, and they discover so many things for sense gratification. They also analytically study all the material elements, but despite their expert knowledge and expert scientific analysis of the whole cosmic manifestation, their endeavors are useless because they cannot understand the Supreme Personality of Godhead.

As far as our senses are concerned, there are many animals, both beasts and birds, who are very expert in exercising their senses more keenly than human beings. For example, vultures or hawks can go very high in the sky but can see a small body on the ground very clearly. This means that their eyesight is so keen that they can find an eatable corpse from a great distance. Certainly their eyesight is much keener than human beings', but this does not mean that their existence is more important than that of a human being. Similarly, dogs can smell many things from a far distance. Many fish can understand by the power of sound that an enemy is coming. All these examples are described in *Śrīmad-Bhāgavatam.* If one's senses cannot help him attain the highest perfection of life, realization of the Supreme, they are all useless.

TEXT 12

किं वा योगेन सांख्येन न्यासस्वाध्याययोरपि ।
किं वा श्रेयोभिरन्यैश्च न यत्रात्मप्रदो हरिः ॥१२॥

kiṁ vā yogena sāṅkhyena
nyāsa-svādhyāyayor api
kiṁ vā śreyobhir anyaiś ca
na yatrātma-prado hariḥ

kim—what is the use; *vā*—or; *yogena*—by mystic *yoga* practice; *sāṅkhyena*—by study of Sāṅkhya philosophy; *nyāsa*—by accepting *sannyāsa; svādhyāyayoḥ*—and by study of Vedic literature; *api*—even; *kim*—what is the use; *vā*—or; *śreyobhiḥ*—by auspicious activities; *anyaiḥ*—other; *ca*—and; *na*—never; *yatra*—where; *ātma-pradaḥ*—full satisfaction of self; *hariḥ*—the Supreme Personality of Godhead.

TRANSLATION

Transcendental practices that do not ultimately help one realize the Supreme Personality of Godhead are useless, be they mystic yoga practices, the analytical study of matter, severe austerity, the acceptance of sannyāsa, or the study of Vedic literature. All these may be very important aspects of spiritual advancement, but unless one understands the Supreme Personality of Godhead, Hari, all these processes are useless.

PURPORT

In *Caitanya-caritāmṛta* it is said:

bhakti vinā kevala jñāne 'mukti' nāhi haya
bhakti sādhana kare yei 'prāpta-brahmalaya'
(*Cc. Madhya* 24.109)

Impersonalists do not take to devotional service but take to other practices, such as the analytical study of the material elements, the discrimination between matter and spirit, and the mystic *yoga* system. These are beneficial only insofar as they are complementary to devotional service. Caitanya Mahāprabhu therefore told Sanātana Gosvāmī that without a touch of devotional service, *jñāna, yoga* and *sāṅkhya* philosophy cannot give one the desired results. The impersonalists wish to merge into the Supreme Brahman; however, merging into the Supreme Brahman also requires a touch of devotional service. The Absolute Truth is realized in three phases—impersonal Brahman, Paramātmā and the Supreme Personality of Godhead. All these require a touch of devotional service. Sometimes it is actually seen that these Māyāvādīs also chant the Hare Kṛṣṇa *mahā-mantra*, although their motive is to merge into the Brahman effulgence of the Absolute. The *yogīs* also at times take to chanting the Hare Kṛṣṇa *mahā-mantra*, but their purpose is different from that of the *bhaktas*. In all processes—*karma, jñāna* or *yoga—bhakti* is required. That is the purport of this verse.

TEXT 13

श्रेयसामपि सर्वेषामात्मा ह्यवधिरर्थतः ।
सर्वेषामपि भूतानां हरिरात्माऽऽत्मदः प्रियः ॥१३॥

śreyasām api sarveṣām
ātmā hy avadhir arthataḥ

sarveṣām api bhūtānāṁ
harir ātmātmadaḥ priyaḥ

śreyasām—of auspicious activities; *api*—certainly; *sarveṣām*—all; *ātmā*—the self; *hi*—certainly; *avadhiḥ*—destination; *arthataḥ*—factually; *sarveṣām*—of all; *api*—certainly; *bhūtānām*—living entities; *hariḥ*—the Supreme Personality of Godhead; *ātmā*—the Supersoul; *ātma-daḥ*—who can give us our original identity; *priyaḥ*—very dear.

TRANSLATION

Factually the Supreme Personality of Godhead is the original source of all self-realization. Consequently the goal of all auspicious activities—karma, jñāna, yoga and bhakti—is the Supreme Personality of Godhead.

PURPORT

The living entity is the marginal energy of the Supreme Personality of Godhead, and the material world is the external energy. Under the circumstances, one must understand that the Supreme Personality of Godhead is factually the original source of both matter and spirit. This is explained in the Seventh Chapter of *Bhagavad-gītā:*

bhūmir āpo 'nalo vāyuḥ
khaṁ mano buddhir eva ca
ahaṅkāra itīyaṁ me
bhinnā prakṛtir aṣṭadhā

apareyam itas tv anyāṁ
prakṛtiṁ viddhi me parām
jīva-bhūtāṁ mahā-bāho
yayedaṁ dhāryate jagat

"Earth, water, fire, air, ether, mind, intelligence and false ego—all together these eight comprise My separated material energies. Besides this inferior nature, O mighty-armed Arjuna, there is a superior energy of Mine, which consists of all living entities who are struggling with material nature and are sustaining the universe." (Bg. 7.4-5)

The entire cosmic manifestation is but a combination of matter and spirit. The spiritual part is the living entity, and these living entities are described as *prakṛti,* or energy. The living entity is never described as *puruṣa,* the Supreme Person; therefore to identify the living entity with the Supreme Lord is simply ignorance. The living entity is the marginal potency of the Supreme Lord, although there is factually no difference between the energy and the energetic. The duty of the living entity is to understand his real identity. When he does, Kṛṣṇa gives him all the facilities to come to the platform of devotional service. That is the perfection of life. This is indicated in the Vedic *Upaniṣad:*

yam evaiṣa vṛṇute tena labhyas
tasyaiṣa ātmā vivṛṇute tanūṁ svām

Lord Kṛṣṇa confirms this in *Bhagavad-gītā:*

teṣāṁ satata-yuktānāṁ
bhajatāṁ prīti-pūrvakam
dadāmi buddhi-yogaṁ taṁ
yena mām upayānti te

"To those who are constantly devoted and worship Me with love, I give the understanding by which they can come to Me." (Bg. 10.10) The conclusion is that one must come to the platform of *bhakti-yoga,* even though one may begin with *karma-yoga, jñāna-yoga* or *aṣṭāṅga-yoga.* Unless one comes to the platform of *bhakti-yoga,* self-realization or realization of the Absolute Truth cannot be achieved.

TEXT 14

यथा तरोर्मूलनिषेचनेन
तृप्यन्ति तत्स्कन्धभुजोपशाखाः ।
प्राणोपहाराच्च यथेन्द्रियाणां
तथैव सर्वार्हणमच्युतेज्या ॥१४॥

yathā taror mūla-niṣecanena
tṛpyanti tat-skandha-bhujopaśākhāḥ
prāṇopahārāc ca yathendriyāṇāṁ
tathaiva sarvārhaṇam acyutejyā

yathā—as; *taroḥ*—of a tree; *mūla*—the root; *niṣecanena*—by watering; *tṛpyanti*—are satisfied; *tat*—its; *skandha*—trunk; *bhuja*—branches; *upaśākhāḥ*—and twigs; *prāṇa*—the life air; *upahārāt*—by feeding; *ca*—and; *yathā*—as; *indriyāṇām*—of the senses; *tathā eva*—similarly; *sarva*—of all demigods; *arhaṇam*—worship; *acyuta*—of the Supreme Personality of Godhead; *ijyā*—worship.

TRANSLATION

As pouring water on the root of a tree energizes the trunk, branches, twigs and everything else, and as supplying food to the stomach enlivens the senses and limbs of the body, so simply worshiping the Supreme Personality of Godhead through devotional service automatically satisfies the demigods, who are parts of that Supreme Personality.

PURPORT

Sometimes people ask why this Kṛṣṇa consciousness movement simply advocates worship of Kṛṣṇa to the exclusion of the demigods. The answer is given in this verse. The example of pouring water on the root of a tree is very appropriate. In *Bhagavad-gītā* it is said:

śrī bhagavān uvāca
ūrdhva-mūlam adhaḥ-śākham
aśvatthaṁ prāhur avyayam
chandāṁsi yasya parṇāni
yas taṁ veda sa veda-vit

"The blessed Lord said: There is a banyan tree that has its roots upward and its branches down and whose leaves are the Vedic hymns. One who knows this tree is the knower of the *Vedas.*" (Bg. 15.1)

This cosmic manifestation has expanded downward and the root is the Supreme Personality of Godhead. As the Lord confirms in *Bhagavad-gītā:*

ahaṁ sarvasya prabhavo
mattaḥ sarvaṁ pravartate
iti matvā bhajante māṁ
budhā bhāva-samanvitāḥ

"I am the source of all spiritual and material worlds. Everything emanates from Me. The wise who perfectly know this engage in My devotional service and worship Me with all their hearts." (Bg. 10.8)

Kṛṣṇa is the root of everything; therefore rendering service to the Supreme Personality of Godhead, Kṛṣṇa (*kṛṣṇa-sevā*), means automatically serving all the demigods. Sometimes it is argued that *karma* and *jñāna* require a mixture of *bhakti* in order to be successfully executed, and sometimes it is argued that *bhakti* also requires *karma* and *jñāna* for its successful termination. The fact is, however, that although *karma* and *jñāna* cannot be successful without *bhakti, bhakti* does not require the help of *karma* and *jñāna*. Actually, as described by Śrīla Rūpa Gosvāmī, *anyābhilāṣitā-śūnyaṁ jñāna-karmādy-anāvṛtam:* pure devotional service should not be contaminated by the touch of *karma* and *jñāna*. Modern society is involved in various types of philanthropic works, humanitarian works, and so on, but people do not know that these activities will never be successful unless Kṛṣṇa, the Supreme Personality of Godhead, is brought into the center. One may ask what harm there is in worshiping Kṛṣṇa and the different parts of His body, the demigods, and the answer is also given in this verse. The point is that by supplying food to the stomach, the *indriyas*, the senses, are automatically satisfied. If one tries to feed his eyes or ears independently, the result is only havoc. Simply by supplying food to the stomach, we satisfy all of the senses. It is neither necessary nor feasible to render separate service to the individual senses. The conclusion is that by serving Kṛṣṇa (*kṛṣṇa-sevā*), everything is complete. As confirmed in *Caitanya-caritāmṛta: kṛṣṇe bhakti kaile sarva-karma kṛta haya* (Cc. *Madhya* 22.62). If one is engaged in the devotional service of the Lord, the Supreme Personality of Godhead, everything is automatically accomplished.

TEXT 15

यथैव सूर्यात्प्रभवन्ति वारः
पुनश्च तस्मिन् प्रविशन्ति काले ।
भूतानि भूमौ स्थिरजङ्गमानि
तथा हरावेव गुणप्रवाहः ॥१५॥

yathaiva sūryāt prabhavanti vāraḥ
punaś ca tasmin praviśanti kāle
bhūtāni bhūmau sthira-jaṅgamāni
tathā harāv eva guṇa-pravāhaḥ

yathā—as; *eva*—certainly; *sūryāt*—from the sun; *prabhavanti*—is generated; *vāraḥ*—water; *punaḥ*—again; *ca*—and; *tasmin*—unto it; *praviśanti*—enters; *kāle*—in due course of time; *bhūtāni*—all living entities; *bhūmau*—to the earth; *sthira*—not moving; *jaṅgamāni*—and moving; *tathā*—similarly; *harau*—unto the Supreme Personality of Godhead; *eva*—certainly; *guṇa-pravāhaḥ*—emanation of material nature.

TRANSLATION

During the rainy season, water is generated from the sun, and in due course of time, during the summer season, the very same water is again absorbed by the sun. Similarly, all living entities, moving and inert, are generated from the earth, and again, after some time, they all return to the earth as dust. Similarly, everything emanates from the Supreme Personality of Godhead, and in due course of time everything enters into Him again.

PURPORT

Because of their poor fund of knowledge, impersonalist philosophers cannot understand how everything comes out from the Supreme Person and then merges into Him again. As *Brahma-saṁhitā* confirms:

yasya prabhā prabhavato jagad-aṇḍa-koṭi-
koṭiṣv aśeṣa-vasudhādi-vibhūti-bhinnam
tad brahma niṣkalam anantam aśeṣa-bhūtaṁ
govindam ādi-puruṣaṁ tam ahaṁ bhajāmi
(Bs. 5.40)

Transcendental rays emanate from the body of Kṛṣṇa, and within those rays, which are the Brahman effulgence, everything is existing. This is confirmed in *Bhagavad-gītā. Mat-sthāni sarva-bhūtāni* (Bg. 9.4).

Although Kṛṣṇa is not personally present everywhere, His energy is nonetheless the cause of all creation. The entire cosmic manifestation is nothing but a display of Kṛṣṇa's energy. The two examples given in this verse are very vivid. During the rainy season, the rain, by rejuvenating the production of vegetables on earth, enables man and animals to obtain living energy. When there is no rain, food is scarce, and man and animal simply die. All vegetables, as well as moving living entities, are originally products of the earth. They come from the earth, and again they merge into the earth. Similarly, the total material energy is generated from the body of Kṛṣṇa, and at such a time the entire cosmic manifestation is visible. When Kṛṣṇa winds up His energy, everything vanishes. This is explained in a different way in *Brahma-saṁhitā:*

yasyaika-niśvasita-kālam athāvalambya
jīvanti loma-vilajā jagad-aṇḍa-nāthāḥ
viṣṇur mahān sa iha yasya kalā-viśeṣo
govindam ādi-puruṣaṁ tam ahaṁ bhajāmi
(Bs. 5.48)

This entire material creation comes from the body of the Supreme Personality of Godhead and at the time of annihilation again enters into Him. This process of creation and dissolution is made possible by the breathing of the Mahā-Viṣṇu, who is only a plenary portion of Kṛṣṇa.

TEXT 16

एतत्पदं तज्जगदात्मनः परं
सकृद्विभातं सवितुर्यथा प्रभा ।
यथासवो जाग्रति सुप्तशक्तयो
द्रव्यक्रियाज्ञानभिदाभ्रमात्ययः ॥१६॥

etat padaṁ taj jagad-ātmanaḥ paraṁ
sakṛd vibhātaṁ savitur yathā prabhā
yathāsavo jāgrati supta-śaktayo
dravya-kriyā-jñāna-bhidā-bhramātyayaḥ

etat—this cosmic manifestation; *padam*—place of habitation; *tat*—that; *jagat-ātmanaḥ*—of the Supreme Personality of Godhead; *param*—transcendental; *sakṛt*—sometimes; *vibhātam*—manifested; *savituḥ*—of the sun; *yathā*—as; *prabhā*—sunshine; *yathā*—as; *asavaḥ*—the senses; *jāgrati*—become manifest; *supta*—inactive; *śaktayaḥ*—energies; *dravya*—physical elements; *kriyā*—activities; *jñāna*—knowledge; *bhidā-bhrama*—differences from misunderstanding; *atyayaḥ*—passing away.

TRANSLATION

Just as the sunshine is nondifferent from the sun, the cosmic manifestation is also nondifferent from the Supreme Personality of Godhead. The Supreme Personality is therefore all-pervasive within this material creation. When the senses are active, they appear to be part and parcel of the body, but when the body is asleep, their activities are unmanifest. Similarly, the whole cosmic creation appears different and yet nondifferent from the Supreme Person.

PURPORT

This confirms the philosophy of *acintya-bhedābheda-tattva* (simultaneously one and different) propounded by Lord Śrī Caitanya Mahāprabhu. The Supreme Personality of Godhead is simultaneously different and nondifferent from this cosmic manifestation. In the previous verse it has been explained that the Supreme Personality of Godhead, as the root of a tree, is the original cause of everything. It was also explained how the Supreme Personality of Godhead is all-pervasive. He is present within everything in this material manifestation. Since the energy of the Supreme Lord is nondifferent from Him, this material cosmic manifestation is also nondifferent from Him, although it appears different. The sunshine is not different from the sun itself, but it is simultaneously also different. One may be in the sunshine, but he is not on the sun itself. Those who live in this material world are living on the bodily rays of the Supreme Personality of Godhead, but they cannot see Him personally in the material condition.

In this verse the word *padam* indicates the place where the Supreme Personality of Godhead resides. As confirmed in *Īśopaniṣad, īśāvāsyam idaṁ sarvam.* The proprietor of a house may live in one room of the house. but the entire house belongs to him. A king may live in one room in Buckingham Palace, but the entire palace is considered his property. It is not necessary for the king to live in every room of that palace for it to be his. He may be physically absent from the rooms, but still the entire palace is understood to be his royal domicile.

The sunshine is light, the sun globe itself is light, and the sun-god is also light. However, the sunshine is not identical with the sun-god, Vivasvān. This is the meaning of simultaneously one and different (*acintya-bhedābheda-tattva*). All the planets rest on the sunshine, and because of the heat of the sun, they all revolve in their orbits. On each and every planet, the trees and plants grow and change colors due to the sunshine. Being the rays of the sun, the sunshine is nondifferent from the sun. Similarly, all the planets, resting on the sunshine, are nondifferent from the sun. The entire material world is completely dependent on the sun, being produced by the sun, and the cause, the sun, is inherent in the effects. Similarly, Kṛṣṇa is the cause of all causes, and the effects are permeated by the original cause. The entire cosmic manifestation should be understood as the expanded energy of the Supreme Lord.

When one sleeps, the senses are inactive, but this does not mean that the senses are absent. When one is awakened, the senses become active again. Similarly, this cosmic creation is sometimes manifest and sometimes unmanifest. As stated in *Bhagavad-gītā:*

bhūta-grāmaḥ sa evāyaṁ
bhūtvā bhūtvā pralīyate
rātry-āgame 'vaśaḥ pārtha
prabhavaty ahar-āgame

"Again and again the day comes, and this host of beings is active, and again the night falls, O Pārtha, and they are helplessly dissolved." (Bg. 8.19)

When the cosmic manifestation is dissolved, it is in a kind of sleeping condition, an inactive state. Whether the cosmic manifestation is active or inactive, the energy of the Supreme Lord is always existing. Thus the words "appearance" and "disappearance" apply only to the cosmic manifestation.

TEXT 17

यथा नभस्यभ्रतमःप्रकाशा
भवन्ति भूपा न भवन्त्यनुक्रमात् ।
एवं परे ब्रह्मणि शक्तयस्त्वमू
रजस्तमःसत्त्वमिति प्रवाहः ॥१७॥

yathā nabhasy abhra-tamaḥ-prakāśā
bhavanti bhūpā na bhavanty anukramāt
evaṁ pare brahmaṇi śaktayas tv amū
rajas tamaḥ sattvam iti pravāhaḥ

yathā—as; *nabhasi*—in the sky; *abhra*—clouds; *tamaḥ*—darkness; *prakāśāḥ*—and illumination; *bhavanti*—exist; *bhū-pāḥ*—O Kings; *na bhavanti*—do not appear; *anukramāt*—consecutively; *evam*—thus; *pare*—supreme; *brahmaṇi*—in the Absolute; *śaktayaḥ*—energies; *tu*—then; *amūḥ*—those; *rajaḥ*—passion; *tamaḥ*—darkness; *sattvam*—goodness; *iti*—thus; *pravāhaḥ*—emanation.

TRANSLATION

My dear Kings, sometimes in the sky there are clouds, sometimes there is darkness, and sometimes there is illumination. The appearance of all these take place consecutively. Similarly, in the Supreme Absolute, the modes of passion, darkness and goodness appear as consecutive energies. Sometimes they appear, and sometimes they disappear.

PURPORT

Darkness, illumination and clouds sometimes appear and sometimes disappear, but even when they have disappeared, the potency is still there, always existing. In the sky sometimes we see clouds, sometimes rainfall and sometimes snow. Sometimes we see night, sometimes day, sometimes illumination and sometimes darkness. All these exist due to the sun, but the sun is unaffected by all these changes. Similarly, although the Supreme Personality of Godhead is the original cause of the total cosmic manifestation, He is unaffected by the material existence. This is confirmed in *Bhagavad-gītā:*

bhūmir āpo 'nalo vāyuḥ
khaṁ mano buddhir eva ca
ahaṅkāra itīyaṁ me
bhinnā prakṛtir aṣṭadhā

"Earth, water, fire, air, ether, mind, intelligence and false ego—all together these eight comprise My separated material energies." (Bg. 7.4)

Although the material or physical elements are the energy of the Supreme Personality of Godhead, they are separate. The Supreme Personality of Godhead is therefore not affected by material conditions. The *Vedānta-sūtra* confirms (*janmādy asya yataḥ*) that the creation, maintenance and dissolution of this cosmic manifestation are due to the existence of the Supreme Lord. Nonetheless the Lord is unaffected by all these changes in the material elements. This is indicated by the word *pravāha* (emanation). The sun always shines brilliantly and is not affected by clouds or darkness. Similarly, the Supreme Personality of Godhead is always present in His spiritual energy and is not affected by the material emanations. *Brahma-saṁhitā* confirms:

īśvaraḥ paramaḥ kṛṣṇaḥ
sac-cid-ānanda-vigrahaḥ
anādir ādir govindaḥ
sarva-kāraṇa-kāraṇam

"Kṛṣṇa, who is known as Govinda, is the Supreme Godhead. He has an eternal, blissful, spiritual body. He is the origin of all. He has no other origin, and He is the prime cause of all causes." (Bs. 5.1)

Although He is the supreme cause, the cause of all causes, He is still *parama,* transcendental, and His form is *sac-cid-ānanda,* eternal, spiritual bliss. Kṛṣṇa is the shelter of everything, and this is the verdict of all scripture. Kṛṣṇa is the remote cause, and material nature is the immediate cause of the cosmic manifestation. In the *Caitanya-caritāmṛta* it is said that understanding *prakṛti,* or nature, to be the cause of everything is like understanding the nipples on the neck of a goat to be the cause of milk. Material nature is the immediate cause of the cosmic manifestation, but the original cause is Nārāyaṇa, Kṛṣṇa. Sometimes people think that the cause of an earthen pot is the earth. We see on a potter's wheel a sufficient amount of earth to produce many pots, and although unintelligent men will say that the earth on the wheel is the cause of the pot, those who are actually advanced will find that the original cause is the potter, who supplies the earth and moves the wheel. Material nature may be a helping factor in the creation of this cosmic manifestation, but it is not the ultimate cause. In *Bhagavad-gītā* the Lord therefore says:

mayādhyakṣeṇa prakṛtiḥ
sūyate sa-carācaram

"This material nature is working under My direction, O son of Kuntī, and producing all moving and unmoving beings." (Bg. 9.10)

The Supreme Lord casts His glance over material energy, and His glance agitates the three modes of nature. Creation then takes place. The conclusion is that nature is not the cause of the material manifestation. The Supreme Lord is the cause of all causes.

TEXT 18

तेनैकमात्मानमशेषदेहिनां
कालं प्रधानं पुरुषं परेशम् ।
स्वतेजसा ध्वस्तगुणप्रवाह-
मात्मैकभावेन भजध्वमद्धा ॥१८॥

tenaikam ātmānam aśeṣa-dehināṁ
kālaṁ pradhānaṁ puruṣaṁ pareśam
sva-tejasā dhvasta-guṇa-pravāham
ātmaika-bhāvena bhajadhvam addhā

tena—therefore; *ekam*—one; *ātmānam*—unto the Supreme Soul; *aśeṣa*—unlimited; *dehinām*—of the individual souls; *kālam*—time; *pradhānam*—the material cause; *puruṣam*—the Supreme Person; *pareśam*—the transcendental controller; *sva-tejasā*—by His spiritual energy; *dhvasta*—aloof; *guṇa-pravāham*—from material emanations; *ātma*—self; *eka-bhāvena*—accepting as qualitatively one; *bhajadhvam*—engage in devotional service; *addhā*—directly.

TRANSLATION

Because the Supreme Lord is the cause of all causes, He is the Supersoul of all individual living entities, and He exists as both the remote and immediate cause. Since He is aloof from the material emanations, He is free from their interactions and is Lord of material nature. You should therefore engage in His devotional service, thinking yourself qualitatively one with Him.

PURPORT

According to Vedic calculations, there are three causes of creation—time, the ingredient and the creator. Combined, these are called *tritayātmaka,* the three causes. Everything in this material world is created by these three causes. All of these causes are found in the Personality of Godhead. As confirmed in *Brahma-saṁhitā: sarva-kāraṇa-kāraṇam.* Nārada Muni therefore advises the Pracetās to worship the direct cause, the Supreme Personality of Godhead. As stated before, when the root of a tree is watered, all the parts are energized. According to the advice of Nārada Muni, one should directly engage in devotional service. This will include all pious activity. *Caitanya-caritāmṛta* states: *kṛṣṇe bhakti kaile sarva-karma kṛta haya.* When one worships the Supreme Lord Kṛṣṇa in devotional service, he automatically performs all other pious activity. In this verse the words *sva-tejasā dhvasta-guṇa-pravāham* are very significant. The Supreme Personality of Godhead is never affected by the material qualities, although they all emanate from His spiritual energy. Those who are really conversant with this knowledge can utilize everything for the service of the Lord because nothing in this material world is unconnected to the Supreme Personality of Godhead.

TEXT 19

दयया सर्वभूतेषु सन्तुष्टया येन केन वा ।
सर्वेन्द्रियोपशान्त्या च तुष्यत्याशु जनार्दनः ॥१९॥

dayayā sarva-bhūteṣu
santuṣṭyā yena kena vā
sarvendriyopaśāntyā ca
tuṣyaty āśu janārdanaḥ

dayayā—by showing mercy; *sarva-bhūteṣu*—to all living entities; *santuṣṭyā*—by being satisfied; *yena kena vā*—somehow or other; *sarva-indriya*—all the senses; *upaśāntyā*—by controlling; *ca*—also; *tuṣyati*—becomes satisfied; *āśu*—very soon; *janārdanaḥ*—the Lord of all living entities.

TRANSLATION

By showing mercy to all living entities, being satisfied somehow or other, and controlling the senses from sense enjoyment, one can very quickly satisfy the Supreme Personality of Godhead, Janārdana.

PURPORT

These are some of the ways in which the Supreme Personality of Godhead can be satisfied by the devotee. The first item mentioned is *dayayā sarva-bhūteṣu,* showing mercy to all conditioned souls. The best way to show mercy is to spread Kṛṣṇa consciousness. The entire world is suffering for want of this knowledge. People should know that the Supreme Personality of Godhead is the original cause of everything. Knowing this, everyone should directly engage in His devotional service. Those who are actually learned, advanced in spiritual understanding, should preach Kṛṣṇa consciousness all over the world so that people may take to it and make their lives successful.

The word *sarva-bhūteṣu* is significant because it applies not only to human beings but to all the living entities appearing in the 8,400,000 species of life. The devotee can do good not only to humanity but to all living entities as well. Everyone can benefit spiritually by the chanting of the Hare Kṛṣṇa *mahā-mantra.* When the transcendental vibration of Hare Kṛṣṇa is sounded, even the trees, animals and insects benefit. Thus when one chants the Hare Kṛṣṇa *mahā-mantra* loudly, he actually shows mercy to all living entities. To spread the Kṛṣṇa consciousness movement throughout the world, the devotees should be satisfied in all conditions.

nārāyaṇa-parāḥ sarve
na kutaścana bibhyati
svargāpavarga-narakeṣv
api tulyārtha-darśinaḥ
(*Bhāg.* 6.17.28)

It does not matter to the pure devotee if he has to go to hell to preach. The Supreme Lord lives in the heart of a hog, although the Lord is in Vaikuṇṭha. Even while preaching in hell, a pure devotee remains a pure devotee by his constant association with the Supreme Personality of Godhead. To attain this state, one has to control his senses. The senses are automatically controlled when one's mind is engaged in the service of the Lord.

TEXT 20

अपहतसकलैषणामलात्म-
न्यविरतमेधितभावनोपहूतः ।
निजजनवशगत्वमात्मनोऽय-
न्न सरति छिद्रवदक्षरः सतां हि ॥२०॥

apahata-sakalaiṣaṇāmalātmany
aviratam edhita-bhāvanopahūtaḥ
nija-jana-vaśa-gatvam ātmano 'yan
na sarati chidravad akṣaraḥ satāṁ hi

apahata—vanquished; *sakala*—all; *eṣaṇa*—desires; *amala*—spotless; *ātmani*—to the mind; *aviratam*—constantly; *edhita*—increasing; *bhāvanā*—with feeling; *upahūtaḥ*—being called; *nija-jana*—of His devotees; *vaśa*—under the control; *gatvam*—going; *ātmanaḥ*—His; *ayan*—knowing; *na*—never; *sarati*—goes away; *chidra-vat*—like the sky; *akṣaraḥ*—the Supreme Personality of Godhead; *satām*—of the devotees; *hi*—certainly.

TRANSLATION

Being completely cleansed of all material desires, the devotees are freed from all mental contamination. Thus they can always think of the Lord constantly and address Him very feelingly. The Supreme Personality of Godhead, knowing Himself to be controlled by His devotees, does not leave them for a second, just as the sky overhead never becomes invisible.

PURPORT

It is clear from the previous verse that the Supreme Personality of Godhead, Janārdana, is very quickly satisfied by the activities of His devotees. The pure devotee is always absorbed in the thought of the Supreme Personality of Godhead. As stated, *śṛṇvatāṁ sva-kathāḥ kṛṣṇaḥ.* By always thinking of Kṛṣṇa, the pure devotee's heart is freed from all kinds of desires. In the material world, the heart of the living entity is filled with material desires. When the living entity is cleansed, he does not think of anything material. As the mind is completely cleansed, one attains the perfectional stage of mystic *yoga,* for then the *yogī* always sees the Supreme Personality of Godhead within his heart. As soon as the Lord is seated within the heart of the devotee, the devotee cannot be contaminated by the material modes of nature. As long as one is under the control of the material modes, he desires so many things and makes so many plans for material sense enjoyment. As soon as the Lord is perceived in the heart, all material desires vanish. When the mind is completely free from material desire, the devotee can think of the Lord constantly. In this way he becomes completely dependent upon the lotus feet of the Lord. Caitanya Mahāprabhu prays:

ayi nanda-tanuja kiṅkaraṁ
patitaṁ māṁ viṣame bhavāmbudhau
kṛpayā tava pāda-paṅkaja-
sthita-dhūlī-sadṛśaṁ vicintaya

"My dear Lord, I am Your eternal servant, but somehow or other I have fallen into the ocean of this material world. Kindly pick me up and fix me as a speck of dust at Your lotus feet." Similarly, Śrīla Narottama dāsa Ṭhākura prays:

hā hā prabhu nanda-suta, vṛṣabhānu-sutā-yuta,
karuṇā karaha ei-bāra
narottama-dāsa kaya, nā ṭheliha rāṅgā-pāya,
tomā vine ke āche āmāra

"My dear Lord, You are now present with the daughter of King Vṛṣabhānu, Śrīmatī Rādhārāṇī. Now both of You please be merciful upon me. Don't kick me away, because I have no shelter other than You."

In this way the Supreme Personality of Godhead becomes dependent on His devotee. The Lord is invincible, yet He is conquered by His pure devotee. He enjoys being dependent on His devotee, just as Kṛṣṇa enjoyed being dependent on the mercy of mother Yaśodā. Thinking Himself dependent on the devotee gives the Supreme Lord great enjoyment. Sometimes a king may engage a joker, and in the process of joking, the king is sometimes insulted. The king, however, enjoys these activities. Everyone worships the Supreme Lord with great reverence; therefore the Lord sometimes wants to enjoy the chastisement of His devotees. In this way the relationship eternally existing between the Lord and His devotees is fixed, just like the sky overhead.

TEXT 21

न भजति कुमनीषिणां स इज्यां
हरिरधनात्मधनप्रियो रसज्ञः ।

श्रुतधनकुलकर्मणां मदैर्ये
विदधति पापमकिञ्चनेषु सत्सु ॥२१॥

na bhajati kumanīṣiṇāṁ sa ijyāṁ
harir adhanātma-dhana-priyo rasa-jñaḥ
śruta-dhana-kula-karmaṇāṁ madair ye
vidadhati pāpam akiñcaneṣu satsu

na—never; *bhajati*—accepts; *ku-manīṣiṇām*—of persons with a dirty heart; *saḥ*—He; *ijyām*—offering; *hariḥ*—the Supreme Lord; *adhana*—to those who have no material possessions; *ātma-dhana*—simply dependent on the Lord; *priyaḥ*—who is dear; *rasa-jñaḥ*—who accepts the essence of life; *śruta*—education; *dhana*—wealth; *kula*—aristocracy; *karmaṇām*—and of fruitive activities; *madaiḥ*—by pride; *ye*—all those who; *vidadhati*—perform; *pāpam*—disgrace; *akiñcaneṣu*—without material possessions; *satsu*—unto the devotees.

TRANSLATION

The Supreme Personality of Godhead becomes very dear to those devotees who have no material possessions but are fully happy in possessing the devotional service of the Lord. Indeed, the Lord relishes the devotional activities of such devotees. Those who are puffed up with material education, wealth, aristocracy and fruitive activity are very proud of possessing material things, and they often deride the devotees. Even if such people offer the Lord worship, the Lord never accepts them.

PURPORT

The Supreme Personality of Godhead is dependent on His pure devotees. He does not even accept the offerings of those who are not devotees. A pure devotee is one who feels He does not possess anything material. A devotee is always happy in possessing the devotional service of the Lord. Devotees may sometimes appear materially poor, but because they are spiritually advanced and enriched, they are most dear to the Supreme Personality of Godhead. Such devotees are free from attachment to family, society, friendship, children and so on. They abandon affection for all these material possessions and are always happy in possessing the shelter of the lotus feet of the Lord. The Supreme Personality of Godhead understands the position of His devotee. If a person derides a pure devotee, he is never recognized by the Supreme Personality of Godhead. In other words, the Supreme Lord never excuses one who offends a pure devotee.

There are many examples of this in history. A great mystic *yogī*, Durvāsā Muni, offended the great devotee Ambarīṣa Mahārāja. The great sage Durvāsā was to be chastised by the Sudarśana *cakra* of the Lord. Even though the great mystic directly approached the Supreme Personality of Godhead, he was never excused. Those on the path of liberation should be very careful not to offend a pure devotee.

TEXT 22

श्रियमनुचरतीं तदर्थिनश्च
द्विपदपतीन् विबुधांश्च यत्स्वपूर्णः ।
न भजति निजभृत्यवर्गतन्त्रः
कथममुमुद्विसृजेत्पुमान् कृतज्ञः ॥२२॥

śriyam anucaratīṁ tad-arthinaś ca
dvipada-patīn vibudhāṁś ca yat sva-pūrṇaḥ
na bhajati nija-bhṛtya-varga-tantraḥ
katham amum udvisṛjet pumān kṛta-jñaḥ

śriyam—the goddess of fortune; *anucaratīm*—who follows Him; *tat*—of her; *arthinaḥ*—those who aspire to get the favor; *ca*—and; *dvi-pada-patīn*—rulers of the human beings; *vibudhān*—demigods; *ca*—also; *yat*—because; *sva-pūrṇaḥ*—self-sufficient; *na*—never; *bhajati*—cares for; *nija*—own; *bhṛtya-varga*—on His devotees; *tantraḥ*—dependent; *katham*—how; *amum*—Him; *udvisṛjet*—can give up; *pumān*—a person; *kṛta-jñaḥ*—grateful.

TRANSLATION

Although the Supreme Personality of Godhead is self-sufficient, He becomes dependent on His devotees. He does not care for the goddess of fortune, nor for the kings and demigods who are after the favors of the goddess of fortune. Where is that person who is actually grateful and will not worship the Personality of Godhead?

PURPORT

Lakṣmī, the goddess of fortune, is worshiped by all materialistic men, including big kings and demigods in heaven. Lakṣmī, however, is always after the Supreme Personality of Godhead, even though He does not require her service. *Brahma-saṁhitā* says that the Lord is worshiped by hundreds and thousands of goddesses of fortune, but the Supreme Lord does not require service from any of them because if He so desires He can produce millions of goddesses of fortune through His spiritual energy, the pleasure potency. This very Personality of Godhead, out of His causeless mercy, becomes dependent on the devotees. How fortunate, then, is a devotee who is thus favored by the Personality of Godhead. What ungrateful devotee will not worship the Lord and enter into His devotional service? Actually a devotee cannot forget his obligation to the Supreme Personality of Godhead even for a single moment. Śrīla Viśvanātha Cakravartī Ṭhākura says that both the Supreme Lord and His devotee are *rasa-jña,* full of transcendental humor. The mutual attachment between the Supreme Lord and His devotee is never to be considered material. It always exists as a transcendental fact. There are eight types of transcendental ecstasy (known as *bhāva, anubhāva, sthayībhāva* and so on), and these are discussed in *The Nectar of Devotion.* Those who are unaware of the position of the living entity and the Supreme Person, Kṛṣṇa, think that the mutual attachment between the Lord and His devotees is a creation of the material energy. Factually such attachment is natural both for the Supreme Lord and for the devotee, and it cannot be accepted as material.

TEXT 23

मैत्रेय उवाच

इति प्रचेतसो राजन्नन्याश्च भगवत्कथाः ।
श्रावयित्वा ब्रह्मलोकं ययौ स्वायम्भुवो मुनिः ॥२३॥

maitreya uvāca
iti pracetaso rājann
anyāś ca bhagavat-kathāḥ
śrāvayitvā brahma-lokaṁ
yayau svāyambhuvo muniḥ

maitreyaḥ uvāca—Maitreya said; *iti*—thus; *pracetasaḥ*—the Pracetās; *rājan*—O King; *anyāḥ*—others; *ca*—also; *bhagavat-kathāḥ*—topics about the relationship with the Supreme Personality of Godhead; *śrāvayitvā*—after instructing; *brahma-lokam*—to Brahmaloka; *yayau*—went back; *svāyambhuvaḥ*—the son of Lord Brahmā; *muniḥ*—the great sage.

TRANSLATION

The great sage Maitreya continued: My dear King Vidura, Śrī Nārada Muni, the son of Lord Brahmā, thus described all these relationships with the Supreme Personality of Godhead to the Pracetās. Afterwards, he returned to Brahmaloka.

PURPORT

One has to hear about the Supreme Personality of Godhead from a pure devotee. The Pracetās got this opportunity from the great sage Nārada, who told them of the activities of the Supreme Personality of Godhead and His devotees.

TEXT 24

तेऽपि तन्मुखनिर्यातं यशो लोकमलापहम् ।
हरेर्निशम्य तत्पादं ध्यायन्तस्तद्गतिं ययुः ॥२४॥

te 'pi tan-mukha-niryātaṁ
yaśo loka-malāpaham
harer niśamya tat-pādaṁ
dhyāyantas tad-gatiṁ yayuḥ

te—the Pracetās; *api*—also; *tat*—of Nārada; *mukha*—from the mouth; *niryātam*—gone forth; *yaśaḥ*—glorification; *loka*—of the world; *mala*—sins; *apaham*—destroying; *hareḥ*—of Lord Hari; *niśamya*—having heard; *tat*—of the Lord; *pādam*—feet; *dhyāyantaḥ*—meditating upon; *tat-gatim*—unto His abode; *yayuḥ*—went.

TRANSLATION

Hearing from Nārada's mouth the glories of the Lord, which vanquish all the ill fortune of the world, they also became attached to the Supreme Personality of Godhead. Meditating on His lotus feet, they advanced to the ultimate destination.

PURPORT

Here it is seen that by hearing the glories of the Lord from a realized devotee the Pracetās easily attained strong attachment for the Supreme Personality of Godhead. Then, meditating on the lotus feet of the Supreme Lord at the end of their lives, they advanced to the ultimate goal, Viṣṇuloka. It is sure and certain that anyone who always hears the glories of the

Lord and thinks of His lotus feet will reach that supreme destination. As Kṛṣṇa says in *Bhagavad-gītā:*

man-manā bhava mad-bhakto
mad-yājī māṁ namas-kuru
mām evaiṣyasi satyaṁ te
pratijāne priyo 'si me

"Always think of Me and become My devotee. Worship Me and offer your homage unto Me. Thus you will come to me without fail. I promise you this because you are My very dear friend." (Bg. 18.65)

TEXT 25

एतत्तेऽभिहितं क्षत्तर्यन्मां त्वं परिपृष्टवान् ।
प्रचेतसां नारदस्य संवादं हरिकीर्तनम् ॥२५॥

etat te 'bhihitaṁ kṣattar
yan māṁ tvaṁ paripṛṣṭavān
pracetasāṁ nāradasya
saṁvādaṁ hari-kīrtanam

etat—this; *te*—unto you; *abhihitam*—instructed; *kṣattaḥ*—O Vidura; *yat*—whatever; *mām*—unto me; *tvam*—you; *paripṛṣṭavān*—inquired; *pracetasām*—of the Pracetās; *nāradasya*—of Nārada; *saṁvādam*—conversation; *hari-kīrtanam*—describing the glories of the Lord.

TRANSLATION

My dear Vidura, I have told you everything you wanted to know about the conversation between Nārada and the Pracetās, the conversation describing the glories of the Lord. I have related this as far as possible.

PURPORT

Śrīmad-Bhāgavatam describes the glories of the Lord and His devotees. Because the whole subject matter is the glorification of the Lord, naturally the glorification of His devotees automatically follows.

TEXT 26

श्रीशुक उवाच
य एष उत्तानपदो मानवस्यानुवर्णितः ।
वंशः प्रियव्रतस्यापि निबोध नृपसत्तम ॥२६॥

śrī śuka uvāca
ya eṣa uttānapado
mānavasyānuvarṇitaḥ
vaṁśaḥ priya-vratasyāpi
nibodha nṛpa-sattama

śrī śukaḥ uvāca—Śrī Śukadeva Gosvāmī; said; *yaḥ*—which; *eṣaḥ*—this dynasty; *uttānapadaḥ*—of King Uttānapāda; *mānavasya*—the son of Svāyambhuva Manu; *anuvarṇitaḥ*—described following the footprints of previous *ācāryas; vaṁśaḥ*—dynasty; *priya-vratasya*—of King Priyavrata; *api*—also; *nibodha*—try to understand; *nṛpa-sattama*—O best of kings.

TRANSLATION

Śukadeva Gosvāmī continued: O best of kings [King Parīkṣit], I have now finished telling about the descendants of the first son of Svāyambhuva Manu, Uttānapāda. I shall now try to relate the activities of the descendants of Priyavrata, the second son of Svāyambhuva Manu. Please hear them attentively.

PURPORT

Dhruva Mahārāja was the son of King Uttānapāda, and as far as the descendants of Dhruva Mahārāja or King Uttānapāda are concerned, their activities are described up to the point of the Pracetās. Now Śrī Śukadeva Gosvāmī desires to describe the descendants of Mahārāja Priyavrata, the second son of Svāyambhuva Manu.

TEXT 27

यो नारदादात्मविद्यामधिगम्य पुनर्महीम् ।
भुक्त्वा विभज्य पुत्रेभ्य ऐश्वरं समगात्पदम् ॥२७॥

yo nāradād ātma-vidyām
adhigamya punar mahīm

bhuktvā vibhajya putrebhya
aiśvaraṁ samagāt padam

yaḥ—one who; *nāradāt*—from the great sage Nārada; *ātma-vidyām*—spiritual knowledge; *adhigamya*—after learning; *punaḥ*—again; *mahīm*—the earth; *bhuktvā*—after enjoying; *vibhajya*—after dividing; *putrebhyaḥ*—unto his sons; *aiśvaram*—transcendental; *samagāt*—achieved; *padam*—position.

TRANSLATION

Although Mahārāja Priyavrata received instructions from the great sage Nārada, he still engaged in ruling the earth. After fully enjoying material possessions, he divided his property amongst his sons. He then attained a position by which he could return home, back to Godhead.

TEXT 28

इमां तु कौषारविणोपवर्णितां
क्षत्ता निशम्याजितवादसत्कथाम् ।
प्रवृद्धभावोऽश्रुकलाकुलो मुने-
र्दधार मूर्ध्ना चरणं हृदा हरेः ॥२८॥

imāṁ tu kauṣāraviṇopavarṇitāṁ
kṣattā niśamyājita-vāda-sat-kathām
pravṛddha-bhāvo 'śru-kalākulo muner
dadhāra mūrdhnā caraṇaṁ hṛdā hareḥ

imām—all this; *tu*—then; *kauṣāraviṇā*—by Maitreya; *upavarṇitām*—described; *kṣattā*—Vidura; *niśamya*—after hearing; *ajita-vāda*—glorification of the Supreme Lord; *sat-kathām*—transcendental message; *pravṛddha*—enhanced; *bhāvaḥ*—ecstasies; *aśru*—of tears; *kalā*—by particles; *ākulaḥ*—overwhelmed; *muneḥ*—of the great sage; *dadhāra*—captured; *mūrdhnā*—by the head; *caraṇam*—the lotus feet; *hṛdā*—by the heart; *hareḥ*—of the Supreme Personality of Godhead.

TRANSLATION

My dear King, in this way, after hearing the transcendental messages of the Supreme Personality of Godhead and His devotees from the great sage Maitreya, Vidura was overwhelmed with ecstasy. With tears in his eyes,

he immediately fell down at the lotus feet of his guru, his spiritual master. He then fixed the Supreme Personality of Godhead within the core of his heart.

PURPORT

This is a sign of associating with great devotees. A devotee takes instructions from a liberated soul and is thus overwhelmed by ecstasy from transcendental pleasure. As stated by Prahlāda Mahārāja:

naiṣāṁ matis tāvad urukramāṅghriṁ
spṛśaty anarthāpagamo yad-arthaḥ
mahīyasāṁ pāda-rajo 'bhiṣekaṁ
niṣkiñcanānāṁ na vṛṇīta yāvat (*Bhāg.* 7.5.32)

One cannot become a perfect devotee of the Lord without having touched the lotus feet of a great devotee. One who has nothing to do with this material world is called *niṣkiñcana.* The process of self-realization and the path home, back to Godhead, means surrendering to the bona fide spiritual master and taking the dust of his lotus feet on one's head. Thus one advances on the path of transcendental realization. Vidura had this relationship with Maitreya, and he attained the results.

TEXT 29

विदुर उवाच
सोऽयमद्य महायोगिन् भवता करुणात्मना ।
दर्शितस्तमसः पारो यत्राकिञ्चनगो हरिः ॥२९॥

vidura uvāca
so 'yam adya mahā-yogin
bhavatā karuṇātmanā
darśitas tamasaḥ pāro
yatrākiñcanago hariḥ

viduraḥ uvāca—Vidura said; *saḥ*—that; *ayam*—this; *adya*—today; *mahā-yogin*—O great mystic; *bhavatā*—by you; *karuṇa-ātmanā*—most merciful; *darśitaḥ*—I have been shown; *tamasaḥ*—of the darkness; *pāraḥ*—the other side; *yatra*—where; *akiñcana-gaḥ*—approachable by the materially free; *hariḥ*—the Supreme Personality of Godhead.

TRANSLATION

Śrī Vidura said: O great mystic, O greatest of all devotees, by your causeless mercy I have been shown the path of liberation from this world of darkness. By following this path, a person liberated from the material world can return home, back to Godhead.

PURPORT

This material world is called *tamaḥ,* dark, and the spiritual world is called light. The *Vedas* enjoin that everyone should try to get out of the darkness and go to the kingdom of light. Information of that kingdom of light can be attained through the mercy of a self-realized soul. One also has to get rid of all material desires. As soon as one frees himself from material desires and associates with a liberated person, the path back home, back to Godhead, is clear.

TEXT 30

श्रीशुक उवाच

इत्यानम्य तमामन्त्र्य विदुरो गजसाह्वयम् ।
स्वानां दिदृक्षुः प्रययौ ज्ञातीनां निर्वृताशयः ॥३०॥

śrī śuka uvāca
ity ānamya tam āmantrya
viduro gaja-sāhvayam
svānāṁ didṛkṣuḥ prayayau
jñātīnāṁ nirvṛtāśayaḥ

śrī śukaḥ uvāca—Śrī Śukadeva Gosvāmī said; *iti*—thus; *ānamya*—offering obeisances; *tam*—unto Maitreya; *āmantrya*—taking permission; *viduraḥ*—Vidura; *gaja-sāhvayam*—the city of Hastināpura; *svānām*—own; *didṛkṣuḥ*—desiring to see; *prayayau*—left that place; *jñātīnām*—of his kinsmen; *nirvṛta-āśayaḥ*—free from material desires.

TRANSLATION

Śukadeva Gosvāmī continued: Vidura thus offered obeisances unto the great sage Maitreya, and, taking his permission, started for the city of Hastināpura to see his own kinsmen, although he had no material desires.

PURPORT

When a saintly person wants to see his kinsmen, he has no material desire to see them. He simply wants to give them some instructions so that they can benefit. Vidura belonged to the royal family of the Kauravas, and although he knew that all the family members were destroyed at the Battle of Kurukṣetra, he nonetheless wanted to see his elder brother, Dhṛtarāṣṭra, to see if he could deliver him from the clutches of *māyā*. When a great saintly person like Vidura sees his relatives, he desires only to deliver them from the clutches of *māyā*. Vidura thus offered his respectful obeisances to his spiritual master and departed for the city of Hastināpura, the kingdom of the Kauravas.

TEXT 31

एतद्यः शृणुयाद्राजन् राज्ञां हर्यर्पितात्मनाम् ।
आयुर्धनं यशः स्वस्ति गतिमैश्वर्यमाप्नुयात् ॥३१॥

etad yaḥ śṛṇuyād rājan
rājñāṁ hary-arpitātmanām
āyur dhanaṁ yaśaḥ svasti
gatim aiśvaryam āpnuyāt

etat—this; *yaḥ*—one who; *śṛṇuyāt*—hears; *rājan*—O King Parīkṣit; *rājñām*—of kings; *hari*—unto the Supreme Personality of Godhead; *arpita-ātmanām*—who have given their life and soul; *āyuḥ*—duration of life; *dhanam*—wealth; *yaśaḥ*—reputation; *svasti*—good fortune; *gatim*—the ultimate goal of life; *aiśvaryam*—material opulence; *āpnuyāt*—achieves.

TRANSLATION

O King, those who hear these topics about kings who are completely surrendered to the Supreme Personality of Godhead obtain without difficulty a long life, wealth, good reputation, good fortune and, ultimately, the opportunity to return home, back to Godhead.

Thus end the Bhaktivedanta purports of the Fourth Canto, Thirty-first Chapter of the Śrīmad-Bhāgavatam, *entitled "Nārada Instructs the Pracetās."*

END OF THE FOURTH CANTO